THE ANCIENT ATLANTIC

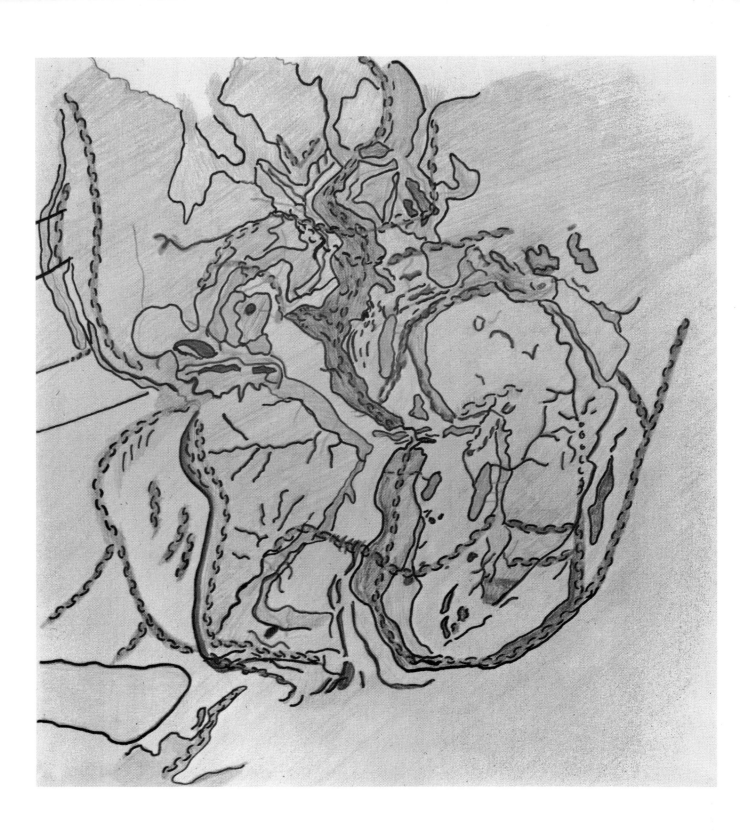

THE ANCIENT ATLANTIC

By L. TAYLOR HANSEN

AMHERST PRESS

Amherst, Wisconsin 54406

Author's concept of the Ancient Atlantic Ocean, prior to the time of Solon, when the legendary continent of Atlantis sprawled almost from pole to pole. (After Rand McNally, 1964 Readers Digest map, and many others.)

◄――――――――――――

This map of the northern Atlantic's submerged lands is gleaned from maps and descriptions in the following books: "The Viking and The Red Man" by R.T. Sherwin, published in 1942 by Funk & Wagnalls, New York and London; "Lost America" by Captain Mallory, published by Dartmouth University Library, (The Portolan Chart); "Map of The Ancient Sea Kings" published by Chilton Books in 1965; "The Earth's Shifting Crust" published in 1958 by Pantheon Books; "Great Mysteries of The Earth" published in 1960 by Pulnam.

LIBRARY OF CONGRESS CATALOG NUMBER : 69-15422

COPYRIGHT 1969
PALMER PUBLICATIONS, INC.
ALL RIGHTS RESERVED
PRINTED IN THE UNITED STATES OF AMERICA

PRINTING   Tomorrow River Printers, Amherst, Wisconsin 54406

BINDING   National Bookbinding Company, Stevens Point, Wisconsin 54481

1618165

I dedicate this book to all those who have preceded me in the enthrallment which the Atlantic has held over the mind of Man, and to all those who will follow me haunted by the earnest desire to fit together the parts of an ancient jigsaw of the past which may lead to a greater perspective of the future.

Roll on, thou dark and deep blue ocean, roll!
    Ten thousand fleets have swept o'er thee in vain!
Man marks the earth with ruin. His control
    Stops with the shore. Upon thy watery plain
The wrecks are all thy deed, nor doth remain
    A shadow of man's version, save his own
When for a moment, like a drop of rain
    He sinks into thy depth with bubbling groan;
Without a grave - unknelled, uncoffined and unknown.
           Byron.

A Cree Indian tracker once explained to me how he had managed to stroll leisurely through the tundra of the Canadian Northwoods, while the men who had hired him struggled frantically to keep themselves out of difficulties, and within calling distance of their guide.

"I have two sights," he explained his ability to me. "I have a near-look and a far-vision."

Most laymen who live within the limited horizon of a daily job can never experience the personal thrill of a scientific discovery which is the "near-look" of science; while by the same token many scientists whose chosen field is the lands facing the oceans may be involved with fossils, plants, animals, climates, undersea maps, insects or Man himself, and through lack of multi-dimensional concept, lose contact with the advanced horizon which is, in essence, "scientific far-vision."

It is in an attempt to capture something of the thrill of viewing both the single discovery, and the magnificent panorama of the advancing horizon, that this book has been undertaken, and why it has become the biography of the Atlantic.

L. Taylor Hansen

Contents

		Page
FRONTISPIECE (Author's Concept Of The Ancient Atlantic Ocean)		2
DEDICATION		5
POEM (BYRON)		6
PREFACE		7
FOREWORD		12
INTRODUCTION		13

Chapter

1	AN ANCIENT LEGEND RETURNS TO HAUNT THE HALLS OF SCIENCE	14
2	THE HAUNTING LEGEND FROM ANTIQUITY	18
3	THE MYTHICAL LAKE TRICONIS OR TRITON LAKE	33
4	DOES HISTORY OPEN WITH ASTRONOMICAL KNOWLEDGE AND THE COMPASS?	38
5	THE PIRI RE'IS MAP	43
6	THE GLACIAL RHYTHM AND THE MEDITERRANEAN VALLEY	47
7	THE AMAZING EGYPTIANS	51
8	DIODORUS AND THE AMAZONS	56
9	THE AMAZING ANTIQUITY OF PERU, SOUTH AMERICA	61
10	AN ANTHROPOLOGIST REPORTS ON THE CHANNEL ISLANDS OF CALIFORNIA - THE SHIPS OF THE DRAGON LAND?	69
11	WHO WERE THESE ANCIENT MEN?	75
12	THE ROUND HEADED LANDSMEN	83
13	THE TRAGEDY OF NEANDERTHAL MAN - THE FIRST EUROPEAN	88
14	THE GREAT DISHARMONIC CROSS	92
15	FITTING TOGETHER SOME PARTS OF THE PUZZLE	101
16	THE PEOPLE OF THE VEIL	106
17	THE BIRD OF THE LIGHTNINGS	111
18	THE PUZZLE OF BRONZE AGE EUROPE	116
19	ANCIENT CLUES FROM SPAIN	122
20	THE DANCE OF THE TRIDENT	127
21	COULD THERE HAVE BEEN A CENTRAL LAND IN THE ATLANTIC?	136
22	THOSE SUBMARINE CHANNELS	141
23	IS THE ATLANTIC FLOOR SINKING?	148
24	THOSE GIGANTIC EARTH TEARS WHICH GEOLOGISTS CALL RIFT VALLEYS	153

25 THOSE ANCIENT CLIMATES
        - AND DROWNED MOUNTAIN CHAINS WHEN CHICAGO WAS THE NORTH POLE   161
26 ANCIENT GONDWANNALAND   166
27 THOSE ANIMAL MIGRATIONS   169
28 THE STRANGE MUMMIES OF THE NORSE   175
29 THE MYSTERY OF THE AFRICAN RIM AND THE VEILED RAIDERS   178
30 THE TAYLOR HYPOTHESIS   188
31 THE WEGENER HYPOTHESIS   192
32 HOW CAN WE EXPLAIN THE PACIFIC CURTAIN OF FIRE?   195
33 PUTTING THE PARTS TOGETHER   200
34 THE BACKGROUND AND PRELUDE AS THE DRAMA OPENS   206
35 THE DRAMA OF OUR PLANET   208
36 THE TIME OF ANCIENT LIFE   210
37 THE GREAT SOUTHERN GLACIAL   214
38 THE DRAGONS RULE THE EARTH, THEN CONTINENTS COLLIDE   218
39 THE CENOZOIC OR THE AGE OF THE MAMMALS   226
40 THE CASE FOR THE MONSTERS   232
41 THE MAMMALS INHERIT THE EARTH   238
42 HOW GEOLOGY IS READING THE PAST   245
43 PERIODS OF REST AND PERIODS OF FIRE   250
44 THE FIERY MIOCENE   254
45 THE PLIOCENE   258
46 MAN'S EARLIER COUSINS, THE APES   262
47 MAN'S OTHER COUSINS, THE SUB-MEN   267
48 THE PLEISTOCENE AND THE COMING OF CIVILIZATION   272
49 THE MAZE, THE LABYRINTH AND THE WALL   276
50 THE COMING OF THE ICE AGE   284
51 WHO WERE THE OLDEST CIVILIZATIONS?   299
52 THE EARLIEST NATIONS OF HISTORICAL TIMES, IN THE MEDITERRANEAN,
        AND THE FIRST GLOBAL WAR   304
53 THE FLIGHT OF THE TYRRHENIANS   311
54 THE MARCH OF THE AR-ZAWANS   317
55 WILL IT HAPPEN AGAIN - COULD IT?   328
56 THE SUNKEN LAND OF LYONESSE   338
57 THE GIANT CRACK IN THE EARTH   344
58 THE GREAT DESTRUCTION   352
59 OUR FANTASTICALLY ANCIENT ALPHABET   367
60 THE KERRIANS OR CARIANS   380
61 SOME RECENT CRACKS THROUGH THE MISTS OF TIME   388
62 THE WAR DOG OF THE ANCIENTS   392
63 A TIME OF TREMENDOUS DISCOVERIES IN GEOLOGY   396
64 THE ANCIENT SUNKEN CITIES OF YS, HEL AND ASGAARD - A SEA BOTTOM MAP?   404
65 THE RING OF FIRE - DOES IT STILL ENCIRCLE THE WORLD?   411
    INDEX   424

Illustrations

Author's concept of the ancient Atlantic ocean	2
Profile of the Atlantic ocean (the sunken land)	14-15
African clues to an ancient sunken continent	18-19
Pelasgian wall	23
Wall of the citadel of Troy	23
Flying serpent of the Venus calendar	32
Scottish bagpipers	33
The Mediterranean world of 13,000 years ago	36-37
Piri Re'is map	44-45
Fossil find linking Antarctica to Gondwannaland	46
A "drowned valley" on the island of Capri	48
Bust of Nefertiti (unfinished)	51
Tokhari prisoner taken by Rhameses III	52
Tokhari prisoner captured by the Assyrians	53
Ceremonial dress of the Kiowa	58
Shooting Star, Sioux Indian	61
Navaho girl - eastern type Cro Magnon	65
Machu Picchu	66
Chumash prehistorical sites	70
Santa Barbara (Channel) islands	71
Long headed Azilian	75
Ancient Indian sculpture	78
Azilian stones	81
A sunken river around Bogoslof island	84
Bogoslof volcano	85
Neanderthal skull of La Chapelle	88
Top view of Neanderthal skull	88
The Weimar valley skull	88
The Australian aborigine	89
Chief Yellow Horse	95
Geronimo	97
The Joy of Returning Spring - Zuni painting	101
Addax	104
Oryx	104
Medallion of royalty	104
The Bird of the Lightnings	111
Map of the British Isles	114
Astarte, the Syrian war goddess	115
Etruscan bronze	116
Apache Crown Dance	118
Bronze age swords	119
Two bronze razors or knives from Denmark	120
Map of Spanish coastline	122
Copper knives from Peru	123
Crown dancer	126
Leader's helmet	127
Head of Amen-em-het III	135
Bust of a statue of Amen-em-het III	135
Grand Canyon of the Colorado	136
The Columbia river undersea gorge	141
Eel river map	146
Hudson river gorge map	147
Downwarp of North America	150
The mythical Mudhead - a Hopi painting	151
The San Andreas fault	154
Great rift valley of Africa	155
The Walking Hills, Yuma desert	159
A sunken mountain chain	162

The sunken Appalachian-English-
    Norse cordillera   163
Ancient Gondwannaland   167
Ancient line of Easter capes   170
Present line of Easter capes   171
2000 year old Tollund man   175
Bronze ibex found buried in Egyptian sands   184
The African shelf   186
Taylor's concept of Gondwannaland   188
The Pacific curtain of fire   195
How land rises from and sinks into the sea   198
Rifts, and how they form   199
Pro and con concerning continental
    drift (chart)   202-3
Chief Crazy Horse   205
Trilobites   210
The archean shield   212
Gondwannaland   213
The great southern glacial   214
Gondwannaland at the time of the
    land-locked Pole   215
Gondwannaland after the continents
    had drifted apart   217
Continental collision   220
Aftermath - Australian collision   221
Aftermath - the great Mesozoic cordillera   222-3
Recently discovered rifts, Mesozoic age   224
The trans-Atlantic trench   228-9
Tyrannosaurus Rex   233
Plesiosaurus   236
The marmoset   240
The lemur   242
The tarsier   243
Entombed leafy plant found at lake Uinta   246
Petrified tree at Ginkgo petrified
    forest, Vantage, Washington   247
Lake Uinta entombed mite   248
How the fire moves north   251
A study of Drake straits   252
The fault along the California coast   253
Young dragon tree   254
Diceratherium and dinohyus   255
Neanderthal, Springbok and
    Strandlopper skulls   260
Gorilla, orangutan and chimpanzee   264
Pithecanthropus Robustus   268
Modern Neanderthal cross   268
The face of Zinj - Olduvai gorge, Africa   269
The London skull   269
Cliff dwellings, Montezuma Castle
    National Monument   273
Maze stone at Hemet, California   276
Examples of ancient mazes   277
Maze coin with human figure   278
Two Pima fret designs   279
Mitla maze   280
Megalithic wall   281
Ancient round towers   283

A modern Cro Magnon (Doepping
    granddaughter)   284
Adopted Mohawk (Doepping daughter)   285
A modern "Nefertiti"   287
Alphabet chart   289
Sumerian writing   290
Dragon ship, either Viking or
    Phoenician trireme   292
Petroglyphs at Tule lake   293-4
Pictographs along the Columbia river   295
Newspaper rock, petrified forest, Arizona   296
Shell disk   296
Sacred evening star design of the Hopi   297
Hawaii and Gila river glyphs   297
Serpent mound, Adams county, Ohio   301
Ancient peoples (a chart) agglutinating tongues,
    matrilinear succession, culture
    traits   (gatefold between pages   304-5
The hero twin dance   308-9
Plains Indian chief   312
Gold mask of a Mycenae prince   321
Sierra Nevada fault escarpment   329
The main street in Compton, California
    (1933 earthquake)   330
Street in San Francisco after 1906 earthquake   331
Volcanic island rising from the Atlantic
    south of Iceland   333
San Andreas fault, crossing Carrizo plain   335
A branch of the San Andreas fault   336
Location of ancient Lyonesse   339
Great Glen fault in Scotland   345
The great earth crack   346-7
Robeson channel separating Greenland
    from Ellesmere island   348
Rifting of supercontinent   350
Wegener's idea   351
Candle of the Volcanoes - Zuni Indian painting   362
Calendar stone   363
Aztec sacrificial stone of Tizoc   364
The Land Has Gone Down - Zuni Indian painting   366
Landa's Mayan alphabet   377-8
Irish (Gaelic) alphabet   379
The (supposedly) extinct Plesiosaurus   380
The water monster   381
The water dragon   381
Mosasaurus   388
"Nessie", the Plesiosaurus   390
Elasmosaurus   391
The Chow (war dog of the ancients)   392
Remnants of the old red land   396
The location of Atlantis?   406-7
Sunken Atlantean ruins?   408
Fine's map of Antarctica   409
Nefertiti   410
Plates from an old Chinese play
    about Atlantis   412-3-5-6
L. Taylor Hansen (a sketch)   423

Foreword

This is the story of an ocean and the facts about it which puzzle us - physical, seismological, biographical and legendary.

The legendary cannot be explained adequately unless we understand the facts, or at least unless we understand how limited our knowledge is at present. In attempting to see the extent of some of these facts we may have to touch upon the global aspect, but this is not a history of the planet - except as that story may influence the solution, or at least the understanding, of the mysteries of the Atlantic.

In our examination of this one fascinating ocean, we will always try to be objective. By this term is meant a non-emotional approach. To insure this attitude, let us review the three main types of "investigators" a true scientist abhors.

First, there is the "vandal". He may not realize that he is one; he may think that he is exploring the past when he digs into an ancient graveyard. Or he may be just a "pot hunter". Nevertheless, he is disturbing the entire picture and its sequence of the past which the true scientific team uncovers layer by layer, keeping copious notes on each layer and marking each find with samples of its own level (or horizon, as it is called by the anthropologists).

The second type is the hoaxer. He usually has already conceived a theory which he pursues avidly. In his desire to prove it he will destroy facts that disagree, bury an artifact (tool of ancient man) or even a skeleton clothed in armor, to prove that a certain type of man was to be found in this place. What he does not realize is that his own time is not the final horizon. The buried facts which will prove or disprove his pet theory will keep on turning up ten years from now or a thousand years from now or any of the million moments in between.

The third type is the rigid mind. This is usually an educated man who, like the hoaxer, has succumbed to the lure of a pet theory learned during his college days and followed ever since.

He will deliberately overlook certain facts, claiming all sorts of reasons, often most absurd, for not recognizing that his pet theory is inadequate.

The truly scientific thinker will yield to a fact when it is uncovered by a team of accredited scientists, as it has been said that Einstein did when confronted by specifics at California School of Technology, then setting about to correct his mistake.

Many scientific names, great in their own time, have fallen into disrepute because they became so certain of their own theories, or some one else's theory, that they refused to allow for later possible contradictions.

However, when a scientist actually buries facts that disagree with his theory, he brings down upon his head the condemnation that he has "---ruined the evidence for a later scholar." There is no greater damnation than that, for this is real vandalism, not the carelessness that is forgiveable in the ignorant.

Upon the other hand, scientists must at all times be careful before accepting a fact. They must be particularly careful of the hoaxer. These are usually publicity-seekers. A striking historical case is that of the cranium and jaw of an early type of man for a long time accepted as a real find. Now it is known that only the cranium is ancient, while the jaw is that of a modern chimpanzee. This is why scientists will not accept as genuine a find made by amateurs. They must be led to the site, do actual digging and find for themselves some of the tools and artifacts of the supposed horizon before the find can be recognized. Many finds are lost thus, being written off as hoaxes, but if the fact is a true one, then there will be other finds elsewhere, for the rock-books of the planet will keep on being opened and read for thousands of years. This is why the hoaxer and the rigid thinker in their impractical pursuit of a theory must presuppose that some day they will be found out, for that is the way of science.

Introduction

Beyond the limits of our present scientific knowledge, except for meagre, tantalizing bits of information, are two mediums - the Air and the Sea. Though we use both for transportation, they are an illusive substance in which, because we are denizens of the land, we must forever remain an intruding alien. Yet, with our insatiable curiosity, we stand pondering inscrutable mysteries, while looking into those forbidden depths.

Someday we may take a trip in a glass-lined submarine whose metal plates roll open at the midnight depths of seven thousand feet, so that in the piercing glow of powerful beams of probing light, we may see for ourselves what lies within the long-lost valleys, along the river-banks and bays of such sunken lands as the mid-Atlantic ridge.

However, until that day of adventure arrives, let us ponder the work being done now by men of science - probing the ocean depths by echoing sound or metal drill or dredging tools. Day by day new evidence is being brought to light, much of which is steadily pushing the "time of Man" back into an antiquity which our grandfathers deemed nonexistent. We know now that Man lived through most and probably all of the glacial periods in his present recognizable form, following the animals which were his food over land-bridges apparently since reclaimed by the sea.

The anthropologists of the 1930's were far too certain of what they thought they knew and even of what later research would reveal, when they argued with such heated fervor about the recent Asiatic origin of all Amerinds, or American Indian tribes. Carbon-14 dating has set supposed dates back about a thousand years, while many artifacts such as certain types of arrowheads are now recognized as of Pleistocene or ice age time.

As Louis A. Brennan in his "No Stone Unturned" has so perceptively said: "This is the very sparkle and exhilaration of prehistory, that its most complacent theories can be embarrassed at any moment by an impudent fact."

Perhaps those men of the thirties should have started their graduate studies under Dean Reiber of the University of California at Los Angeles. I am certain that no student of his will ever forget how we were greeted.

"Young people, you are probably rather proud of that degree under your arm, or in your pocket - or wherever you have it. You are also undoubtedly pretty proud of yourselves. You are thinking" - looking from face to face - "how much more you know than your young brother still in high school, or the clerk at the dry goods establishment where you bought that coat. Let me tell you that before you remain in this class one more day you will have to reorient yourselves."

"Knowledge, my young friends, is a ball floating in a sea of ignorance. While you have been spending your few short years accumulating this much knowledge," - touching his slim fingertips together - "I have had the benefit of so many more years, that along with these white hairs on my head I have accumulated all this knowledge," - touching his fingertips above his shock of silver hair which stood out above his face like a corona - "but don't let that awe you for one moment. Just consider all my exposure to ignorance!"

Thus spoke a great teacher of the thirties - adding (as though he meant to say it to himself) these words; which I am certain none of his students ever forgot: "It is only when you begin to realize how much you do NOT know, and in fact how little ANYONE knows, that you have earned the right to consider yourself an embryo scientist."

Chapter 1

An Ancient Legend Returns To

Out of the profundity of antiquity and through the vandalistic burning of ancient documents, rising like a ghost from their ashes, comes a legend of a sunken land long lost to volcanism and subsidence which once existed in the center of the Atlantic ocean; a land which from almost impregnable ports, ruled the earth.

Science has tried to lay this spectre, as St. George slew the dragon, but somehow it manages to return. Each time it does, science is a little less certain of its ground, for a multitude of puzzling facts keep stealing its weapons. The most potent sword the scientists carried was rusted away by the discovery of an old parchment map; while tiny microscopic animals, eleven thousand years after their death, point like the hands of a giant clock of the ages to the "Date of the Cataclysm."

Now, to live in the musical world of one's grandfather might indicate a good musical education, and to live in the literary world indicate a fair general education, but to live exclusively in the scientific world of the last thirty or forty years stamps one as a poorly educated man; yet there are scientists who are doing just this. Furthermore, they are teaching the youth without having kept up with the advancing horizon of their subject; and for the purpose of showing them how they have fallen behind the general march of new facts, I have chosen to write this book on the most

controversial of all scientific subjects - the Atlantic ocean.

The story originally came down to us from the writings of Plato, who definitely was not a writer of science-fiction, although his history of Atlantis has been treated like a fairy-tale told to beguile children. It was never meant to be that. Solon, who first heard the story from the librarian of the incredibly ancient collection of papyrus manuscripts which made up the Alexandrian library, was a law-maker of Athens and far more interested in local politics than ancient history. However, he left notes and a manuscript which he had partly finished. Neither survived to our time. The notes were inherited by Critias (pronounced Cree-shus), then in turn handed down to his grandson, Plato, who was also interested in law. Plato started a manuscript but never finished it. He deserted it for a dry dissertation on law and a just state. Both have survived, but one only wishes that he had a bit more of the historian in his makeup and less of the philosopher. Neither Solon, Critias nor Plato were fools and the Greeks of the golden age were hardly to be compared to children. Nor can the ancient knowledge of the Egyptians (from whom the story came) be written off as inconsequential. Egypt is the one great bridge leading back from historical times into the legend of prehistory.

14

Haunt The Halls Of Science

Thus from voices over two thousand years old comes a story translated from an ancient history which no longer exists. Just because we no longer have this book, should we say that it never was? Or should we withhold our judgment until all the scientific facts are in, even though that may take many years of research? So far, the ancient legend is winning. If you do not think so, then you are not as informed as you should be on recent scientific discoveries.

During the eighties of the last century Ignatious Donnelly wrote a book called "Atlantis and the Antediluvian World." It was excellently researched for its day and the mistakes it made were due to the fact that science had not yet enough material to entertain a different viewpoint. However, Donnelly tried to do a scientific work which certainly is more than many writers upon the subject of the sunken land have done. Most of them veer away from oceanography and prefer to get their facts either from a medium or an ouija board. Such "facts" convince no one except spiritualists and even their points of view will differ.

However, when Donnelly tried to get answers for his questions from scientists, they covered up their ignorance with laughter. The book promptly became the butt of endless caustic classroom wit. And Donnelly, completely frustrated, fell silent.

Since the time of Donnelly, science has moved forward, as it always does, treading upon the fragments of exploded hypotheses. Why? What explodes a chosen hypothesis? Facts. Newly discovered facts. Any hypothesis must fit facts or it goes into the discard. Some of our scientists are not even aware of these facts and therefore they are not aware that their pet theories are no longer admissable. It is time that these men came out of their ivory towers. In fact, ivory towers have no place in science. That is its challenge and its glory.

In this book we shall discuss some of these facts - the great sunken land on the floor of the Atlantic and other mysteries of that ocean such as overwhelmed fossil rivers, and immersed cities, submerged water falls, and the strange planetary features which we call rifts, as well as the curious change of climates and water levels throughout the ages. We shall inevitably raise far more questions than we can possibly answer for science has not as yet unearthed all the evidence. It is finding more answers every year, and it will continue to find them. Yet it is also true that too often an answer to an initial question raises half a dozen new questions, for which science now has no clues.

Here, working in laboratories and in ships sounding the ocean floor, or drilling into it, are the oceanographers of today, and their adventure into the unknown is twice as fascinating as the adventures of our exploring ancestors of a few hundred years ago. Nor is it all arm-chair discovery. Sometimes it entails great dangers; but the lure of the unknown is an ever-present lure. Science has no place for the mind which knows all the answers, for as some wit once said; "if you know all the answers, then it is obvious that you do not know all the questions."

For example, if you are one of the scientists who acquired your viewpoint upon water-lockup in ice from a teacher who in turn was taught during the eighties and has not studied much since, and you begin to argue against the possibility of an Atlantis upon the three hundred foot level which was supposed to have been the water withdrawal at that time, you may be asked in turn to explain: 1) the lava which solidified under air, torn from the ridge at the nine thousand foot depth, or: 2) the tremendous rebound of glaciated lands which is far greater than it should be considering the presently estimated ice weight, or upon the other hand: 3) asked what about Daly's remark in his "Floor of the Oceans" that a Russian scientist had confided to him that an immense sheet had once covered Siberia and cartographers were just now discovering its range?

The latter statement reminds me of the time when the present writer was in a party coming up the Mackenzie river from the Circle in Canada and had met just such a group of cartographers.

These Englishmen were jolly fellows with whom we shared our food and exchanged ideas. One of our party asked them: "Tell us the name of that large river which we just passed."

"It has no name as yet."

"Oh, come now - it must be the size of the Columbia river"

"Yes, it probably is. We are on our way to survey it. We have it marked as about five hundred miles in length."

"Where does it rise?"

"We are not certain of that. Two old miners or part-time trappers were our informants, only they could not agree about the source. One said that it arose from a large lake and the other said

it began in a spring on the side of a mountain."

"It could be that both are right," one of our men observed, "perhaps one had penetrated the country farther than the other."

"That is also possible," the Englishman conceded, "however, our worry is whether the river is frozen solidly enough so that we lessen the chance of breaking through, and are able to cover as much territory as possible before the spring thaw."

Yes, there is unknown territory in the vast stretches of Canada, without considering Siberia. It all contributes to our problem of the Pleistocene ice age (pronounced Ply-stoh-scene) ice sheets and the amount of water which they drained out of the oceans. Up to the time that Daly dropped this bombshell, no geologist had dreamed that Siberia might have had an ice sheet! And considering the rapidity with which information trickles out of Russia, it may be some time before we find out anything more on the subject.

Only one fact is certain, as sunken bank after sunken bank is discovered to have had its own Pleistocene sheet, or have been covered from the nearest land - the estimated water level in the time of the Pleistocene is steadily going down.

Up to the time of Donnelly's book, science had not known about any land in the Atlantic, and was only amused by the legend. Not only was a land to be found there, but running as it does, from five hundred to a thousand miles wide, and the entire length of the Atlantic from its head, Iceland, which is still out of the water, to where it curves around Africa, the ridge made it obvious to Donnelly that the Egyptian priest could not have been so far wrong when he said that once it was as large as Libya and Asia put together. By this he meant Asia Minor, since it is to be doubted if the Egyptians were acquainted with Asia proper, or called by that name. Yet, if Asia Minor and Libya (the land from the borders of Egypt to the Atlantic) are moulded slightly, they will not only fit upon the great central ridge of the Atlantic but leave enough room for an England, Japan and Ireland also - laid end to end. How science began to combat these facts, until new discoveries silenced their voices, will be taken up by later chapters in this book.

There was also the problem of the Biblical Flood. For this, Donnelly received no help from the scientists of his time. Since the day of "Atlantis and the Antediluvian World" science is discovering much about the Flood. There was indeed a deluge of cataclysmic proportions which ended the Pleistoscene. However, there were also floods which heralded each retreat of the ice, although not of the cataclysmic type of the final one. For the evidences of this Donnelly made a masterly work of researching world legends, but he forgot or ignored the evidence of paleontology. If he had looked into this, he might have gotten the uncomfortable feeling that the calaclysm of the Pleistocene is not yet over.

When Donnelly was researching his book, anthropologists and archaeologists did not dream that the ice sheets with their advances and retreats took place in the time of man. But then, these are the laggard sciences. Whenever man is concerned these sciences become ridiculously conservative. Perhaps this is because they are themselves emotionally involved or the pressures from an emotionally involved public limit their scope of research until facts are thrust down their throats, as it were.

Take for example the case of Mt. Mazama or Crater lake, Oregon. Geologists had just gotten out a bulletin on the subject, which I have in my possession. The bulletin insists that the great Mt. Mazama (Indian name for the fire-god) blew its top into the clouds long before the time of man - probably during the Mesozoic or very early Cenozoic (the time of middle-life or the days of the dinosaurs, and late-life respectively), therefore it was not to be considered as part of the Pleistocene diastrophism. Then the remains of man were found. The burned mummy was sealed in a cave by the outpouring of lava from Mazama. Immediately another bulletin followed saying that the mountain erupted very late and therefore this body could not be considered too old. We are awaiting the results of carbon-dating on this one.

There are many other questions which will be taken up in turn as we try to see, scientifically just what happened in the Atlantic ocean. However it is true that the men of anthropology and archaeology (from the Greek words anthropos or man and ology, study of, as well as archae - ancient - in this case cities), are shielded by the other scientists from the shock of new facts. This is not exactly in concern for their feelings, but due to a sort of conspiracy. As one geologist put it: "We never learn anything new from them and some are even so far behind the times that they don't believe in carbon-dating. It might upset their ivory tower, you know. So when they come into the room where one of our debates is in progress, we simply postpone the arguments and discuss the weather. That is a good

non-controversial subject. As a result they learn very little from us. Too bad in a way, but natural."

"How about excessive rain caused by rapid glacial retreat, or earthquakes along rifts?"

"We never discuss such things with them."

"Have you ever hinted what might happen if an ice sheet suddenly melted because of the outpouring of lava? Or if Japan, which leans precariously over one of the greatest deeps on the planet, should slide in on one of her rifts?"

"Oh no! Those are strictly for us - not them."

"I should have thought the subject might naturally come up in the discussions of the Alaskan shake of 1964."

"And the tidal wave? No, we do not discuss either rifts or tidal waves."

"No wonder they seem to pass over the eight-foot drift of gravel which separates some of the ancient ruins in the Mediterranean as a normal geological occurrence."

"It wouldn't be worth an argument with them. They are still living back in -"

"- the Eighties?"

"Remember, you said it, I didn't."

"They have never discovered that over the debris of exploded hypotheses, science advances?"

"Very well said; I must remember that."

"And they are still clinging to the theory before the theory before the last?"

"Remember, you said it. I didn't."

"All this reminds me of a professor I once had named Reiber. He was a most inspiring person and a privilege to have known."

"Ah yes, we have all had a few like that. And it is too bad, isn't it, that we can count them on the fingers of one hand?"

"That is all too true."

"But I interrupted you. What did he say?"

"The Bastile Mind sometimes fancies that he is a scientist. He may even have a doctorate in his specialty, which on occasion he dusts off and wears like a shining medal. Unfortunately, however, he has the type of intelligence which has come thus far and no farther. Once he has discovered an idea which his emotions tell him is favorable to the retention of all the creature-comforts that he enjoys, he grooms it, manacles and blindfolds it, and entertains it listlessly to the end of his life. Of course, he never changes his mind or reevaluates his primary ideas. His is the true Bastile Mind into which it is most difficult to get an idea and almost impossible to get it out."

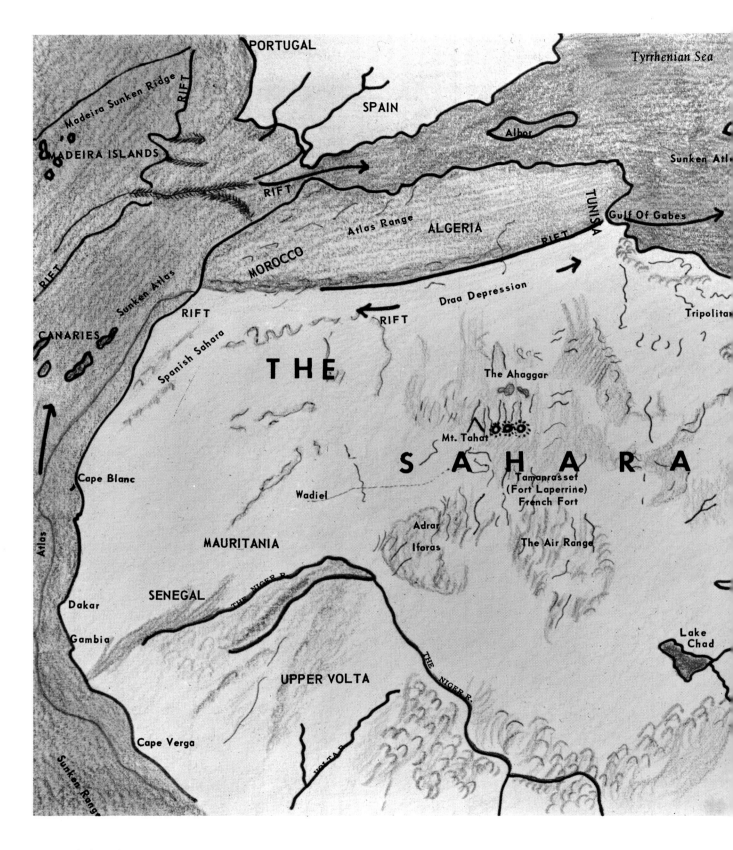

One of the charges levelled against the legend of Atlantis is that Plato authored the story out of whole cloth. It is to be suspected that the people who made this charge were not too well ac-quainted with the Greek philosopher.

It is true that his character of Socrates was one of the most entertaining intellectual rascals in literature. Yet he wrote about Socrates when

Chapter 2

The Haunting Legend From Antiquity

African clues to an ancient sunken continent. Author's map after Readers Digest, Colliers, Atlas 1964.

he was young, for the beloved scamp was Plato's teacher, and witnessing the last moments and death of Athens' "gadfly", as he so often called himself, left a traumatic effect on the young mind

of Plato which he finally eased by writing all of the Dialogues. They were often written tongue-in-cheek because Socrates argued with a crazy kind of logic which was never really meant to unwind mysteries but to tangle, tease and entertain.

However, it was not a young Plato who wrote the Timaeus or the Critias. Socrates had vanished from his pages except as a listener who did not enter the conversation, much less monopolize it as he was wont to do when Plato was young.

A delightful wit of my college days, who happened to be my Professor of literature, was Dr. Spaeth of Princeton. He once characterized the men of the classical era as follows: "When the Romans came into Greece as conquerors, they physically walked as men among children, but they soon learned to their chagrin that mentally they were but children among men."

It must have been a very stimulating time and place to have been alive - this beautiful marble city of Athens. Here were more gifted men gathered in one place in the span of TWO CENTURIES, than have been known since to any people. The ratio of one genius known to history (excluding those whose names were lost) - either in science, architecture, painting, sculpture, drama (tragic or comic), law, oratory, sports, poetry, and teaching - to every three hundred and seventy of the population, has never since been equalled and probably never will be. It was from this land that we received our constitution and the foundations of our government and our courts. It was here that we received the words democracy as well as autocracy. Here was born our modern tragic and comic dramas, the most elegant standards for beauty in public buildings, the understanding of the grace of bodily movement in sculpture, the laws governing logic in· law. Here was suggested, for later scientists to discover, the circulation of the blood, the atomic structure of the universe, the discovery that the sun was a body of fire and a glass would concentrate its beams to flame, the discovery that air has a body and must be displaced when water is poured into a container. One of the greatest minds of the day was Pythagoras who suggested the Copernican theory of our solar system long before Copernicus himself. Cadmus helped to give us our alphabet (which is a Greek word), and Euclid our geometry. Here were born the methods of teaching which are still practiced in our best colleges. The population of Athens during the golden age was one of great sophistication.

The legend of Atlantis, carried to this city by Solon, from Egypt, was not told to beguile children. The Greeks of the golden age were anything but childlike. Nor for that matter, were the Egyptians.

Almost typical of the Athens of this era was Socrates. He probably would not have become famous at any other time or in any other land.

Socrates was a sort of intellectual pixie. It was his joy to wander about the streets of Athens barefoot, and not well-dressed but on the whole shabbily, seeking arguments. He was never alone. A dedicated court of the youth, teen-agers if you please, always followed at his heels. Why? Because they found that Socrates provided them with unfailing entertainment. One of the youths was Plato. Socrates himself never wrote a book. He lives today mainly because of that admiring young man who followed him until he was condemned to death for corrupting the youth of Athens and was forced to drink the hemlock poison. If it had not been for that youth, the old rascal would only be remembered as a minor character in one of the comedies, and by the words of a man who reported that Socrates' excuse for wandering the streets of Athens was that his wife was a shrew and made his home so unbearable. Some Athenians thought she had reasons.

When Socrates walked the market-place, trailed by his court of the mischievous young, he would accost the general, the famous philosopher, the physician or the man of wealth. His method was usually the same. He would humbly ask them for information. Being shabbily dressed the famous man could not see that this apparent mendicant would pose a threat to his prestige. So invariably he stopped when the old fellow begged for information on how the man of wealth obtained his money. Socrates would say that he too would appreciate having an income, so the trap was sprung on the unsuspecting victim. It was, of course, not long until the master had the rich man so entangled in a web of logic that he became utterly confused. "Was that method of making money entirely desirable? Was it actually moral? What constituted the moral man?" Finally the wealthy victim, enraged and frustrated left in a fury. When he did, the court was delighted and convulsed with laughter, for losing one's temper always signified defeat.

Not that the logic which Socrates used was always the best. One has the feeling that he often argued with tongue-in-cheek to see if the victim could ensnare him as he was ensnaring. It is no wonder that he made powerful enemies; that he was forced to drink the hemlock poison for leading astray the youth of Athens. Yet, actually, viewed from the distance of two thousands years, he did not lead them into corruption. He only honed their wits to razor-sharpness, and his contribution to the study of debate and how to torment an opposing witness before the bench in court, is endless. His would have been the mind to have in a law suit, with his clever logic - that is, provided he was on your side.

Thus it is that a condemned prisoner is teaching all of the young lawyers of the world. To take logic is one of the requirements of law courses, and one can hardly study that without meeting Socrates. So today the youth of the world are still arguing with Socrates - or each other - such questions as: "would it not be possible for an immoral physician to be as good a doctor as a moral one?"

This slight digression from our search after authenticity of the Atlantis legend was necessary to show why some people might have reason to believe that Plato was still writing with Socratic humor when telling the story of the sunken land. However, Plato did not put the story in the mouth of the pixie of his youth. It was a sober and almost rigid middle-aged Plato, far more interested in the laws of a good state, who wrote about Atlantis. The old "gadfly" had long left his pages and now appeared only once in a while as a spectator. With that rascal, had gone much of the color and entertainment which still makes Plato a must for youth learning logistics and the law.

Upon the contrary, the Atlantis legend was told to Plato by his kinsman Critias. It is interesting that our English pronounciation of some of these old names differ from the way they were pronounced in their own land. For example, our Plato (Play-toe) in Greek is Plah-toh, the same as Spanish plateau and strangely enough that is its meaning, but was a nickname designating his wide forehead. Aristophanes, the dramatist, pronounced by us as we read it - Aris-toff-a-ness is pronounced by the Greeks - Aris-toh-fay-nees. Diogenes, the cynic philosopher, whose sculptured face peers from the facade of one of the colleges of University of Southern California holding up his lantern and looking quizzically into the eyes of every student ascending the stairs, in his eternal search for an honest man, is pronounced by us Die-ah-juh-knees but by the Greeks - De-oh-gay-n-yees. With most of the Greek pronounciation, I believe it is the more euphonius on the whole, but as far as the names for Socrates is concerned the Greek Soh-crah-tees does not fit him as well as the English - Sock-ra-tease. Need I say why?

That the story of Atlantis was told to Plato by Critias who had it from his great-grandfather who was related to Solon, the original carrier of the story from Egypt, lifts it out of the realm of the Socratic humor which sparkled from Plato's pen when he was young. Solon was no comedian. He was a great law-maker and a famous Greek statesman. He would not have allowed his name to be attached to nonsense.

The Egyptian priesthood from whom Solon heard the story had been the keepers of the immensely ancient collection of priceless manuscripts coming down from antiquity which is known to us as the Alexandrian library. The histories, one of which held the records of Atlantis, were to be viewed and read by the serious scholar accompanied by either one or several members of the priesthood. Solon evidently saw this book and kept notes concerning the laws and customs of this interesting civilization. Apparently he had intended to write a book, and may have almost completed it, but the press of official business had prevented him from presenting it to his fellow Athenians. Critias inherited the notes, and in time they came down to sober middle-aged Plato who was too much interested in writing his treatise upon law to be intrigued enough to finish the legend. Possibly he decided to drop it when the gods and the goddesses of the day were mentioned, feeling that its historicity had been damaged. Today we no longer regard these creatures as imaginary divinities, but as ancient kings and queens of prehistory. But Plato did not suspect that there might be an even earlier history than that with which he was concerned, so we inherit an unfinished manuscript from a long lost history, and a very dull, lengthy discussion of laws for an ideal state.

Perhaps we should only be glad that we inherited the legend at all. The supposedly well-educated Julius Caesar put the torch to the unguessably ancient Alexandrian library. Could this be one of the reasons why Cicero said: "The world will not always admire your type, Julius Caesar."

We can be quite certain that Solon brought back the story, and not Plato, although the latter may have checked on it in later days. How do we know this? Herodotus, the historian, having heard the legend from Solon, became intrigued and wished personally to research the authenticity of the tale. Accordingly he went to Egypt and talked to a number of the famous sages of the Egyptian priesthood. Finally he discarded the story as fantastic and destroyed his notes. Why? Because of its ancient dates? No. Because of the manner of the kingdom's doom? No.

Herodotus died two years before Plato was born.

Solon was not given to ridiculous stories. He realized that from the depths of antiquity his city state had celebrated a festival to Athena-Minerva concerning an Atlantis war in which the Greeks had triumphed. He was obviously intrigued with the ancient legend but not enough to give it the necessary research time, so his notes were inherited by Critias who in turn gave them to Plato. Neither of the latter two men took the time to finish the story from the notes, yet it is through these three most casual men that we inherit the ancient legend, and not the history, due to the short-sightedness and stupidity of a general named Julius Caesar.

Even then it might have eluded us, never reached our century, for when Constantinople fell to the Turks after they had thrown fresh battalions of troops (captured in childhood and raised as soldiers) at the tired Greek defenders for nine days and nights of steady fighting, they again put libraries to the torch. One expected this from uneducated conquerors, and this is why the Greek scholars fled with their precious manuscripts to Europe, breaking down the walls of ignorance which we know as the Dark Ages. One of these was the Plato manuscript and evidently another was the Piri Re'is map. Apparently a part of the later was spared by its captors because it intrigued them. Both hark back to Atlantis. Of the two, undoubtedly the map is the older.

In tracing the authenticity of the Atlantis legend we must not fail to mention Homer. He probably had not seen the books of Egypt but he had heard the historical chants whereby many ancient peoples handed down the stories of the past. These were remembered by minstrel after minstrel who went about repeating them in return for food and lodging. We are grateful that Homer took the time to collect these ancient stories and write them down for posterity. We have no more right to say that they were all fictional than we have to dub Herodotus ''The Father of Lies'' as he is so often called. Both men were dealing with symbolical situations the real meaning of which has been lost. What would we not give today for a Homer who had taken down the sagas of the Norse and saved them for us?

Homer also wrote of a strange city upon an island. During the Nineteenth Century the professors of literature were certain that Homer was writing fiction. One man decided that he was not. Heinrich Schliemann was not an archaeologist. He was a German business man who had become enamored with Homer. He lived a rather uninteresting life during the day, but at night, beside his lamp, he fought through the battles of Troy and sailed with the Greek heroes around the seas. As he read, his heroes came alive, and for him they had once lived and died. He began to conceive the wild idea that there once was a Troy. He began to make maps, and these led to the desire to look for the lost city of Illium. If he had gone to college, he would have had the idea laughed out of his brain. Fortunately he had never been to college.

Heinrich Schliemann went into business for the purpose of making enough money to find Troy. His compensation for all the amusement which his dream was causing when he finally proclaimed it to a startled world, was seeing enough money from his business enterprises pile up to pay his way to Greece.

It made not the slightest difference to him that both the professors of archaeology and literature were having so much fun over the idea that a layman had believed the fiction of Homer. To him these were historical happenings compressed into rhythm for a better aid to memory. The professors laughed at the thought that Hercules had fought birds with metal heads. Schliemann wondered if this just might mean the metal helmets of the ancient Greeks with the bird-like crests? Because Heinrich Schliemann did not discuss his ideas with any of the recognized authorities upon the subject of ancient cities, or of Greek literature, he did not become disenchanted with Homer. He was certain that his favorite poet wrote of prehistoric events and that Troy had never been found. In fact, no one had ever bothered to look for it. He didn't know that it couldn't have existed because Homer was writing fiction, as everybody else believed.

Finally he sold his business enterprises and began to prepare for his big adventure. Archaeologists and others in the colleges burst into laughter. There was no Troy because there never was a Trojan war! Schliemann heard what the papers were saying and smiled. So these men of antiquity were but the figment of a writer's imagination? Perhaps - and perhaps not.

Taking a ship to the Turkish port, he sailed along the coast to the place he had marked out from his studies of Homer. There he hired help from the natives for the purpose of excavation. Again taking his Homer, he studied the ground and comparing it with the directions he had gained from the printed page, he began to dig. He found Troy. Not only the Troy of Homer, but the Troy of before the time of Homer, and the

Pelasgian Wall - remains of a Mycenaean citadel on the
Acropolis, Athens, 13th century, B. C.

Wall of the citadel of Troy with bastion,
South Gate. Probably 25th century B. C.

Troy which followed, now also turned to rubble and dust.

When this news broke across Europe, taking the banner headlines of the papers, one of the scientists who had laughed the loudest and longest was so mortified that he committed suicide.

Undaunted and still uninterested in all this commotion, Schliemann took the treasures of the Trojans and sailed for Greece. There again, he got out his maps, and followed foot by foot the printed page and uncovered the graves of his heroes.

It is a sad comment upon the egotism of the rigid mind of a supposedly brilliant scientist, that he could not stand the shock of facing the fact that he was wrong. Perhaps it was not so much that his theory was overthrown, but by a Homer-loving layman. Did someone hear Homer laughing?

Thus began a new horizon of prehistory.

For the lover of Homer, it is pleasant to know that there once existed a Helen of whom another poet wrote:

"Is this the face that launched a thousand ships
And burned the topless towers of Illium?"

And for the lover of the French capitol on the Seine, it gives one more understanding of its never-ending youth, to realize that there was a real Prince of the Trojan House of Priam, charming but indiscreet, who finally escaped the flames of the burning city and made his way to France, where according to legend, he bequeathed to his many sons and daughters that deathless personal magnetism and carefree nature which was his - in Paris - the city which still bears his name.

Most of the people who regard the ancient legend as a fable have never read it. There is something convincing about the description of Atlantis, the most vivid painting of a living city of that time which we possess. The noise of the traders where the ships came in to tie up to the docks, the homes of the wealthy and their sports, the manner in which the city-state provided for surprise attacks, the manner of living for the great majority of the people, how the army and navy were maintained, and even the magnificence of the temple, undoubtedly almost unbelievable to the Greeks of Plato's city is not strange to anyone who has read of the city in Prescott's Conquest of Peru. In the latter city it was all duplicated - the painted columns, the great sculptured figures of the past, the lavish use of silver gold and jewels, even to the splashing of blood of sacrifices on the temple columns, all this was Peru. The main difference seems to have been that Peru did not have the horse and chariot, nor the ships of Atlantis. Both locations were noted for the variety of foods which they used, and in this field certainly there is a fertile realm for future research.

As we read what has come down to us of the tale of the lost land, remember that the histories which once existed have been burned and this story itself escaped the flames when Constantinople fell to the torches of the Turks. Attempt to read it with an open mind and ask yourself as you read: is this a fable; or did Plato write the story with the notes of Solon before him, careful notes on details of a city-state, foreign to the author but interesting, not so much for its final doom as for its living construction as a state? Is this a wild tale; or the details of how a city of antiquity once lived - such details as a future man of the Athenian Senate who was interested in a prosperous city, might note down, given the opportunity to pursue their ancient history?

Let us keep in mind that the very name Atlantic is neither an Aryan nor a Semitic word, nor is it to be found in any of the languages of Europe or Asia..Yet in most of the languages of the Eastern tribes of the Americas "atl" is "water". The k sound always stands for "people" in most Amerind (American Indian) tongues, which would make "Atlantic" mean "the people of the sea". "Antis" often means either "eastern" or "copper", which could make Atlantis - "the eastern copper land".

Coincidence? Perhaps. We know of the Atlas range that bends around the shoulder of Africa, and the old Mediterranean god Atlas who balanced the earth on his shoulders, shaking it with earthquakes every time he shifted his position. Yet the word is not a root word except in America.

One wishes devoutly that Plato, or perhaps Solon, had been more careful about the original names. However, it was the custom of the day both in Greece and Egypt, to find out the meaning and then to translate them. Perhaps Atlas had no meaning for them, nor did Atlantis, nor the Atlantic ocean.

Now as to the Atlantis legend. The setting is in the oldest temple of the city of Sais (today's Port Said) Egypt, namely the fire god Volcan. The date was about 600 B.C. Strange it is that Egypt, which had no volcanoes, should build a temple to the fire god, yet she continued to do so as long as she was a free land. Was it because it was Volcan's people (Egyptians) who came up the Nile from the Mediterranean in the forgotten past?

Here in the temple of Volcan an aged sage, priest and librarian waited to speak with youthful Solon who had been sent to Egypt to complete his education. Solon had sought out this temple because he knew that there were the ancient books carrying the history of the ages. Our books today are as yesterday compared to the antiquity sought by young Solon, for somewhere in the vast cool recesses of this giant building was the library which linked his world with that of forgotten empires.

Walk with him into the torch-lit twilight of the soaring columns whose painted scenes lose themselves in the darkness. Surrounded by the paintings of what even in that day was tremendous antiquity (we possess nothing to compare to it today), it is no wonder that the mind of the young traveler should be on the past. We have advanced over his knowledge in one respect - when these men of two thousand years ago speak of "goddesses" they are thinking of actual divinities, for this was their religion and religions are always somewhat insulated from the mind and its reason; but to us these so-called divinities of theirs have too many human traits to be actual creator gods. Historians are beginning to think of them as prehistorical kings and queens; although it is possible that one name may be a title and stand for an entire dynasty. Especially is this true when they divide or proportion the land and make laws governing it. This is true of Atlas and Uranus or Oannes, and the names for him. Poseidon is the Greek name of Oceanus, and Neptune, the Latin. These may have been the titles for the kings of various islands in the great oceanic league. Possibly the first was Uranus-Oannes-Oceanus and following the invasion by another people who then rebuilt the land, the leader became Atlas, and this title continued down through the dynasty.

It is also to be doubted that these well-fortified cities could have been conquered by normal methods of war. The invasions probably followed tremendous natural catastrophes when great portions of the various islands were lost to the sea, and the resultant tidal waves wiped out the population, for it is probable that the ridge had been crumbling off along its rifts for millennia. It is normal that on such an unstable portion of the earth, the main diety should be the fire god.

Under these circumstances it would appear that the city-state pictured by Plato was not one of the early powers, for not enough importance is given to the fire god. Also cattle were hunted in the temple and eaten. This then is an enemy totem, for no people eats its own totem animal. The fact that these Atlanteans have horses would point to a late conquest - probably the last before the destruction. The use of "twins" is symbolical as no man has five sets of twins. This would refer to the twin-star or Venus calendar so widely used among Amerind tribes from the top of North America to the snows of the South American Andes. With the calculation of time by the Venus calendar and its necessary astronomical observations, comes the "double rule" of almost all Amerind tribes - vested in a Peace and a War chief always conferring together. The use of the number ten is alien to this culture, and indicates the later one which came in with the horse and wheel. With these patterns of culture fairly well understood, return to Sais Egypt in the year 600 B.C. and listen to what the famous priest Senehis (or others?) has to say to the youthful Solon:

THE TIMAEUS BY PLATO

CRITIAS: Then listen, Socrates, to a strange tale, which is however, certainly true, as Solon. who was the wisest of the seven sages declared. He was a relative and a great friend of my great-grandfather, Dropidas, as he himself says in several of his poems, and Dropidas told Critias, my grandfather, who remembered and told us, that there were of old great and marvelous actions of the Athenians, which have passed into oblivion through time and the destruction of the human race - and one in particular, which was the greatest of them all, the recital of which will be a suitable testimony of our gratitude to you.

SOCRATES: Very good, and what is this ancient famous action of which Critias spoke, not as a mere legend, but as a veritable action of the Athenian State, which Solon recounted?

CRITIAS: I will tell an old-world story which I heard from an aged man, for Critias was, as he said, at that time nearly ninety years of age, and I was about ten years of age. Now the day was that day, the third of the Festival of the Apaturia, which is called the registration of youth, at which according to custom, our parents give prizes for recitations, and the poems of several poets were recited by us boys, and many of us sang the poems of Solon, which were new at the time. One of our tribe, either because this was his real opinion or because he thought that he would please Critias, said that in his judgment, Solon was not only the wisest of men but the noblest of poets. The old man, I well remember, brightened up at this and said, smiling: "Yes Amynander, if Solon had only like other poets made poetry the business of his life, and had completed the tale which he brought with him from Egypt, and had not been compelled by reason of the factions and troubles he found stirring in his country when he came home to attend to other matters, he would have been as famous as Homer or Hesiod or any other poet."

"And what was that poem about Critias?"

"About the greatest action which the Athenians ever did, and which ought to have been most famous, but which, through the lapse of time and the destruction of the actors, has not come down to us."

"Tell us," said another, "the whole story, and from whom Solon heard this veritable history."

"At the head of the Egyptian delta, where the river Nile divides, there is a certain district which is called the district of Sais, and the great city of the district is also called Sais, and is the city from which sprang Amasis the king. And the citizens have a deity who is their foundress. In the Egyptian tongue she is called Neith, but she is asserted by them to be the same whom we call Athene. Now the citizens of this city are great lovers of the Athenians, and say that they are in some way related to us. Thither came Solon, who was received by them with great honor, and he asked the priests, who were most skilled in all such matters, about antiquity, and made the discovery that neither he nor any other Greek knew anything worth mentioning about the times of old. On one occasion, when he was drawing them on to speak of antiquity, he began to tell about the most ancient things in our part of the world - about Phoroneus, who is called the First, and in whose time occurred the flood of Ogygia, and about Niobe, "Mother by Zeus of Pelasgus (man of the sea)" and after the deluge of Deucalion to tell of the lives of Deucalion and Pyrrha (fire goddess) who landed from a vessel on Mount Parnassus after nine days, and then he traced the geneology of their descendants, thus attempting to tell how many years old were the events of which he was speaking and thus give the dates. Thereupon one of the priests, who was of a great age, said "O Solon, Solon, you Greeks are but children, and there is never an old man who is a Greek." Solon, hearing this said: "What do you mean?" "I mean to say that in mind you are all young, for there is no opinion handed down among you by ancient tradition, nor any science which is hoary with age. And I will tell you the reason. There have been, and there will be again, many destructions of mankind arising out of varied causes. You have preserved a story that Phaethon, the child of Helios, the sun, having yoked the steeds of his father's chariot, because he was not able to drive them in the path of his father's usual path, burned up all that was on top of the earth and was himself destroyed by a thunderbolt. Now this has the form of a myth, but really it signified a deviation from their courses of the bodies moving around the earth, and in the heavens, and indeed a great conflagration of things upon recurring at long intervals of time. When this happens, those who live upon the mountains and in dry and lofty places, are more liable to meet destruction than those who dwell by rivers or the sea shore. From this calamity the fact that we live on the low-lying land by the Nile, who is our savior, we are delivered. When, on the other hand, the gods purge the earth with a deluge of water, among you herdsmen and shepherds on the mountains are the survivors, whereas those of you who live in cities are swept away by the waters into the sea. In this country the water comes not from the heavens but up from below and these are predictable and help the crops, for which reason it is said that the libraries preserved here are the oldest.

"The fact is, that whenever the winter frost or summer sun does not prevent, the human race is always increasing, and when nature does interfere it diminishes. Whatever has happened to your country or to ours or to any other region of which we are informed, if any actions which are noble or great, or in any other way remarkable have taken place, it has been written down of old in histories, and is preserved in our temples. Whereas, you and the other nations having just provided yourselves with letters and other things which states require, the stream from the heavens descends like a pestilence, and leaves you with only those who are destitute of letters and learning, and thus you must begin all over again as children who know nothing of the past, or what has happened in ancient times either among other nations or among yourselves."

"As for those geneaologies of yours which you have recounted to us Solon, they are no better than the tales of children, for in the first place, you remember one deluge only, where there were four with many lesser ones. In the next place, you do not know that there were dwelling in this land of yours one of the noblest races ever to have lived of whom your land and your people are only a remnant. And this was unknown to you because for many generations the survivors of that destruction left you no histories. There was a time Solon, before the great deluge, when the city of Athens was the first in war and was preeminent for the excellence of her laws, and is said to have performed the noblest deeds and have the fairest constitutions of any of which history tells upon the earth."

Solon marvelled at this and earnestly requested the priest to inform him exactly and in order, about these former citizens of his land. "You are welcome to hear about them, Solon, both for your own sake and for that of your city, and above all for the sake of the goddess who is the common ancestor, mother and guardian of both our peoples. She founded your city a thousand years before ours, when Gaea and Hephaestus (Greek name for Volcan or Vulcan) established your race, and then she founded ours, the constitution of which is set down in our sacred registers as eight thousand years old. As touching the citizens of 9000 years ago I will briefly inform you of their laws and of the noblest of their actions; and the exact particulars of the whole, we will hereafter go through at our leisure in the sacred registers, themselves. If you compare these laws with your own, you will find that many of ours are the counterpart of yours, as they were in the olden time. In the first place there is the caste of priests, which is separated from all the others. Next there are the artificers who exercise their several crafts by themselves, and without admixture of any other, and also there is the class of shepherds and of hunters, as well as that of husbandmen; and you will observe too, that the warriors of Egypt are separated from all the other classes, and are commanded by the law only to engage in war; moreover the weapons with which they are equipped are shields and spears, and this the goddess taught first among you and then in Asiatic countries, and we among the Asiatics first adopted." (Note this implies that weapons were first of the sea peoples - the lance being a serpent instrument, and that the first Egyptians were farther to the east - this being their name for that location - Asia. Thus weapons went from west to east.)

"Then as to wisdom, do you observe what care the law took from the very first, searching out and comprehending the whole order of things even down to prophecy and medicine with a view to health, and out of these divine elements drawing what was needful for human life, and adding every sort of knowledge which was connected with them? All this order and arrangement, the goddess first imparted to you when establishing your city; and she chose the spot of earth in which you were born, because she saw that the happy temperament of the seasons in that land would produce the wisest men. Wherefore the goddess, who was a lover of both war and wisdom, selected, and first of all settled that spot which was the most likely to produce men like herself. There you dwelt, having such laws as these and still better ones, and excelled all mankind in virtue, as became the children and disciples of the gods. Many great and wonderful deeds are recorded of your state in our histories, but one exceeds all the rest. These histories tell of a mighty power which was aggressing wantonly against the whole of Europe and of Asia. To this invasion you put an end. This power had landed on the Atlantic coast, for in those days the sea was navigable from an island which was west of the straits which you call the Pillars of Hercules. The island was larger than Libya and Asia combined and from the island you could reach other islands, and from these islands you might pass through to the opposite continent, which surrounded the true ocean; for this sea which is within the Columns of Hercules is only a harbor, having a narrow entrance, but that other is a real sea, and the surrounding land may most truly be called a continent. Now this island was called Atlantis and was the heart of a great and powerful empire which had rule over the whole island and several others, as well as over parts of the continent, and, besides these, they had subjected parts of Libya as far as Egypt, and of Europe as far as Tyrrhenia." (Note - Tyrrhenia, the ancient name for Etruscan Italy.)

"This vast power, now gathered into one, endeavored to subdue at one blow our country and yours, and the whole of the land which was within the straits. Then Solon, your country shone forth in the excellence of her virtue and strength, among all mankind for she was the first in courage and military skill, and was the leader of the Hellenic allies. When the rest fell off from her, being thus compelled to stand alone, after having undergone the extremity of danger, she defeated and triumphed over the invaders, and preserved from slavery those who were not yet subjected, and freely liberated all the others who dwelt within the limits of Heracles.

"Then afterward, there occurred the most violent of earthquakes and floods, in a single day and night of rain and horror all your war-like men in a body sank into the earth, and the island of Atlantis, in like manner disappeared beneath the sea. And that is why the sea in those parts is impassable and impenetrable, because there is such a quantity of shallow mud in the way caused by the subsidence of the island."

FROM THE CRITIAS BY PLATO

"But in addition to the gods whom you have mentioned, I would specially invoke Mnemosyne; for all the important part of what I have to tell is dependent upon her favor. If I can recollect and recite enough of what was said by the priests, and brought hither by Solon, I doubt not that I shall satisfy the requirements of this theatre. To that task I will at once address myself.

"Let me begin by observing, first of all, that nine thousand was the sum of years which had elapsed since the war which took place between the people who dwelt outside the Pillars of Hercules and all those who dwelt within them. This war I am now to describe. Of the combatants on the one side, the city of Athens was reported to have been the ruler, and to have directed the contest while the combatants of the other side were led by the kings of the island of Atlantis, which, as I was saying once had an extent greater than that of Libya and Asia, and afterward, sunk by an earthquake, became an impassable barrier of mud to voyagers wishing to sail from hence into the ocean. The progress of history will unfold the various tribes of barbarians and Greeks which then existed, as they successively appear upon the scene, but I must begin by describing, first of all the Athenians as they were in that time, and then their enemies who fought with them. I shall have to tell of the power and form of government of both of them. Let us give precedence to Athens.

"Many deluges have taken place during the nine thousand years for that is the number of years which have elapsed since the time of which I am speaking, and in all the ages and changes of things there has never been any settlement of the earth continuing to flow down from the mountains, as sometimes in other places. It has always been carried round in a circle, and then disappeared in the depths below. The consequences of this, in comparison to what once was there are remaining only small islets which are the bones of a wasted body, as they may be called, all the richer and softer parts of the soil having fallen away and the mere skeleton of the land remaining. . .

"And next, if I have not forgotten what I heard when I was a child, I will impart to you the character and origin of their adversaries. Friends should not keep their knowledge to themselves, but share in common. Yet before proceeding farther in the narrative, I ought to warn you that you must not be surprised if you should hear Greek names given to foreigners. I will tell you the reason for this. Solon who was intending to use the tale of his poem, made an investigation into the meaning of the names, and found that the early Egyptians, in writing them down, had translated them into their own language. He then recovered the meaning of the several names and retranslated them, copying them down in our language. My great grandfather, Dropidas, had the original writing, which is still in my possession, and was carefully studied by me when I was young. Therefore if you hear names such as are used in this country, you must not be surprised.

"The tale which was of great length, began as follows: I have before remarked in speaking of the gods, that they divided the whole earth amongst themselves in portions differing in extent, and made for themselves temples and sacrifices. Poseidon, the god of the sea, receiving for his lot the island of Atlantis, begat children by a mortal woman, and settled them in a part of the island which I will proceed to describe. On the side toward the sea, and in the center of the whole island, there was a plain which is said to have been the fairest of all plains, and very fertile. Near the plain again, and also in the center of the island, at a distance of about fifty stadia (author's note: one stadium (singular of stadia) is one eighth of a mile, or 606 feet 9 inches. Its use began in the foot races) there was a mountain, not very high on any side. In this mountain there dwelt one of the earth born primeval men of that country whose name was Euenor. He had a wife Leukippe, and they had an only daughter named Cleito. The maiden was growing up to womanhood when her father and mother died. Poseidon fell in love with her, and had intercourse with her and, breaking the ground, enclosed the hill in which she dwelt all round, making alternate zones of sea and land, larger and smaller, encircling one another. There were two of land and three of water which he turned as with a lath out of the center of the island, equidistant every way, so that no man could get to the island, for ships and voyages were not yet heard of. He himself, as he was a god, found no difficulty in making special arrangements for the center island, bringing two streams of water under the earth, which he caused to ascend as springs, one of hot water and the other of cold, and making every variety of food to spring up abundantly from the earth."

"He also begat and brought up five pairs of male children, dividing the island of Atlantis into ten portions; he gave to his first born of the eldest pair, his mother's dwelling and the surrounding allotment, which was the largest and best, and made him king over the rest; the others he made princes, and gave them rule over many men and a large territory. He named them all. The eldest who was king, he named Atlas, and from him the whole island and the ocean received its name. To his twin brother, who was born after him, and received as his lot the extremity of the island toward the Pillars of Hercules, he called Gades and the region is still called Gades, which in the Hellenic language is Eumelus, and in the language of the land which was named after him is Gadeirus."

"Of the second pair of twins he called one Ampheres and the other Euaemon. To the third pair of twins he gave the name Mneseus to the elder and Autochthon to the one who followed him. Of the fourth pair, he called the elder Elasippus and the younger Mestor. And of the fifth pair he gave to the elder the name of Azaes and to the younger Diaprepes. All these and their descendents and inhabitants of divers islands in the open sea, and also as has been already stated, they held sway in the other direction over the country within the Pillars as far as Egypt and Tyrrhenia. Now Atlas had a numerous and honorable family but his eldest branch always retained the kingdom, which the eldest son handed to his eldest for many generations. They had such an amount of wealth as was never before possessed by kings and potentates, and is not likely ever to be again. They were furnished with everything which they could have, both in city and country. For because of the greatness of their empire, many things were brought to them from foreign countries, while the island itself provided much of what was required by them for the uses of life. In the first place, they dug out of the earth whatever was to be found there, mineral as well as metal, and that which is now only a name, and was then something more than a name - orichalcum. This was dug out of the earth in many parts of the island. With the exception of gold, it was esteemed the most precious of metals among the men of those days. There was an abundance of wood for carpenters' work, and sufficient maintenance for tame and wild animals. Moreover, there were a great number of elephants in the island and there was provision for animals of every kind, both for those which live in lakes and marshes and river, and also for those which live in the mountains and on the plains. Therefore the animal which is the largest and most voracious of them all was to

be found there."

"Whatever fragrant things there are in the earth, whether roots, or herbage, or weeds, or distilling drops of flowers or fruits, grew and thrived in that land. The cultivated fruits of the earth, both the dry and edible fruit and other species of food which we call by the general name of legumes, and the fruits having a hard rind, affording drinks, and meats, and ointments, and good store of chestnuts and the like, which may be used to play with, and the fruits which spoil with keeping - and the pleasant kind of desserts which console us after dinner when we are full and tired of eating - all these that sacred island lying beneath the sun brought forth in fair and wondrous abundance. All these things they received from the earth, and they employed themselves in constructing their temples and palaces, and harbors, and docks."

"They arranged the country in the following manner: First of all they bridged over the zones of sea which surrounded the ancient metropolis, and made a passageway into and out of the royal palace. Then they began to build the palace in the habitation of the god and of their ancestors. This they continued to ornament in successive generations, every king surpassing the one who came before him to the utmost of his power, until they made the building a marvel to behold both for size and beauty. Beginning with the sea, they dug a canal three hundred feet in width and a hundred feet in depth, as well as a length of fifty stadia which they carried through to the outermost zone making a passage from the sea to this, which then became a harbor, and leaving an opening sufficient to enable the largest vessels to find ingress. Moreover, they divided the zones of land which parted the zones of sea, constructing bridges of such a width as would leave a passage for a single trireme to pass out - one into another - and roofed them over so there was a way for the ships, because the banks of the zones were raised considerably above the water. Now the largest of the zones into which a passage was cut from the sea was three stadia, and the one which surrounded the central island was a stadium only in width. The island in which the palace was situated had a diameter of five stadia. This, with the zones and bridge which was the sixth part of a stadium in width, they then surrounded with a stone wall on either side placing towers and gates on the bridges where the sea passed in. The stone which was used in the work they quarried from underneath the center island and from underneath the zones on the outer as well as on the inner side. One kind of stone was white, another black while a third was red. As they quarried, they at the same time hollowed out docks - double within, having roofs formed out of the native rock. Some of their buildings were simple, but in others they put together different stones which they mingled for the sake of ornament, to be a natural source of delight. The entire circuit of the wall which went around the outermost one, they covered with a coating of brass, and the circuit of the next wall they coated with tin, while the third which encompassed the citadel, flashed with the red light of orichalcum."

"The palaces in the interior of the citadel were constructed in the following manner: In the center was a holy temple dedicated to Cleito and Poseidon, which remained inaccessible, and was surrounded by an enclosure of gold. This was the spot in which they originally begat the race of the ten princes, and thither they annually brought the fruits of the earth in their season from all the ten portions, and performed sacrifices to each of them. Here too, was Poseidon's own temple, of a stadium in length and half a stadium in width and of proportionate height. It had a barbaric splendor for all of the outside of the temple with the exception of the pinnacles, was covered with silver, while the pinnacles were of gold. In the interior of the temple, the roof was of ivory, adorned everywhere with gold, silver and orichalcum. The other parts of the walls and pillars as well as the floor was lined with orichalcum. In the temple they placed statues of gold: the god himself standing in a chariot - the charioteer of six winged horses of such a size that he touched the roof of the building with his head. Around him were a hundred Nereids riding dolphins, for such was thought to be the number of them in that day. There were also other images that had been dedicated by private individuals. Around the temple on the outside were statues in gold of the ten kings and of their wives. There were many other great offerings both from kings and private individuals, coming both from the city itself and from foreign cities over which they held sway. There was an altar also, which in size and workmanship corresponded to the rest of the art, and there were other palaces in like manner which answered to the greatness of the empire and glory of the temple."

"They used fountains both of cold and hot springs which were very abundant, and both kinds were wonderfully adapted to use by reasons of the sweetness and excellence of their waters. They constructed buildings about them and planted suitable trees, also cisterns, some open to the heavens and others roofed over to be used in winter as warm baths. There were the king's baths, and the baths of private persons, which were kept apart. Also there were baths for women and others again for horses and cattle and to these they gave as much adornment as was suitable. The water which ran off, they carried, some to the Grove of Poseidon, where were growing all manner of trees of wonderful height and beauty owing to the excellence of the soil. The remainder was conveyed by aqueducts which passed over the bridges to the outer circles. There were many temples there built and dedicated to many other gods, also gardens and places of exercise, some for men and some set apart for horses. In both of the two islands formed by zones and in the center of the larger of the two there was a race course of a stadium in width, and in length allowed to extend all around the island, for horses to race in. Also there were guard houses at intervals for the bodyguard, the more trusted of whom had their duties appointed to them in the lesser zone, which was nearer the Acropolis, while the most trusted of all had houses given them within the citadel and around the persons of the kings."

"The docks were full of triremes and naval stores, and all things were quite ready for use. Crossing the outer harbors which were three in number, you would come to a wall which began at the sea and went all round. This was everywhere fifty stadia from the largest zone and harbor, and enclosed the whole, meeting at the mouth of the channel toward the sea. The entire area was densely crowded with habitations and the canal as well as the largest of the harbors were full of vessels and of merchants coming from all parts. From their numbers they kept up a multitudinous sound of human voices and din of all sorts both night and day."

"I have repeated Solon's descriptions of the city and the parts about the ancient palace nearly as he gave them, and now I must endeavor to describe the nature and arrangement of the rest of the country. The land was described as being very lofty and precipitous on the side of the sea, but the country immediately about and surrounding the city was a level plain, itself surrounded by mountains which descended toward the sea. It was smooth and even, of an oblong shape, extending in one direction three thousand stadia, and going up the country from the sea through the center of the island, two thousand stadia. The whole region of the island lies toward the south, and is sheltered from the north. The surrounding mountains were celebrated for their number and size as well as beauty, in which they exceeded all that are now to be seen anywhere on earth. They had in them many wealthy inhabited villages, and rivers and lakes. The meadows supplied food enough for every animal, wild or tame and the wood of various sorts was abundant enough for every kind of work."

"I will now try to describe the plain, which had been cultivated during many ages of numerous generations of kings. It was rectangular, and for the most part straight and oblong. What it wanted of the straight line followed the line of the circular ditch. The depth and width of this ditch were incredible, and gave the impression that such a work, in addition to so many other works, could hardly have been wrought by the hand of man. I am saying exactly what I heard. It was excavated to the depth of a hundred feet and its breadth was everywhere one stadium. It was carried around the whole of the plain and was ten thousand stadia in length. It received the streams which came down from the mountains, and winding around the plain, then touching the city at various points, was there let off into the sea. From above, likewise, canals one hundred feet in width were cut into the plain and again let off into the ditch toward the sea. These canals were at intervals of a hundred stadia, and by them they brought down wood from the mountains to the city, and conveyed the fruits of the earth in ships, cutting transverse passages from one canal to another and on to the city."

"The fruits were gathered twice a year for in winter they had the benefit of the rains and in the summer water was introduced from the canals. As to the population, each of the lots in the plain had an appointed chief of men who were fit for military service, and the size of the lot was to be a square of ten stadia each way, and the total number of lots was sixty thousand."

"As for the inhabitants of the mountains and the rest of the country there was also a vast multitude having leaders, to whom they were assigned according to their dwellings and villages. The leader was required to furnish for the war potential, the sixth portion of a chariot, so as to make up an army of ten thousand war chariots. Also two horses were required and riders upon them, as well as a light chariot without a seat, accompanied by a fighting man on foot carrying a small shield, and having a charioteer mounted to guide the horses. Also he was required to furnish two heavy-armed men, two archers, two slingers and three stone shooters, as well as three javelin men who were skirmishers. He was

also required to furnish four sailors for the complement of twelve hundred war ships. Such was the requirement for the war potential in the royal city. Each of the other nine governments which went into making the Oceanic league was each different and it would be wearisome to recount them all here."

"As to offices and honors, the following was the arrangement from the first - Each of the ten kings in his own division and in his own city-state, had the absolute control of the citizens, and in many cases of the laws, punishing and slaying whomsoever he wished."

"In regard to the relations of these ten governments to one another, they were regulated by the injunctions of Poseidon as they had been handed down in a covenant of laws. These were inscribed by the first men on a column of orichalcum, which was situated in the center of the island, at the temple of Poseidon, whither the people were gathered together every fifth and sixth years alternately, thus giving equal honor to both the odd and even numbers. When they were thus gathered, they consulted about public affairs, and inquired if any one had transgressed in anything, and passed judgment on him accordingly. Before they passed judgment, however, they gave their pledges to one another in this wise - there were bulls which had the range of the temple of Poseidon, and the ten who were left alone in the temple, after they had offered prayers to the gods that they might take the sacrifices which were acceptable to them, hunted the bulls without weapons, but with staves and nooses. The bull which they caught, they led to the column, and the victim was then struck on the head and slain over the sacred inscription. Now on the column, besides the laws, there was also inscribed an oath invoking mighty curses on the disobedient. When therefore, after offering sacrifice according to their customs, they burned the limbs of the bull, they mingled a cup and cast in a clot of blood for each of them, the rest of the victim they took to the fire, after having made a purification of the column all round. After this they drew from the cup in golden vessels, and pouring a libation on the fire, they swore that they would judge according to the laws on the column, and would punish anyone who had previously transgressed, and for the future they would not, if they could help, transgress any of the inscriptions, and would not command or obey any ruler who had commanded them to act otherwise than according to the laws of their father Poseidon. This was the prayer which each of them offered up for himself and for his family, at the same time drinking and dedicating the vessel in the temple of the god. Then after spending some time at supper, when darkness came on, and the fire about the sacrifice was cool, all of them put on most beautiful azure robes, and sitting on the ground at night near the embers of the sacrifice on which they had sworn, and extinguishing all the fire about the temple, they received and gave judgment. If any of them had any accusations to bring against anyone, they gave judgment. At daybreak, they wrote down their sentences on a golden tablet, and deposited them as memorials along with their robes."

"There were many special laws which the several kings had inscribed about the temples, but the most important was the following: that they were not to take up arms against one another, and they were all to come to the rescue if any one in any city attempted to overthrow the royal house. Like their ancestors, they were to deliberate in common about war and other matters, giving the supremacy to the family of Atlas, and the king was not to have the power of life and death over any of his kinsmen, unless he had the assent of the majority of the ten kings."

"Such was the vast power which the god settled in the lost island of Atlantis. This he directed against our land on the following pretext, as traditions tell. For many generations as long as the divine nature lasted in them, they were obedient to the laws and well affectioned toward the gods who were their kinsmen, for they possessed true and in every way great spirits, practicing gentleness and wisdom in the various chances of life, and in their intercourse with one another. They despised everything but virtue, nor caring for their present state of life, and thinking lightly on the possession of gold and other property, which seemed only a burden to them. Neither were they intoxicated by luxury, nor did wealth deprive them of their self-control, but they were sober and saw clearly all these

goods were increased by virtuous friendship with one another, and that by excessive zeal for them, and honor of them, the good of them is lost, and friendship perishes with them."

"By such reflections, and by the continuance in them of the divine nature, all that which we have described, waxed and increased in them, but when the divine portion began to fade away, and became diluted too often, with too much of the mortal admixture, and human nature got the upper hand, then they, being unable to bear their fortune, became unseemly. To him who had an eye to see, they began to appear base, and had lost the fairest of their precious gifts, but to those who had no eyes to see the true happiness, they still appeared glorious and blessed at the very time when they were filled with unrighteous avarice and power. Zeus, the god of the gods, who rules with law, and is able to see into such things perceiving that an honorable race was in a most wretched state, and wanting to inflict punishment on them that they might be chastened and improved, collected all the gods into his most holy habitation, which being placed in the center of the world, sees all things that partake of generations. When he had called them together, he then spake as follows . . ."

Here the manuscript of Plato ends.

It is almost tragic to realize that the book of Solon called "The Atlantikos" never came down to our time. It was last heard of in the early part of the second century when Plutarch, a Greek historian, mentioned it in his "Life of Solon."

So ends the strange legend which has haunted men for over two thousand years. Remembering that Zeus may have been a very early king of Crete, one seems almost to grasp a lost history that fades between the fingers like smoke, and disappears.

Flying serpent of the Venus calendar

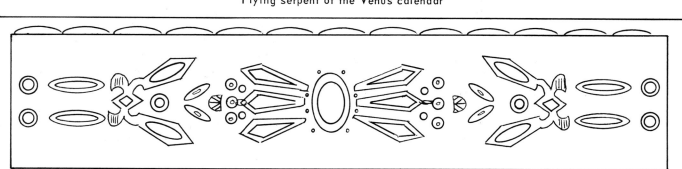

Chapter 3

According to the earliest myths and legends of antiquity there was once a lake Triconis or Triton lake where today is the Sahara desert.

Science does not disagree with this fact but first placed it before the time of man. They cannot easily deny the fresh water fish caught in the deepest wells, the few crocodiles which are still to be found on some of the oases, or the very interesting pictures drawn by early man of the creatures who once inhabited the lush swampy land of the Sahara. Since the discovery of the petroglyphs, science has again revised its view and now admits that early man apparently hunted in the Sahara.

Not only this, but the geologists admit that the Sahara may have been a lake. This happened before the time of the subsidence of the southern part of the Atlas chain. The massif can be traced from the bay of Gabes, running around the shoulder of Africa and dipping into the sea near Agadir. From there it can be traced to the Canaries and a few other islands to the south. When did the chain go down? That is the question! The people of Morocco and Algiers tell strange legends of their sunken land which went down in one day and night of horror with the torches of two hundred cities burning and the volcanoes belching forth fire.

The eyes of the Berber people become misty when they speak of these days. They will very frankly tell you that they are the survivors of the great destruction. Their land was known as Atlantis and they owned not only the Atlantic ocean but also the Mediterranean. One stares at them thoughtfully as one asks if they have the histories? No, the books were all lost but anciently they had books and writing.

They are definitely of the white race, and the eyes of many are blue or grey. Red hair is common. Some of the costumes have a strong resemblance to the kilts of the Irish, Scotch and Greeks. They also have the bagpipes. In their dances, it is to be noted that they point their two hands above their head as is so typical of the Scotch and Irish. I once met a Berber who was willing to give me some information on this. He was a big fellow, blond and more like a displaced Goth than a type to be found so far south.

"What is the meaning of the two hands pointing up and held high above the head? Is it a relic of bull worship?"

"I do not believe so, although we had cattle in ancient times. No, I conferred once with a

Scottish bagpipers.

Basque. They also have the kilts, the pipes and some of the same type of dances. He told me that the gesture stood for the trident. Since that time, every time I see it, I can think of nothing else."

"The symbol of Poseidon, the sea god!"

"Or Atlas," he corrected me.

"Or Volcan," I suggested. "Or the Roman Neptune?"

"Or Vodan whom the Germans call Wodin? Or Odin?"

"Then you believe that the Canaries are a part of old Atlantis?"

"Yes, certainly."

"And there was no island west of the straits

as Plato told about in the Timaeus?''

"I didn't say that. We had a powerful league of many islands. There must have been some powerful ones near the Azores. It is so long ago - all we have are legends and they tell us we were all a part of the great sunken land.''

Thus we strike a blank wall and remember sadly how Senehis said that men without their books become children, when the most learned of their people are swept away by disaster.

The legends of the "gods" and their lives, of both the Greeks and the Phoenicians, after a study in comparisons, become constantly more recognizable as garbled ancient history. How ancient? Just before the dawn of historical Egypt? Or before the time of the great flood which is the cataclysm that seems to be a dating period for all legends? And who were the gods and the Titans who fought in these legends of the old Mediterranean? Apparently this also is historical, for we even have locations given to us for the prison where the captive Titans died. Tartarus is referred to as a city of the "gods" and by the later Romans as Hades existing in the abyss, or again, a sunken city of the Mediterranean, the location of which is somewhere around Italy, apparently in the sea of Tyrrhenia.

It is to be noted that Zeus is sometimes spoken of as the king of Atlantis but more often as the king of Crete and that the great flood took place in the reign of his son. (The name of the son (or sons) changes, depending upon the people telling the story.)

As we continue to read about the ancient war of the gods and Titans, we become increasingly suspicious that they are earthly peoples - but who?

Then Baldwin and especially Boeckh (commentary on Plato quoted by Humboldt in History and Geography of the New Continent - Paris) writes:

"In the greater Panathenaca, there was carried in procession a peplum of the goddess Minerva, representing the war with the giants and the victory of the gods of Olympus. In the lesser Panathenaea they carried another peplum of Minerva, whose symbolic devices showed how the Athenians, supported by Minerva, had the advantage over the Atlantes." This shows definitely that the Titans were the Atlanteans or the Atlantides as some ancient writers call them, and the "gods" were the ancient kings of the Mediterranean league, or as we know them - the Pelasgians. The words on the peplum of the goddess Minerva in the lesser Panathenaea were "The Athenians, supported by the goddess Minerva were able to overcome the armies of Atlantis." This festival was celebrated long before the time of Plato and even of Solon.

The mystery then is why did the goddess Athene (who was constantly spoken of as "Titan born", the daughter of the sea god and carried on the foam of the waves) and Neith (who apparently was also of the Titans, bringing her laws and weapons to eastern groups) lead these groups against her homeland? Is the answer not time, and the rebellion of a lesser league of Mediterranean trading states against a more powerful and tyrranical Oceanic league? Perhaps they were partially related, and intermingled from many centuries of contact. Or if the westerners were the aggressors as Senehis said, then the invasion may have been a last desperate effort to obtain more land for conquest and colonization before the sea took all of their homeland. Undoubtedly on such an unstable location as was theirs, they had suffered many warning earthquakes with continual loss of land.

To bring this down to the scientific thinking of today, let us discuss the possible racial types involved.

First let us clarify two phrases this book will constantly be using to distinguish early wandering tribes: one is Aryan speakers and another, Semitic speakers. The latter, being predominantly easterners and coming into the Mediterranean in the Assyrian and Arabian invasions during the Second Millenium BC will not have too much to do with the book except through the interest of the Assyrians in the people who came previous to them - the Sumerians.

The Aryan speakers, on the contrary, show some very interesting signs of great antiquity, although not as great as the people who went before them into the Atlantic coastlines, and therefore will come in for their share of attention.

What is meant by these terms? Both these groups are of the bearded white race and suggest an original Asiatic homeland, to the north of the Mediterranean. However, the names Aryan and Semitic are both language terms, as is the word Berber.

It has been argued that these names mean nothing because a group of races as divergent as the Indian, European white and the Negro can all be using English. However, this is not exactly fair. It is a contact language in most of these cases and not an ancestral tongue. Even when two languages have a great many words in common, they still may be only contacts, showing a long history of living close to each other, and meeting the other language in trade. For example,

Phoenician and Assyrian have been thought to have a single origin. This I doubt strongly since the Phoenicians have the legendary name of Tyrrhenians, called one of their main cities Tyre, and had the secret of the purple dyes of the ancient sea peoples. Furthermore, there was a legend that Tyre or Tyr, who was the son of Votan, a Titan, decided to leave Tyrrhenia on the Tyrrhenian sea, and lead part of his people east to a distant part of the Mediterranean because of crowded conditions. The name Phoenician was not their name for themselves, but a Greek nickname, meaning "redskins". For these reasons I believe that in time the two languages will be found to be very ancient contacts and not of common ancestry.

How do we know when languages are ancestral, and of related peoples? Let us take the Aryan tongues: ancestral languages have the similarity in very simple words; contact languages in longer words. The Normans, when they invaded England, brought in some interesting long words, and these were soon copied. The same is true of the Latins when Julius Caesar went through Europe. Thus even though Latin is an Aryan tongue, the other Aryan tongues soon began to add Latin words for sophistication. The same is true of Greek. Thus almost our entire English language of more than a single syllable is either joined words of Latin or of Greek. (Microscope - Greek - micros, very small - scopis, to see. Or telescope - tele being Greek - long distance. Or Latin - interurban meaning between cities in that order.)

The one syllable words spoken often and constantly are the ancestral words. Let us take a few - mother, English, mutter, German, mere, French, mater, Latin, metera, Greek; or church, kirk, etc.; or night, nacht, nichta, etc. Very similar words will be found for father, sister or all family relations, many foods, etc. You can make up your own lists from Russian to Spanish and from Norwegian to Austrian, skipping then to India which was conquered early by Aryan speakers and through Armenian to Persian. Very often you even have the location. Russian da to German yah to English yes. The people who study languages can even tell the amount of time separation there is between the various groups. The three thousand year figure which is the most often given for most of the Aryan tongues seems very inadequate for some of the fringe languages such as the Norse, and Scotch-Irish, or possibly there is an early conquest indicated here over another people?

Returning then to the ethnic background of the people of Algiers and Morocco, we must remember that they have had contacts not only with the Crusaders of the Middle Ages, but also lately by the roving eye of lonely French men of the Foreign Legion. There may be reasons later than the legendary kingdom of Atlantis for the grey and blue eyes and the blonde and red hair. However, it is there as well as the occasional negroid type. Of the later, we know that Negroes have been drifting north ever since Egypt, and later the Arabs brought them up as slaves from the rain forests of the south.

Yet nowhere are the legends of the sunken land more convincing or more universally believed, than along the curve of Africa where the Atlas range runs out and dips down under the sea.

Geologically speaking, most scientists will agree that during the great time clock of the glacials, the Sahara probably went from a swampy region to desert and back again, according to the advance and the retreat of the ice. However, that is not what the old legend itself insists upon in this country. This was once a lake. It was held in by the curve of the Atlas range like the rim of a cup, and the water thus held covered the land from the Gulf of Gabes where it entered the Mediterranean to the mountains south of dry Lake Chad. Only after the sudden sinking of the southern arm of the Atlas, did the Niger river break through these southern mountains and tear its way out to the Atlantic. The giant lake thus formed, had made an island out of the Ahaggar mountains and those of the Air just south of them.

Upon the probability of this legend, geologically speaking, scientists are actually awaiting more facts upon which to judge. Survey teams are rare in the killing heat of the vast Sahara, especially when facing the possible harassment of viciously hostile tribes. Negroes? No. Arabs? No again. Of the people, the most feared are tribes which strike suddenly out of nowhere and leave dead or looted caravans behind.

The description of these people is curious and the very name enough to bring up the hackles of the hair of Arab camel drivers or guides who cross the Sahara. They are described as very tall men with relatively petite but lovely women who often have blonde or red hair. The faces of the men are never seen for they are swathed always in blue or purple robes, which leave nothing but their grey or blue eyes showing. The Arabs, who have probably never read Plato, shudder at the mention of them and speak in whispers of the "Blue Vengeance".

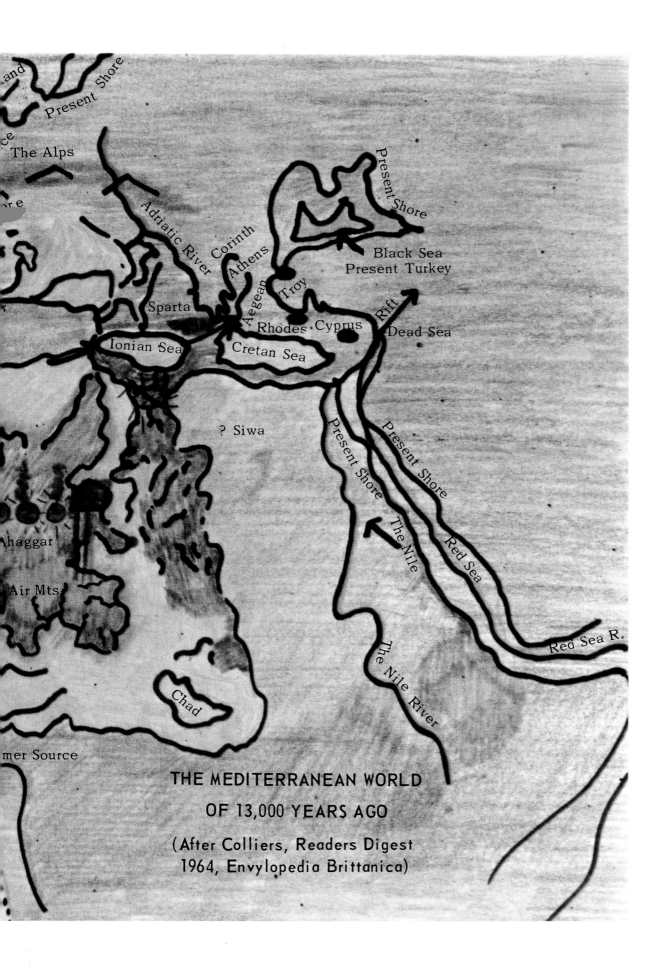

Present Shore

The Alps

Adriatic River

Corinth

Athens

Present Shore

Black Sea
Present Turkey

Sparta

Aegean

Troy

Rift

Rhodes · Cyprus

Dead Sea

Ionian Sea

Cretan Sea

? Siwa

Present Shore

Present Shore

The Nile

Red Sea

Ahaggar

Air Mts.

Chad

Red Sea R.

mer Source

THE MEDITERRANEAN WORLD

OF 13,000 YEARS AGO

(After Colliers, Readers Digest
1964, Envylopedia Brittanica)

The Nile River

Chapter 4

Does History Open With Astronomical Knowledge And The Compass?

"TWINKLE, TWINKLE LITTLE STAR, HOW I WONDER WHAT YOU ARE - "

This nursery rhyme might be satisfactory for children and primitive peoples, but - were the ancients all primitives?

Science would like to explain away the interest of the ancients in the sun and stars as mere superstition and worship of the heavenly bodies, but there are a number of facts which make such an explanation too simple, although it may be probable that sun worship began with the advance of the ice sheets when primitive men saw their world freezing up. Also it is possible that sacrifice, as such, had its beginning at this same time, when seeing the sun apparently becoming more feeble in the power of its rays to warm the earth, man began to experiment, in his desperation, with "feeding" an image of the solar disc.

Let us consider a few of the reasons why it is probable that some early civilizations, prior to the dawn of history, not only observed the stars, but also had the compass.

For one example, let us take the Great Pyramid of Egypt; the sides are exactly oriented to the four cardinal points. This is also true of the two pyramids which accompany the great masterpiece. We know that the Egyptians had a calendar as far back as we have been able to investigate the great civilization of the delta. History begins in Egypt with writing, star observation and ships. It is now being planned to start a large operation of digging in the bay of Port Said, which is the modern name for Sais. With modern pumps to get down below sea level, we may discover a great deal about the civilization of the ancients, although papyrus books, unfortunately, would not have survived the inundation.

In addition to this, it is now believed that some of the ancient monuments of the early Britons were for the purpose of star observation. When I was in London during the early part of 1963, I met with and stayed briefly at the home of the Honorable Brinsley Le Poer Trench and his charming wife, Millen. He had then just finished his book

"Men Among Mankind", and he convinced me that the great ruins of Stonehenge, England were calendrical. The rising and setting of the moon around 1500 B.C. when the giant stones were supposed to have been laid out seemed to indicate that they were so placed for the purpose of solar and lunar observation. Also, hiring a plane to fly above this antiquity as well as the very ancient site of the first Christian church - Glastonbury - he discovered what were giant zodiacal figures. (They are further described in his book published by Amherst Press.)

Dr. Gerald S. Hawkins of Smithsonian Astrophysical Observatory has offered a theory on Stonehenge which is very similar. His correlations taken on site of the antiquity of various stones and holes were then fed to the computer at Harvard university and the results showed that ten correlations with solar directions had an accuracy of one degree, and 14 correlations with lunar directions were within 1-1/2 degrees.

Dr. Hawkins also discussed the rock called the "heel-stone". This is situated where a long avenue crosses the outermost circle. The surprise in this stone lies in the fact that the line which joins the center of this rock and an indentation, shows the sunrise in midsummer. However, if the builders did have an astronomical purpose, the average horizontal error is eighty inches, which is much more than is to be found in the Americas.

On the steppes of Peru and Bolivia, great surprises are still awaiting the explorers. At one point on the Peruvian coastline three giant crosses are cut into the cliff face of the rock. tied together with lines. The tall center one is 500 feet high and the others to either side are proportionally smaller to give a sense of perspective. They are exactly oriented and no compass of today could have done a more perfect job for a surveyor. They were carved approximately two thousands years ago.

In the high plateaus to the east where today no one goes except perhaps a wandering Indian or an animal, are long perfectly laid out lines many miles in length. They are new to science because they have just been discovered - not by men on horseback or afoot, but by the only means in which they could have been discovered: from the air. Without doubt their purpose is star observation.

The ancient city of Mitla in Oaxaca, Mexico, is exactly laid out to the points of the compass. There are three hundred and sixty-five and 1/4 designs of pyramids - all different. There is no need to remind anyone that this is the number of days in our year.

The pyramids of Teotihuacan are probably for star observation. This ancient city of Mexico is a fantastic place to see. The city we call Monte Alban in Oaxaca, not far from Mitla, is just being dug from the ruins. The pyramids and plazas appearing from under the rubble are all oriented exactly to the points of the compass. Besides you will not wet your shoes if rain pours down on you while you are standing in the plaza. The giant sewers will take care of that, although we do not yet know where they empty because they have not all been uncovered, even though they are working perfectly. When I asked the professor of Mexico university who was with our party, if they had carbon-dating on this city, he answered:

"Oh yes, certainly. From 700 to 750 AD was the date of its fall to barbarians coming down from the north. Of course, we do not know the founding date."

"Are the sewers unusual in these ancient cities?"

"No, many in Yucatan have sewers; and in South America, as you probably know, Chan Chan had hot and cold piped water to its tiled baths as well as sewers. These cities also had roads, walls, roofs, etc. greater than those of Rome. The goldwork was equal to that of Egypt or Peru and the mountains were believed to have been terraced and irrigated as in Peru."

I was not surprised when later I saw a Peruvian vase being excavated from the ruins. Any archaeologist who was not emotionally involved would suspect trade. In the Mediterranean archaeologists would date the ruin by that vase's date in the land from which it came; but Dr. Espejo simply shrugged and said: "The Americans won't believe it!"

Nor are we through yet, with these oddities. In Ohio alone among the Mound Builders there were according to Bancroft, who wrote while the great mounds could still be counted, over 10,000 tumuli and from 1,000 to 1,500 enclosures. All the pyramids were, like the works of the Egyptians, oriented so that their sides corresponded precisely with the cardinal points of the compass. No modern cartographer could have done a more perfect work of surveying. They were able to form perfect circles and perfect squares of such accuracy that in one case, a square and a circle contained exactly the same amount of acreage - 20 each, or forty acres. Bancroft tells us that the Great Mound of Cahokia in East St. Louis was the size of Egypt's Cheops, and similarly oriented. It once had a terrace on the south side 160 x 300 feet. My grandfather remembered when it was torn down. Some men from New York had bought it and they ripped everything out, piling it about and selling everything at auction. He said that there were all types of articles including the most beautiful golden jewelry and parchment which seemed to hold writing. There were various types of cloth and clothes, all embroidered, which were torn to bits for their jewels. There were a great many articles of copper, a good many of silver and a considerable amount of gold worked in the finest artistic manner. My grandfather was a musician, and at the time not a wealthy man. He turned away, sickened.

It should be noted that the Mound Builders were river people. They definitely came up from the south and followed the rivers. They never seemed to have gotten over the eastern mountains, but they did go west, and pilots flying over Arizona and New Mexico have seen their handiwork in giant mounds which would be unrecognizable to a man on a horse. They not only laid out squares and perfect circles, but also pentagons and octagons of giant dimensions.

They also had weights, for bracelets of copper have been found on the arms of skeletons which are identical, each measuring two and nine-tenths inches and each weighing precisely four ounces.

They built giant forts surrounded by walls and ditches, with artificial lakes in the center. One such fort on the Little Miami river, Ohio, called Fort Ancient, could have held a garrison of sixty thousand men with their families and supplies. It is interesting that the Mound Builders had lines of these forts stretching across the land from New York through Central and Southern Ohio to the Wabash. Now that we have the tool of carbon-dating, there is much for our young archaeologists taking their degrees in our universities to learn. It is to be hoped that they learn of the mounds (what are left of them) before they spend all the rest of their lives in the region of the Mediterranean - interesting though that may be.

Did these people have a compass? If the mass of pyramids stretching across both North and South America as well as Egypt are all coincidences, then indeed we have a miracle. I prefer to think that they had not only weights for their massive work in copper and other metals, but also compasses for their surveying.

Now if these antiquities were oriented exactly to the four points of the compass for star observation - what stars were they observing? Ask any Amerind who knows the old chants and legends and they will very quickly tell you that it is the "twin-star" - or that which shines for part of the year in the morning and part of the year in the evening - namely Venus.

From the north of North America to the south of South America we find strong traces of the Venus calendar. Sometimes it is lost and garbled, and the people only remember the childish legends concerning the twin-star boys who slew the monsters in the "ancient Tla-Pallan" or the "old red land". If you take a course in the calendars of the Americas from Dr. Lizardo in Mexico university you will learn about the Venus calendar. I warn you that his courses are not sinecures. You need at least a minor in mathematics - advanced - and several courses in astronomy to keep up with his lectures. However, you will finally come out of the semester with the knowledge that the planet Venus, circling about the sun on an internal orbit, makes thirteen revolutions to eight of the earth. Thus eight thirteens brings the planets back again to the starting position. This is the full cycle of one hundred and four years. The half cycle is fifty-two years. If anyone tells you that the Aztec cycle of fifty-two years was pure nonsense and had nothing to do with astronomy, you can just smile like the kitten who was caught over the whipped cream jar with a face-washing task being hurriedly finished. Or you can gasp with amazement at the statement I once read in an early edition of an Encyclopedia (I won't mention its name) which defined the American Indians as "an interesting people with many fanciful stories but absolutely no talent for mathematics".

Of course, there were other calenders which the Mayans had - our simple one of 365 1/4 days a year, the Lunar calendar and the Tropical calendar - or the swing of the sun from Capricorn to Cancer. Every date is written in all four. They had a tremendous knowledge of astronomy, used the zero centuries before Europe; they weighed the earth - etc. Did they have the compass? It would be a simple instrument for the Mayans, so we may presume they did.

Then since the Mayans and probably the Toltecs (the great nation preceding the Aztecs, recognized by the university of Mexico as much farther advanced than the later warrior tribe) understood the precession of the Equinoxes (the shifting from east to west of the equinoctial points along the ecliptic), were the Americas ahead of Egypt? Probably they were not; especially since we realize that the great mind of Imhotep apparently guided the building of the pyramids. Was it coincidence that he should place the Great Pyramid at the point which is the center of the earth's land masses? Or, was it another miracle? The Egyptian priesthood were the guardians of tremendous amounts of secret knowledge. The Greeks knew that, and this is the reason why they sent their promising sons to Sais. It was their way of giving their youth a course at an Oxford or a Harvard.

The young men of Athens had grown up with the acceptance of an ancient war as today we accept the wars of the Roman empire. The festivals celebrating that victory had been celebrated before the birth of Plato. Besides, if there was any reason to doubt the knowledgeability of the Egyptians, the youth of Athens, trained in the technique of argument and enjoying the game, would have certainly challenged the story. In fact the erudition of the Egyptians concerning the distant past would not surprise them a fraction as much as they would have been amazed, if anyone had been around to inform them, that over two thousand years in the future, the young lawyers of many different nations, speaking various other languages unknown to them, would be, with Socratic humor, arguing out the premises and conclusions advanced by a certain snub-nosed, round-faced, stodgy figure whose delight was to seek out arguments in the Agora (market place) of Athens.

However, since Herodotus went to Sais to authenticate the story before the time of Plato, it would be well to pause a moment in our search for astronomical knowledge among the ancients, and check on Solon's informers, since he was a contemporary of the historian.

That Solon should visit Sais was nothing unusual for the youth of means and promise during the golden age. Sais, the great trading city of the delta of the Nile, was ruled by a king who kept Greek mercenaries to maintain order, and Greek tutors for his children. Sais had its period of greatest affluence between 697 and 524 B.C. The visit of Solon took place at the peak of this prosperity. The two peoples had a great deal of feeling for each other, believing as they did that their mother-goddess was the same. Actually the Greeks were only related through the Pelasgians, or the people of the sea, who had inhabited the Mediterranean before the invasions of the Aryan speaking Hellenes or Greeks. There were three Aryan speaking tribes to come into Greece - the Ionians, Corinthians and Dorians. They were so named for the style of the columns upon their temples. The Ionians lived in or near Athens, the Corinthians in or near Corinth and the Dorians in Sparta - the three main city-states of Greece.

Dr. Blanchard of UCLA, with a twinkle in his eye and his tongue in his cheek, once remarked: "One might try the experiment of making another golden age. All you need is some Aryan speakers who have a keen curiosity and love to argue, and mix them up generously with some trading-pirates for about a thousand years while you cull out the unfit. You might get another golden age. But on the other hand, you might get better pirates - who knows?"

Of course we must admit that when Dr. Blanchard was classing the Egyptians who were probably Pelasgians as "pirates" he may have been stepping slightly out of line. They undoubtedly did have pirates among them as the Pelasgians seem to have been a rough group of seamen on the whole, but there were two groups of people in Egypt. Upper Egypt consisted of the ones who may have been the "easterners" mentioned by Senehis. Perhaps they had drifted in from the direction of India, while the men of Lower Egypt definitely came in ships up the Nile from the Mediterranean. How do we know this? Because in the glyphs, the symbol for "east" is a drop of metal falling from a perch - or what seems to be a perch. The symbol for "west" is a feather resting on what appears to be a curved perch. Now the sign for "left" coincides with the symbol for "east" while the one for "right" is the same as "west". Since the men of the Delta brought in ships and writing, we have the picture of their entrance, as they faced up the Nile. This orients the ones who brought in the glyphs, but further than that we do not know. Up to now the archaeologists have been frustrated by the fact that we can not dig far below the water level of the sea through the Mediterranean mud and therefore we can not get down to the early civilization. However, as we are hoping, this may soon be changed, and a real attempt will be made to find the start of delta civilization and possibly the source. We do know that the delta civilization came in before the time of the invasion of the Semitic speaking Hyksos kings who were subsequently driven out. These "shepherd kings" in-

vasions were apparently the first glimpse a beardless people had of the heavily bearded Asiatics. But what was the homeland of the erudite "people of the sea"? We only know that with them came the pyramid, writing, ships, the study of medicine, and undoubtedly the study of astronomy and the compass. They brought in the worship of the fire god, Ammon, whose name was subsequently joined with the name of the sun god of Upper Egypt - Ra. The name of a fire god would immediately point to an unstable homeland where for untold centuries a desperate people were wont to placate the red fury which came from below.

This is why we are hoping that within the next decade the archaeologists will be able to get through the mud which the flooding of the Nile has deposited through the ages. This is not easy when the mud that the scientists are trying to penetrate is all below the level of the sea.

Also there is the difficulty in trying to penetrate the civilizations of the various branches and colonies of the people of the sea, and of meeting the inevitable wall of secrecy. The wisdom was taught to only a select few, to be passed on by them to others and to be filtered out when given to the people. This may have been necessary in a trading world of ships where locations of various lands were the secrets of the sea captains of the great league - or at least so they thought. The pattern is so strong that it follows us even today in certain rituals which no longer have life and death meanings. It is extremely strong in the Americas with the Amerinds. There are whole tribes which remember animal stories, but have forgotten the meanings through centuries of war and conquest, so that they have the tales of the Twin-Star boys and their adventures, as the Europeans had the tales of the adventures of Hercules and his twelve "tasks". Behind those tales which were told to children, the initiates in secret ceremonies learned the real meaning - usually bits of an ancient history. We are hoping that the archaeologists of today will be able to keep the water out as they dig through the layers of ancient mud to what may lie below, in the tremendously promising delta of the Nile.

Perhaps it is a commentary upon our times that so much of the dawn of civilization is again in danger of being lost in this very age in which we are living! The great dam which the Russians are building in Egypt for the Egyptians, to be completed in 1967, will cover priceless paintings on temples which have come down to us through the millennia of the ages. When the green waters of the Nile creep over them in that year, they will be forever hidden to the eyes of our children's children. When that happens our last touch with the Oceanic league or the great colossus of the sea - the power long before the rise of a land named Egypt, or one named Greece, will once more be submerged by the green blanket of water. And the tragedy of this is that the mud which the Nile carries to the sea will in a few years fill the dam and make it useless; but the antiquities - the paintings which Rhameses had made of the people of the sea - will be gone forever.

To return to the story told in the Timaeus, the Roman, Proclus, stated that Plato himself had visited Egypt. This would suggest that Plato made either an attempt to check Solon's story or perhaps, to add to it by seeking out his own information from the same temple and library. Proclus further adds to our knowledge by telling us that the priest Pateneit at Sais, Ochlaip at Heliopolis (Greek - sun city), and Ethimen at Sebonnytus were also visited by Plato. It may be doubted however, that the aged Pateneit, who was probably among those who talked to Solon, would still be alive in the time of Plato.

There is also another interesting bit of information coming down to us through the Romans. Without either mentioning Plato or Solon, (and it is possible he never heard of either), Ammianus Marcellinus, in his eighteenth book said flatly that the destruction of the empire of Atlantis was an historical fact. Was he able to see the books from the Alexandrian library?

Cranter who died thirty three years after Plato, and was one of his best known commentators, stated that the Egyptian priesthood was very much interested in the youth of Athens, generally speaking, and whenever they had the opportunity, they would take them to the pillars of the temples, and with torches show them not only the pictures but also the writing concerning Atlantis - as it had been left for the ages of the future.

Of course, behind the invading Ionians were the immensely ancient conquered Pelasgians who revered the mother goddess of their city and who had fought the Atlanteans in what would appear to be an inter-tribal war between two great trading leagues of the time. It is very much to be doubted that the Athens of today is the city which figured in this war. That city of the past may have existed upon one of the wide fertile fields of the ancient Mediterranean valley. Where is it today? Probably its wide streets and marble columns are under a watery sky where the octopus lurks in the ruins of the temple, while above,

the bottoms of the ships are to be seen passing, which undoubtedly still carry the great-great-grandsons of the lost Pelasgians of the Atlantic and the Mediterranean valley. It was not the Ionians in whom the Egyptians were interested - it was the Pelasgians who were the mothers of Athenian youth.

The Pelasgians were also in the ancestry of the Phoenicians, for the war of the "gods" and the "titans" is also all through their mythology. Just what triggered this war and where it was fought, as well as the location of the city, Tartarus, with its terrible prisons, will have to be left for the archaeologists of the future. Doubtless they will use some kind of diving bell which will allow them to excavate the Adriatic and Tyrrhenian seas. However, the entire answer will finally have to be sought on the ancient lost peninsula of the Atlas range, and the central ridge of the Atlantic ocean.

Pure fantasy?

Plutarch in his "Life of Solon", as well as his "De Iside et Osiride" states that Solon visited Egypt and spoke with the immensely erudite Senehis of Sais. Now, looking up this priest, we find that Clemente of Alexandria, Egypt, tells us that it was Senehis who was the instructor of Pythagoras of Greece.

Pythagoras, the man who first gave to the world the Copernican theory of the heavens! Centuries before Copernicus himself gave it to a startled world and began the renewal of learning which was to crack the wall of the dark ages for Europe! The knowledge that it is the planets which circle the sun and not the sun which circles a flat earth! The knowledge upon which all of our modern astronomy has been built and has been shown to be correct by thousands of telescopes!

Senehis taught Pythagoras? And the same man Senehis, as well as others talked to Solon in Sais?

So Senehis was the center of all this ancient knowledge?

That should pin-point, dead center, the great colossus of the sea as the power which mapped the earth in three sections (the sacred number of the trident) so many thousands of years ago that the U.S. Hydrographic Survey Office cannot believe what its cartographers have held in their hands. For this map of antiquity (one bit of parchment) is so far ahead of us today - in our twentieth century - that it has the whole world of science holding its collective head. This ancient and confounding relic is the Piri Re'is map.

Chapter 5

The Piri Re'is Map

Piri Re'is was a Turkish admiral who may have been one of the most widely traveled sailors of the Columbian era, or he may have been one of the luckiest "arm chair" explorers of all time - if we are to judge by the now famous (and also most mysterious) map that bears his name. Also, he must have "gotten around" in other ways with equal success, for the map was found in an old harem of the Sultan of Constantinople, located in the abandoned ancient imperial palace. It was while an inventory was being made of the relics of this old palace in 1929 that the yellowed fragment of parchment was found. The inscriptions on it were in a Turkestani idiom, written in Arabic script. It was dated in the 16th century and was labeled as the work of the admiral.

There are a great many maps of this period (notably another by Oronteus Finaeus which is probably of equal importance) showing what we know today to be quite fanciful lands and seas which do not really exist. However, the Piri Re'is map cannot be said to fanciful in the slightest degree - for, while drawn in 1513 A.D., it locates the continent of Antarctica even more accurately than our most modern maps drawn by our research expeditions at this very moment on the scene. It locates the south polar continent in correct relationship to South America also; but more than this, it shows as open land areas portions of the continent now under 10,000 feet of ice! This map could not have been drawn from explorations by Piri Re'is in 1500 A.D., nor by any other contemporary explorer, but must necessarily have been copied from a far more ancient map, one that was the result of exploration before the formation of the Antarctica ice cap! How long ago would this be? Present research on ice core borings made in the ice of the cap indicate that at least 10,000 years must have

passed since the first snows fell that began the build-up of this enormous two-mile thick cap over the now invisible continent.

There are other things peculiar to this map which astound cartographers, among them the use of longitude (correct usage!) in locating the various features of the continent. The ability to discover longitude was not achieved until the chronometer was invented during the time of England's George III.

But the most interesting fact concerning the admiral's map is that the shore of the south polar continent is shown as being free of ice, while today it is covered deep with ice, and furthermore, shows the areas to be inhabited by various fauna not suited at all to a continent not in a temperate or semi-tropical zone! In short, the originator of this map drew a concept of a continent that was comfortably warm at the time, and located much nearer Earth's equator! Since that map was drawn, a whole continent has "drifted" from two to six thousand miles! It would be too much to credit the arctic location to a tilting of the Earth on its axis; and it is theories such as this that tend to confuse the thinking of those who would research into the dim past to the realities that caused our continental locations today, with their very confusing magnetic lines that do not match nor confirm with the realities of the magnetic fields of the planet.

By means of "echo-sounding", and "seismic profile" of the areas shown in the Piri Re'is map along the coastlines in question, our scientific expeditions of the 1960s have almost precisely duplicated the coastal features shown in the map. They do exist, precisely as the ancient and unknown cartographer depicted them to be!

Antarctica was not even discovered until

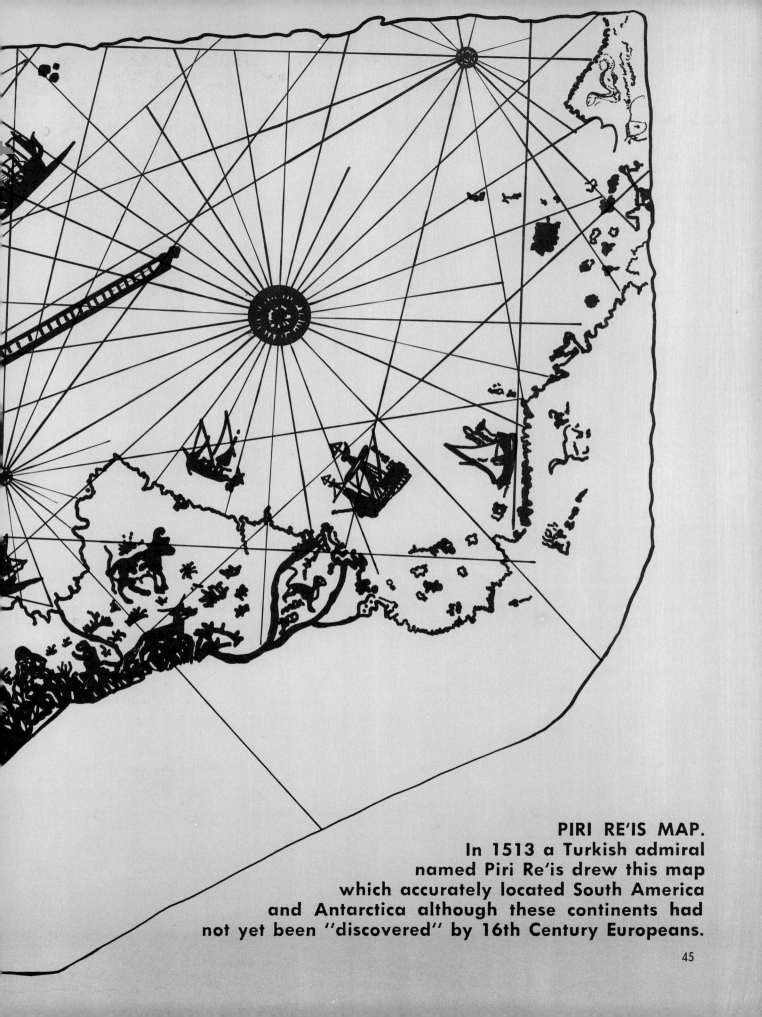

PIRI RE'IS MAP.
In 1513 a Turkish admiral
named Piri Re'is drew this map
which accurately located South America
and Antarctica although these continents had
not yet been "discovered" by 16th Century Europeans.

300 years after Piri Re'is. And when it was discovered, the theory was advanced that the ice cap covering the continent was millions of years old. Thus, no explorer who visited its tremendous ice shelf shoreline even considered the possibility that life of any kind, and particularly human life, ever existed on the soil beneath that tremendous mass of "deep freeze". Today, however, we know that this figure of millions of years is fanciful, and that the facts are much closer to 25,000 to 10,000 years as a date for an ice-free continent.

There have been studies made of sediment cores made along the coast which reveal "run-off" from the continent during more temperate ages. According to the dating methods used by the Washington D.C. Carnegie Institute, one such period existed some 6,000 years ago. Apparently, in its drifting around, the continent several times emerged from the south polar area and experienced periods of temperance. At the very least, the original of the Piri Re'is map was drawn under that last period of emergence, 6,000 years ago. We would have to give the dating a bit more antiquity to account for the fauna (and therefore the flora) of the area as depicted on the Piri Re'is map. In my own opinion, I would accept the date of 10,000 years as very reasonable.

The proof that the continent was moving is enhanced by the discovery that the very peculiar "projection" employed in the map does not today orient itself with modern projections. Yet the projection used is in perfect accord if the map is "twisted" about so that its scientific factors become readily apparent when compared with the best scientific projections of today's cartographers. In other words, the map's creator was a scientist of no mean ability, and one who possessed positive knowledge of the true shape (and size!) of the globe, and of astronomy, and of the best principles of navigation.

The shoreline features of the Antarctica continent are shown in their proper relationship to the South American continent, particularly the Cape Horn area, and this in itself, on the Piri Re'is map drawn in 1513 A.D. and showing South America with an amazing degree of perfection, gives solid basis to the non-fantasy nature of the Antarctic continent geographical features. South America also was unknown at that time, and no current maps of it existed. Yet, thousands of years ago, perhaps tens of thousands, the entire Earth was accurately mapped, but in continental relationships that seem more perfect than in modern maps. An example of this is the Oronteus Finaeus map, drawn in 1531. For instance, it shows the Ross sea area as charted by the United States Navy in 1960-61 with incredible exactitude, depicting each inlet correctly even though portions of them are today under the ice cap, and identifiable only by soundings through the ice.

Here, beneath two miles of ice, we may someday find the ancient relics of the mysterious peoples whom we will see come and go strangely without explanation or rhyme or reason in this book in the environs of the ancient Atlantic. But with the Piri Re'is map to ponder, a gigantic missing piece to the puzzle falls into place, and we know that great adventure yet awaits us in our search to solve the mysteries of the amazing ocean from which so many fables spring. To me, they are no longer fables. In this book I am attempting to convince you to believe as I do. You will find the evidence overwhelming!

Fossil fragment of jawbone of Labyrinthodont found in Antarctica in December 1967 in sediment layers of once subtropical stream bed about 325 miles from South Pole provides firm support for the Gondannaland continental breakup and drift theory.

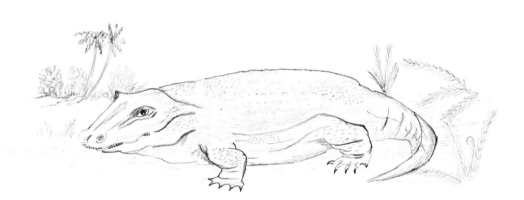

Chapter 6

The Glacial Rhythm And The Mediterranean Valley

From the knowledge brought to us by the Piri-Re'is map, civilization began during the glacial age before the interglacial time of the map-making. The old legends of the Mediterranean tell the story of a great leader who, finding his people surrounded by ferocious animals and even more ferocious tribes of men, gathered together tribe after tribe and welded them into a nation because he felt that strength lay in numbers. Then he had even a better idea. He told his men how they could clear a long peninsula of enemies, and since the front to be defended would be smaller, they could hold their land more easily. This led to the experiments with boat building. Doubtless the first boats were great logs hollowed out by fire, and moved with poles or (later) paddles. Once this art was mastered, it became easy to establish themselves on islands where they could not be attacked except by sea. This great leader's name was Orannes, or Oannes, or Urannes according to the people. Greek and Phoenician names are very similar for this lengendary history.

Probably this first attempt in communal living and communal defense by man began during the 50,000 years of the third heavy glacial when the land about the islands of the Atlantic was many times more extensive than it is today. On such a location, man's caste system, carried on down through the centuries by these people who built themselves into the most powerful sea-power on earth, was probably first established in the division of work.

Here too, began agriculture, in their attempt to be self sustaining. Some men were given the task of hunting, some of always being alert for the defense, some of finding plants which could be grown for food, and some for herding such edible animals as could be kept in captivity. Later other castes would be added - the caste of the mason or builder would be one of the first of these, those who were best at making houses and those who would be the best at making ships, etc.

Thus it is easy to understand why the first civilizations, and the most powerful, would begin on islands. There would probably be four of these locations - those colonies which began in the Atlantic and neighboring peninsulas; those who learned to colonize the Mediterranean valley. For at this time, the geologists tell us, the Mediterranean was a valley with a large river and two small lakes. The river wandered slowly toward the Atlantic where it dropped over a very high falls to continue down the Atlas valley to the south between the high peaks of the Atlas range and the equally high peaks of the central Atlantic ridge, finally emptying into a large lake. The falls can be followed today by oceanographers mapping the Atlantic, as well as the bed of the ancient river between the mountain ranges - now far below the sea.

Were there cities in the Mediterranean valley? According to Plato the Greece left today is but the wasted skeleton of the land which once was owned by the Pelasgians, or people of the sea. According to legend there was a city of Tartarus in the Tyrrhenian sea, an arm of the Mediterranean into which empties the Po river at the top of Italy. This has been partially explored, and definitely shows signs of the 300 ft. sea withdrawal, but has not been explored to the 600 ft. level. Suppose we call this the Tyrrhe-

Painting made from vantage point of the Roman Emperor Trajan's ruined palace on the island of Capri, Italy, showing how the land is sinking. Geologically, this is a "drowned valley". Artist E. C. Ripley won gold prize for this painting at 1893 Chicago Exposition. (Courtesy Elaine Beam)

nian valley. According to legend it was founded by Tyr, a son of Votan, emperor of the great sea power based in the Atlantic. According to Norse legend he is the son of Odin or Woden, and lost his arm in a battle with the great wolf. According to another Mediterranean legend the Tyrrhenians once divided, one portion seeking more fertile land, and sailing across the Mediterranean, and up the river, founded another city called Tyre, which with Sidon, became the strongholds of the Phoenicians. The Phoenician language at the time of Athens' greatness shows many similarities to Semitic, but this may well have been the result of borrowing due to much contact between the two peoples. There are too many other culture traits to class these sea-rovers with a land based group like the Semitic speaking tribes. The name "Phoenician", in Greek, means "red skin", a nickname which the Americans going west gave to the Amerind. Thus although the Phoenicians were completely

surrounded by Semitic speaking tribes, I doubt if later language students will find them to have language similarities any deeper than early and persistent contact; while, on the other hand, their ships, religion, clothes, use of the purple dye, historical legends, etc. all mark them as Pelasgians - kin of the early Greeks, Egyptians and Etruscans - the red skinned people of the sea.

Was there once another Athens down below the waves of the blue Mediterranean? The Greeks have always been men of the sea, and since so little scientific exploration has been done, I attempted to do a bit of investigation on my own.

One day, reading of new arrivals in the shipping section of a Los Angeles paper, I determined to follow this column until a Greek ship arrived.

Finally my ship was listed. I drove to the harbor at San Pedro and started engaging the sailors in questions. I found that I had a language handicap. However, I soon located an interpreter.

"How many of you men are divers?"

Several indicated that they were.

"What do you dive for?"

The answer seemed to be sponges, although evidently the demand is dropping because of plastic sponges now on the market at lower prices than they can meet.

This settled, I plunged right into the subject near to my heart.

"Why don't you Greeks who are divers know more about your own antiquity? Now you probably had cities before the deluge of Deucalion. Why don't you find them?"

I received some blank stares. I tried again.

"Let us take the Adriatic valley..."

"You think that the Adriatic is a RIVER?" the interpreter asked.

I saw I had a problem. Language was not the only barrier. There was a little thing called oceanography.

"No. I mean the valley below the sea. Now the Italians are getting ahead of you in exploring these undersea lands around their country. Di Marchi has mapped a great deal of the Adriatic river valley. He found one resting stage at three hundred and sixty five feet below, and it gave a very plain beach line."

As I waited for this to be translated, I watched the men's faces. They were becoming interested. I continued.

"The fisherman about Tunis say that a certain city below the waves ensnarls their nets. There are other cases. I met a captain of a submarine who, in World War I, was in the Caspian sea."

I glanced around again and watched the faces as my words were translated. The men were not speaking. They were looking at me with deadly sort of interest.

"This man told me that at one place, when they surfaced, they stopped for about a whole afternoon. The day had been cloudy and the men had been swimming. Then suddenly the sun came out at a low angle. There in the sea below them was a broken city. There were giant columns of a great Greco-type of building. Some of the columns were down. The strange thing about it was that the marble was pink. In the golden glow of the sun it was magnificent. The men wanted to dive down, but one found it was deeper than he thought and came up pretty well winded. The captain thought of how a report would look to the war office if he had to mark a death down as due to swimming to see a sunken city! The other men were now giving him a bad time be-

cause each one wanted permission to go all the way down. The only way out of this predicament, said the captain, was to give orders to move. The next day he was shown the wisdom of his move. A German ship saw them and gave chase, dropping depth bombs. Their sub went down and rested on the sea floor. Finally after hours and hours with their air almost out, they decided to come up. They couldn't. They were stuck in the mud of the bottom. When he found he couldn't move front or back, he gave the order to spin. They began to move but this was only digging a deeper hole. The men were gasping for breath. Finally they threw the spin into a forward lunge and broke free. Reaching the air, the men burst out of the hatch and threw themselves on the deck or along the water line."

As I waited for this to be translated, the men looked at me with intense faces, almost anticipating the next words.

Then the translator broke in: "Did anyone ever go back?"

"I don't believe so. He was living here when I met him and I am sure he would have mentioned it if he had."

"How long did he stay in the Caspian?"

"He was ordered out because the Germans had reported his submarine had been sunk, so the Navy made use of it elsewhere. By the way, there was an interesting sequel to that. At a dinner of the submarine branch of the Navy, a German captain was brought in during the last thirties to speak as guest of honor. My friend said that his breast was covered with medals. After dinner, he approached the captain of the German destroyer and asked about the medals.

"Did you ever work the Caspian?" my friend asked of the guest.

"Yes, once. I sank a particularly bad one which had been giving us a great deal of trouble. I got this medal for that sinking. It was the ..." and he named my friend's ship, who laughed and told him that he had not been sunk.

"How did you ever get out? The mud there is almost a quicksand!"

"I know. I found out."

"Then how did you get out?"

"As I told him, he shook his head and gave a sympathetic whistle. Then he took off his medal and with a laugh, pinned it on me. I'll show it to you sometime if you are interested."

The men gave a chuckle as the translator told about this incident. Then one asked a question which the translator propounded to me next.

"I do not know about too many other sunken cities," I answered, "but looking for them could be a fascinating hobby, far more interesting than fishing or roaming just anywhere. For example, if one could find an old beach line and followed it below the waves, one might find artifacts - I mean the tools of early man such as arrows and hand axes. Any museum should find these interesting, provided, of course, that you knew the exact location.

"As for cities, I believe that Sodom and Gomorrah on the Dead sea are now below sea level and may some day be found. (At the present time two excavation groups, one from each side of the Iron Curtain are excavating this interesting site below the Dead sea.) However, I was thinking of Greek cities - very old ones. It is my belief that there once was an earlier Athens - before the flood of Deucalion and accompaning earthquake dropped half of your land - the most anciently fertile part - into the Mediterranean."

As I watched their thoughtful faces while this was being translated, I suddenly exclaimed: "Talking to you like this, I feel like Diogenes seeking an honest man."

There was general laughter at this even before the translator got around to the translation. So they knew about Diogenes?

"I see you know about that old Greek. It might interest you to learn that at the university of Southern California, as one enters the portal of one of the colleges, the very lifelike statue of Diogenes peers down from the roof, holding his lighted lantern before him and looking with a most quizzical expression into the eyes of each student coming up the stairs."

When this was translated there was general good humored laughter. I was interested in the way they spoke the name - not as we have been taught in our colleges. It was "Dee-oh-gain-yees". I found their spoken language more beautiful than our manner of speaking the classical Greek.

"There are lost cities," one man volunteered.

"But we never go there," another said shrugging his shoulders."

"Why?"

"Because of the rivers."

It was my turn to become puzzled.

"He means currents," the translator said.

"Oh. Tell me about any of them that you can."

"There are whirlpools."

"But one of you must have seen one at least?"

They looked at one old bearded fellow who stepped forward.

"Yes. I have seen them - these cities of the dead. They have wide streets, many with wagon or chariot ruts. But they are like spiderwebs luring men where the sea can suck them down."

"Describe to me just one city."

"Once Creon and I, when I was a youth, were fish-swimming toward this forbidden place. We had heard stories - the kind that grandfathers tell around the fire on winter nights and we learned the location. It may have been your earlier Athens. We just wanted to see for ourselves - we were not going to stay long . . . we were foolish."

He stopped a moment as if biting his lips. One of the other men said: "You hear a tale no one hears any more."

"The city was enormous. The streets very wide. There was a building with great marble columns like the Acropolis - only the roof had fallen and the columns were scattered everywhere as if it had been a toy city broken by an angry child. Above us the watery sky was green and tall plants swayed lazily as here and there a big fish swam by. We began to forget the depth. Then it happened . . .

He waited for a few moments for the translator to catch up to the story. Not one of the Greeks moved a muscle or spoke a word.

"I was staring at some of the great columns. There were a few standing as if a giant of so long ago had not cared to push them down. I was coming to the end of my breath and I had to go up. I turned around to motion to Creon. He was not there!

There was another moment while he waited for the translator. I noted that he was biting his lips. The memory must have been very vivid to him.

"I had to go up to get my breath. I waited for a moment on the surface looking for him, but he did not come up. Then I went back. I had to. He was my friend. I came down to the giant scattered columns and the many buildings of the city below me. Then I saw Creon. He was being swept along around columns and down a road running into deeper depths. It was as if the sea, like a giant cat, had shot a lightning fast claw and snatched him like that - like a broken, tiny mouse." He made a swift clawing motion.

"I went up again to get another breath. Then several times I returned, but I never saw him again. One time the claw of the sea tried to catch me, but I am a strong swimmer and I twisted about until I shook the claw and came up. Now I could hardly breathe at all so I went home and told the men. They looked with boats, but Creon was never seen. I don't ever again want to see the city of the dead."

Archaeologists have acquired a fondness for the Egyptians. It is easy to become enamoured of a people whose remains one has been excavating in an effort to reconstruct a factual history. This is natural for the archaeologist. He reads their private letters. He enters the tomb where the young girl has hurried so fast to be in the procession of slaves that goes to its death with the king, that she forgot the wreath of flowers she was supposed to wear in her hair and crumpled it in her pocket instead. The scientist wonders as he tests to see why it was, millennia later, that she crumpled it in her pocket? Was she late because of one last goodbye to the lover she would never know again because she was to be buried alive with her king?

On entering another tomb, the archaeologist sees an obstinate donkey being pulled and pushed by two very annoyed and perspiring porters while the animal looks about with an unmistakeable twinkle of mischief in his eye.

There is a great deal to admire in amazingly modern ancient Egypt. Their life, we find, was in many ways not too different from ours. They painted themselves as slender and graceful with long slightly tilted eyes of exotic beauty. Their clothes are always a dazzling white. Their women lacquered their pink nails, curled their long hair (we have found the curlers), and dressed in graceful filmy gowns of almost veil-like transparency made of the finest of white linen, usually 365 threads being used to a bolt of cloth - one for each day of the year. We see them at their banquets being served by youthful maids and porters, eating delicately or sipping their wine or beer. About them play their pets: cats and dogs - usually greyhounds and daschunds. We see their musicians making merry with music on all types of instruments - guitars, drums, harps, double pipes, cymbals, lyres, flutes, castanets and the sambric.

We know that they had a talent for jewelry equalled only in the beautiful work done by ancient Chan-Chan in South America. Like the latter people, they did plating, as well as the most intricate gold and silver work. They carved carnelian, lapis lazuli, made glass and even filled teeth with gold. Their talent for magnificent and lasting masonry was topped only by the ancient Peruvians who lived in the High Andes long before the rise of the Inca empire.

Their early medical knowledge was amazing. They even performed delicate eye operations such as removing cataracts. It is a most fascinating fact that a papyrus of medical treatments was transmitted to King Sent, after whose

Bust of Nefertiti
(Unfinished)

Chapter 7

The

Amazing

Egyptians

death it was restored to the place where it had been discovered - under the feet of Anubis in the town of Tet (or Taaut? or originally Thoth?). Here again is great antiquity pointing to a time or a power previous to the chronology of Egypt. Let us glance at this manuscript. It had been rolled up in a case and was very ancient at the time of the Second Dynasty. King Sent lived in 4751 B.C. Was this a treatise on charms and incantations? It was not. It was an entirely medical treatise dealing with draughts, unguents and herbs. Many of them we do not know. Later papyrus rolls, purporting to be medical, were of charms and incantations. Here we have a strange degeneration of medical knowledge which is puzzling archaeologists today in Egypt.

They had other strangely modern knowledge. They knew how to temper iron to the hardness of modern steel. They used chemistry. They had single threads that could be subdivided into 365 other threads of almost spider-web fineness. They used both linen and cotton. Their cotton is of the long-thread variety to be found in the Caribbean sea and now believed to probably be a native plant of the Americas. They had the sun-dial, used gold and silver money, and raised all of the cereals of the old world. They had horses, cattle, sheep and chickens - sometimes using artificial heat to incubate the latter.

Their slaves were treated with kindness compared to the other nations of their time. The statement mandatorily placed in the tomb of every man was: "I swear that I have never incriminated a slave to his master." That was the first statement which he must face when he passed through the portal of death to meet his judges upon the other side of the veil. Egyptian slaves were taken in war as was the custom of all of the nations of antiquity. Many of the Semitic speaking slaves were taken during the Semitic invasions of the Mediterranean lands. After they drove out the Semitic speaking Hyksos kings who overthrew their government, they then kept the invaders away from their borders to prevent another inroad.

They were never as cruel in war as were the Assyrians. We see the latter in their pictures of their conquests, torturing their prisoners most brutally. The Egyptians, on the other hand, often rescued drowning adversaries in sea fights - especially in the great wars of the invading people of the sea. Also we see the great colossus struggling for land - which will not be lost to the invasions of the ocean? In all probability that is what is pictured. The Philistines, with their feathered head-dress so typical of the Sioux and the Aztec are depicted, after such a battle, as asking for land from the Pharaoh. Their plea was that the ocean had taken their homeland, and their main argument was that the Egyptians were actually their relatives, who should not drive them back to the ocean where they had no land any more. The Pharaoh, realizing that there was an ancient relationship, agreed to allow them lands, and gave them Palestine with their promise that they would help him protect his borders from the Semitic speaking invaders from the east.

The costume of these Philistines is to be seen again in the feathered head-dress of the Tokhari who were taken prisoner by the Semitic speaking Assyrians, pictured in the chained lines of Assyrian captives. Were these the

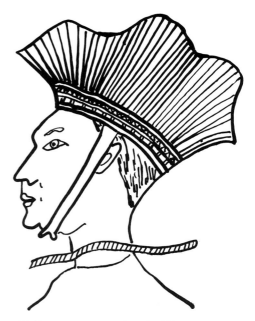

Tokhari prisoner taken by Rhameses III in a sea battle while fighting Atlantic invaders. From 13th century B. C. Egyptian monument.

Tuaregs or Tuarak tribes of the Sahara whom some archaeologists have called "the very ancient Libyans (world power before the rise of Egypt), preserved as if under glass," the same shattered people of the sea? The time of the invasions of the sea people from the west was when Rhamases III was upon the throne of Egypt. Among the pillars of the temples built by him are the frescoes and the pictured columns where again and again are pictured the sea fights with the ocean-going ships and armies of the people of the sea.

This claim of land lost to the sea made by the Philistines may have been true. Herodotus tells us of a giant labyrinth which he wandered through in the delta. Perhaps today it is under the water level which seems to be rising, or the land is sinking. This massive structure aroused the amazement of the old Greek historian who tells us that it "has" over three thousand chambers, half above ground and half below. These "are" a combination of puzzling courts, colonnades, statues, great halls and pyramids.

Of the things which we may see today, the temple at Karnak is so large that the whole cathedral of Notre Dame in Paris could be placed inside one of its halls. For that matter the whole valley of the Nile is one great vault of antiquity, while the delta from the catacombs to the sea was once filled with palaces, tombs, great squared pillars and pyramids covered with inscriptions.

There are other suggestions of western antiquity in the dress of the Egyptians. The costumes of the men who went to war have some links to the Libyans. The stiff skirt of heavy linen or animal skin to the calf of the leg, undoubtedly to protect the genitals, is called the "Libyan sheath" wherever it is found. Perhaps this was the ancestral garment of the Celtic kilt and the Greek kilt-like skirt. It is to be noted on certain ritual costumes of the Amerinds in America, when dancing ancient dances. In these costumes of the American Indian it is often fringed on the bottom.

Imhotep, one of the greatest architects and sages, was the designer of the first stepped pyramid of Egypt. Later, it became fashionable to make the pyramid solid with a shining cover like a giant four-sided cap, but one feels that the knowledge of Imhotep, perhaps learned through books of history and science, guided these later builders into making their monuments exactly oriented to the compass. The great pyramid seems to hint at other geographical and astronomical knowledge which later Egypt had lost. To have oriented these pyramids so exactly, both in Egypt and in the Americas, the ancients of the great colossus must have had the compass. These monuments in America, at least, are far too numerous to be written off as coincidences. They run into the hundreds when one takes both Mayan antiquities and also those of the Mound Builders. They go far beyond the law of the average.

The Egyptians also were astronomers. They probably no longer used the pyramid for its original star observational use. As time went by, this use was also lost in the Americas, but there is no doubt that in antiquity this was the main function of the pyramid.

The Egyptians had the ancestor of our calendar. The only way in which these calendars differ is that we have a five hour difference per year while they had six. One hour in over two thousand years!

There is another hint that Egypt - at least the delta - was peopled by refugees from another land. They arrived apparently with a court system, a full set of history books, and much other wisdom, yet not showing the signs of decadence which is observed in the Mayans, and in some

Tokhari prisoner captured by the Assyrians as depicted on one of their monuments. Was he a torchbearer? Date, 700 B. C.

degree, in the people of Chan-Chan, Peru. All three of these nations arrived in ships. The Egyptians show pictures of ships in their prehistoric graves.

Thoth was the god of letters and history in Egypt. This is simply a carry-over from a migration. No man invents history - not even Herodotus or Homer, though they have both been accused of this. Certainly they do not invent history and letters. (The latter seems to grow from signs and these later became condensed into letters.) Thus apparently Thoth was the leader of the great migration. How does this square with queen Neith? Apparently there were two migrations, perhaps of two different peoples. According to what Senehis told Solon, the queen found her people to the east. This would make them the Dravidian underwash of all the Mediterranean peoples - the men of the South of Egypt where they were driven by the later invasion up the delta of the Nile, by those who brought in the pyramid and all the vast knowledge of building and history which made up the Egypt of Greece's golden age.

Let us take a look at Thoth. We have to agree that no man invents history. All he can invent is fiction. Homer took down historical chants already ancient in his time. Herodotus took down legends which were told, often in symbolism. Both were historians. If he brought in with him the history books which were the glory of Sais during the time of Solon and Plato, where did he come from?

The Phoenicians declare that the Egyptian civilization was derived from their own. Historically this is extremely unlikely; unless we are mistaken about the Phoenicians. As science knows them now they were a Semitic speaking people living along the African shore of the Mediterranean, in the cities of Tyre and Sidon. They were famous for their purple dye, the manufacture of which was a Phoenician secret. But was that language of fundamentally root words that were Semitic, (as some have claimed) words that are due only to long contact and borrowing? The name of their city, Tyre, (they will tell you) was taken from their distant ancestor Tyr. According to Norse sagas, Tyr was the son of Odin who lost his hand in a battle with the wolf, Fenir. Mediterranean legends tell us that Tyr, who lived in Tyrrhenia, probably an early monarch, fought in the last great antediluvian war with the Titans against the gods and was thrown into prison in Tartarus, where he lost his life. Since the Titans were defeated, he was a Titan. Here we have an actual place. Tyrrhenia was where today the Tyrrhenian sea lies between Spain and Italy. The name which the Italians gave the Pelasgian people of Italy is Etruscan. The Greeks called them Tyrrhenians. Here we find a legend that Tyr once split their people and led a portion of them away in ships to found other cities. One of these must have been the Tyre of the Phoenicians. This would make the Phoenicians, Pelasgians or Tyrrhenians. As time goes on, let us see how this theory works out. History dawns with these Tyrrhenians known as Phoenicians (Greek - meaning red skins) using ships as skilled mariners should. I see no reason why a Greek nickname

should continue to follow a people historically. Therefore I shall call them Tyrrhenian-Phoenicians until we find a better name.

Let us see if there are any racial characteristics for this distinction of the Tyrrhenian-Phoenicians as other than Semitic speaking invaders from the east. When the Hyksos Kings invaded and conquered Egypt, the amazed Egyptians described them as "men with hair on their faces". This would suggest that the original Egyptians, both of the north and south, were beardless. They painted themselves always as having red skins. For example, when describing the four races of mankind, they took themselves as the men with red skins; the Persian as the bearded white men (they are Aryan speakers); the Assyrian or another bearded Semitic speaker as the yellow race; and a typical Negro as the black men.

Now the Tyrrhenian-Phoenicians could not have given Egypt the calendar, for it was calculated in the delta. Therefore, it is interesting to hear just how the Tyrrhenian-Phoenicians thought they sired Egypt. They explain in detail that Taaut (Thoth), according to their legends, was a child of Misor. In turn, Misor was a child of the Phoenician gods Amynus and Magus. These names sound very much like Anubis (The Egyptian god who had the medical papyrus) and Magog - the British goddess of the deluge - a queen who lived in the sunken land of Ogygia. Misor also has a familiar sound. Could he be the king Mestor mentioned by Plato?

When Chronos visited the Mediterranean country, say the Tyrrhenian-Phoenicians, he gave all of Egypt to Taaut for his kingdom, and Taaut came in with his people. This has all the appearance of an historical legend of the delta invasion. Chronos, we know, was one of the early Titan monarchs of the sunken colossus. Did this happen when the old land was in imminent danger of breaking up?

There are in historical Egypt some strange customs which hint of a homeland across a western sea. As R. S. Poole has pointed out in the "Contemporary Review" of London of 1881 and noted by Donnelly, the Egyptians always kept their city of the dead WEST of a body of water. For example, as a funeral procession moved to the tomb, they kept up the chant: "To the west". A model of a ship was always carried in this procession, and if the Nile itself was not crossed to the tomb (which was the most desirable condition), then it was proper for the procession to cross some artificial lake. Thus it is very apparent that the

Land of Blessedness was supposed to lie to the west; and to reach it, one must cross a body of water in a ship. Is this the direction from which Thoth, well versed in writing and books of history, once brought his people to the mouth of the Nile?

There are a few descriptions of this Land of the Blessed, the ancient homeland. The Egyptians thought of it as a mountainous land - a strange memory for a people of almost a flat river valley like that of the Nile. This land of racial memory was very mountainous, with high snow-capped peaks. A river ran through it which they said was named Uranes. This sounds like the name of the first man to collect the wandering tribes. It also reminds us of the God, Uranos and the Sumerian god, Oranos - the ancient king who led them from their flooded homeland. He was sometimes pictured as part fish and became the later Poseidon or Neptune (Poseidon of the Greeks and Neptune of the Romans). He may even be the Varuna of India - also an oceanic deity. He is sometimes thought of as the giver of laws and codes. Some legends say that he slept at night on the water. Apparently from this symbolism this leader led the Sumerians, and perhaps others, out of the flooded lands with a ship or fleet of ship; placing them on unoccupied but fertile land, thus once again restoring some of their lost civilization. Did this leader of the refugees from the destruction take his name from the river of the lost land? This is more likely than the story that Sumerians "crawled out of the mud of the Mediterranean, led by a creature which was half fish."

There are a few more interesting points before we leave the amazing Egyptians. M. Opert read a paper to the Congress of Science concerning the calendars of the Assyrian and the Egyptians. This was some time ago and thus was included in Donnelly's book. However, since that time we know from excavation that Assyrian and Babylonian learning was actually Sumerian - a language which had been dead for a thousand years when the Assyrians were in their prime. The amazing knowledge of the Sumerians was probably thus due to the books of antiquity with which they had been entrusted. These have been found and are now in the process of being translated in many parts of the world. When the translators have finished and given these books to the world, apparently literature and history will have to be rewritten.

M. Opert gives the following figures: The Egyptians calculated by a cycle of 1460 years.

Since they lost one day every four years (as we do, but make it up on leap year), in 1460 years the time is made up again and the calendar back to where it began. The Assyrians calculated by the moon or lunations. 1805 years is 23,325 lunations. The Chaldeans, he recalled, said that between the date of the deluge and their first dynasty was 39,180 years. This date, according to Dr. Opert, was in reality 12 Egyptian cycles plus 12 Assyrian lunar cycles. Thus 12 x 1460 equals 17,520 and 12 x 1805 equals 21,660 or 39,180 years. He continues: "These two modes of calculation are in agreement with each other and were known simultaneously to one people."

He then continues his argument by building up the series from our era and the results are as follows:

Zodiacal Cycle	Lunar Cycle
1,460	1,805
1,322	712
2,782	2,517
4,242	4,322
5,702	6,127
7,162	7,932
8,622	9,727
10,082	11,542
11,542	

"At the year 11,542 BC the two cycles came together and consequently they had on that year their common origin in one and the same astronomical observation."

Where was that observation made?

Perhaps we shall never be able to answer this question. However, it is certain that Egypt is the solid bridge of history leading beyond the time of our known earliest history, and if the answer is to be found it probably will be in the mud of the Nile valley - perhaps below the level of the sea. We have complications in what we have learned. There are either two dates for the deluge or there were two catastrophes. The priest who talked to Solon mentioned that there were four. (This has since been translated as "many".) Undoubtedly the answer was not only in the destroyed Alexandrian library. There must be other answers in the thousands of inscriptions on temple columns.

One fact is bitterly certain: if these antiquities are allowed to disappear forever without being copied again and again - then for a few years modern Egypt may be the winner of better food for awhile - but the entire world will be the loser in knowledge.

Chapter 8

Diodorus And The Amazons

Every year, during August, generally from the 13th to the 16th, thirty-six tribes congregate at Gallup, New Mexico, to perform their tribal dances. The gathering is popularly known as "The Ceremonial". It was there that I ran into some old friends, the O'Donnigans. I was in the great hall where the American Indian exhibits and judging on crafts are held, and where I have often found things of extreme interest. I heard Pat's voice behind me:

"I knew we'd find you here! We've been looking for you."

After all the greetings were over, I asked him why he had been looking for me.

"We had an experience last night," Pat's wife whispered mysteriously.

"Here at the Ceremonial? You are liable to - remember you are among the Indians."

"That's just it. We heard some Indian singing to the beat of tom-toms and . . ."

"Wait," Pat put in, "this is my story - but let's get away from here; too many kibitzers."

I glanced around, and saw some Navaho edging toward us.

"Very well. Let's have lunch somewhere."

We crossed the main street, elbowing our way through men with their long hair done up in the tight Navaho knot on the back of their neck, and Hopis with their raven-black bobbed hair held out of their eyes with the traditional red silk sash of these people. Lovely sloe-eyed Navaho maidens dressed in the ankle-length full skirts and colorful velvet blouses, set off with the beautiful silver jewelry which only the genuine handcrafted Indian work can set off to the best advantage, came giggling by while two young Sioux braves let out long wolf-whistles.

Finally we stopped. When we were inside, Pat said:

"You know I heard a cute remark behind us - did you?"

"No, I was watching the play between the Navaho and the Sioux."

"I saw that too! But this was an Indian talking. I turned around. He did not have on any tribal dress so I couldn't have told which tribe. He was talking to another Indian."

"And?" I prompted as we reached a table.

"He said: 'The Negro and the Indian will never get together. They've got two different goals. The Negro wants to be a white man while the Indian is too busy just trying to keep on being Indian!' "

"There is a lot of truth in that!" I said.

Then after we ordered our lunch, I asked: "Well, what was the problem?"

"No problem. As I said, we heard sort of a sing-song chant out past the Ceremonial grounds last night when everything was over, so we elbowed our way through a mob of Indians - Navaho mostly - to where a sort of dance was going on . . ."

"The Squaw Dance! I forgot that the moon is full!"

"Are you listening to me, or have you 'flipped' your lid'?"

"You came on the Navaho Squaw Dance! Did one of the maidens ask you to dance with her?"

"Yes. She pulled my arm and my wife pulled the other arm; I was torn between two determined females!"

I threw back my head and roared with laughter.

"That's just what all the Indians did! They were all around us slapping their thighs with glee - and we were the butt of the joke!"

"Certainly, Pat. You should have gone with her."

"Gone with her!" his wife turned on me.

"Yes . . . gone with her. She was only asking you for a dance."

"The women ask the men?"

"Absolutely. The woman has the choice among the Indians."

"How mixed up can you get?" Pat's wife asked with a puzzled frown.

"You two are college people - at least Pat is. Did you ever read about the Amazons in school, Irene?"

"Yes, I had a high school class in which they were mentioned - ancient history, I think it was."

"Well, we are dealing with a custom which harks back to the Amazons."

"Here in the Americas?"

"Yes. Apparently so. Here in the Americas." Pat began to laugh.

"Well - I'll be - Amazons and the full of the moon. That puts me in mind of a story about them. These were some which had been taken by the Greeks. I think that they were taken somewhere around Spain or Italy. Well the Greeks had them hog-tied and were going back to Greece when someone passed around the drinks. While the Greeks were celebrating the Amazons got loose. They threw the Greeks overboard and sailed the ship on to the shores of the Caspian where they got out and went to tearing up the country. This was in the land of the Scythians, who are either Germans or Russians - I don't think that the archaeologists have made up their minds yet. Anyhow, the Scythian king led some men into war with them. Imagine his surprise when he saw he was fighting women! He retreated, because his men were just bent on getting prisoners - the younger ones. He called his wise men into council and one came up with a good idea. He found about twelve very personable youths and sent them to the Amazon camp with presents, and told them to hang around. If they were chased, to run away, but go back again. This went on until one night the moon was full. The Amazons came out with long dresses on and took the men to a dance. After the dance they kept the men for four days. At the end of that time they sent the men home and told them to return in one year. At the end of that year, the men received their sons. The women kept their daughters. Some women left the Amazon camp. So when the king found out that the full moon was their weakness, he got the women away one by one until all the Scythians had Amazon blood."

I laughed. "That isn't the way I read it. The Scythians found that the Amazons just kept the men for pets and went right on raiding as before. But I like your story the best. Of course, you know it was Hercules who finally defeated the Amazons. He killed some and married off the others to his men."

"Are you quoting Diodorus Siculus of Agyrium, Sicily? He has a yen for Amazon stories."

"No," I answered, "but Diodorus is one of my favorites because he told so many stories of the Atlantides, as he called them. Remember the one about the city of Cerne in the Atlas peninsula where it curled around the Triton sea?"

"I probably never read that one. Besides, where is the Atlas around the Triton sea?"

"The Atlas peninsula was supposed to run from the sunken portion of the Atlas range eastward into the Triton. And the Triton sea was the lake which was once to be found where today is the Sahara desert."

"Oh come now . . ."

"For that we journey back to the time of the last glacial."

"Oh? Real antiquity . . ."

"Yes. The time of the Libyan empire when the Mediterranean was known as the Libyan lake - before the rise of Egypt."

"The time of the 'two swords of the bronze age', attached to the upper arm-band - the time of the Libyan war sheath?" Pat stopped suddenly. "Say, some of this reminds me of American Indian dance costumes!"

"Yes, I know. But don't ask me the reason - I have not figured out the connections - as yet. However, to get back to the Amazons, Diodorus said that there were two groups: the Gorgons who lived near the west coast of Spain, and the Amazons proper who lived in Hesperia. This had once been a large land in the Atlantic, but the sea had broken it into many small islands which, nevertheless, were famous for their minerals and jewels. They became known as the Hesperides."

"Sounds like Atlantis."

"They may have been part of the Atlantis chain. But the fighting which both the Gorgons and Amazons were doing seems to be tied in with the fact that the sea was taking their ancestral homeland. So they began to fight the Atlantides or the inhabitants of the Atlas chain. These people had apparently the same trouble with losing land to the sea and were seeking territory further east. While the men were away to war, the Amazons raided and carried off the women and children."

"Did they keep the boys?"

"Apparently. Perhaps they were trying to become a nation."

Irene broke in thoughtfully: "At the bottom of all this trouble was the inroading or eroding sea?"

"It would seem so to me," Pat nodded.

"Probably so. Perhaps the ice was beginning to melt on the ice caps, and in the recurring earthquakes of readjustment, the leaders all saw the handwriting on the wall as it were - in

The full-costume shield dance of the Kiowa eastern tribe - Oklahoma.

this case - in the waves of steady land loss."

"But you started to tell us about the Amazons," Irene insisted.

"Well, according to Diodorus, both the Gorgons of Spain on the west coast of Spain, and the Amazons of the Hesperides (which were breaking up) began to war for land on the Atlas chain beside the Triton sea. The Atlantides had their hands full trying to get land further east from the Tyrrhenians to Greece, and on down the Mediterranean which, apparently, then was a rich valley with two lakes and a large river. While the Atlantides were away, the Amazons took some cities and the Gorgons others. Finally the Atlantides, returning from an unsuccessful war, made a compromise with the queen of the Amazons, agreeing to accept her into the league of city states which comprised the Atlantic empire, if she would protect her border against the Gorgons. She agreed, and in the great war of the Amazon tribes, queen Merina (or Merynia) defeated the Gorgons. She had an army of 20,000 foot soldiers and 2,000 horsewomen. When they went into battle, they clad themselves in serpent skins and wore helmets. They carried javelins, bow and arrow and the short sword. Queen Merynia took 3,000 Gorgon prisoners and drove the others into the forests of Spain, where they disappeared forever from the pages of history.."

"No. Wait a moment," Pat said. "The Tyrrhenians, whom the Romans called the Etruscans, wore serpent skins and carried live serpents into battle, didn't they? Some Gorgons were mixed up in this outfit!"

"That's right. I'll bet that they were. Besides the Tyrrhenians admired their women and gave them a voice in affairs, as did the Egyptians. Remember, Egypt allowed the women to keep their own money accounts, and if they were unhappy in marriage, it could be dissolved and the husband was honor bound to give back the dowry."

"Women's rights back then!" Pat said. "Was that why Cleopatra ended her life with a serpent bite?"

"There may have been something ritualistic about it, like the serpent head coming from the crown of the Pharaoh."

"Let's get back to the Amazons," Irene suggested.

"By the way, wasn't there a Frenchman named Felix something or . . .?"

"Yes, Felix Berlieux," Irene noded. "He found a ruined city where the Sahara becomes a salt bog. I believe it was on a sort of mound that runs out from the Atlas mountains. He thought it was Atlantis, and ended up by calling it 'Cerne - a city of Atlantis'."

"It may have been Cerne, all right, but I doubt if it was Atlantis, unless you consider that the Atlas range is the lost Atlantis. Some people do, you know," I said.

"I thought Atlantis was out in the ocean," Irene protested.

"Well if you put a Triton sea over the Sahara, then the Atlas would become an island or peninsula. I don't really believe that it was Atlantis, but I do believe, or I am beginning to think, that the Atlantides were part of the great Atlantic league of city states."

"And the Amazons?" Irene reminded us.

"Did live in Cerne, didn't they?"

"Yes. The Atlantides rebuilt this city which Merynia had over-run and gave it to her for a capital. She was so pleased she populated it with the prisoners of war which she had taken."

"That reminds me," Pat said. "Wasn't there a claim that someone found some Atlantean ruins in Nigeria?"

"Oh, there are some unidentified ruins there, but they have not been excavated, much less identified as Atlantean," I said. "But there is a legend that somewhere in Nigeria a people named Gaetulae stormed and took a capital city there while Atlanteans were away fighting in the Mediterranean. It does fit the story of Plato, but I do not believe it unless this was a colony. Of course, the trading empire had many colonies. The story goes that the army returning was taken prisoner and subsequently mingled with the population."

"No," Pat continued, "this story is about an island in the Atlantic - not Plato . . . Aha - this time I stopped what you were about to say!"

"Go on," I said.

"It was about Atlantis. Pomponius Mela, born about the time that Vesuvius erupted and covered Pompeii, said there was an historical Atlantis; only he placed it in the southern hemisphere."

"Which hardly agrees with Plato, does it? Remember Plato said that Atlantis had higher mountains toward the north, shielding it from the cold winds, and that it "faced south", or in other words its capital or main port opened to the warmer seas of the south."

"But there was someone who told about visiting Atlantis."

"You mean the Phoenician story by Diodorus? He claimed that the Phoenicians discovered an island in the Atlantic while coasting along the west coast of Africa, and were driven westward for days by winds. After a long time they came to a large island. The land was crossed by winding rivers and the valleys thus formed were wide and fertile. The sailors saw many cities rich with public baths and beautiful buildings. During the heat of the summer, the inhabitants went to villas of great luxury built along the many beautiful lakes. Metals were in abundance and gold was no more important than copper."

"Didn't that story come from Plutarch?"

"Yes, you are right; but it was about Diodorus - I believe in his fifth book."

"Well now," Pat said, "wouldn't you say that they had reached Atlantis?"

"Perhaps. But it sounds very much like ancient Cuba or Yucatan, to me."

It could have been, especially as the argument over settling the place and making a colony of it was vetoed by Carthage. Yes, Carthage makes this close to the time of Rome rather than the time of Atlantis."

"By the way, Pat, isn't it interesting that the Phoenicians told the Tyrrhenians 'because they were related to them,' and they both conferred with Carthage for the same reason? It is another point in my belief that the Phoenicians were Tyrrhenians."

"And for that matter, so were the Carthaginians."

"Right . . . and that is why Caesar burned the Alexandrian library! These were the remnants of the Atlanteans!"

Pat said: "Poor ole Julius. He didn't dream that we moderns would have the blood of both peoples - I mean the modern Italians. Walk up and down the streets of Rome today and you see as many Tyrrhenian faces as typical Romans!"

"True enough."

"What about the Amazons?" Irene asked.

"They disappeared after Herodotus began swinging his big sword."

"Except in the Americas."

"You are joking," Pat said.

"No. When Pizzaro went into South America the natives told him of the tribes of warrior women who wore snake skins and had metal heads which they took off on occasion and carried under their arms (helmets?). These women told of a sad story of how the sea had completely covered their islands, and asked for land. The natives directed them to the great river running through Brazil and they took their ships into the jungles and disappeared. Hearing this tale, the Spanish called this magnificent river 'Amazon'."

"And the Navaho are their descendents?"

"No, but the Navaho have conquered and intermarried with many tribes and have taken over their legends. However, everywhere in South America the full moon is connected with women in some way, and in the southern part of Mexico, dwell a race of very lovely women who are extremely wilfull. They wear a long, lacy, ruffled head-dress and dance interesting dances at the full of the moon.

"The story goes that these white starched head-dresses are in reality baby dresses. Once a ship load of baby dresses was wrecked on the shore and the chests full of these dresses were washed ashore. The women finding them put them on and now they wear them for ornaments. Whether the story is true or not, I do not know, but the lacy frills set off the moonbeam delicacy of these women to advantage.

"The beautiful Tehuanas live in the isthmus of Tehuantepec. The Indian meaning of this word is: 'the people of the land of ancient glory' which is suggestive of its origin. If these are Atlanteans, or even the mixed children of the Amazon branch, they must have been very beautiful. They are indeed not unlike the charming Egyptians of antiquity as painted upon the olden frescoes when suddenly lit up by the light of torches in temples or tombs."

"What is the dance like? A modern twist?" Pat asked.

"I don't know if the dance is old. It is more like a stately Napoleonic waltz. But the swaying of the long dresses of the women remind me of what I have read of the dance of Tuarak women. I believe their Egyptian-like gowns with the right shoulder bare, just as we see in the tombs of the ancients, causes the onlooker to remember the motion of the sea."

"We must go to Tehuantepec someday," Pat looked at his wife. "But, how will we handle the episode of last night, should we ever desire to attend another Squaw Dance?"

"Go with the girl to the crowd where couples are shuffling about in a circle, one behind the other. After awhile, give her a quarter, and thank her. Then you are free to leave, unless another girl grabs you."

"So it is a money making scheme!" Irene said. "Well, Pat, two can play at that game. I'll just tag a good-looking Navaho while you are dancing, and then what will you do?"

"Yes. How would I get her to quit and come home?"

"I really don't know the answer to that. But remember this, Irene, if he doesn't pay you off and leave you, but elects to keep on dancing instead . . . well, you are engaged then, according to the Navaho custom . . ."

Chapter 9

The Amazing Antiquity Of Peru, South America

Shooting Star, a typical Atlantic or Cro Magnon facial and skull type. The makeup is for the Sun Dance. Sioux tribe.

When we try to determine the antiquity of the old colossus of the sea, we must turn to the clues offered by a study of the ancient boat-builders, which inevitably leads us to Peru, South America. The Pan's pipes of the Amerinds could in all probability be ancient Peruvian. Thus Peru becomes the next site of the hunt for the extremely ancient culture complex of the old colossus of the sea.

Peru is a land of great contrasts, not only in the abyss between riches and poverty, but also in the amazing difference in the elevation of arable land. To find the ancient cultures, one must go to the heights of the Andes. There the lungs labor to overcome the lack of atmospheric pressure, and one of the most undeniable signs of the antiquity of the Amerind here is the tre-

mendous power of his lungs. It is not surprising that Yma Sumac can sing through four octaves - she is a Peruvian Indian. The rumor that she is a Jewish girl from New York whose real name is Amy Camas is utterly absurd. I heard her discussing some root words with a select few of our Atlantic tribes who went in a delegation, and the reverential courtesy they accorded her convinced me immediately of her authenticity. The Dacotah told me afterward: "She is of our people far back at the dawn."

All of Peru is "far back at the dawn". One of my friends, Shooting Star of the Dacotah (the Sioux), a tribe whose culture is definitely Atlantic, gave me an Amerind's impression of Peru and its red skinned ancients. I will repeat it here:

Shooting Star's story. "The land is almost haunted. You don't sense it in the lowland cities of white man, but around Lake Titicaca it thrusts

61

icy fingers into your soul. The fire god stares at you out of square eyes and speaks from an angled mouth while he holds up the arm daggers of the ancients in the old gesture of friendship. Yet, he stands in a giant doorway which leads nowhere! (If he held up crossed swords, it would mean keep out!)

"You look around at the land with almost a racial memory. The mountains are terraced from top to bottom as our legends tell us they were once terraced by the ancients, but now the terraces are overgrown with bushes and the land is so high that it will no longer grow the plants which we knew once grew there.

"Our group climbed to the old fortress high on top of the mountain peak. I am a strong man, but my lungs labored, and some get the dreaded mountain sickness (sirroco), yet our Indian guide strode up easily.

"There we could look over the vast expanse of the land, at the terraces in every direction below us. The stones which built this magnificent city were of tremendous size. One, they told me, was supposed to weigh one-hundred-sixty tons, yet they were lifted and fitted like diamonds, beveled and shaped one into the other. A white man with the party asked:

" 'How could they possibly build like that up here - on top of the Andes? I have seen Egypt and all the Mediterranean - I have never seen anything like this.'

"Our guide answered: 'They say that once giants came up here and threw rocks at each other.'

"Everyone laughed. The white man gave him a disgusted look, but later, when I caught the guide's eye, he winked at me. I did not lose that opportunity, but stepped up toward him:

" 'Is this the city of the thunderbirds?'

"He looked at me sharply and then answered: 'It is the city of the bird of lightnings. Every street is a feather, but one does not see that is so unless from an airplane."

" 'Where are the caves where people lose themselves?'

" 'They are under the city. Some of the entrances are secret. Others are closed.'

"'Have you ever been down in them?' I asked.

"He shook his head. 'It is forbidden.' That answer I expected, and he knew that I did. We smiled our recognition.

" 'Where is your tribe?' he asked.

" 'Thousands of miles to the north, through the United States and almost to Canada.'

" 'It is well,' he said, and we clasped arms in the ancient manner. (This is a grasp of the right forearm above the wrist.)

"A few days later, after the ceremonial length of time, he brought an old man. I had expected him. Altogether there were eight of us. We spoke of legends and words. I tell you, my friends, this is the land of our beginning, where we went from the old red land even before it sank, because this land is as old as the dragon land of the fire god."

That is the gist of the story as Shooting Star told it to me.

After this conversation, I went to the library and studied scientific ideas on the antiquity of Peru. There is some belief among zoologists that the fauna (animals) of the region suggest a steady rise of the mountains since the Pleistocene. One reason is that the ant eater, a tropical creature, seems to have been trapped (like man) in the great valley of Titicaca lying between Peru and Bolivia, and still manages to survive.

The botanists point to the amazing differences here in corn. This domestic plant is to be found in two strangely different varieties. One is very tiny like a berry, while the other has such enormous kernels that they must be eaten separately like nuts. Furthermore, the antiquity of the cereal corn, or maize, is not to be doubted. There are other manners in which the Amerind has been able to train this vegetable through uncounted millennia of time. He has a special type corn with very long roots which has adapted itself to the desert of the Hopi tribe who grow it in Arizona; and a kind with a very short season which the Canadian tribes have been able to grow in their short summers of the Canadian and Alaskan north. The other kinds - the black corn, blue and red corn may be purchased from the Hopi, Navaho, Apache and other western tribes. All this amount of breeding in a vegetable which has long ago lost the ability to plant itself, shows an antiquity which easily goes back to the postglacial or even the interglacial. Both Peru and Mexico have been mentioned as the place where possibly corn was first domesticated, but most authorities believe that it actually was Peru.

From 1913 through 1916 Yale university, together with The National Geographic magazine sent a team of scientists to South America. In a fascinating article called "Staircase Farms of the Ancients", the scientists told some very interesting facts.

Huge step dams (and we think of step dams as very modern) were rediscovered whereby the water was conserved thousands of years ago. That it must have been thousands of years ago, was determined by the scientists in a very ingenious manner. After tracing out the ancient stepped farms and sampling the soil in these artificially terraced masonry, they then discovered that the soil was sorted as carefully as the most meticulous greenhouse owner would sift soil for his finest orchids with drainage and richness in mind, because these terraces contained almost entirely imported soil! The scientists then began to trace out the irrigation systems used. Imagine their amazement to discover that the ancient pipes ran not to the present glaciers, but to the ancient glaciers of the Pleistocene!

Who built these staircase farms? How many thousands of years ago were they abandoned? These questions they would not answer. The learned men from Yale would only go on record as saying that thousands of years ago agriculture as a science reached a very high level in this land, then entered a decline, and only recently has made an attempt to return. Then concluded that the various levels up the mountain took plants through all of the climatic zones from tropical to frigid, and the variety of plants raised in this extensive nurseries has probably never been equalled upon the globe.

Furthermore, there were other surprises in this most amazing land. Great roadways were discovered. These ran for thousands of miles. Many led to tunnels through the Andes which had caved in perhaps thousands of years ago and therefore could not be followed in safety.

The scientists from Yale university came back humbled and thoroughly puzzled at what they had seen.

One of the most interesting facts about the giant rocks with which the ancients built the cyclopean walls and masonry is that these boulders are not of local rock, but were brought from quarries in Ecuador, almost fifteen hundred miles away! Water was carried by aqueduct for hundreds of miles to irrigate the fields. Their bridges and roads are amazing. Often mountains were bored through, and deep canyons filled with masonry for a solid bridge or swung with a suspension bridge. They were expert in the ceramic arts and the textiles are without peer. Cotton was grown in all the colors besides the white.

The cyclopean stonework is a subject for future scientists to study, and that study should add to our knowledge of the earth's past. For example, there are no remains of an archaic or earlier form. These people seem to have arrived in the remote past with a vast scientific knowledge to aid them in their work, No cement or mortar is used in their building. The enormous blocks of stone are cut, faced and fitted so perfectly that even today one can not slip the blade of a knife between the giant blocks. Not only that, but the scientists could not slip a six-thousandth of an inch guage between them either. No two blocks are alike. Yet all fit perfectly. It has been stated that no modern mechanic with the aid of metals and tools of the finest steel, and using micrometer guages, could produce results more accurate. Each individual stone must have been planned long before hand. Twenty-ton rocks can not just be dropped into position and hope to obtain such superhuman accuracy! And that so many thousands of years ago! In addition, the rocks, despite their size, are locked and dovetailed together in many cases. Many of the stones are square or rectangular, yet some have as many as eight or thirty-two sides.

These massive buildings are all over Cuzco. The Incans, finding them, simply made use of them, and the Incan work, often on top of the ancient or added to it, is startlingly inferior.

One of the most amazing buildings on this entire planet is the temple of the sun. Today it is a church with European embellishments, but its giant blocks of stone, no two of which is alike, is an engineering marvel. These boulders are so perfectly cut and designed that the circular interior with its radii is mathematically and geometrically perfect. As Verrill states in his "Old Civilizations in the New World": "No engineer of our times equipped with the most delicate of instruments and the most modern of appliances and mathematical tables could excel the work of these long vanished designers who conceived and constructed this remarkable temple."

Verrill's picture of the temple of the sun when first seen by the Spanish has strange Atlantean echoes to anyone who has read Plato.

"The walls outside and inside were covered by plates of gold. The gardens were filled with trees, shrubs and plants of silver and gold. Among the leaves and limbs of metal were birds, animals and insects of gold and silver, and even the fountains, the tools and the implements of the gardener's trade were of the same metals."

This is his description of the temple interior: "Upon one wall, above where the Christian altar now stands, was an immense sun of massive gold studded with jewels which flashed and scintillated in the sunlight until the eyes of the marvelling Dons were almost blinded with their brilliance. Opposite this sun was a huge representation of the moon wrought of polished silver, while about these two chief luminaries were the stars of silver and told, with an arching rainbow of gold tinted in some remarkable manner to imitate the natural prismatic colors.

"Beneath the wondrous image of the sun were seated the mummies of the Incan emperors wrapped in their robes and mantles of tapestry and feathers, their false heads adorned with golden crowns, golden masks representing their features, gold and jeweled ornaments upon their breasts, and with ornate staffs and symbols of their office before them."

He continues with a description of the queens and princesses seated before the silver moon. Then comes the sentence which brings such a striking resemblance of that other temple lost so long ago below the green waves of the sea: "There were twelve golden statues of the deceased Incas standing in life-size poses."

His other descriptions of the draperies and textiles end with the rather revolting story of how the Spanish fought with each other over the loot, melted down into ingots these priceless antiquities from who knows how long before, then using the royal robes as wrappings for the ingots. Much of the wealth never reached Spain and, of course, never will. My Amerind informers tell me that they have legends that it is hidden in the miles of labyrinths which network the Andes, and is still guarded by the ancient priesthood.

Although the gold was stripped from them, the massive walls withstood the desire of the Spanish to topple them. Using great hordes of Indian slave labor they were able to knock a few holes, or topple sometimes the top layer of the giant blocks, but the work which had defied the earthquakes and the untold millenia of time, in the end defied their efforts, and they gave in to the ancient walls which still stand.

Outside the city is the fortress of Sacsahuaman, built of blocks of stupendous size. It stands on the summit of a high hill frowning down upon what remains of the ancient glory.

Ollantay Tambe is built of blocks from twelve to eighteen feet in height and from six to eight feet square. As in the temple, these blocks have been trued like metal, showing the same fantastic engineering knowledge in both locations.

There is also Machu Picchu long hidden from the eyes of man as well as from his memory; the temple of the white god, Viracocha, and the palace of Manco-Kapac. There are also strange round towers of perfectly fitted stones. These are to be found in North America as well. One is in Colorado, and another, now half submerged in New England, was the subject of Longfellow's poem "A Skeleton in Armor". (The poet thought it was Viking-built.) What it may have been originally, we have no idea. These mysteries are all about ten to thirty feet high and about ten to twelve feet in diameter. Although mummies have been found in them, we do not know for certain that these "mulpas" are burial places. It is possible that they may have been signalling towers or used for observatory work. Curiously enough, they reappear in Ireland.

One of the most interesting descriptions of Verrill is that concerning the inscription which he copied from the ancient fortress of Sahhuayacu.

"Notable among these are the sculptured stones of Sahhua-yacu, about one hundred and eighty miles northeast of Cuzco, in a district probably never under Incan dominion. In one of these there are twenty-four characters, all but seven of which are repeated two or more times, much as if they were true letters, and formed words." The letters do not form a repeated sequence. From such a repetition, the scholar might discover the word and thus the language group.

The two lines which Verrill did copy are as follows:

In Fate Magazine for May 1962, there is an article entitled "Mar-cu-huasi, the Stonehenge of the Andes" by Dr. Marcel F. Homet, French field archaeologist, at present based in Brazil and sponsored by various French organizations, including the Societe E'thnographique, Ecole d' Anthropologie. Dr. Homet's reply to criticisms that he is placing the Amerind too far back in time, is: "We have been on the spot and have studied the available literature and the practical material for generation after generation. This has made it possible for us to build up a body of observations of which Europe is scarcely aware."

Dr. Homet is of the opinion that about thirteen thousand feet high in the Andes, east of Lima, Peru, are gigantic roughly carved statues which date to twelve thousand years ago. Here he found statues carved from the native rock. First there was a tremendous head which he believes to be the head of Cro Magnon man, an early cave man of Europe. Local Amerinds referred to it as "the head of the Inca." (In Peru the

Miss Anna Mae Begay, Navaho,
an Eastern type Cro Magnon.

word Inca is a title to be used similarly to Emperor, King, Pharaoh, etc.)

On the high plateau, says Dr. Homet, is a collection of statues which resemble a Stonehenge in the sky. There is a cave constructed of giant blocks in the fashion of the ancient Britons. Upon entering the cavern which was placed over a cliff, the scientists found a peaked rock which marked the center of the giant blocks. Measuring with the best modern instruments, they found that this was the center of the cavern which had been formed by the boulders. Then in attempting to measure the angles of the cyclopean blocks, forming the walls as they leaned inwards, the scholars discovered that both of the walls measured forty seven degrees, or each one was twenty-three and a half, which is the annual variation of the sun due to the angle at which the earth leans.

Farther along through the cavern there is a huge rock of sacrifice. This stone was twenty-one feet long and three feet high. Both the table and its substructure are exactly the same width, and both slope at the same angle. Above the table and

its substructure was a hexagonal form very similar to the three thousand dolmens near Constantine in North Africa. In both of the Americas such rites were carried out, and the blood thrown upon the idols, the columns of the temple and upon the sacred fire. (Like Plato's Atlantis except oxen blood was used.)

All this has a haunting likeness to ancient Europe and to the Mediterranean. The Etruscans; Phoenicians; the early Celts of Brittany, Scotland and Ireland; the Carthaginians and others practiced these ritualistic murders, tearing out living parts of the body in order to read the "portents", or the future. Did it stem from a similar ritual in the Atlantic homeland?

That Plato describes a much less vicious type of ritual, may mean that Plato's Atlanteans were a civilization of conquerors who overthrew the original fire god. That the volcanic deity would be the most important is what we would expect in an unstable homeland where man's very existence, according to his beliefs, depended upon the goodwill of an ever-growling terror.

Returning, however, to the scientists of France, we hear that they discovered, as they moved about the giant sculptured head, that another head appeared. Even farther around this eighty-foot-high statue, a third face appeared. All three faces are carved from the same giant boulder. The strange thing about them is that one is a perfect duplicate of the giant faces carved in rock which stands on mysterious Easter Island and face out to sea. This face with its stone eyes is staring toward Easter Island. On the back of the rock is a zodical sun with twelve rays. This faces toward the east.

Dr. Homet says that there is also a lion - a perfect African lion with mane, tail, mouth, eyes - all remarkably carved. The lion is lying upon a pedestal, and about sixty feet away a seat is carved out of the cliff. If one settles into the seat, one soon realizes that this is the place for the spectator to be while looking at the lion. From here the light is just right to bring out the intricacies of the carving.

One has the impression as one finishes the article of Dr. Marcel Homet, that this is not an isolated group of giant statuary. Upon other plateaus, perhaps now inaccessible or simply undiscovered since the death or abandonment by the ancient builders, other cyclopean statuary exists by the hundreds.

A memory comes to my mind of Death valley near Bad Water. Standing at the site of this poisonous pool ringed around by the bones of birds and animals who had been unwise enough

Machu Picchu, terraced city high in the Andean peaks.

to quench their thirst, one of our party called to another member who had climbed toward a cliff of the Funeral range. The voice was echoed and re-echoed. Delighted at this discovery, everyone began to call. One woman wailed, and the eerie sound was repeated again and again among the cliffs. Glancing toward the sound, I suddenly noticed that the cliffs had weird gargoyle faces. Strange imps, witches and grotesque creatures grinned and grimaced at us with smirking smiles.

When I pointed them out, everyone was quiet and all eyes were studying the cliffs.

"Those faces are too real and there are too many of them to be natural," one man remarked.

"You read my thoughts," I said.

"Are the Indians known for this sort of thing?"

"No, not particularly. But there is a people who are known for their carving - sometimes whole cliffs."

"Who are they?"

"Ancient boat builders who built with giant stones. Science calls them the megalithic builders."

"How long ago did they live?"

"Perhaps from the time of the last interglacial on through the last glacial. They could have come here in ships when this was a lake."

"That is putting it far back in time," my friend said, "but then, I knew a spot which really puts it back."

"Where?"

"There is a town named Keeler. Near it is a road toward Lone Pine, Inyo County, California, where petroglyphs are on a whole mountain of marble. The huge hill, hundreds of feet high, was once a river bed with water polished stone and what had been whirlpools and falls. Travertine had formed over it from the incrustations of the water being dried in the sun. Under the travertine, and therefore put on before the stream had dried up, were all kinds of figures and drawings."

"What kind?" I asked curiously.

"There were many of these sheep or goats from the Pyrenees mountains - the kind with the long horns . . ."

"The ibex. A strange animal to be copied so often on rocks in a land where it does not exist, isn't it? I have seen it often."

"Then there was a sun with twelve rays and guess what?"

"I give up. What?"

"A dinosaur."

"Are you sure?"

"Absolutely. It was perfectly carved and the travertine had preserved it very well."

"What kind was it?"

"One of the big fellows that look like a kangaroo. He was walking on his hind legs, but you couldn't mistake the short front arms nor the long teeth in his open mouth. He had something in his front claws that might have been a man."

"Well, this could have been reconstructed from a fossil. And the time of the stream could have been post glacial."

"Possibly. But the mountains which made the stream were gone - entirely gone - on both sides. Rivers don't run over the top of marble hills - not a big, fast one like this. So I know that it was away back."

"Apparently you are right. But as you were talking, I began to remember. That was the place where someone shot at Dr. Harrington. Since then, I understand the owner sold the marble for bank fronts in Los Angeles; so Dr. Harrington of the American Indian Museum told me. Who

knows where your dinosaur is today! Perhaps we walk over him every time we make a deposit in our bank."

"To bad! But there is a site where there is writing under travertine in the old shoreline of Salton sea. There are lines and lines of inscriptions on one of the high boulders."

"I saw that one myself. I don't seem to be able to find it again. Can you remember any of it - or better yet, did you copy it?" I asked hopefully.

"No. But I can make several of the letters." He thereupon drew the following for me:

"Yes. I remember those too. Also the cross as well as the Maltese cross. I had an excellent photograph, but a supposed friend was stupid enough to tear it up. You know, these letters are very much like those on the 'lost city' of Peru."

"You tell me about this city and I will tell you about a place where some living people have similar writing."

"That is a deal. I have been searching for people who write like this."

"You start first."

"Very well. A man named Bingham made the discovery of Machu Picchu. He had heard rumors. There may be many other lost cities in the Andes of Peru. Most of the rumors he had followed were duds. Then came the great find. It happened after all of his party were ready to give up. He climbed dizzy heights, clung precariously to trails where often the mules had to be rescued and dragged back from the edge of the depths below them. Sometimes these men crossed flimsy bridges of vines which swung in the breeze over river-cut gorges. They crossed one at a time with a mule, because of the weight. Then as they were about to give up, an Indian came to tell them of the great city of the ancients. Bingham started out the next morning with only one friend and his Indian, leaving the others in camp. Around an Andean peak, down a gorge, across another bridge of vines and up still another peak. And there it was, as he said: 'Like the Great Pyramid and the Grand Canyon, rolled into one.' He returned the following year to bring the scientists of Yale and the photographers of The National Geographic Society. Thus Machu Picchu was presented to an amazed world."

"Isn't that the pre-Incan city which has stairways for streets?"

"Yes. Over a hundred of them. Some of the top ones lead to what must have been great public buildings, with porches and balustrades carved from great blocks of granite."

"What were their tools?"

"Apparently an exceedingly hard bronze."

"From the bronze age?"

"That is my opinion. And I believe they were the Master Builders."

"The water supply?"

"An ingenious procession of fountains. Their water was the best."

"I wonder if this all ties in together?"

"That is what I was wondering. The giant carvings, the staircase farms, the magnificent masonry, perhaps even the ibex wild goat of the Pyrenees mountains which dip from the border of France and Spain into the sea. We know that the writing does, for we found some carved there too."

"What else do you know about them?"

"Let us say I am only searching. However, there are some interesting loose threads which lead to question marks. These people played with Pan's-pipes. In fact that musical instrument may have originated here."

"You forget the great god Pan, of Greece."

"No I haven't. He is part of the mystery. According to Herodotus, the great god Pan, who was pictured as half-goat, and playing his instrument so sweetly that none could resist him, was one of the 'early eight gods, out of whom the twelve gods were made.' This sounds like the break-up of a land into islands . . ."

"Or a conquest?"

"Or both. And the strange thing is that among the Amerinds over here Pan stands for an ancient land in the Atlantic, lost long ago in what they call the great destruction."

"Who were the Eight?"

"I don't know. But Hercules was one of the Twelve!

"Hmm. What makes you say that Pan's-pipes may have originated on this side of the Atlantic?"

"Because you see them, from tiny ones held in one hand, to large ones played by as many as eight men. In the latter case they sound like an organ."

"Did you ever hear them?"

"Yes, once in Mexico City. A group of Peruvians were playing and the Mexicans were reciprocating with a concert played on twenty-six marimbas. It was played one night in the plaza of Oaxaca (pronounced Wah-ha-cah)."

"What other instruments did the Peruvians have?"

"There was a harp very much like the ancestral harp of Ireland, a strange guitar, a trumpet, flutes and many-toned drums which were the background for the hauntingly mellow tones of the Pan's-pipe organ. The Peruvians, with their tremendous lung power, are remarkable on this instrument. By the way, I have heard that they have an opera or play which is pre-conquest and is enacted at Ollantay Tambe, which is the original setting. The actors are all Amerinds and the orchestra is probably the one I heard while it was on tour. Verrill mentioned it in one of his books and was so much impressed that he copied some of the ageless melodies."

"I have heard that some of these melodies have reappeared in a half-hundred songs in various languages around the world."

"Very well," I said. "My part of the bargain has been fulfilled. Now how about yours? Who are the mysterious people who write like these mysterious inscriptions?"

"Have you ever heard of the Tuaregs?"

"If I have, it hasn't registered on my memory."

"They are a wild people of the Sahara. They are savage and fierce, and the Arabs are terrified of them. They have blue or green eyes. That is all you ever see of the male face. These people may be all that is left of the ancient Libyans."

"The Libyans? The great world power before the rise of Egypt?"

"The same. The women often go unveiled. The men - never. I understand that the women are pretty. Some have ivory skin and red hair, but during the war I was warned against looking at them. You could be found with a bronze arm-dagger sticking out of your ribs."

"Bronze?"

"That's right. The Arabs have nicknamed them 'Blue Vengeance' because of their blue or purple robes."

"Purple robes?"

"Yes! Page Plato expounding the Timaeus. Well, happy hunting!"

One of the women of the party came up.

"What in the world are you two gabbling about?"

"We were talking about a few lines from Kipling -" I said.

"Go and look behind the ranges -
Something's lost behind the ranges!
Lost - and waiting for you - Go!"

An Anthropologist Reports

On The

Channel Islands Of California--

Chapter 10

The following is taken from the book written strictly for scientists - "Early Man on the Santa Barbara Coast" by David Banks Rogers, Curator of the Santa Barbara Museum of Prehistoric Man. (Published by the museum.)

"At one time, preceding the close of the Pleistocene period" (the ice age probably dated from 15,000 BC to 7,000 BC) "there occurred a tremendous remodeling of the coastal region of California. Areas approximating, in some places one hundred miles in width, were suddenly swallowed by the ocean, and at the same time, a line of low-lying hills that had formerly straggled through the interior were now raised to a range of low-lying mountains which bordered the new coastline.

"At the close of this movement nothing remained of the fertile lowlands except a dozen or more islands. These still mark the places where volcanic outbursts had anchored small bits of land during the catastrophe which engulfed the neighboring land. Of these remnants, the channel islands are the most northern representatives. From the period of this major convulsion to the present time, there have apparently been no more eruptions of igneous material" (lava) "along any of these shores.

"In parts of Santa Cruz island, as in Santa Rosa island, we found deep deposits of terrestrial origin of Pleistocene age. In the formations near the western extremity of the island are huge legs of Douglas Fir" (which no longer grow on these volcanic fragments) "imbedded beneath many feet of sandy clay which antedates the present era." (Our era is post glacial.) "I found no authentic records of Pleistocene animals in this material, but have little doubt of their occurrence if more excavation is undertaken.

"In the interim to the present time the islands have been raised about forty feet. This movement has been slow and steady, for the beachline from the disturbance to the present is without a sudden break."

From Page 280:

"In a few sites we noted the devastation wrought by these former earth movements, during which villages were torn apart and whole sections of others hurled into the sea."

From Page 292:

"The examination of the mass of wreckage below the break was anything but satisfactory, everything being in such confusion that only the most painstaking care could discover any meaning. It was not unusual to find great blocks of sub-soil resting above masses of camp refuse, the original structure of the land having been completely inverted. In other places these formations lay prone with the original horizontal stratification now standing in a perpendicular state and greatly distorted.

The Ships Of The Dragon Land?

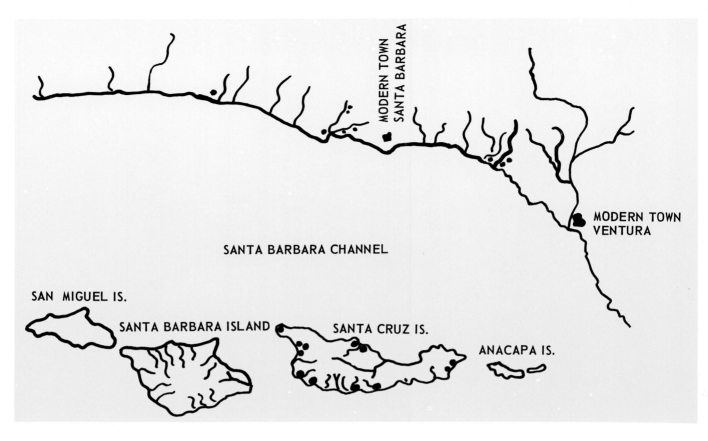

Best known Chumash prehistorical sites on mainland and islands are marked on this map by the author of the Santa Barbara coast. Other sites are to be found on Santa Barbara and San Miguel islands, though not important. Anacapa consists only of precipitous cliffs rising from the ocean. After a map by Ronald Olson.

"At one part of the wreckage near the southeastern angle, a great many disassociated fragments of human bones were unearthed. This we took to be the remains of a former cemetery which previous to the time of the land-slip had been on a much higher level and farther inland."

(Dr. Rogers showed me photographs of large columns of land standing out in the sea with human bones protruding from the sides in the upper level, which had once been part of this cemetery.)

Page 311:

"This site outranked all others examined by us in the number of vestiges of ships. The planking was decayed, but the fragments of wood still retained enough of their original shape to identify them as having been parts of boats.

"These boats had not been placed in the cemetery entire. In two instances there were parts of the prow or stern in another part of the section while others had small portions.

"Skeletons were buried flexed with their faces down to the earth with the heads to the

north and some vertebrae bones of the Sperm whale marked this as a probable Catalina site.

"Two types of unusual domestic dogs were buried with care."

(Dr. Rogers explained that one type of dog was a large hound type and the other a very small toy type sometimes found in South America in pre-Incan sites in Peru.)

Page 319:

"On the northern side of Cerbada creek, an acorn eating site was found." (This was on the continental beach where he showed me photographs of burials thirty-six feet below the present land level.) "Flagstones were uncovered with wide eliptical grooves, and vestiges of planking showing a boat-building site. Dogs were buried with reverence by the oldest inhabitants. One skull was found with a spear or dagger imbedded in it, penetrating the frontal bone."

Page 285, on Santa Cruz:

"A ridge drops sharply to the second terrace some eighty or a hundred feet lower. This island also once bore a heavy population. However, the earth-movement here almost com-

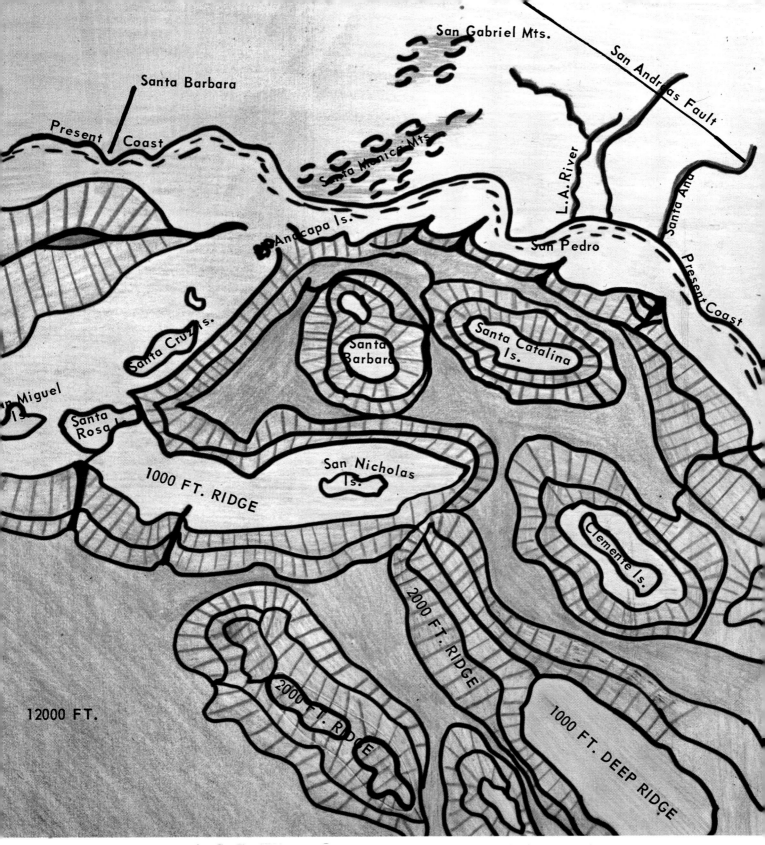

The Santa Barbara Islands (mountains) sometimes known as the Channel Islands. Depths in feet. Ridges 1, 2 and 3 thousand feet. Deeps three or more. After Reed and Coast Geodetic Survey. Size of islands is exaggerated. Santa Catalina is 25 miles from shore.

pletely destroyed everything. Yawning fissures of considerable depth criss-cross the former site in every direction giving to it a miniature 'bad land' effect.

"Upon the crest of these monument-like fragments which are still standing upright, one may see the stratified debris of a former village."

Page 291:

"About one-third of a mile east of Valdez cove is an enigmatic site of a rounded ridge which ends in a sea cliff.

"One quarter of a mile northwest of this, on the crest of a cliff, was a deep accumulation of a village site. Standing on it, one is able to see what happened. There is a deep diagonal rent to the cliff, dividing the village in half and hurling the outer half seaward. This jumbled mass now lies at a much lower level in a distinct heap down-stepped into the sea. From the ruined cemetery we recovered incised stones, strange pipe-like stones and what had been Pan's -pipes similar to those to be found in pre-Incan Peru. The writing is of an unknown script or chirography."

The most interesting fact told me during this summer at the end of the war when I went to see Dr. Rogers at the Santa Barbara museum, was his description of the boat-building center. He said that there were several partial impressions of ships and one full impression which measured one hundred feet long. When I asked him how he knew considering the wood had decayed, his answer was most amazing: "They were built of planks caulked with tar - like the Phoenicians and others in the early Mediterranean." Opening an album, he showed me photographs taken at the site. The long lines of tar were very plain, and I could easily see what he meant. "We had to uncover them with great care," he added.

I was still puzzled.

"All other ships in both the Americas, as far as we know, were hollowed out of giant logs by means of burning and chipping. Who then taught these people such a radically different method?"

He shrugged his shoulders.

"Where did they get the tar?"

"There are a number of tar pits which were active in the Pleistocene and are still active. The best known, of course, is the La Brea pits where mastodons, saber-toothed tigers, the dire wolf, the American lion, the giant condor and many other animals were trapped as they waded in to drink. The top, of course, was covered with water."

"Yes, I know. The trap preserved the bones.

Did you know there was also the skull of a woman?"

"Modern?"

"Yes and no. They say she is of the modern type, but the skull is thick and the jaw as heavy as some early types of modern man - Cro Magnon for instance."

"Dr. H---- would strongly disapprove of that opinion. He is determined to keep the Amerind a very recent invader from Asia."

I laughed.

"You can ride a hobby in science just so long. Then that impudent fact uncovered by the spade catches up with you and 'pfft' goes your reputation."

Dr. Rogers reached over and squeezed my arm with silent understanding, adding:

"That fact should be the recovery of planked ships at an early date level, say at the close of the Pleistocene?"

He shook his head. "Right now, facts are being laughed off with derision because certain circles will stop at nothing short of . . . . well, let us say they will not recognize any antiquity in the Americas or any fact which suggests that the Amerind is not a late invader from Asia, and from there alone!"

I nodded, and decided to change the subject.

"If this boat-building center was an ice age port, during the wet period or pluvial which closed the ice age, why is it not at the end of the shelf if that was the shoreline before the subsidence movement? Therefore today it would be some thirty miles further out to sea than Catalina or your islands. Or wouldn't it?"

"Yes, except for one thing. You have forgotten the great rivers which cut the coastline of the pluvial, or, let us say, the present shelf."

"Oh, I see. You believe that the ships came up the rivers?"

"Why not? The Los Angeles river alone, now only a joke, was then one of earth's mightiest rivers."

He pulled down a book of the undersea soundings along the shelf, showing the old river channels as they would run out to sea.

"Look at these winding channels. There must have been much room for harbors."

"What a challenge to skin divers except for the fact that the currents make those old river channels a death trap."

"Yes, I know. The lure is almost unbearable for the adventurer."

"Coming back to our early adventurers - how would they get the tar, for I suppose they were after tar?"

"Undoubtedly tar was the trade object. They may have ridden almost up to the La Brea tar pits in their ships at that time. Or they may have carried it otherwise. However, the ships seem the most likely method of transportation."

"And the La Brea tar pits have been working a long time judging from the mastodons, camels and other odd skeletons in the museum on Vermont Avenue. But what did they bring in return - these traders of the close of the Pleistocene?"

"Perhaps the Pan's-pipes, or these Peruvian dogs?"

"Oh certainly. Both are a link to Peru - pre-Incan Peru - the most ancient civilization - the men who built with the giant stones."

"These Phoenicians may have really gotten around?"

I laughed. "Oh come now, Dr. Rogers. Phoenicians back at the time of the pluvial? These traders must have been Atlanteans . . ."

"Sssh! That is a naughty word. If certain parties heard you say that, my reputation would be gone. Perhaps it is gone already because I have dared to publish what I found, and date the finds to and before the land subsidence."

Underneath his joking protest I sensed the bitterness at the rejection of factual evidence. A tremendous scientific discovery laughed away - once more I decided to change the subject.

"These Pan's-pipes are, of themselves mighty intriguing. The goat-god who is always pictured by the ancient Greeks as playing them - the great god, Pan, according to Herodotus, was one of the ancient eight gods who ruled before the later twelve."

"Whatever that means I wouldn't know - would you?"

"Not now, but someday, if I keep on trying to fit pieces together, it may turn out to be a missing part to some scattered picture of long ago."

"And you figure the Pan's-pipes would be a link? Wait a moment - have you ever worked among the legends of the eastern tribes?"

"You mean along the Atlantic coastline? I have read a good deal and yes, I have. Why?"

"Then you must have heard the repetition of Pahn used often to designate an eastern land. For example: Panuco, Mexico is the place where the people landed who came from Pahn."

"Oh, then the Pauns - the Algonkin ancient name, is a link?"

"And also perhaps the Pahnee or Pawnee?"

"And with them are connected goats and Pan's-pipes?"

"Perhaps in a way we don't know, as well as the number eight. If I remember right, the earliest peoples of the Mediterranean counted by eights instead of tens."

"Oh thank you - this seems like the pattern of a culture-complex - an exceedingly old one. These must have been the people of your planked ships."

"I wouldn't know that. It is too small a number of facts as yet. Could be just coincidences."

"Very well - think hard. Were there any ceremonial burials of goats?"

"No, only dogs. Perhaps the goats got away," he said.

"I wouldn't blame them if the ground was heaving like that. I had enough in the 1933 quake. But this - could the tidal wave and the earth readjustments have been triggered by the Atlantean disaster?"

"And the herds of mammoths who were drowned in Alaska with their last meal undigested?" he added. "Are we talking about the bibical flood?"

I nodded. "Call it whatever you wish: Gilgamesh or Deucalion or Noah. They were all survivors."

"Small elephants were to be found on the islands. I thought they were small because of the lack of food."

"They may have come from Atlantis. A dwarf elephant was to be found in the Atlas mountains of North Africa, where they were hunted to the ultimate extinction for their ivory by the Romans".

"You are putting words in my mouth - interesting, but we shall never know unless we could obtain one of the skeletons of these North African elephants for comparison."

"I just had another interesting thought. I have seen the ibex on the rocks north of here."

"We don't have the animal over here! If you saw one, you will have to make the flying saucer contactees move over!"

"Not in the flesh of course! In petroglyphs."

"Say - so have I! Many times - on the rocks north of here; in Inyo County . . ."

"In Imperial County! In New Mexico! In Arizona!"

"Did you by any chance hear about Dr. Harrington's find in Inyo County where someone peppered him with shot?"

"Yes, I heard. The marble river with no mountains near it? Did he see the ibex there?"

"Not only the ibex with horns back to the flanks, but also the Troy-Town maze, the twelve-rayed sun and a Tyrannosaurus Rex with something in his front claws! The something (a man?)

was so unbelievable that he may not have made a record of it. However he did say that this was, in his opinion, the oldest site of the work of man upon the planet."

"This was the site that was quarried for building blocks?"

"Yes."

"There is another magnificent site in the craters of Coso - a sleeping volcanic boiling lake in Inyo County. The Air Force was going to use it for a bombing range. In those corridors where the lava had once flowed were giant paintings in color. One was of a man with a trident upon his head. I had no camera when I saw 'The Gallery' as it is called. But when I heard what was going to happen, I marshalled all the scientists to write to have the gallery photographed. They did, I understand, before it was sacrificed to the war god."

After a moment of silence he asked: "How do you account for the giant reptiles?"

"I wouldn't know."

"Well, let's draw on our imagination. If this land in the sea was half-sunken, there may have been swamps. . ."

"And perhaps warm ones, as the lava was close to the surface."

"That is right. Plato spoke of two fountains - one hot and one cold."

Dr. Rogers nodded thoughtfully.

"And of course, early man would have considered the creature to be a god. Undoubtedly he fed it too. Perhaps at first animals and later on people. I have often wondered why the Vedas of the Aryan-speaking conquerors said 'We have conquered and killed the dragon of the eastern sea.' "

"That could have meant China."

"True. But the Norse symbols are older than the Scotch, Irish and English if you follow me. The latter people all killed the dragon - like Beowulf, but the Norse used his image on their ships."

"That is curious, isn't it?"

A long silence followed - we were both pursuing our own thoughts. Finally he broke the quiet.

"I want to find out about the script which seems to be found at these most ancient sites. Remind me to give you a sample from the Santa Barbara islands."

"Writing?"

"It looks almost like Egyptian with some reminders of very early Chinese. There is another element of this culture of the Amerind which is curiously unlike that of the Aryan speaking and Semitic speaking peoples. And Egypt is closer to the Americas in this. The white man is patrilinear while the red man is matrilinear."

"You are right; the women owns the house and children - they must not marry into her clan. For an emperor to insure that his son instead of his grandson succeeded him, he had to marry his sister as did the Incas and the Egyptians."

"The earlier people of the Mediterranean were matrilinear - as proof we find there were fighting women. With white man comes the beard, and the customs of children who carry the father's name."

"Then we have the importance of the date of the separation - or the big break between Atlantis (or the Atlantean league) and her American colonies. I speak of the Aryan conquest. The horse and wheel did not really enter the Americas from Plato's Atlantis. Perhaps the Tyrrhenian-Phoenicians kept it out for their own devious reasons."

"I like the way you link those names. I have always thought of them as the same people. So there was an invasion and conquest by the Aryan speaking horsemen? During the bronze age of course. Plato paints with an artist's brush a metropolis of this era." Then giving me a quizzical look, he asked: "What about the Norse with their dragon ships?"

"I don't know. They do not fit the pattern, do they?"

Suddenly another question hit me.

"What was the skull type of these people?"

"Dolicephalic - the ancient long head and long face. Also they had the usual burial-in-crouch position. The face was turned down to the earth. Sometimes a long stone pipe stem was placed in the hand. The long heads of the slender build usually had ships."

"But Cro Magnon, who went before, may have had them also."

"Perhaps. Then also, these men may not have been the traders."

"That too, is possible. We know so little, don't we? Perhaps our children's children will have more of the illusive answers."

So with a warm handshake, we parted. I never saw Dr. Rogers again, but I consider him one of the great scientists of the type which unfortunately we have too few. Most of them today walk timidly when it comes to going against group opinion, as did some of the great names of the past. Long after I was on the train, speeding away, a searing thought struck me. I had forgotten to ask for a sample of that writing!

Chapter 11

Who Were These Ancient Men?

"There is a principle which is a bar against all information, which is proof against all arguments, and which cannot fail to keep a man in everlasting ignorance: That principle is contempt prior to investigation."

Herbert Spencer.

In this book, we have run across our first example of truly ancient man: buried below overturned mountains or parts of mountains on the channel islands, or thirty-six feet below the present level of the soil in Santa Barbara and its environs, Dr. D.B. Rogers, curator of the Santa Barbara museum, tells us that he was

undoubtedly Pleistocene in origin and vertical placement. And we found this man with the knowledge to make and to sail ocean-going ships. In order that we can discuss this in Dr. Rogers' own language, let us go back to the four main types of ice age men.

When we come across a grave of this antiquity, we do not have the color of skin, eyes or hair to guide us. We have something far more fundamental - skeletal difference. For, strange as it may seem, the modern races at the time of the ice age were far more differentiated than they are today. There are four types: the dolicephalic harmonic; negroid; brachycephalic harmonic; neanderthaloid-Cro Magnon (the great disharmonic cross). I will treat with these in that order, in this and succeeding chapters.

The dolicephalic harmonic - this means the long head with the long face. He is not a large man. His hands and feet are small and delicate. His frame is slender. His nose is medium to medium long. His hair is straight or with a very slight curl. The Egyptian, called by some anthropologists "the slim-hipped Egyptian (Leonard Cottrell in his "Anvil of Civilization".), is a typical member. We may take his picture of himself as a correct one - the males beardless with red skin; the women lighter skinned - a golden tan. He usually buried his dead in the crouch position with face down. This is the manner of the earliest Egyptian burials. With them also there is the evidence of ships, and there is a slight suggestion that these ships may have had sails.

(2.) The second type to mention here, although this book will not deal with the type because we do not take up their continental habitat, is the negroid type. This may be a branch from the ancient longhead raised in vast time separation or perhaps intermingled with another type of man. The main skeletal difference here is in the difference of thigh as compared to leg bone, a similar difference in the arm and a different type of jaw. The skull is long, but thicker than the dolicephalic harmonic. The teeth are much larger than the dolicephalic harmonic and set forward, giving a more protruding lip. The nose is shorter and wider with spreading nostrils. The type is an excellent tropical one and is adjusted by nature for intense heat, the heat of tropical islands and Africa.

The dolicephalic harmonic, on the contrary, has thin lips, thin nostrils and instead of the somewhat receding chin of the negro, the chin is protruding and in many cases pointed. The teeth are small. The habitat is India or the Indian ocean and the ancient Mediterranean, although they are to be found all over the earth along sea coasts. For this reason, their blood is in us all.

One of the earliest groups of the dolicephalic harmonic is what are known as the Kitchen-Middens. These people lived in the lakes of Europe, building their houses on stilts where the waves would flow under the dwelling. We find them in almost world-wide distribution, although they have been best studied in Switzerland and along the Baltic coastline. They are also to be found on Asiatic isles - and always along the coasts of the oceans. They had dogs, the ox, the deer, perhaps bison, the pig, and perhaps types of elk which may have been domestic. Their name Kitchen-Midden, comes from the large amount of refuse they left behind. They lived not only in Europe, but also in Japan, Norway, Sardinia, North America, South America along the coastline of Chili, Brazil and Egypt to mention only a few locations. Again their origin points to India and the Indian ocean for it was there that the ox was first domesticated, and it is there that even today the cow is sacred, being no doubt an ancient totem animal and not edible therefore for them. Of course, it does not follow that the ancient dolicephalic continued to respect this religious ban or taboo after they lost contact with their homeland. However, the domestication of the ox follows the rovings of the ancient dolicephalic across and along the world's oceans. The chicken, which was also domesticated first in India, is not always carried by these sea rovers, but was carried by them throughout the Pacific islands as well as the dog and pig. Perhaps the ox was too large for their ships.

It is significant that near their communities they had flint mines which were always well worked. Apparently with their hunters came the bow and arrow. At least one ceremonial habit was always theirs - that of placing very tiny ceremonial flint weapons and utensils in the grave of the dead so that the spirit would find artifacts for his needs in the life beyond the medium in which we live. These tiny ceremonials follow the rovings of the long heads.

Also, they were the first historical people to place feathers in their hair and wear feathered head-dresses. We see these marks of identification on their pictures of themselves in the caves of Spain, and again on the historical pictures made of the Philistines by the Egyptians. Of course, between these ancient people and the Egyptians with their captive Philistines are many thousands of years, yet the old ancestral type is there and the ancestral traditions still persist.

These people of the ice age are known to anthropologists as the Azilians. They always bury their dead in the crouch position as was mentioned by Dr. Rogers, but the position of the skull is not always down. Sometimes it faces west and sometimes east, but almost always toward the nearest ocean.

In Tule Lake, Northern California, along the Oregon border, where the United States government drained a lake to obtain land to put the Japanese camp where groups of these people could be held for the duration of World War II, some children were digging one day in the sand under one of the barracks. They brought up some tiny flints to amazed and puzzled parents. An anthropologist was called and salvaged two skeletons of the dolicephalic race, together with their ceremonial flints. The only unusual fact was that one was carrying a long stone in one hand which was fashioned like a pipe stem. The children had disturbed the skulls and they did not remember how the heads had been originally placed. The Modoc tribe, native to the region, were called upon to explain the burials. They were amazed and declared that as long as their people had lived in this region - from "way-way back" - "this site had been a lake, and how could anyone be buried at the bottom of a deep lake?" The Modocs glanced sidelong at the Japanese children as if they suspected that the youngsters were playing tricks. However, the anthropologists recognized the ancient dolicephalic, dug further and uncovered one more grave. After that, the government asked them to stop, as the Japanese people were getting nervous at the idea of living in such close proximity to the dead. This long stone was purchased by me and later taken to England where at present it rests in the Oxford museum.

The distribution of the ancient long head not only carries with it the suggestion of oceanic travel, but also possibly man's first attempts to write. Perhaps because of his distribution, is this the basis of numerous writing systems? For the long head is to be found on such isolated islands as Easter - far from the way of ocean travel, and which long ago lost its forests to boat builders. Today there are no trees on Easter Island, in the Pacific off South America. The ancient dolicephalic type is sometimes also seen in the Philippines where he has intermingled long ago with other people; in the Mediterranean below the time of either the Semitic speaking or the Aryan speaking invaders; along all the coasts of the Atlantic and many of the Pacific, and in fact, even among the Eskimo.

His skull capacity is equal to and sometimes better than modern man. Because of his long thin nostrils, he is suited to cold climates as well as semi-tropical, for the nostrils can heat the air on its way to the lungs.

In recent years there has come to light an increasing number of skulls or graves which are to be found in the terraces of lost or dead rivers such as for example - the Mimembres of the southwestern United States. These people lived when the air was humid with water and the rivers were full. Today the land is a barren desert. Did the Mimembres come up these full rivers so long ago in ships? We do know that the lush land held no enemies for them. Their homes were not fortified, and they lacked weapons.

Yet even in those days when climatic conditions were so reversed that we cannot assign it a recent date, the Mimembres had vegetables and grains as well as cotton. They grew their food, ground their grain and made delicate pottery so lovely that the museums of the world have treasured any work of theirs. Strangely enough, the repeated motif is fish and the swaying lines of sea plants. The ibex or long-horned goat, no longer to be found in the Americas (if indeed it ever did live in that land) is one of their favorite subjects. They also often delight in drawing the stylized dragon. Strange creatures indeed for the time and location of the Mimembres.

Or could it have been a racial memory kept alive in chants? Or carried down through legend? I determined to find out. The nearest neighbors of these ancient peoples are the Keresian speaking modern Pueblos. They differ from Pueblo to Pueblo (those pyramid shaped towns where one man's roof is another's garden or porch) by several thousand years of language separation - probably as far as German and Italian or Russian and Spanish.

One happy afternoon I chanced to meet one of their "sachems" - the men who knows the legends. He had been down to the corn field and the bright lad I paid to translate for me, introduced us.

After the presents and ceremonial small talk, which is very necessary in the slower moving world of the Red Man, where undue haste shows bad taste, I noted that the dragon motif on the women's pottery was somewhat in the style of the Mimembres. I spoke about the time when they lived and how the land had changed. He listened with interest. I mentioned the fish designs and the sea plants. Then I asked the big question: "Could this be because of your homeland? You seem to look as I imagine the Mimembres looked. They may have been your ancestors. Where was your distant homeland?"

"I will deal accurately with you if you will contribute to our knowledge. I wish to know more of these homelands so many thousands of winters ago."

"Very well. Tell me the name."

Ancient Indian sculpture.

"First there was Hawaiku. It lies to the sunset. Do you know of it?"

"Yes indeed. It is the ancestral name for the land which today is only represented by the Hawaiian Islands. When Hawaiku was entirely in the sun it was much larger - perhaps during the time of the ice mountains in the north?"

"That must be right. There were many fish, and the sea plants were easy to reach and see."

"You say that there was another homeland?"

"Yes. Itzamana lay very long ago in the sunrise ocean. It is no more. Do you know of it?"

"I certainly do. The name comes from the Mayans. Itzama was the leader of their migrations and he was pictured as coming in a boat from the direction of the sunrise."

"Ah you do know! Tell me more about these people."

After I had talked a long time on the Mayans,

I asked: "Now you tell me of this land, for your memory is longer than mine in the story of this land - it was before the time of our histories and few men have the legends any more."

"I will tell you. Friends should not have secrets from one another. The land was high and built like the pueblo - with set back gardens up the high peaks. It was a wonderful land. Everyone was very happy. There was food and clothes for all - much of all different kinds of food. There was hot and cold water which ran in rivers. There were many ships, and in those days - books."

"Where did you get the ibex - I mean the goat with the long horns of which you make pictures? Here in this land?"

He shook his head. "No, they came from Itzamana, where they ran in flocks. There were many kinds of animals there. That is where we got the big lizard, too."

A miniature Tyrannosaurus Rex, about 8 inches long, dashed across the sand in front of us, holding his tail up to keep it off the hot sand. The old man motioned toward it.

"He is but the tiny child of those monsters. They were large - very large. One could leap over the whole pueblo."

"Where did they live?"

"In the swamps toward the sunset of Itzamana. There were many swamps, some quite warm with hot springs. We had to push our boats through . . ."

"Wait a moment. I thought the dragon was from China. In their mythology the dragon is supposed to carry little children to heaven."

"I suppose they did in a way, but we had to throw them as sacrifices to get through the swamps - "

"How horrible!"

"Yes - the Twin Star boys killed them finally. It took a brave man. Spears could not pierce their skin. It might have been done with fire. I do not know how exactly."

"You are certain that you are not talking about alligators in Florida?"

"I am most certain. These people - the Mayans - they should be able to tell you."

"They speak little of their legends. They came, it seems, with a civilization already very old indeed. Besides they did not keep their books in their memory. They wrote them down and the Spanish threw the books in the fire."

He closed his eyes and bit his lips silently. After a moment he asked: "How do you think that we got here?"

"The Mayans live down where Mexico juts out into the Atlantic. You must have come north and up the Rio Grande. It would not be hard for people with boats."

He nodded. "Do you know that some of the people go courting with robes or blankets wrapped around them up to their eyes so that only the eyes show?"

"Yes, the Sioux or Dacotah do."

"No, I do not mean the eastern plains tribes, though that is interesting. It is an old custom with some of our people."

"Now that you mention it, so do the Mayans at night. They have an idea that the night air is poison."

"Because the Breath Master can get into one's lungs better at night."

No matter how foolish the superstition seems to us, I have found that everything is a link to put away on the memory shelf and some day it will light up another fact half a globe away with a sudden light. So I merely nodded, with a murmured: "Thank you."

He took this for a sign that our conversation was at an end and rose. I too, arose and we shook hands warmly.

"You will always be welcome to come to our dances and you may learn much more."

"Thank you. I shall do that. One thing I do know. You use short kilt-like garments when you dance and sometimes tie an animal tail behind. That costume is on very early pictures in Upper Egypt where are the graves of the long heads of greatest antiquity . . ." my voice dwindled away as I saw that I had lost both him and my translator. I tried again, but he could not enlighten this puzzle after I showed him on a world map the location of Egypt.

So we parted company in friendly promises to meet again some day at one of the dances, a promise which I have not fulfilled. But then I have not learned enough to contribute greatly to the council, so I wait for added knowledge before I go back.

I have found however, that some Amerind tribes have the most amazing knowledge of Egyptian gods, and if you spread a tableau from the temples of the Egyptians before them, they will quickly point out the Breath Master or god of life (Osiris), the Pharaoh (the emperor) and the wolf-headed Set (god of death) by the garments each is wearing. As one Amerind sachem said to me: "The god of life holds out the drink to the emperor, and behind him stands the death god just waiting to snatch it away. How do I know that this figure is the emperor? See the medallion of office hanging on a chain around his neck? That is how I know. The way the collar is made on these others say that they are of royal blood."

These words were not spoken by Sedillio, great war chief of the Yaquis, who had studied with the Egyptian priesthood and had other degrees from European universities before he lost his life in a small tribal war against the Mexican government, but by a Choctah, possibly unlettered, who did not know anything about Egypt, but was intensely interested when pointed out its location on an atlas world map. He had never heard of Sedillio.

Returning to the ancient dolicephalic, there is another interesting burial location. While taking graduate work in anthropology at the university of Mexico, the professor one day asked casually how many had studied geology. A number raised their hands. Choosing one young German, he said: "Our new and beautiful university is resting upon an old lava flow. You have no doubt noted that the university is surrounded by parks with all types of trees and shrubs. The setting was especially set out by designers to place the buildings of glass and steel, (sometimes with one wall done in murals or mosaiced in semi-precious stones) in the most beautiful settings as one would mount jewels. We are very proud of this university. Now tell me about the lava flow upon which it stands."

The youthful blond German began quietly: "The university is indeed magnificent. The lava flow, I judge, is about the thickness of a four-story building. It is very extensive and intrigues me a great deal. I would judge it to be Pleistocene - meaning from the time of the ice age. My reason for this is that lava does not dessicate enough to allow so many plants and trees to be grown in it before a number of millennia. I would say it came from the Xitli (pronounced Sheetlee) volcano sometime during the latter part of the Pleistocene or from 8 to 12,000 years ago."

The professor nodded and thanked the young geologist.

"Your answer is what I usually receive when I ask this question. Tomorrow we are going to take a trip beneath the mass of this old rock. Be sure to dress warmly. It will be cold down there. We will meet here and go in a bus. Bring flashlights."

The following morning we were taken to the edge of the "Pedrigal" as it is known to the Mexicans. We climbed down several flights of stairs and began our guided tour underground. Imagine our consternation when we came to graves. They were lighted with electric lights so that one could look upon these ancient people. Here again, in the typical crouch burial, was the ancient dolicephalic. With many were the scattered dust of red ochre and the ceremonial flints. I stared at them in amazement and then around at the roped rock above us.

This cemetery, I found out later, was discovered by chance not too long ago when the Mexican government was taking some of the rock for building blocks for the paving of streets and the building of homes. (American millionaires with their magnificent mansions comprise about one quarter of Mexico City's building problems and her subdivisions. Many of these are located on the Pedrigal.) The homes are exquisite with gardens and fountains. Sometimes the living room has a glass floor so the goldfish swimming in the surrounding pool can be seen. I wondered idly if the occupants ever thought of that cemetery below them - as yet hardly disturbed.

Two facts were added here to our knowledge of the ancient dolicephalic. Their pottery in this location sometimes consisted of three-legged pots, but there were no colors left for us to see. The temperature below the lava blanket was over 700 degrees! Also there was a pyramid. The lava had flowed around it and the rock bound it tightly. With the rest of the class I climbed it and collected a few rocks. Some had insects turned to crisp stone by the heat as they settled here in this sea of bubbling fire. I also found a bone which I picked up and took to class. A young doctor sat next to me and I saw him staring at it. Finally he said:

"That is a human bone. Probably some priest stayed behind to act as a sacrifice. Please let me bury it."

I did. This was the summer of 1955.

In 1859, Retzius, in his report to the Smithsonian Institute on his research among the Amerinds, made this statement which was amazingly keen considering the time at which it was made: "With regard to the early dolicephalae of America, I entertain a hypothesis still more bold, namely that they are related to the Atlantic populations of North Africa (along the Atlas) - namely the Moors, Tuaregs, Copts and others which Latham comprises under the group name of the Egyptian-Atlantidae."

While this was a very keenly analytical report, yet later discoveries show that the type is too world wide in distribution to be entirely Atlantic or Egyptian. Their trail of flints, which we think of as typically Azilian, gives us another clue to the origin of these ancients. Apparently there was a time before they had ships. During this time they walked. This trail stretches from

Spain along North Africa on the tops of the Atlas mountains, from thence to the Sudan and finally across to the Caspian and from thence to India. Spence and others believed that these Azilians came from the Atlantic to Spain, but there are arguments against this proposition. The domestic animals which they usually brought with them ran wild in India and were of Indian origin, therefore probably first tamed in India, or on islands in the Indian ocean. Which way did the Azilians go?

Dr. Frank Buck in his book "Vikings of the Sunrise" makes some interesting comments. As curator of the Bishop museum of South Africa, and a Polynesian by birth, his notations are pertinent to the subject. He points out that these Polynesian navigators travelled thousands of miles across the Pacific, back and forth from island to island, carrying the chicken, pig and dog as well as innumerable edible plants, or plants used for cloth or weapons. They guided themselves by the stars, a subject in which they had made some lengthy and interesting observations. They had undoubtedly reached the Americas in antiquity because the plants which they brought are to be found there. Also, from one of the educated Amerinds of Mexico university came this corroborating comment: "The Polynesians undoubtedly reached Central America in antiquity. Not only do the Amerinds have dozens of the plants under Polynesian names, but bark cloth is prepared as they do today in the South Seas with the same beaters, and antioch is prepared as they do to take out the poisonous fluid so that it can be eaten. Furthermore, in Brazil and other points in the jungle the Amerinds had the chicken and dog at the time of the conquest - and there these animals had been bred entirely mute to insure quiet so that the camp would not be betrayed to enemy tribes."

Dr. Buck is of the opinion that these invasions of the Pacific did not take place until after the Aryan speakers invaders over-ran India and had mingled with the original inhabitants. If this is correct, then these Polynesians are not true Azilians, but only a much later mixed group, which we today call by the name of Polynesians. However, he does place for us the domestication of the dog, pig and chicken, found with the Azilians long before the Aryan speakers were on the move from their Asiatic homeland; again - India.

If the Azilians went in vast antiquity from India or the Indian ocean along the Mediterranean toward the Atlantic, it was during an interglacial when the water was very high. It is also entirely possible that the caves of Spain, where we find

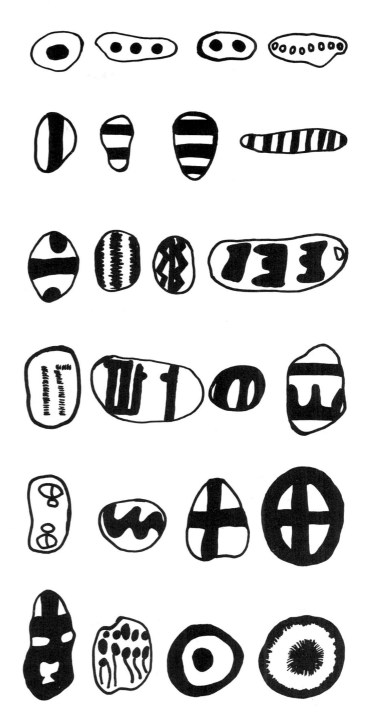

Azilian stones perhaps 200,000 years old. Colors were red on white stones.

the Azilian burials and also the pictures they made of their life, were made at a much later date, when after reaching the Atlantic islands and the shores of the Americas and establishing colonies, they were again driven back to the continent by the rising waters of another flood. These pictures have certain Amerind characteristics which it is very hard to understand otherwise. True, they bury their dead in the crouch position, with the usual heavy sprinkling of red ochre and flints, building a fire above the grave either for ritualistic reasons or to hide it from enemies, but the pictures they make of themselves on the walls are most surprising. We see them in typical Sioux or Aztec feathered war bonnet, while the women dress in skirts of fringed buckskin. We see them hunting the bison exactly as the Amerind does in the Americas, by stalking it - dressed in a skin of the animal and mingling with the herd. We see them dancing as the Amerinds dance or indulging in tribal battles. In one painting we see what apparently is the face of a Neanderthal man. Perhaps we should not be too surprised then to see the Tokari in Assyrian drawings and Philistines in Egyptian drawings with war bonnets on their head, nor be too much amazed when the Egyptian priest tells Solon many thousands of years later that their two peoples were once the same stock, having been led from the east by the same goddess and assigned their separate lands. We know that the Azilians brought in the bow and arrow, for we see them hunting with that weapon on the walls of the Spanish caves, while the animals they are hunting are those of the Pleistocene.

However, the most fascinating thing about these slim hipped people of so very long ago are the Azilian pebbles. These are always rounded and painted in red. The symbols are unknown. A tribe in Australia voluntered the information that the stones stood for people who were missing. This, of course, may be true or may not. However they are often found in groups, and sometimes there are a few intentionally smashed.

Yet the pebbles in themselves are fascinating to anthropologists because there is the ever-present suggestion that here we have the basis of all the written languages of today. In these symbols we seem to recognize a letter or part of a letter, or the part of a glyph. It is a fascinating subject for some aspiring young person seeking an upper degree, say a doctorate (Ph.D) in anthropology or linguistics to undertake. The jig-saw puzzle facing this future genius is hoary with age and hauntingly intriguing.

Before we leave the subject of the ancient dolicephalic or the Azilian, let us note two possible dates given us by two different branches of science. Dr. Pliny Goddard, during the last century, noted not only the twenty-two languages of California to be found in islanded remnants far more widely separated than Arabic and English, but also the wide time separation of all the languages of the Americas, and pointed out that it would take two hundred thousand years to bring them into any type of harmony. That reminds one of the legend of one of the early Mexican books which declared that the "great suns" (emperors) of the tribes from the old red land in the sunrise sea promised to meet once every tying of the Venus cycle (one hundred and four years) to talk over their adventures, and correct their calendrical observations. However, they found after a certain number of meetings that this had to be abandoned because their languages were steadily growing apart, and finally they could no longer understand one another.

There is another check on the antiquity of man in the Americas. That is the insect which lives upon the spider monkey, possibly also brought originally from India? The spider monkey was revered by some jungle tribes and hunted as food by others. This parasite was discovered sometime during the last century to have originally been a parasite of man and not the monkey upon which it was living. However, this contact was so remote that the creature was no longer able to live upon man. The parasitologists inform us that because the environment of the parasite is so even and constant, the evolutionary process is greatly slowed down. Therefore, taking this into consideration, it is necessary to assign at least two hundred thousand years to the first association between this monkey and the man in Central and South America.

Before we leave the ancient dolicephalic, let us note one more discovery. Sometime after World War I, in dredging the English channel, the dredge brought up a coffin. The eminent British anthropologist, Sir Arthur Keith, was summoned at its opening. It was found to be the ancient dolicephalic buried in crouch position with the usual flints, red ochre and weapons of the warrior.

Sir Arthur, shaking his head in amazement, remarked that "Anthropology to adequately keep up to date, should be completely rewritten every five years."

One wonders what this ancient man's friends, standing in their lush green forest as they lowered his coffin into the grave, would have thought if someone could have told them that someday ocean-going giant ships would pass far above their heads in a future world that they would consider pure fantasy if they could look upon it? And one wonders, also, how these ancient ancestors of ours would evaluate our progress - physically, mentally and morally? Perhaps it is just as well that we cannot ask?

Chapter 12

The Round Headed Landsmen

The third type of antediluvian, or Pleistocene man is the brachycephalic harmonic, or the round face type. He is a landsman and he stems from Asia, probably the steppes of Russia, through Turkestan. Again these skeletons are very old and we have no skin or hair, but from the skulls and skeletons we know that he had a stocky frame indicating strength and endurance. His nose was short, and this is interesting since the land where he apparently lived for many thousands of years is cold. His upper lip is long as compared to the short upper lip of the Azilian long head. The hair, judging from the great mass of brachycephalic men living in the Asian well of the ancient type, is straight, and in the cross-section is round (as compared with the softer hair of the long head which is inclined to curl slightly and in the cross-section is oval). His hand is on the square. He is apparently lighter-skinned than the long head, and the beard, which is evidently a brachycephalic trait, may have been a mutation kept because it was functional in a cold climate, as peppercorn hair was functional to the tropical negro.

The pure round headed type gradually disappears as one approaches the sea coasts of either the Atlantic or the Pacific today, in Eurasia. Another characteristic of the brachycephalic harmonic is the heavy eye-fold of the upper eyelid. This apparently has no functional value, but it is a dominant characteristic and long retained. I remember that my mother remarked that she had once asked of her grandmother, a Prussian countess, where the family got the heavy Asian eye-fold. The old lady drew herself up to the full height of her stocky figure and answered: "Well, my dear, at one time the Huns overran Germany to the Rhine river, and most Germans bear their mark. Now don't tell this to your uncle Gearhart, because it will only make him angry, but I have read history." If the old lady had only known, that mark was older than the invasion of the Huns.

The same fact is true of peppercorn hair. It is undoubtedly a mutation, for it is to be found in many Norse families who have no historical trace of Negro blood. As for the beard, it is a very dominant characteristic of the white man, and if the Amerind has one drop in his veins, he has to shave. In the lands overrun by the Spanish, part of the conquest was to rape the women, and there are hardly any Indians left who are free of

facial hair. On the contrary, in the reservations of the United States and among the tribes of Canada, the sight of facial hair on the face of a red-skinned Amerind will be the cause of unending teasing during his entire life, from his fellows. The Athapascan speaking tribes of Amerinds, the last tribes to come over from Asia - apparently about 800 to 100 AD, show traces of facial hair which they often pull out, and there is a very light beard on some of the Chinese and Japanese. The Hairy Ainu with their long beards, to be found in the north of the Japanese islands, and now almost extinct, have sometimes been considered to be a lost tribe of white men. This however, has only been a speculation as no notable scientific investigation of these people has apparently been undertaken.

There is no doubt that the brachycephalic harmonic is a landsman. The well of the pure type disappears as it reaches the coastlines, and on the sea shores of the Pacific, it often gives away to the slighter and more delicate figure of the long head.

In order to cross into the Americas, the brachycephalic used the Aleutian bridge, when the bridge was open to traffic. Of course, that traffic was a two way stream. The horse, an American animal, was first to be found in the lush forests of the Eocene where he is known as Eohippus (the dawn horse), has five toes and is no larger than a dog. At this time he ate forest leaves. The

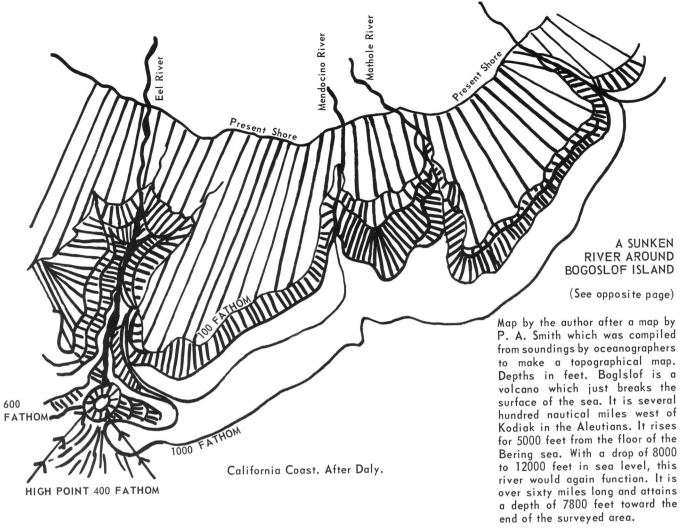

Eel River

Mendocino River

Mathole River

Present Shore

Present Shore

Present Shore

100 FATHOM

600 FATHOM

1000 FATHOM

HIGH POINT 400 FATHOM

California Coast. After Daly.

A SUNKEN
RIVER AROUND
BOGOSLOF ISLAND

(See opposite page)

Map by the author after a map by
P. A. Smith which was compiled
from soundings by oceanographers
to make a topographical map.
Depths in feet. Boglslof is a
volcano which just breaks the
surface of the sea. It is several
hundred nautical miles west of
Kodiak in the Aleutians. It rises
for 5000 feet from the floor of the
Bering sea. With a drop of 8000
to 12000 feet in sea level, this
river would again function. It is
over sixty miles long and attains
a depth of 7800 feet toward the
end of the surveyed area.

animal which we have today apparently crossed in the Pleistocene to Asia. He walks on only his middle toe, and the fingernail has toughened into his hoof, while his taste in food, and his teeth, have both undergone change.

There were times when this road from continent to continent was broad and firm for both plants and animals, including man. The horse which came from America during the Pleistocene, was finally able to go into Asia, where it was tamed by the brachycephalic harmonic man: in this case the one who spoke the Aryan tongue. Upon his back, the Aryan speakers rode to victory both in the Mediterranean and throughout Europe. We find him in the Mediterranean as the Hittite and the Persian. We find him throughout Europe as our own ancestors, or perhaps I should say one of them, as many of us show mixing of types through these long millennia since the ice mountains of the north began to retreat.

On the shores of the Americas he came in waves - sometimes, apparently many many mil-

lennia apart. And as he came he flowed around and islanded some tribes of long heads, or pushed them to less desirable locations. How long ago did he come and in how many waves? That will take a great deal of future study. In California alone, there were at the time of the coming of the white man, twenty-two languages, many of which were farther apart in time separations than Arabic and English.

We know that at one time the Aleutian bridge was very wide, allowing for the passage of many plants and animals. Dr. Tokuda, a Japanese geologist, points out that the islands of Japan are Tertiary in age. This means that they are about as old as the horse and were probably raised from the sea when he was a small five-toed creature, or shortly thereafter. Botanists of all nations have been noting a similarily between the plants of the islands off California and those of Japan. Perhaps in its early phases these were connected, because plants do not cross the ocean. But the major traffic across the Aleutian bridge

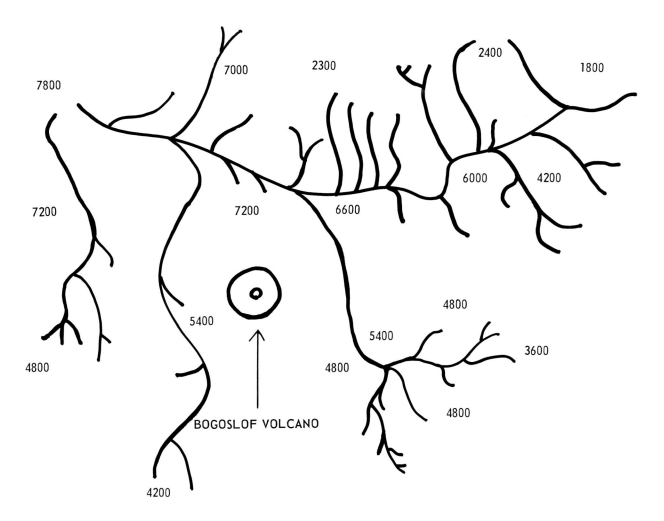

7800

7000

2300

2400

1800

7200

7200

6600

6000

4200

5400

4800

5400

4800

3600

4800

4800

4800

4200

BOGOSLOF VOLCANO

seems to have occurred during the Pleistocene when both plants and animals were migrating to seek warmer lands as the ice caps moved down from the north. Not that they were in a hurry. These movements were slow, for the ice perhaps moved only a few inches a year, but the animals were following the plants and the plants were following the climate.

The Aleutian bridge has, by some scientists, been compared to a busy drawbridge. For a number of millennia it was passable and the traffic flowed across it back and forth. Then it became flooded and the traffic stopped for even more millennia, the plants and animals awaiting the return of the passageway.

When was the bridge open? Perhaps for a few millennia when the ice mountains were on the march and the sea level of the oceans was falling. For some of the time it probably was warm enough to have rivers of its own. This may have occurred when the ice was heavy and the magma was flowing away from below the ice sheets to locations of lighter load. One of these may have been the bridge. We know that at times it was

wide enough to have a large river, because we have found it - on the bottom of the Bering sea!

Dr. P.A. Smith in The Geography of Review (a scientific magazine) reported the river in an article titled "The Submarine Topography of Bogoslof" and with its publication (see vol. 27, 1927 pp 630-636) gave the scientific world much food for thought. Under the old methods of under-sea mapping of fifty years ago or even less, the ancient river would never have been discovered. However, using a modern device to record the height of the ocean floor by the means of sound, and using it often enough, so that a complete map of the region in relief showing heights and depressions could be made, the long lost river came into being upon the drawing boards of the amazed oceanographers.

The river, which we may call the Bogoslof river, is very close to the volcano known as Bogoslof island, a cone rising from the ocean floor some five thousand feet and breaking the surface, often smoking and sometimes erupting. Yet the river has no connection with the volcano. It winds its quiet way around the volcano as it must have done in past ages from an unknown source to an unknown destination. It winds its way familiarly, with typical dendritic entering streams, from 1,800 feet below sea level where it first comes upon the drawing boards to an ultimate 7,800 feet below, still dropping fast as it goes off the drawing boards, with a tributary hurrying to meet it at some unknown bay or lake. With a raise of 10,000 feet, if we can imagine such a raise, we would have a river. If some unknown genii, such as a mass of magma under the mantle were to come in, the land would again rise, and the river - all sixty miles of it - would again begin to drain the land. And the land would be warm and pleasant from the furnaces below its feet, and the tropical plants and warmth-loving animals would once more come into this Eden.

Is there any other undersea suggestion of a once higher land or lower ocean drop - or both? Yes, in the channel islands of California not far from the place where Dr. Rogers found the tar caulking of the Azilian ships. It is the Eel river canyon. (See map in Chapter 22, page 146 Those Submarine Channels.)

Today the Eel river is a small unimportant stream in California, on the Mendocino strip, making its way to the sea; but there was 'a time when it was one of the large rivers. Then it had many tributaries which today make their separate ways to the sea. It is only when one looks at the relief maps below the level of the sea that one begins to see the massive cut which this river and its tributaries made in the past. About halfway down the shelf, one can see the last resting stage of the drop in sea level. It is at 600 feet. This is a sharp and well defined beach level. The Eel however, makes it curving way on down the canyon and then around a sunken island, before it finally empties into the sea at 6,000 feet below sea level. This island is flat-topped, showing that it was once eroded by rain. The lost island is found now 3,600 feet below sea level. This might suggest that the magma rise in the Aleutians was considerably greater than in California and undoubtedly lessened as one went south, thus deforming the entire continental block, when ancient drainage patterns are considered.

To the south, we find the great sunken Santa Barbara coastal strip, with the giant Los Angeles river of forgotten days. Today that river is almost nonexistent, but settlers of the seventies and eighties tell one that it was once a river, even in modern times. During the Pleistocene it was a mammoth waterway, and indeed it led not too many miles, about ten, from the La

Brae tar pits.

Today one may visit these pits where the great animals of the Pleistocene have been dug out of their sticky graves, the tar blackening their bones, but preserving them to almost the hardness of rock. The tar lies thickly below the surface, with a thin covering of water above, through which escapes an endless chain of bubbles from the gasses below. Thus for the thirsty animal coming to the deadly trap, he would undoubtedly mistake it for a lake, wade in for a drink, and immediately begin to sink in the tar. Undoubtedly the cries of anguish from the trapped ones lured the carnivores such as the dire wolf and the saber toothed cat or tiger to their death in turn. Leaping upon the trapped meal, and thus pushing it down faster by the extra weight, they would in turn be entrapped and the bait for other meat eaters. The tar pits became an endless museum of camels, enormous condors, huge wolves (the dire wolf) the saber toothed and other cats, the great sloth (as large as a grizzly bear), the tribe of the rhinoceros, the horse, the mastodon, the mammoth, and innumerable others, as well as an ancient woman and a cypress tree, to be dug out by modern scientists.

Today the cries of anguish and snarls of the fighting carnivores has given away to the roar of the traffic on Wilshire Boulevard, which skirts around the edge of the ancient trap. Yet, there is something ominous about this place. The present writer, as a child was not forbidden to go here and watch the scientists digging, perhaps because my mother, busy with bridge clubs, had never seen it. However, one day my strolls there were stopped. That happened when the papers were filled with the story of the boy who fell in, trying to save his pet dog, and was only saved in turn when his cries attracted some passers-by. They had to throw in planks and then make a human chain to reach him.

The place has an unholy fascination for children, but it is not as thrilling today since great wire cages are made of the pits which keep animals and children out. When I was a child, the sight of the half buried bones of a mammoth coming to light was a source of unending wonder at the size of the creature, and how he got there. I remember staring at the enormous molar teeth being handed up and placed just before the crowd, of which I was usually a member.

One can no longer see the scientists digging. Mr. Hancock, of Hancock Oil Company, the owner, undoubtedly plagued by the scientists rushing to get a particularly desirable skeleton for a particular university museum, decided to close the pits forever to anyone outside the city, and preserve the site for the education of the people. A park was then made, filled with statues in metal of some of the monsters which once roamed these grounds. A building was placed above one of the pits to keep out the rain, and one can go in and see what I watched as a child - the half buried mammoth which was then being dug out of the pit. Farther on is the still untouched main lake. One may even yet stand beside it and wonder just what it may hold in its eternal grip of tar. Perhaps even some of the tools of the Azilian-Tyrrhenians who came here so many thousands of years ago to obtain the tar with which to caulk their ocean-going ships? According to the Sumerian library, there was a tremendous demand for tar in the Mediterranean valley before the time of the great destruction. One stands before the ancient trap, and suddenly the past becomes very much alive in a ghostly way, as if one were standing in a place that is haunted.

Another animal in addition to the horse was found in the ancient trap, and with the horse crossed into Asia. That animal is the camel, now believed to have been of American origin since the variety of woolly llama and other types are to be found in the South American Andes of the present day. This animal, like the horse, crossed during the Pleistocene into Asia where he was tamed by another group of bearded white men - the Semitic speakers. On his back, as the Arab rides today, their early tribes rode into the Mediterranean to conquer and intermingle with the Azilian long heads. Besides their particular mounts of the horse and the camel, the two bearded types also brought sheep with them and dressed in clothes made of sheep's wool.

In the Americas, the brachycephalic harmonic began to cross upon the Aleutian bridge into the new world on the flanks of the animals which he sought for food. Which came first - the round head or the long head? There is one fact which argues the most strongly for the Azilian. The Mimembres people, living in the lush forested land which today is a desert, upon the banks of rivers long dried up and gone, are to be found quietly cultivating their grain and finding no use whatever for weapons. Were the round heads coming down through the centuries from the north to lands further south, then locked up here by the sinking of the ancient bridge - not necessarily the first sinking nor the last? Was this the place where Cro Magnon man was evolved - the big man - the first disharmonic cross type who had consolidated his mixed characteristics for so many thousands of years in isolation that he had

become a true race? If one insists that he is not an American, but a European, then how did he come out of a well of long heads such as the Mediterranean was when he evolved, or - in Europe - a well of round heads bordering a lost race of men - Neanderthal - the only true European?

Considering the two great ancient harmonic groups of which we are all descended - which had the greatest intelligence? That, I believe is a tie. There is no answer to this. Both types are too ancient in the pure form to judge. Are some of the great round headed musicians of Germany greater than England's long headed Shakespeare? It is significant that Greece of the golden age was a thousand-year mixture of the round headed Aryan speaking invaders coming on horseback and intermingling with the people they called Pelasgians, whom we know today to have been the long headed Azilians or Tyrrhenians, moving, trading and colonizing by means of their ships. This mixture of races was the most fortunate the earth has known to date.

We must remember that when we are pursuing the subject of race, it is difficult to be objective because, even though the investigator or commentator may not know it or realize it, every man prefers his own type and thinks of it as the greatest, even as one prefers one's own children. For example, when one investigator into the past of the Americas insists that all the civilizations of South America were started by white man with long noses, one may be quite certain that the author has a prominent probosis. Or when another supposedly scientific man declares that the golden age of Greece was entirely due to the invasion of large armies of round heads led only by a few long headed blonds, no comments by anthropologists are needed. Any good psychologist would understand this author's problem.

It is not too hard to be objective when one thoroughly realizes that these men of yesterday are back untold thousands of years. Today there are no more pure types of the harmonics unless one finds isolated groups in fossil cultures, and even then, they may have taken captives.

As far as the aforementioned supposed anthropologist or archaeologist is concerned, I would rather get into an argument with any of the long headed blonds of ancient Greece than one round headed harmonic who enjoyed wandering through the Agora, or market place with his court of teen-agers or laughing Athenians in tow. (And though my great-grandmother was undoubtedly a perfect brachycephalic harmonic - I am not.)

Chapter 13

The Tragedy Of Neanderthal Man-The First European

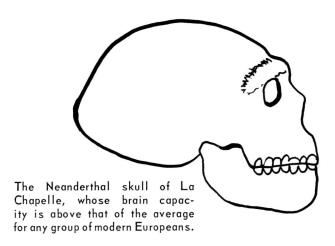

The Neanderthal skull of La Chapelle, whose brain capacity is above that of the average for any group of modern Europeans.

Top view of Neanderthal, showing the peculiarly typical growth of massive bone ridges over the eyes.

After Keith

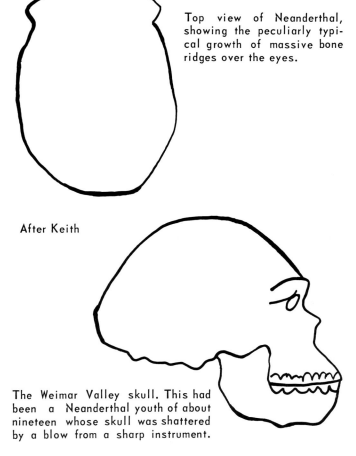

The Weimar Valley skull. This had been a Neanderthal youth of about nineteen whose skull was shattered by a blow from a sharp instrument.

To look at Neanderthal man, we are repulsed by his simian characteristics. He looks stupid; but do not let that fool you. Apparently from his skull, he was not. In the latest dating of his skeletons we find that the early Weimar skull of Germany dates back to the first interglacial. This skull is not that of a smart man, but it is considerably higher than the apes.

First let us get one fact straight - Neanderthal man is not our ancestor; he is not even on our stem. His teeth proclaim him a vegetarian while we retain the canine teeth of the meateater. It has even been suggested that Neanderthal man chewed from side to side. The teeth, a very strong skeletal feature, separate him from modern man. The teeth of most of the ancient types of modern man are larger than ours, with the exception of the Azilian. The jaw has been shrinking in modern man and the teeth have been growing smaller throughout the ages since the Pleistocene. It's hard to tell where we seem to be going - to a pill taking, sucking jaw? However, joking aside, this does seem to be a physical fact, whether it may be desirable or not.

The skull of the Weimar man is that of a youth of probably eighteen or nineteen. His head was shattered by the blow of some sharp instrument, perhaps a club, which undoubtedly caused his death.

Between the time of the Weimar skull and that of La Chapelle (both these have been named for locations) there is a curious change in the facial structure. Undoubtedly a great number of millennia have passed, for the change toward modernity is most striking. The jaw has shrunk and the face is straighter. The heavy ridges of the eyebrows, the mark of his race, is, however, retained. The man of La Chapelle, a much older man than the Weimar youth, is certainly not stupid. He has a better brain capacity than any modern race, or any group of modern Europeans. Of course, much of this is taken up with muscle control, for his stocky figure was one of a powerful man. This does not mean that he was in any way related to the brachycephalic harmonic, even though he held the land to the west of that type for untold ages. He was a long head, but there the similarity to the Azilian stops. His head was set down very low on his frame, giving him practically no neck, and the nose was short, and probably wide. The arms were very long and he walked with a shuffling, swinging gait. He was in fact a tropical type, even better prepared for the rigors of a hot climate than our modern tropical - the Negro.

He must have separated from modern man very early - probably during the long fiery, hot Miocene period of earth's history when our own ancestor was quite simian, and lived in the dank tropical jungles of Spain, where he was recently found in the coal beds. Even then our ancestor shows a straighter face and a reduction of eye-ridges beyond that of Neanderthal man. For this reason, many scientists are now placing the separation in early Miocene times. Yet it is possible that even then these animals may have captured some of each other's females. Some anthropologists believe that a few modern Europeans sometimes show a slight Neanderthal characteristic in their heavy eye ridges and deep sunken eyes. However, this is not a characteristic of any modern type of man with a single exception - the Australian bushman, who with his wild dog, hunts his meat with the boomerang and eats his meat raw. His deeply sunken eye is the only characteristic he retains as evidence of his contact with Neanderthal man. He is very tall and slender with a short nose and curiously enough, has a bushy beard on his chin. For this reason he has been noticed by some anthropologists as a possible lost tribe of the white man. If so, the contact is very remote.

The Miocene of the time of Neanderthal man's beginnings was a lush warm paradise for animal life. At this time and up through the last interglacial we know that the continent of Africa included the Canary island chain which was a part of the Atlas range. Certain plants including Canary island buckthorns have been found in the glacial moraines of Switzerland. Also, it is possible that the Atlantic may not have been the ocean it is now, for trees passed back and forth from Europe to the Americas and vice-versa on a broad front. Louis Agassiz was the first geologist to discover this fact when he found in Swiss Miocene beds the fossils of trees which are today flourishing in New England America, instead of Europe. However if the oak and other trees

THE AUSTRALIAN ABORIGINE

Pen sketch by the author, after an illustration from The Blue Of Capricorn, by E. Burdick, published in 1961 by Houghton Mifflin, Boston, Mass.

went west, undoubtedly the fig, maple and other species went east to Europe.

The Mediterranean at this time was a river draining its two lakes and dropping into the Madeira gorge in a magnificent waterfall. Then turning south between the ranges of the Madeiras and Canaries, it met the West Atlantic river coming down parallel to the Atlantic ridge, and finally entered the great lake of the southeast Atlantic basin. Later in the geology chapters of this book we shall discuss the facts which lead us to reconstruct such a picture.

Neanderthal man, having teeth of the vegetable eater, makes us believe that this fact, together with his thicker skull, would suggest an evolution in a more tropical setting than that of modern man. We have not only the molar of the vegetable and fruit eater, but also the canines of the flesh eater. These would place us as a more general type, and actually closer to the ancestral stem. If the Europe where we find him at the start of the glacials was the homeland to which Neanderthal man had learned to adjust his tropical body, then certainly tragedy awaited him, for his world was growing colder all the time, and surely in his eyes, with what legends he carried of the past, he must have viewed that world as slowly turning to ice.

We know that he did carry some legends, for he buried his dead and therefore must have believed in an afterlife. It was part of the tragedy of this human creature that he lived to see the paradise which had nurtured him turned into an eternal land of ice and snow. At least it seemed eternal, for untold millennia passed before the ice began to melt. One can imagine the sun-loving tropical creature hugging the fires in his cave home while he watched the advance of the ice mountains with those eyes that looked out from under his craggy, beetling brows. Did he tell his young stories of other times which were handed down through his ancestors? Did he turn to the worship of a sun god, as apparently did Azilian man, facing the same incredible slowly changing weather pattern? Is this how sun worship really began? Surely, in the last analysis, we must find that sun worship was the product of the ice age. Was the attempt to feed this failing divinity also the start of the practice of sacrifice?

There is one strange thing about this religion of his. He used red ochre to powder his dead much as did the Azilian, and the tools which he enclosed with the body in the grave always marks his passage even if no skeletons have been found. The name for his culture and the types of tools which were his are called Mousterian from the location where they were first found. The red ochre carried a strong suggestion that Azilian, the canny trader, may have made an early contact with these distressed people, to whom, coming as he did in ships, Azilian must have appeared as a god. Perhaps the Azilians were called that, answered to the name and played the part, not only in Europe but also in other parts of the world. What greater article of trade could these early sailors offer than "red dust from a sacred land" which was supposed to have omnipotent power? And what cheaper article of trade could they find than the red dust from some ancient mine, perhaps now long lost on some sunken island? What else is one to think when one sees the people of such vastly different races all using the same dust of the red ochre? It would be most interesting to find out someday whether or not this is of the same composition as the massive belts of red clay upon the bed of the Atlantic not far from the Atlantic ridge. Is this the origin for the almost intertribal ritualistic name given to a lost homeland by the Amerinds, namely "the old red land?"

Undoubtedly when Neanderthal man in his European caves, hugging his furs close to his body by the fire, listened during the nights to his story tellers describe earlier days, he may well have concluded that compared to the heavenly days of the past, his world was freezing up and everything would eventually end in ice.

Yet the story of Neanderthal man does not end on this note. The red ochre worked its magic. The sun grew stronger, the birds came back to the trees which were almost gone, the frozen streams began to flow again, at first slowly, and then faster and faster. A flood of terrible proportions was in the making. It was probably not the last one remembered in the legends of the Mediterranean as the flood of Noah, of Gilgamesh or Deucalion and in the Americas as the great destruction, but it caused lands to be flooded and tribes of people to move to better locations.

With this flood of readjustment when much land was being covered with water, a new type of man invaded Europe, apparently from the west. He was not a pure harmonic. He was definitely a type which was crossed between the two harmonics, but he had been isolated for thousands of years, apparently through the entire glacial which was now passing, and this isolation had caused him to interbreed with his own until he had consolidated his type to the point where it was a distinctly separate race. Science has called him the great disharmonic cross. His skeletons were first found in cave at Cro Magnon, France. From that location we get his name: Cro Magnon man.

When this new breed of homo (Latin for man), first saw the long armed Neanderthaloid, he was evidently repulsed, for he immediately began a war of extinction. He took no prisoners. Neanderthal man - what remained of his people - began a headlong flight to the south. Evidently he did not go east to the well of the harmonic round head. He may have had age long clashes with this ancient harmonic type. He could not go north because of the retreating ice, so he took the only direction still left to him - south. We find his remains in the caves of France. From there we trace him to Syria and in a cave we get our first big surprise. With the Neanderthaloid we discover the skeleton of a type which was evidently the issue of a cross with a modern - probably a captive. Scientists were indeed amazed at this discovery. Many had predicted that the Neanderthaloids were too different to be able to cross with modern man and this was the reason why none had ever been found. But this skeleton stopped any such speculation. He had definitely crossed with modern man.

From this point he disappeared (probably still further south) into the heart of Africa.

Returning again to our possible descendent of another modern cross with Neanderthaloid, let us look again at the Australian aborigine.

Recently an interesting book has come from the press giving a good picture of this strangely isolated creature who is now suspected of being a Neanderthaloid-Modern. Reaching Australia many millennia ago, probably from Asia, along with his wild dog (the dingo) he lives in utter isolation from the invading white man, upon the most undesirable land possible from the point of view of earning a living. Running naked through the eroded, moon-like landscape of an utterly barren desert, he manages to find good food in everything which moves - reptiles and insects as well as such mammals as the kangaroo and a few rabbits or birds. There is no water, except what he can obtain when a thin shower manages to scatter some drops over the parched surface. This storm he can smell and feel even before he can see it, and he makes a mad dash for the falling silver drops, dancing in it with high glee until a few puddles are to be found. Then he bends down and sucks them dry.

His thin canny dog, the dingo, suggests that he originally came from Asia, for it has the tawny color of the wolves and other old canines of that continent. The dingo helps him hunt and then patiently awaits its share of the entrails or skin. The dingo looks like a coyote. It ranges in color from a russet brown to yellow, and its eyes are like tiny lemons set on a slant. It is a quiet animal, showing its wild nature much like the almost extinct chow of China, both breeds of which the present author has had the pleasure of owning. In a way it is not as cat-like as the chow, but just as fiercely loyal.

The Australian aborigine is not a true Neanderthaloid. His thin body is not stocky. He is in fact, surprisingly tall. His hair, as we might expect from an Asian, is straight, but is so dirty and unkempt that one cannot be certain. He is probably earth's most primitive human being. Yet there is something about him that seems hard to believe, unless one grants that he is a long way off the stem of modern man. His lashes droop over his eyes like miniature curtains, but it is the eyeball itself that is strange. He does not seem to blink. He stares at you underneath those craggy brows in an unblinking manner, and when one sees a fly or ant crawl down the cheek and cross the open eyeball, one wonders.

He builds no villages and lives only in a lean-to where he can find refuge from the wind driven sand. There with his naked wife and bedraggled children he manages to stay alive. He has even learned to handle a poisonous yam and prepare it for eating by pounding it over a rock and baking it out in the sun where he leaves it for the next storm of raindrops to purify. The youngsters catch ants, but they don't dig for them. They allow the ants to come to them.

There is an interesting account in "Blue of Capricorn" condensed in the Readers Digest for March 1962, describing how the aborigine threw the boomerang. The rancher telling the story asked the Australian for a demonstration and he had one of his boys put a dead rodent on a distant bush. Then he threw once missing the target, and taking a single step forward, he caught the weapon.

"Now he'll throw and hit," the rancher said.

"Idje threw again. The boomerang spun out, seemed to come to a standstill, and whirled back. This time it dipped just before it came to the saltbush, came up savagely and slashed into the dead body of the rodent, almost tearing it in half. Idje grunted. One of the boys got up and brought the boomerang and the rodent back."

The description of the possessions of the aborigine are interesting. "I turned to look at the lubra. Like the man, she was entirely naked. She was squatting among the family possessions: two rubbing sticks for making fire, two stones shaped roughly like knives, a container woven of roots which held a few pounds of dried worms, and the dead body of the rodent. There was also a long wooden spear and a woomera, a spear throwing device which gives enormous velocity and high accuracy. And there was the boomerang, elaborately carved."

The thought strikes one that here might be a cross type from the Neanderthal-Cro Magnon war of antediluvial times - the tall one who got away? But if so, how did he get to Australia? In all probability we shall never know.

Thus Neanderthal man leaves the story of man's struggle for survival on a moving and changing planet. It is a story which both begins and ends in a question mark.

Cro Magnon man now took the Neanderthaloid's place in the European caves. His own campfires are only a short distance above the campfires of the former tenant. One wonders if Cro Magnon, in turn, did not watch the slow return of the ice mountains in terror - seeing the streams which were freezing earlier and staying frozen later with each passing season? Or did he have legends of his own homeland and how the sun god grew wan and almost died once before, but that wise men had learned how to feed the divinity so that there would come a day when at last he would return? And was the magic which they used the blood of sacrifices, or a pinch of sacred red powder, or both?

This too, perhaps we shall never be able to learn.

Chapter 14

The Great Disharmonic Cross

Dr. Clarke Wissler, world famous anthropologist, and curator of the Heye museum for the American Indian, once quoted a colleague as saying that no scientist ever actually convinced his opponents. They simply died off and the newer generation, having different ideals or prejudices, or lack of them, began to think for themselves.

Sometimes this observation seems closer to the truth than one would like to believe, but occasionally a student, completely won over to the outmoded views of a professor, continues to fight savagely for them against even such modern tools as carbon dating. It reminds one of a grown tiger fighting for a loved parent. The situation only becomes tragic to science when the student in turn becomes instructor to the youth.

It was once suggested that the two wells of the harmonic types of early modern man were separated by the rise of the Himalayas. This was immediately frowned upon by the anthropologists (from the Greek anthropos - man and ology - study of) because they did not wish to think of man as a creature as old as the animals. Since this view was proposed, many finds have shown that modern man is not the last creature of a long branching stem, but of the stem himself. His tools and skulls have been found below those of Neanderthal man both in England and in Africa. The antiquity of modern man is continually being pushed back in time. His teeth are less specialized than those of some other types, and therefore apparently more primitive. Or, he may have retained the canines for eating meat by living in a cool climate, while Neanderthal specialized his by remaining for untold millennia in a tropical land and eating vegetables. Neanderthal of course, is not the only so-called "missing link". We will take the others up in time. What these finds have done for us is to prove that canines are not a late evolvement or a mutation. They are very ancient to the stem. With these finds comes the discovery of the antiquity of modern man. Nor do we any longer believe with Dr. King

of the earlier days of the discovery of the Neanderthaloids that this early man, even though he did have a forward bending frame and long arms as well as a low brow, had "died off from a lack of brains". The Weimar skull is about the capacity of many moderns while the skull of the old man of La Chapelle had a brain capacity of 1,625 cubic centimeters, or in other words 145 cubic centimeters above that of the average white European. From this, Sir Arthur Keith, a very conservative anthropologist, has stated that the old man of La Chapelle showed an advance which must have taken two hundred thousand years to accomplish, even though that advance was along the low browed, heavy eye-ridge face so typical of his race. Of course, much of this was taken up in muscle control, for he had a large frame.

Thus science has had to concede the antiquity of the skull from Weimar valley. It was found in a very much petrified and fragmentary condition in what had been the gravel of an ancient stream. With it were the remains of such extinct animals as the Rhinoceros Mercki and the Elephas antiquus (ancient elephant). Both of these animals became extinct before the last glaciation. Now, unless we find the body in a burial, we cannot be certain that it belongs to that period. It may have been washed down with the stream gravels from a very much earlier strata of rock. However, the same is true of many other skulls of vast antiquity - Heidelberg man, the ape man of Java, Sinanthropus (China), and the still ape-like (but more intelligent skull than the modern apes) Taunge skull of Australia all belong to this list of gravel finds washed along in a petrified and fragmentary condition.

Another fact moving the horizon of man's antiquity backward, is the discovery that wisdom teeth are as rudimentary in these ancient jaws as they are in the jaw of modern man, which points definitely to a time when the jaws of our ancestors were even more massive and have since then made a steady decline.

Furthermore, in the caves where the races of ancient man built his fires and buried his dead (Neanderthal man did both), why must science always take the last possible date rather than the time when the animals which man ate and tossed their bones upon his pile of kitchen refuse were the most plentiful, for the time of the caveman's occupancy? The answer is, of course, the great caution of science. The man in question must be dated as "he could not be later than the last glaciation" rather than "he probably lived during the long cooling Pliocene when the hot jungles of the Miocene were becoming conditioned slowly to the advent of the ice sheets". Is it not possible that man is as old as the horse? If he is, then someday, somewhere, there will be more finds between the creature of the hot Miocene and the later types, for the books of the rocks have only just been opened for study.

Let us take a close look at this man who is known as the great disharmonic cross. He very plainly shows his ancestry. We know that he was a creature of the Pleistocene, when the ice sheets were either advancing or retreating. Keith, by the way, as well as some others, prefers to refer to only two glaciations, the first and the third, which were the heaviest, and to regard the second and fourth as mere fluctuations of climate.

At the close of one of these glacial periods, the great disharmonic cross poured into Europe and began his war upon the Neanderthaloids. He came on the flanks of the ancient ox and the bison or American buffalo. He was wide faced with high cheekbones. He carried the bow and arrow, and wore feathers in his long braided hair.

Some authorities would like us to believe that these men chased the herds of early ox and bison from the edge of Asia where they came off the Aleutian bridge, through the entire land of Asia where the round heads were busy taming the horse and camel without acquiring either domesticated animal, and what is still stranger, without taking any captive women.

Other authorities would have us believe that they migrated from the well of the long heads - namely the Indian and Mediterranean regions, even though what history we do have tells of massive invasions from the Atlantic into the Mediterranean both before and after the deluge. Up to the time when their main cave at Cro Magnon, France was found, there was a calm of contentment among the anthropologists. It was the calm of ignorance and had in it the ominous quiet of a coming storm.

Then one day a child chased a rabbit into a bush and beneath it found a hole. He crawled in. Suddenly he found himself in a large cave filled with pictures of strange looking animals. He went home and told his parents, and Cro Magnon has been stirring endless debates ever since.

Let us take a look at this interesting skeleton. Definitely he is a modern, and all the scientists recognized him as such. He strongly shows his ancestry. His skeleton is a combination of the doli and brach (cephalics). For the sake of brevity I will abbreviate the two as we did in college. The correct spelling of the first is dolichocephalic but we abbreviated it to the spelling I have been using. In our papers we abbreviated the terms even more. As long as we understand the matter under discussion, I do not see that it matters a great deal.

Let us begin with the skeleton of the great disharmonic cross. He has the slender build of the doli but the ruggedness of the brach, making for a very large, strong man. He has the long head of the doli but the broad face of the brach. He has neither the short upper lip of the doli nor the pointed chin. Instead he has the long lip (upper) and round chin of the brach. He has the very high broad cheekbones which seems to be a recessive characteristic of the brach and the heavy fold over the upper eyelid, especially as the type blends outward toward the Pacific Orientals. Yet he has the long nose of the doli. In fact he has exaggerated the characteristic, and often the nose is hawked. He has a curious feature of his own in that his forehead is slender and often retreating to the hair line. This, together with the very high cheekbones gives the impression of a face built upon the diamond, with the chin rounded off. His other feature which is distinctly of his race is that his woman usually comes only to his shoulder.

He is definitely a racial cross, but he has lived for so long in isolation, interbreeding with none save his own, that he has consolidated his type into a true race of his own. Where was this homeland? That was the location about which the arguments began, especially when the scientists learned that his skull capacity was somewhat better than ours today, even allowing for the necessity of muscle control for such a big frame, for these were big men averaging six feet or over and well over the heads of either ancestor. What isolated land, cut off perhaps through an entire glacial, yet with lush forests for an abundance of game would have nurtured this big fellow? A child's curiosity had led to a scientific storm. The cavern where he was found could give us but few hints. The walls were covered with pictures of the animals which he hunted. Many of them were undoubtedly American animals. They were done with definite artistry and even below them were other animals moulded from the rocks which were lying about.

For the tall disharmonic these paintings were obviously functional. He wished to control the destinies of the game which he hunted, and so he drew them with an arrow through the heart. When he wished to hunt another type of animal, he whitewashed out the first scene and drew another picture over it. Throughout the ages, the whitewash has weathered away and the result is the animals he drew are one upon another in a welter of confusion. Most of the pictures are in red - the brilliant red of ancient man. (For example the Azilian pebbles are in a red which has never faded through these many millennia since they were made.)

From what isolated place did this tall hunter-artist enter western Europe on the flanks of the herds of the bison, ox and other Pleistocene animals? Europe? Not only was it half covered with ice, but also occupied by Neanderthal man and had been for over a hundred thousand years. It seems unlikely that he would not have found the round headed women attractive enough to have stolen enough in all these untold centuries to forever break up his racial characteristics. Or that he would have waited for over a hundred thousand years to kill off the Neanderthaloids after living with them peacefully for over a thousand years in untouchable isolation. But where did he live? The harmonics and the Neanderthaloids had the caves. Apparently the scientists who are proposing this theory are either not thinking straight or they may have a touch of emotional bias. I suspect the latter.

However, there were a few anthropologists who suddenly began to take a hard look at the tall bodies and lean faces of the American Indian of the eastern Atlantic tribes. If other Europeans looked, they quickly looked away. Wishing to claim Cro Magnon for an ancestor, they refused to study the similarities in the faces and skeletons. The geologists backed them up, denying that it was possible that a bridge between Europe and the Americas had at one time been passable during the Pleistocene. Since that day, geology has been slowly changing its combined mind. Anthropology, on the contrary, is still tapping its collective fingers.

However, there were a few anthropologists who suddenly began to take a hard look at the gaunt faces of the Atlantic tribes - Iroquois, Sioux, Comanche, Cheyenne, Blackfoot, Osage, etc. They saw a man with a face built on the diamond. They noted the firm chin, the prominent cheekbones, the hawked nose, the long upper lip, the long head, the big frame and that strange curiosity - the relatively shorter woman. They noted the similarity of the ritualistic painting to control the destiny of food animals, the use of ochre paint, the braided hair, bow-arrow weapons, etc. They even noted the unusual capacity in that long skull with the diamond face and the forehead narrowing as it retreated slightly to the hair line. As in both cases, much of this was taken up with muscle control for a big frame. There was still another curious individuality of both races - the pelvis was so shaped that they could squat upon their haunches for hours at a time without, in the least, tiring.

Dr. Clarke Wissler was one of the first scientists to see the Amerind in a new light. With characteristic scientific caution, he wrote: "Cro Magnon man has in his disharmonic face one of the most prominent of New World characteristics".

However, it was Huxley, with the boldness of this great scientific thinker, who turned the full light of his scrutiny upon the American Indian of the Atlantic tribes. Finally he suggested, not that Cro Magnon invade the Americas, but that here was the homeland of the great disharmonic cross. It was from here that Cro Magnon, crossing upon an old sunken land bridge, invaded, along with so many animals of the Americas, the European shores of the Pleistocene.

He further postulated the manner of the mixing of the two harmonics. The dolichocephalic came around from the region of the Indian along with the animals of that part of the world by way of Antarctica. (I have an idea he would have welcomed the later discovery of Dr. David Banks Rogers) namely the planked ships of the Azilians. About this same time, said Dr. Huxley, the round heads came down from the Aleutian bridge, along with their Pleistocene animals. The two races met and fought. In the meantime the ice returned and they were trapped. Throughout the following glacial they captured each other's women and amalgamated. Thus the great disharmonic cross. Both of these men pointed out the fact that there were no skeletal differences between the two types.

If Huxley had only known about the Azilian ships and the probable seeking of tar, according to Sumerian documents, a trade object in the Mediterranean before the flood, then he might have suggested that the earlier towns of such

Azilians as the Mimembres living with no weapons were surprised by waves of round heads coming down the Aleutian bridge, and made captives. The return of the ice then would have isolated them and the mixing of the great disharmonic cross began. Furthermore, future waves of the round heads coming again and again down the Pacific after other glacials would have driven the Eastern tribes toward the Atlantic, or the disharmonic cross gives away to the round type along the shores of the Pacific. Perhaps this mixing was as early as the curiously early

This way of very easily losing their skin color makes one believe that white is a recessive characteristic far back in their ancestry. Almost any young Indian child standing in the sunlight, the deep red-gold of the hair gleams with color and the blue of the raven shade only comes later in life. Also all of the Atlantic tribes, if posing for artists, always warn the painter to color the skin more red, for it fades out to an old ivory shade in the light of the city. Also they are very prone to sunburn. It was the joke of the Universal City studios, filming a western and using

Chief Yellow Horse. The tall hunter-artist type, illustrating the true, Indian (Amerind) face.

giraff found in the La Brae tar pits.

At any rate, the Atlantic tribes are a handsome people, very definitely talented as artists and showing signs of an ancient civilization. There is something else about them. When one of them marries a white skinned American the offspring are usually blonds, although they carry some of the Indian features and, of course, the men have to shave. In two generations one would not recognize anything Indian save the size and perhaps the high cheekbones which, in the woman of mixed marriage, makes for an exotic beauty.

Dacotah tribesmen for their ancestors in the Custer fight, that they had to close down for two days while the Indians recovered from a bad case of sunburn!

For a moment let us digress and discuss skin-color. Hitler was not the first one to start a fad on hair color by sending his women to the drug store for peroxide. Of course, he was not aware of this and they probably sneaked the bottle home with the groceries. But ancient Egypt so admired red hair that an extensive trade was carried on in henna. Turks have admired fat women, the early Greeks straight profiles from nose tip to forehead until one suspects that they may have tried to mold the nose bridge of the babes. The Incas admired big ears and hung heavy pendants to make them long; the San Blas Indians admire long noses and hang heavy pendants in the child's nose with this result in mind. The length of these national fancies could go on indefinitely. Today we no longer admire excessively long necks as did medieval artists and indeed wonder what a woman would look like if her "neck was like a swan".

Yet it is true, at least among children, that blondes are concentrated in the northern countries of Europe. Dr. Huntington in his "Human Geography", believed that skin color was purely a matter of the ultra violet sun rays and gave for his reason the manner in which the northern blonds darken to brunettes in the Mediterranean and then to black skin in Africa. Of course, his attention should be called to Asia and the Americas. However, this fact is so noticeable in Europe that Dr. Dixon wondered if indeed there were not something about the food which had these effects. He pointed out that he had kept track of blond families who had left for Africa and had learned they could expect only brunette children within two or three generations. He furthermore found blonds among long heads, round heads and a close resemblance of what is left after much admixture of the great disharmonic cross in Europe. As to which group of harmonics was the original stem, there are some differences of opinion, and one might point out in passing that there are both types among the primates (apes).

Dr. Clarke Wissler in a letter to the present writer suggested that the round headed white race had lived very near a glacial in an isolated valley, and there developed facial hair as a protection to the cold. This is possible as a functional mutation, but as I pointed out to him in one question he could not answer: "What about the Eskimo?"

I asked one time of a very old and knowledgeable sachem of the ancestor chants of one of the Atlantic tribes: "Did you by any chance, once have red headed people, or did you take red headed captives?" pointing to a small child who was standing close to me in the sunshine. His answer was quite surprising.

"Yes, we did. Yet if you are thinking that we are your grandchildren, you are wrong, although you and the Irish may be our grandchildren."

"What is your reasoning on this?"

He pursed his lips and gave an almost imperceptible shrug of his shoulders.

"The beard," he said simply.

When I wrote this to Dr. Wissler he commented: "I too have noted the red lights in the hair of some children. Have you also noted how they become less evident as one goes toward the western tribes? One wonders if it is an purely Atlantic trait?"

It was in answer to my letter about the remark on the beard that Dr. Wissler presented the idea of the possibility of glacial nearness as a reason for the retention of excessive hair as a functual mutation. He had no answer to my question about the Eskimo. Who knows how it happened, but Dr. Wissler was convinced that the old sachem was correct in saying they were the older race - or should one say the elder race? Or as he said in his own picturesque way - we were his grandchildren.

The following letter from Dr. Wissler is most interesting: "By the way, have you read the Smithsonian Institution's report on the white San Blas Indians of Darien, Mexico? If not, I will be sending you a copy."

While awaiting his answer and the copy, I began to look up the San Blas in the library. I found one small book the name and notes of which I seem to have lost. One scientist from the Smithsonian went on a trip to their region to look up the legends about white Indians in the jungle. He found that the regular red skinned San Blas called them "moon children". He found that he seemed to be up against the proverbial stone wall whenever he mentioned the pale skinned San Blas. So he tried another method. He noted that the San Blas had great admiration for long noses and tied metal on the babe's nose to lengthen it. He also noted certain diseases carried by the bite of a large beetle (the cone nose bug). Beaching his yacht he lived with the San Blas, making friends with them. Instead of trying to convince them that he had any magic, he allowed them to look through his microscopes and see the composition of insects, the germs in a drop of infected water, etc. The San Blas were fascinated. He tried and was able to cure some of their jungle diseases.

One day he saw a captive white child. Probably the mother and father had been killed. He asked that he should be allowed to take the little red haired boy back with him as his son. The San Blas were amazed and skeptical. He promised that he would give the child an education in medicine. If he decided later, he could then return to his people and give them the results of his knowledge, but if he did not want to do this, he could remain a white man.

Geronimo (or Gheronimo)

The San Blas agreed to this proposition and then they began to tell about their own "moon children". Once there were many. Also they were accepted, and the tribe was in the process of turning white, for they found that white skin was a dominant trait. However, then came the Spanish conquest. Horrified at the savagery of the conquering whites, they turned against their own and attempted to massacre them all as "children of evil". Some escaped into the jungles where they became, in turn, relentless savages. Now they were hunted and killed on sight.

He found that the San Blas were actually deeply touched by his evident desire to adopt the little red headed waif. Then he made them a bolder proposition. Could he take back with him many whites? They would be shown American cities, fed American food and bring back American presents. The San Blas agreed. They went toward the jungles with "talking drums" and soon the whites began to come in - timidly at first as if they feared some kind of trick. He saw that they were not albinoes. They did not have pink eyes. Their skin was not colorless nor was the hair. They simply looked like whites.

True to his promise he was able to take them to the Smithsonian Institution at Washington, D.C. where they were to be housed and fed - all to be paid for by some questions to be answered about legends and particularly words of the language. He was able to entice thirty to return with him.

Dr. Wissler sent me his copy of the Smithsonian report which I read through and returned. There was a good deal of interesting material especially in the field of language. The white San Blas referred to themselves as "Yahpisahs" which meant "hairy ones", and pointed to the light colored fuzz on their arms such as most of us have. The surprise to the scientists was the discovery that they had many words of very early Gothic which can today only be found on remote islands off the Norwegian, Scotch coasts or other isolated Atlantic positions, in mountain villages. The San Blas were enchanted by the wonderful world they saw and the scientists found out that their guests showed good intelligence, and were in no way to be considered albinoes. However, they hardly knew what to write in their report on these blue, grey or green eyed people with their light brown, blond or red hair. So they finally decided to call them "partial albinoes." One wonders how these learned men would classify the rest of us?

The child adopted by the scientist soon adjusted to his white school, was quickly accepted, was good at his lessons and at making friends.

Further than that his adjustment was instantaneous and successful, one learned no more. Apparently he was not a part of the report and so whether he ever became a physician and went back to the San Blas is not told.

To these bits of help from Dr. Wissler, I replied with two stories of my own. The first had happened a few days before. I had been eating at a restaurant in Los Angeles when a man sat down beside me who looked like a tanned Irishman with red hair and freckles. He was much amused at something he was reading in the paper. He had a most infectious laugh. Then another man came by who was distinctly an Amerind of the disharmonic type with the high cheek bones and hawk nose. He sat down on the seat to the other side and they spoke quietly together in an unknown tongue. Finally the Amerind arose and left, leaving the "Irishman" with his paper. I could contain my curiosity no longer.

"Pardon me for being so bold, but what was that language? I couldn't place it."

"Yaqui," he answered with a slight smile.

"Yaqui! (pronounced Yah-kee) That is an Indian language."

"Right. It is my native tongue. That man was my brother."

"Oh, you mean half brother."

"No. I mean full brother. You see at one time, very long ago, a long ship came to our village bearing white men and women. The wife of the captain was a red head, and they put in to our village because he was dying from the infected bite of some kind of fish. We could do nothing for his ailment, for we were not acquainted with the poison, so all we could do was to give him a good burial. But we fed the people and they remained with us for four years. The red haired woman became "queen" and ruled the rest, choosing a new captain. Then she married an ancestor of mine. When they finally left, they had all intermarried and many stayed with us and many of our people went with them. So we have red heads in our village. I am one."

"What was the ship like?"

"It was about a hundred feet long with a serpent or dragon head and tail. Some of the men wore helmets with horns."

"Did they carry guns?"

"No, this must have been before the time of guns. They had bows and arrows - big ones."

"Did they tell you anything about their homeland?"

"Yes, they told us two stories that we didn't believe until our people began to go to school. They said that their streams and lakes got so hard in winter that they could walk over them."

"And they weren't joking," I chuckled.

"They also said that they had an elk which had horns larger than the animal itself."

"The caribou or reindeer?"

"No, some of us have looked it up and we believe they must have meant the extinct Irish elk."

"Why did they come? Tar?"

"No, but they were interested in oil. They had been whaling for oil."

I nodded.

"When our people sailed away they promised to return, but we never saw them again. And ever since then there has been red hair in our village."

"And the beard?"

"Yes, but not as heavy as white man."

The other story had to do with the Sioux. I had met one in a book store where he was buying a book which I was after.

"I really have more right to it than you do," he said half jokingly as he refused to relinquish this fascinating dictionary of Gothic words in use among the Amerinds of the eastern tribes: "The Viking and the Red Man."

I looked at his blond hair and his blue eyes, and asked: "Why?"

"Because I am Dacotah."

"You mean half Dacotah."

"No. I am full blood Dacotah," drawing himself up to his full six feet.

"I would have taken you for a Dane - of typical Cro Magnon stock."

"I don't know the Cro - whoever they are - but I am Dacotah."

"Which tribal group?"

He was beginning to show real anger until I asked that. Then in a softer voice he answered: "Hunka-pah."

"I have a Hunka-pah friend . . ."

"Then ask him," and bending over the book he scribbled down a name.

The next time I saw Shooting Star, I showed him the torn bit of paper. He took it and smiled.

"Oh yes, where did you meet him?"

"He bought a book I wanted and gave for his reason that he is Dacotah."

"He is."

"Does he shave?" I asked suspiciously.

Shooting Star laughed.

"You have been around Indians too long, asking too many questions and getting too many right answers." Then, shrugging his shoulders, he said thoughtfully: "A baby is born to our people and we do not ask if it is white or red.

We treat it as one of us, and sometimes the white ones are more red than the red ones. This boy is a red one. Do you understand?"

When I wrote this story to Dr. Wissler I received a letter asking me to do a bit of research for him.

"I am very much interested in this ceremonial rite of the Amerind of the Atlantic tribes, called Secondary Burial. You will understand when I tell you it is a Cro Magnon rite. In the graves which have been unearthed, Cro Magnon paints the bones of his dead with red. Now I want the steps between the death and the painting of the bones. Something very similar is being observed in many of these people, but I have been told that two or three groups have the entire long rite. From the southern portion of the High Andes among the Aymaras certain portions were observed, where the dead are first placed on platforms as among the Dacotah. Among the Rama the bodies are then taken down in a partially mummified condition. This may have been the start of the mummification process as it was practiced among the Incan people before the conquest. However, there are three tribes who have the entire rite - the Aurakians of South America, the Bribir of Central America and the Choctah of the United States. Now I am in touch with a certain sachem of the latter tribe who might talk to you. Please go, and try to take your friend, Shooting Star. I have typed out some questions for you to ask and left a space for the answers. Please say yes. You have quite a way with them which is most unusual."

So in the company of Shooting Star I met the Choctah. After the preliminary small presents and small talk which always allows for getting acquainted and giving the informant the opportunity to size up the questioner and appraise the worth and reasons for the questions, we finally got around to the subject. He was pleased when I explained how old this burial rite really was, and why both Dr. Wissler and I were interested. I could see that both of the Amerinds were becoming very much interested themselves, and then I knew I would have good cooperation. So we got around to the subject.

With my first question the Choctah said: "Our burial rite comes down to us from the time of the dawn. When a warrior has left the lodges of the living, we dress him in his best clothes and place him high on a platform in the woods. Then we go away and leave him. This is so that the spirit might learn its directions from the birds. You see the spirit will be earthbound for one year. We of the living wait for a year before we say the final farewell. In fact, you do not do anything more than that, do you?" he asked the Dacotah.

"That is not entirely correct," Shooting Star answered. "We reverently gather the bones at the end of the year and we bury them in crevices in the rocks even as our ancestors were once buried during the horror of the great destruction."

"You have not forgotten as much as I thought you had," the Choctah observed.

"Is there any other reason than the one you have given, as to why you expose the body for a year?" I dutifully read from Dr. Wissler's list.

"Yes. The birds are sacred to the sun. The great sun must see the dead warrior and know him. The place is forbidden to the living so that this recognition will not be disturbed."

"Our idea is similar," the Sioux noted with a touch of surprise. Then leaving his "white man chair", he took one of my empty sheets of paper, pulled a pencil from his vest pocket, and placing it on the floor, squatted down on his haunches and began to draw.

"Our platform looks like this. Do you recognize anything?"

The Choctah immediately left his chair also and squatting beside the Sioux drew his own burial platform below the other.

I sat back and watched them, realizing how much pleased Dr. Wissler would be with these drawings. Then suddenly I remembered something. Here were two good specimens of Cro Magnon man squatting easily on the floor, conferring together in a language foreign to them, because their own tongues were no longer mutually understandable. How many thousands of years of time separation, I wanted to ask, but knowing that would only bring blank stares, I dutifully read: "What happens at the end of the year?"

"The time has come for the spirit to take his departure," the Choctah continued, turning his head slightly. The bones are gathered and polished and painted red for the journey. There is singing and ritual dancing - or there used to be. We are fast forgetting."

"But what happens in war or if you cannot go through this long ceremony - say on a trip?"

Shooting Star answered: "We gather the bones at the end of the year and we bury them in crevices in the rocks even as our ancestors were once buried during the great destruction."

But the Choctah saw that this was not the answer I wanted.

"When the brave is killed in war, or during a long migration, then the full ceremony is not possible. He may be placed in rocky crevices or given after due ceremony, to the sacred fire."

"Is that because the fire is red or because you wish the spirit to look ruddy and full of health? Some scientists have been told that this is the reason," I read from my list.

"No. The colors of the fire and the sun are both red, but that is not the reason."

"Is it not because of the ancient homeland?" Shooting Star asked.

I suddenly sat up very straight. The ancient homeland? What did he mean? He turned and saw my expression.

"You have been around Indians these many years and you have never heard of the old red land?"

I shook my head. It was true. Since then, I have often heard it mentioned by many tribes, but this was the first time. They looked at each other and I saw a few swift hand signals pass between them.

"I read your paper," the Sioux nodded to the test which Dr. Wissler had typed. "That about being pale and wan is not the reason."

The Choctah uncoiled his frame from the floor and the Sioux followed suit.

"Your Dr. Joyce was not told correctly down in the jungles of Mexico, and those Indians were smiling behind their hands when they told him. The real reason is that red is the aristocrat of all colors. The great ones will never recognize their own. Now you look as if you wanted to know something else - something which is not on that page you are holding. Is there?"

I nodded, but my voice was almost dry and gone from a dry throat.

"The red land! Where is it?"

The Choctah pulled out a most interesting old ceremonial pipe from his pocket, passing it to my friend, the Dacotah, who put in a few pinches of tobacco. The Choctah took it back then, put in a pinch of something else and taking a few puffs, waved it to the four directions. Shooting Star did the same and then certain ritual chants were said. I was asked to stand between them and face east. I did. I heard the voice of one of them chanting behind me as I was pushed forward: "Long ago at the dawn there were four bacabs who upheld the heavens before their power broke and was scattered. There we had all in our hands. Everything was settled there. Then came the terror. The sacred caves fell together and became the tomb of our ancestors. Far out there it lies, but down low - very low - beneath the green waves of the sea."

Chapter 15

Fitting Together
Some Parts Of The Puzzle

"What is truth?" - Pontius Pilate.
This question may be said to be both the inspiration and quest of all science.

Not exactly disbelieving what the Amerinds had told me, yet I was skeptical, for it did not seem probable that an island had been the homeland of isolation where the great disharmonic cross had consolidated its racial type. I haunted the shelves of the public library for days. Then I began searching through the rare book sections of book stores. One day I was rewarded. It was a fairly thick book, in a dark red cover with gold lettering - The Traditions of Decoodah. In gold on the cover was the etching of a proud Indian sachem of more than a century ago. I bought it and took it home. Reading it took my night which should have been spent sleeping.

Instead, in breathless imagry I roamed through the dark woods just beyond St. Louis, Missouri where a young surveyor had become intrigued with the "earthworks" of the Amerind. He wandered over them and finally began to survey them. He carried no food or other equipment except his survey tools and papers, a gun for obtaining food, a pan to cook it and a blanket for sleeping.

One day while working he was startled to find an Indian standing beside him silently watching what he was doing. The Indian was a tall man, straight as an arrow, though a few streaks of white in his hair showed that he was not young. Both facts here are typical of the Amerind. You will think that you are alone - perhaps even entertaining the intriguing delusion that you are the first human being to have stepped upon this lonely mountain ledge or to have knelt down to drink of this lovely spring, when suddenly there he is, as if he had materialized from the mist of the morning. To your surprised greeting he will simply nod, or perhaps if you are more lucky he will smile and tell you that he has been following you for hours.

Pidgeon was not entirely naive in the ways of the Amerind, and he knew that a streak of white in the hair meant that his observer was near the century mark. I personally have seen such men

"The Joy Of Returning Spring". Original painting by Harry Epaloose, Zuni Junior High School student.

as old Marksman of the Chippewa whom, I was told was "over eighty winters" shoot a rabbit with deadly accuracy at fifty yards, run over with the agility of a youth to reach it, and hold it up grinning, showing all of his white teeth while he flung his dark braided hair from his face. However, the red man does not fare so well in our cities. He ages the same as we do. Asked why, he will usually remark: "The air stinks, that is why."

The elderly man was intrigued with the drawings Pidgeon was making. Finally using his poor command of English, he asked: "Why do you draw pictures when your people destroy?"

Pidgeon answered simply that there would come a time when men would want to know about these giant mounds. "I want to put it down in a book for that time. A book talks on paper," he explained. "It goes on talking after I am dead. I wish to talk to the people who live after the time of the destroyers." (I do not have the book before me and am quoting from memory, but in general, this is the thought he conveyed.) The old man nodded his interest and asked Pidgeon to follow him. This turned out to be an invitation to have dinner and meet his tribal friends.

That night Pidgeon learned that his new friend was Decoodah, the last living man of the extinct Elk nation of the Algonkins. He was the keeper of the histories which went back for over a thousand years. His sons had died in the Black Hawk war fighting the white invaders. He had found no youth among the red men who was worthy of receiving the traditions, so he had intended to take the chants to the grave of his people.

Pidgeon decided right there and then that he would learn the old man's language and try to learn more than he could at the white universities. So he invited Decoodah to go with him as he continued to "map the earthworks". Decoodah accepted, and for four months they wandered through the forests together. Decoodah led him to the most important mounds, sketched for him the parts which had been eroded away by streams, and then began to explain the meanings. Finally after the "time of waiting and knowing", Decoodah ceremonially took young Pidgeon for his son and began to give him the histories. He learned that Decoodah's detailed knowledge of these past civilizations was due to the fact he was "reading the mounds". They were indeed histories, to be read from the center outward, and the story of that city had been ended with "the mound of extinction".

Each animal pictured stood for a tribe of people. One mound, or rather set of mounds in

Wisconsin, was a capitol city whose historic dynasties had a past as brilliant and checkered as that of London - where incidentally, Pidgeon finally published his book over a hundred years ago.

Decoodah began to tell his "son" of the people who lived in peace along the rivers, the mound builders, trading even with distant nations in their longboats. Their religion was peaceful, since it had been brought to them by a long-dead saint. Together with what he told and what one can learn from some of the explorers who first talked to such extinct nations as the Natchez of the Mississippi river, and the tribes of Louisiana, one can picture these cities very well. They were built in the shape of a wheel with streets for spokes. The government buildings were on the central mounds. When the city was captured by enemies, those mounds were closed and the mark of extinction added. They were never destroyed. In them were the tools and the clothing and utensils used at that time. These large buildings were built of hewn whole logs, painted or gilded. The grounds about them were covered with strawberry bushes as today we use grass. Some trees were used for shade and some for their good nuts or fruits. Built thusly, the pyramids extend all the way into the land bordering Mexico.

About the year 700 A. D., a tremendous invasion took place from the south up the Mississippi. Four (the sacred number) tribes came up the river. The Turtle (the Dacotah) was leading the Snake (Iroquois) and probably the southern tribes such as Choctah, Chickasaw, Creek Cherakee (ra meaning sun), or Muskogian speaking and perhaps the Caddoan speaking tribes. Today we classify them as the Atlantic tribes. They had cities on islands in the Caribbean sea which were being devoured by the ocean. Also, one of their group were setting themselves up as "Lords" and capturing the others as slaves (Aztecs?). They were originally the "seven families who fled from the old red land in the destruction" the Dacotah tell as a supplemental story to fill out the picture. They fled north, preferring to learn the knowledge of the woods to living in slavery. They were fire worshippers. They remembered a sacred dragon and giant caves where he had once lived. Was he the personification of lava? Perhaps. They brought with them the memory of pyramids and of ancient writings. They carried fire in their long boats which they burned out of a single giant tree trunk. They carried their history in the form of chants and sometimes in the knotting of colored threads. They held sacred the memory of a giant bird who had a tuft of white feathers about his naked neck, because they had once been told to wear these above the eyebrows, so that long after the terror, they might recognize one another. This bird had a dolorous cry, as if weeping for the lost land, and it flew through the lightnings. They carried the memory of a sacred calendar and a reverence for the twin stars of night and morning or summer and winter. All these things were carried in the chants of the tall, powerful red-skinned people who were coming up from the south in the year 700 A.D. They drove the Algonkins, with their guttural language, farther north. (Not that Decoodah remembered all these cultural details about the invaders - they themselves have helped me out with these memories.)

Decoodah tells how the great mound of the serpent being led by the oval symbol of the turtle was built along the banks of the Mississippi, "the father of waters", to commemorate this invasion. The Algonkins simply moved further north and established another capitol city while the black tortoise emperor took over their old capitol at St. Louis, Missouri. The Algonkins closed their mounds and the tortoise began their own from this point.

The black tortoise had a very beautiful court and the people dressed in great elegance. (Why was he called "black"? Because that is one of the colors of the fire god. It is the shade of very ancient lava.) The emperor then divided his kingdom into four parts. The Mississippi was the dividing line. Two parts were north and two parts in the south. These he put into the hands of his four sons, and about their necks was hung the "badge of royalty" which made of them one of the "great suns".

All went well then until in the southern court was born a grandson who was much like the black tortoise himself. As he grew up, another wave of southerners was welling up the Mississippi in their long boats. The youth saw these people being peacefully absorbed by the other kingdoms and realized that they were of his own people. He listened to their stories of their troubles in the southland. He also listened to scouts coming in from the west where small islands of very ancient people were being surrounded and over-run by invaders coming down the sunset ocean from the north, aided in their marching by fierce brown dogs with bushy outstanding fur and black mouths. (Curiously enough, some of the Atlantic tribes still have some wild descendents of these mongrelized chows, whom they call "dog soldiers" since their ancestors were captives of battle. They are sometimes ceremonially eaten

to thus gain the courage of their ancient enemies).

The young man then tried to overthrow the kingdom by conspiring with these new refugees. He did not succeed, but threw the kingdom into a turmoil because the four sons were faithful to the old emperor. However, there was in the court of the aged black tortoise, a brilliant captain of the armies, named Dacotah. He had a much better idea than the youth from the south. He took a leave of absence and went to the Algonkins. His idea was to weld them into an army, capture the old kingdom and then turn his entire attention upon the west, making one powerful kingdom from sea to sea. This happened about the year 900 to 1000 A.D.

Dacotah was able to weld the Algonkins into a fighting force and by the brilliance of his military strategy to take the black tortoise capitol. However, the sub-kings began to rally their troops and the most fierce type of civil war broke out. It finally went into complete anarchy, and in order to exist, the people had to abandon their cities and join the guerrilla bands who were sacrificing captives to the old fire god. When the white man came, this had been going on for several hundred years.

When I closed this most enlightening book, I wrote a long letter to Dr. Wissler. He had been ill, but his letter was full of the old enthusiasm. "That is the find of the century!" he wrote. "Don't send it to me as you said that you wished to do. I will come to Los Angeles and pick it up. I want to republish it, of course. Suddenly the language map of North America begins to make sense. The Algonkins obviously once held the land and there were obviously some invasions from Asia down the Pacific bringing in the Athapaskan speakers. But these Atlantic tribes were a great mystery. There is a very old similarity in tongues, but it is of tremendous antiquity - so old that they must communicate by hand signs. Dr. Hrdlicka has spent his life insisting that they all came down from Asia - broke through thousands of miles of enemy tongues without leaving any islanded groups like the Asiatics did to trace them back to their source. Besides where did the Chickasaws get their South American plum? And where do they all get their worship of what evidently is a South American bird - the condor - sometimes seen as far north as New Orleans, although there are some smaller descendants in California? How much more obvious to say that they came up from the south, than to try to insist that they broke through thousands of miles of Athapaskan and Algonkin speakers without leaving a single clue behind?"

ADDAX

ORYX

It was the last letter I ever received from Dr. Wissler. His death came as a real blow to me, and although we had never talked face to face, I think of him as one of my best friends and one of the most inspiring minds it has been my great pleasure to know.

So I continued my search of the truth and a lead through the labyrinth of Atlantic mysteries without the keen insight of Dr. Wissler.

However, I did find a real legacy among his writings. In studying his method of finding the center of the sun dance rite or the pole dance, which not only spills over into Mexico as he once pointed out to me, but also into our own May pole dance, I found his method a very good pattern to follow. He found the sun dance was used and apparently revered as an ancient rite by two or three unrelated language groups. He began to list the steps of the rite, making note of all possible parts. For example, one part concerned a girl who was called "beautiful enemy". Another part was that the tree which was to become the

MEDALLION
OF
ROYALTY

Found in Texas by Mrs. Frank Kidd. Enlarged twice size.

pole had to be scouted for by a certain number of warriors. His reasoning was this: that if tribe #1 had traits A and B, tribe #2 had A and E, while tribe #3 had B and D, these scattered parts had once fit an entire ancient rite. Thus the tribe which had the most and was the closest to the center was certainly nearer to the origin point than the tribes which were apparently but fringe contacts.

Therefore he began; 1) the tree was scouted for; 2) there had to be a specified number of warriors doing this; 3) there must be a lovely young girl in the party who was to be called "beautiful enemy". etc. The end of this long piece of research was that although the Dacotah-Sioux were the best known for this colorful rite, the Algonkin speakers were closer to the center and therefore he decided it was an early Algonkin ritual, while the Sioux was an early contact. It is interesting that my Siouan speaking friends deny this, saying that it was theirs "way back at the dawn!" It is just as possible that like the secondary burial rite, much was forgotten in the interceding years of war and migration. However, the method is quite excellent in tracing down people and their animals.

For example, many races had domesticated animals. Who had them first and what animals did each group have? Of course there is the almost unanswerable argument that they were to be found wild at such and such a location, but beyond that one has to "peel back the onion", as he once wrote to me - look at the previous people. Whatever culture traits they had, or animals they had are theirs and become just contacts when taken over by the conquerors. The conquerors are seldom the civilizers. They only absorb the civilization which they find - unless this trait is not to be found in the conquered people. Thus we do not become bogged down in an embarrassing morass of culture traits. Especially when we are seeking the nation of the greatest antiquity as we are attempting to do in the Atlantic puzzle. Who first tamed the mysterious ibex and brought the animal itself or the memories of it to the Americas? Where is it to be found wild today? On the Atlas range is a species, but the main animal is to be found on the Pyrnees mountains (Greek - fire mountains) which extend to Switzerland and the Alps. Then which was the earliest group in the Swiss Alps who had goats? Apparently the long headed harmonics who lived in the Kitchen Midden villages above the lakes during the Pleistocene.

There is, however, a similar animal which was tamed by the ancient Egyptians and kept in herds to be milked and used for meat. This long horned elk today runs wild in herds above the Ah Hoggar mountains of the Sahara. Coincidence? Not entirely. The Egyptian was a dolicephalic harmonic. We must therefore place this as a doli tamed animal unless later finds contradict this conclusion. The scimitar horned golden animal of the Saharan desert is the oryx. Near it, and sometimes sharing the same desert foliage, is the addax. This is a long horned animal also, except the horns have waves in them.

One of the most interesting and puzzling culture traits of both the Cro Magnon type Atlantic tribes of the Amerind and the Azilian - Egyptians is the circular medallion worn around the neck of the great sun, or the emperor of the tribe. It is hereditary, and is passed down from generation to generation from an unknown antiquity. It is usually fashioned of bronze.

After I had published my last book (He Walked the Americas - Amherst Press, 1963), I was fortunate enough to receive a letter from a woman living in Texas who had found such a medallion on her land near what remained of an Indian mound. Mrs. Frank Kidd, Box 950, Brady, Texas, wrote me a long description of the medallion and finally sent me two photographs. The most fascinating aspect about this object is the writing which is similar to Egyptian hieratic and also similar in the seated figure to some Mayan types of drawing with the war bonnet feathers streaming down the back. The main figure is apparently seated in a chair with cat (or tiger) arms and carries the sun disc enclosed within horns upon his head. The other side of the medallion seems to resemble a sphinx-like animal with three pyramids in the background, and a rainbow-like fire, perhaps the rising sun, to the animal's back. The medallion was, as I had suspected, made of bronze, Mrs. Kidd assured me. The only reason I could imagine for the medallion being cast aside into the dirt was the fact that the young chieftain who was wearing it, fearing death or capture, did not want to be found with it upon his body and hurriedly cast it aside where he thought he might retrieve it on a later date. It was found, I understand, well over half a century ago.

Now here is a puzzle - the medallion, claimed by both the Atlantic tribes and by the Azilians, is the symbol of royalty. Which had it first? Is there any way we can obtain even an educated guess? Let us go on farther into the puzzle of the ante-diluvian world, and see if we can learn more.

Chapter 16

The People Of The Veil

The Arab with whom I had contracted for an interview, entered the lobby of the Del Prado hotel in Mexico City, and walked toward me, bowing with cold politeness.

I appraised him thoughtfully. I had been told by friends that he could add to my knowledge of the "people of the veil", those mysterious raiders of the Sahara. He was dressed in the swathing white of his native costume, but that might mean nothing.

I invited him to sit down.

"I have been told that you know something of the Tuareg or Tuarak people. The spelling, I have read, varies from tribe to tribe, but the pronunciation is similar. Is this true?" I asked by way of introduction.

"I have seen them. However, they are not my people."

"I understand. Yet, it would seem that they are almost impossible to contact - especially half a world away."

"Even close, you leave them alone. Many an Arab, or a Frenchman, finding their women lovely, ends a mild flirtation with a dagger in his back."

"I have read that the women are not veiled - only the men. Is this true?"

"No, not entirely. When they raid, the women often fight with the men. One never knows, under those purple veils, until the dead are counted."

"Warrior women! Do the women seem to rule?"

"I am not sure. Some tribes have a queen, others a king. I do not know who is the head over all."

"About this king - how does he inherit his chieftainship?"

"From his mother, and it goes on down to his grandson through his daughter."

"You know - this sounds like the Amazons!"

"Who are they?"

"A tribe of women warriors. Once a year they met men, chosen ahead of time, at a designated place and mated with them. Then the sons of this meeting were returned to the fathers and the daughters were kept and raised as warriors."

"I heard a legend like that. There is a stronghold near In-Salah long fallen to ruin which is supposed to have belonged to them. The walls are high and circular - so high that no one has ever been able to get inside."

"Are there any inscriptions there?"

"Inscriptions?"

"I mean writing or pictures."

"No, only the carving of an axe with two heads."

"The symbol of the Amazon queen!"

"What was it used for?"

"It was their weapon."

"Then they are not the Tuaraks. These people carry the arm dagger or short sword - one on each arm. They are fastened with a metal or jeweled band above the elbow. How they can use them!"

"The ancient arm dagger! How about the shields? Do they carry shields?"

"Sometimes. Long triangle ones with a red cross on them. That doesn't mean that they are Christians. They say that they worship Allah, but I don't believe it. They worship some old sea god who carries a pitchfork."

Into my mind leaped the word trident!

"How do you know?" I asked.

"It is whispered in the Sahara that the Tuarak sacrifice people to this god - warriors taken in battle."

"How unbelievable!"

"Maybe, but true. If they take away a captive, you never see him again."

"By the way, can you describe this pitchfork?"

"It has three points - like the peaks which mark the Tuarak land in the Hoggar."

"Tell me about this land."

"Near In-Salah there are three high peaks of the Hoggar. No Arab will go there if he can help it. These peaks touch the sky with claw-like fingers. Once a friend of mine got lost and saw the ruins of one of their cities on the Atlas. It was built of giant stones - each one the size of an Arabian tent. In the front is a great circular wall. But in the desert they live underground. I have heard that under Ah Hoggar are many galleries deep in the earth around an underground lake. These galleries are filled with paintings of the long age."

"What kind of paintings?"

"About elephants, and strange looking cows with long horns and an odd looking bull which could be your American buffalo. Please tell me why you are asking all these questions?"

"Because I wish to learn about the Tuaraks."

"Why?"

"Frankly, I think that they might be the last remaining pure strain of the old Atlanteans. All that you have said really strengthens that belief. It is fantastic that they could have come down to the twentieth century, but . . ."

"Who are the Atlanteans?"

"The people who lived on an island in the Atlantic which sank into the sea about twelve thousand years ago."

"Oh. You said that you were writing a book in the note you sent. Is that book about this island?"

"Yes."

"Then you really are interested in the past of long ago and you do not have other reasons?

"There could have been other reasons. Very well. If you will not print my name in this book I will really tell you. I lied before. You will not print my name?"

"Not if you do not wish me to. But what did you lie about? So far the whole picture is getting clearer - Poseidon or Neptune, the underground galleries, the arm daggers, the manner in which the throne is inherited. Did you lie about these?"

"No, not those things. Only about not ever being there. You see, we have been on the same side of a few battles. On one of these times I took a message from my sheik to Tamen-Ra-Set - that is the Tuarak capitol city. That is where Amen-Okhal - their king - lives."

My eyes must have widened in surprise at the names of these Egyptian gods who were already ancient at the dawn of history.

"Yes, I can see now that this is what you really are interested in. But there are older people than the Tuaraks. The Tibbesti who look like the Dravidian peoples of India with straight noses and straight hair were the first in the Mediterranean. They were related to Dravidians and come with their cattle, colonizing all the Mediterranean when the Tuarak tribes invaded from the ocean and then settled on the Sahara when it was the Triton sea."

"How do you know?"

"They told me - the Tuaraks."

I could hardly believe my good fortune.

"Did the Tuaraks say where they came from - or which direction?"

"Yes, they came from the ocean. Tuarak means "the people of the sea.""

"So the underlying blood of the Mediterranean is Dravidian and the Tuaraks are invaders?"

He nodded.

"That must have been what the priest of Volcan in early Egypt meant when he told Solon that the Greeks and Egyptians were really brothers in the days when the Mediterranean was a valley filled with cities! Yes, that is right. The people of the sea invaded and they were stopped by the Greeks."

"I couldn't say about all that."

"Probably it was Hercules who stopped the invasion of the Atlanteans - I mean the people of the sea."

"Oh no, you are wrong about that. His name was Heracles and he was a Tuarak - their greatest emperor."

"How do you know?"

"They told me. On my way back, I passed the ruins of his capitol city."

"What? Why that is fantastic! A prediluvian city? Where is it?"

He ignored the question, asking instead: "Do you know why Gibraltar is called the 'gates of Heracles'?"

"No."

"Because he controlled all the commerce and shipping going in and out of the Mediterranean. I have argued with many Greeks on this. They have some very silly stories about Heracles, but the Tuaraks have the truth."

"Perhaps so. How long ago did he live?"

"In the time of their greatness before their cities crumbled in the light of flaming volcanoes and sank into the sea."

"If they know all of that, then they would know about your people too, wouldn't they?"

"They do. We came about two thousand years before Christ, they told me. All our tribes - the Assyrians, Jews and all other peoples speaking our kind of languages."

"The Semitic tongues?"

"Yes, we all came from the direction of Arabia upon our camels - an animal they said they never saw before we came."

"All right, now let us go back. You were

speaking about the time you brought a message to the Tuarak monarch. Tell me all about the journey."

"The land I speak of is beyond the Mya river - one of the great dead rivers of the Sahara. The terraces rise from its ancient bed in colors of red and white. Once it emptied into the Triton sea and carried ships up to the great cities of the Tuaraks on top of the Atlas and the Hoggar mountains. I believe the Mya emptied where the dry lakes of the Chotts are today. As the sea level of the Triton sank in long dry spells, another lake was where Lake Chad is now with a waterway in between. That land was green then. Ostriches, buffalo, deer, tigers reamed the woodlands and crocodiles slept in the rivers."

"How do you know?"

"Tip an Arab guide sometimes and he will take you to some oasis where there are pictures perhaps on the rocks and perhaps underground. You will see."

"I suppose there are some pictures under the Hoggar peaks?"

"Miles of them, so it is whispered, but no one ever sees them but the people of the veil."

"Let us go back to the trip you took."

"Oh yes. Well, before you get to the real Tuarak country, you come to the land of fear and the valley of the monsters."

"What in the world is that?"

"This place is called the land of the monsters because the cliffs are shaped like monster animals - such as you have never seen. There are enormous shaggy elephants and a giant lizard that sends your hair arising when you first see it. In the heat of the Sahara, they seem to come to life and move. I tell you that it is enough to drive a man mad."

"I can imagine - especially if one is low on water, and the heat is beginning to affect the eyes."

"The Tuaraks say that when they first came to the land the living monsters really gathered here to fight over their feeding grounds, but of course, that was untold ages before my people appeared."

"And the land of fear?"

"That lies at the gateway of the Hoggar. There is a narrow gorge one must pass through, and here the rocks explode in the sun with the rattle of machine gun fire. Then from time to time small avalanches tumble down from the peaks above. There is a good reason for that name and it takes a brave man to keep on going through the land of fear."

For a moment a silence settled over us and I was beginning to wonder if he was planning on ending the interview just as he was about to enter the forbidden city, when his voice began again.

"After I had talked to king Amen-Okhal, they invited me to dine with them. We ate by torch-light, reclining on divans while servants brought the food."

"Could you understand them?"

"No. To me they have a heathenish tongue, but when I hinted that, the king through his interpreter told me that to them Arabic sounded like a stallion approaching a mare."

At this we both laughed. He had a good sense of humor. Perhaps that is why he had been chosen for this important errand. As the laughter died down, he continued:

The woman are very lovely - especially some of them. I remember one with creamy skin, grey-green eyes and hair like flames. They dressed in long garments of some soft purple material that fell from the shoulder, being fastened on the left side, thus leaving the right arm bare. Their hair was either worn in one long curl or was looped up at the back of the neck in a loose knot. They wore a few red or turquoise jewels."

"What did they do for entertainment?"

"When we had finished eating, a full moon arose, and with the light of the torches it gave the whole scene a sort of weirdness. One by one, some of the women came forward and chanted something which sounded like poetry. I couldn't make anything out of it, but it may have been a story. Everyone was listening very intently."

"The women chanted the legends?"

"I suppose so. I couldn't understand them. One woman said this poetry with gestures and two others played on the amzaad."

"What is that?"

"A curious old long-necked sort of violin. You see them painted on the galleries where the animals are and the women playing them dress just like the women at that party. I was sort of glad that everyone was listening to that story because it gave me a chance to look around without everyone watching me to see where I was looking. The men are big fellows. Those in the bodyguard of the emperor are all seven feet tall. Yet, strangely enough the women are not tall. They come only to the shoulders of their men, but I have heard that they are strong willed. I dared not look at them too closely, for I knew how dangerous that can be."

"I wonder if the men always wear the veil."

"I don't know. They may have just worn it because I was a stranger, but maybe not. At any rate the weird rhythm of the story and the amzaad playing and the lubki, or palm wine which they were serving were making me dizzy.

"Then suddenly the story stopped. There was a sort of silence as if everyone was expecting something unusual. From somewhere drums began to beat. A big fire was lighted. Then out of the darkness of the night from the direction of the distant Atlantic, came a masked figure. His body was all rubbed in black with funny marks on it painted in colors. On his head was a black mask which came to his shoulders with only slits for eyes. On his head was a tall peaked white hat with a bunch of feathers at the top. He stopped and bowed low to the fire. Behind him came four other figures one at a time in single file. These men had on masks like his, but their head dress had flaming pitchforks on top. They all bowed low to the fire, and then they began to dance with those arm daggers. Drunk as I was, my tongue became glued to the top of my mouth. That was a sight. I'll bet I was the only stranger alive ever to have seen this dance. I have never heard of another."

"Please tell me some more details if you can."

"After I got my voice back, I whispered to the interpreter asking what it meant. He whispered one sentence: 'That is Heracles and his warriors coming from the old homeland in the ocean. They are called the men of the mountain'."

"I would have given my right arm to have been there."

"That is about all I do remember, because I was becoming very drunk. I remember seeing an ouran - that is the huge green poisonous lizard walking around among the watches like a pet dog. I tried to sit very still so that he would not see me. The Tuaraks paid no attention to him at all."

"He must have been their totemistic animal."

"What do you mean by that?"

"All very ancient people seem to have totems. It was some animal which stood for their homeland. They never killed or ate these animals. They used weapons of the totem's element. For example, all around the earth, the serpent stands for water or the sea, and these people use lances which they threw. It surprises me that the Tuarak do not use them as well as the arm dagger, since they call themselves the people of the sea."

"Oh, but they do! That is why no one will follow those galleries very far. A poisoned lance may come hurtling at you from the dark."

"I can see why it might be dangerous to explore these most fascinating galleries."

"There are other dangers, too. They seem to be a favorite haunt for the ourans. Do you know what the Tuaraks called that one at the party?"

"Their maternal grandmother?"

"How in the world did you know?"

"That is the pet name with most ancient people for their totem animals. I only hope that you did not laugh. That might have been very dangerous."

"I suppose I was too frightened - and drunk. I just thought I must have misunderstood them."

"Tell me, do the Tuaraks ever eat fish?"

"I have heard not, because they believe that fish are their ancestors! Could that be true?"

"I heard a similar story from a tribe of American Indians who remember the great tragedy of Atlantis. They told me that their ancestors who sank beneath the waves when their homeland went down were eaten by fish. Therefore if they ate fish they would be eating their ancestors. Not very scientific or logical, but I have actually seen fright in their eyes if they saw blood on a fish."

"Do you think that these American Indians are from Atlantis also?"

"No, not as directly. I believe this ancient power of the early world was a sea power with many colonies. These distant 'children' in the language of the legends were kept for many ages or until the homeland sank. Then the various tribes went their ways in the new land, warring and being conquered perhaps many times."

"But then how would they remember?"

"The women carried the legends, and the women are usually spared in a war, to be carried off by the conquerors."

"Oh, yes."

"I have a book called Ancient America which was written some ninety years ago. The author tells of a ceremonial in which the Indians tell the story of the deluge and the sinking of the homeland and pray that the great spirit will never allow such a tragedy to ever happen again."

"I came here to answer questions and not ask them, but I find this very interesting. I cannot help asking them."

"That is all right - we must share our knowledge so that we both will benefit. However, I do have another question. If these green poisonous lizards like to live in the galleries, then they must have good air and not bad air, for no animal would stay where the air is foul."

"They do have good air."

"Ah. That means there are openings to bring down ventilation. Where are they located - do you know?"

"Some are on the peaks of the Hoggar. My friend slipped upon one when climbing these peaks once and almost fell in. The opening was like a window with bars across it. He leaned upon it and looked down. There was a shaft leading down - he could not tell how far. He was tempted to drop a pebble, but that might bring some of the veiled raiders. So he thanked Allah that he had not fallen in, and started back. If he had fallen, he would either be killed in the fall or would find himself in a prison - who knows? At any rate, he had suddenly lost his curiosity. After that experience, I believe that he was actually afraid of that country. He thought that it was haunted. I am inclined to agree with him."

"Oh, come now - that I do not believe."

"Very well. I shall tell you. Once when the two of us were young, we went there. We were afraid to go in the daylight because we would be seen, so we chose a moonlit night. That way, we would not be so easily seen, and besides the part-light would help us to find our way. . ."

"And?"

"We saw a troop of horsemen ride past not far from us. For a few minutes they seemed real enough. Their veils floated out in the moonlight and the horses' hooves kicked up the sand like miniature whirlwinds. Then we saw some other horsemen waiting to meet them. These were Tuaraks also. The two lines met and began to fight. It was a fast, hard battle. We watched with our tongues stuck in our throats, crouched down low in the sand. Then as soon as it had begun, it was over. The other group rode away and our group came back, carrying their fallen, and leading the riderless horses. We made ourselves into rocks, and again they did not see us. They passed, and when the last had gone, and we felt it was safe to turn around and look after them - they had just disappeared. There wasn't a thing moving on the desert anywhere. Now do you believe we saw ghosts?"

"No."

"But I tell you we saw a battle."

"I do not doubt that, I do not think they were ghosts."

"Then why did they disappear?"

"They used an old Indian trick - an American Indian trick. Somewhere there was a cave opening, and they rode in."

"Oh? Perhaps you are right. We were near the opening of some of the galleries?"

"Certainly."

"But why were they fighting?"

"Once more, they were doing something the American Indians did for thousands of years. It was just a ceremonial war."

"Not a real battle? But it was! I saw some who looked mighty dead being brought back."

"Of course it was a real battle, but only a ceremonial one."

"What do you mean?"

"You said that these people sacrificed human beings to the fire god?"

"No, an old sea god with a pitchfork on his head."

"Very well, the sea god with the trident - that is a three pronged pitchfork."

"Oh yes, now that you put it like that. We know that captives fallen in battle never return."

"Very well, the American Indians, especially the Atlantic tribes, sacrificed warriors to the fire god, and to get sacrifices they fought ceremonial wars. This was a ceremonial war for sacrifices."

"They have strange ways, do they not?" he said, staring off at nothing.

"Yes, very strange, and very ancient - down from the very dawn of civilization.

"The loser is sacrificed. Perhaps that is why they are so tall and so strong - the men I mean."

"Perhaps. Yet, I must ask another question. These people, from your description of them, are like the Cretans who lived on the island of Crete in the Mediterranean some seven thousand years ago. The hair is done like them, though the arm dagger is like the Libyans or the Atlanteans - the people of the sea."

"That is why they are called Tuar. . ."

"Wait, I haven't finished my question. The Cretans have a writing. There are two kinds evidently. We have so far only learned to read the kind which deals with money and trade, such as invoices and bales of goods. The kind which tells of drama and of history - that we cannot read. Do you know if the Tuaraks . . ."

"Yes, they have writing." he said.

Then he dropped the bomb.

"Down in the miles and miles of underground galleries, where it is said that they wander about a beautiful artificial lake, and then pass along torch lighted passageways looking at pictures painted of their cities so many thousands of years ago - are their libraries. There are kept the books which are the oldest libraries on earth. There are the histories which go way beyond the great deluge, to the times when the Tuaraks ruled the seas. How do I know? They told me, that is, the emperor did. But save your next question. I could not get to read them. Neither could you, or anyone else - no one will ever read them except the people of the veil."

Chapter 17

The Bird Of The Lightnings

I was sitting in a restaurant on Avenida Juarez in Mexico City, so deeply engrossed in my own thoughts that I scarcely heard the very attractive "musica" being played and sung by a group of cabaleros with sombreros, fancy high boots and colorful blankets tossed carelessly in a folded manner over their shoulders. They were singing the plaintive songs so typical of the Mexican Indians. Even though they were one of the at-

tractions of this small cafe, and I often went there to hear them, yet on this afternoon I was scarcely aware of their jokes and their harmony. Suddenly a hand was laid over mine.

"Why Joe!" I exclaimed in surprise. "This is a pleasure."

"I was almost afraid to interrupt the seance," he said, pulling up a chair.

Joe Martin was taking his Ph.D. at Mexico

university where I was enjoying a few wonderful courses in antiquities - not as much for the credits, as for the bus trips and the learned men who went along to answer questions and give us the carbon dating.

"I do have a problem," I nodded. "It has me baffled."

"Then it will probably baffle me too."

"Well Joe, I don't know who said this, but someone once noted that when you think you have learned all the answers, you simply haven't been asking enough questions."

He grinned. "Go ahead," he said, meanwhile pointing to an item on the menu to the waiter and then leaning back expectantly.

"Very well. Did you hear all that racket last night?"

"You mean noise?" The fun had suddenly drained from his face.

"Of course I mean noise - crying and screaming like some woman was in terrible agony - running down one street and then another?"

"Yes. I heard it," toying with his water glass.

"Well?" I questioned.

He did not seem to anxious to continue the conversation as if he really did not want to talk about it.

"They say that it is a ghost," he finally said.

"Nonsense. No ghost has vocal chords that powerful."

"Then what do you think it was?"

"It is a bird."

"A bird?"

"That's right. And furthermore, I am certain."

"I suppose you went out and saw it!"

"I would have like to have done so but I got stopped."

"Then how do you know?"

"I saw it."

"How? Where?"

"Through the window of the Del Prado Hotel. You know how long and wide the big windows are before the lobby? Well I heard it coming and I rushed over to the window. The place was empty because the hour was late, but I caught a glimpse of giant wings and the spread of a white tail edged with black. The wing spread must have been fifteen feet."

"What kind of bird is that?"

"A South American condor."

"Here in Mexico? Impossible."

"Improbable perhaps, but not impossible."

"Well, could be, but . . ."

"I started to rush out to get a better look, and would you believe it, all the men about the office

came alive suddenly, and stopped me."

"That was probably a good thing. You have them to thank that you are alive."

"Why?"

"You would be by now no more than some bloody clothes. La Llorona is a killer."

"Who is . . .?"

"La Llorona - the crying woman."

"And you are trying to tell me that your La... something is a Mexican legend?"

"I'll say she is. And pure Indian too. The Spanish cannot be blamed for La Llorona, although recently I have heard that she is really the Indian mistress of Cortez wailing for her ravaged people."

"That doesn't sound very old."

"But La Llorona is. Originally she was the female serpent - the mother of men - Co-hua-co-huatl. (Co-serpent - hua-ancient - l-majesty) Sometimes she is called Quilaztli, meaning 'the one who always bears twins, and lives over the water.'"

"In the old red land?"

"I don't know what the color of the land is, but it is supposed to be an island to the east."

"Go on. I am learning more than you think."

"Old Mexico is full of ghost stories, you know. La Llorona is supposed to dress in white with a black cape, and when she runs, the white lining floats out behind her. She sometimes carries a crib on her shoulder and can always be heard sobbing and shrieking."

"Like last night?"

"Yes, like last night. Have you ever heard a condor? Does it scream?"

"No, but I have heard a mountain lion out hunting. If you ever heard that, it too would curdle your blood."

He shook his head.

"Would you know a condor if you saw one?"

"Yes, I saw one once at the San Diego zoo. There is a pair in a giant cage that is about a city block in length. The male was sitting in a large tree growing in the cage, and was preening himself. I knew that he was sacred to the Indians and I was anxious to get a feather. I wondered if he could be sweet talked into a less distrustful attitude. So I began. No one was around to consider me mentally deranged, and I had the place to myself for my little experiment. I talked to him in the coaxing tones one might use to a strange animal and he turned that big head around and stared at me. His eyes were as red as two rubies. Finally a feather fluttered down. I started to reach for it and I saw him stop preening himself and study me. I began again with the coaxing sounds. There appeared to be no sticks handy with which I could reach it. Finally I knelt down and put my arm under the wire - reaching the entire length of the arm to get the feather and zip it out.

"That was a mighty silly thing to do!"

"I suppose it was. But he didn't seem alarmed."

"No. But this giant bird is lightning fast. If he had chosen to do so, he could have gobbled your arm up like a robin eats a worm."

"Really?"

"Do you still have the feather?"

"No, I sent it to a Hopi medicine man who wanted it for the rain dance. He thanked me profusely, but later I received a letter through friends saying that they had to bind the feather up and put it away. It caused the worst flood in years, and so many autos were overturned that people grew afraid."

"Yes. That is Llorona. She is a very powerful lady. You don't play around with her. Did you ever read the poem The Ancient Mariner? That albatross has nothing on La Llorona."

"Someone has taken a shot at her?"

"Has? You should hear the stories of what happened afterward! Talk about curses! No Indian in his right mind will fool around with her."

"Do you think that this legend goes back to the time of Plato? I was just digging up some strange stories myself."

"Mexican? Stories about La Llorona are many. In 1585, Father Bernardino de Sahagun told the people that their ancestors were worshipping a devil named Cioacoatl who dressed in black and white and ran around at night terrifying people with her screams. Evidently a very evil goddess is living on into modern times - and you believe she is a bird!"

Our food was brought in and we stopped talking while the waiter was placing it down and pouring the coffee. I finally took up the conversation again.

"How about the Irish banshee? She runs around at night shrieking. She carries news of death. And the name interests me - ban is very close to Pan, the Algonkin name for the island with which they traded - out in the Atlantic. And she - well that should mean woman."

"In Aryan."

"Atlantis may have had its greatest days before the Aryan invasions but it certainly (that is a portion of it) must have lasted through that time, especially with the Irish because of the location."

"Those are some mighty interesting ideas,

but how in the world could you know for certain?"

"Perhaps never for certain. But do you remember Astarte? She bewailed the death of mankind when she looked down on the flood, saying: 'These are the tribes of men I bore, and now like the fishes, they are filling the seas!'"

"There was an even earlier goddess. Her small brother was killed by his uncle who wanted the throne. She became insane and ran through the streets sobbing. . . Wasn't that woman you called Astarte also called Ishtar - the goddess of the moon?"

"Yes. That was the Chaldean version of the same story. When these goddesses moved from one country to another, they changed their names."

"Like modern criminals?"

"I admit that they did not act like gods and goddesses."

"Who were they, then?"

"The kings and queens of pre-history."

"Is this your idea?"

"No. Many historians are finding this increasingly probable. They are not creator gods. They act too human - with all the frailties of our type of animal."

"When they married, they really made alliances? And when they had children?"

"They probably founded colonies. But I am interested in this earth mother of the Aztecs. Perhaps she is the mother goddess of the Cro Magnons - the fat one - remember? You said that she only bore twins?"

"Yes, that's ridiculous now isn't it . . .? Plato again! The twin children of Poseidon!"

"And the mother is the one they remember? Matriarchy? Or a people who were conquered? And this, in turn, harks back to the double rule of almost all of the Atlantic tribes - peace and war chiefs. Actually it has spilled over into many other types."

"The Aztecs are hardly Atlantic."

"They could have been in the beginning, when they migrated from that island with the palm trees which they picture as their homeland."

"Was human sacrifices Atlantic?"

"Undoubtedly. But under the Aztecs it ran wild. It has been said that they set back the scientific skill and knowledge of the Toltec empire two thousand years."

"But don't all civilizations retrogress about a thousand years after each bitterly fought complete conquest? Look at Constantinople? And the Vandals?"

"And Julius Caesar?"

"I have read that the Assyrians set the world

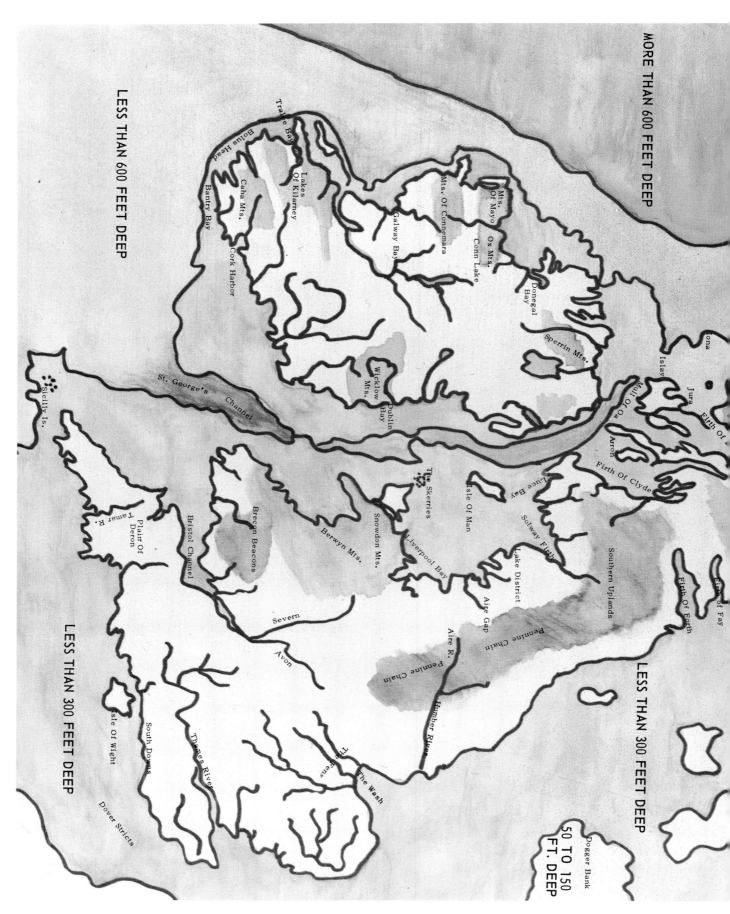

LESS THAN 600 FEET DEEP

Tralee Bay
Bolus Head
Bantry Bay
Caha Mts.
Lakes Of Kilarney
Cork Harbor
Galway Bay
Mts. Of Connemara
Conn Lake
Mts. Of Mayo
Ox Mts.
Donegal Bay
Sperrin Mts.

St. George's Channel
Wicklow Mts.
Dublin Bay

Islav
Jura
Iona
Mull Of Oa
Arron
Firth Of Clyde

Sicilly Is.

The Skerries
Isle Of Man
Luce Bay
Solway Firth
Southern Uplands
Firth Of Fay

Tamar R.
Plair Of Deron
Bristol Channel
Brecon Beacons
Berwyn Mts.
Snowdon Mts.
Liverpool Bay
Lake District
Aire Gap
Pennine Chain
Firth Of Forth
Firth Of Fay

Severn
Avon
Aire R.
Pennine Chain
Humber River

LESS THAN 300 FEET DEEP

Isle Of Wight
South Downs
Thames River
The Fens
The Wash

Dover Stricts

LESS THAN 300 FEET DEEP

Dogger Bank

50 TO 150 FT. DEEP

114

back two thousand years. That means that they did a more thorough job of vandalism."

"Yet, Joe, it was their king Ashurbanipal who discovered the Sumerian library and sent his wise men out into the land to make dictionaries so that he could read the dead language. The first real scientist!"

"That is right - and he was an Assyrian."

"Isn't it the irony of all conquerors, that they destroy their own roots in the mistaken belief that they are destroying those of their enemies? 'Ah, would some gift the giftie give us, to see ourselves as ithers see us!' "

"Especially after a thousand or more years?"

"Joe, you are a philosopher."

"Greek - philo - lover of the sophis - wisdom?"

"I was about to say that conquerors, per se, are not usually well educated men, are not acquainted with long vistas of history and not gifted with profound insights. However the great flood did more than its share of destruction without even being human - perhaps more than all the conquerors of history."

"You really believe in the flood, don't you?"

"Have you ever thought of the adjustments which took place during the Pleistocene and . . . oh, oh . . . we are about to be pleasantly interrupted," seeing friends about to enter. Then as they stopped to chat with two other friends along the street: "Perhaps we have a moment to finish up La Llorona . . ."

"Yes. The condor would hunt in Ireland? What would it get - children?"

"Perhaps a pig - who knows? You know the condor can fly in the teeth of the strongest winds and sail for hours on updraughts. He may be the Phoenix of legend - the bird who built its nest in volcanic peaks which periodically caught fire, burned up and then again rose to power."

"Are you talking about a bird or empire?"

"Perhaps both. One may be the symbol of the other."

"Well, I suppose it is possible that he may once have nested in Atlantis - since he likes the highest peaks of the Andes. I have heard that Seminoles say that he warns them of coming hurricanes."

"I know that they have a way of disappearing weeks in advance. The people watch the Indians rather than the weather reports."

"His warning may be only his knowledge of wind currents?"

The British Isles and the water depths around it, with ancient St. George's channel.

Astarte, the naked Syrian war goddess, on her horse, as depicted on an ostracon from Thebes.

"At any rate, the effect is the same. The Seminoles, especially under Chief Jimmy Bowlegs, disappeared long before any great hurricane, but then Florida has great limestone caverns, doesn't it?"

For a long time Joe was silent. Then: "Well, I am convinced. The great mother who bears only twins is not a ghost. She is a condor, and she is connected with the great flood."

"By the way, isn't there a festival in Spain in which they remember every year the insanity of one of the goddesses who ran through the streets screaming for her lost children? Wasn't this one the daughter of Atlas or some other emperor of forgotten times? That is the one I was trying to remember before. I believe she also sang weird songs, and the people of Spain get some young woman to play her part at this festival. That legend is previous to the flood."

"Here they come," Joe announced. "Tell me quick - did you ever see a condor chick?"

"Yes. At the San Diego zoo they had a chick that was two years old. It was grey and the size of a turkey. The adult black and white bird is almost four and a half feet tall - perhaps even more. He strides along with the long step of a big man. The youngsters, though are only the size of a large turkey."

Our friends came up overhearing the last.

"Imagine a youngster the size of a large turkey! How old is this curiosity?"

Another one added: "Yes, does he gobble, too?"

Amid the general laughter, the subject of La Llorona, a legend which runs through mankind from the very depths of time, came to a sudden conclusion. But I was glad I had talked to Joe. Another link was forged in the long search for the lost colossus of the sea.

Chapter 18

The Puzzle Of Bronze Age Europe

"No one was more dogmatic in subscribing to the idea that enough planets had already been discovered than the fledgling philosopher Georg Wilhelm Hegel, who in his dissertation published at Jena proved by impeccable logic that the number of planets could not exceed seven. Thereby he disposed once and for all of the future of astronomy."
James R. Newman in Scientific American.

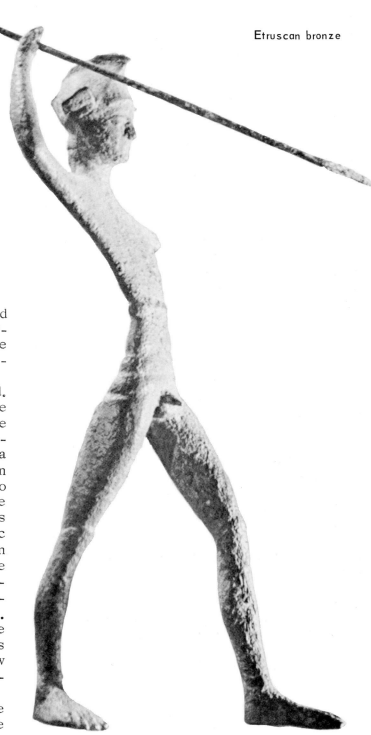

Etruscan bronze

Bronze is composed of two metals - copper and tin. For this reason, a copper age, and the knowledge of moulding tin should precede a bronze age. It does not in Europe. Nor in the Mediterranean.

Furthermore bronze is not an Aryan word. It came through the Roman "bronzo" from the Iberian "broncea" through the Etruscans, the conquered people of Italy. Probably the Etruscans were the Tyrrhenians or the Pelasgians (a Greek name for them, as Etruscan is the Roman name). These Tyrrhenian people of the sea, who spoke an Iberian tongue, are related in language to the Basques and the Finns, islanded tongues pressed along the north Baltic and Atlantic coastline by the Aryan speakers who came in from the east, and flowed around them. The Norse also, show an amazing affinity for these pre-Aryan words, which incidentally, are closely related to the Atlantic languages of the Americas. (See the amazing dictionary of "Red Man and the Viking", in two volumes, which gives thousands of these words.) Furthermore, the Basques show many Amerind likenesses, even having a pre-conquest game with the same name.

Furthermore, there is a dance done with the bronze age arm dagger, wearing kilts, to the music of bagpipes which is not only done by the Basques, Celts and the Iberians, but according to some ancient books, had once been known in the Americas. In this dance the short swords were held, one in each hand, either at right angles to the shoulders or above the head, thus making, with the head as the center blade, a trident. This also may have had something to do with the cult of the bull, which was strong through the Mediterranean in ancient times and along the Atlantic. For example, this may have been the reason for the horns on the helmets of the Norse.

There are some strange facts about this bronze age in the old world, and some very curious ones which seem to dovetail with facts about the Americas of a comparable date. The people who do have copper in the European continent are the Basques. There is very little in the Alps - not nearly enough to handle all the bronze used by the hinterland. Nor were there any notable tin mines. However, we must immediately correct this, because if one rolls back the water level to the 600-foot depth, then the fabled tin mines of England again come to light off the coast of Cornwall. Were these the mines of the earlier people taken over, toward the end of the bronze age, by the Aryan speakers? At the present date, scientists do not believe that the Aryan speakers came into the region during antediluvian times. However, the picture which Plato paints of the Atlantis described by the Egyptian priest is definitely an Aryan city because of the horse and the interest in horsemanship.

That is not saying that it was originally an Aryan speaking power, for the ancestor worship would suggest a conquered location. So we have a mystery within a mystery. If the Goths, Celts, Basques and Finns were the remnants of the previous people, then it is possible that they, and not the Aryan speaking invaders, were the makers of bronze. If so, did they have enough of the raw metals to supply both Europe and the Mediterranean? Besides, why is the bronze of Europe so much more pure than the bronze of the Mediterranean, which is not only often diluted with lead, but also, sometimes, silver? Because of this fact, many investigators do not believe that the same power supplied both locations. Could it be that the Atlantic power which may have supplied Europe got their metals from the land where they were both plentiful - namely North America for copper and Peru for both copper and tin? There was a flourishing copper age in both of these locations. The finest bronze

also seems to be centered in the Americas, for the memory is still carried by all the Atlantic and Peruvian groups of the bronze which was "harder than white man's steel". Yet the problem of the white man's beard prevents any vast amount of trading during and after his conquests.

Similarly, in the Mediterranean, the traders, though diluting bronze, yet provided these Mediterranean nations with swords of iron before they were known in Europe. We know that the men which Homer wrote about had iron swords about one thousand years before Christ. Yet strangely enough, the chants which are thought of as Aryan sagas are probably a borrowed form of historical story telling to verse or to music as noted by the Finnish kavella, and the innumerable chants of the Amerinds - even to the animals mentioned with human characteristics and the four trochaic beat, to eight beat measures. (One might suspect from the Arab's description, that the verses by which the women in the Tuarak or Tuareg city told stories for the entertainment of people at the banquet may have been such a series of sagas.)

Some investigators have believed that these horse riders who came into Europe from the well of the round heads, and carried bronze swords or arm daggers, also brought in the ox, sheep, goat and pig. Let us check back. The Azilians, who built their towns out in the Pleistocene lakes of Switzerland (and around the earth) who may have been known as the Kitchen Midden people, had, among other animals, the goat, the pig and the ox. This leaves the sheep and the horse which were definitely the property of the Aryan speaking round heads. The dolicephalic Kitchen Midden people may have been conquered and absorbed as the brachycephalic tribes swept westward, but they did not bring the ox and pig from their homeland. Incidentally the Semitic speakers, who swept into the Mediterranean about this same time or shortly thereafter, came in with the camel and the sheep, both of which they also brought from their homeland.

Let us take a second culture trait: clothing. The earliest pictures of the Semitic speaking invaders into the Mediterranean show them with very long robes, while the Egyptians picture themselves as wearing the short sheath which could easily become the kilt of the Celts. We are told that these long robes of the invaders were made of wool, the wool of sheep, which the shepherd kings brought with them. The clothing of the Egyptians, on the contrary, was made of linen (flax) and cotton. The longest threads of the

- FRED BEAVER -

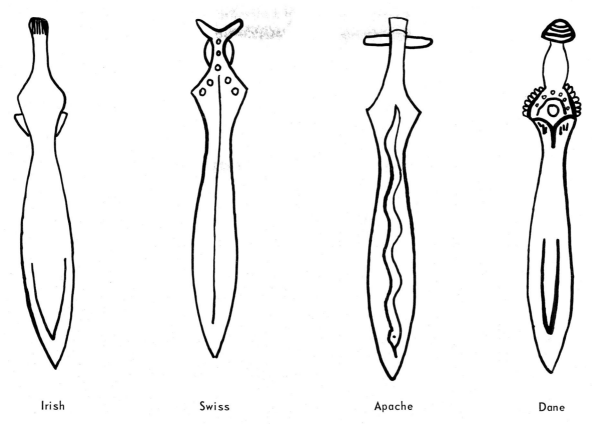

Irish   Swiss   Apache   Dane

BRONZE AGE SWORDS, partly after Donnelly.

cotton are to be found in two places: the cotton of Egypt and that of the Caribbean. The cotton must have been an American plant, for it does much better in the Americas then in Europe or Africa. Furthermore, the Amerinds have legends of cotton grown in color. This was thought to be a mere myth until Dr. Harrington of the South-west museum, Los Angeles, tested some of the cotton found on Peruvian mummies (in the 1940's) and found no trace of dye. Of course, the Aryan-speaking invaders such as the Romans and the Grecian tribes, found these garments to be both cooler and more comfortable and soon adopted them.

It is interesting to note that while flax does not seem to be known in the Americas, cloth spun from the "seed silk tree" was used for very delicate wear, while the wool of both the vicuna and the llama were used in South America. The Mayans had their own silk made from the cocoons of caterpillars which lived on their own

APACHE CROWN DANCE

Note trident headdress or "crown" of the old red land. Original Indian painting by Fred Beaver.

mulberry trees; and while it is not as delicate as the oriental variety, yet it is just as lustrous and probably as old. This was much used in embroidery. One of the facts which one learns in the university of Mexico antiquities, is that the Amerinds all had embroidery before the Spanish conquest. In fact, the Aztec girl was prized for her ability to embroider, before her beauty was considered. This was because her husband desired a beautifully embroideried gar-ment. Embroidery was a status symbol with the Aztecs and other Amerind tribes. Even in the north, where skins and furs were used for cloth-ing, embroidery was done with porcupine quills and other materials. Dr. Patricia Ross, who teaches in the university of Mexico, brings out many of these facts in her book, "Made in Mexico".

There were many things made of bronze in Europe. Not only weapons, but also cooking pots and jewelry. There were two general types of swords. First, the short swords which we have been discussing. These were made for small hands. However, there was another type: the big sword with a blunt end for slashing. This was made for a big man with very big hands. One remembers king Arthur and his famous sword when one reads of this type.

In looking at the skulls of the round head invaders we come to realize that the skeletons are not large and their hands are definitely small. These swords are to be found in either Switzerland, Sweden, Norway or Ireland and are everywhere very similar except in the decorations. Were they trade articles, and if so, who was the trader? Was he from beyond Europe? This possibility seems to be strengthened by the fact that they are far more numerous along the coastlines than in the interior, although the Baltic river was evidently navigable at times. This seems to point to a shipping trader.

Besides these, there are the razors. They are an almost unknown item among the Egyptians and other pre-Semitic and pre-Aryan peoples such as the Sumerians. We do not find them among the artifacts of Crete, for example. The Cretans, like the Egyptians, picture themselves as beardless and with red skin while the women are the shade of old ivory. Nor are razors to be found in the artifacts of the Chaldeans previous to the invasions of the Semitic speaking tribes.

Two bronze razors or knives from Denmark. Note in upper, twin stars over ship, eight other stars. Lower, apparently a fleet of ships. After Donnelly.

Yet these razors of Europe are most interesting. Engraved upon them are ships with lifted prows and sterns in the shape and style of the later dragon ships of the Norse. Were the traders these big men who themselves used the slashing swords? Could they have been the men who built the cyclopean walls which were found with Cro Magnon artifacts in Spain? Could these have been "the Titans" of mythology? And if so, who were "the gods" who defeated them and threw them in prison at Tartarus, probably today somewhere in the Tyrrhenian sea? Were the "gods" the Azilians who had for thousands of years carried their red ochre everywhere - perhaps in their planked ships? The Azilian culture was found above the Cro Magnon and showed much contact and absorbed characteristics.

Yet if this was true, then why were the big men defeated? Is the answer the iron sword which the canny Phoenicians sold throughout the Mediterranean, but which was not found in Europe until very much later?

Let us examine one fact closely. Where did these people get their metals? Apparently the Titans had access to the greatest number of mines? Apparently the Titans, based on the Atlantic isles, and perhaps on northwestern Africa along the Atlas range and the long lost Lake Triton. Was this what the two people had fought about?

But what if the bronze was mined somewhere else - say in Switzerland and England, as some authorities have suggested. It is wishful thinking that does not seem to square with facts. Dr. E. Deser in "Lacustrian Constructions of the Lake of Neuchatel" says: "We are asked if the preparation of bronze was not an indigenous invention which had originated on the slopes of the Alps?" Then he gives his reason why, after first agreeing, he later changed his mind. "In this idea we acquiesced for a moment. But we are not by the objection that, if this were true, the natives, like the ancient tribes of America, would then have commenced by manufacturing utensils of copper. Yet thus far no utensils of this metal have been found, except a few in the strand of Lake Garda. The great majority of metallic objects is of bronze, which necessitated the employment of tin, and this could not be obtained except by commerce, inasmuch as it is a stranger to the Alps. It would appear, therefore, more natural to admit that the manufacture of bronze was of foreign origin and importation." Admitting that there is some copper in the Alps, nevertheless, he goes on to say: "Even the copper may be of foreign importation. Now, in view of the prodigious quantity of bronze manufactured at that epoch, this single branch of commerce must itself have necessitated the most incessant commercial communication."

After discussing why he does not believe that

the traders were Etruscans or other Mediterranean groups, Dr. Deser then ends the discussion with: "It will be the province of the historian to inquire whether, exclusive of Phoenicians and Carthaginians, there may not have been some other maritime and commercial people who carried on a traffic through the ports of Liguria with the populations of the age of bronze of the lakes of Italy before the discovery of iron." He became intrigued with the picture of the Tokhari vanquished in a naval battle with Rhameses III in the 13th century B.C. and whose likeness is upon the Egyptian temples. He quotes Morton, who believes they are Celts (or Tuaraks?). He believes that these men may have been the traders, and if they were, "the age of bronze may thus ascend to a very high antiquity, doubtless beyond the limits of the most ancient European races."

In this latter conclusion he may be wrong. The Europeans of round head extraction and speaking the Aryan tongues, may themselves be older than hitherto believed. They may well have been a group who not only traded with the people of the sea (the Titans of mythology), but also fought taking over their main capitol. This state of affairs would undoubtedly have been brought about in a nation of this antiquity and entrenched strength only by a series of seismological disasters which all but destroyed their power. Then after the combined Atlanteans were defeated by the Azilian powers in the Mediterranean because of the advent of the discovery by the latter of iron, and before the Atlanteans had time to search out their own iron mines and develop the new weapon, the great destruction came which demolished both of these powers of antiquity. Fanciful? Yes - perhaps, but impossible - no.

It is greatly to be doubted if the ancient bronze age sword dances in kilts are any more Aryan than the horned helmets or the dragon ships of the Norse.

In this discussion we have left the missing copper age of Europe the mystery which it must remain if we are unwilling to believe that the "people of the sea" have not only mingled their blood and their strength with us all, but also are the traders who worked the mines of Michigan during the age of bronze, and then late in that time started to work an iron mine in Peru. Any people who had enough knowledge to draw the Piri Re'is map, would have enough knowledge to know where to look for the newly discovered metal of iron.

The copper mines were worked for centuries,

and perhaps for thousands of years in northern Michigan. That the traders were foreigners is probable, because they brought their own miners. These men lived near the mines, and there grew their own vegetables. However, we never find their graves. Some of the mines are more vast and clever at following veins of metal than our best mines in the region today.

Then in Peru, where the copper and tin mines were worked avidly while gold and silver was only looked upon as an ornament, an interest suddenly developed in iron. There is an iron mine. There is an official Peruvian name for the new metal. It was "Quillay." In old Chilian it was "Pan-ilic." This name, with the inclusion of Pan, is most significant.

There is another point one might mention in passing. The Atlantic tribes usually designed with crecents, triangles, diamonds, etc., while the Algonkin designs were always floral. The bronze jewelry of Europe repeats these floral designs. Did they get them from the place where the copper mines were located - among the Algonkins? According to Algonkin legends, the great serpent always came up the Mississippi searching for copper, for which it had an enormous appetite. No wonder they had this opinion. At Isle Royale the works reached a depth of sixty feet and the individual drifts ran for miles. Intelligence was shown by the engineers in following always the richest veins or drifts, even when interrupted. On three sections of this island the amount of mining exceeded the amount mined in twenty years by one of our best and most modern mines with a large force constantly employed in shifts of continual work. The ancient mines also had drains and other advantages which we think are very modern inventions.

It is to be noted in passing that there are very few bronze swords to be found in Roman graves or associated with Roman coins. On the contrary, they are to be found in far greater abundance in lands never occupied by the Roman legions - such as Ireland, Scotland and among the Norse. Thus the mystery of the bronze age in Europe begins to take on worldwide significance. One is haunted by two questions as one closes the page on this time of tremendous world impact: why do the words which go to make up the peculiar non-Aryan name Atlantis, the city of horse racing (Atl and Antis) have the meaning in Peruvian of water, eastern, copper land?

And why was the iron mine of Peru so anxiously sought and then so suddenly abandoned? Is this date of abandonment the date of the great destruction?

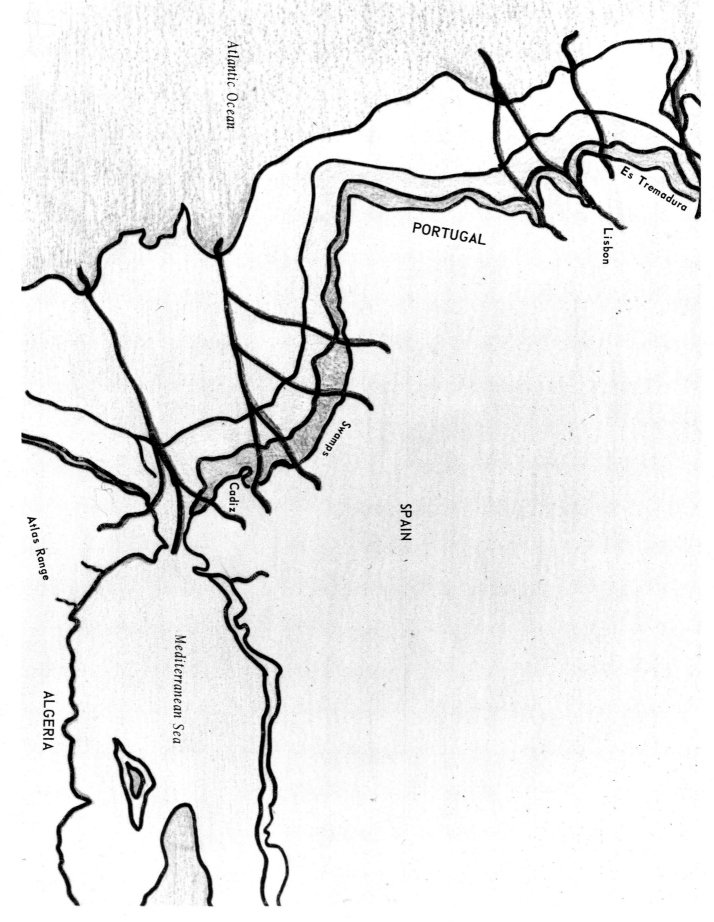

Atlantic Ocean

PORTUGAL

Es Tremadura

Lisbon

Swamps

SPAIN

Cadiz

Atlas Range

Mediterranean Sea

ALGERIA

122

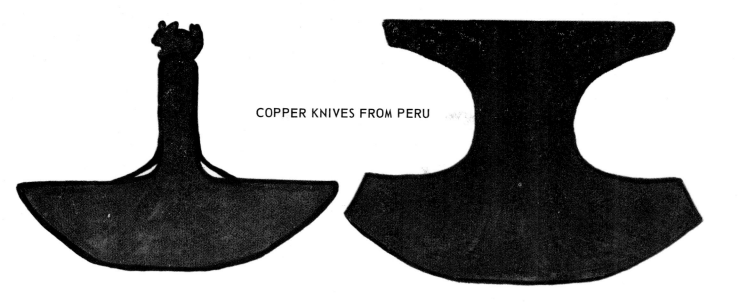

COPPER KNIVES FROM PERU

Chapter 19
Ancient Clues From Spain

In the legends of the Greeks and Phoenicians as well as the Egyptians, certain gods are now recognized as prehistoric figures. The wars they waged are now beginning to be thought of as wars between what are called by all of these peoples as "the gods and the Titans". Who were the "gods" who defeated the "Titans"? Of that we cannot as yet guess, but after more excavations, our guesses may get closer. We do know that Tarsarus or Tartessus was one of the cities they fought over, and the place where the victors threw the vanquished into prison. Where was this Tarsarus or Tartessus? We were told that it was either in or near Spain.

In 1914, a woman scientist by the name of Mrs. Elena Wishaw founded the Anglo-Spanish School of Archaeology, and then with a grant from king Alfonso, began excavational work to try to find Tarsarus. She was almost convinced by Spence's theory that the "Titans" were originally of a western island off of Spain and

Map of Spanish coastline and offshore depths. Sea level to 150 feet deep indicated by red; 150 feet to 600 feet by green; 600 feet to 6000 feet by blue. Depth of river channels exaggerated to show their location.

that they were the Cro Magnons, while the "gods" were the smaller long headed Azilians who invaded Spain from the direction of the Atlantic, probably a few thousand years later, carrying much of the Cro Magnon culture, and thus showing conquest and absorption.

First in Seville, and then in Neibla (a name that is most reminiscent of the Egyptian goddess Neith) she found objects from both the old stone age of man and the new stone age - or that of polished stone. These objects ran from the very early times to the invasions of the Moors in historical days. Among the neolithic or new stone objects she found fragments of pottery exquisitely polished which bore designs in relief. Pottery always suggests that the culture leaving it were tillers of the soil and had grains and other vegetable foods. Most of the objects, according to the authorities working at the site, were ancient - being of old stone age which is the very earliest time of man. However, the flints of these early times were supplemented here by beautiful work in quartz, slate, and porphyry - some of which were found in the drifts of the last, or warm glacial. This should be kept in mind when we speak of an Atlantic island which may have been the seat of these two empires.

It has been suspected for some time that this was the location of ancient Tartessus. However at the date of these artifacts, the last glacial, the land should run much further out to sea, since so much water of the period was locked up in the great mountains of ice moving down from the north upon both sides of the Atlantic. Therefore Mrs. Wishaw was lucky to find so much at the present sea level.

One of the greatest finds was near Seville, where pottery tiles were found of a funerary nature among remains which were classified by the authorities as Cro Magnon.

Because it has been known that Tartessus was occupied not only before the time of the Romans, but probably also before the time of the Carthaginians, and well into the time of the Etruscans, and an early seaport, was one of the reasons that Mrs. Wishaw had for excavating at this site. The Etruscans, it will be remembered, fought the invading Aryan speaking Romans for centuries from city to city until finally conquered and absorbed. (The Etruscans had many Atlantean culture traits which we will take up in another chapter.) Therefore the choice of this site for excavation was not entirely a fortuitous one. It was a well thought out plan for reaching pre-diluvian material.

Not only must we suspect the Etruscans, but also the Tyrrhenians, the Carthaginians, the Philistines and the Phoenicians of being people of the sea, or rather, refugees from Atlantic disasters. Carthage had certain culture traits, one of which was the purple dye of these peoples, admired in ancient Egypt and used by the aristocrats of the Mediterranean for millenia. In fact it is the reason why purple is the color for so many traditional royal robes of the present day - or up to the turn of the century when there were traditional royal robes and thrones.

The Phoenicians, whose language has been classified as Semitic, probably show strong early contact, but I prophesy that with greater study their language will be found to be Atlantic in basic root words even as Basque and Finnish. I base this belief on the fact that the Phoenicians considered themselves Tyrrhenians, a land situated just west of the Etruscans, and which Plato said was overrun by the Atlanteans. Tyr (incidentally one of their cities) was, according to the Norse Edda, one of the sons of Votan or Odin, god of the sea. His other son was Atl. This name undoubtedly was Atlas. Thus the Atlas range of mountains now running into the Atlantic was probably either a part of the sunken land or a bridge to it.

This belief that the Atlas was a part of the original oceanic empire was apparently started by Diodorus, who called the people of that sec-

tion - Atlantides. It is to be noted that the authorities who were investigating the excavations made in Spain found so many ancient Libyan characteristics that they reported a great fusion of Libyan culture.

And where was ancient Libya? To the west of Egypt - in what today is the Sahara desert.

Libya was the great power of pre history - suspected of being the homeland of the Egyptian delta culture from whose city of Sais, Solon heard the story of Atlantis. The delta culture was the civilizer of Egypt. It was the delta which raised the great pyramids and introduced writing. History began with the delta using ships.

Thus when the authorities at the excavations of Spain saw a fusion of the Libyan culture of the Atlas in what they were finding, they were pointing at the Egyptian delta of the dawn of history and the rumored prehistoric magnificence of the Atlantidae of the Atlas.

Though these remains - especially those of Cro Magnon burials, and the obviously Aurignacian culture, must be placed as Paleolithic or old stone age time, yet, they found walls with an amazing amount of engineering skill. The excavations uncovered harbors and walls of cyclopean blocks along with strongholds, the remains of which constitute the background of the work. They exhibited many facets of being pre-Tartessian. Perhaps this was the ancient Libyan influence.

At Neibla, soundings were taken down through thirty feet of very rich soil without coming to the bottom of the deposits. A museum was built to house the artifacts, and great enthusiasm was expressed at this rolling back of the historical horizon.

For some time Mrs. Wishaw and the authorities with her were puzzled by the lack of typical caves for the remains of Cro Magnon man, in a region so rich with the artifacts of these early Europeans. Beautifully chipped quartz and porphyry fish hooks were found, along with giant grain crushers, showing beyond doubt that Cro Magnon harvested grain. The crushers were made from local black quartz. All these objects were stratified and therefore could not have been carried down by the flooding of the river, from other levels.

There were indeed some caves not far away, but they showed remains much more recent than those of Cro Magnon. Then well below the foundations of Neibla a wall was uncovered made of chopped local limestone, very near Cro Magnon remains. The association of this wall along with the implements of Aurignacian culture, leaves little doubt now for science that Cro Magnon was a builder in stone. This is particularly interesting to archaeologists for it suggests that Cro Magnon was the builder of the walls fashioned of cyclopean rocks which line the shores of so many continents. These people have been up to now a mystery. Was Cro Magnon man then indeed the megalithic builders? Wherever these walls are found, they always precede the earliest known civilizations. This, then was a tremendous step in rolling back the historical dawn.

In 1923, nature herself gave a helping hand to the work. A series of floods along the Rio Tinto river washed away a great deal of earth, and uncovered a wall composed of cyclopean blocks, rough hewn, and held together with Hormaze mortar. This is a local name for a coarse variety of concrete which later became known as Hormigen, peculiar to Andalusia.

This wall was apparently part of a harbor where the river had been artificially deepened. Furthermore, a stairway of the width of thirty feet had been cut into the rock so that the passengers from ships could alight and go to the city. The wall had evidently been built so that the silt of the banks would not fall into the harbor. Perhaps also it was meant to strengthen the defenses of the ancient city.

The most interesting part of this revelation was not only that Cro Magnon man must have lived here in this city, for again his artifacts were found in connection with the wall, but also that Azilian artifacts followed, thus probably suggesting conquest. The later culture had undoubtedly made use of the earlier work. Perhaps they had built the city. However, the most amazing aspect of all about this wall was that some of the building blocks were constructed of the curious polygonal or many-sided masonry which has so amazed the engineers of the world when they visit pre-Incan Peru.

That the Cro Magnon and the Azilian were separate races there is absolutely no doubt. The first is the disharmonic cross and the latter the ancient long head. Yet, the conquerors may have intermarried with the Cro Magnon women.

However, both carried small statuettes of the mother goddess or great earth mother, and apparently both were matrilinear. We are told that the Atlanteans regarded the throne as going down through the woman, so a man had to marry the daughter of the monarch to be legitimately recognized as king. This is actually why so many of the monarchs of nations in the line of descent from the sea empire, married their sisters. This would be one of the strong culture traits to be watched for in any nation in the old line of descent, even as the Incans and the Egyptians.

In recognition of the strange likeness of the building blocks of the early Spanish city to those of Peru, it is curious that such nations as ancient Egypt of the Mediterranean family should follow the old way of inheriting the throne as did the later Incas of Peru. Connection? Not necessarily. These are just two culture traits, and could have been coincidence. We shall have to find many more before we can suspect a connection.

As far as the old city of Spain is concerned, frog-men swimming about the ancient site of Syracuse on the island of Sicily off the toe of the Italian boot, were amazed to find a harbor many fathoms under water. Massive walls and docks built to accomodate hundreds of triremes were found during diving operations in 1961. The extent of the ancient port far exceeded that of the modern city, and once more underwrites the greater interest of the ancients in the sea.

The information which we have gleaned from Spain seems to link Cro Magnon man with the first sea empire, and point to the long heads of the early Mediterranean as the first conqueror, and then inheritor, of the culture. If Cro Magnon man was indeed "the Titans" and the long heads were "the gods" who overthrew the ancient sea colossus, and then by marrying the daughters of the deposed or slain monarch, followed as the emperors in a new dynasty, we are making a long step toward understanding the picture which Plato painted for us of a bygone age.

However, there is one flaw in this story. As Cro Magnon man was the dominant figure of the old stone age of earliest antiquity except for the long heads who founded colonies along the shorelines, and then at the end of that period, overthrew the old colossus and founded the new stone age, did they continue into the bronze age the city which Plato was describing?

The answer is probably - no.

The reason? The horse and the wheel. These came in with the earliest invasion of the Aryan speakers into the Mediterranean. Therefore, this may have been a third invasion into the shrinking land mass of the old colossus, and a new flowering of civilization before the substructure collapsed into the sea. The name "Atlantis" may have been only the last name given to a very old and well loved homeland of two previous races. It will take much more investigation by scientists working both in languages and other sciences during centuries still to come before we can really know for certain, or place the idea in a book called "History."

CROWN DANCER. After notes taken at dance and sketches. Swords are of bronze age shape. Note star mirrors on chest with white down feather edge. Buttons on belt are silver. Leather sheath is gold with black fringe.

LEADER'S HELMET. Note significance of 13 red pyramids over top, 8 red pyramids across bottom, five crescents. Also, white condor feathers at peak (explained as power of twin-stars).

Chapter 20
The Dance Of The Trident

It was one of the most memorable nights of my life; I was about to see the Apache crown dance. All my other Amerind friends had pointed out that the wild Apaches were of the wolf totem - and my scientific friends had noted with erudition that the Apaches spoke Athapaskan. That was the last language to come from Asia, and it spread all the way up to the Aleutians, if there was to be any suspicion that they were not recent invaders from Asia.

Then I saw a picture of one of the dancers in a magazine. When I pointed it out to a certain scientific friend, he shrugged and said: "So, he is dressed up with a trident on his head. It won't mean a thing. The dance is called the devil dance because these strangely dressed figures are supposed to be chasing the devils out of the camp. A sort of childlike magic. You are an incorrigible romanticist, imagining something ancient in the hodge-podge of these savages. Go on and see it like I did once at the Indian festival. There won't be much of it, but you won't be bored either. You will find the Pueblo dances more beautiful."

I took his suggestion and turned my car toward Arizona. I had chosen to see the wildest of the tribes of Apaches - the Mescalleros. They were the people of Geronimo, the terror of the west for decades when they made monkeys out of both the American and Mexican armies at once. The Apaches only had eleven to sixteen warriors and were burdened with women and children besides, yet outnumbered hundreds to one they kept up a guerrilla warfare for over a decade and then were only captured by the treacherous use of the white flag as a means of bringing them close enough to be surrounded.

I came in as quietly as possible and slipped up to the edge of a crowd where the great fire was burning. A strangely haunting song was being sung, and it continued throughout the dance. There was a certain air of expectancy. Somehow I thought of the Arab's description of the dance of the men of the mountain which he had witnessed in the Tuareg camp. He said that they had entered in single file with flaming tridents on their heads from the direction of the Atlantic. Imagine the manner in which I caught my breath when I saw this identical sight. The figures danced into view in single file from the east, the direction of the Atlantic, the trident very prominent on the heads of all four of the dancing figures except their leader. His head-piece was a pointed helmet with a tuft of feathers on top. How were the helmets of Atlanteans described? Like a mountain with smoke on top - denoting the volcano!

In each hand they held the ancient arm dagger of the bronze age so often mentioned as Atlantean. Above the elbows of each arm was the band to which the daggers could be chained. The next article of clothing I noted was the Libyan sheath used by the peoples of the sea when they went in to battle. Then as the dancers moved, I began to notice other things: the two whirling circles with a mirror background painted and embroidered on each breast. The Venus calendar of the old red land!

The dancers came up to the fire and stretching forth their arms, bent low and backed up in unison. In the second figure of the dance, after going south and again worshipping the fire, they appeared to be building walls. The monotonous song of the dance seemed to become one with one's blood as the tom-toms pounded out the rhythm and the rattles on the dancers' soft boots shuffled out their insistence.

The third part of the dance was a battle. The swords were used simultaneously as they clanged against each other. Was this, too, a part of the Tuareg dance? What a sword dance this was!

Then a large woman arose and stood before me, and I lost my patience that she ever intended to sit down again. I was missing great portions of the dance. Trying to see around her was impossible. When I moved to the right, she also moved and again after a glimpse of the veiled figures, I had to sit back. I decided to stand also. The veils intrigued me. They were black to the line of the eyes and below that, red. Was this the original dress of the Tuaregs? Now I knew that I had to talk to the leader of this ritual. The most burning questions were simply tearing up my insides.

Finally, after what seemed like hours, I had my chance. I arose and followed the figures as dawn was coming over the mountains.

I had not come unprepared. I had borrowed large prints from the library on the "devil dances" of the Orient where the figures are devils either chasing or being chased - I was not certain of which.

But just in case my scientific friends were wrong - I had borrowed large pictures from other directions. First from Egypt - some well done copies of the ancient rituals to the fire god. Then, remembering my friend, the Dacotah and his description of Peru, I borrowed some large prints of the fire god upon the great gate which went nowhere, and also some of the giant walls with the cyclopean building blocks. The best picture was one of the city which my Dacotah, friend had said was the city of the bird of lightnings, with every street a feather, and from its height, one could look down on other peaks and the terraced land. Also in my pocket was a lid to a jar. It was from Egypt, and the writing underneath was full of red dust. The lid represented what I had taken for the fire god, with his two horns, but a slave, or someone was bending before him with his two hands on the calf of the god's leg. I had been told that it was probably the lid of some woman's rouge jar. However it dated back to the First Dynasty, and so I had it wrapped up very carefully indeed. The rest of the jar had been broken, so the scientists had put it among things to be mended, and since the two had been separated, I was able to buy the lid.

It was early morning when I caught up with the dancers and stopped where they were washing off the black paint with which they had covered their faces even under the veil. The zig-zag marks of the serpent up and down the arms were also being washed off. The clean-up was being done with much horseplay. I stepped up to the older man wearing the peaked helmet with the feathers on top.

"Please tell me something about this dance," I said. "I feel it is very ancient and I would like to confer with you so that we both may increase our knowledge."

The younger men had stopped laughing and joking and were listening. The older man turned and surveyed me coldly with great hostility in his narrowed eyes.

"No savvy the English language," he grunted, turning his back on me.

This is as much an insult as an Amerind can give to an outsider, and I realized that the only way I could reach him was through the young men with whom he had been dancing. I pulled out first the pictures of "Yama" the Oriental fire god represented in the dances of the Tibetians. Long ages ago they consigned him to the underworld (even as we have consigned him in the Christian religion) and now regarded him as the spirit of evil. This was the picture with which, according to my scientific friend, these Apaches were supposed to have vague connections.

The young men took it with whoops of laughter. The leader, finding that his insult had not gotten rid of me, glanced over his shoulder as his curiosity got the better of his antagonism. I saw him laughing silently and making some remarks in Apache.

So they thought that was funny? Very well. I would try Egypt. I pulled out the copy of the ritual which had been painted on the ancient temples. There was a fast intake of breath all around. Some of the young men called out for various other young men in civilian clothes of the twentieth century to come, apparently, for this is what happened. At this point the leader turned around, and the picture was willingly released into his hands.

"Where do these people live?" he asked of me quietly in the language he did not "savvy".

"In ancient Egypt," I answered. "That is upon the other side of the Atlantic ocean, and these pictures were painted on the old temples many thousands of years ago." I continued passing out some other pictures, which he in turn

passed to the younger men.

"I recognize the figure," he said. "The clothes are entirely correct, which is not true of the first figure you showed us. Where was that from?"

"Tibet, in Asia."

"The manner of dressing the figure was intentional to make him ridiculous - the one from Asia."

"I see," I answered thoughtfully. "Tell me, do you regard this god as good or bad?"

Suddenly all the old antagonism was back. Lightning shot through his dark eyes as he drew himself up to his full height and folding his arms said coldly: "Only enemies regard him as bad."

"Now wait a moment," I replied, "I am asking to learn and not to try and change your religion. You see this god is before all the others upon earth, and every religion coming since has consigned him to the underworld - that is, had made of him the spirit of evil. This is true of Buddhism, Confucianism, Taoism, Judahism (of the Hebrews), Christianity - even the many gods of the ancient Greeks, Romans, Sumerians and others."

"Oh. Now I understand. His worship is very ancient?"

"Yes."

"Perhaps it began on an island where there was a great mountain of fire?"

The young men were crowding around us, listening intently.

"That is what I believe, although I may be wrong."

"You are not wrong. That is correct."

"And that land lay in which direction?"

"You saw us come in tonight to the fire. From which direction did we come?"

"From the east?"

"You are observing well."

"Now I would like to know the name of this god."

"I am sorry. To speak the name aloud is forbidden. We never speak the name aloud."

"There is a book of rituals in Egypt called the Book of the Dead. In those rituals the name is given. If I speak the name, will you tell me if I am correct?"

He shrugged his shoulders and laughed softly. "Do you know how small your chances of speaking the correct name will be? Almost impossible - with so many miles and so many centuries of time like a haze separating the homeland? However, if you desire, I see no harm in allowing you to tell us what these people called him."

The silence was almost deadly. The ring of intent Apaches were holding their breath.

Softly, but very distinctly, I gave the name.

There was a sharp sound of indrawn breaths almost like a cry. The young men looked at the ground and around at the tops of the mountains. I did not need to have the leader say:

"That is the name. Now in deference to us, please do not use it again."

My pulse was pounding at this revelation. But how could it be? Apaches - the last tribe over from Asia - speaking an Asian tongue?"

I gave vent to my thoughts.

"Yes, they tell us that our language is Asian. Yet we drank in these traditions with our mother's milk."

"Oh - your mothers carried the traditions?"

"You understand much."

"Your mothers were captured by the invading Athapascans - of course, the women carry the traditions - I remember now. I learned that while studying some of the people close to the Egyptians of long ago named - Tuaregs."

"You mean Tuaraks?"

"You know about them?"

"No, but in the old language that would mean 'people of the all-glorious fire god.'"

Then glancing at the other pictures I still held, he asked: "Do you have more pictures to show us?"

I pulled out the picture of the fire god on the gateway which led nowhere in Peru.

He took it almost reverently, nodding his assent.

"This is the figure. We recognize it. Where is it from?"

"Very far to the south - in Bolivia along the border of Peru, South America."

The young men were crowding around and pointing out features to each other which he, too, was discussing with them. In order to get the conversation out of Apache and into English again, I asked a question:

"If the figure is the one you believe it to be - why is he holding up the two swords on high? Is it because he wishes to represent a bull?"

"That is one meaning. However, the one here, being on a doorway, tells the stranger to enter, but to be careful even though he be a friend. If the swords were crossed before him, that would mean - 'stay out'."

"And why is he crying? There seem to be tears."

"Do you not know? You do know so much. Do you not guess the secret sadness at what has happened?"

"Oh - you mean the destruction of the old red land?"

"You know about that, too? Where did you of white skin learn of all these things?"

"From tribe to tribe - fitting together the pieces like bits of a puzzle. Then there still remains parts of the old books. These people, the Tuaraks, as you call them - they have some but no one can read them - they are unfriendly to strangers."

"I only wish I could go to them - alone and unarmed."

"They might make a sacrifice of you," I smiled with a touch of banter.

He answered softly and seriously: "No. They would not. We would talk for many days, and I would go down into their galleries, if they live in the mountains, and we would exchange the old greetings."

I felt like saying as he did: "You know about that, too!" but he was holding his hand out for the last picture as he handed back the one of the portal which went nowhere.

I handed him the picture of the old city on top of the Andes with the view below of the terraced land.

There was almost a yell from the young men as they saw it, and as he passed it to them, there was evidently an admonishment in Apache not to tear it in their anxiety to see.

"It does exist then! Our city on the mountain tops where the land is terraced. This is our city! We built it! Now see -" to the young men "tell that to your teachers! It never existed - huh? It is all a fairy tale! There is no place where the city was made of giant stones on top of a mountain and the sides of the great peaks are terraced!" Again the words went into Apache, tumbling from him in a torrent of pent up emotion. Again I had to get this frantic exchange of words back into English.

"Not so fast," I said. "I half agree with your skeptics. First the island in the Atlantic and then a city on top of the Andes in faraway Peru, South America! You are - how would you say it in Apache? - you are walking around the earth with very long strides! Very long steps indeed."

He smiled. "Very well," he conceded softly. "I, too, like to get my facts straight. I will describe this city. You will nod if I am right, and shake your head if I am wrong. The stones are fitted exactly - the stones in the walls." I nodded.

"There are four galleries under the city which go far into the mountains."

"So they say, but only two have been found, and these have been walled up because too many people went in and none ever came out again."

Now it was his turn to nod.

"The terraces of the lands were used for farming and some of the dirt was brought from a long way?"

I nodded.

"The land was irrigated by tile drains which went to the ice on top of the peaks."

"It did when the peaks had ice that low. Now the ice is much farther back."

"It was many many winters ago that we lived there. Then we built dams to hold the waters of the rivers."

"You are very correct. This is leaving me speechless."

"I will tell you something. Indian tribes can almost be divided into those who bring down the water from the mountains to their fields, and those who pray for rain. The last ones are not so old."

"If you mean the Hopi, there is a great civilization behind them too, I am sure - perhaps two - one in Peru and one in old Mexico, but they are not your people."

He nodded with a great deal of interest.

"What you say may be true. It would be interesting if we could know all of this for certain, wouldn't it?"

"Of course. But returning to the city - there is something else about the city. You can see that from an airplane.

"Oh. You mean the plan. It is the city of the bird of lightnings; is that what you mean?"

"Yes, with every street a feather - like Cuzco."

Again the conversation broke like mad among them, and I had to do something desperate to get it back into English. They seemed to be largely talking to one young man in particular who was dressed completely in "white man clothes" without even the inevitable touch of turquoise.

"How did you get out of the city - through the galleries when the enemies stormed it?"

"You know that too?" he asked with almost unbelief.

"I told you that other tribes were with you, or you split up later when you went north in your dug out boats. I have learned it from others."

"Then do you know what these mean?" looking down to the two stars upon his breasts. (Incidentally Amerinds do not point. That is an insult.)

"Oh you mean Venus. That is an old calendar."

"A calendar?"

"Yes, you see Venus is a planet like the earth, but closer to the sun. . ."

The young skeptic among the Apaches gave out a long satisfied gutteral grunt, that was almost a derisive laugh directed at the old leader. I ignored him and continued:

"Now it swings around the sun on an internal orbit to us," illustrating with my fists, "while we go around like this. Venus, which is the morning and evening star, depending on the time of the year, makes exactly thirteen revolutions to eight of ours, so when eight thirteens are up, the planets are again in the starting position and this would be one hundred and four years - or one complete cycle of the calendar. The half-cycle would be fifty-two years." The figure on your helmet I have counted, but it has only twelve appendages instead of thirteen."

"The center circle is thirteen," he said simply. "Also there are thirteen points

on the figures of each arm because everything in the old red land was in doubles - even to the rulers. In those days of our greatness, we had the twin stars on our horns. Does that have a meaning to you?"

"It certainly does. The cult of the bull, which was carried everywhere by the people of the sea."

"Or: the men of the mountains," he corrected me - or added to what I had said. I thought again of the Tuaregs; that is what they called themselves.

"Did you know all that about Venus?" the young skeptic asked of the leader.

"I do not tell you everything," he answered coldly and then to me: "Would you say that we once had cities either in the south on mountains, or out in the seas before the destruction, in order to know this about the twin star - Venus - as you call them?"

"I certainly would. To learn about the movements of the stars, they must be watched from one exact spot for hundreds of years, and no hunting tribes could do that."

"But the teachers of these boys, like the one with white man hat, have told them that we never had cities; that we were always savages and always would be; that our traditions were fairy tales told by children for children; and that there never was a city of the bird of lightnings, or an old red land."

"Then I say to your young men this: I have as much education as your teachers, probably more - much more, and I am still learning.

There is a friend of mine - a supposed scientist - who told me a story something like that when I asked him about this dance of yours: the dance of the trident."

"We call it the crown dance, because in it we wear the ancient crown."

"My friend," I continued, acknowledging his correction with a nod of gratitude, "told me that your dance was a chasing of devils out of the camp - a sort of childlike magic. I will go back and tell him: 'You looked on this dance and you did not see the trident; the Libyan sheath which is the long skirt worn to the calves of the legs during war; the symbols of the Venus calendar; the bronze age swords fastened to the arm band; and the peaked helmet of the sunken land - you look and you do not recognize? You are blind. You have wasted your father's money going to college. You should have stayed home and milked cows.'"

The Apaches broke into long and loud laughter and the skeptic looked puzzled. Then I added:

"No, I wouldn't say it like that, but jokingly and more politely. However, he would understand me, even though he might not change. It is hard to change opinions gathered over a long time and bound up not with reason, but with feelings perhaps of distrust.

"I say this to your young men: Your traditions - these chants - they are your books. Once you had books, but mostly they have been burned by ignorant and distrustful people. Your chants are the oldest histories on earth. They are your heritage. Learn them. And teach them to your children. Was it not Votan, the last great emperor who said: 'Recognize each other and never forget your chants, or you would be like ships without a rudder or an anchor, for remember, you once had ships in the days of your greatness.'"

The old man grasped my arm and said softly: "Thank you."

I started to go, and then I remembered the old Egyptian lid.

"Oh yes, by the way, I bought this from a scientist who found it way down among the things of the First Dynasty in Egypt. I would like you to see it," unwrapping the little porcelain lid which just fit in the palm of the hand.

He took it and gasped.

"Oh! I have a very strong wish to own this."

"I am sorry, but it is expensive - you know being so old."

He turned it over reverently and held it up for the young men to see. Then he said: "We will try to get enough money to buy it - we will give you twice what you paid."

I shook my head. "Sorry, but it just isn't for sale," taking it back and wrapping it up again.

"Then I will ask you this - come back late this afternoon or better yet - tomorrow."

"No I have to leave for business reasons."

"Please come back this afternoon."

"Very well, if it pleases you, I will make arrangements and return."

So I walked away. Two of the young men accompanied me back to the car.

"I have never seen him talk like this before to a whiteman," one said shyly. "It is easy to see that he likes you."

"He is hard for one to become aquainted with him?"

"Yes. Do you know who he is?"

"No."

"That is Asa Delugie. His mother was Geronimo's sister."

"Oh. And if Geronimo did not leave a daughter, the chieftainship would then go to him?"

"You know a great deal about us," the other one said wonderingly. "You may become an Apache legend."

I smiled.

"You are very kind, but I have learned a great deal today. Your leader is a very wise man. I talked to him because I know that helmet from pictures of long ago. You learn those chants. I meant that. They should never be lost and if they are - all mankind will be the loser."

That afternoon when I returned as I had promised, imagine my consternation to see everything the tribe owned laid out on a table. First there were beautiful blankets, hand made, and on them lovely baskets - jewelry of all kinds of the heavy turquoise and hand hammered silver type which is so lustrous on Amerind arms.

Asa Delugie was waiting, and when I came up to him he made a sweeping gesture: "All this for that lid to the jar."

I smiled and shook my head. You want it very badly, don't you?"

"Yes. Very badly. Yet this is all we own. We are not a rich people."

"Very well. I will tell you what I will do. You tell me what it means and I will give it to you, because it is more yours than mine."

"You do not want these things which represent money?" in a voice full of amazement.

"No."

"You are no white man. Your heart is as ours."

I smiled my gratitude for the compliment.

"Here it is. Now tell me the meaning."

"First tell me what was told to you by the men who dug it from the dust of the ages."

"They said it was the rouge jar of a woman."

"That is not true. Was it found in a chest or a metal box?"

"Yes. I believe so. It was full of red sand. Some of it is still on the lid."

"I knew that. What happened to the sand?"

"It was probably dumped out when the box was put with other things to go to the museum."

He gave a sigh of resignation.

"That was some of the sand of the old red land."

"Oh no!"

We looked into each other's eyes. My feeling was almost akin to his.

"Now I see why you wanted it so."

"Not only that, but because of the picture on it."

"It is the deity whose name must not be spoken?"

"Yes. It is."

"Then what was kept in the jar?"

"Black paint."

"What for?"

"To paint the figure for the ritual dance. You see, the priest is putting the paint on the deity's leg."

"Oh yes. Now I do see. I am glad that I gave it to you. It should have been yours. Only I ask that it be passed down among your people from generation to generation to remind them that the legends are not fairy tales for children."

"Your wish will be followed."

"Are there any other answers we could give you in payment?"

"Yes. Is the tuft of feathers above that ritual helmet taken from the neck of the giant bird called the condor - the bird of the lightnings?"

"I am really sorry, but that I cannot answer. It is forbidden."

Unbeknown to him behind him, however, half a dozen youths were nodding a vigorous "Yes!" I smiled my gratitude.

If they are the fluff feathers of the condor, then your last emperor - Votan, the master metalworker, who limped slightly in one leg and whose sign was the large ram, told you to wear it above the forehead as a sign of recognition. If you see it, you are to make an alliance with these people, as the men of the sea were allied, island to island. Do you know that?"

The leader nodded silently, staring at me in almost a puzzled manner.

"Tell me more of this bird."

"He is as tall as a man, can kill an ox with a stab of his bill or carry off a calf. His wing spread is ten to fourteen feet. His feathers are black and white."

"Have you ever seen one?" he asked.

"Yes, there is one in the San Diego zoo. He lives in a giant cage about a block long, and small animals are thrown in for him. Full sized trees are in the cage and a pool of water."

"There are some smaller ones in California."

"Yes I know. I believe there are some of them too. There is a large fine for killing one. They seem to be dying off, and the state is trying to protect them."

"What fools would ever kill this ancient bird?"

"Some might, thinking it is sport."

"They do not know about the curse. But in time it will catch up with them, and then they will wonder why they are having such bad luck - not only them, but all their party with them in body or spirit."

I thought of the Ancient Mariner and the albatross.

For few moments he was silent and then:

"Are there any other answers I might give you in place of that one I could not answer?"

"Yes. Please speak to me of the old red land."

"We do not speak of these things to white man. In the early days they laughed. To us this is not funny. We have lost some of the meanings, but I do not speak lies. I know that I speak the truth, even though I may not always understand."

"Perhaps between us we can grasp some of these meanings, but if I do not know, I will say so."

"Then listen. In the times of the dawn there were FOUR. He nodded to the head dress held by one of the young dancers. I know not what, but I know that after many ages eight more were added because the four lost their strength. Then there were twelve. In those days the twin sparkling star was upon our horns and there was a place where ships came in . . ."

"A harbor?"

He nodded.

"It had a puzzle at the entrance where enemies lost themselves. In the days of our greatness, when we wore the stars upon our crowns, everything in the world was straightened out there like today small quarrels are straightened out in Washington, and what the great emperor of the horned ram said was law."

"Was there a dragon?" I asked.

"In the times of the dawn, the fire god himself took this form sometimes and lived in the swamps. At other times he crawled through our galleries, for we had miles of painted galleries. He shook the land with his anger and left the galleries burned with his breath."

"Did he sometimes take the form of the condor also?"

"Sometimes, I think."

"Another question. Before the final destruction, were there still the eight who came in when the first four lost their power?"

"Do you understand the meaning of that?"

"No, not yet. But the answer might help me to find out."

"And if you do, will you return and tell us?"

"Yes."

"Before the great destruction there were twelve. What could it mean?"

"Perhaps mountains - the break-up of the land surface - or perhaps new calendar systems with new invaders - I don't know yet."

"After that the people became afraid and ran away. We went to the south, to the mountain tops, for we are the men of the mountains. There we built our cities. The oceans ran away and we did not see them any more. What does that mean?"

"Probably that you gave up shipping, since the homeland had sunk."

"We have spoken of our cities and how we left them through the caves - each clan following its own token, or totem."

"Was the land in the south new to you, or was it an old colony?"

"I believe we knew of the land, but we fashioned other cities."

He turned and raised his arm to the sun.

"He arises high, and my memory fails me of the things of long ago."

I realized that he was giving me his dismissal speech, and I saw the golden opportunity fading away.

"One thing more," I pleaded. "Speak of the great destruction."

"Very well. It began with a tremendous cloud of black which spread over the heavens. The earth had been shaking from time to time for days. Now the sacred mountain began to spurt fire like a giant fountain, and the fire god crawled through the caverns, roaring and thrashing the land about like a wolf shakes the rabbit."

"In the . . . .(something) Katoun, Ah-Musem-Cab crawled out of the underworld in order to close the eyes of the thirteen gods. His name was not known. Only his mother and sisters spoke

it sometimes among themselves."

What the leader had been saying was so much like the ancient Chilam Balam that I almost subconsciously began to quote, hardly realizing what I was doing or even that I could remember so much of the antique phrasing of this ancient Amerind book.

Suddenly I was aware that dozens of eyes below which was the ancient horizontal band of the serpent across the cheeks and the bridge of the nose were staring at me as if seeing a being from another planet. I stopped in confusion.

"Go on," the leader whispered.

"My memory fails me - truthfully. I simply cannot remember."

"Where did you learn these lines?"

"An ancient book. The original was thrown into the flames by the conquering Spanish, but one man, a priest of the ancients, had remembered much of it by heart, and he wrote it down in his own tongue, using Spanish letters. Thus it was saved."

"I would hear more from this book. Perhaps then, together, we could understand much."

"I have copied some and I will bring this when I come again."

"To make it certain that you will come again, I make to you an invitation. For you alone, in four years, we will dance the original crown dance as it was before it was changed."

"You changed it?"

"The government of Washington would only allow us one dance, so we had to put two together to save them both. Now all other dances are being forgotten."

"I could wish the men in Washington more wisdom in the appreciation of what is so old."

"It is said among all the Indians that white man is smart, but not wise."

I nodded thoughtfully.

"As I said, we will dance for you the ancient crown dance of the trident. And to be sure you will come and bring more of the book, I will promise something else - I will speak aloud to you the last speech of the emperor before, standing on his pyramid, he sank below the sea with his old red land."

"You know that?"

He nodded.

"Nothing will be able to keep me away, unless death steps between us. But if it does," turning to the young men, "learn this. Do not let it die. These things are true. They are your histories. Do not let ignorant speakers turn you from what is rightfully yours. If you lose these books, all of mankind is the loser. None of us know all of the meanings because some are secret, but by conferring from tribe to tribe we will someday learn - but only if the people have not forgotten. There is a Socsa-hu-man city formed of the most perfect buildings the earth has ever known, on top of the high Andes. Nor is it the only ancient city in the peaks of the Andes. These are not fairy tales; these are facts. And I believe that the old red land was also a fact. I am going to write a book to try and pin down the facts so that others will begin to see the shadow of the past arising from the sea as I see it. I will send you one of these books. But hold on to your legends at all costs."

"Thank you for your words to my people. When next they doubt that once the 'twin stars were on our horns' I shall only answer: 'The numbers speak for themselves.' "

"And thank you, my friend, for all the help you have given me last night, and today. And again to your people: when next you are inclined to doubt, remember all those thousands of years of wandering, war and capture. Remember your mothers who, even though captured by the strange tribe of your fathers, remembered the legends and taught them to you. They would not have been so insistent that you remember lies."

A young man said: "Our teachers have been telling us that they were child stories for fifty years. They told him," nodding to the leader.

"And he knew better," I answered him. "They have been telling this for fifty years? The legends have come down - garbled perhaps and with parts missing - but they have come through the mists of centuries that pile into thousands of winters. Remember that, and learn them, not only from your people, but other people - learn all you possibly can. And if you are able to go to college to learn even more, perhaps from such people as the Tu-ar-aks in the Sahara who have the books and the painted galleries - that would be even better, but at all costs - keep on learning."

Delugie stepped up to me and gripped my arm in the Amerind sign of friendship.

"Do not forget to come," he said as I nodded "yes" and bowing to the young men, walked away.

As for the anthropologist who told me with such erudition that the dance was a hodge-podge of child-like magic, I carefully avoided seeing him again. If I had, I most surely would have said some of the insulting things which were on the tip of my tongue. However, since his death, time is not dealing with him kindly, because his fellow scientists are noting that he was a careless worker and more intent on putting over a theory of his own than following knowledge for its own sake.

Head of Amen-em-het III from a sphinx fround at Tanis.

Bust of a statue of Amen-em-het III in the Lenigrad museum.

This is the most damning comment which could be made about a man's life-work in science. To paraphrase Dr. Reiber: "There are, unfortunately, Bastile minds!"

Yet for me the memory of that night and the following day will never be forgotten. The beauty of the dance of the trident in the light of the great fire, with the sparks spurting out to the stars, the pungent odor of burning cedar, the red glow on faces which looked like copies of Pharaoh Amen-em-het III, and the weirdly haunting melody of the chanters which beat itself into your very soul, are the background for the soft voice of the man in the peaked white helmet who spoke of events millenia beyond our histories.

Wherever he walks now in the land of shadows, as the Chippewa, Navaho, or Dacotah would say: May this man who so loved his people, walk the paths of beauty forever.

Chapter 21

Could There Have Been A Central Land In The Atlantic?

Grand Canyon of the Colorado.

During the Eighties when Donnelly brought the laughter of the scientific world down about his head for suggesting that there was at one time an Atlantis in the center of the Atlantic ocean, he had little scientific evidence to answer his critics. On the other hand, they were too sure of themselves and their ideas to rate the name of scientist. They had not glimpsed the expanding horizons of investigation. They had no idea how their pet theories could ever be tumbled into dust by the accumulating information being brought in by research in the decades following their statements of what they considered to be fact.

For a moment let us pause and look over the field of this expanding horizon which has to deal with the oceans of the earth. It is a fascinating field - mankind's actual last frontier of exploration of his own planet. We are upon the threshold of magnificent discoveries, and I, for one, would like to be there in spirit, if not in the flesh, when they are being made.

Just as the archaeologists of the last century did not believe that there could have been either a Trojan war or even a Troy, so the oceanographers and geologists completely discounted the possibility that there was sunken land in the center of the Atlantic. Then when the English research ship Challenger, discovered the Mid-Atlantic ridge with its mountains and valleys, they insisted that this was but a sub-oceanic area of volcanic activity. They were quite right. It was and is, but they did not go far enough. The reason for this was, of course, that they did not have access to the information which is compiling year after year for us to peruse.

Since the time of Donnelly, point by point their arguments are being nullified. Take for example their prolonged insistence that the central ridge, being newly discovered, was volcanic entirely and only of volcanic origin. Today no scientist would make such a statement unless he had gone over the ground of existing islands such as the Azores, which are the tops of the mountains of that central ridge. Dana and Daly did discover that there were granite bombs in the lava of these islands. In other words, fragments torn from a deep base and hurled by the volcanoes into the air with their lavas during eruption contained chunks of granite. Where did that come from? Naturally this could only come from a granite base and granite is a continental rock.

After this discovery, the scientists then hedged, insisting that if the central ridge was ever land, it must have been land when the earth was young - billions of years ago - long before the time of man. Thus the Atlantis legend was but a fairy tale told for the benefit of children. Again they repeated the antiquity angle of the land, when Beno Gutenberg discovered the pattern of continental rock in the debris of the central ridge of the Atlantic.

Beno Gutenberg, head of the seismological department of California Institute of Technology and co-worker with the brilliant Dr. Richter of the Richter scale for evaluating earthquakes, was an humble man. When I interviewed him, I found him far more impressed by the extent of man's ignorance of the ocean beds than he was by his own discovery of continental rock in the three great oceanic bodies of water. By using the seismograph for recording earthquakes, he was able to discover that continental rocks which he called sial made a distinctly different pattern than the ocean bottom which he call sima. Thus he was able to say with certainty that the Indian ocean contained a great deal of sial, the Atlantic a lesser amount, while the Pacific had the least. However, there was once a sialic base upon which the chains of the South Sea islands rested, although it has now become sunken to plutonic depths. The names sial and sima have filled a distinct oceanographic and geological need and are at present in constant use by modern scientists. (In his book "The Earth" Beno Gutenberg

went into this subject more thoroughly.)

Geologists and oceanographers have to admit now that the oceans do have some continental rocks along the strange structures which are known as ridges. Each ocean has its ridges and in every case they are the site of seismic activity - of tremendous earthquakes and of eruptions. Should such an undersea volcano erupt while a ship is passing over it, the resultant monster wave would undoubtedly overwhelm the unsuspecting traveler.

As in all sciences, once you have the answer to one question, you immediately have half a dozen new questions arising from that answer. Why do the oceans have ridges? What causes them? How old are they? If they ever were continental land, then how did the land get out there in the center of the ocean? Are there similar features to these ridges on the continent? Why are they always the site of intense earthquakes and volcanism?

Even the one possible exception brings its questions. In the Pacific there do seem to be some rises that may be entirely volcanic and without a sialic base, but then, why?

Before we become overwhelmed by questions, let us return to the Atlantic and note that Donnelly was perceptive enough to recognize the fact that an ancient empire of states which were islands, and were banded together in a league from an unknown antiquity, based on trade and defense, would be almost impregnable as a power in the ancient world. When he attempted to show that the legends of all peoples tended to underwrite such a power, he was met with scorn and laughter by the scientists of the day. Their arguments were 1) that there was no such land in the Atlantic ocean. When the central ridge of one thousand miles in width and the entire length of the Atlantic was discovered, their arguments shifted to 2) that this was only volcanic cracks perhaps due to a shrinking globe. The book of Donnelly was silenced. Then came Dana and others who found granitic bombs and Gutenberg who discovered sialic rock along the mid-Atlantic ridge. The arguments then shifted to 3) that this land was of tremendous antiquity - long before the time of man. Now let us see; what has science to say about that?

At one time scientists who were out learning about glacials by counting the varves, believed that those of Europe and the Americas did not match and that they were global features of tremendous antiquity - long before the time of man. They did not dream that man may have lived through all the glacials of the Pleistocene in more or less his present form. Glaciologists are now learning that the glacials were a global feature and the advances and retreats in Europe do match those of the Americas.

Do we have any radio carbon dates on these great global features of our planet? And what do they have to do with the mid-Atlantic ridge, or with the emergence and sinking of large mid-Atlantic islands?

Dr. Cesare Emiliani of the university of Miami, Florida, has become very much interested in the cores which research ships have been bringing up from the ocean bottoms. He has found that the skeletons of tiny animals and plants which fall in a rain to the bottom of the seas can tell with a fair amount of assurance whether the temperatures during their span of life has been either warm or cold.

Using the Pacific as a start, near the equator, and choosing the center in order to get away from any rivers which might muddy up his findings, Dr. Emiliani began to outline a temperature chart for the Cenozoic era - or the time of warm-blooded animals and of man, particularly the former - usually known as the age of mammals.

First, he charted the long-time trends. He found these on the bottom waters. Here he discovered that polar trends would quite easily make themselves known. For this purpose, he had to study the bodies of the creatures themselves as well as their fossils. He then discovered that thirty-two million years ago, the Pacific bottom was about 51 degrees Fahrenheit. One million years ago it had fallen close to the present temperature of the bottom. Thus the entire global Pleistocene was not any longer ago then one million years. Also thirty-two million years ago the temperature of the bottom of the Pacific was about the same as our temperate water at the top is today. By one million it had fallen to the present temperature, which is only a few degrees above freezing.

A new method of dating now began to help with this work. Developed by Dr. Willard Libby when with the university of Chicago, it is still so new that it has not as yet been applied to the waves of advancing and retreating glacial ice. However, a word to show how this time-clock works: use is made of radioactive ionium found in sea water; by comparison with earlier and later material in cores, the date can be learned. The concentration of this material at the surface gives the rate at which the isotome is incorporated in the sediments on the bottom. Then, since we know its rate of decay, its concentration in the core becomes an atomic clock dating the layer being studied.

In order to date the ice fluctuations, Dr. Emiliani sought the help of Dr. Hans Suess and Dr. Meyer Rubin of the Radiocarbon Laboratory of the U.S. Geological Survey, choosing cores from the Caribbean, the Mediterranean and the Atlantic. He chose to test for animals which would most clearly show the temperature change - the foriminifera. With the help of these scientists, he found that the peak of the ice age (when the ice mountains covered half of England and reached Chicago, U.S.A.) was about eighteen thousand years ago. When the ice was down to its deepest southern penetration, the temperature at 15 north latitude was 68 degrees to 72 degrees as compared with the present 84 degrees.

Furthermore, using the oxygen temperatures found by Dr. D. Ericksen of Lamont, and carbon dates worked out by Drs. W.C. Broecker and J. L. Kulp, he succeeded in further pin-pointing the temperatures. These scientists together found that the Atlantic and Caribbean waters warmed up suddenly and significantly about eleven thousand years ago.

Could this have been due to an out-pouring of lava along the central ridge? And if so, is it not remarkable that the date of Plato for that "day and night of horror" should match the best efforts of our scientific carbon dating?

In looking over these dates, we find that Solon was talking to the Egyptian priest of Volcan about the year 600 B.C. Plato, undoubtedly using Solon's notes, quotes the Egyptian sage as saying: "Let me begin by observing, first of all, that nine thousand is the sum of the years which has elapsed since the war which took place between all those who dwelt outside the Pillars of Hercules and those who dwelt within."

The exact date of the deluge and destruction is after this date, which is about eleven thousand five hundred from our time. Furthermore, there is always the "give-or-take margin of error" of a few hundred years either way in carbon dating.

There are some other interesting dates. There is the paper read by Dr. M. Opert at the Brussels Congress to show, from astronomical observations of the Egyptians and Assyrians, how they came together at one time and perhaps had an identical starting time and place. He wished to show astronomically that 11,542 years before he read the paper, man not only existed upon the earth in his present recognizable form, but had enough intelligence and experience in astronomical observation to form calendars, and thus calculate with accuracy the length of the year. The Egyptians calculated by zodical cycles of 1460 years. Their year consisted of 365 days, which caused them to lose one day every four years (our Leap Year) and consequently 365 x 4 equals 1460 or the number of years needed to bring the cycle around again to its starting point. Their zodiacal cycle ending in the year 139 of our era, began in the year 1322 B.C.

On the other hand, the Assyrian cycle, which was calculated by the moon, and was undoubtedly inherited by them from the conquered Chaldeans, consisted of 1805 years or of 22,325 lunations. The Chaldeans stated that between the time of the deluge and the beginning of their First Dynasty (historic), 39,180 years had elapsed. "What does this number mean?" asked Dr. Opert.. Then after pointing out that an Assyrian cycle began in 712 B.C., he continues by stating that these two methods of astronomical calculation were known to the same people. The number 39,180 years stands for 12 lunar cycles and 12 zodiacal cycles. Running the two cycles backward from our era we finally get to the year 11,542 which is an amazing similarity to the date given to Solon. Taking the date of 1965 and adding to it the number 600 which is the time of Solon's talk with the priests of Volcan, and adding to that the date of 900 which is the number of years which have elapsed since the war of the Atlanteans or people of the sea, with the Mediterranean league we have 11,565 years ago.

Thus:

Date of Atlantean War	11,565 years ago.
Date of intercalation of the calendars	11,542 years ago.
Difference	23 years.

Accordingly the calendars were intercalated 23 years after the Atlantean war. Is it not possible that a desperate people, seeing the signs about them of the coming destruction of their land, and having suffered defeat in their attempt to conquer other lands, give in this intercalation of calendars a strong clue to massive migrations to more stable lands for colonies? Such a migration probably took place after the intercalation of calendar systems. It may have been carried on for many years and points to an almost pathetic desire that the colonies do not forget the mother land? It almost suggests that the homeland, suffering from continuous earthquakes and displays of volcanism, had ample time to escape the final horror, and that the first migrations were probably an orderly and planned dispersal of ships carrying people and their foods as well as their libraries and other cultural pleasures. Perhaps there were pitiful attempts to keep in touch, and even long-line

plans from the leaders to continue the league for trade and defense through which they had gained their domination and power. It would seem the natural and human thing for a civilization facing destruction from natural forces to plan.

How do we know that they had such warning display of volcanism? In 1898 when a French ship was laying cables about five hundred miles north of the Azores, on the central ridge, at about 1500 fathoms or 9,000 feet, fragments of tachylite, or vitreous lava, which can only be formed under the air and upon land (since lava, formed under the sea, or under water, has a different structure) came to light. This was a tremendous surprise to both geologists and oceanographers. Of course we do not know if these fragments were from the mountain tops or the valleys of the sunken land, but the haunting thought persists that a drop of sea level of nine thousand feet would dry off the entire central ridge, and give ample room to support many Japans and Englands.

Furthermore, tachylite decomposes in less than 15,000 years and therefore it was spewed out into the air less than 15,000 years ago. The French geologist, Pierre Termier, as well as others, were much intrigued with these fragments which are now in the Paris museum. Papers were written upon the subject, and some of these thinkers feel that the fragments may have been submerged shortly after or even immediately after cooling. Otto Wilkins, the German geologist, joins Termier in his interest over these fragments and suggests that not only the central ridge, but also the northwestern part of the African shelf may have been submerged about the same time. (See Termier in Smithsonian Report 1915; Otto Suess "Are Ocean Depths Permanent?" Natural Science, 1893; Termier: "The Derivation of Continents", Paris and Smithsonian 1924; Wilkins: "Atlantis", Leipzig 1913.) These men point the way for both Taylor and Wegener.)

It should be noted that Emiliani was a very meticulous thinker in his researches on dates. With the dates for the last part of his chart thus checked, he worked through the first thirty-five thousand years and then on down into the earlier parts of his cores. One method of double checking was by comparison of the dating with other cores, using different techniques. By careful study of fossils, he also cut down on possible errors.

After pin-pointing the time which some paleontologists have called "the great destruction" (because so many of the Pleistocene animals were wiped out to extinction) and Emiliani chose to call "the end of the ice age", he then studied the fluctuations of temperature caused by the advances and retreats of the ice sheets. He found that the cores correlated with other land evidence for the past one hundred thousand years. Apparently the present northern glacial began about three hundred thousand years ago. This is about two hundred thousand later than has hitherto been believed by glaciologists. However, even more exact dating is on the way.

The maps of the sea bottoms which are now coming from the drawing boards of the oceanographers are a tremendous improvement over the grappling methods of the last century. One scientist likened those antique methods and their frustrations to a man running through a forest with a butterfly net. However some interesting articles have been recovered. Take for example the pile of ancient kiln dried bricks brought up from the central ridge. However, the disappointed men watching, and judging them to be ballast from some antique ship, promptly threw them back. One wishes that they had been saved, if only to be sold for souvenirs. I would have appreciated one for a paperweight, and I doubt if I am alone in ths viewpoint.

Now the oceanographers use the sound and echo system, which brought up the ancient Bogoslof river and placed it on the drawing boards of the cartographers. If a profile is desired, the ship moves in a straight line, but if a more thorough study is required, then the ship stays in the general vicinity and moves about slowly. Not only are these new methods and techniques with later instruments helping us to see through thousands of fathoms of water, but volcanology and the seismograph are doing their share in furthering our understanding of our planet. Thus due to the help of better tools and the patient labors of such outstanding scientists as Hull, Shephard, Daly, Joly, Schuchert, Du Toit, Willis, Crool, Brooks and many many others, we are beginning to have a much clearer picture of not only the composition of the earth and the curious features of the oceans but also mountains, valleys and rivers are beginning to appear on the drawing boards of the cartographers when the research ship is over the great central ridge of the Atlantic ocean.

Before closing this chapter, there is one more interesting fact which will throw additional light upon the date when the great central ridge met its final death throes. Dr. Maurice Ewing is a very brilliant oceanographer who is at pres- ent connected with Columbia university, but was formerly at the university of Southern California. It was during those days that I met Dr. Ewing and heard him discuss the trip on a research ship over the central ridge. After the lecture, I walked with him back to his office and there looked at some of the specimens which he had salvaged from the depths. One was particularly fascinating and he saw me eyeing the core of the driller.

"Beach sand," he volunteered. "And not composed of coral or lava fragments, but of granitic rock."

"Sialic rock from over a thousand miles from the nearest continent! What a find! Where was the drilling done?"

"Just south of the long valley - toward the edge of the ancient shelf." (The long valley is a feature of the ridge - six hundred miles in length and sixty miles wide.)

"Do you have the carbon dates?"

"Certainly. About ten thousand years B.C. - give or take a few hundred. But this isn't all. Here is a lower drilling, and you see again we have the beach sand. This is 20,000 B.C. The debris in between would suggest ash and submersion."

"I wonder what children played here, and what lovers strolled along these sands..."

Dr. Ewing smiled.

"You are a romanticist!"

"Undoubtedly, but the basis is pure science. And you know," I continued thoughtfully, "this reminds me of a popular book I was reading about the adventures of a skin diver. It seems that he discovered a road which ran into the sea off the coast of France. On the land it was not very plain, but once in the water the old cobble stone highway was very obvious - even to the ruts of the wagon wheels. The further he went from the shore, the plainer it became. He followed it easily as it wound its way around old bluffs and onward down the shelf. Suddenly he stopped. There was such a thing as "the rapture of the depths". Ahead of him the road continued. Regretfully he stopped on an ancient bluff above it and stared as it wound almost hypnotically below him and lost itself in the sinuous emerald mystery we call the sea."

Dr. Ewing shook his head and asked quizzically:

"Suppose he had followed it. What would he have found - besides death?"

I made an imperceptible gesture and answered:

"Who knows? Perhaps our...past?"

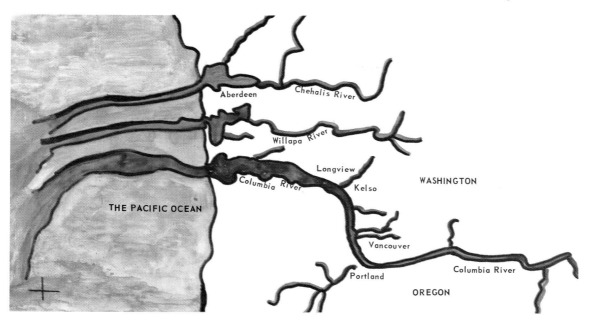

Chapter 22

Those Submarine Channels

If an anthropologist and a geologist were to be placed upon a ship bound for an unknown destination from an unknown port, the anthropologist would probably begin studying his fellow passenger, and the geologist would attempt to find out where they were at the time, where they had been as an indication of the direction which the ship was going, in order to learn what was to be her final destination.

Curiosity about the oceans of the earth has caused more hot debates than any other subject among men who follow the earth sciences - with the possible exception of continental drift. The subject causing the hottest debate is the channels of the world's rivers which run down under the sea. There is no doubt that they are there. Most geologists have, up to the present time, resisted the idea that these canyons are drowned river valleys. They are in the state of the man who saw an unwelcome ghost, and closing his eyes, wished it would be gone. To paraphrase a nursery rhyme: "I saw a ghost on the chart today! I am well aware that it isn't there, but it isn't there again today. Oh, how I wish that it would go away!" To admit these strange curiosities are really ancient rivers is to entertain a romantic idea, and geologists are constitutionally opposed to romantic ideas about their work.

For the layman these channels of long dead rivers, if that is what they are, can be one of the most fascinating subjects of oceanic research.

Suppose in our imagination, we equip ourselves with one of these vehicles of the future which can travel under the sea. Much as we might enjoy the thought, we cannot follow the old French road for we do not know its destination, and since we are on a scientific trip, let us stay as close to facts as possible. However, we will stay with France where the legends of a continuation of the land under the sea are as strong as they are along most of the Atlantic coastline, especially in Europe. Let us take the Adour river. It is a fairly large one, and as it goes under the sea, the old beach lines are well defined. We pass numerous lines of former seashores as we proceed down the shelf, and it will no doubt be upon these terraces that the anthropologists of the future will hunt for the artifacts of ancient man.

The river which we have chosen does not run right down the shelf and dump into the sea as we might imagine. No, it winds around like many rivers upon the land. It cuts canyons as it goes, passes over waterfalls and here and there joins with a tributary. Were these channels cut under the sea? Most geologists and oceanographers would like to pretend to think so. Let us glance at some of their theories before we go on.

The great argument against sub-aerial (under the air) erosion is: "Very well: Granted that these channels do resemble fossil rivers - exactly. But if they are, then where did the water go?" Is that an easy question to answer? It is not. Therefore, we will listen to some of the ideas that scientists have elaborately prepared to explain the undersea channels.

To say that the sea floor sank is possible only to a slight extent. It is not the answer. The reason for this is simple. These channels are not entirely an Atlantic phenomenon. They are worldwide. Not only do the rivers of the Atlantic, such as the Gironde, Adour, English Channel, the Baltic river, and the Mediterranean river, make their way through their own huge submarine channels, but so do the Ganges, Amazon, Lima river, the Mendogo, the Taugus and others pursue their own ways to the abysmal depths of ten to fourteen thousand feet. Also they usually turn and enter the deeps which, if the water is drained out, would then become lakes. Especially is this true in the Atlantic, and probably the unexplored Indian.

Nor is this all. We find undersea rivers in the South Seas, in Japan, Korea, eastern and western coasts of Formosa, off the mouths of the Ganges where a long lost river seems to join the Ganges canyon, the Indus and off the coast of Ceylon where a giant canyon lies. They are to be found around Zanzibar, the Gold Coast and Cape Verde. They are around the Philippines and numerous other places. This is a world wide puzzle.

The coast of California, which is the home of the Scripps Institute of Oceanography, has a great deal to study. However, as I was told at a meeting of the American Association for Advancement of Science, there would be much more study if only it were not for the deadly currents in the canyons. I remembered the Greek who lost his friend in such a current.

One of the most interesting is the Eel river canyon, mentioned before, with its sunken island which the river circumambulates even though the flat top of this island is now sunken to 2,400 feet below sea level. That is a question to counter the one about the water and where did it go. How does it happen a submarine canyon makes its way around a long lost island?

Most of the ideas which are put forth to explain these canyons are often exploded quickly by another geologist or oceanographer so that he can then put forth his own theory. This is natural,

for these men are after facts, not fiction - and rivers under the sea do resemble science fiction! However, there is one fact to note about the Eel before we go on. The resting stage of 6000 feet is most plain here and along the coast as one resting stage. However, since the International Geophysical year (IGY) when the ice of the Antarctic cap was found to be so much heavier than expected, this has become the more or less accepted level of ice withdrawal during the Pleistocene, when the great sheets were advancing.

Further along the coast the rocky gorge of the Mendocino river joins the gorge of the Mathole river some ten miles out to sea. We have already discussed the Santa Barbara coast with its overturned cemeteries on what were once mountain tops and are now islands far from shore.

With a eye on these puzzling facts, Dr. Ralph D. Reed, in an article upon the California coastline, published by the American Association for the Advancement of Science section of American Association of Petroleum Geologists, remarks: "The arguments just cited (concerning the canyon) is enough to convince many of the geologists interested, but not all, that the California mainland stood some thousands of feet higher than at present during a portion of the Pleistocene epoch. There may even have been several such periods, corresponding, possibly, to the different stages of glaciation. Whether the uplift amounted to twelve thousand feet in central California, is a matter of less import. The chief objection to this conclusion is that it seems 'unreasonable'. Perhaps it will seem more reasonable, or less so, when more facts are known about the Pleistocene diastrophism." The word diastrophism is a geological term applied to the end of an epoch of time when catastrophic outbreaks of volcanism over all the earth cause the end of many ruling groups of animals and the stage is set for a new breed of animal to gain the ascendancy. For example: the Mesozoic diastrophism closed the long reign of the giant lizard population (the dinosaur) and cleared the way for the rise of the mammal. The epoch of the Pleistocene has not been thought of usually as having a diastrophic end. Of course it is possible that it is not entirely over and the worst is yet to come.

When the channels were first discovered, Dr. F. A. Forel remarked that these trenches might have been dug by bottom currents. Recently others have revived this theory. Walter H. Bucher in "Submarine Valleys and Related Geological Problems" outlined the idea that earthquakes could start waves which would cut these gorges.

A. Lindenkohl was of the opinion that the continents were raised in a tremendous uplift and then submerged to the same depth they were at the beginning. Dr. Reginald Daly, one of our foremost modern geologists in his "Floor of the Oceans" and also "Our Mobile Earth" discusses these submarine channels at great length. He is of the opinion, and it would seem rightly so, that Lindenkohl's theory, because of physics, would fall by its own weight. That all of the continents on earth would be raised at the same time and then be lowered again to the same original elevation seems most improbable.

Daly did not believe the theory of Bucher was possible either, because "the laws of hydrolics demand that even the mightiest seismic waves cannot give a reflux current rapid enough to erode the lower half of the continental slopes, with sufficient friction along the sea bottom to tear up the clay and sand and ultimately excavate canyon and furrow."

However, Drs. Ewing and Heezen of Lamont did not agree. They looked around for evidence and found that in the severe earthquake which shook the Grand Banks south of Newfoundland on November 18, 1929, cables lying within 60 miles of the epicenter were instantly broken. Daly returned with the argument that many of the canyons were at places where there never had been any history of seismic activity.

Daly then mentioned the theory of W. D. Johnson that undersea springs eating back caused the gorges. If this were true, said Daly, one of the main premises is that clay is soluble in water - a fact that is contrary to physics, and therefore would eliminate this theory. (Daly continued to explain that for soluble clay to be carried in water is practically impossible.)

Then Daly proposed a theory of his own. If the rivers running down the shelf carried silt in solution, this would make the river water more dense than clear water, or the water of the ocean. Heavier water would sink to the bottom while the silt would act as an abrasive agent which would then cut the walls of the canyons. Shortly after Dr. Daly of Harvard put forth this theory, Dr. Kuenen of Holland began experiments with Daly's theory. He built a very large tank half filled with mud to represent the continental shelf and slope. A small stream of water was allowed to trickle over the slope. This was a muddy stream, and from the pictures, one gains the impression that it was being shot into the mud with some force, perhaps because the walls were gutted. Admittedly this is a difficult experiment, because even though the mud of the incoming stream is fine,

and the mud of the slope has been packed in some way, concerning which we are not told, nevertheless the grains of sand coming down in that "river" would be like giant boulders tumbling over each other as they crashed their way down the slope. Furthermore, how does Dr. Daly explain the curving canyons and the manner in which they turn into closed basins? Or the bay on Corsica which continues under the sea? Or the way the Eel river turns around a long sunken island? Or a few other curiosities of the Atlantic? For example, there is a river on the floor of the Atlantic similar to the Bogoslof. It comes down from the north on the west side of the ridge and some of its "tributaries" are from lands which are themselves now sunken below the waves. This river was once a long and powerful one, being several miles wide and a few hundred feet deep. It bends around mountains and enters the basins of what may once have been lakes.

On the other hand, Veatch and Smith in "On the Congo Gorge" have come out flatly with the declaration that geomorphic evidence found by them at that location warrants the assumption that the Atlantic ocean waters dropped ten thousand feet not any longer ago than about twenty-five thousand years.

What did happen? If the water was drained out, where did it go? Even allowing for the drop in sea level and the bulge in the crust, this seems a tremendous amount of water to be locked up in ice unless there are many fields of which we know nothing, not only in Siberia but in the Andes and elsewhere? Or is the bed of the Atlantic sinking? And if it is - why?

Furthermore, we have another problem. The Atlantic is more heavily gutted on the western side of the ridge than on the eastern side, where some of the continental shelves run almost to the edge of the ridge, leaving a sort of fossil river in between. Why is the western basin so much deeper than the eastern?

Now that we have discussed our problems, let us go back and finish our ride across. We reach the bottom of the abysmal slope and we find that our river turns and dives for what may have once been a lake, but now is a basin or deep.

We turn here and drive toward the west. Imagine our amazement when after crossing the abysmal plains with a few little hills, we come upon another continental shelf. It looms up above us - half the depth of the ocean itself up to within six thousand feet of the top. Upon this ancient land we see the old volcanoes as they once stood there. We know that this was land because some of the lava that was scraped from the sides of these volcanoes by a research ship during the last century, scientists found to their astonishment had been cooled under the air and not under the water as they had expected. Besides, there is the beach sand from just before the great destruction. These continental shelves at one time may have been much higher. For example, the shelf off Peru to the bottom of the trench just beyond is a distance of nine miles. This is not normal to the rest of the planet and may indicate a very unstable region. The average shelves are about forty miles from the present shore, and the depth before they plunge down to the ocean basin is from 150 feet near Europe to over 200 feet. At the outer edge of the slope the depth is usually about 400 feet. The inclined areas that slant down to the ocean floor are called continental slopes. These are the greatest escarpments we have on our planet. Where the plunge is too great however, like that of Japan, then we have an area of instability. Such may once have been the slope of the "old red land" in the Atlantic.

What makes us think that this land in the Atlantic is a fossil land? Since World War II many fossil islands have been discovered throughout the oceans of the world. They were not all of continental rock base. Many undoubtedly were of lava origin. This is how it happened. During the war, Dr. Harry Hess, serving as a Naval Reserve officer on board the USS Cape Johnson, and making many voyages across the Pacific, became interested in the radio log of the bottom. In spite of his other duties, he kept a record of its findings. Before long he discovered that there were flat topped mountains which he reasoned were sunken islands because the ocean must have at one time eroded them down to the surface, or the weather must have eroded them down to sea level. Completely sunken mountains can no longer be eroded.

Dr. Harry Hess named these mountains guyots after the 19th century geographer, Arnold Guyot. Hess himself believed them to be very ancient indeed - perhaps five hundred million years old. However, Dr. Edward Hamilton of the Naval Electronics Laboratory found with further study, that they were a chain of volcanic islands which sank rather rapidly during the Cretaceous period. Since then many other guyots have been found.

Hamilton's theory about these mountains is very suggestive. At a time in the past which is as yet undetermined, a crack in the ocean floor brought forth much volcanic material. This grew into a chain of mountains along a massive rift. Some of them lifted their peaks above the level of the sea and existed for a considerable time as islands. The weight of these structures is borne partly by the crust, and partly by the buoyant isostatic pressures (of mantle and sea level). The crust under the sea is strong and compensates for the weight placed upon it. Thus the islands flourished for many centuries and were eroded by the elements. Then something happened which upset the balance between the mantle and the crust. Perhaps a sudden dumping of water into the sea. Deep cracks developed to either side of the mountain chain and the whole range began to go down, melting rather quickly from below until it again reached a point of new equilibrium where it lies in a fossilized condition upon the ocean crust. The general depth of guyots is about 6,000 feet - or the present depth of the Atlantic ridge!

This theory seems very sound and may not only explain many sinking islands, but why they always seem to rest at 6,000 feet below the surface of the sea.

Our vehicle of the future has now climbed up the massive shelves of the sunken land. Once on the top, we see volcanoes, what would appear to have once been lakes along their valleys where fossil rivers made their way seaward. There is a long valley of some two hundred miles in length and one can be certain that this will be the focus of much research and speculation in time to come. It would be interesting to know if the ooze of this valley floor is red as the clay deposits to the west of this ridge on the floor of the ocean? The ridge, apparently once a continental fragment, is from 500 to 1,000 miles wide and stretches like a sinuous dragon along the entire length of the Atlantic. If one closed the ocean to the edges of the old land, and drained out the water, then the old rivers of the shelves would again begin to drain their lands, including the West Atlantic river which drains the great banks where today the fishing ships congregate off the North American shore, but which is striated by the marks of its glacial cap. Were the shelves once together? Were the Americas against the sunken land to the west and the European and African shelves against it to the east - leaving the two great Atlantic rivers flowing south to their central lakes? The ancient fit is most thought provoking even to the most skeptical geologists.

Leaving the ancient land mass, we start down the slope to the deeper red channel of the western part of the Atlantic. Here, too, we pass our guyots or the abysmal hills, as we follow to the south of a sunken range, across to the American shelf. The five- to six- thousand foot shelf of the land of mystery has been left behind. In passing we noted the granite boulders which have most often been lifted from its lost valleys, but that may mean nothing. The bergs which crack off from the northern glaciers and drift south in our modern Atlantic often grip boulders of granite in their icy fingers which they have scraped off the the mountains of the north, and melting here, release them to fall through the oceanic depths. There were even some kiln dried bricks once dredged up from the ridge by England's research ship, Challenger. However, in the belief that these bricks were merely the ballast from some passing ship, they were thrown back. At least that is probably what happened, as the ship's record does not say what happened to them. Today they would at least be handed over to a radio carbon dating laboratory - we hope. But in the time of the Challenger, this tool of science was still in the future. And incidentally there are one or two so-called scientists still teaching, who "do not believe in it". Let us hope that their students have a few more forward instead of backward looking minds to guide their own studies, and balance this worship of fossil ideas.

After crossing the abysmal plains, we begin to ascend the great canyon to the Hudson. It turns south to empty into its fossil lake, now a deep, but we will start up its winding course. It is a giant canyon. From its walls Tertiary rocks have been dredged. This Hudson canyon runs for one-hundred and eighty miles beyond the present beach line. Several tributary streams enter it through rock walls which sometimes reach 4,000 feet in height. In the closed basin where it finally dumped its load at one time, the deepsea fan of alluvial deposits is 14,000 feet in depth. Thus we come out again into the sunlight from our trip across the ocean.

However, perhaps one of the most intriguing features we have no more than barely touched upon - and that is the two rivers which lie in fossil form to either side of the northern ridge. From the tip of Greenland they start, and branching, go down to each side of the ridge. This system was discovered and partly surveyed by expeditions from Lamont from 1949 to 1952. It is a complete branching system such as one would expect to find on any land which had water draining from icy peaks. The rivers run for nearly two thousand miles and end in the deep basins of the central Atlantic. The western river, which

was apparently the most alluring to the scientists for more work was done upon it, is from two to four miles wide and from 150 to 600 feet deep. The tributaries pour down to these rivers from both shelves of the Atlantic and from both sides of the mid-Atlantic ridge.

Dr. Daly, what is your explanation for this fact?

When the oceanographers and geologists are studying the very beginning lessons of their chosen science, one of those lessons is to chart a river. A topographical map is given, with the figures of land heights and some peaks, which because of their elevation are certain to be ice-capped. At one corner is a lake or a bay. The problem is to chart the stream and its tributaries from the icy peaks to the bay. It is not too difficult if one remembers that water seeks the lowest point, in its passage.

When these scientists took their first look at the relief maps of the North Atlantic, they were due for a shock. Here was not a single oceanic basin like the Pacific, but a double valley - each side of the central land had its own drainage system and lakes.

The only part of the picture which was wrong was the height of the peaks in the central land. According to the width and strength of their rivers, these peaks should have ice caps, but they were too short. Even though they appeared to be rugged and tall, they were too short to reach the heights necessary for ice caps. It was like having the Alps on too low a base.

Strangely enough the strength of the rivers were there - showing that these peaks should have been as high as any on the slopes to either side. Yet the fact is that they were not. What happened to this land of the center?

Except for this one error, the picture before them was an excellent presentation of the river problem. All of the rivers coming down into this system of double valleys turned into their lakes or bent to the south to enter the great rivers on the bottom which evidently were also flowing south.

Then one of the geologists took some of the boards out of the middle where the five hundred miles of mud flats were placed to each side of the central ridge. Thus the two sides could be pushed together, shelf almost touching shelf except for the rivers between. Now the picture became a perfect example of a great double rift-valley. This was understandable in every way except two: First, the central land was still too low unless it had sunk. And second - it was the bottom of the Atlantic ocean!

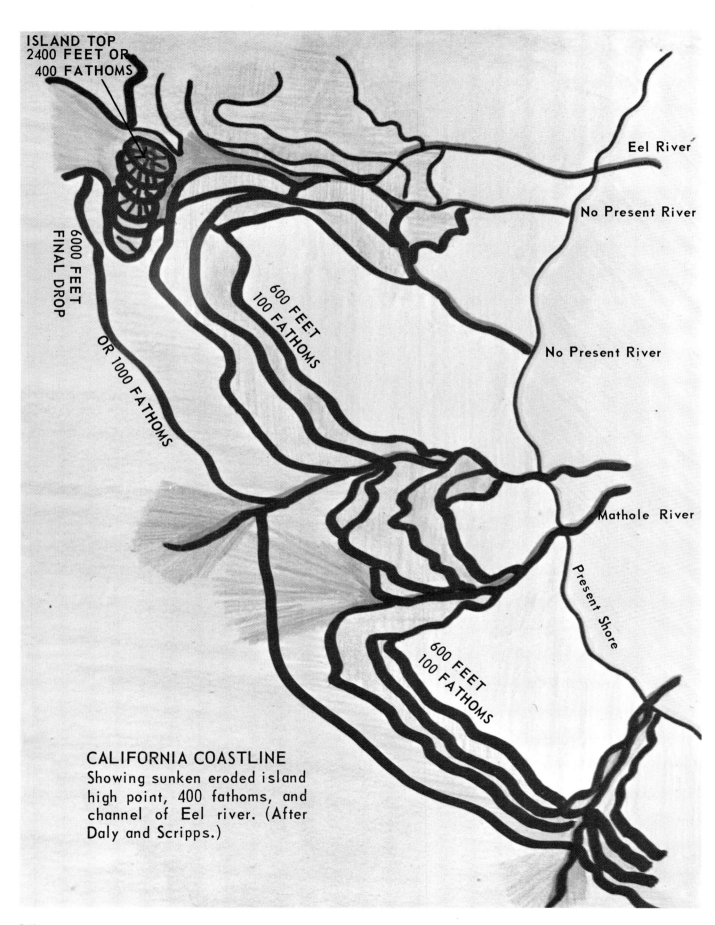

ISLAND TOP
2400 FEET OR
400 FATHOMS

Eel River

No Present River

No Present River

Mathole River

Present Shore

6000 FEET
FINAL DROP

OR 1000 FATHOMS

600 FEET
100 FATHOMS

600 FEET
100 FATHOMS

CALIFORNIA COASTLINE
Showing sunken eroded island
high point, 400 fathoms, and
channel of Eel river. (After
Daly and Scripps.)

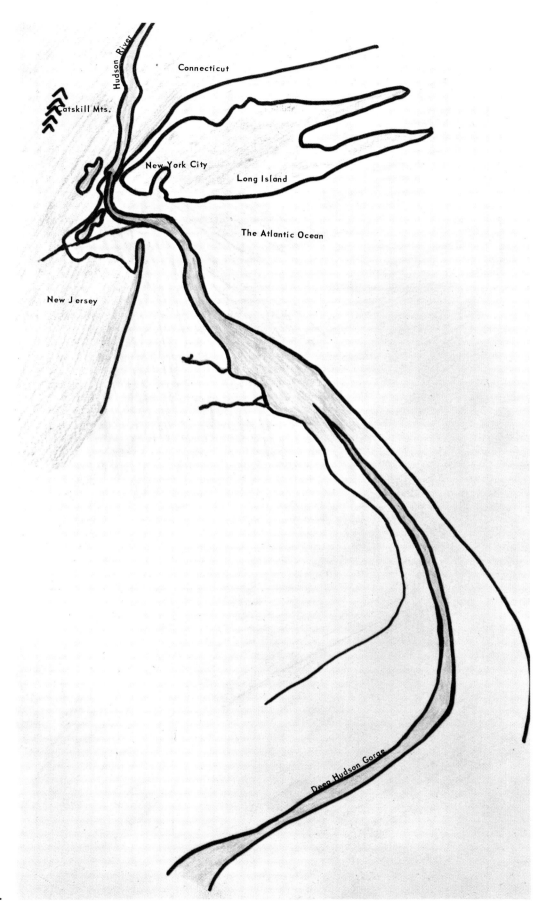

Catskill Mts.

Hudson River

Connecticut

New York City

Long Island

The Atlantic Ocean

New Jersey

Deep Hudson Gorge

Undersea channel
of the Hudson river
gorge, after Dana,
Daly, Readers Digest Atlas.

Chapter 23
Is The Atlantic Floor Sinking?

Scientists have been studying the Atlantic bed too short a time, inquiring whether or not the Atlantic floor is sinking, to give a definite answer to this question. We know that part of the Atlantic near the Gulf of Mexico probably is sinking, and perhaps the down-warp runs across the ocean bed and up the Mediterranean. This is a future field of study, and there are many avenues for the scientist of the next few generations to explore. In many ways this exploration of the unknown, reasoned out in the mind, is even more intriguing than the physical exploration of new lands.

First, there is the obvious rise of previously glaciated lands such as the Baltic and Hudson bay. This rise is from a foot to a foot and half per century, and increases rapidly toward the north. The rise is due to the fact that when the continents were loaded with ice, they sank to the depth of about one third of their load. Where did the lava go from beneath them? To the south - to unglaciated lands which then were bowed up in a false rise lasting during the ice advance. When the ice melted, the lava flowed back under the crust and the newly freed lands started to rise to their former level while the bowed-up lands began to sink to theirs. Of course, there was a long time lag. We do not really know how long. We previously thought they have been rising for fifteen thousand years; now we know a more probable date is eleven thousand. We also know that the ice advance on both sides of the Atlantic was simultaneous, as was the retreat.

This information, together with the fact that Antarctica is carrying far more ice than we had thought before the discoveries of the IGY (International Geophysical Year), means that scientists must make a complete re-evaluation of the extent and depth of the ice. However, until we can get more information on the extent of the Siberian ice sheet, and the rebound rate of the lands which it had basined, we must face the possibility that the ice during the Pleistocene was far heavier than we have hitherto believed.

It is completely understood by scientists that the amount of water taken out of an ice sheet and restored to the ocean would greatly contribute to the instability of that ocean bed, especially since, as some geophysicists have computed, the ice in its final retreat probably reached

a thousand feet or more a year. Also, if there was any undersea volcanism, this retreat would have been much faster, and the instability that much greater.

The full reaction from the ice load has not been completed as yet, and it is to be wondered if the rising glaciated lands will be able to check the incoming magma as it returns to its former position under the crust, or will that crust crack under the incoming pressure, allowing outwelling of lava? After all, the crust is only about twenty-five miles thick.

There is another question which confronts us. The British isles were partly glaciated, as this was the extent of the great ice sheet. We would expect them to be rising along with other glaciated lands. However, they are not; they are sinking at about a foot a century. Why?

The same amount of subsidence is taking place on the American side. The rock where the Pilgrims landed to walk dry-shod to the woods where they were to try living, is now half-submerged in the sea. Cosmul island in Yucatan, to which the White Prophet walked to the ship which awaited his coming, and to which the crowds of the Amerind nations followed, some two thousand years ago, is now over twelve miles out to sea. (He walked the Americas, L. Taylor Hansen, Amherst Press, 1963) The Round Tower whose antiquity so intrigued Longfellow that he wrote "The Skeleton in Armor", is now half submerged in the Atlantic.

Some of this is a rebound from the ice load. As was stated, when the land is basined by the weight of the ice, the magma flows slowly away from the weight, raising the lands which are beyond the ice as it comes under the crust. Then as the basined lands are freed of the ice load, the magma flows back, and the raised land descends to its former position. How much were these lands raised by the weight of the ice sheets to the north? We do not know because the weight and extent of the ice sheet is unknown. The only fact which we do have is that it was greater than we had thought some thirty years ago.

By now it has probably become obvious that the sea level during the time of the glacials was intimately bound up with the extent and weight of the ice. If we must take out two-thirds of the ice load from the sea's water to make the ice, and then raise the lands south of the ice another third for magma bulge, we are lifting them falsely from the sea for the time of the glacial sheet's advance. Dana, who wrote his geology books many years ago, had an unusual scientific mind in that he was able to understand this possibility when the first hint of a sunken ridge and the sunken river channels were called to the amazed attention of his puzzled fellow geologists by the English ship Challenger and other pioneer vessels of undersea research. Dana argued with his puzzled co-workers that these channels were apparently eroded under the air, and instead of denying the possibility of sub-aerial erosion, reasons should be sought for the immense lowering of the sea level which they demanded.

This is, as we have said before, not an Atlantic problem. It is world-wide. Charles Darwin, famous for the shaping of the theory of evolution, is equally famous in the field of submarine exploration. On his trip with the HMS Beagle (1831-36) to the Pacific, he became interested in the coral reefs which he was able to observe on the islands, and deduced that they were formed by a sinking Pacific floor (a rise in sea level would produce the same effect). Since coral is an animal which needs sunlight for its life and growth, as well as fairly warm water, he visioned in his mind's eye a discrepancy between the depths from which coral was being dredged in the Pacific and the impossibility that coral could grow at such abysmal depths. His theory was that a volcanic peak, thrusting its head above the waves and living for many centuries as an island, would form a coral reef where its slopes were the correct depth below the waves for the coral animal to live. As the mountain sank slowly (or the water rose), the coral would build upon the shells of its ancestors, thus making a rising reef to match the subsidence of the volcano. This would continue as the mountain sank, until nothing was left of the original mountain except the reef of coral upon which the waves broke. During his lifetime, Darwin had many arguments upon the subject with those who could not accept either a sinking floor or a rising sea level to the amounts needed. Dr. Daly of Harvard and Sir John Murray of the Challenger expedition disagreed, although the theory did seem to explain both the fact that some coral reefs seemed to arise from plutonian depths, and also the expanse of barrier reefs. Up to this time, these formations had been believed to be based on some existing rock formation. Darwin accepted the fact that corals could become established on previous rock formations,

but this did not obviate his theory. In spite of the support of Dr. James D. Dana of Yale, a sub-aerial erosionist, he met criticism from other quarters.

For one premise, geologists wanted to know how the sea bed could subside. Dana pointed out that sunken river channels ran to the bottom of many barrier reef encircled islands. On the subsidence of the sea, no one had an answer because the modern knowledge of crustal adjustment or isostacy was not yet known. We understand today that the lighter rocks of the continents float on the mantle at a higher level than the heavy sea bottom, but this was not then understood with sufficient clarity. We know that it is quite possible there may be a general adjustment of the sea bottom, involving large areas upon which had existed sialic strips, or islands. In other words islands can sink.

Sir John Murray gave the view that corals did grow from either rocks or extinct volcanoes, which if not high enough for corals, could be built up by the deposition of floating sediment. The German geologist, Albrecht Penck, on the other hand, suggested that the reefs could be explained by the upgrowth during times of lowered sea level, upon very low rocks, and following the rise in sea level growth would continue upward during such epochs as the changing levels of the Pleistocene. This very excellent suggestion has since been incorporated with Murray's ideas upon Darwin's original theory.

However Daly had taken up the argument of the skeptics. He built Penck's idea into a theory of reef formation based on what he called "glacial control". He argued that the lower sea levels and turbulence of the water would erode the exposed coral and kill them, thus implying that coral reefs were all of Pleistocene age. Of course, coral grows so slowly that geologists could not tell by watching, just what had happened. The Royal Society of England in 1897 commissioned some drilling to settle the arguments. The drilling was done to the depth of 1,100 feet which was considerably more than the five or six hundred asked for by Darwin. This core, which brought nothing but coral from the Funafuti atoll in the Ellice islands, was regarded by the Darwin camp as triumph, but the opposition argued that sea weed and debris at the top of the mound should not count, as this is where the drilling had been done. The skeptics refused to recognize the subsequent drillings by other lands because it was done on the mound and not the main reef structure.

This argument reached a climax during World

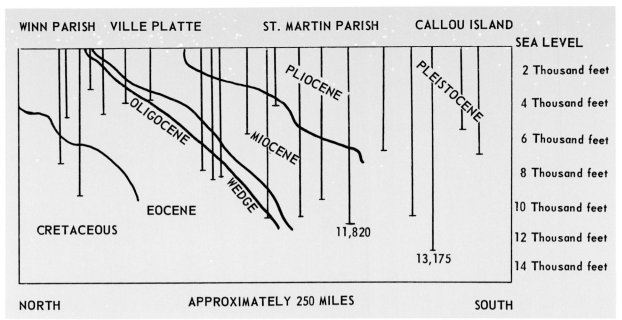

WINN PARISH VILLE PLATTE   ST. MARTIN PARISH   CALLOU ISLAND

SEA LEVEL
2 Thousand feet
4 Thousand feet
6 Thousand feet
8 Thousand feet
10 Thousand feet
12 Thousand feet
14 Thousand feet

PLIOCENE
PLEISTOCENE
OLIGOCENE
MIOCENE
WEDGE
EOCENE
CRETACEOUS
11,820
13,175

NORTH   APPROXIMATELY 250 MILES   SOUTH

Map showing downwarp of North America to south-south-east as shown by deep boreholes. After Daly.

War II and was taken up by the American, William Morris Davis. He showed that Daly was partly right, especially in the coral reefs of the Atlantic. However, in mid-Pacific the picture was somewhat different. In the Atlantic the living reefs were no more than thin encrustations over old water-worn or eroded terraces, but in the Pacific, the effect of the glacials had been slight. In other words, Darwin had his eyes on the Pacific and Daly on the Caribbean.

The arguments came to an end when the United States' 2700 foot drilling of the Bikini atoll began in 1947. Then the argument was renewed by the Daly school because the drill had not as yet gotten through the coral. However their voices were silenced at last in Eniwetok. Harry Ladd of the U.S. Geological Survey made a major effort to get through the coral. Bores were drilling on both sides of the atoll, and they finally hit lava at 4,222 and 4,630 feet below sea level. All the way down they drilled through coral. Drill cores showed that they had gone through the reef and an orderly array of coral skeletons which dated back some sixty million years. Thus Eniwetok has been subsiding at the rate of two millimeters a century. As far as the Pacific was concerned, Darwin had won.

However his theory has not yet been accepted in entirety, for Shepard pointed out that the reefs would undoubtedly have been affected by the glacial changes in sea level. Atolls would show this in the narrowness of the encircling

reef. Also when the water was low, the reefs would be eroded by the waves, but with the rise in sea level, the growth would begin again. Guyots might be explained in the same manner. Also modern oceanic studies have shown that water connections were maintained between the Caribbean and the Indian by way of the Mediterranean until the Miocene, and since then coral reefs have been on the decline in the Caribbean. It is interesting that there may have been extensive reefs in the central Atlantic before the great earth-building period of the Tertiary, because much of the central American land seems to be built upon over two-and-a-half miles of limestone rock, a formation often found under coral reefs. Yet with the Indian ocean being cut off by a rising land mass (probably the Himalayas during the early Miocene), and then the Isthmus arising and cutting off the Caribbean from the Pacific during the Pliocene, the Caribbean became a land locked sea or large lake upon what had been a shoreline some ten to thirty millions of years ago, running from Florida to the Indian ocean.

In the desert cliffs east of San Diego I once came across a giant oyster shell embedded in the sand of an old sea beach. Taking it to Dr. Clements of the university of Southern California geology department, he placed it as of Atlantic origin and probably Miocene in age, an animal which had lived its life on the old sea beach of the tropical to semi-tropical Miocene (or possibly earlier) which once extended from San Diego to the Indian ocean, a creature of that vanished tropical ocean which the geologists have named the Tethys sea.

Thus although the various parts of other

Original painting "The Mudhead And The Water-snake" by Kyrate Tuvahoema (Hopi). The mudhead was a mythical creature of the old red land who lived in the sea. Note painted and masked figures.

theories have been incorporated with that of Darwin, to explain various phases of coral reefs and guyots, yet, in Robert Owen's words (Frontiers of the Sea): "Darwin's early understanding of the role of subsidence, his grasp of this important geological phenomenon and the imaginative use of it in his coral reef theory - was the flash of genius that has illuminated this difficult geological puzzle for over a hundred years."

Darwin's theory of the coral reef has been also used to explain the Blake plateau just east of Florida. This body of sunken land is almost as large as Florida itself and is as flat as if it had been cut with a scythe. There is no debris atop the Blake plateau, probably due to the sweeping action of the gulf stream, that warm oceanic river which sweeps from the Caribbean to the coast of Europe, making it more pleasant to live in than its position on the map and its nearness to the arctic would indicate. The Blake plateau may be an old coral reef or it may be a guyot or a part of a sunken land. Its outer or seaward side plunges down in cliffs that are in places entirely vertical. This would suggest the shearing look of the rift - those great earth-tears. It is one of the Atlantic mysteries about

which oceanographers must do more exploratory search for facts before we are able to understand what it may be.

Is the bed of the Atlantic sinking? As far as the Gulf of Mexico off the coast of Texas is concerned, the answer is a definite yes. The petroleum geologists who do much for the study of the earth in their cores from their drillers for oil, have some very interesting information from both the fields of Louisiana and Texas.

The oldest formation recorded in Texas is called the Yegua. It is Cretaceous in age. It was a hot swamp land through which the giant dinosaurs roamed and filled the humid air with their cries and roars. It is made up of typical peats and clays which are the debris of the strange trees and animals of the period. It runs down at a steep angle to the south and east before being lost at eleven thousand feet below sea level. This one instance alone should forever answer the question as to whether a region which was once land can sink to oceanic depths. When it is lost by the drill cores, the Yegua is still

151

running very steeply down toward the mantle.

With the great down-warping of the swamps, the sea invaded this land, and the Paleoscene, with its beginning of the time of mammals, was a resting stage.

This was ended with a tremendous bowing of the crust. The pressure was from the same direction, southeast. Now came the Eocene. For a long time there had been stability. The lands were eroded as the rains washed the hills, which had formed in the previous epoch, into the sea. The horse at this time was a small animal which ran around on five toes and was no larger than a whippet dog. Finally the period ended in a blast of volcanism and the land was pushed down steeply. This horizon (the Jackson) is finally lost by the drill cores at ten thousand feet below sea level.

Following the Eocene Jackson, came the Frio sands of the Skelley well at Van Vleck. The Gulf plate was first pushed up and then later pushed down. (At another well the Jackson ran out of the cores at eleven thousand feet below sea level.)

Then a strong shale ledge showed another long resting stage during the placid Oligocene. This was followed by what has been called "the fiery Miocene". The start of the Miocene was recorded by Harrison and Abercrombie in well # 4 of the Bernard River Land Company. It was found at from five to six thousand feet below sea level and it was a time of disaster. This is called the Catahoula formation and the clay and sand of what had been a peaceful land was filled with the ash of volcanoes and the glass of burned sand intermingled with the silicified wood of burning forests. The Miocene came in with the thunder of volcanoes from mountains which no longer exist. Plant remains badly burned and vast quantities of volcanic ash fill the cores. There were no marine fossils, so no sea here. The Gulf Coast had been a wide and heavily forested land before the pressure from the south became too strong for the rocks to withstand, and the old plate was down-warped very sharply. Above the Catahoula was the Oakville sandstone which lies upon it unconformably showing long erosion and then sinking, as the sea invaded. This contains Miocene fossils. Next is the log of well # 15 which shows the epoch to follow the period of volcanism is the Flemming beds of Wharton and the log places them at from two thousand to thirty-seven hundred feet below sea level. However they rise rapidly and outcrop on the surface some hundred miles to the north where they are known as the Lagarto formation. They carry the vertebrate fossils of animals which roamed the land with primitive man during the Pliocene. It is interesting to note that Catahoula underlies and overlies marine wedges showing sea invasion, but farther north, where it outcrops, it overlies unconformably upon the old Jackson, showing intense mountain building and pressure. The Pleistocene itself, the time of man, when his cities flourished upon the not so stable lands of the Atlantic, is found to run down in some wells as deeply as seven thousand feet below sea level. Seven thousand feet! This would dry off a good deal of the mid-Atlantic ridge.

We know that some of the Atlantic lands have already sunk at least to the depth of the shelf. Roman travellers spoke of Insulum Illurian as a land connecting England and France and which was a pleasant countryside during the second and third century AD. This would be the present location of the Scilly Isles where it is said that when the tide is very low, one is able to see the hedges of piled stones from the farms long sunken. Judging by the shelf, one wonders if at an earlier period this land was not connected to Spain as the shelf went south, and from there via the Madeira peninsula to the very gateway of - Atlantis?

Is the bed of the Atlantic sinking? That is a problematical question. However, there is one incontrovertible fact. When the theorists of the United Nations wish to get consent to bomb the northern and the Antarctic ice caps in a plea that it would make for milder weather, the people of London and Los Angeles, as well as other low lying cities should remember what that raise of two hundred feet or more in the level of the earth's oceans might do, and consider this step for at least the length of time that it will take to obtain a great deal more data on the subject.

Is the bed of the Atlantic sinking? Perhaps I can answer that question no better than by quoting from the Introduction to Robert Cowan's book "Frontiers of the Sea", written by Dr. Roger R. Revelle, director of the Scripps Institute of Oceanography:

"We don't yet know from whence the ocean waters sprang, although we have searched for some of the depths. We know why the sea's proud waves do not cover the earth - the waters are encircled in deep basins, underlain by heavy rock, above which the comparatively light rocks of the continents float like giant rafts. But no man knows how the continental rafts rose from the seas or why areas that were once dry land are now deeply covered by the ocean."

Chapter 24

Those Gigantic Earth Tears Which Geologists Call Rift Valleys

What do geologists mean when they say that the Atlantic bed looks like a double rift valley? And the question which naturally follows is - are there others?

There are indeed. Yet they are such a recently recognized feature of earth science, that as yet we are not certain what may be their meaning or import. We do know that any theory which bids for future recognition must explain them or fall into the discard of exploded hypotheses. The patterns of these strange features of our planet present a challenge as another field for scientific exploration opening to the future scientists. Are the great trenches on the bottom of the oceans really rifts? Their patterns are essentially different from land rifts, yet they have certain features in common.

These features of the land rifts are similar. Tracing one across the country is easier to do by plane than by car and far more simple by car than by walking. The reason is that all rifts are giant features, often running for thousands of miles. Yet knowing these features makes a trip twice as interesting.

First, the giant rift has a number of lakes laid end to end, although often separated by hundreds of miles. Between these lakes, are marshes or very soft sand. To either side are cliffs with sharply sheered faces like lips thrust forward and held open. If there are streams coming down into the rift, they cut deep trenches or fall from great heights. Very often, however, the streams go the other way, for the true rift has little to do with the drainage of the land. There is a probability, of course, that the rift was once a part of land drainage in which the streams or rivers cut very far down toward the mantle, but once the crust begins to tear, the rift seems to become divorced from drainage and the lakes of the rift apparently have no outlet.

Other features of the typical earth tear are the fact that the rift valley is straight for hundreds of miles and then runs in giant curves or arcs; and the fact that they are often marked by hot springs, mud volcanoes or sulphur springs. It is interesting to recall that Plato mentioned the hot springs of Atlantis which were a main feature of the central island.

We know that rifts are the focal point for earthquakes, and are often lined with volcanoes either upon the lips or along the center, if the rifts run in pairs. Furthermore they are often marked by previous out-pouring of lava, or the presence of geysers. Geologists find them a fertile field for oil wells, as often the oil will filter into the giant crack.

The only rift which has been given a good deal of global attention is the great rift valley of Africa. It follows the pattern of all land rifts - the pattern of tension and sheer, or the tearing apart of a land mass into smaller fragments. It is not too difficult to follow it across the map of Africa. It apparently starts at Lake Nyassa and continues northwest through Lakes Tanganyika, Lifu, Albert Edward, Albert Nuanza. Then swinging in a typical arc to the northeast, it continues through Lake Rudolph, which is salt, and thence to Stephanie or Basse Naeber. From here the great gorge goes into the Red sea where one fork turns to the Dead Sea. It is thought that another fork cuts past Greece to the west and into Europe, while a third fork swings up the Adriatic where it branches into a pronged rift, one prong of which goes through Holland and the other through Germany.

It will be noticed here that these African

Death Valley Sink
Salton Sea Sink
Saluda Mexican Sink
Coso Crater (Boiling Lake)
Mt. Lassen Volcano
Goose Lake (Periodically vanishes)

lakes do not seem to form an essential part of the drainage system, but take on the aspect of water gathered at the bottom of a crevasse. Furthermore, these lakes lie end to end as rift lakes do, as they swing around their great curve across the continent.

In his brilliant studies in the Dutch East Indies, Brouwer found that in such an arc, the pressure was coming from the inner side.

Looking at the map of Africa, and using this information, the eye travels south and east for the focus of the pressure. What happened at one time in the Indian ocean to cause this rift?

Although the rift of Africa is perhaps the best known, it certainly is not unique, nor perhaps does it end in the Mediterranean, as Tabor, Van Der Graff and others are interested in following it through northern Europe.

Dr. Robert T. Hill sees the California gulf as a giant rift. Incidentally peninsulas are often to be suspected as rifts. In this regard, both the Canary peninsula of the Pleistocene and the Madeira peninsula were known to be connected with the African rim and Spain respectively be-

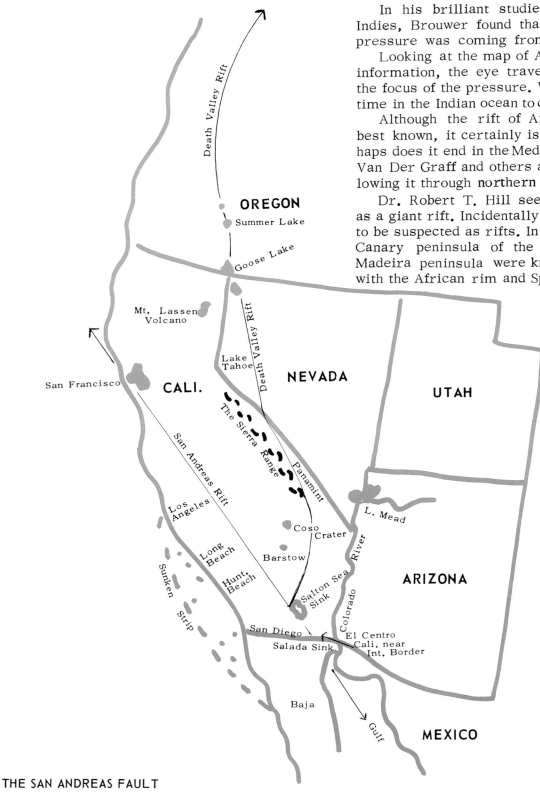

THE SAN ANDREAS FAULT

154

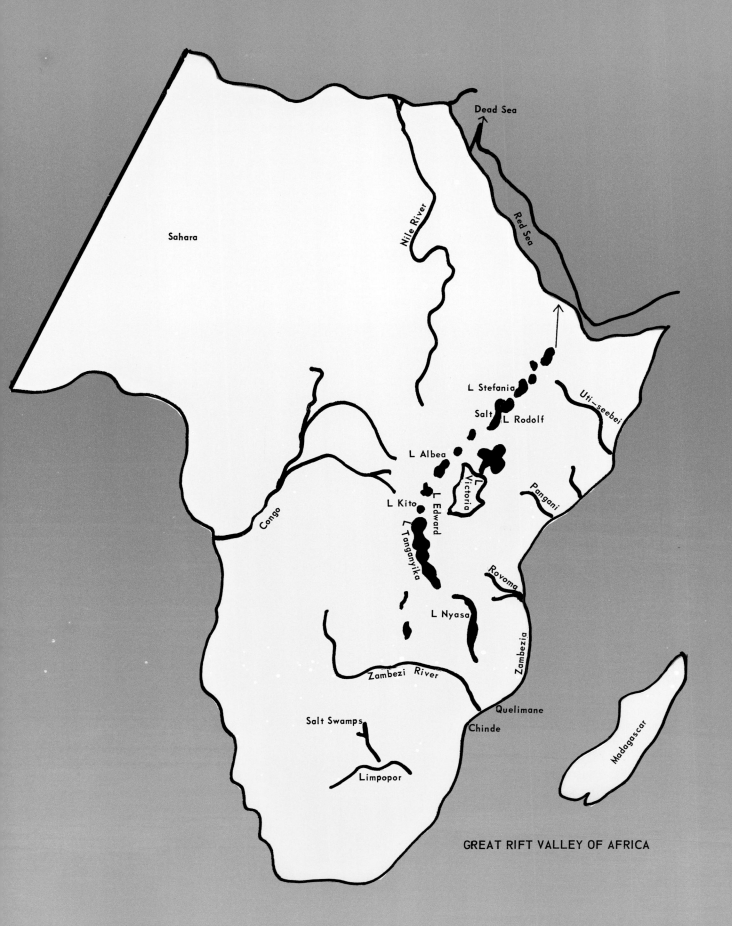

Sahara

Nile River

Dead Sea

Red Sea

Uti-seebei

L Stefania

Salt   L Rodolf

L Albea

L Victoria

Pangani

L Kito   L Edward

L Tanganyika

Rovoma

Congo

L Nyasa

Zambezia

Zambezi River

Quelimane

Chinde

Salt Swamps

Limpopor

Madagascar

GREAT RIFT VALLEY OF AFRICA

fore the end of the last interglacial and probably during the last glacial as well, since plants found in these islands are also to be found in glacial varves in Switzerland. Looking at the map of the Atlantic bed it can easily be seen that these ancient peninsulas may have been double rifts running toward the mainla d.

Dr. Robert T. Hill also calls attention to the Colorado depression of over a thousand miles in length and a hundred miles in width. He finds it the region of many transverse faults.

The San Andreas rift of California is more of a fault actively becoming a rift. Entering California from the Gulf of California and the Mexican border, it bends past the towns of Mexicalli, Callexico, El Centro and Imperial where it swung highway 99 (going to Los Angeles) in a wide arc during a major earthquake. It was easier to leave the highway thus than to resurvey all adjacent property, so the great curve of the highway for many miles remains a monument to the power of the mighty San Andreas. Turning through Imperial county, the fault runs to the large lake of Salton sea which has been suspected by some geologists of having underground connections with the Pacific since many oceanic forms of life have recently entered mysteriously into this desert-bound lake which marks the lowest point in the sunken rift valleys of Imperial and Coachella. Continuing up Coachella valley the rift heads toward Los Angeles along highway 99, but turns in a wide arc at Mt. San Gorgonia pass and continues to San Francisco where it goes out the Golden Gate into the Pacific. Flying over it by plane, one is able to see how streams have been diverted from their courses and old roads cut off by the movement of the earth along the giant crack. Where it runs through the desert it resembles a long low mound. Usually one can hear nothing by lying upon it prone and putting one's ear to the ground, but just after a slight tremblor, if one hurries to the fault, a low growling and grinding coming as if from miles below the surface is quite audible.

Earthquakes running along the main fault or the transverse faults which branch from it are typical of the rift. These with the deepest focus seem to be located about two hundred miles inland. For example, in the Andes in South America the deepest focus shocks, sometimes of over a hundred miles down in the mantle, are to be found on the eastern side of the Andes where the mountain range presents its more vertical and unscalable cliffs.

Rifts seem to be of three types: the continental type such as the giant rift of Africa; the intercontinental type such as the Mediterranean; and the coastal type such as that which dropped the channel island strip from the coast of California. It is obvious that one type can run into another as is indicated by that of Africa and the Red sea, or turn into another as the San Andreas may one day become coastal.

We know that the movement may be very slow, lasting thousands, or perhaps even hundreds of thousands of years, and possibly even millions, yet the end, when it comes, is catastrophic. Witness the manner in which an entire hill of older rocks was dropped upon the wrecked cemeteries of the channel island villages; the manner in which one part of a village was upon one cliff, and another edge apparently of the same village upon a distant cliff with nothing but sea in between; or the manner in which a mammoth had scrambled to safety upon a small island and then had probably died for want of food.

Did a tremendous pressure once come from the north and from the Atlantic during the end of the Pleistocene, as witness the arc effects of the coasts of California and the swing from north to northwest and back again to north with a slight western angle in the arcs of the San Andreas rift showing pressure from the north and east. Do you remember the old physics experiment of putting a piece of lead through a block of ice and of water? It will go through both but it will take longer to go through ice. In fact you would be foolish to put it on top and then wait. The lag in the movement is different than it is for water. Perhaps we have not as yet felt the crush of the Pleistocene pressure nor the final end of such tears as the San Andreas.

However, the earthquakes set off and triggered by this rift and its branching cracks in the crust are experiences to remember. I was motoring to Long Beach for dinner on the evening of March 10, 1933 about five-thirty. I was supposed to be there by six for a dinner party, but a soft tire probably saved my life. Pulling into a gas station to have it attended to, and fretting because I would be late, I did not again get started until about ten minutes to six. At five minutes to six I was on the center of the bridge running from Sunset Beach across a partly dry wash toward Long Beach when I felt a bumping in what I thought was the same tire. I opened the car door to lean out and look again at the tire, when suddenly I saw the entire Long Beach horizon sway crazily with neon signs running across one of the main streets snap and fly up into the air. Instantaneously, I slammed the car door and tried to race the coming shock across the bridge, but I could not beat the shock. Like great waves running under the earth it came toward me, hurling cars from the highway and toppling buildings. One policeman riding toward me on a motorcycle was hurled into the air for what seemed like two hundred feet and landed in the marsh below the bridge. I noticed that he did not move. Probably he never knew what killed him.

When it hit the bridge, I strained every muscle to hold my light car. The lights on the bridge came crashing down and the center opened in great gaping jaws running the length of the bridge and then slamming shut again. I succeeded in keeping the wheels out of this trap, but the bridge now was almost two and a half feet above the land and I had to jump off to reach the highway again. The car bounced about, but again landed on its wheels. Great geysers of oil and water were spurting here and there from broken pipe lines.

Then in a wave from the stricken city came the cats and dogs, rabbits and chickens running neck and neck in terror and not even glancing at each other. As I could not go back home, I continued on to Long Beach. Automobiles were tearing here and there down the road. I saw a woman carrying a baby run out of a brick structure some three stories high and leap into a car only to have the entire side of the building come crashing down upon her, before she could close the car door. In a second only a pile of bricks and red dust was all that was left of the street where the car had been.

Arriving at the site of the apartment house where I was supposed to have dinner, I found it in a shambles and no sign of the people who had been expecting me. Later I found that some of them had been killed and injured and the others were with the injured trying to find a hospital. Most of the markets were open when the shock came, but fortunately the schools were closed. Many of the casualties were from markets. Glass, radios and vegetables littered the streets. Screaming women were running down the streets and men with dazed looks were leading crying children.

On the Richter scale (an earthquake measuring scale devised by Dr. Richter of California Institute of Technology) the 1933 earthquake of Long Beach was supposed to be only a little over six, much less than the San Francisco disaster (7+). However, the first jolt was strong enough to hurl a piano half through a wall of our neighbor's home in Huntington Beach, a wall which was more than twenty feet away from the

instrument. The shock snapped off an entire grove of trees from one to two feet in diameter at the base as if they had been cut with a great knife and left them (more than sixty of them) all pointing toward Huntington Beach. From this evidence it is presumed that the focus was in the sea beyond Huntington Beach. However, the waves came down the highway from Long Beach toward Huntington Beach which I had just left to keep my dinner appointment. It is therefore my belief that the first shock was from Long Beach and the second, probably triggered by the earth waves from Long Beach, came from the sea off Huntington. The fault which caused this earth adjustment is called the Compton fault and is undoubtedly one of the forks of the San Andreas. In this earth shock the beach cities of the adjacent coast to Long Beach and Huntington lost much of the long sloping sand which went to the sea in the evident drop of the land level.

The aftershocks from this disaster continued for a week during which everyone slept on their lawns, and the ground felt like quivering jelly. I noted that filled-in ground suffered the greatest destruction, although one street might have every house wrecked and the next street show little damage. Brick houses, if not built with the best mortar, showed the most damage while stucco and wood showed the least. Steel frame structures held together well.

The difference between the shocks from earthquakes and from volcanism is the intensity. In the former the initial shock is usually the worst. In the latter, the shocks build up in intensity until the volcano breaks forth. In the Caribbean, the Caribs seemed to know weeks in advance of the outbreak of Mt. Pelee volcano. (The name of the mountain given to it by the Amerinds is identical to the fire goddess of Hawaii - coincidence?) They left the island in every way possible until forbidden to go (by the tourist bureau) and then sat about awaiting the end with resignation.

Dr. Becker of Redlands university smiled when I handed him the article from the Reader's Digest which told this story. "That reminds me of a favorite story of some geologist friends. They were in Mexico trying to trace out the southern end of the San Andreas. One night, their Yaqui helpers all left the old ruined church where they had received permission to sleep in case of rain. When the geologist asked the reason they replied 'Sachem say torramote tonight'. The geologists were amused. One said:

" 'Oh that is absurd. He cannot predict a tremblor. They run in fault lines . . .' but his audience was leaving, carrying their blankets outside.

"The man turned to his fellow geologists: 'What does that sachem fellow know anyhow?'

"His co-worker grunted: 'Obviously nothing but superstition. Better save your lectures for the classroom.'

"The speaker shrugged his shoulders.

His wife and children, who saw in this trip a perfect vacation, spread their sleeping bags along with his on the worn floor of the old church. They had no sooner closed their eyes than the tremblors began. Snatching up the children they ran for the outside.

"The Amerinds were sitting about a campfire talking.

" 'Well you men were right about the tremblor. However now you had better go inside with us.'

" 'No Senor, there will be another.'

" 'Oh rubbish. The aftershocks will always be lighter, and that was not a bad tremblor. You had better come in. It may rain.'

" 'No Senor. We stay.'

"The geologist induced his half reluctant wife to accompany him and his fellow scientist back into the church. However, they had gotten only to the location of the sleeping bags when the floor began to heave and a corner of the old ceiling fell. When they reached the open air, they found the Amerinds picking up their blankets preparatory to going in.

" 'Now you fellows had better stay here! If the waves keep getting stronger it may mean real trouble.'

" 'No Senor, we go in now. Later it will rain.'

"Giving her husband a look of profound disgust, the geologist's wife herded her two children inside with the workers. The geologists lay for some time outside talking until rain drops began to splash their faces, then with mutual consent, they picked up their sleeping bags. As they entered sheepishly, where many sleeping forms were lying peacefully, one of the learned geologists remarked: 'You know when you asked me what does that sachem fellow know, you emphasized the wrong word? You should not have stressed the word what, but instead, HOW does he know? I would like to take a class under him!' "

Let me say right now that I do not believe that these children of the forest and desert have such an amazing amount of "ESP", but that they have fantastically keen senses. Perhaps our eardrums are dulled by the constant noises of the city, but I have had Amerinds tell me in confidence that the men "of the old days", when they lived free, were able to tell the amount and direction of troop movements by listening on the ground at "certain places". The children of the wild red men are far less sensitive to sights sounds, and smells than their ancestors. From the scent of a page, the old men could tell whether the letter had been written in springtime or not, and other surprising facts. When the Amerinds start wearing hearing aids, that will be the day we can seriously question the advantages of civilization. James Fennimore Cooper in his "Leather-stocking Tales" and "The Last of the Mohicans" has been accused of absurd exaggeration, but the criticisms, I have found, are all from men who do not know the American Indian.

Shortly after World War II, a group of geologists, honoring Dr. Henny of Holland who was studying the California Pleistocene, rode with him in an auto caravan following the San Andreas fault south to the gulf from San Gorgonia pass. After visiting the mud volcanoes at Salton sea, our party turned toward the gulf. During the ride, Dr. Henny talked freely about his interest in the "great American rift" as he called it, and suggested further study of Mexico and possibly also Canada and South America. He described various points along the coast where he had followed it south, noting the out-welling of lava over Pleistocene sediments. At one place he picked up a green rock on one side of the rift some two hundred and fifty miles from the outcrop on the other side. The rock had been glazed to a brilliant shiny lustre from being dragged along the great crevasse. He broke the rock into small pieces and gave a piece to everyone in the party. I still have mine.

We crossed the border at Calexico and inquired of a Mexican attendant in a gas station concerning the condition of the road.

"It is very good, Senor. It is wide and level and very fine for travel as long as you do not leave the highway. But do not go down to the sand. It is very soft like mush and you may sink down in it. We lost many men and bull dozers. They were working on the road, pushing the sand up high to make the highway safe. They just sank out of sight."

As we started down through the below sea level wasteland, it was like travelling below the sea itself, for that day a greenish haze hung in the air. To the right, several miles away, were the sharp cliffs of the lip of the rift. They were a combination of reds from russet to gold and one of the scientists informed us that they had

been known to produce very good opals. No one had an inclination to explore.

The Mexican in the gas station was correct. The highway was excellent. It had been built up some twenty to thirty feet above the sand. One of the strangest sights of the entire trip was the rare elephant trees. They received their name because the thick reddish trunk resembles the leg of a pachyderm. To me, however, they looked more like giant red spiders or denizens from another planet because of the manner in which their many red roots gripped the sand in a very wide arc or circle while their thorny tops, innocent of leaves, looked like some kind of a strange comb. I had heard from such well-known desert men as Shorty Harris, that if you broke off one of the twigs, bright red sap like blood would drip from the wound. I took a look at the sand and decided to forego the experiment.

My memory of Shorty Harris also made me glance toward the sand dunes several miles to the left. The sand dunes blocked the entrance of the water of the gulf into the sunken valleys of the great crevasse. Harris had told me that there was a ship in these dunes. His description tallied with what could have been a vessel of great antiquity. The planks of the ancient wreck had once been caulked with tar. He had judged it to be about sixty feet in length with a six or eight foot width. The wood in the terrific summer heat of the desert had hardened to a rock-like state of semi-petrification, and near its smashed

timbers were still to be seen human bones which had probably been scattered long ago by packs of desert wolves or coyotes. However, Harris warned: "Don't you or your friends go looking without a good guide! The sand has soft places, you know. Besides the Indians call the dunes 'walking hills' for a mighty good reason. What you found yesterday will be covered in the next sandstorm and not see the light of day again perhaps for a hundred years."

I knew that he was right. I had met the man who found the pioneer caravan while riding over the dunes between El Centro and Yuma Arizona. His description of the experience was that of a never-to-be-forgotten day.

"Here I was riding over the dunes on my horse when I saw the pioneer caravan. I shook my head and rubbed my eyes. It wasn't a mirage. It was real. Then I saw that the horses were slumped down in the sand, which was over the hubs of the wagon wheels of the canastogas. I rode closer. A man and a woman were sitting propped against what must have been a trunk just staring ahead at the horses. I rode up from behind and touched the driver on the arm of his checkered woolen shirt.

" 'I don't know how you got here, Mister...'

Then my voice died away. The figure slumped over. The heat of the sun and sand had almost mummified him. I turned and rode to the Yuma museum. They gave me two hundred and sixty dollars for taking them to the wagons. They buried the people, but the wagon can be seen just outside the museum door, and most of the clothes inside in glass cases. But I will never forget the moment that the mummy slumped over."

There is another arm of the giant rift which most geologists do not have a chance to study, but it should be pointed out to them as a future field of investigation. It is apparently another prong of the San Andreas coming in from the Gulf of California, but running up on the eastern side of the Sierras. Near it is the boiling lake of Coso crater and large hills of volcanic rocks from which boulders are always tumbling down from the top. The Sierras present a very steep face to the east even as do the very high Andes of South America.

If one fork of the rift runs along the eastern face of the Sierras, other forks run along the parallel valleys of Panamint and the sink of Death valley. In the latter, Bad Water, the lowest spot on the North American continent, seems to cast a spell over the visitor. Against the backdrop of the Funerals are strangely carved rocks looking like gargoyles or imps staring down at you, while your voice is repeated numberless times among them like strange creatures gossiping among themselves.

From Zabriskie, where the gods must have mixed their paints, to the salt fields which hide a lake beneath their salt crust and where one's footsteps echo hollowly, to the salt marshes toward the almost impassable and extremely dangerous pass to the south, Death valley is a true earth crevasse. Even the salt marshes where Shorty Harris once almost lost his life trying to see if a pair of boots with the soles up had a man below them, and the salt pools where the cover of salt, like glass, is said to hold the body of a pioneer woman perfectly preserved in her red calico dress, and in another, a child's toy grasped by a small hand reaching through the salt marsh below, Death valley is at once not only a very good rift, but unless accompanied by many cars, a good place not to explore, at least without a guide.

Yet for those who love its beauty, the evanescence of the changing lights of the day, the dawn or sunset, the unscalable Panamints with their strange Piute legends and weird smoke trees (those wild denizens from a bygone age with their thorns of blue-grey for leaves, so beloved by artists for their beauty and so impossible either to transplant---because of its tap root ten times its height---or to grow from seeds), Death valley from October to May has a fascination of its own. After that, the temperature gauge on the sand runs above the $140°$ to $150°$ mark. There are, however, deep salt caves below the valley were the pioneers could have retired when the lure of the rugged salt flats looking like waves in the sunlight induced them to enter its trap. One wagon load died within 300 feet of a spring.

From Death valley with its modern crater, the great rift runs north and west to Goose lake where the water has been known to disappear over night and return a few days later. When this happened the first time, residents were amazed to see the wagon ruts of the pioneers across its bottom sands. The rift may be traced through Long valley, Lost valley to Summer lake, and perhaps into Canada. Near Goose lake, the rift may be seen quite easily by plane as a long winding crevasse.

My thoughts, when the rift of the San Andreas is mentioned, leaps to such things as giant spiders with their tufts of thorn and their long red legs (misnamed elephant trees) perched delicately above the treacherous sand as if to spring to safety, and the pitiful bawl of a cow some half a mile from the highway who had sunk to her shoulders; the earth waves coming from Long Beach to kill the unsuspecting policeman and strike the bridge; and the strange fascination of Death valley.

Shorty Harris was buried where they found his body, near the whispering sands of his beloved Death valley. Somehow, I cannot accept the coroner's verdict that he had died of thirst, and was one of the latest victims of the infamous death trap. Yet if there was foul play in that long wasteland where his animals were not found, we shall probably never know.

I, for one, mourn a most colorful character of the old west, who might have been induced to one day lead me to the ancient ship with its tar caulked planks and its lost crew in the "walking hills". Now the ship will have to remain for the explorer of the future, but I hope that when at last it is found, a new chapter may be written in Pleistocene exploration, for these valleys of the rift were inland seas when such seamen as the Atlanteans, and later the Phoenicians, rode the ocean waves. May the explorer who finds it remember: Shorty Harris found it first.

Chapter 25

Those Ancient Climates -

And

Drowned

Mountain

Chains

When Chicago

Was The

North Pole

One of the greatest surprises which came to the geologists during Antarctic expeditions, was the discovery of coal under the ancient Antarctic ice. This was almost unbelievable. Coal meant that the land once lay in the tropics, and a lush jungle, growing in the heat, had died and left its skeletal pattern - coal. But a jungle on Antarctica? When could this have happened? Especially if continents were always where they are now?

Nor was this all: probably not too far distant from the time when Antarctica was sweltering in the tropical sun, Canada and the northern United States was the scene of a heavy glacial - so heavy that they must have been very close to the north pole, if indeed that pole did not cross Canada. This was not the last glacial age of the Pleistocene, but one immeasurably distant in the past.

If continents were always where they are now and oceans the same, we might attribute the two ice ages to some fluctuation of the sun's heat, as numerous scientists have suggested while seeking the reasons for glacials. However, there is another fact which always intrudes to upset these theories, and that is: between these two northern glacial ages, the northern continents lay also upon the equator - in fact, that line crossed Pennsylvania to Spain and England where the lush jungles again lost their skeletons in the heavy veins of coal. Also, about the time when England was at the equator, Africa, India and Australia were bearing Earth's heaviest glacial load of ice. The enormous southern glacial was exceptionally wide spread, and Antarctica may even yet retain some of its ice-load from this far off time.

So the difficulty which many theorists searching for the reason for glacial ages have to hurdle, and the one which negates most of the theories is simply this: why is only one hemisphere at a time glaciated? Of course, there was some glaciation during the Pleistocene in South America on the heights of the Andes, but it was not a great cooling of the planet any more than was the great southern glacial. Also, why were England and Greenland in the hot, tropical rain forest with the dinosaurs roaming the Wyoming swamps

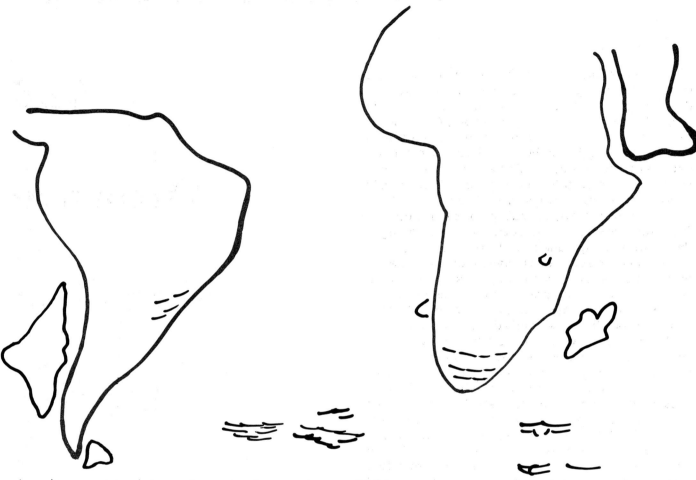

A sunken mountain chain running under the sea. Age, pre-Permian.
The Afro-Lemurian-Australian chain.

at the same time India and Africa were glaciated?
Can those geologists who still adhere to the
contractionist theory (that continents were always where they are now) answer this? Most of
them cannot, nor do they try. For this reason
the theory is losing advocates with each passing
year.

Or, if you happen to be among those who
believe that Earth swung around in her orbit,
and thus the tropics and the poles changed position, then answer this one: Why is Antarctica
still bearing its load of Mesozoic (middle-time-
life when the lizards were dominant) ice? Why
did Antarctica not move from its position under
the South Pole? Would one large continent have
retained its same position in such a spin of the

Map compiled by Du Toit, Daly, the
Challenger expedition, and others.
Depicts the Pyrenee-Alps range,
the Appalachian-English-Norse
cordillera, and the Atlas range.

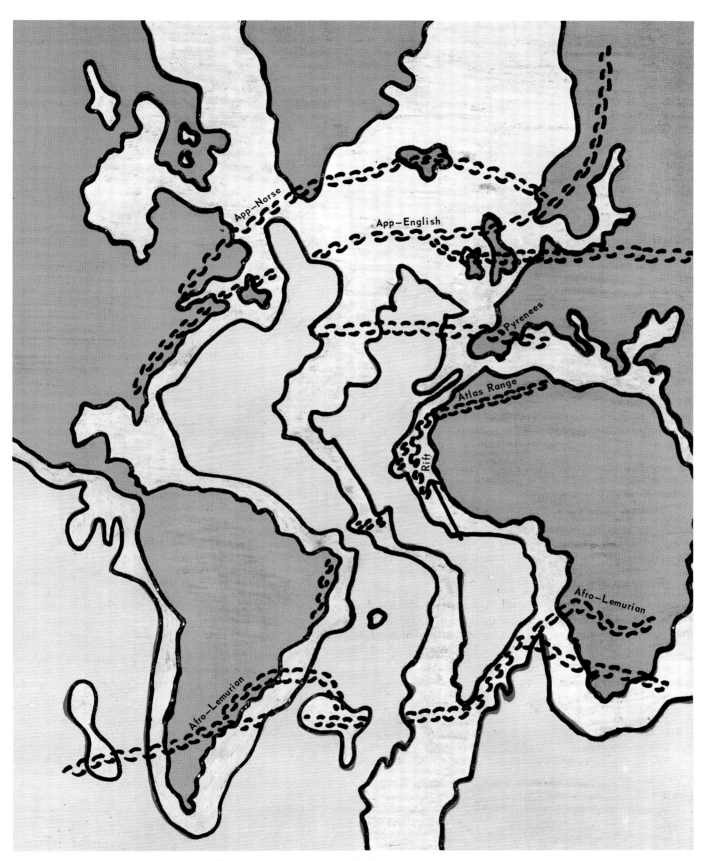

The sunken Appalachian-English-Norse cordillera.
Pyrenee-Alps range. Atlas range. Compiled by
Du Toit, Daly, Challenger expedition and others.

entire globe?

These are not the only questions with which geologists are struggling. There is also the matter of mountain patterns which modern geology has called cordilleras. There is one cordillera which runs from Alabama up the coast of the United States to Maine and the Canadian coast where it dips into the sea. Here it is known as the Appalachians, consisting of the Smokies, Alleghanies, Blue Ridge, Cumberland, Catskills, etc. This range crosses the Atlantic ocean and reappears in England where one stem turns up the Baltic peninsula, while the main stem crosses to France and eventually becomes the Urals of Russia. These are among Earth's oldest mountains. Apparently they were raised when there was but one continent from North America to Asia, and no north Atlantic ocean. Formed of the same rocks during the same time, there can be no doubt of the relationship. During the hoary ages which have passed since they were first raised, they have been worn down and raised again, sometimes from the opposite direction. Geologists call them the Appalachian-English-Urals, or App-Eng-Norse. Today they are one of Earth's great partially drowned cordilleras.

In South America there is a transverse range which starts in the drowned plateau of Easter island, crosses through Argentina into the south Atlantic, reappears in Africa as the Cape Range on the southern tip. From there the cordillera runs into the Indian ocean through a number of islands, reappearing in Kerguelin island and turning down the great ridge of the Indian ocean, to India. This partially drowned cordillera is known as the Argentine-Cape-Kerguelin cordillera or Afro-Lemurian cordillera. It is somewhat later than the Appalachian-English-Urals, but again the relationship is undoubted. It too was raised in the same epoch from the same rocks when there was apparently neither a south Atlantic nor an Indian ocean.

Again we have the great cordilleras of the Tertiary, formed at the end of the Mesozoic or time of giant reptiles, and the start of the age of mammals.

These mountains were all formed at the same time during great earth disturbances. It is the business of the hypotheses to discover what caused them to wrinkle up. One cordillera is the Himalayas to the Alps with a possible branch of the Atlas which curls about Africa and loses itself in the south Atlantic as it dips under the sea. Some geologists have believed that the Antilles may belong to the same cordillera, but others believe that the Antilles off the coast of Central America are the relics of an older range. The interesting fact about the Alpine-Himalayas is that the highest peaks on Earth, north of India such as Everest, are composed of an ancient sea bottom, and upon the tops of these almost inaccessible mountains one may find shells from the bottom of what geologists call the Tethys sea which once separated the northern continents from the southern. (The name Tethys, incidentally, is one of the names given to the ancient sea god we know as either, Uranus, Chronos, Oannes, Poseidon or Neptune.) We know that there was a Tethys sea and that at one time the marine animals were able to travel from California to what are now the Himalayan peaks. One of those which did was a giant oyster of some ten inches in length which I once picked up in Painted canyon, which may be entered from the highway running from Yuma, Arizona to San Diego, California. The results of my search there now rests in the geology collections of the university of Southern California, and England.

Another giant cordillera, perhaps the longest one on Earth, is formed of the Rockies running from Canada through the United States and the Mexican Sierras to the South American Andes where they turn about the continent of Antarctica to reappear about the Pacific side of Australia. It is a very active cordillera with many faults and volcanoes along its vast length. It may even be found later that it dips into the Pacific only to continue along the eastern shore of Asia through such partially submerged lands as Japan, the Phillipines etc., circling through the Aleutians to meet again its starting point in Alaska and Canada. This is now known to geologists all over the world as the Pacific's curtain of fire. Any theory which would explain what has happened to our Earth, must not forget the curtain of fire, for this is not only the present - but the future.

Are these strange patterns to be explained only by the wrinkles upon the skin of a drying apple (the contractionist theory)? Every year the number of geologists who are shaking their heads with a negative reply is growing. The patterns of Earth's cordilleras are apparently far more significant than geologists of a few generations back believed them to be.

Are they, furthermore, not connected in some way with the giant earth tears or rifts? Is it not strange that both in the line of the Death valley rift and in the Andes of South America a tremendous sheer face of mountain range is presented to the east while to the west of it the range seems still to be building? The coast ranges of the Pacific through California northward may someday in the distant future rival the mighty Andes, considering the rate at which they are rising. Before both coastlines, the sima of the sea bottom is wrinkling, showing perhaps a steady advance of the continental prow. Of course the advance is older in South America ---the mountains are higher and the deeps more profound, which would suggest that the pressure hit South America first from the east and millennia later the force from the east struck the North American block. In both regions long tensional cracks like the San Andreas run parallel, or roughly parallel, to the coastline. In the San Andreas the continental movement of the eastern section is south compared to the western section. This too, must be explained.

In Panamint valley, lying parallel and to the west of Death valley (the colors of which are the ecstacy and despair of artists), a drilling company driving a core down through the valley floor, searching for minerals, lost their instruments at two hundred feet. The drillers stared at each other aghast.

"It was as if we struck a vast hole or the end of the crust," one man said, shaking his head. "We can't understand it."

I watched them for a moment in silence as they began to tear down their drill. Who could explain that? Was the crust here only two hundred feet thick instead of the customary twenty five miles? One is almost tempted to believe so when standing near the boiling lake of Coso some fifty or seventy miles to the southwest. Here the houses of many occupants pipe up the boiling water for heating their homes in the winter and keeping the cottages warm where people come to bathe in the steam caverns.

If the army is using the practice bombing range in Nevada, the ground at Coso gives a rumble, and for a short time nothing seems to happen. There is a lag - sometimes of twelve hours. But then come the deep growls from below and the steam jets start hissing. Looking at the boiling lake of the crater, one's scalp seems to crawl. Perhaps that is why the army closed the springs to the public and moved the people out? Did they wish to study the reactions of the boiling lake around which run huge polished coridors of black lava upon the sides of which in some places are life sized paintings of the fire god done in colors as exquisite as any of the temple paintings of Egypt? "Coso" I understand from the local tribes means "fire dragon". The army promised the many famous an-

thropologists who wrote to them when the announcement was made, that Coso would become a bombing range, but that they would photograph the huge paintings and the strange script writing to be seen at some places in the corridors. I hope that they kept that promise.

To me the paintings were a magnificent surprise. I had no camera with me. The writing, I was told, was several miles more distant and as the hour was late, our party would not go on. I fully intended to return, surely within a year or so. In the meantime, the gates were closed.

From the road leaving Coso, the hills seem to be formed of a ropy sort of lava from the top of which rocks are always tumbling down. I suspect that they are building rapidly from below and that boulders from the top are thus being sloughed off. As one winds out upon the highway of Owens valley, one can see to the north and west the snow capped pinnacle of Mt. Whitney, the highest point in the United States. It is one of the mountain peaks which forms "the scarp", or the geological name for the lip of the rift.

What do these strange patterns of mountain ranges and of profound rifts, as well as the ancient climates, mean? At present we do not know. Yet we do know that any geological theory of the future which hopes to survive must give them an adequate explanation.

We do know that an increasing number of scientists from various fields are becoming impatient with the contractionist "Fixity of Continents and Oceans." As an example, Dr. George Simpson, writing in the Smithsonian Report for 1936 (p. 289) remarks acidly: "It is of great importance to notice that as far as the evidence goes, the ice at this time (Gondwannaland glacial) was all situated well within the forty degrees of latitude of the equator, and mainly in the southern hemisphere. Most geologists consider that, at the same time, the north polar regions had much higher temperatures than at present, luxurious vegetation growing in both Greenland and Spitzbergen.

"This would mean that while there was glaciation within the tropics leading to vast ice sheets at sea level, there was an almost sub-tropical climate in polar regions. This is a reversal of the climatic belts which no meteorologist can accept. Owing to the shape of Earth, the equatorial region must always be warmer than the polar. The only explanation which the meterologist can give or accept . . .is that the continents were not then in the same position relative to the pole as they now occupy. In other words, continents have moved since Permo-Carboniferous times."

Chapter 26

Ancient Gondwannaland

Alexander Du Toit did not have a doctorate in his favorite scientific subject: geology. However, this did not keep him from becoming one of the great scientific minds of the age.

He was tremendously interested in the rocks across the south Atlantic, tracing them out from age to age and from one side to the other. For example, when he discovered that the rocks containing the fossils of certain animals or plants were to be found on the shores of Africa, he traced the same strata in South America to see if it bore the same fossils, and if it did not, how the fossils differed. Sometimes it occurred in debates before the forums of scientists he was asked how it happened that the strata containing certain small dinosaurs were to be found in Africa, but were missing in South America? His answer, which shows how thoroughly he knew his subject, was: "That strata itself is missing." Then he went on to explain how apparently the strata had been eroded away.

It is due to the untiring efforts of such investigators of fact as Alexander Du Toit that we know so much about the south Atlantic, and which in fact allowed Alfred Wegener, in giving his famous hypothesis, to liken the rocks across the Atlantic to "writing across a torn page".

We know today that the southern continents had the same experiences. They lay under the tropics about the same time. They became glaciated at the same time and they bore the same species of animals and plants. Therefore, the consensus of opinion is now beginning to place these continents together through most of the long history of the planet.

The geology of the future is going to have to explain how South America, Africa, India, Australia and Antarctica not only bore the same types of plants and animals, but also had the same experiences in ancient climates, and carry the same cordilleras. Are they the fragments of one great southern sialic mass which were torn apart in some tremendous disturbance, and are now pursuing separate paths?

Many geologists and geophysicists as well as botanists and zoologists believe this to be the case, because only thus can they explain the ancient migration of the plants and animals which they are studying, with comprehensive adequacy. Otherwise, they are facing ridiculous situations. How did the tree frog get from Australia to South America? Certainly the animals did not swim! Did their eggs float on a stick across two oceans? Or was there a bridge between Australia and South America by way of Antarctica?

Of course the tree frog is only one instance. There are many others and the list grows yearly. There are ants, worms, fresh water fish, animals and plants of various kinds.

There is one new check which generations preceding us did not have. These men were allowed to be skeptical without being annoyed by the parasitologists. Today we are not able to think comfortably that the eggs of some tree frog managed somehow to cross two oceans. The parasitologist steps in and announces with finality that eggs do not carry the opalind parasites (worms), to be found in the similar types of tree frogs, so we are face to face with the fact that somehow, the tree frogs crossed from Australia to South America. It is a fact and must be explained.

Not only are the zoologists annoying the geologists for explanations, but so are the botanists, and these questions multiply every year. And, not only are the southern continents the

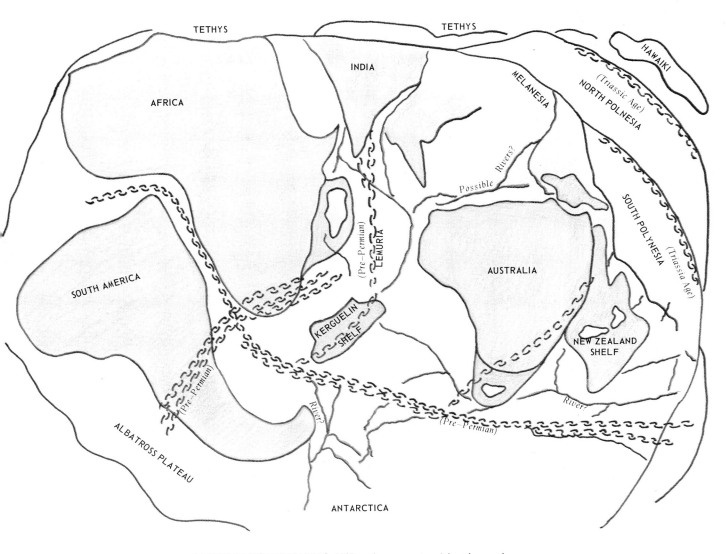

ANCIENT GONDWANNALAND - As conceived by the author.

target: the fringe of islands running from Japan to Southern California, for example, have an old related flora (plant cover), and the botanists are wrinkling their brows and staring at the geologists for an explanation. Nor can they comfortably believe that the seeds floated. Once more the parasitologists are reminding us that rusts or certain insect borne diseases do not float over vast stretches of ocean. "When was there a connection between Japan and the coastal islands of the Southern California coast?" The parasitologist taps his fingers on the table. "You fellows should stop this foolish arguing and figure this thing out. There was a connection. That is a fact."

During the Miocene there was a huge invasion on a wide front of American trees into Europe and an invasion of European trees coming to

America. The first easy suggestion is erased by a glance at the parasitologist. This was a dry land invasion. That is a fact.

But let us return to our southern continents. Have you ever stared at the shorelines of the Atlantic on a globe, thinking how they seem to fit together if the water was taken out and the continents to either side pushed back to make this curving contour a valley? You may be surprised to know that is just what the scientists are doing. First you must take a globe and trace off the continents. Allow for the ridge. Wegener and other geologists did not do this and immediately became involved in trouble, as we shall see later. Then you push these sialic masses together and you suddenly receive the surprise that many amazed geologists have received - the great partly drowned cordilleras match.

Not only the cordilleras match, but so does the glacial till from the ice sheets, and also the seams of coal from the time when the land lay under the tropics and bore a jungle cover. In fact geologists are so used to looking at a reconstruction of the early land mass that they have a name for it which geologists all recognize. After a very primitive tribe of Africans named Gonds, a geologist before the time of Taylor or Wegener named it Gondwannaland. The name has remained, so that certain rocks etc., are called "Gondwannaland series". When the name is mentioned in scientific debates, everyone knows exactly what is meant as much as if one would say Africa or India.

There is another name which science has coined for a postulated land of the past. The great sunken ridge of the Indian ocean, running from Antarctica to India, was eyed by a zoologist by the name of Sclater. He contended that the lemurs, or dog faced monkeys, which are now to be found on all lands that surround the Indian ocean "as if they once scampered away from a sinking homeland" had at one time an island home which sank during their evolutionary life. He postulated for this land the name Lemuria, or land of the lemurs. Among scientific circles the name has clung, in spite of the fact that science fiction writers have chosen to use this euphonius name for lost kingdoms - usually in the Pacific! Knowing the real meaning of the name, its use in such stories becomes not only absurd, but also a confession of ignorance.

The great ridge of Lemuria is however, made up of sialic rock and undoubtedly was at one time a part of Gondwannaland. It bears a heavy ridge of early mountains along its spine, similar to the ridge of the Atlantic. Kerguelin island which is situated on this Lemurian ridge is composed of continental rocks, even though it is seven hundred miles from the nearest land. Also the whole extent of Lemuria has been shown to have been composed largely of continental rocks, or lavas solidified under air - such as the Seychelles banks and Murray banks which are lost sialic fragments. Thus in a reconstruction of Gondwannaland, the Lemurian ridge as well as the south Atlantic ridge, are necessary parts. Indeed Kerguelin is but the dry top of one of Lemuria's larger highlands, while there are many others - some are only four hundred meters below the surface. (The nearest continental neighbor of Kerguelin is Antarctica.)

To reconstruct this old land surface of Gondwannaland, we must push South America against Africa, allowing for the south Atlantic ridge, pull India down between some lost island fragments and Africa, partially over the northern end of Lemuria. Then by giving Australia a half-turn, closing the Red sea, and pulling Australia against Lemuria, and rounding off the southern coast with Antarctica, we have ancient Gondwannaland.

Suddenly we see that the old sunken cordillera falls into place across the old land mass, and even the later Pacific cordillera outlines the coastline so well that some geologists suspect that it was once raised before the Tertiary, and in fact, that this time of general mountain-folding was a second orogeny (mountain building) on top of the first. A great deal more study of the cordilleras now on three continents will be necessary before we can say for certain.

The ancient gneiss shield with which all these continental fragments are underlain, now fits into place, with the overlying coal beds, and on top of those, the ancient glacial till, all matching in what are called the Gondwannaland series.

The Carlsberg ridge, part of the Lemurian ridge from which the John Murray expedition dredged fragments of basaltic lava, as well as the Murray bank are all necessary to the construction of the old land. The Seychelles bank is composed of granite similar to that of Kerguelin island, and is three hundred miles wide.

With the help of bathymetrical maps and reports of various ships, the reconstruction of ancient Gondwannaland gains unexpected headway. Once more we are startled by the apparition of a double rift valley with Lemuria as the central sialic block. Is this the pattern of a torn ocean? Otherwise why is there such a strange similarity - in both cases the double-rift and then the central land carrying a mountain range, probably heavy with volcanoes, whose width in both cases is from three to six hundred miles?

Kerguelin must have been the highlands from the general point of which four rivers took their rise - two coursing down to either side of Lemuria, north to the Tethys sea, and two coursing south to the Pacific, marking the points at which the old land mass was to split. Perhaps the eastern Lemurian river, running north, later divided into two prongs - one seeking the sea through a channel to the north and east of Australia.

At any rate, it is necessary to understand what happened here in Gondwannaland before we can begin to understand what happened millions of years later in the Atlantic.

As the witty Dr. W. E. Prouty once said: "Geologists, like Gaul, may be divided into three parts: those who believe in the fixity of continents and oceans; those who build bridges; and those who believe in some kind of continental displacement." (continental displacement is the geological term for the slow drift of the continents.)

Charles Schuchert was one of the second type. He gathered animal and plant evidence for migrations, and explained them by means of sialic bridges. Not only the very obvious Aleutian bridge where Alaska and Asia are so near, but a bridge across the south Atlantic and the north Atlantic probably along the old Appalachian-English-Urals and the Antarctica bridge from Australia to South America.

On the subject of Gondwannaland, the parasitologists were beginning to ask why the opalind (worms) were to be found in only the animals who had evolved apparently in the southern sialic masses? That is a particularly bad question for the contractionists with their fixity of continents and oceans to answer concerning the Americas. Schuchert on the other hand, simply sank the bridges. Schuchert fought hard for bridges, putting his evidence in book after book. Though he probably did not entirely realize the fact, each book was a harder blow at the contractionists than it was against those who were seeking some kind of continental movement through the uncounted millions of years in the past.

Without doubt, in some ways he was entirely right, for Charles Schuchert knew his animal migrations. It is the new knowledge of these migrations, always checked by the parasitologist, which is tearing the once comfortable contractionist theory full of holes. Each new scientist, usually young and eager, pursuing his chosen plant or animal, and checked by the parasitologist, is driving a new nail into the coffin of the conservative world of our fathers and grandfathers. Schuchert was one of these men. In his "Gondwannaland Bridges" published by the Bulletin for the Geological Society of America, Vol. 43, pp. 775-916, he takes up the fight over the southern continental mass, showing the necessity for migrations. Yet he thought that he was one of the main opponents of continental displacement or the slow drift of sialic masses. He could not see why it would be necessary to have continental masses move over the crust in order to explain the migrations of plant and animal life. He was right. His only trouble was that he was not looking any farther than

Chapter 27

Those

Animal

Migrations

migrations. Other geological problems he simply chose to ignore. Thus his perspective was limited. He was the father of the idea of bridging masses of sialic rock, and he pushed the idea all during his life. There are too few geological forums where the geophysicist, meteorologist, and paleontologist among the geologists can get together and argue out their differences. Schuchert was a paleontologist.

For example, let us take up the problem of the northern continents from the viewpoint of a paleontologist such as Schuchert. It has been said that a sialic bridge, say across the Aleutians, was to be likened to a giant drawbridge on a busily traveled highway. When the bridge is down and ready for traffic, the animals and plants cross, going both directions. When the bridge is out of use, the traffic waits patiently for the time when it will again be open. The only difference is that so many thousands and even millions of years have gone by that the horse, or the camel, would never recognize his distant progeny. However, this timing is a great help to the paleontologist, botanist and zoologist, for the change in the traffic helps him to classify the ancient animals and plants. Also it helps to estimate the millennia since the bridge was last used.

Bound up in this story are many surprises

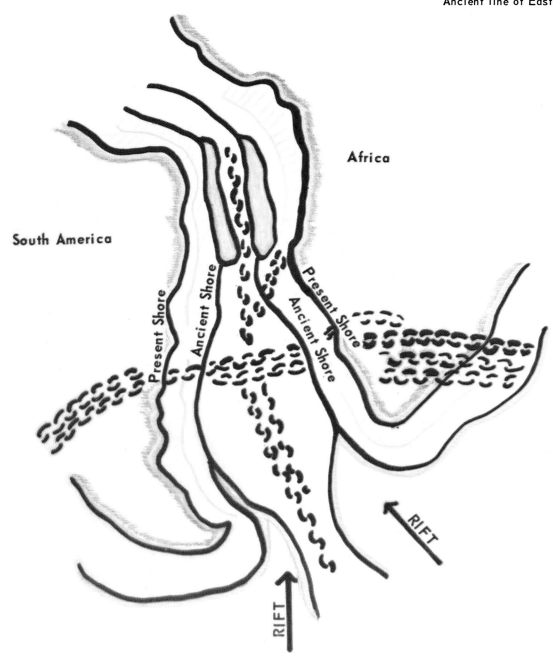

for the average man. He may not be aware that the horse originally evolved in Wyoming and South Dakota when these places were warm luxurious forests, and that the animal at that time was only eleven inches high, walked on five toes and ate largely a diet of leaves. Scientists have named him Eohippus Borealis or the dawn-horse of the Eocene. (Incidentally, Greek and Roman names are given to various species so that scientists, writing in any language, will know exactly the plant or animal under discussion.)

Eohippus grew to the size of a small pony during the Miocene and walked on three toes, each with its hardened nail. During the Pleistocene or ice age, he had grown to the present size, ate grass and walked on one toe, the hoof being an adaption of his nail. It is strange that the horse should die out in the land of his birth, but he did come down to fairly recent times. It may have happened because the Amerinds hunted him for food to the point of extermination, or there may have been other reasons. We know that the civilizations of Mexico had never heard of the horse before the arrival of the Spanish, because in Bernal Diaz' book "True History of the Conquest of Mexico" this doughty old conquistador tells of how a sick horse left behind for the red

170

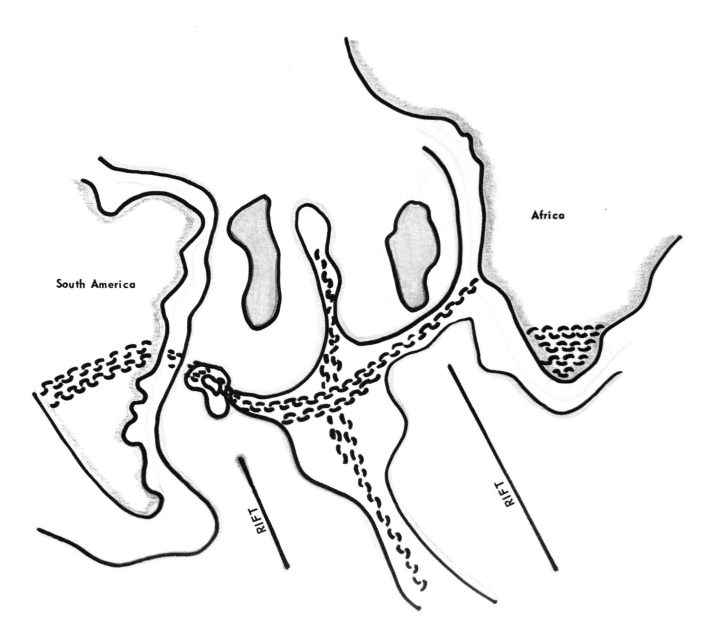

South America

Africa

RIFT

RIFT

men to care for, probably died of starvation because its solicitous hosts tried very hard to feed it chickens. However, there is one strange fact which rules out an entire ignorance of the horse by the Amerinds unless, somehow, it can be explained. The Nez Perce, who fled to Canada on their horses from their lands in Oregon and were captured only a mile or so from the border, used the grey Appalousa which has spots on the flanks. This animal, sacred to some very old nations of antiquity was not brought here by the pioneers. The Nez Perce say they have owned the breed from "the time of the dawn", and who can gainsay them? This is one of those riddles we cannot say them? This is one of those riddles we cannot fathom. The Spanish never heard of this breed. Also on the travertine covered rocks of Salton sea, California - high above the old Pleistocene beach line are inscriptions, also travertine-covered, of some nation fighting from the backs of horses. They do not resemble the Spanish Dons, but the inscription is so extremely old that it is almost impossible to tell for certain. This inscription is not more than two hundred feet from the one with the ancient letters - apparently previous to the Phoenicians, and similar to that in Peru. One letter repeated often is the five pointed star, one the maltese cross and others similar to Pelasgian (pre-Greek) and old

Phoenician.

To return to the migration of animals: if it was the Amerind who killed off the horse, this dim memory of his past and perhaps similar instances has taught him his strict conservation of food resources practiced by all tribes with appropriate religious ceremonies. The horses he later learned to tame and ride were taken from the wild herds of the prairies which grew from those which escaped from the rancheros of the Spanish.

There is some basis for the belief that the dog and possibly the cat evolved in the Americas. (The wolf which science does not distinguish from the dog, both being canis, the latter word Roman for dog, used here will be understood to include the wolves.) Both appeared rather early on the eastern coast of the Americas, or more particularly, North America. Were these animals actually evolved on the ridge, and is that why the domestic cat as well as the large cat was so much admired in early Egypt? We shall probably never know these answers. They may be buried under unmeasured masses of lava.

Apparently dogs and cats crossed in large numbers when North America was still in actual contact, with no more than a river or so between New York and London - say in the Miocene? The cats soon evolved many species, the greatest of which were the saber tooth monsters - Smiledon and Machairodus. Both the cats and dogs reached their culmination in the Pleistocene.

The rhinoceros also probably evolved in North America. They have, of course, completely died out in the land of their birth and now are only brought back for zoos.

The camel is another North American animal which migrated during the Pleistocene and earlier to Asia. In the La Brae tar pits of Los Angeles, now to be seen to one side of busy Hollywood traffic laden boulevards, are the skeletons of the Pleistocene camel. Of course the domesticated llama of South America and the vicuna are a breed of camel which the Amerinds have owned for untold thousands of years.

On the other hand, the deer was probably evolved in Asia. The elephant came from Gondwannaland - possibly Lemuria because the two types of elephant living today, Indian and African, are so different. Incidentally the elephant shows that a connection existed between India and Africa in the Eocene and is the reason that many authorities believe that this is the era in which the Lemurian ridge finally sank.

In the realm of the plants, many trees go back to the wetter and warmer climates of the Cretaceous in the northern continents. The maple, for example, first found in the Cretaceous of North America, would seem from the number of varieties found growing in Japan to have originally evolved there, or at least to have crossed very early.

Other strange locations for familiar plants during the warm Cretaceous when swamps were still echoing to the cries of the dinosaurs are the eucalyptus, now an Australian tree transplanted to the Americas, which was also to be found in Europe. The lotus, beloved by the early Egyptians, once grew in Greenland, Iceland, Europe and North America while the magnolia ranged from Europe to North America. The fig tree may be thought to be Mediterranean by the average modern man, but it was to be found in the lakes of Eocene Oregon and probably evolved in North America along with the oak tree. It is interesting that the latter is sacred to the peoples of both shores of the Atlantic during the Pleistocene. Was it evolved on the ridge?

It will be noticed that our trees are older than our animals. Many of the trees such as some of the weird desert cacti and the palms (cycads) are even previous to the giant dinosaurs, as is the South Sea island tree fern. Among the great plants of our planet we have many living fossils.

Now let us see how men like Schuchert traced the migration routes. The elephant family entered the northern continents sometime during the Miocene, perhaps through the forests which grew across a closed Atlantic, moving from Europe to North America. From these parts they also invaded Asia, moving from continent to continent. It will be too bad if the newly freed negro nations of Africa exterminate this ancient animal which so anciently antedates mankind. There should be some kind of reserve set aside so that these creatures may be preserved - not to be hunted down, but to live into the future.

The horse which we have discussed began to populate Asia during the Oligocene, while during the Miocene, Myohippus (the Miocene horse) ranged only from Europe to North America and back with the forests which crossed the Atlantic at this time. During this fiery period, the sabertooth roamed across all the northern continents - particularly Europe and America, and the rhinoceros crossed to Europe where he evolved the Brachypotherium, an animal which shows distinct relationship to its North American cousins.

However, during the Oligocene the Aleutian bridge was as active as the Atlantic was during the Miocene. The rhinoceros had crossed the Aleutian bridge in the Oligocene into Asia where he developed the thirteen-foot giant Baluchiterium during the Miocene. Evidently during that epoch the bridge was again down, for the monster as far as we know did not return.

The story of the rhinoceros in Asia is one of interest because it tells us something of the earth. The type known as the Amnodont of Wyoming and South Dakota apparently crossed into Asia and even reached Burma and India. This would indicate that the Himalayas were not yet very high. However the lush forests of the Gobi desert were soon to begin drying up. This tells us that the great mountain range of Earth's highest peaks were on their way up - thus cutting off the moisture from the Asian Gobi desert. The moisture loving animals could not tolerate the changing climate, and the end of the Oligocene saw their extinction. May one draw the inference here that the Oligocene saw the separation among men of the round heads and the long heads, and that the stem of modern man was living through the Oligocene as well as the elephants and the rhinoceroses?

It was also during the Oligocene that the cousin rhinoceros of South Dakota, the Casnopus, entered Asia, for the following Miocene shows rhinoceroses of this breed in Asia. Today these animals are confined to India, China, Sumatra, Borneo and Africa. This would certainly indicate a separation of these lands during the following Pliocene at the latest.

When the rhinoceroses were going into Asia during the Oligocene, they met the Asian deer coming to America. He remained for a few thousand years, or a few million and then in the Miocene, he crossed to Europe. As the deer crossed the Aleutian bridge in the Oligocene, he met the camel going to Asia.

Now it should be increasingly plain that during the Oligocene when the Atlantic was quiet with an unusual spread of seas, the Aleutian bridge was dry, while during the following Miocene when the Atlantic was practically dry, the Aleutian bridge was flooded. Would this not seem to indicate a rocking movement of the crust?

There is one rather startling exception. Among the dogs, we find Cynodictis living in both France and North America during the Oligocene. Could he have found a precarious way over the icy and high Appalachian-English-Urals or across the Pyrenees in some manner? As the latter chain touches France, it seems the most likely, but the connection was certainly of a very short duration.

It would seem from this crustal oscillation that the magma or lava in the mantle might flow in giant waves from a center of disturbance such as the Indian ocean, and that the Oligocene was a low point for the Atlantic, allowing spreading seas, while the Miocene lifted the Atlantic over a wave that brought volcanoes and lava, and the spread of warm forested land encouraging plant and animal migrations.

Of course there is much work to be done in following out this possibility, but it is an intriguing path of investigation for some future scientist.

This was in my mind one day (I believe it was in the late thirties) when I found one of Charles Schuchert's books on the shelf in the Los Angeles public library. I carried it over to a table and began to thumb through the pages, preparatory to making notes, when a good looking white haired gentleman stopped at my chair and looked over my shoulder. I looked up. Thinking that I had chosen the book for which he had been searching I said: "I won't keep it long, if you are waiting for it. I wish to check something."

He smiled and pulled out the chair next to mine.

"Oh that is quite all right. I just wished to see which book you had taken."

"It is Charles Schuchert. I was checking on the Aleutian bridge."

"Its animal traffic is most suggestive of how the bridge works, wouldn't you say?"

"Yes, I agree. However, bridges, though necessary - particularly this one---are not the whole story."

"I might infer that you believe in some sort of continental displacement?"

"Yes, it seems the only way of explaining certain facts."

"Then you do not believe in bridges?"

"I did not say that. The two are not mutually exclusive, you know."

Suddenly we both became aware of a tapping of a pencil from an annoyed librarian.

"We are being reprimanded for talking in the holy precincts," he whispered. "Come, let's find a coffee shop. Do you mind? I find your challenge stimulating."

I nodded and picked up the book, stopping to check it at the desk. We walked to the corner and entered a coffee shop discussing our problem. As soon as we had gotten inside, he met my challenge.

"So continental displacement and bridges are not mutually exclusive?"

"No they are not. If you take two parts of a mud pie - the kind which children make and pull them apart, you will not have a clean break. There will be strings of mud connecting them for a time - or let us say a short distance."

"Yes, I can see the logic of that. But if you admit the bridges, you do not need continental displacement."

We sat down and ordered coffee while he asked the girl to call him a taxi.

"It will be here in a moment, Mister. The stand is just around the corner."

"Very well. I have to make a plane, so that is well." Then to me: "We are going to have to talk fast. I have tossed the challenge right back at you."

"You must be a follower of Schuchert all the way," I laughed. "That is what he believes, you know. The trouble with him is that he needs more meteorology and geophysics. A course in oceanography might help too."

"You don't think much of him, do you?"

"I didn't say that. He has a great scientific mind, but it is confined to paleontology. There are problems which bridges will not explain."

"What else do they say about Schuchert?"

I laughed. "Oh I have heard that he is an irascible old codger, but . . ."

"From his best friends no doubt," he laughed.

"Do you know him?"

"Only a speaking acquaintance, but I am interested in your reasons. You threw down a challenge and then you didn't follow through."

"What I meant is simply this - let us take Schuchert for example. He has held the subjects of animal and plant migration so close to his eye that he cannot see around them. There are other problems which bridges simply can not explain - ancient climates, the world's cordilleras, the Pacific curtain of fire, the deeps of the oceans, the great rift valleys - need I go on?"

He gave me a long look.

"You see no need for bridges?"

"Of course there is a need. The Aleutian traffic for example. Furthermore, there is one bridge which tells us a great deal about continental displacement."

"Indeed? Which one?"

"The one which runs from the Argentine to Africa. Have you noticed that both the Argentine and the African anchors are north of where it crosses the ridge?"

"True. What of it?"

"This plainly shows that South America and Africa moved northward faster than the ridge.

Like the heavy truck and the light child's car, there is a difference in momentum. This difference is what may have caused the rift to either side of the ridge."

"That is a most interesting idea. We must get together . . ."

"Your taxi is here, Mister."

He had been toying with the book of Schuchert I laid down, probably looking for a map of that bridge - if there was one, which I doubted. Absentmindedly, he picked the book up and carried it to the counter. There he stopped and wrote something, evidently asking for some directions. I waited and wondered about him as I sipped my coffee. Undoubtedly he was a paleontologist, or possibly a botanist. He could be a parasitologist. He was definitely not a geophysicist or a meteorologist. He came back to the table.

"I was about to depart with your book," he smiled, putting it down on the table. "I am dreadfully sorry that I have to go and end this stimulating talk. I have enjoyed every bit of it and particularly your frankness. However, I intend to return this time next year and often drop in at the library. Would you please leave your name and address with the librarian so that I may contact you at that time? In the meantime, goodbye, and may I say once more your thought provoking suggestions have given me much to think over on the plane tonight."

We shook hands warmly.

Four weeks later when I returned the renewed book to the library the young lady behind the desk said:

"Did you know there is a card with some kind of message on it behind your library card in the holder?"

I took the calling card - for that was the size of it, in puzzled amazement and read: "When I return, call me on the phone at this number. Do not forget. I will be expecting to hear from you. If I have stepped out, please leave a message."

I tapped the card against my other hand. Who? Where? Male or female? Perhaps it wasn't meant for me at all. Possibly it was for the previous borrower. It did look like a calling card.

I started to turn it over when it slipped from my fingers and fluttered to the floor. As I started to pick it up, all of my breath left my lungs. Staring up at me was a very famous printed name -

Charles S. Schuchert, Paleogeographer.

With this card I now have a clipping from a newspaper.

"Death came to Chas Schuchert, one of the greatest names in paleontology when he - - -"

Thus it is with Fate . . .

Chapter 28

The Strange Mummies
Of The Norse

2000 year old Tollund Man, a Dane, found in peat bog. From a photograph in "Buried Treasure" by Paul Johnstone.

In 1797 near the town of Jutland, some peat diggers seeking fuel came upon the body of a man. He was a middle aged man clad in a leather coat or cape, and lying under three branches of myrtle. They stared at him with their hair rising. Then they quickly pulled him out and frantically buried him. That was one of the early finds of the Norse mummies.

One of the latest happened in May, 1950. Some peat diggers working in a bog near Tollund had uncovered the body of a man clad only in a leather cap and a belt. He had been strangled with a leather thong. The peat diggers called the police to report the murder. The police took one look and phoned Dr. Peter Glob who was lecturing at the university of Jutland. This famed archaeologist immediately left his class and hurried to the peat bog. Then he announced that in spite of the natural look of the man, the "murder" was at least two thousand years old. Another famous mummy of the old Norse had been found.

Altogether there have been over one hundred of these mummies. Apparently they were sacrificial victims to the old gods. They had usually been strangled, though one had evidently had his throat cut. One was a young fourteen year old girl with half of her hair shaved off. Almost all had been placed naked in the bog.

Curiously enough, the tannic acid of the peat had tanned the skin perfectly, although it had turned it to the black color of the peat itself. Yet in the case of Tollund man, his hair strayed out under the leather cap which he was wearing, and although he had evidently been laid in the bog clean shaven, there was a stubble of beard evident on his face - possibly having grown after death.

Professor Glob describes the man in this manner: "In the peat cut, nearly seven feet down, lay a human figure in a crouched position, still half buried. A foot and a shoulder protruded, perfectly preserved, but dark brown in color like the surrounding peat, which had dyed the skin. Carefully we removed more peat and a bowed head came into view.

"As dusk fell, we saw in the fading light a man take shape before us. He was curled up, with legs drawn under him and arms bent, resting on his side as if asleep. His eyes were peacefully shut; his brows furrowed and his mouth showed a slightly irritated quirk as if he were not over pleased by this unexpected disturbance of his rest."

The noose which had been used to strangle him, like several others, had been made of two leather thongs. Professor Glob judged that, from the seven feet of peat which had gathered above him, the man must at least be two thousand years old. Possibly he had seen Julius Caesar campaigning in Gaul. Or, if he had been given to even more distant travel, he might have glimpsed a slender white robed figure humbly walking about Jerusalem.

In 98 A.D. the Roman, Tacitus wrote about executions among the Norse: "Traitors and deserters are hanged on trees; cowards shirkers and the unnaturally vicious are drowned in miry swamps under a cover of wattled hurdles. The distinction in the punishment implies that deeds of violence should be paid for in the full glare of publicity, but that deeds of shame should be suppressed."

Now either the Norse were lying to the Romans, or these mummies are much older than the time of Tacitus. Probably the Norse were lying since they did not want the conquering Romans to be prying into their religion, and perhaps be trying to convert them to the Roman pantheon.

One must note that only after the adoption of Christianity was hanging, or the cutting off of the breath, regarded by the Norse as fit for criminals. Therefore, the incoming religion must have placed the old method of killing a sacrificial victim in the line of disgraceful acts. Every incoming religion places the old gods among the damned. Christianity was not the only religion to do this. Buddahism, Brahmanism, the Hebraic faith, Shintoism - all are inclined to down grade the previous religion. The ancient fire god is the devil in almost all of these religions. Sin, the name of the Summerian moon goddess, is used in a different manner than formerly. Hel - meaning light originally, has at present another meaning.

In the most ancient Norse legends, hanged men belonged to Odin or Woden. One of the earliest legends tells that for a favor done to King Vikar, Woden demanded as payment the sacrifice of the king's life. Since, understandably, the king was unwilling to comply, Woden persuaded the king's brother to place a noose of leather upon a young tree and then coming behind King Vikar to put the noose around the monarch's neck and let the tree go, saying: "I thus give you to Woden." With a reed, the brother then pierced the king's body. As he did, the reed was transformed into a spear - the symbol of the god Woden.

The archaeologists are beginning to wonder if this legend may not also account for the many reeds or sticks found with these corpses. Why was the man of Borremose, found in 1946, a seemingly ascetic type with soft uncalloused hands in these times of the warrior type? Was he a priest? And why are most of the mummies found with no clothes, especially when regular Norse burials were either in ships put out to sea, or interned with all their worldly goods? And why were the thongs put around the necks of the victims often twisted to resemble horns? Was it because the fire god Ammon, with whom Woden or Votan is so often associated, is called "the two-horned"?

Professor Glob is of the opinion that these naked victims were perhaps the sacrifices offered to the gods during the spring festivals. Today the Shrovetide of Denmark and the Fasching carnivals of Germany are vestiges of these pagan festivals, as is the English Maypole dance around a "sacred tree". Originally a fertility goddess named Nerthus presided at these festivals and was supposed to insure a replenishment of the Earth's crops. Possibly she was even older than Votan or Odin. Certainly there was a fertility goddess worshipped by almost all of the cave men.

Tacitus has a passage describing the rites of this goddess in his book "Germania". "The (people) believe that (she) enters into human affairs, and travels about among them. In an island of the ocean, there is her sacred grove. In it is a holy chariot covered with cloth. Only the high priest is allowed to touch it. He knows when the goddess is present in her consecrated bower, and in reverence, he accompanies her as she is drawn about by cows.

"These are very joyful times, and the places which the goddess honors with her presence, make her visit into a holiday. No one is allowed to begin a war or take up arms and all weapons are hidden. Peace and happiness only are known until the priest takes the goddess back to her holy bower. Then the wagon with the covering cloth and the divinity herself are taken to a hidden lake and washed. These services are performed by slaves whom the lake then swallows. Hence springs the secret terror and sacred ignorance about something which is seen by those alone who then are damned to immediate death." (This has a strange likeness to the Aztec festival where a beautiful youth is entertained for a year as a god and then at the end of that time is sacrificed.)

It is interesting that many small bronze figurines of Nerthus have been found and about all of them are certain characteristic. They are naked; the female parts are exaggerated; about the necks of these figures are twisted double tongues much like the nooses found on the mummies, including Tollund man.

Professor Glob says of Tollund man: "It is the face of the man who in supernal exaltation took the noose around his neck knowing that he went to his great goddesss, to Nerthus and her fair handmaidens and that by his death he ensured the life of his people for the coming year."

Personally, I can see no joy or supernal exaltation in the face of Tollund man. There is instead, sadness, pain and fear. There may be fatalism, but, at least to me, the way the brows are drawn almost speaks of agony.

In our present state of knowledge on how to preserve these mummies after they have left the peat, the cost is rather prohibitive. Therefore the head and feet were kept and the rest of the body turned over to the National museum of Copenhagen for study. Among the facts which they learned is that Tollund man had a last meal still in his intestines. He had eaten it from twelve to twenty-four hours before his death. He had eaten no meat. If we are to judge from his last meal, the food was rather poor in ancient Denmark. They had little of the food we enjoy today. For example he ate some things we never touch. He had barley, but also such grains as flax (which has a strong laxative effect if not soaked and drained) also camelina (one of the mustard family), white goosefoot (a wild turnip), wild pansy and bits of sphagnum moss.

Paul Johnstone who arranged the BBC portrayal on TV of Tollund man arranged for the last meal to be cooked and eaten. He had to call on pet shops specializing in bird food finally to get all the ingredients. A gruel was made of the seeds. His description is amusing in his book "Buried Treasure."

"The most unattractive part of this was its color, a greyish purple flecked with orange and black of the smaller seeds, but the actual taste, though unexciting, was quite reasonable. An indignant Dane wrote denying that his ancestors could possibly have existed on such disgusting food, after Sir Mortimer's cheerful comment that 'Tollund man probably committed suicide to escape his wife's cooking.' "

I could no better close this story of Tollund man and the story of the mummies of the Norse than the end with Paul Johnstone's description of Tollund man.

"to us this extraordinary face, so remarkably poised between the remotest past and the present, is essentially that of a fellow creature. It is no way strange, alien or barbarian. More than most things it brings the past alive to our imaginations, and reminds us how close to us and how much a part of us it is. To study it is to know ourselves better, and if we know clearly whence we came, there is more chance we may see a little less dimly where we are going."

Chapter 29

The Mystery Of The African Rim And The Veiled Raiders

I was leisurely eating dinner in Louise's Pantry in Palm Springs, California, when I met the Johnsons. I was eating in a booth by myself which is more or less frowned upon since there is always a line waiting to enter this popular eating place; unless you are willing to have a couple seated with you. I had asked the waitress for an extra paper napkin and was sketching a map of Africa upon it while I nibbled at my food, when Louise herself came up bringing a pleasant looking middle aged couple. She has the charm and graciousness of manner which sets off the honey colored blonde beauty of her Scandinavian ancestry.

"This is my favorite customer," she said to them by way of introduction, "always using our extra paper napkins to sketch maps or exotic types of people."

After the orders were taken, I was aware that the strangers were intently trying to see what I was doing. Finally the man spoke.

"Isn't that a map of Africa?"

I nodded.

"Don't you have the shoulder extended too far out? And what is that land lying out there in the Atlantic?"

"I suppose it is a weird looking map at that," I admitted. "You see, it is supposed to be Africa during the Pleistocene ice age. The land to the west is the Atlantic ridge, which may have been partially out of water."

"How intriguing!" Then reaching for it he asked: "May I?"

"Certainly," passing it across the table.

"We were there about seven years ago," he informed me. "The name of this mountain range is the Ahaggar and not Hoggar."

"Oh, so glad you told me. I know that it is so marked on the maps, but the Arab from whom I received much of my information told me that name was wrong."

"The Arabs have different dialects. Undoubtedly it was Hoggar in his language. In fact the spelling is different so much of the time that a stranger can become very much annoyed."

"I imagine. Something like Indian names over here."

"Exactly. By the way, I see you have the Triton sea on your map; isn't that a mere legend?"

"It may be, and then it may not. You see, it may have been down-stepped in a widening of the Atlantic rift."

He regarded me suddenly as someone who might have escaped from the men with the white coats from an institution. I laughed at their expressions.

"Sorry. I was using geological language. There is a possibility that the Atlantic was torn open in a rift or earth tear at the end of the last ice age."

"Oh - really? How did it happen?"

"To explain it all would take hours. However, let us say the crust, I mean earth, beneath the Triton may have been tipped toward the sea during great earth readjustments, and then the Triton would have been poured out, and perhaps at the same time the Atlas range beyond the rim went down."

"Why, that is what the legends say! Has this ever actually happened elsewhere?"

"Yes. There has been block faulting many times during geological history, and mountain chains have been partly sunk . . ."

"During the time of man?"

"There was at least one instance---here on the California coast. The San Andreas is pretty active, and you probably know some points which are slumping into the sea yearly---that is, if you have lived on the coast for a long time and have watched, or know people who have."

He nodded thoughtfully. Then his wife leaned

forward, addressing him:

"Joe, do you remember the old stone quays which ran out into the Sahara, and you remember the Arab guide who told us that some of the rivers which now run to the Atlantic, once ran the other way---into the Triton?"

"Yes. How about that? Could it happen?"

"In block faulting, rivers can be made to run in the opposite direction. In fact, that would seem to pin down the fact that the area was step faulted or block-faulted into the Atlantic. We do not know for certain, because so little geological research has been done. A man by the name of Campbell said that he found fossil sponges and coral south of the Draa depression, but he was no geologist, unfortunately."

"I can well understand why no one wants to go out there," the woman volunteered. "You never saw such a land! High above you to the north are the sheer cliff faces of the Atlas range; I am sure no one ever has climbed them. Then ahead of you are strange dry salt lakes with long dry rivers emptying into them."

"The lakes are sort of laid end to end?"

"That is right. Some don't even have dead rivers - they look like a dried up arm of the sea."

"Is there quicksand?"

"Is there? If one only knew just where it is, the trip along that way would not be so dangerous, but even the best guides don't seem to be very certain."

"I know that sounds like a woman's description," her husband intercepted, "but actually the guides did not give one a great deal of confidence about their certainty of the road. It was supposed to be marked by buoys, but the things are never where they are supposed to be. I asked the head guide why all the conferences and he answered that the buoys were gone. When I suggested that they should post guards about them, he shook his head and said that no one took them. They just sank out of sight..."

"And that wasn't all either," his wife added. "Those fellows kept telling you that it was here that a camel caravan sank out of sight in such and such a year---until you become so nervous that you could bite off your tongue for having listened to the travel bureau that suggested it as a 'fascinating trip of exploration, and not too dangerous if undertaken during the winter.'"

"Why didn't you turn back?"

He made a gesture of frustration.

"We never could have found our tracks, if that is what you had in mind. They have a way of flattening out behind you like tire tracks do when you are driving over wet sand at the beach."

"Oh. That rift then is in the late stage, and mighty dangerous. It is below the sea level, is it not?"

"Yes, I believe so. There were some dunes off in the distance to the south and I finally persuaded the guides to take our chances on the dunes and circle back as soon as they thought they knew the way well enough ..."

"I never prayed so loud and long in my life," his wife broke in. "Finally they thought they saw a way and they took us safely out over the dunes ..."

"That is when we saw the Tuaregs ..."

"Tuaregs!" I exclaimed.

"Yes. You have heard about them?"

"I should say I have! I paid an Arab who was supposed to know a good deal about them to tell me, and I learned enough to whet my appetite for more to the point of going there one of these days."

"Say, why not come over to our place and we will show you some films. We have very little of the veiled riders, but you would enjoy the dune pictures perhaps, and those of that awful Draa depression."

"I would love to go. I had a sort of partial engagement for the evening, but anything can wait for this."

"That is the way with us. Perhaps you can help to explain what we saw."

I followed the Johnson car over to the Sahara Mobile Home Park. I smiled to myself at the name and afterward the Johnsons told me that the name had "sold them on the location". The Sahara is one of the most beautiful trailer parks in this town of beauty spots. The mobile homes are all of the luxurious type ten and twelve feet wide by fifty and sixty feet long, parked in terraced and landscaped settings. In the distance, the Sahara dance floor was crowded with couples swaying to the Tennessee Waltz, and the lights, reflected in the large swimming pool among the palm trees, were very attractive. We parked the cars in the driveway of one of the large new trailers and went inside. My hosts turned on the lights inside the long living room, drawing the drapes across the full length French widows.

Johnson wasted no time in setting up the screen, and soon we were deep in the Sahara desert. The pictures in color gave a vivid idea of the scarp face of the Atlas range whose peaks seemed to soar up to ten and twelve thousand feet above the sunken Draa depression with its dry wadi fossil rivers and its dry salt lakes.

One of the camera shots showed a buoy half submerged in the sand.

"Uuuh . . ." Mrs. Johnson shuddered. "That god forsaken place!"

Johnson then flipped the pictures to another roll. The camera was sweeping the dunes, apparently taken from camel back, as the pictures were rather swaying and jerky.

"This is where they come in. I wanted to get off and set the camera up to get good shots, but the Arabs wouldn't hear of it. They are really terrified of the Tuaregs. Watch!"

"How did you know they were coming?"

"The guides began looking back. I heard the word 'Tuaregs' and that was enough. They sometimes stop you and demand a toll, you know. It is cheaper to pay them what they ask than to fight with them. Even the French pay, and I was told that the Romans did also. Here they come..."

Over the top of a nearby sand dune came the veiled head of a rider upon a camel, and then the rest of the flowing garments swept into view as another appeared behind him. There were three in all. The eyes of the first one swept along the caravan briefly, and apparently did not seem to see the camera. I mentioned the fact.

"It is a good thing that I had the camera partly hidden, as the Arabs insisted that I do. Look, I had the few shots of his face blown up, and you will get a surprise."

The face of the man behind the veil suddenly loomed large in a close-up as the eyes moved swiftly in our direction and then turned away. It was a surprise.

"Why, the robes are blue! I thought that they were black."

"No blue. Wait I will run it again. Look at the eyes."

The eyes were definitely blue---almost a pansy blue.

"Blue eyes! And he looks like he is wearing blue eye shadow or some kind of eye make-up."

Johnson laughed.

"That is what I thought also, but the Arabs told me that it rubs off from the dye on the robes - some kind of vegetable stuff, I suppose."

Johnson started the machine again and the three Tuaregs rode majestically off the dune in single file, one after the other, and the last shot of them was as they were silhouetted in the distance along the top of a dune against the sky.

"We followed them. My Arabs were very nervous about doing so, but I insisted. I even gave them an extra tip to calm their fears. This helped some. However, as I learned later, the fears are real. We came to this village near an oasis."

The film showed a wretched group of palm-thatched huts with naked children running hither and yon among standing and resting camels.

"Then I saw them again - look."

The camera swung to a group of palms and there were the three camels and two Tuaregs sitting, apparently on their haunches, beside the peaceful creatures. The camera clicked off.

"I wanted more pictures. So I started toward them. Suddenly my Arab guides began to walk backward as if I had the plague or something. I realized that their fears were probably more than just pretended. I rolled up the films which I had taken, put them in my pocket, and reloaded the camera. As I approached the veiled riders, I realized that they were big fellows, squatting there indifferently and turning their heads casually as I walked toward them. As I approached them I desired more than anything I know to look at the whole face instead of just the eyes. But that was not to be.

"I had been told by my Arab guides that they believed that the men whom they called 'Blue Vengeance' thought all white men were robbers whom it was clever to rob first."

"No wonder, after the visit of De Provok to their land! He actually was able to see some of their cities and gain their confidence. However, his sole purpose was to find the tomb of their legendary queen, which he located and excavated, carrying everything away - including her mummy and jewels." I said then added: "I understand that after many years of indecision, the savants now agree that the mummy was really that of Queen Tinian - or whatever they called her. At first they had thought that the circular tower where she was buried was only a sort of out-look for raiders on a trade route."

"Carbon dating should tell the story of that mummy with finality," I went on, "but those round towers do run all the way to Ireland and from there down through New England to Colorado and into Mexico. They are too similar not to be of the same people. The one in New England is now partly under water and some day the Atlantic will take it all."

He sighed and shook his head thoughtfully.

"You believe these people are ancient, don't you?"

I nodded.

"It might interest you to know that I do, too, but probably for another reason. I'll tell you how I found out. As I said, I kept on walking toward them until I came up pretty close. Then I held out a small group of bills. These would buy the world with a fence around it from the Arabs.

"The one closest to me looked at the money curiously. I said: 'Not French money - American money - worth more than French money. Please - some pictures . . .' with a pleading expression.

"He turned from the money to appraise me. His expression at that moment was not particularly friendly or unfriendly - only curious. I added: 'I am an American. I come from across the ocean.'

"Then I lifted the camera to show him what I meant. I will never be able to tell you how swift was the movement which followed. He rose to his feet and with a lightning movement whipped out an arm dagger about two feet long that neatly took my camera and flipped it a good fifty to seventy-five feet away. I heard it shatter against some rocks.

"For a second my throat went dry. Not from the loss of the camera, or the way the money was tossed about, but because of the arm dagger which that motion revealed. You see, I am a collector of them, and this one was of bronze - leaf-shaped. If you know your bronze age daggers, you know how I craved that weapon. I looked at the dagger in amazement and from the dagger to the arm which held it. Above the elbow was the arm band with which the ancients could chain these daggers to their arms to use in war or let them hang if they wished to use their hands for a moment. And that arm band! How can I describe it on that muscular arm, faintly tinged with the blue dye. It was worked exquisitely, and mounted at the center was a red gem stone of some kind. Perhaps it was a large ruby. I could not say, but its beauty scintillated strangely in the sunlight. I found myself wondering if this could be the orichalcum Plato spoke of when he described Atlantis."

"I can certainly understand your interest. What did you do? Try to buy it from this man who cared so little for your money?"

"What else could I do? Would you just look at it and forget it? Yes, I suppose you would..."

"Let's put it this way. I am not a collector of daggers. I would rather have a few of their books and a dictionary to read them. I would like to just borrow them for a short time. Yes, I am convinced of the antiquity of these people. However, I did not mean to interrupt. What happened?"

"Well, I started putting more bills on my hand, pointing to the dagger and the armband. I tried to let him know how many camels each

bill would buy. He watched with an almost, let us say, sardonic glint of amusement. I am certain that he understood. I would have traded this trailer for it, but when I finally came to the last of my bills, he looked up from the money into my eyes. If I had been the most menial servant on the face of the Earth, and he the most powerful monarch looking at a man who had dared to hold out a trinket to trade for his palace, the look could not have contained more contempt. Then abruptly he turned his back. There was nothing for me to do but retrieve the bills which lay scattered by the wind and pocket the other bills. I walked over to the shattered camera, then leaving it for the oncoming children, I walked back sheepishly to where my Arab guides awaited me. That was my one and only interview with a Tuareg."

"Could you describe the design on the armband?"

"There was a sort of pyramid design and the maltese cross. That is all I remember. Perhaps some of it was a kind of writing. I really don't know."

"What was the design on the dagger?"

"It looked like a Troy-town maze on the handle and a sort of serpent design on the blade. It was very antique, I am sure, yet it shone with polished care. I will never forget it. Never."

"That is interesting. Both of those symbols exist here in the Americas. The Troy-town maze is on many Indian baskets and on the rocks in Oregon. The maltese cross is on a script inscription under the travertine at Salton sea. They are both clues to something I feel just beyond my reach at present. Perhaps the meaning may be clearer some day. But please go on; what happened from that village?"

"We have no more films to show. The Tuareg ended that."

"I know. But tell me about the land."

"Well we started back out, that's all."

"Did you receive any of these Tuareg legends about the Triton from your Arab guides?"

"Yes, come to think of it, we did. Sally, you took down some of the names. Could you find them?"

"Perhaps we are boring you?" she asked.

"Not at all. I would like to hear these legends. Every one helps a little."

She rose and went to the other room. While she was gone, probably looking for the book or notes she wished to find, I asked:

"Where did the road lead from this village?"

"All the way back to the starting point. But I have a question: who are the Tuaregs? They look something like what one might expect the ancient Egyptian to look if he walked out of a time machine into the twentieth century. I confess sometimes I felt that I was the one who walked out of a time machine into the distant past."

"One scientist has been quoted often as remarking that they are the ancient Libyan preserved under glass."

"Brief me on the Libyans."

"Apparently the pre-historical world power preceding the Egyptians."

"Aha! That is why you were drawing the map of the Triton. Were they the Atlanteans?"

"I am inclined to believe that they were one of the league - the Atlas group. You know that there have been many suggested locations for Atlantis. Crete is one. It has immense antiquity, but may it not have been a colony, perhaps founded by Zeus who was related to Atlas and Chronos? (Chronos - connected with Ireland. An Irish king? - Author) Perhaps another name for the Tuaregs is the old Roman name, Atlantides, who once held the strategic Atlas peninsula and the Triton - thus the waterway to the Mediterranean."

"And about this time the ridge was dry?"

"Let us say, partly dry. Plato's Atlantis would have been the island based on the ridge which would be opposite the Madeira peninsula of Spain." I pointed to the map on the paper napkin.

"I just remembered something---he had a trident on that dagger, pointing toward the blade."

"I thought it would be there, and was almost disappointed when you didn't mention it. Yes, there were at least three large islands, according to traditions and legends of various nations. Another was toward the Americas perhaps in the Caribbean, and was ruled over by Pluto. Was this Bermuda? Or perhaps the very interesting Blake plateau just east of Florida? You know, there is much red clay on much of the Caribbean floor. All of these islands mentioned are or were on a very unstable part of the Atlantic."

"When did this enormous sinking happen?"

"When the water which had been locked up in ice was returning to the sea. According to the latest estimates, about eight thousand B.C."

"Plato said ten thousand B.C. and some have estimated the destruction of Deucalion as 9600 B.C."

I added: "And would you believe it, some modern authorities would like to set up the sinking of the Atlas range as much more recent?"

"Really?"

"About the only scientific investigators who have been in the land of the Triton sea, Drs. Hermann and Borchard, have come forth with the statement that the rim was dropped into the Atlantic not further back in time, but between 2000 and 1250 B.C. with the final drying up of the great lake to be placed at the latter date."

He opened his eyes in amazement and I added: "Personally I am more inclined to give the disaster the date the oceanographers decide on for the final retreat of the ice, whenever that may have been; because of unbalance of weight. However, wasn't it Strabo, the Roman historian who, writing in the second century after Christ, spoke of England's Sillurian Insulum - or the Sillurian peninsula or the Scillies which today is only a group of islands where the population grows flowers? It would seem therefore that this land and the coast of France sank in the third century A.D. These may have been a succession of disasters running from south to north a few millennia apart. However, it would seem to me that the sinking of the Atlas peninsula, the emptying of the Triton, the sinking of the Spanish peninsula which paralleled the Atlas, and the submergence of Atlantis were all related disasters perhaps occurring at about the same time, possibly separated by only a few months or days. The last one was probably the cracking open of the Mediterranean valley, its sea wall being weakened by the former disasters."

"Do you think that this whole Atlantic ridge went down at this time?"

"Oh no. The sea had probably been eating it away piecemeal; especially so after the end of each ice sheet when the retreat began in earnest. Thus the original extent of Plato's Atlantis as 'larger than Libya and Asia Minor' referred to the original legendary land of the first glacial and not the islands left during the last glacial."

"That sounds reasonable. Now what about the double axe symbol on the arm band?"

"You didn't mention that."

"I just remembered. Did that refer to queen Hippolita of the Amazons whom Hercules conquered?"

"Perhaps, if he was the Tuareg monarch as the Arabs say. Also it is interesting that the symbol also occurs at Crete, along with the Troy-town maze and the trident. Carthage had it, too, didn't they? And the Etruscans of pre-Roman Italy?"

"What a league!"

"Some were the inheritors, I suppose, like the modern Tuaraks. It is even evident in the heraldry of Europe."

"Meaning that there is a little Amazon and a dash of Atlantean in us all?"

"Undoubtedly."

Mrs. Johnson's voice echoed from the other room, almost plaintively: "Did I put that in the steamer trunk?"

"I wouldn't know, dear."

Then to me: "How about the blue eyes? Isn't it possible that they might have come from the Crusaders? I understand that they brought some mighty attractive women back with them . . ."

"And left some offspring behind? It could be." This reminded me of something and I laughed. "Do you remember the story of the Amazons who were being taken to Greece as captives, and in the middle of the night got loose, dumped their captors overboard, and sailed on without a pilot? Their ship came to rest on the shores of ancient Scythia. They piled out in the morning and stole some horses. Then they began to raid the countryside. The king of the Scythians waged war upon them when, to his amazement, he discovered that they were women. He then withdrew his forces. Seeking out his most attractive young men, he gave them goods to trade to the ladies---materials and trinkets designed to attract their eyes. The young men were instructed to go to the camp and sort of hang around. The king's scheme worked only too well. The Amazons captured the young men and the materials. The kept both, and went right on with their raids. History does not record what the king did then."

"Who were the Scythians?"

"Either the Germans or the Russians, or a group in the ancestry of both. Most authorities believe Scythia was in Russian territory. However, I just thought of something: these Amazons were not Atlanteans. They did not know how to handle a ship. Besides Diodorus said that there were three groups. These must have been the eastern group and not those who came from the Hesperides."

A triumphant voice from the other room called:

"I have it - at last."

"Bring it in. Our guest is interested in these Tuaregs and I didn't pay too much attention to the legends the Arabs told us."

Mrs. Johnson came in holding up a small dark leather note book. "Now we will go on with the trip. I have a note here about the depression ---'I only pray that this ancient car they rented to take me will not get engine trouble, or a flat

tire. What ever would we do?'

"Here is another note---'Ahben keeps talking about the Triton sea. He says that when it sank, many cities went down on it because it was about a hundred miles wide . . .'."

"How do you geologists know that it was ever connected to the land?" Johnson cut in.

"The same way that we know that Catalina island, thirty six miles out from the California coast, was once a part of the land - by the plants. They are related to those of Baha California. The Canaries have plants which migrated to Switzerland during the third glacial - Switzerland and France I believe. A paper was written for Smithsonian on the subject. And in 1946 Dr. Coleman wrote a paper for the American Association for the Advancement of Science, showing the relationship of the South Sea island orchids with the fossil orchids on the rocks of Antarctica. Plants prove many interesting facts - to which, however, some geologists are still hiding their eyes, like the ostrich, in the sand."

Mrs. Johnson continued to read: " 'Ahben said that the Tuaregs say the Triton carried the commerce of the whole world. It was the way from the Atlantic to the Mediterranean valley. This was long before the rise of Egypt. In those days the Atlantic was a double much of its way, and goods could be carried from Africa to England and even to the continent beyond. I sat wondering if he meant America, but did not like to interrupt him.' Do you wish me to go on?"

"Very much indeed."

" 'He told us about an old Arab who could tell us a great deal. I tried to persuade Joe to see this fellow . . .' "

"For a time I was not sold on the idea of going out of our way, but it wasn't too far," Johnson nodded. "Sally had her heart so set on it, so we . . ."

Mrs. Johnson glanced up from her book.

"Oh here is about our trip to Siwa. It was smelly, dirty and altogether unattractive."

Johnson nodded.

"The negroes had come up from the south until the population today was almost entirely black, and they did not seem to be interested in bathing."

" 'Siwa is a disappointment,' " Mrs. Johnson read. " 'It is so shabby and filthy that one can hardly believe that Cambysses, when he was engaged in conquering and plundering Egypt, met his defeat here. Of course, that was 524 B.C. when he gazed with greedy eyes upon the temple of the fire god and the palaces of the Ammonian kings. He sent in his army by way of

Exquisitely worked hollow bronze ibex from the prow of a ship found buried in Egyptian sands, taken from the prow of a ship. Work of the famed Saite sculptors, unrivalled even by the Greek. Now in the Berlin museum.

Thebes. The army surrounded the ancient temple, all right, and decided to wait until morning. According to the legends of the Arabs, the priesthood began an ancient chant. The army laughed and went to sleep leaving guards on duty. That night, very suddenly, a sand storm came upon them, and not a man was left alive of the fifty thousand iron clad men and their horses. No one ever found them to this day.' ''

She looked up at me, then without a comment, continued:

" 'Passageways run from below the temple of Agourmi for about two miles to Djebel Muta. The temple was most remarkable, even in ruin. The circular walls had a sheer lustrous red beauty, but it was the galleries which really intrigued us. We had to give the Arabs a large extra tip, but it certainly was worth it.

" 'We followed the Arab guide, who carried a torch. The gallery seemed to have a stone floor and smooth walls. Before we had gone over two city blocks, we came to the paintings. I suppose the torches have done them no good, but the colors did seem to be quite brilliant. First there were animals. They must have been from ice age times. There was an American buffalo, or something that looked like one. Not far away was a very large elephant - perhaps a mammoth. He was pulling some fruit from a tree. There was water everywhere, and ferny forests beyond the stream. Crocodiles were in the water. Beautiful birds sat in the trees, and strange animals peeped through the shrubbery.

" 'We went on and came to the paintings of a city on the shore of a sea. The guide told us that this was the Triton. Many square-sailed ships were about. We didn't know whether they were Libyans, Cretan, Pelasgians, Etruscans, or Egyptians because neither Joe nor I was familiar enough with the clothes. The quays were wide and well made - apparently of stone. Just then Joe started down another passageway which crossed ours. The guide followed him and then asked him not to go wandering off because this was a labyrinth and many people have died because they could not find their way out.' ''

"I'll tell you why I wandered off..."

"I know," I laughed. "You saw a dagger."

"You are so right. There was a picture of a fight of some kind. One army - the ones who carried the daggers, the bronze age leaf shaped ones---wore peaked helmets with a tuft of feathers on top; I suppose like a mountain. There was a mail woven chain down the back of the neck so that it was protected. They wore skirts to the calves of the legs like our Apache Indians. Funny - some of them seemed to be carrying snakes, and others were holding up burning torches. The boots seemed to turn up a bit at the toe."

"Atlanteans!" I found myself exclaiming.

"How do you know?" he challenged.

"They were so described on the columns of the temple at Sais. Didn't they carry triangle shields or hour glass type like two triangles put together?"

"Yes, they did. But wait a moment---so did some of the Crusaders: How did they get these things in Europe?''

"I wish I knew."

"Sally, this passageway reached a dead end. How about the next group of pictures before we came out into the light. Do you have them on the paper?"

"I don't have them all. Someone seems to have used this for scratchpaper and has torn most of them out up to the part about the old Arab..."

"Never mind. I can remember. There was one of a very long swinging bridge over a ferny chasm wasn't there?"

"And off in the distance were the ships again on a blue sea. Then there was one of castles on the side of a high cone shaped mountain. The castles had curving walls and turrets. The mountain was cloud tipped. But oh, Joe, how could these pages have been taken?"

"I don't know, but read those pages about the old Arab."

"Before we do go on, I must tell you that after Joe and I came into the light, the Arab took us to the old stone quays stretching way out into the desert sand. So the picture must have been of the city when it was a trading center of the ancient Triton sea. And the quays proved that there must have been a Triton sea."

"During the middle ages a ship was found not too far from the Draa depression in which the skeletons of the rowers were lying with the chains still around their bones. The Arabs, I understand, charge a very high fee to take you there. It still must be in existence."

"We didn't hear about that," Mrs. Johnson said with a note of regret in her voice.

"And I am glad," her husband added, "or we might just be there yet and in not a very good condition either."

She smiled at him wistfully and again began to read:

" 'He was a very old man, but seemed to be immensely pleased by our presents.' Joe, where is the first part of this?"

"I don't know, but we heard about this fellow and so we had our guides take us to him with all kinds of presents - food and other commodities. He looked as if he needed the food badly. Sally did most of the talking. The first part was about how his caravan became lost and his struggle to stay alive on the desert. We'd have to skip it anyhow. It wasn't a pretty story. Do you have the part where he wandered up the Igharhar dry wadi?"

"No."

"Or the part where he climbed the Ahaggar mountains at the place where three peaks form a trident? He said that the mountains were hollow because he seemed to hear voices and couldn't tell where they came from. He seemed to see the blue robed Tuaregs riding and then suddenly they would disappear. For my part, he had too much sun! Perhaps we had too much, too, when we saw those stone quays. Who knows?"

"If you think so," I answered, "then how does it happen that when the French bore through the desert for artesian water they find fish? Furthermore, the wells so long isolated across hundreds of miles of burning sands still support some of the larger reptiles. There are many types of fish and besides that mollusks and crabs. The fish are fresh water varieties, if you think they are coming from the sea."

"How far down do they have to bore to get this result?"

"Three hundred feet."

"Could the Tuaregs have a lake below the surface?"

"That is certainly possible. Yet you must admit, from the Draa depression to the Egyptian border the whole Sahara is a mass of giant dry rivers very often running in the very opposite direction from the present short trickling streams - especially to the south. Yes, geologically, there was a Triton sea."

"What is that Draa depression - the old bed?"

"No, a rift. The Atlas range is cracking off. Put one finger on Agadir on the Atlantic coast and the other on the Gades bay off the Mediterranean, and you will see the line of the Draa depression on any map of the Sahara. Also the Igharghar river is one of the mightiest fossil rivers in the world. It takes its rise below the tropical line and flows---or once flowed---almost six hundred miles in a straight line to the mountains of the Tuaregs. At the time of Tuareg greatness these mountains were islands. They were one nation which did not change---the geography of the land and the nations of the people changed with it while they were left behind - a fossil nation living in dreams of the past. There is something very pathetic about them."

"One of the tragedies is what happened to the books at Siwa."

"Don't tell me that there were books at Siwa!"

"Were. You know that the Negro is usually followed by their witch doctors . . ."

"Oh no!"

"That is right. The fellows with the magic powders ground them up with hairs, etc., and then used the ashes for their formulas."

"I wonder if there are any left? The Arabs are missing a gold mine if there are. Just think what the Dead sea scrolls sold for, and then think of the age of these!"

THE AFRICAN SHELF

Compiled by the author from studies by Du Toit,
Johnstone, and the Challenger expedition.

Johnson laughed.

"I wonder what this fossil nation of yours would become if once they ever found out about the money involved in the tourist business?"

Mrs. Johnson cleared her throat as a lawyer might when the jury was getting too noisy.

"Would you really like to hear the rest of this?"

"Certainly," I nodded.

"Before I begin, I would like to know why it is always speaking of ancient ruins on top of mountains? Would that be the place to look for ruins?"

"It would, in the Sahara. One begins searching on the top of the mountains for the flints of the cave men and the cities which thrived at the same time. The fossil rivers tell us how the Sahara must have bloomed at one time. As the water table dropped, the human and animal inhabitants followed it down until now the Arabs pitch their tents by the well in the oasis at the bottom. But the last page has not been written in the story of the Sahara. Someday the rest of the Atlas range will also rift off. Then perhaps the mountains of the Tuaregs will again become islands."

"You don't have to convince me. I saw the quays at Siwa where neither sea nor commerce has existed since long before the time of the would-be conqueror and his buried fifty thousand. But this will interest you from the diary:" she said, and read:

" 'The old man told me that above a mighty gorge in the very heights of the Atlas is the ruins of the city of Khamissa. It has towers of marble which have been deserted for untold thousands of years. Yet at certain times, when the weather is just right and the atmospheric conditions are perfect, especially if one has had a sip of wine and a smoke on the pipe, then the gorge doesn't have the blue-purple veils of evening at all, but is deep purple-blue water upon which are a tumbled mass of shipping going to and from the teeming city. It becomes a kaleidoscope of galleys, triremes and ghost ships from long forgotten nations. And the beauty of the rounded towers are reflected in the sea like those from a never-never land.' "

"He made it sound like the place was haunted."

"You know I believe that the Arabs think the places of the Tuaregs really are haunted."

"I am sorry that I interrupted you. Is there any more, especially such intriguing passages as that?"

She smiled and again began reading:

" 'In the galleries which are not lakes, or places for the storage of water, the unimagined splendor of the Tuaregs in the full pride of their power is still pictured in endless gallery paintings.

" 'The city of Khamissa is not the only ruin lost in the vastness of this little-explored land. Between the ranges of the Air and the Ahaggar, is once proud Tafassaset, and southeast of the Ahaggar range is Essouk, the imperial capital of Heracles, once the most important city on Earth.' "

"What I wouldn't give to explore it!"

With an impish grin Johnson warned:

"And you would end on the point of the antique arm dagger."

"It might almost be worth it. . ."

Mrs. Johnson closed the book.

"I'm sorry, but the witch doctors got the rest, for some inscrutible reason of their own," giving her husband a sidelong look.

"Very well. The lawyer wanted some more paper when we were figuring the income tax. I couldn't figure out what the scribbling was about on the other side of the paper at that moment."

I looked at my watch. (I felt it was an auspicious time to be leaving.)

"Do you good people realize how late it is? I know that I didn't for I had such a wonderful time exploring the Sahara."

After the usual cordialities, I drove away from the beautiful mobile home park. The recreation hall was now empty and dark, and the only lights were those which Palm Springs places at the base of the palm trees - the indirect lighting of the green spotlight thrown up into the branches, being the street lights in this artistic decorator-planned town.

Yet, once more at home, and in bed sleep would not come. Finally, when it did I wondered restlessly across vast sand dunes where blue-veiled figures blended with their camels, or moved through endless labyrinthine galleries with the Johnsons, pausing before island scenes which I suspected had descended thousands of years ago to the green plutonic depths of the ocean; or else, we stared unbelievingly at a teeming and noisy seaport where busy men hurried about stone quays - a seaport which had been a shabby desert village for untold millenia; trying to make out the costumes of the people we saw engaged in trade. In the painting, they were so active that they almost seemed to move, yet our history books had told us that some of them had never really existed - except, of course, in a legend of hoary antiquity . . .

Chapter 30

The Taylor Hypothesis

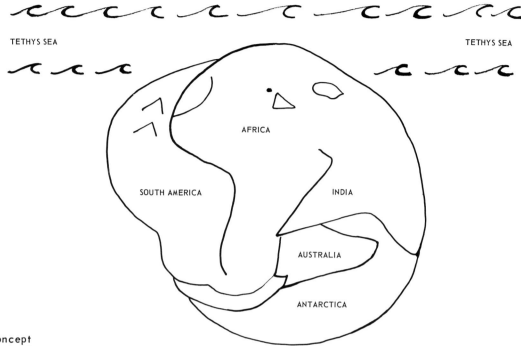

TETHYS SEA

TETHYS SEA

AFRICA

SOUTH AMERICA

INDIA

AUSTRALIA

ANTARCTICA

Taylor's concept
of Gondwannaland

Before we get more involved with ancient civilizations, let us go back through time and see what the rocks tell us about this ocean - the Atlantic. We will have to go very far back - before there were any plants or animals as we know them now, and of course, before the time of man. This history is very important if we would understand this planet upon which we find ourselves passengers, following our sun through space. What went before, millions and even billions of years ago has a bearing, as we shall see, not only on the present, and the historical past leading up to the present, but also on the future. Without this knowledge we cannot adequately discuss pre-history.

When I was attending high school, geology and geography were lumped together in something called "climatic geography". I have since come to suspect that my teachers had little interest in the subject, and therefore neither did their pupils. In college the professors did better, but they themselves had not been too deeply bitten by the bug of curiosity. As far as most of them were concerned, lands were always lands and oceans always oceans. That is how they had learned their science, and they passed on just what they themselves had been taught. We had not been given any problems to solve which might tend to make us question this. We were told that Earth is like a drying apple. As the globe loses water, it shrinks and mountains are pushed up. The apple dries, of course, with wrinkles. The likeness was simple. Mountains were Earth's wrinkles.

However, even then, there were thinkers abroad who had challenged this idea. There was a tremendous revolution sweeping the science against the old "contraction hypothesis", but I did not hear about it until I started reading a good deal and as a result began asking embarrassing questions.

Why did so many mountain chains form along the edge of continental masses? Why did some chains cross oceans? Why were these submerged chains once raised from pressures in one direction. What causes rifts? Why are fossils of ferns and tropical plants found at both the poles? With these questions I was only beginning. Eventually some of my professors became annoyed; others started reading.

That's when I learned about the theories of "drift" or "continental displacement" and our geology classes became interesting debating sessions. I soon found that the scientists in their geological forums were not only asking my questions, but were asking many others even more intriguing.

Why do earthquakes and volcanoes run in certain belts? And the prize question of all: why did the great glacial ages refrigerate only one hemisphere at a time?

Strangely enough, as more field geologists study the rocks, the questions multiply yearly. And yearly it becomes more apparent that the contraction theory is unable to give the answers. The old belief in the stability of continents and oceans, or Earth's supposed wrinkled skin (like the drying apple) is yearly becoming less tenable. For most modern geologists, geophysicists and meteorologists, the facts can no longer be fitted into this comfortable old fashioned frame. The migration of certain species of animals and plants are difficult to explain - even with the help of land bridges; and if the oceans were always there, then how did land bridges come into being?

Finally, as the popularity of the old theory began to slide, other scientists began to attack it from the affirmative as well as the negative angle. One maintained that according to geophysics there was not enough power in mere crustal shortening to raise half of Earth's mountains. This inspired Joly to bring out the theory of "crustal eruption which was brought about, he said, by stored radioactive heat. Yet, that still wouldn't answer most of the questions.

Another geologist asked by what right should we say that Earth is drying? Is it not even possible, from the mixture of gasses thrown up by volcanoes during an eruption, that Earth is actually gaining water?

Beno Gutenberg of the California Institute of Technology, in his book "The Earth", suggests that if the continents had always been where they are, they should have slumped out over the ocean bottoms. In fact, said Gutenberg, that is probably what is happening and he put forth his theory of "sialic creep". Undoubtedly this is a factor. It may explain the shattered bits of sial which are the islands of the south Pacific, covered by some of the oldest living fossil plants on Earth. Yet there are other questions which sialic creep does not answer. Perhaps it is just as well for us that this is not entirely what is happening. If all the continents were spread out over the ocean bottoms, they would today lie as low as the Atlantic ridge.

Has your eye ever been halted by the strangely parallel Atlantic coastlines of Africa and South America as you stood idly twirling a globe of the world? Perhaps you have even remarked aloud that these two continents looked as if they had once been one, and had since been pulled apart like two slices of a mud-pie?

You may be surprised to find that you were not the first to voice this opinion. As far as we know, that man was a geologist by the name of Snider who, in 1858, published a map showing the Americas pushed up against Europe and Africa.

Contemporary with Snider was another geologist named Suess who saw rather significant patterns in Earth's mountain ranges. The maps of these two men, together with the immense amount of work done by Alexander Du Toit (not a professional geologist, but one of the most honored men in the science), and other thinkers, led to one of the greatest revolutions to sweep a science against long accepted views.

Of course, it is true that no matter which one of the sciences is one's field of study, no man stands alone. What he has learned is made possible by the previous detailed study of hundreds of experts. Even the questions which have come up to challenge a theory are made possible because such students as Du Toit compared in detail many outcrops of rocks across the South Atlantic, or studied the similarity of fresh water fish, or insects, or mammals, or plants. The theory with which a man tries to explain these facts may have a partial truth because he had certain facts in mind, to the exclusion of other facts.

In the forums where knowledgeable men of many sciences meet to discuss the new theory, the hypothesis meets its baptism of fire. The skeptical listeners will soon point out the parts of the theory which do not coincide with facts. Yet there is often an element of truth which the facts cannot entirely contradict. For example, the theory of sialic creep may explain the South sea islands. They may once, long before man, when trees were great ferns, have been the mountain tops of a continental mass. Darwin, better known to most men as the father of the theory of evolution, is known to geologists for his work on coral reefs. As explained before, he found that in the South seas, coral reefs extended down to depths where no coral could grow, thus showing a slow sinking of all the South sea islands. Were they remelting under the crust, or was this creep?

The questions which any new theory must meet are the questions which make the contraction theory seem more improbable with each passing year. It is unable to answer why sunken ranges raised in the same long distant epoch of the past are composed of the same rocks; or the distribution of ancient climates compared to present climates (to mention only two).

The first guns fired in this revolution against the contraction theory were the "equatorial drift" ideas of Kreichgauer and Frank Taylor. Of the two, Dr. Taylor, a geologist of Indiana university, was the most specific. In 1910 and 1911 he put forth his hypothesis of equatorial drift, postulating two masses of sialic rocks - a Holarctica in the north and a Gondwannaland in the southern hemisphere. These masses, because of the rotational forces of Earth, began to move. They slid into each other during the end of the Mesozoic era, closing the ancient Tethys sea which had lain between them. The bed of the sea was pushed up by the tremendous forces of the collision to form the peaks of the Alps and Himalayas. The collision caused Gondwannaland to crack at the southern end, tearing open the Indian and Atlantic oceans; and the force of this collision also pushed up most of the other ranges of this age.

Taylor made allowance for the similarity of the continents in the southern hemisphere, as he placed them in a single mass. The name he used was not his, but that of a fellow geologist, who had seen the need for such an early center grouping and had named the postulated mass after a primitive African tribe, the Gonds, who lived along the shores of the Indian ocean. The name is so much used today in all the sciences that most any geologist, botanist etc., who has heard of the drift theories, knows exactly what is meant by ancient Gondwannaland.

Taylor was neither the first to use the name, nor the first to note the likenesses across the Indian and south Atlantic, yet he was the first to study just how this ancient continent should look. By pressing South America and Australia back against Africa to close the Indian and south Atlantic oceans, and then by pulling Antarctica back to touch the southern tip of those continents, and India back to Africa's east coast, he had his ancient Gondwannaland. In this he made one mistake. He did not allow for the sunken ridges in the south Atlantic and Indian oceans.

The same gneiss shield lies below all these continents and can be made to fit, if the partly rotational manner in which South America and Australia have drifted away is corrected as done by Taylor. Above this gneiss shield (Earth's most ancient rocks called shields underlie the sialic masses of both hemisphere), are the southern coal bearing rocks of Gondwannaland. Here Taylor made his second mistake. He did not allow for these rocks. Coal bearing rocks are laid down in the tropics. Therefore Taylor should have had his Gondwannaland in the tropics before it drifted south to be glaciated. That these continents were glaciated at one time is not to be doubted. His third mistake is insufficiently to explain the sunken Easter island---African capes ---Kerguelin island range of mountains which crossed the ancient continent and then continued on down the sunken Lemurian ridge in the center of the Indian ocean. (The name Lemurian ridge, was given to it by a paleozoologist named Sclater who was searching for a home for the lemurs or dog faced monkeys which surround the Indian ocean as if they had scampered to their present homes from a land rapidly becoming unliveable.)

Some of the arguments in the forum for the American Association for the Advancement of Science were most interesting when Gondwannaland came in for its share of discussion. Geologists, noting the likeness of the flightless birds family of animals, including such members as the ostrich, the cassowary, rhea and extinct groups such as the New Zealand moa, argued that they must have migrated from a center in order to get to such now distant lands as Australia, Africa and South America. They could not fly. Neither could they swim, and it was very doubtful if their eggs could float across the Indian or south Pacific oceans. The ornithologists who make a life study of birds refuted this possibility immediately by saying that they were not even of the same genus or species, but were curious products of similar lines of evolution having taken place at distant points. The ancestor was undoubtedly a type of pigeon which flew to those locations many epochs ago. At this point the parasitologists came into the argument. The flightless birds, said the parasitologists, are definitely related. They have related parasites, and these creatures do not live on the pigeon. With that, the argument was closed.

Again, when the subject of the tree frogs came up, the parasitologists checked the interrelation of types living across vast stretches of ocean. The parasites settled that: the tree frogs were related.

Nor is it only the flightless birds and tree frogs which argue for a connection between the now widely separated continents of Australia,

India, Africa and South America---there are the members of the parrot family, various cranes, numerous types of insects, fresh water fish, crocodiles, etc., and a great number of plants, to mention only a few. The lists lengthen with every passing year, and with more students seeking doctorates. Du Toit, who did so much in matching the rocks across the south Atlantic (finding in many cases the same beds on each side with the same fossils; or if they were missing on one side, that was due to the fact that they had been eroded away), was the master who pointed out the pattern of this work.

Yet, Taylor ignored one of the most interesting facts: the long winding ridge on the floor of the Indian ocean. It is composed of sialic rock. It will show up if you have a contour map of the Indian ocean which will indicate the one thousand fathom line---the depth at which submerged fragments seem to come to rest. Like the north and south Atlantic, the Indian ocean shows a double rift valley whose turns fit the continents to each side. Also like the north Atlantic, and the south Atlantic, the ancient river channels of the Indian turn from the highlands and run down the old valleys to the sea. The highlands in the case of the Indian ocean is the Easter island--- Kerguelin range which bends and follows the Lemurian spine to the ancient Tethys. At one time this range carried very high peaks which were the fountainheads for the glaciation. Unlike the river channels of the north and south Atlantic, much of this evidence has been lost by the glaciation, as glaciers gouge out the valleys they follow down to bed rock.

Kerguelin island, which is situated upon the Lemurian ridge, is composed entirely of continental rocks, although its nearest continental neighbor, Antarctica, is now seven hundred miles away. The Seychelles banks, like the Murray banks, are also composed of granite and other continental rocks.

In our reconstructed ancient Gondwannaland, we note a strange fact. The Andes of South America blend into the ranges of Antarctica, and they in turn bend to meet the high mountains of Australia. Nor is this all: the Alps seem to be a western extention of the Himalayas, while to the east, the high mountains of northern India turn and run southeast into the Pacific where the South sea ridges seem to be long lost fragments, finally disappearing in the ocean, with their tiny inhabited tops which are the South sea islands, bending away to the southeast. All of these cordilleras of mountain ranges are apparently of the same age, dating their greatest folding during the end of the Mesozoic era when the ancient Tethys became the tops of the Himalayas and the giant dinosaurs which had ruled Earth for millions of years, became extinct.

Thus the Taylor hypothesis was considered by the American Association for the Advancement of Science forum to have been refuted because it could not answer certain very important facts:

1) Why were the glacial rocks or till underlain by coal if the mass was at the south pole to begin with?

2) If it did move from the tropics where the coal was laid down, what caused it to move? In fact, just what caused it to move from the south pole? (Some geophysicists thought that the rotational forces were inadequate.)

3) What caused the rise of the Easter island ---capes---Kerguelin cordillera?

4) Why was Antarctica left behind?

However, the theory does explain a tremendously important fact: it explains the closing of the Tethys sea and the twisting upward of the bed to make the Himalayas. That there was an early Tethys sea is a fact. That the bed was folded up to make the peaks of the Himalayas is another fact. For this the theory has a reasonable explanation.

We do know that the end of the time of the dinosaur reign was the most violent which Earth has seen. Basaltic lavas of great depth have been dredged from the Carlsbad and Murray banks, while the capes of Africa were inundated by tremendous sheets of lava. This "curtain of fire" was, of course, not seen by modern man. Yet the rocks silently tell the story of the intense fury of the period.

The book of Frank Bursley Taylor of Indiana university in 1910 was the most comprehensive published to that date which made an attempt to explain two facts - the Gondwannaland glacial and the collision of continental masses along the Tethys which could have been the cause of the Mesozoic diastrophism. Thus we owe a debt of gratitude to his foresight in outlining his theory in "Bearing of the Tertiary Belt in the Origin of Earth's Plan". He may not be entirely correct in all details, but he has given the scientists who will follow him a platform to stand on while they repair some of the details. His name could never be dropped from any final theory of continental displacement which so many scientists such as Dr. Clements, head of the Department of Geology at the university of Southern California (in speaking to the present writer) called: "the geology of the future".

Chapter 31

The Wegener Hypothesis

If Taylor fired the first shot into the sleeping camp of the world's geologists, Alfred Wegener blasted a whole broadside. Not only did he do a massive amount of research in assembling evidence, but, leaving his native Germany, he demanded and got a forum debate from the American Association for the Advancement of Science.

The contraction theory (of the drying apple) under which most geologists had learned their science, now really came under the shrapnel of the theories of continental displacement, or "drift". Many geologists were taken unaware, and were suddenly unable to answer the barrage of questions.

The forum became warm and at times almost personal, which, of course, has no place in a scientific discussion. The manner in which the hypotheses of Taylor and Wegener were discussed in opposition would lead a listener to suppose that they were mutually exclusive. They are not.

Geological theories are hardly prize fighters entering a ring. They are logical attempts to explain certain facts and should be examined as such. No man's theory is wholly a product of his own brain, to be guarded by his friends with a sort of fierce paternal jealousy, but rather a plank to be built into a platform upon which future scientists can orientate themselves as they push back the mists from the unknown with which we are all surrounded.

Alfred Wegener's hypothesis, put forth in his volume "Origin of Continents and Oceans" translated from the German in 1924 by Brownjohn, so completely complements the hypothesis of Taylor that Reginald Daly of Harvard, recognizing this fact, suggested that they be incorporated in a single theory called "The Taylor-Wegener Hypothesis". It is to be regretted that he did not follow up this suggestion with a book showing in detail exactly what he meant.

I shall not repeat all the scholarly arguments of these two scientists in defense of their theories nor the arguments of the forum of petroleum geologists called up to discuss the subject, in detail. I feel that the reader, if sufficiently interested, may read the volumes for himself, but I shall try to sum up as briefly as possible Wegener's hypothesis and the main arguments, for and against it, used at this interesting meeting of minds.

Wegener postulated one massive continent surrounded by the Pacific ocean which he named Pangea. This mass of continental rocks (the name meaning "whole earth" in Greek) did not take into consideration an ancient Tethys sea which once flowed where the Mediterranean is today, and being a geological fact was the first mistake to be pointed out against his theory.

In order to arrive at his Pangea, or mother-continent, Wegener tells us that he joined the geological, faunal (animal) and floral (plant) evidence across the Indian and Atlantic oceans which are like "writing across a torn page".

In some manner, said Wegener, possibly because of Earth's rotation, this mass began to move westward. As it started sliding, it began to tear at the south, first with the southern end of the Indian, and then followed with an almost simultaneous tearing of the Atlantic, also starting in the south with fragments showing where South America left Antarctica. This rifting in the Indian reached the Mediterranean at the end of the Mesozoic, when India was forced into Asia and the dinosaurs died in the earth convulsion which followed. In the Atlantic, the rifting reached the Mediterranean at the same time, but did not reach the Arctic until the last great northern ice age - or the Pleistocene. This timetable calls for a closed Atlantic in the north until the time of the glacials, when the widening began. Its breakthrough to the Arctic would be one of the facts which would have ended the glacials.

Chambers, Allen and others in agreement with this timetable of events, pointed out that the Shetland and Faroe islands were ground, polished and striated, showing that they bore a very heavy sheet of land ice. Geike then expressed the opinion that in view of this fact we can hardly contend that the Atlantic was filled with floating ice during most of the Pleistocene. He reasoned from the fact that in Scotland he found ranges of one thousand feet which had been completely buried, and from the fact that the Canadian shoreline had been invaded by ice grinding against it from somewhere to the east. These authorities agreed with Wegener's timetable on the final rifting of the Atlantic, placing it in the days of the great northern glacials. Geike also contends the glacials were heavier than we had believed.

That the ice load was much heavier than had been thought possible was the opinion of Daly in his book "Our Mobile Earth". In his "Floor of the Oceans" he quotes an apparently authentic statement by a Russian scientist that indications of a massive glacial sheet had been discovered in Siberia, which up to now has been believed to have been free of glaciation. Also in accord that the glacials were far heavier than has up to now been thought possible is Lambert's contention that if the weight of H rocks would basin Earth's crust to the extent of H/3 and take a lag of from ten to one hundred thousand years to return to normal again, then the actual rising rate of Hudson bay and the Baltic, from only eight to fifteen thousand years ago (as has been figured by many geophysicists for the final disappearance of the ice) is too short a time for the small load we have thought probable. In other words, the rising rate is far too sharp, and we must refigure on the basis of a much heavier glaciation. This of course, would mean more water locked up in ice during the advance of the ice sheets. These contentions seem to be factual and therefore will be accepted. Wegener's timetable seems very reasonable.

Wegener's matching of the shores across the north Atlantic was criticized by the statement that the glacial moraines of Canada and England do not match, nor do the folds of the mountains between England and America of the Appalachian-English range. He was told that a land of a thousand level miles or a mountainous land of five hundred miles was needed. Wegener should have looked at the bathymetrical maps of the north Atlantic for his answer. It lay on the bottom of the sea. Undoubtedly the high ridge range argued for by Kober and R. M. Field, were also fountainheads for the glacials.

Bowie, the geophysicist, criticized Wegener's conception of a Pangea or "whole Earth", saying that the construction of the globe would not allow such massing of rocks in one hemisphere.

Since this and the need for an ancient Tethys sea (which is a geological fact) demand it, we must accept Taylor's conception of two original continents---Gondwannaland and an Amer-Eurasia---separated by a Tethys sea and surrounded on all other sides by the Pacific ocean.

At this point Van Der Gracht shows a need for another continental mass which, in the very beginning of geological history, came riding out of the Pacific and crushed the western coast of North America and Mexico. Its main point of contact seemed to have been an old land shield south of Mexico which may have been part of Amer-Eurasia, but which he calls Antillia. The contorted ancient crystals of the mountains of the Antilles argue for such a clash, says Van Der Gracht. Therefore let us accept this and agree that some unknown land mass struck Amer-Eurasia from the southwest at the beginning of what is known of geological history, closing perhaps a very ancient Atlantic sea and pushing up the giant mountains of the ridge range. This collision may have been the force which sent Amer-Eurasia under the pole and brought on the first northern glacial when Canada was the north pole and Chicago bore a frigid climate. What this land mass was or where it came from we have no idea, but it is possible that parts of Mexico, California and other west coast States as well as Alaska, may have once been a part of this continent.

These scientific criticisms are not negative and personal. They are based upon scientific facts. For a hypothesis to be workable, it must meet the facts. If it does not, it must be changed or amended to meet them. We are not being scientific if we attempt to make the facts meet the hypothesis. A workable hypothesis must explain all of the facts - not just some of them. The facts come first.

Let us continue in the light of the facts to see how complementary these two great theories are. If there are other facts which neither one meets and another theory does, let us see if that also can be worked into our structure.

The fact known to seismologists that sialic or continental rocks make patterns distinctly differentiated from simatic or ocean bottom patterns on seismographs is a well accepted fact, as is Gutenberg's discovery that the Indian ocean had the greatest amount of sialic rock upon its floor, while the Atlantic is second and a small amount in a scattered condition is to be found in the Pacific. This will be one of the basic elements of the combined hypothesis, even though neither Taylor nor Wegener paid as much attention as they should have done to the bathymetrical maps of the "torn" oceans. Gutenberg's theory of sialic creep is undoubtedly a factor which takes over when a continent is at rest. There would be a tendency for it to flatten out over the ocean bottom unless interrupted by other forces.

One of Wegener's greatest contributions to the problem of our understanding Earth's history, was his discussion of how a continental mass can move or slide. He pointed out that there are many kinds of movement. For example, a weight can move through both ice and water. Only, the rate of movement will be different. Continental movement may be so extremely slow to our tiny gnat-like lives that it will be completely unnoticed for the very short range of our present written history, going back only some six thousand years. The continental slide, said Wegener, takes place on hot glass and can be measured best in geological epochs. This manner of movement was unchallenged by our present state of knowledge and seems reasonable.

However, his direction of movement---all continents going west---came in for much criticism, and seems to be against some facts. That Wegener considered the Americas were going west and thus pushed up the western cordillera of mountains which garland the west coast of those continents, was not challenged. But the mountains on the continent of Australia were questioned. If the cordilleras on the Americas were pushed up, he was asked, how about the folds in Australia? How could they be pushed up on the east coast if Australia was going west? Wegener answered by saying that the mountains of Australia were raised by being dragged. Of course, the question which followed was: how could mountains be pushed up on the edge of one continent and contrariwise, folded upon the edge of another by being dragged?" Geophysicists immediately noted that according to recent studies of the folding of ranges, the pressures were upon the inside of the arc of a garlanded range. Therefore the mountains of Australia were being pushed as Australia rode into the Pacific.

Thus, apparently a fact which tripped Wegener's belief that Australia was going west, reinforced Taylor's belief that Australia was going east, or rather, away from the Mesozoic point of contact, which was India. Daly's objection to all continents moving west seems to have been justified.

Another point which pinned down what had happened in Gondwannaland was the discussion over India. When Wegener was asked how he would fit India into the Indian ocean in order to reform his supposed Pangea, he answered that if all the mountains on the north of India were ironed out, India would be back where it once belonged. This was about the same as Taylor had said concerning Gondwannaland, except for one fact: namely, the Himalaya cordillera of mountains is largely composed of the bed of the ancient Tethys sea. Therefore, if these mountains were ironed out, we would again have the ancient Tethys sea running between Gondwannaland and Amer-Eurasia as Taylor had postulated. We would have Taylor's Gondwannaland and not Wegener's Pangea.

Furthermore, when Bowie asked Wegener how he could explain the rifting of the Atlantic during the last northern glacial period, in view of the fact that if all continents were moving west at the present time, as postulated by Wegener, why had North America moved farther and faster than Eurasia from the aforementioned tear, when Eurasia being heavier, should have moved farther and upon a deeper plane? The great geophysicist was immediately answered by Taylor. Eurasia did not go west, said Taylor, it went southeast from its point of Pleistocene contact, which was Greenland. Thus it is moving faster and upon a deeper plane than that of North America which is going southwest from the Greenland contact.

Since Taylor's answer was not challenged, it seems admissable that we accept his view of the Atlantic tear during the Pleistocene and its contact point of Greenland.

There is one fact which neither the theories of Taylor nor Wegener sufficiently explained to the satisfaction of the scientists. This is the fact of the "Pacific complex". What is the Pacific complex? It is the curtain of fire, so well-known to seismologists, volcanologists, geologists and geophysicists as well as oceanographers. Most of Earth's volcanoes as well as the deep focus earthquakes are located upon the shores of the Pacific ocean. It has been called the "sea which is ringed with fire". Since neither Taylor nor Wegener seems especially concerned with this strange global condition, let us go beyond them to the theories of rifts and rifting for our answer. Again, with the help of these, worked into our combined complementary Taylor-Wegener hypothesis, we may find the answer to most questions of how the crawling rock crust upon which we live out our lives has moved in the past, and apparently is riding at present toward some inevitable destination while we build cities, wage wars and record the rise and fall of civilizations.

How Can We Explain The Pacific Curtain Of Fire?

Chapter 32

The Pacific Curtain of Fire
(After Daly, Cowen and others)

For any hypothesis to be workable, there must be an explanation for the unrest of Pacific shorelines, especially as that unrest is worldwide. What is happening to our planet? Is the shell cracking with giant tears, as some geophysicists have suggested when they followed the profound rifts through the Atlantic and Indian oceans and thence through the land masses to continue through the Pacific, like a cracking eggshell?

It might be asked what this has to do with the ancient Atlantic? Possibly what once happened in the Indian ocean and later in the Atlantic, partly explains what is now happening in the Pacific. At any rate let us briefly examine the Pacific complex and its possible explanations before we continue with the history of our planet, as worked out upon the plan of continental displacement.

As the beds of the Atlantic and Indian oceans follow the pattern of giant earth tears, the pattern of the Pacific ocean is one of the compression. The bed seems to be wrinkling before the push of the continental masses into its waves. For example, take the deeps. In the Atlantic the deeps are to be found to either side of the ridge, and when they do occur, they resemble closed basins or ancient lakes which gathered during the long ages of a slowly widening tear. On the other hand, the deeps of the Pacific resemble great wrinkles near the shores of the continental shelf. Their position would seem to indicate that the continental masses were bending the sea bottom before them as they shoved their way through the sima.

This wrinkling of the sea bottom is typical of the Pacific. For example, Japan leans over one of the most tremendous deeps of the planet. If we will take a closer look at the sunken ridge of Japan it seems to be an arcuate mountainous range showing pressure from the Asian coastline. Will Japan ever plunge into that deep? In our present state of knowledge, we do not know.

The Tonga islands are another example of this strange Pacific topography. These arcuate islands, perhaps once a part of fractured Gondwannaland, are now leaning over the abysmal Tonga deep, as if poised on the edge of a terrible plunge.

Over in South America the giant Andes cordillera of mountains look down upon another deep wrinkle - an Andes beyond the continental shelf - only in reverse - in depth instead of height. Also in South America, Beno Gutenberg and other seismologists have discovered that the earthquakes have various focal points in depth, and here are some of the deepest - one to two hundred miles below the level of the crust. These deepest focal points are all to the eastern side of the great Andes cordillera. What does this mean? Are the Andes getting ready to crack off from the rest of South America and start a ride into the Pacific?

In all of these cases it is evident that there must be a connection between the ride of the continental masses into the Pacific, and profound rifting. However this is a subject which takes in many theories, each of which apparently holds a partial truth and therefore at times must influence the flow of events, but on the other hand, since time and space are important, only the most obvious will be discussed. Other theories may be noted by the more interested student in the Notes on this chapter to come, then if he wishes, he may obtain the original volumes and go into them at his leisure. Only the theories having to do with volcanism and rifting will be discussed here.

What is known of the red hot mass under our thin crust?

The convection theory of Homes postulates that there is a probable uniformity from the 2900 kilometer level to the core of the planet, with convection currents transversing this space. These currents are the reason why the masses of the crust are dragged apart, said Homes.

The seismologists are not in agreement with this idea of Homes. James E. Macelwane insists that the earth has six shells. Gutenberg also says that there are several shells - three main ones with other lesser levels. Adams says that there are three main shells - Macelwane then specified the types. There is an outer mantle and an inner mantle of about six hundred miles thick whose density increases with depth. There is an intermediate core whose increasing density is doubtful, and an outer and inner core. Hodgson, in "Structure of the Earth as Revealed by Seismology", says: "we may consider Earth to be a sphere consisting of three main divisions: a central core with a radius of about 2,200 miles; surrounded by a mantle, a concentric sphere of less than one thousand miles thick; which in turn is surrounded by a crust of varying thickness which may be set down roughly as twenty-five miles."

Although these seismologists do not exactly agree with Homes, nevertheless Daly finds some reason to believe that lava could be conveyed upward in step by step convection. That the magma does come through a profound active rift when that tear reaches the mantle seems to be a geological fact. It has happened too often.

Joly believes that there is a west to east drive of the magma in the mantle due to Earth's rotation. This is borne out by the fact that the western lava flows of volcanoes always seem to be heavier than eastern flows.

Joly has a further theory which he calls "thermal release". In this he postulates that Earth carries within it a heating process due to accumulated radioactivity. The time of heat storage is thirty million years, says Joly and then when the melting point of basalt is reached, there is a great outbreak of volcanism which causes the continents to drift. As the crust cools it shrinks and mountains are folded with high peaks, which brings on a glacial age. The spreading of seas follows. This may be a factor, as according to Homes there can be heat storage due to stored radioactivity.

Joly was criticized by Daly and Jefferies as needing too many periods of thermal release, which are unwarranted by facts.

Pertinent to this theory of Joly is the Smithsonian Report of 1937 by Leason Adams, pp. 255-268, that below three hundred kilometers the temperature of Earth is nearly as hot as it was originally.

We now come to the Daly-Willis theory, which seems very necessary to our reconstructed hypothesis, especially when considering the "torn" oceans.

In metamorphic orogeny (mountain building) and continental genesis, Dr. Willis puts the stress upon the growth of crystals as a source of lateral compression and without doubt some of the missing motive power to start the continents splitting along the rift.

He points out that tidal and rotational forces have developed diagonally oriented zones of strain in the mantle and crust of Earth. This may well be an explanation for some of the great crustal tears. Many rifts have diagonal trends.

Willis finds that these strain zones are favorable to the welling and ponding of lava beneath the crust. Such local pockets could well reach the hundred-mile dimension. The stresses incident to the growth of such asthenoliths would ultimately cause eruption along the borders of a profound rift, and a central collapse. Probably this is the story of the Atlantic and Indian oceanic deeps. They are extinct asthenoliths from the collapse of the ridge.

Active asthenoliths, on the other hand, are characterized in their later stage by much lava, and are bounded by great mountain chains of volcanic formation. Because of the heat of these pockets, the rocks are metamorphized, which entails the formation of new crystals. As these minerals grow, largely upon the horizontal plane, they exert a tremendous pressure upon the sialic blocks to either side of the rift and pry them apart.

This seems to be a remarkably clear explanation for the great tears of the Atlantic and the Indian oceans and how two small beautiful streams grow to rivers and thence to rifts of the most profound type, finally turning into great sialic tears which give birth to oceans and sink the central land. Certainly, we also have a partial motive power for the prying apart of the lips of the rift and finally for the movement of the two sialic masses. The direction of movement would be away from the rift.

If this is the true picture of the birth of the Indian and Atlantic oceans, then the hardening and growing crystals from many remelting and cooling stages would certainly be some of the missing motive power which pushed the continents to either side farther away from the widening ocean.

However, this does not explain the Pacific, and so we have to search further among the theories of the experts. Finally the theory of Reginald Daly of Harvard, in which he discussed rifting with his eyes upon the ocean of compression rather than upon the disjunctive oceans which had attracted Willis, seems to be our answer. In his "sinking geosyncline theory", Daly tries to explain the Pacific complex. Geosynclines are river beds which, through thousands of years of silt and gravel deposit, gradually place a weight upon the crust which causes them to sink, pushing the crust down into the hot, glassy magma of the mantle and bringing on the tensional cracks of rifts. These become zones of weakness and when earth stresses become too sharp, rifting will take place at the geosyncline. When the rift reaches the mantle, the hot liquid will work through the crystalline belt, finally causing the geosyncline to founder by remelting at its base. The lighter sediments then resting upon the heavier cooled magma, become deformed by the advancing sialic masses toward such oceans as the Pacific. As those lands which are nearer the sea advance more rapidly than those farther to the rear, profound tensional cracks develop parallel to the shorelines, with block faulting. This is the term for such straight cliffs facing a profound rift as the Atlas range of Africa, or the eastern face of the High Sierras of California. Similarly, as the Draa depression is the line of the rift in Africa, so the lines of Death and (parallel) Panamint valleys is the rift line in California. These straight lines of cliff walls will always face the profound rifts.

According to Daly, as more sediments are

folded by the continuing pressure, the crystalline structure below is lost by remelting at the base, and the advancing coastline is raised as it rides over the foundered material. This is true of the California coast. There will be long periods of slowly rising beach. For example, the present writer inherited an oceanfront lot first bought in 1911. By 1931 the beach line had become so long that an organized company was fighting for squatters' rights between these lots and the sea. Also, in Long Beach, after the earthquake of March 10, 1933, which the present writer was fortunate enough to witness personally, and which came down the highway toward our car like giant earth waves, hurling some machines off the road, the beach line evidently sank a foot or so, for the sea invaded for a distance and much pleasure beach was lost to the public.

Also pertinent to the same subject was the rifting off of a strip of land some one hundred miles in width during the Pleistocene. As we know, at one time Catalina island, now thirty-six miles out to sea, stood in the center of this strip, while the shelf about that jutting island, as well as the rest of the shelf, is most interestingly deformed by the tremendous ice age rivers which poured down their channels during the time when this shelf was land, and a part of the coast of California.

Again we have here two very helpful theories of rifting. They are not mutually exclusive. Each contains certain facts which seem to explain other facts. True, Willis has his eye upon the Indian and the Atlantic, while Daly is studying the Pacific, but together they make a large scientific advance possible. Together with the revised Taylor-Wegener, and the help of Joly and Marsden Manson, the confused picture puzzle of our planet's history seems to be slowly coming into focus. Let us try out these theories against the known facts, and see if we do not have now some explanations for what have been seeming contradictions.

As for the name of this revised hypothesis, Taylor-Wegener-Daly-Willis being a little top-heavy with names, suppose we call the new hypothesis, thus revised with the help of many other scientists who must remain remembered but silent, the TW-DW hypothesis.

Thus, upon this platform let us review the magnificent drama of the past, played out upon the stage of our third planet circling a minor sun, lost in a swarm of other suns, swimming in a wheel-like formation through the spangled voids of limitless space.

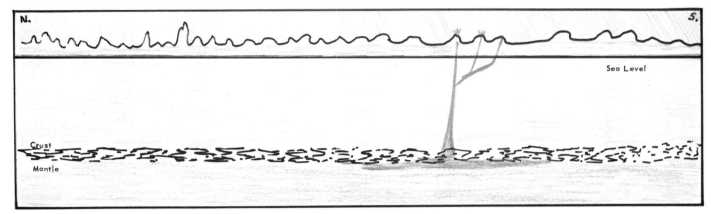

HOW LAND RISES FROM AND SINKS INTO THE SEA

Normal crust, north to south. Mountains have folded, inviting snow on peaks. The alternate periods of lava and ice begins with snow gathering on the northern mountains.

(Drawings are approximations, not intended to be geophysically exact.)

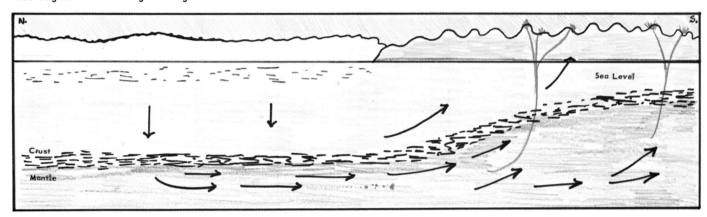

Ice sheet forming in north, wears down the mountains, and crust sinks under the tremendous weight. The sea level has been lowered by the amount of water locked up in the ice sheet. The magma in the mantle cools by the refrigeration above it, thus further sinking because of displacement of magma flows toward unglaciated land, causing it to rise as magma seeks release. (The same principle that causes a floating board weighted on one end to rise on the other.) As the magma is released in volcanism, the oceans and land warms. At this stage the magma returns northward.

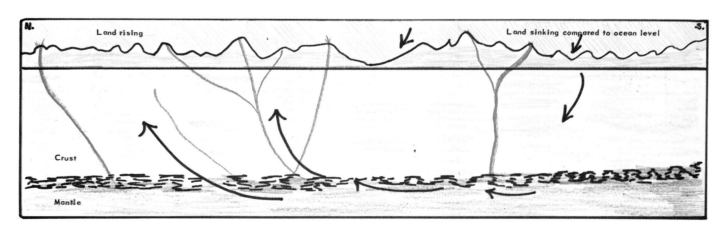

Now the interglacial begins. (The stage of our planet at present.) The glaciers are melting, seas becoming warmer, and its level rising. Land area shrinks, except in the north. There the magma is gathering for intense volcanism as it seeks release through the northern crust. The cycle will end when the hot interglacial is over and snows gather on northern mountain ranges to form another ice pack. Alaska and Hudson bay are now rising, the Baltic sea is shrinking, and perhaps the ancient forest which was once the source of the world's amber will grow again. The Scandinavian lands are rising and volcanism is already evident in Iceland (last remnant of the old red land). Mountain building will begin here.

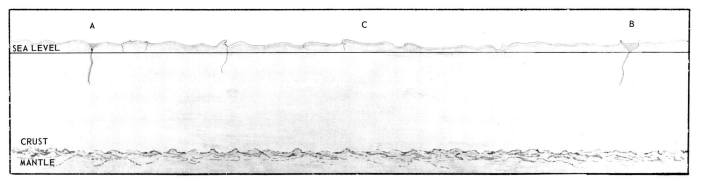

RIFTS AND HOW THEY FORM

A and B are rivers. C is a pleasant valley. Sea level line runs east and west. The crust is placid and normal in this stage.

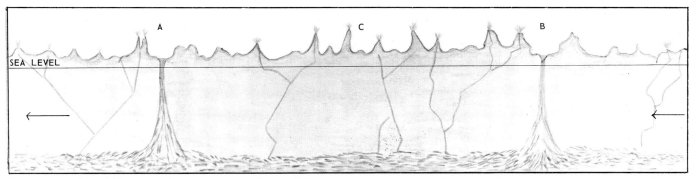

Here rivers A and B are reaching magma as lines of fracture. Pressure from east to west has been folding high mountains. Active volcanoes are in eruption, showing pressure of mountain-building.

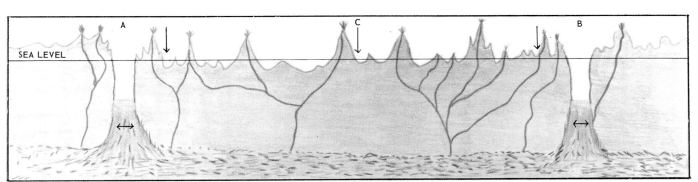

The rivers have reached magma as the site of profound rifts. The central portion, having lost its crustal anchors to either side, begins to remelt at the base, the sinking begins, volcanic activity is at its peak. The rifts widen, bases crumble to either side of rifts A and B. Valley C becomes a lake. Central land is still warm and fertile.

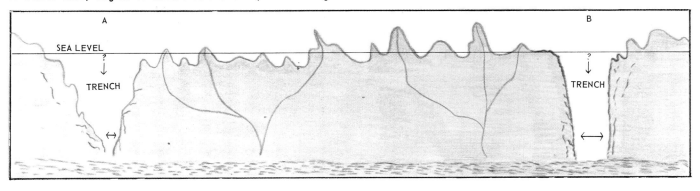

Hardening mantle under widening sea shores anchors further apart and central portion founders, where it remains submerged in isostatic adjustment about a mile below the surface. Scattered islands remain, with dying volcanic activity. The central portion has permanently foundered.

Chapter 33

Putting The Parts Together

The easiest way to follow the facts is to make a list of them and then see how the three competing main theories fit or do not fit the facts and the criticisms. Upon this basis a new hypothesis can be framed which will attempt to follow the facts, but use the good points of the competing theories, showing how the theories meet these points:

The following graph will illustrate how this may be done:

THE ARGUMENTS

1) The early northern glacial is not actually explained by any of the three. Wegener did not find it necessary to discuss it, but actually began his sequence of events with the Permian when the southern continents were glaciated.

Taylor placed the northern mass in the north, but how far north, and when, was not sufficiently discussed. Therefore the answer could be no more than partial.

The contractionist took it for granted that the first northern glacial was similar to the Pleistocene and from their point of view, needed no explaining. Therefore their answer is satisfactory according to their hypothesis.

2) The ancient gneiss shield of Amer-Eurasia now shows that North America has made a partial clockwise turn away from the point of separation. However, the ridge is needed for a perfect fit.

Wegener recognized the drift of North America west from the point of separation and the partial turn. His answer was satisfactory therefore.

Taylor also recognized the western movement of North America and the partial turn due to rotational forces. His answer was satisfactory. The question which was directed largely to the exponents of fixity of continents and oceans, were thus taken by surprise and had no answer.

3) The glacial moraines of the Pleistocene do not match. They need a folded land of five hundred miles between the shores of Europe and North America or a level land of one thousand miles. Also mentioned along this same line was the fact that the folds of the Appalachian-English-Urals are much more contorted in Labrador than they are in England, thus needing a missing section. The question was addressed to Wegener, but it was not answered by either Taylor or the contractionists. Wegener and Taylor should have been consulting the oceanographers at this point. Their answer was the Atlantic ridge - a folded mountainous land of five hundred miles breadth. According to their own belief in the fixity of continents and oceans, the contractionists felt that the question was a score for them and their silence was a satisfactory answer.

4) Shrinkage alone from the time of the Cambrian to the present, could not build Earth's mountain ranges.

The fact put forward by the geophysicists was meant as a blow at the contraction hypothesis. Both Wegener and Taylor had the pressures of movement on their side, while the contractionists, who were apparently somewhat stunned by this information, had nothing to say.

5) The Tethys sea was a Mesozoic fact.

This criticism of Wegener's Pangea found Wegener without an answer. Taylor had allowed for a Tethys with his two continents. The contractionists did not appear to realize that their explanation of sinking crust enough to allow a shelf sea was actually insufficient for the Tethys, as this was a real oceanic sea up to the end of the Mesozoic.

6) The biological distribution of plants and animals in the southern continents was one of the arguments put out by Wegener for his theory of Pangea. He did not seem to realize that in Pangea, with no barrier of a Tethys sea, his southern animals and plants could get into the north where they were not found until much later. His argument was actually for a Gondwannaland rather than a Pangea. The contractionists thought that they had won this one when the ornithologists declared the flightless birds were all descended from the pigeon. It was later that the parasitologists ended this idea forever and established the identity of the flightless birds as creatures of one family due to their insects, and totally unrelated to the pigeon. The unity of ancient Gondwannaland is a curious biological fact which is one of the greatest arguments against both Wegener's Pangea and the contractionists.

7) How were these theories to explain the pre-Tertiary, now partly sunken, ranges of both the Appalachian-English-Urals and the Easter-Capes-Kerguelin cordilleras?

This question was one which neither Wegener nor Taylor tried to answer, probably believing that their drifting continents had at some time in the past pushed them up, as well as afterward tearing them apart. The latter rifting was obvious, according to their theories, and therefore the answer was only a partial. The contractionists again had no explanation at all.

8) The pattern of the Tertiary cordilleras was given by Wegener as an argument for his Pangea. It is true that they do fit when the continents are pushed together. However the geophysicists such as Brower and Van Der Gracht were quick to point out that the cordillera faced the Pacific to the east in Australia and to the west in South America. Wegener answered that according to all continents going west, the American cordillera was being pushed up by pressure of a ride into the Pacific while the Australian one was being dragged. The answer brought him trouble from the geophysicists. Van Der Gracht, who had spent many years studying the folds throughout Dutch possessions before World War II, immediately informed him that pressure came from the inside of the arc. He was then, of course, asked the obvious: how could mountains be built up in one place from pressure and in another place from the tension of being dragged? This was one of the greatest blows which Wegener received.

Taylor did not sufficiently realize his advantage here to point out that he believed that all continents were riding into the Pacific, and therefore only scored a partial. Furthermore, none of the competing theorists seemed to recognize the relationship between the rise of the Tertiary cordilleras and the Pacific curtain of fire. Therefore both Wegener and Taylor should have been given a partial on this one instead of an entire unsatisfactory as many geologists believe. They were not entirely wrong. The contractionists on the other hand have no answer at all.

9) The twisted gneiss shield of Gondwannaland was mentioned by Wegener, who had done a very scholarly amount of research in defense of his theory. It was a partial to satisfactory for him due to the apparent eastern movement of Australia which he denied, but a blow at the contractionists.

10) The Cenozoic distribution of trees and animals in Amer-Eurasia (especially during the Pleistocene) was a blow at the contractionists who wished to bring some types found only on the two shores of the Atlantic around through Asia where they were not found. The march of the forests was a botanical Miocene fact which caught many contractionists by surprise.

11) The fit of the southern continents during the Permian was a fact brought out by Wegener against the contractionists. If Taylor and Wegener had allowed for a South Atlantic and Lemurian ridge they would have had a better fit and a more understandable rifting pattern.

12) The explanation of the Gondwannaland coal series was a fact which Wegener had noted as a continental match, but did not attempt to explain. Neither did the others.

13) Explanation of the sialic masses on the bottom of the Indian, Atlantic and South Pacific oceans was a fact which none of the contesting theories attempted to explain. Since the time of this general discussion in the American forum, and especially since the geophysical year, sialic fragments have been found upon the bottom of the Arctic ocean also. These may help to explain the heavier glacials during the Pleistocene.

14) There is a botanical fact which demands explanation. The South sea islands are covered by Triassic plants. These living fossils, not found elsewhere, demand some type of explanation. No theory was prepared.

15) Bowie's geophysical objection to the massing of continental rocks in one hemisphere was directed at Wegener, who was unable to give a satisfactory answer.

16) The metorologists' objection of Permian climates as opposed to present climates was directed at the contractionists. The placing of present tropical lands under glaciation while still in the tropics and the tropicalization of presently glaciated lands such as Greenland, at the same time, as the contraction theory demands, was found to be a geophysical and metorological absurdity. The contractionists did not have an answer.

17) The patterns of rifting were not too much discussed. It is a phenomena too newly discovered to have brought out many theories besides those of Daly and Willis.

18) The sunken river channels should have been one of the main questions, but was neglected. Before we can formulate any answers, we need more information as to the extent and weight of the Pleistocene ice load and the ability of the mantle, when punctured in a volcanic eruption, to manufacture new water.

19) The geophysical fact that a heavier mass moves faster upon a deeper plane was directed at the western drift of North America and the supposed western drift of Eurasia by Wegener. When Wegener was unable to answer, Taylor stepped in and explained that according to equatorial drift, Eurasia did move faster and upon a

The Chart

CRITICISMS OR FACTS	WEGENER WESTERN DRIFT	TAYLOR EQUATORIAL DRIFT	CONTRACTION FIXITY OF CONTINENTS AND OCEANS
1 Early Northern Glacial	unsatisfactory	partial	satisfactory
2 Gneiss shield of Amer-Eurasia now twisted	satisfactory	(for perfect match, ridge needed) satisfactory	unsatisfactory
3 Glacial moraines of Pleistocene do not match	needs ridge unsatisfactory	needs ridge	satisfactory
4 Shrinkage alone from the Cambrian on would not build present ranges	satisfactory	satisfactory	unsatisfactory
5 The Tethys Sea was a Mesozoic fact	unsatisfactory	satisfactory	unsatisfactory
6 Biological distribution of plants and animals of southern continents needs a route of communication before end of Mesozoic	partial	satisfactory	unsatisfactory
7 Explanation of Pre-Tertiary Ranges partly sunken	partial to unsatisfactory	partial to unsatisfactory	unsatisfactory
8 Tertiary Cordilleras pressure to Pacific and Curtain of Fire	partial	partial	unsatisfactory
9 Twisted Gneiss shield of Gondwannaland	partial to satisfactory	satisfactory	unsatisfactory
10 Biological distribution of trees and animals during the Cenozoic in Amer-Eurasia	satisfactory	satisfactory	unsatisfactory
11 Fit of South Glaciated lands in Permian	partial to satisfactory needs ridge	partial to satisfactory needs ridge	unsatisfactory

CRITICISMS OR FACTS	WEGENER WESTERN DRIFT	TAYLOR EQUATORIAL DRIFT	CONTRACTION FIXITY OF CONTINENTS AND OCEANS
12 Explanation of Gondwannaland coal	unsatisfactory	unsatisfactory	unsatisfactory
13 Explanation of Sialic contents on bottom of the Indian, Atlantic and So. Pacific	unsatisfactory	unsatisfactory	unsatisfactory
14 Explanation of Triassic plants on South Sea Is.	unsatisfactory	unsatisfactory	unsatisfactory
15 Bowie's geophysical objection of massing rocks in one hemisphere	unsatisfactory	satisfactory	satisfactory
16 The Metorologists objection to the distribution of Permian climates	satisfactory	satisfactory	unsatisfactory
17 The patterns of rifting	(as far as our present knowledge goes) satisfactory	satisfactory	satisfactory
18 The sunken river channels	needs more study of glacial load and also of the mantle and its ability to add water		
19 The fact that a heavier mass moves faster on deeper plane	partial	satisfactory	(addressed to drift geology only)
20 The problem of spreading seas following volcanism	partial	partial	unsatisfactory
21 How did the continents move?	on hot glass but not enough to initiate move, partial	rotational pulls but not enough to initiate movement, partial	(addressed to drift geology only)
22 What was the original motive power?	unsatisfactory	unsatisfactory	(addressed to drift geology only)

(Daly and Willis on this have partial answers. Also Manson) Daly—movement and rifting into Pacific; Willis the tearing of disjunctive oceans such as Indian and Atlantic by lava hardening; Manson by ice pressure; Joly by lava movement.

23 What causes Glacials?	unsatisfactory	unsatisfactory	unsatisfactory

(See notes on partial explanations from other theories)

24 What causes the Diastrophisms which change animal domination?	partial to unsatisfactory	partial to unsatisfactory	unsatisfactory

deeper plane than North America moved west. This pinpointed the fact that Wegener was wrong concerning Eurasia and Taylor was right.

20) The problem of the spreading seas throughout history is a strange one. During one period whole parts of Europe will be under water and later the wandering Tethys will be back in its equatorial bed. We have seen how lost islands are usually at the same level on the bottom of most oceans, just as the mid-Atlantic ridge is now located. We have also seen how Darwin proved that the Pacific bed is sinking - or the water level is rising, which gives the same effect. Whether this is caused by a wave-like motion in the crust in the case of the continental shelf seas we do not know, and more research is needed before we fully understand the problem. The answers of the three theories can only be partial to unsatisfactory. It is as much a problem for the volcanologists as any other scientific group. However, there is a strong tendency for modern theorists to suspect that the mantle is responsible for continually adding water to Earth's oceans.

21) How did the continents move? This question was directed only to the exponents of continental displacement.

Wegener believed that the mantle was a sort of hot glass upon which, given an initial shove, the continental mass would slide.

Taylor was of the opinion that rotational forces would cause the continents to slide toward the equator. Both may be partially right.

22) What was the original motive power? This was directed to the two theories of continental drift, and neither Taylor nor Wegener could answer. Since the time of the American forum, Willis seems to have come up with a partial answer in the growing crystals of a lava flow filling a rift. Manson seems to have a partial answer in the pressures of an ice sheet during a glacial. Perhaps if we follow the history of Earth briefly, we can see how this might happen.

23) What causes glacials, especially on one hemisphere at a time? This question was better met by the drift exponents than by the fixity of continents and oceans. However the place of the continent may not be the whole story. There are many minor glacial theories which certainly have partial truths, and for a major glacial to take place, there evidently needs to be many conditions which are just right for the growth of the glacial.

24) What causes the diastrophisms which end geological periods, and from which the dominating animal does not survive?

The exponents of continental displacement are in a better position to explain many of them than the contractionists. However, there is much research needed before this problem will be even partially understood.

From the expanse of the foregoing it will be seen that the problems of geology need a platform which makes use of the good points of these theories and casts out the ideas that clash with facts. In the cause of diastrophisms, for example, Joly suggested his theory that radioactive heat was stored in the crust until such a time as thermal release took place, and it was during this time that continents moved. Favorable to Joly is the fact that there is a good deal of radioactive heat being stored in the crust, but against him is the fact that he would need too many periods of thermal release to be warranted by facts, as pointed out by the geophysicists. Therefore we have here a partial truth which must be noted.

Any platform which is built upon the researches and partial truths of dozens of scientific thinkers must be pliable enough to meet new facts and at least partially explain some of the problems harassing botanists and zoologists as well as other groups.

The hypotheses herein discussed are not mutually exclusive, and in working them together, we may find a new platform. Probably where the hypotheses overlap, the truth may lie. It is a vast subject, and the number of interlocking causes perhaps contribute to the final effect. Undoubtedly no man can sum it up with finality because the intricacies of the various types of scientific knowledge needed are quite beyond one man's lifetime to acquire. Furthermore there is still so much to be learned that no hypothesis can be written which future information may not explode. Yet, the platform must be built so that future scientists can test out its planks as they push back the shades of the unknown. Science moves ahead across the stepping stones of its exploded hypotheses.

Therefore, taking the apparent truths of many theories, let us see how they may explain events, not only for the epoch we are discussing, but how they effect the next epoch to come. Only thus can we bring order of a sort out of chaos so that some day we will not only be able easily to read the past, but with a fair amount of accuracy, predict the future.

The most obvious names for this new combined hypothesis are the names of those who have given the great partial theories - we shall use Taylor-Wegener-Daly-Willis, or TWDW. The theory could become top-heavy with names (Joly, Manson and many others), but in recognition of brevity, they must be limited. Thus we will try to test this TWDW hypothesis against the facts as we know them. It is the hypothesis which Dr. Daly recognized as needful when he said there "should be a Taylor-Wegener hypothesis".

At least it will satisfy some scientists that something is being done to solve their problems, for as Dr. Camp, well known botanist and head of New York's Botanical Gardens, in a letter to the present writer, remarked tartly: "The geologists enter the forums with their cloaks of their own prejudices folded about them, and, like Omar the tentmaker, after hearing great arguments, evermore go out by the same door wherein they entered."

The TWDW hypothesis may not be the final answer, but as many geophysicists, geologists, paleontologists, zoologists, etc., from whom I have sought advice, have remarked in so many words:

"Some type of continental displacement is without doubt destined to become the geology of the future."

CHIEF CRAZY HORSE

War chief of the Dakotah (Sioux) in full war chief costume (Note exquisite feather and bead work.)

Original Indian painting by Fred Beaver

Chapter 34

The Background And Prelude As The Drama Opens

"In the beginning God created the Heavens ..."

Several scientists have remarked that the Bibical story of creation in the first few sentences of the book of Genesis is essentially correct if only the word "epoch" were to be substituted for the word "day". Both words stand for a period of time, the term "day" regulated by our day-star, while the other word signifies a period of unknown duration and to be measured only by events.

The prelude and background of this drama of our planet is more magnificent than most men outside the circles of professional astronomy are aware. In this regard it has also been said among men of science that if the studies of the chemist or physicist have caused him to doubt the existence of a Creator, the more the skeptic is exposed to astronomy, the more he will be driven to revise his opinions.

When Milton wrote "Paradise Lost", it was in bitter protest to the spread of science. He believed that the new subject was ruining the story of the Bible. How tragic that dogma closed his eyes! It is unfortunate that he wasted his magnificent style retelling an allegory very well done by the Bible, when the stupendousness of the actual facts, as recorded by the telescope, silence the tongue of any writer of lesser stature.

The day after the Mt. Wilson telescope was unveiled for the eyes of waiting astronomers, I was in my astronomy class at the university of California at Los Angeles, as usual. We felt something electric in the air when our professor walked up to the lecture platform. He seemed to be staring into space, touching our text absent-mindedly with his slender fingers. A hush fell over the murmuring students which lengthened into an almost embarrassing silence. Finally he spoke

"Young people, I do not know how I can begin to convey to you the turmoil of my feelings this morning. Yesterday, we were studying from this text. It was the best available. Today it is obsolete.

"Yesterday, we learned that there were a certain number of fuzzy stars which astronomers had reasoned were suns in the making - probably a collection of gases slowly condensing into the birth of a sun. We did not know for certain; that was a learned guess. We were wrong.

"Last night I was given the rare privilege of looking through the new giant Mt. Wilson telescope. I saw the heavens explode. I closed my eyes in unbelief, but when I opened them again, I saw the same unbelievable sight. My throat went dry and I could hardly breathe.

"Those fuzzy stars which we had thought were gasses of various colors condensing into suns, instead are island universes - some lesser and some greater in extent than ours. Nor were there only a few! they extend as far as the great telescope is able to see into the abysmal void of space. Like our own universe whose swarm of multicolored suns are as numerous as the grains of sand upon the desert, so each of these is composed of countless suns, some of which are so far away that if their light had been extinguished in the time of the dinosaurs, yet for us last night they were still shining.

"Two of these vast island universes I saw in collision. Also there is one where all of the suns seem to be falling into a central fire. What hells for a condemned soul to be born into - if the mystics of the far east and our own American Indian seers are correct in their belief that we return again in another body after the death of this one - but not necessarily to the same planet.

"Like spangles on black velvet, the suns of our own galaxy are beyond my own poor ability to describe. Not the pen of the finest poet could do justice to that sight, billions of stars flung in a massive swarm, all sizes and colors, some doubles and triples while still others with four partners of various shades, moving about each other in the slow, eternal dance of the heavens.

"Is it reasonable that only our sun should have planets? Only ours among these uncounted billions? Apparently not. In the island universes which are in collision, the space which has already been passed is brushed clean of all dark matter such as planets and satellites, while the part still to know its bath of flame is dusky with unburned matter.

"On the other hand, certainly not all suns have planets; yet, if only one in every five-hundred-thousand has a family of cold satellites such as ours, there would be civilizations out there somewhere greater than ours or lesser, younger or immeasurably older, and therefore, we hope, wiser. Fantasy? No. Who knows but what that strange civilization you conjured out of a cigarette and a flight of fancy is in existence somewhere at this very moment?"

Similar thoughts along these lines were voiced by Dr. Harlow Shapley in an article appearing in the February 1961 Coronet magazine. This ex-president of the American Association for the Advancement of Science believes that we give a bit too much grandeur to our place in the scheme of things.

"I would estimate that there are more than one hundred quintillion radiant stars in the sky - 100 followed by 18 zeros! Suppose that only one star in a million has a family of planets. And suppose that only one in a million of these stellar families has a planet like Earth. There would still be one hundred million planets suitable for life - one suitable planet for every trillion stars."

Farther he speculates upon life saying that "we are now confident that life will emerge whenever and wherever the physics, chemistry and climate are right." After discarding suns as being too hot and many planets as being too cold, he continues with the conditions necessary for the rise of life:

"1) Water must be available in liquid form - not cold ice nor hot steam. Therefore the distance of a liveable planet from its star - its source of light and heat - cannot be too great or too small.

"2) Some atmosphere is necessary. Therefore the planet's mass must be large enough to retain important gases. Hence we must eliminate all comets, meteors, asteroids, small satellites and wandering atoms and nebulae.

"3) The atmosphere must be oxygen rich, if air breathers are contemplated, and it must not contain poisons in sufficient abundance to kill off the air breathers. Hence no more strontium-90 than we now nervously endure, nor too much carbon monoxide." (Note the warning here against centuries of gas burning engines and the destruction of forests which change our own foul air to oxygen).

"4) The planet's orbit must be approximately circular; otherwise the temperature range throughout the planet's year would be unendurable.

"5) The planet's rotation must be such that the nights are not too long and cold, and the days are not too long and hot.

"6) The nourishing star must be reasonably constant in energy output. An exploding star would kill the organisms on its planets."

Then Dr. Shapley voices a most intriguing thought.

"But planets are not the only possibilities for life in outer space. There must be millions of astral bodies bigger than the largest planet and smaller than the smallest star. I call them 'Lilliputian stars'; and some of them could be of the right size and temperature to retain liquid water on their surfaces. They also could be massive enough to hold a life sustaining atmosphere.

"If life inevitably starts when the physical conditions are right, then some of these Lilliputian stars may have life on their watery or rocky surfaces. If so that life must be vastly different from that which we know. There would be no natural violet-to-red light and, therefore, presumably no sense of vision. The surface gravity would be great and any living organisms would have to adjust to enormous pressures."

What weird life form might inhabit such a dark, warm world? He continues: "We recognize (today) that we are acting in a play far grander than foretold in bygone times. Reverence then had to be supported with imaginings and superstitions. The facts of today far transcend the fictions of yesterday. To be reverent, we no longer need the crutches of supersition. Now many of old dogmas seem too earthbound, too egotistically man centered. With our Earth, moon, planets and bright stars exposed as motes in one star filled galaxy among millions, is it not foolish to cling blindly to the notion of a one-planet God?"

The astronomer continues: "After a half century of studying the heavens, I am struck by the inescapable conclusion that there is life in outer space; there must be. The laws of science leave me with no other rational belief." And he ends with the words: "We cannot escape humility. And as groping scientists and philosophers, we must be thankful for the mysteries that still lie beyond our grasp."

Upon such a spangled background, and with the symphony of galactic motion for a prelude, is the drama of our planet enacted.

Chapter 35

The Drama Of Our Planet

I remember that when I once asked Asa Delugio, sachem of the Mescallero Apaches, why they dance to the fire god who was old before the dawn of Christianity, he answered; "All begins and ends in fire." This might in a sentence, be the history of our planet. As yet, we do not know.

How Earth came to be, we can only offer theories which are learned guesses. I will mention three that have been given some credence. You may take your choice.

First there is the possibility that as the flaming gases which finally formed the sun began to condense, there were minor condensations from the center which formed the planets. Or we have the idea that Earth, as well as our sister planets, was formed by the attraction of cold debris of space such as meteorites. This flotsam thrown off by exploding volcanoes or colliding suns then is attracted by the force of gravity into again becoming part of a larger mass. If our Earth is thus slowly growing, it is also then becoming warmer, according to geophysicist Joly, because cosmic rays and other media bring with them radiation to be stored in the crust.

Finally we have the theory that in the distant past, some huge sun passed close enough to our day-star to break its envelope and pull out balls of burning metal, because of its gravitational pull. This theory might account for the various sizes of our planets. The ones at the greatest distance are the small ones, while those occupying the central position in distance from the sun are the largest, and those nearest the sun are again very small. Thus Jupiter, the largest planet, would represent the nearest approach of the visitor, and the four small planets near the sun - Mars, Earth, Venus and Mercury - would represent the lesser gravitation as the intruder sped away into space.

We do know that the earliest rocks of which we have any record are all igneous, or fire rocks. The igneous shields of gneiss upon which the continents rest are all volcanic. These oldest of rocks outcrop at many places: in Canada, upon the top of the Wasatch range; at the bottom of the Grand canyon; and apparently metamorphosed at other places. From this we have deduced that the early history of our planet was mostly written with volcanic flame and fire. When at last water did condense, it returned from warm rain to steam.

As we will be talking about the apparent ages of various rocks, it would be well to understand how today rocks are dated by science. This is called the uranium transformation method. When both lead and uranium occur together in the same piece of rock, otherwise free of these elements, it may be presumed that the lead is transformed or decomposed uranium. It is known that one million grams of uranium yield 1/7600 grams of lead per year. Hence the age can be determined from the proportion of these elements, or:

Age of rock equals weight of lead over weight of uranium times 7600 million years.

This gives a fairly accurate estimate, but when taking such hoary ages as various rocks of Earth, the differences could range within several millions of years.

When Albert Einstein was postulating his theory of relativity, he tried to imagine himself an impartial observer from another planet or sun system. Taking into consideration that the light from distant island universes dipped toward the red end of the spectrum, he suggested that space is a giant globe and that light is actually curved. This brings with it a very fascinating idea; that if we were borne away in a space ship moving faster than light can travel, we would be looking back, see the history of our planet run backward; or returning, we would see the whole drama reenacted before our eyes. With our magic mirror of imagination, we will try to capture this drama as it unrolls. In this we have the advantage of those distant island universes, whose astronomers, if there were some with instruments powerful enough to see our speck of dark matter, would be looking upon the great monsters such as Tyrannosaurus Rex in the jungles of tropical Pennsylvania, and telling each other that this world might be a very dangerous place to visit. The king tyrant with his thirty-six-foot length, eighteen-foot height and his meat eating four-foot jaw would be quite a discouraging host for visitors, especially since from his build, he was probably able to jump not unlike the kangaroo and also, like the Australian mammal, perhaps used his tail as an additional weapon.

There may be two other explanations for the dip of distant light toward the red. Light may just "get tired" after travelling for so many hundreds of millions of years, or the distant island universes may be exploding away from us; racing off at incredible speeds.

Returning from astronomy with our magic mirror of the past, let us view the history of our planet as far as it is generally known and see how this fits into the platform we have built out of six geological theories.

The curtain rises upon our drama to the accompaniment of exploding volcanoes upon the west coast of North America, Mexico and throughout the Antilles. Before the curtain rose they may have been four main continents. In the southern hemisphere there was a large Gondwannaland with a Polynesia attached, lying along the tropical line, where the warm swamps stirred with the first crude plants, one-celled animals, worms and perhaps other simple creatures.

In the northern hemisphere Amer-Eurasia had lain not too far from an Antillia consisting of much of Mexico and the gulf plate continent. Then a strange land came crashing in from the west. Where it came from we do not know. Nor do we know what had caused it to over-ride the west coast of Amer-Eurasia. Some authorities (such as Kober) have believed that this diastrophism closed an ancient Atlantic sea from now to the Jurassic, raising the high mountains upon the Atlantic ridge as North America bumped Europe. Apparently part of this unknown Pacific continent attached itself to the Amer-Eurasian mass - such as California and other states north to Alaska, as well as parts of Mexico. We will have to leave these studies to the work of young scientists following in both time and interest.

We do know that the thrusting from an overriding mass seems to continue its power for many millions of years, coming spasmodically and even deflecting later movements of the crust. Possibly the ancient direction of this crash is the reason that today California seems to be cracking in half.

Following this diastrophism, Amer-Eurasia, probably now with Antillia attached, drifted under the north pole - that location coming over Canada. This heavy icing was called the Proterozoic glacial.

Then the ice sheets ended with tremendous outpourings of lava about Lake Superior. Many very early forms of life died off in the warm seas. This was called the Proterozoic diastrophism. Earth now was ready to enter the time of the Paleozoic or "ancient life" epoch.

Thus with the fire of the Proterozoic lava sheets, and the renewed thunder of volcanoes, we will end the first act of Earth's story.

From the time when the curtain rose on Act 1 of the Proterozoic, until it fell, we have lived through between nine hundred to a thousand million years.

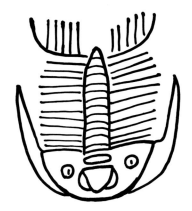

Chapter 36

Trilobite trail on mid-Cambrian sandstone.

TRIBOBITES
Four fossils from over five hundred million years ago. After Hussey, from "Historical Geology" published by McGraw-Hill Publishing Company, New York, 1947.

The Time Of Ancient Life

The Paleozoic (Pale-ee-oh-zoh-ik) opened with the thunder of volcanoes in the Appalachian-English chain running from west of Alabama through England to Asia. The pressures, if we run them back, point to the Proterozoic ice sheet. Was this what was causing the continents to move? The direction was toward the south-east. Possibly a south direction was given an eastern movement by the continued thrusting from the Pacific.

The great continent of Gondwannaland, lying in the tropics, now began to feel a shove from the northwest.

In the massive seas of this period we have our first real fossil. This little animal is called a trilobite. The name is made up of the Greek words for three and parts. Its body has three parts.

When I was attending the university of Illinois, I was lucky enough to find one of these strange little creatures on a geology field trip. With a pen-knife I dug it out of its encased matrix of rock, and with careful scratching, finally had it free. It was about an inch and a half long, curled up about a hole in its body probably caused by some ancient worm which killed it. To me the most amazing thing about this more than five-hundred-million year old fossil is the fact that it has a face. Of course the bumps which look like eyes are probably the place where feelers are attached to the head, but it has a definite mouth, which in my specimen is turned down with an expression of perpetual disgust.

There is something else curious about this little animal. I once heard a high school teacher say that after the rains at Tule Lake, California, the puddles which form on the old lake bed are filled with trilobites. This sounds fantastic and probably the man was not acquainted too well with the structure of the trilobite, but I urge some student of biology to take a trip to Tule Lake after a rain, preferably if he lives in northern California anyway, and wishes a Sunday outing. The trilobite has been extinct since the long-distant Paleozoic. Tule Lake, the scene of a Japanese camp during World War II, has been dry for many years.

After the raising of the Alabama-English cordillera of mountains, Gondwannaland began to feel its first bump from the northern sialic mass. To get a picture of what was happening, suppose we think of a boy tossing a rock into a lake very thinly coated with ice. The lake is our Earth, and the paper thin coating of ice is the sialic crust. As waves move out from the point of contact, they tend to move in ripples, some at greater and lesser distances from the main ripple. Where the ice is the thinnest, the ripple tends to break through. There also are usually one main ripple and several lesser ripples. Under the crust, these magma ripples are vast time epochs apart.

The next sign of our crustal lava ripple was the rising of the great central range of Gond-wannaland. This is the now sunken range running from Easter Island in the Pacific across South America and the South Atlantic, through the African capes out into the Indian to Ker-guelin on the Lemurian ridge. Here the central range turns and runs down the Lemurian spine into India. This ancient cordillera of mountains was also raised by pressures away from the Canadian ice center and toward the southeast just as the Alabama-English-Asian range was raised before them. The magmatic wave causing them did not stop here, but perhaps spent itself in the outward ranges of Australia and Antarctica as those continents were pushed from behind toward the Pacific.

Gondwannaland was riding, with high mountains and air filled with the ashes of volcanoes, toward its destiny with the south pole.

In the meantime, Amer-Eurasia was slowly drifting south. Apparently, judging from the deposits of the epoch, this drift was intermittent. A shove from the original center of the disturbance moves the mass forward, and then after its volcanism, it slumps into a sort of waiting period when perhaps a sialic creep takes over and the low worn land sinks to the level of shelf-sea invasion until the next thrust from the area of disturbance again sends it forward.

The Cambrian was a period of sea life only. The lands were barren. The sea animals were simple sponges and mollusks, brachiopods as well as other creatures starting to evolve into more complex forms. This period lasted about five hundred million years.

The Ordovician period followed with the first primitive fish. The period was relatively quiet. It lasted about four hundred million years.

This period was followed by the Silurian. The euphonious name came from a Celtic tribe living near Wales known as the Silures. Sea scorpions have now arrived. And even more interestingly, the first strange land plants. During this period and the preceding Ordovician, Amer-Eurasia was becoming warmer and water was spreading over the land. For example, during the Ordovician one could have sailed a ship over most of the United States and Canada. Unlike the very early seas which had no lime, corals were now able to make reefs. Most of the salt which we use on our tables today is from these early seas of the Silurian.

During the following period, the Devonian, California was shaken by earthquakes and rained with the ashes of volcanoes from another crush of western pressure. This is the period of the old red sandstone, a famous landmark of Amer-Eurasia. In the great stretches of Arizona and New Mexico, one may still see the remains of the turmoil of the time in the volcanic vents thrust through the picturesque buttes of the old red sandstone, and often weathered away until only the lava throat of an ancient volcano is left standing starkly against the sky. The volcanism also shook the Appalachians and the mountains of the central ridge, which were high, judging from the amount of Paleozoic detrials. In between the times of volcanism were periods of quiet in which a shelf sea existed from Maine through much of Europe and eastern Russia. Small animals crossed back and forth upon the shoals.

The Tethys was a wide sea at this time, flowing over Italy, Spain, Panama and the northern part of South America.

On the land strange plants were living along the marshy shores of Amer-Eurasia. Some were almost rootless. Some were leafless and yet from them we can trace many of our plants of today. Our small ferns and club mosses were towering trees in the weird Devonian forests. If you live near Albany, New York, you will be able to see some of these plants in the state museum and ponder upon the forests which once grew on the land which you now own for your short lifetime and perhaps where you have built your home.

As far as the west is concerned, the weird

The Archaean shield and Proterozoic cordillera of Appalachian-English-Urals.
(Compiled from Daly, Dana, Chamberlin and Salisbury)

blue-grey smoke tree with its needle leaves seems to be a living relic of these far off times. It is indeed an irony that this charming plant so loved by the artists is rapidly becoming extinct due to its almost fantastic sensitivity to being "raised" from seed by despairing nurserymen, while transplanting on account of the tap root (ten times the height of the plant) makes the procuring of a large tree almost an impossibility. No wonder there is a two-hundred-dollar fine for taking samples from this rare wild plant!

Apparently the Devonian was a sort of resting stage in general. Gondwannaland had pulled away from its first great push while Amer-Eurasia was gathering its forces for another shove toward the southeast.

The Devonian lasted between three and four hundred million years.

The Devonian, when Amer-Eurasia went through temperate climate and desert, was followed by the hot Carboniferous. The northern mass was now under the equator. Pennsylvania was sweltering in a weird jungle of tree ferns and mosses. Insects had arrived and with them their enemy, the spider. Reptiles filled the hot forests while dragon flies almost two feet long floated lazily above the swamps. Some cold winter night when you go to the coal bin, pick up some of these fossil remains of this jungle and

see if you can trace the outlines of a fern or insect. The long Carboniferous of over two hundred and fifty million years accumulation of trees and animals rotting in the hot swamps of so many aeons ago, has kept our modern world warm for well over a century. The coal belt runs from Pennsylvania to Spain.

Toward the end of the Carboniferous there was an increasing see-saw movement of the Amer-Eurasian crust. The swamps would dry off and grow a forest cover only to submerge, and the process would then be repeated. There may be two explanations for this long repetition starting in the mid-Carboniferous and then becoming even more pronounced with the approach of the Permian: either the pressures which apparently closed the Tethys sea at the end of the Permian were gathering power in the old northern center of disturbance for the final tremendous shove to the southeast or, Australia having now moved under the vicinity of the pole, was becoming glaciated with the inevitable remelting of the ice with lava outflows and thus causing a fluctuation of sea level. Or both of these factors may have been at work and probably were to complicate the picture.

The hot Carboniferous was followed by the cooling Permian. The period only seems explainable by suggesting that Amer-Eurasia was

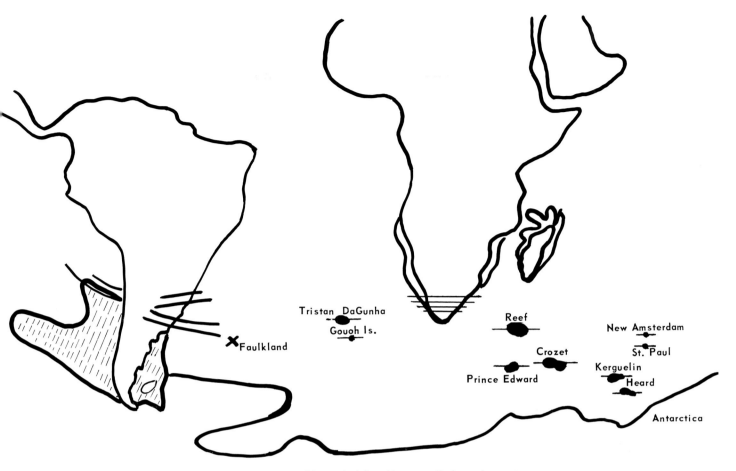

GONDWANNALAND (Compiled from Wegener, Daly and Dana)

beginning to feel the first nudges of the coming thrust from the southeast not to be actually manifest in full for the next epoch of time, the Mesozoic. The south pole was now drifting over the northern Indian ocean land - or in terms of the time, the bend of the great central range of Lemuria was drifting under the south pole. Thus the polar region was presented with a continental mass for the base of one of the planet's greatest glacials, known as the great southern Permian glaciation.

In the meantime, the forces of the old disturbance in Canada were gathering for another great magmatic wave which was now about to shove Gondwannaland again to the southeast and close the Tethys sea. The magma had apparently reached the Mediterranean line of weakness and the first volcanism hit the Antilles and then the Alpine cordillera as the Tethys began to close from the west to the east. This Paleozoic bump probably bowed up both continental masses of the north and south while the volcanoes lit up like a string of roman candles along the Mediterranean cordillera, starting with those of the Antilles.

Thus in the rain of volcanic ashes both Amer-Eurasia and Gondwannaland were further cooled. According to Schuchert the very early Alps, Atlas, Antilles and Saharides were raised with great volcanism at this time and many authorities believe that the Tethys was closed now with pressure again to the southeast. The insects who had lived in the hot swamps either learned to live in cooler air or perished. Amphibians, those creatures which live in both land and water, began to spread widely over the lands. On the other hand, the trilobites which had lived in the seas for untold millions of years now became extinct. Was it because lava flows had heated the waters past the point of their endurance? And if so, why did the fish and some other animals escape? Was it because some types were able to flee the area of danger?

Before we bring the curtain down upon the Paleozoic or time of ancient life, let us take one last look at the massive glacial of Gondwannaland with which the epoch closed. Then the second act of our planet's history will be over.

Chapter 37
The Great Southern Glacial

As Gondwannaland had ridden south during the long Paleozoic, the pressures which had folded up the great central range returning intermittently from the northwest to the southeast had kept the land fairly high, while the volcanism of the highland peaks had probably screened the suns rays much of the time with volcanic ash.

Perhaps all the needed factors worked together to make this one of the planet's greatest glacial periods. There may have been a stray visiting sun to cause more than the usual number of magnetic storms. Undoubtedly our Earth had entered her eliptical orbit placing the maximum coolness upon the southern hemisphere at the most strategic period possible, while certainly much ash screened the rays of the sun. Perhaps our sun had carried its family of planets through a dark matter-dusted area of space, while the crust of the southern mass, moving toward the pole with one of the highest chain of mountains in the world, had been cooling for untold millions of years. The details of these factors I leave to later students.

For a moment let us look at the geography of this land. The river systems are extremely important, for as the drainage followed the deeply dug geosynclines to the sea, so the ice moved later, and still later this would be the pattern of rifting.

We know that the rivers moved as all rivers

The Great Southern Glacial--
Its probable extent in ancient
Gondwannaland.

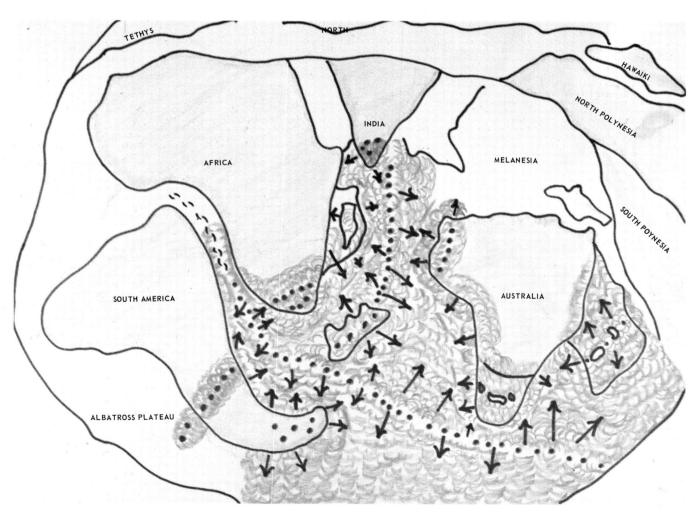

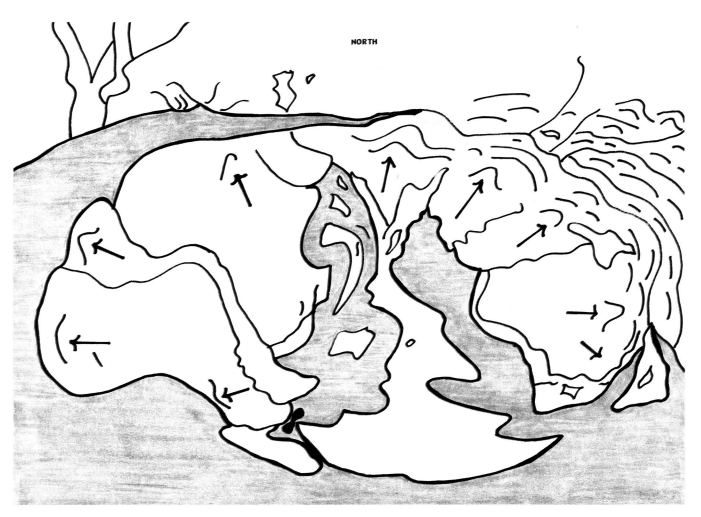

Gondwannaland at the time of the still land-locked pole,
showing the possible fresh water lake north of Antarctica.

do, from the highlands to the sea. In the Atlantic, that is the southern Atlantic, rivers must have moved down either side of the south Atlantic ridge from the great central range to the Tethys sea. Let us call them the southwest Atlantic river and the southeast Atlantic river. The southwest must have drained South America and the ridge from the highlands north while the southeast river must have drained Africa and the ridge north to the Tethys sea. Upon the southern side of the great central range, there must have been a west Gondwannaland river running from the range with tributaries from either side of the ridge and making its way to the Pacific between the tip of South America and Antarctica. It may have had eastern tributaries also draining the northern side of Antarctica.

In what is now the Indian ocean, there were probably two rivers running to either side of the Lemurian spine from the curve of the great central range to the Tethys sea. Let us call them the west Lemurian and the east Lemurian rivers. The west Lemurian must have drained eastern

Africa and the west side of the Lemurian range while the east Lemurian must have drained Australia and the eastern side of the Lemurian range. To the south of the great central range, there must have been an east Gondwannaland river, flowing from the great central range between Australia and Antarctica to the Pacific. Possibly as the land wore down there may have been a fresh water lake on Gondwannaland to the north of the present shores of Antarctica.

During the time that the old continent rode toward the south pole, these rivers must have cut very deeply as the height of the land continued to rise from the intermittent pressures from the northwest toward the southeast. Possibly these geosynclines reached or even cut into the gneiss shield.

As the continental crust continued to cool, the magma base was evidently hardened to some depth, and the vents of the volcanoes upon the great central range frozen under impacting ice. We all know how a glacial starts. Snowflakes, swirling down through millions of winters, pack upon the high points of a range where the temperatures stay below the freezing point. In time these peaks become the fountainheads of a glacier moving down the side of the mountain range into the valley below, carrying everything movable with it, and scouring its way through the accumulated sediments of the ages to bedrock.

However, when this ice front reaches the valley, if it should meet another ice front coming from the opposite direction, the embattled fronts must exert upon each other and the rock upon which they are riding a tremendous lateral pressure. I believe this lateral pressure is one of the main causes for the inception of a rift.

After many thousands of years of such pressures the rock base may start cracking. When this crack finally gets deep enough, and the magma wells out, then the ice will melt back rapidly in steam and warm rain. It might be argued that the embattled fronts finally join to continue down the valley as one mass. Of course, this is true, yet the original embattled condition of the ice fronts continues because of pressures from the fountainheads behind, and this pressure does not stop until the magma wells out of the rift and melts back the ice thus temporarily destroying the fountainheads.

As an example of what happened, let us take the west and east Lemurian rivers making their way upon either side of the Lemurian ridge with its very high mountains, from the African capes to the Tethys sea. Most authorities agree that during the Paleozoic era this was probably the scene of the planet's highest mountain chain. As the pole invaded Gondwannaland from the direction of Australia; or rather, as Gondwannaland drifted under the pole; these mountains must have carried the fountainheads of a very heavy ice load.

At the same time, the high African capes must have had their own fountainheads which poured down the southeastern part of Africa and into the west Lemurian river to meet the battlefront of the west Lemurian sheet. Even though this mass of ice apparently merged to move down the valley toward the Tethys sea, nevertheless, at the base where the two sheets continued to collide directly for untold thousands of years, the lateral pressure could have knifed its way finally through the crust, starting a rift at this point which would slowly tear its way both north and south.

If at the same time the sheet coming down the eastern side of the Lemurian range was meeting in the eastern valley a wall of ice coming from glaciated Australia, we have the embryonic condition for a profound double rift running parallel down the entire land which today is the Indian ocean.

This picture of what happened will probably have to await further corroborating evidence from studies made in Antarctica during the geophysical year of 1961 on the ice sheets. However, from what information has leaked out, there are vast earth crevasses below those of the ice.

When this rift finally reaches the hot magma of Earth's mantle, and it wells up upon the crust, then obviously the ice will melt back rapidly in steam and warm rains, while the mountains upon the lip of such a rift will again become active with volcanism. Then if Joly is right that this thermal release is the time of continental displacement, the direction of that movement must be away from the area of the rift, thus following the tendency to retreat from perhaps a million-year pressure. Also if Marsden Manson is correct, this outwelling of the magma will so heat the crust that for thousands of years the ice will not re-form. Warmth loving plants and animals will return (after the pluvial when the ice is returning to the seas to raise sea level) and a full interglacial will be in progress. As the magma cools in the rift, the same direction of drift, away from the rift, will continue to be felt throughout the continental mass because of the growing crystallization in the hardening magma.

However, it is obvious that this interglacial, although thousands of years in length, is still a temporary condition. The continental mass is still too close to the vicinity of the pole, and in the case of Gondwannaland, that pole is still land locked. The mountain ranges are still high, especially on the lips of the rifts, and as the crust gradually cools, the conditions for another glacial sheet will gain headway. Finally when the crust has cooled enough to retain its ice, the second sheet will begin to form, like the first sheet, upon the fountainheads of the high peaks.

All conditions now will be repeated. The ice fronts will again meet in the rifted valley, wider of course from the first rifting, but the pressures will be identical when the opposing battle fronts of ice meet once more. When the old tears reopen, they will travel further north and south with each new convulsion.

This repetition of ice and lava should continue until at last the sialic anchors of the various continental parts have been knifed asunder, and the continental parts slide away from the rift toward their own directions.

What has happened to the deserted sialic

Gondwannaland, after the continents had drifted apart.

fragment of the Lemurian ridge? Each time the profound rift to either side of the ridge opened and filled with magma, some of that burning rock came from under the base of the ridge itself, as well as from the lips to either side. Thus when these rifts to each side of the ridge again began to cool, the sialic fragment between would be left lower in the crust, and much of its old territory would be lost through remelting.

That is why, after many openings of the rifts with their out-welling of lava sheets, and the retreat of the continental masses to either side of the double rifts, the sialic fragment which had been the ridge with its high mountains will lie along the floor of the widening ocean in a fragmentary and submerged condition.

But now for a moment let us back up. This rifting which we have been explaining probably took place during the next epoch, the Mesozoic. Some authorities would even place the final submergence of Lemuria at the very end of the Mesozoic, and we are talking about the Paleo-zoic, or the second act of Earth's drama, not the third act.

Our second act ends with the Tethys sea closing from a last shove to the southeast raising the ancestral Alps, Saharides, Antilles and others along the transverse cordillera, the action moving from the Antilles east, while Gondwannaland was under one of the planet's heaviest glacials.

The question which seems to be posing itself is: does it take one entire epoch for the magmatic crest from a disturbed glacial center to reach the Tethys sea? If this is true, then we should expect the aftermath of the Permian glaciation to strike the Tethys at the end of the next epoch, the Mesozoic, or the age of reptiles.

Thus although the fiery curtain of our second act comes down with lava and flame, it leaves us with an impending sense of coming drama, or great climax, terrible in its fury to be visited upon the Tethys at the end of the next epoch - the time of the Earth's great dragons.

Chapter 38

The Dragons Rule The Earth, Then Continents Collide

As the curtain goes up on Act Three, the background of plants would be something more like what we would recognize today, yet the animals which wandered below their shade might be denizens out of a nightmare world. One could well imagine landing on Venus with its always-cloudy skies, its sultry humidity and enervating heat and find waiting a Mesozoic Earth, reincarnated with all its dangers and blood curdling sounds.

The Triassic saw the rise of the dinosaurs (the terrible lizards), the strange leathery flying lizards called pterodactyls (the finger-wings) and primitive mammals (those creatures on our stem), with hairy bodies and warm blood, who bear their young alive and suckle them with milk.

The Triassic was also the time of giant fern forests, with trailing mosses and exotic plants which today we find largely in the lovely South sea islands of Polynesia. No wonder that this is true, for the "Islands of Paradise" are botanically Triassic fragments. At the end of the ancient Triassic, they were rifted off from the other sialic masses of the planet, and so today in their isolation they carry the strange plants and lovely ferny forests of that long past era.

Thus botany, the study of plants, comes into Earth's story to tell us that Polynesia was once a part of Gondwannaland, probably connected to Australia, but sometime during the Triassic it was cut off, and began a journey into the Pacific. It had evidently been a fairly good sized continental mass, of which only the tops of its mountains show above the sea today. Yet its remains still carry the ancient plants which tell its story. From them we know that it was a part of Gondwannaland and that it lost its connections during the Triassic.

In fact it is hard to think of the Triassic without thinking of Polynesia: the so-called "Triassic fragment". As mentioned before, the extensive work of Charles Darwin upon the corals of the Pacific islands has given us a much clearer view of this sialic remnant than we would otherwise have. Not only did he find coral reefs at depths which were beyond the liveable limits of the coral animal, but he also found that many of the bombs thrown up by island volcanoes were partly composed of coral, thus implying a great amount of subsidence into the sea since the lava had carried coral up from almost plutonic depths. From these facts, Darwin deduced that there had once been a much more extensive land exposure than these islands carry at present. He placed the time of this larger continental mass in the Pleistocene ice age, or within the last million years.

There is of course, another explanation for this land exposure which does not demand the sudden sinking of this sialic mass of Triassic times into the magma during the last million years. There may have been a vast retreat of sea level due to Pleistocene lock-up of the water in ice. This would have the same effect of exposing greater tracts of land, and the exposure of the land between the old mountain tops would encourage a redistribution of the Triassic flora. Here is a field awaiting the studies of some upcoming young botanist interested in this ancient flora. The present distribution of plants should tell us a great deal about the extent of this old Pleistocene land and also give a fair idea of when the Pacific claimed most of its surface and thus again isolated the species. To encourage that scientist to step quickly forward, the present writer would like to add that there is only one specimen of one ancient tree type and only two of another in Hawaii alone which will soon be lost to science. Of course we also need the help of the parasitologist to reinforce the dates given by the plants. These studies should add significantly to the geological and oceanographical knowledge of the planet.

It seems to be a fair question to ask if the fact that Australia was the first part of Gondwannaland to be glaciated was not significantly connected with the fact that it was also the first part to be rifted off?

It seems to be also significant that during the Triassic the small reptiles of the period, according to Du Toit, were wandering back and forth across the south Atlantic from Africa to South America with the ease that a land animal only obtains upon dry land. Thus we are quite certain that the cracking of Gondwannaland began in the east and at this time had not yet reached any part of the Atlantic.

The Triassic, (pronounced Try-ass-ik) lasted about two hundred million years. It was followed by the Jurassic (pronounced Jure-ass-ik), famous for the entrance upon the world scene of the giant lizards.

The pterodactyl, whose leathery wings were joined to the little finger of its front claws, now flew from land to land. This strange flying lizard probably unwillingly shared its feeding grounds with the toothed bird, whose front feet were still to be seen at the bend of his wings. Possibly he used them as a balance when running after his prey. That prey must have been the insects of the period and perhaps even the small primitive mammals.

Australia in the start of the violent closing of the Tethys sea had been thrust into Asia, before its northern rifts knifed it free. During this period, some of its plants migrated through Asia and into both Japan and the Philippines. It seems more reasonable to assume that the Australian plants migrated through Asia than it does that these large islands of the northern Pacific came from a Gondwannaland connection. However that may be, before the end of the Jurassic both Japan and the Philippines had been isolated and now carry a Jurassic flora, with some interesting minor complications which I leave to a later student to unravel. For example, the tarsier (tarsius spectrum - the tiny mammal with front eyes giving three dimensional sight, and the opposite thumb similar to the other primates who have hands) lives in both the Malay archipelago and the Philippines, yet these creatures did not arise until the Paleocene. Is this due to another case of lowered sea level during the Pleistocene? And how about the migration of such trees as the maples from Japan to America? What land connections did these Jurassic fragments have during the Pleistocene?

In this strange world of the Jurassic, which lasted over a hundred and fifty million years,

trees apparently learned to grow tall to escape the jaws of such reptiles as the Brontosaurus (the herbiferous thunder lizard). He usually liked to lie in the water of swamps, half submerged, all sixty feet of him, perhaps because the water helped to support his twenty tons of weight. When he did wish to eat of the succulent leaves of a tree, he undoubtedly balanced on his hind feet, using his powerful tail as an additional support. It is wrong of course to say that the trees "learned". What happened instead is probably that the tallest trees were more often spared to scatter seeds than the smaller trees which had their foliage eaten.

In this curious world of the Jurassic, the seas of the time held a swimming reptile which indeed was a monster. The animal had a small body, relatively speaking, with flippers, but the long neck with its serpent like head and the very long tail made it resemble the sea serpent of legend. These creatures have been thought to be extinct, yet the oceans of the earth have such a variety of climates and depths, that it is not beyond reason to believe that a few may still be alive. Certainly the sight of one lying dormant or asleep on the top of the waters could well start the sea serpent tales with which our childhoods were enchanted by some sea going uncle while the rest of the family listened very skeptically, or on the other hand, would cause a celebrating tourist upon the deck of a pleasure ship to swear off liquor forever. More than one so-called extinct creature has turned up in the nets of oceanographical expeditions.

In the lush swamps of Wyoming where the dragons of the Jurassic and Cretaceous fought and mated, the jungles of the day must have indeed been a nightmare world. One can well imagine how the small animals of the period had to learn to live on the high mountains, growing a heavier coat of fur to keep warm, or burrow deeply underground to escape the monsters. Even the tops of trees would hardly be safe from the gigantic meat eating Tyrannosaurus Rex (the King Tyrant lizard), terror of the Mesozoic. He could easily have pushed over a tree or with his powerful tail, slapped unfortunate occupants out of it to their doom.

My grandfather, who had ridden much of the western part of the United States on horseback before there were good roads, told of coming to the top of one mesa and facing a stretch of unbroken desert - I presume in Arizona or New Mexico. Leading to a distant craggy hill the sand had been whipped from a long clean bit of sandstone which evidently had once been a Jurassic

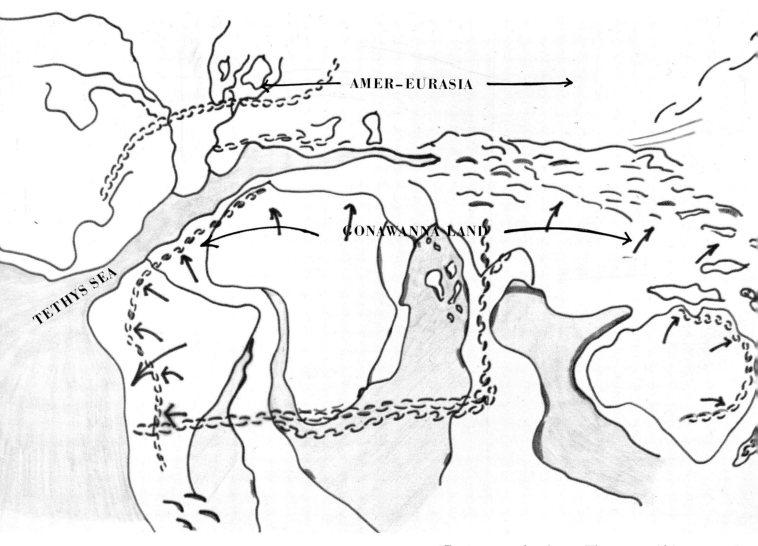

AMER-EURASIA

GONAWANNA LAND

TETHYS SEA

COLLISION!
The Tethys was closed from the east.
Compiled from studies of Wegener, Taylor,
DuToit, Schuchert, Daly, Joly, Gutenberg
and others.

or Cretaceous horizon. There, as if it were only yesterday, a huge reptillian monster had walked over what had once been wet sand, leaving very plainly the enormous tracks of his bird-like toes and the drag of his heavy tail.

Undoubtedly between that day when my grandfather rode to the mesa and today, the prints have been dug up by curio seekers or possibly have found their way into museums. Perhaps this may have been the location from which came the huge print that is to be seen today beneath the dome of the state capitol building in Salt Lake City, Utah. At any rate, it is amusing to watch the eyes of children as they try to match the lengths of their hands to the toes of the extinct monster.

In the present dry Gobi desert of Asia, where once the dinosaurs flourished in the

Aftermath - Australian collision.

swamps of the Mesozoic, Roy Chapman Andrews made the discovery of his lifetime. He found their eggs. Until this discovery science was not certain that the monsters had made nests of eggs like the turtle and other living fossils of the period, and had wandered away, allowing the sun to hatch them.

Incidentally the eggs of these creatures are rare and therefore a highly desirable rock. They are to be valued even above the meteorites, those metallic substances which strike our planet from outer space and make us wonder from what exploded sun or ancient planet they originated. The dinosaur egg is not a large rock for such a gigantic animal. It can be held in the hand. However, if upon slicing one open lengthwise, the fortunate "rockhound" who found it should see therein the skeleton of a lizard, he should not try to sell it as a curiosity, or cut it up for color, but take immediate notice of the exact location with as many samples of different kinds of surrounding rocks as possible, and then com-

municate with the nearest geologist or paleontologist to be found at the local museum or university. We hope that in the future there will be more such finds, when those who make their week end hobby of finding and then polishing beautiful rocks into attractive jewelry, become fully alerted to these scientific treasures.

It seems hard to believe that the small lizard which scampers across the hot floor of the desert from Death valley to Montana, from one rock to another, holding its tail high to keep it from the hot ground, is the distant cousin of these monsters. Yet the dinosaurs, whose armored hides could easily turn a rifle bullet, are strictly the denizens of the Mesozoic, (pronounced Mess-oh-zoe-ik) or time of middle life. From the Triassic when they arose, through the Jurassic and Cretaceous when they were the monarchs of their world and dominated all living things, indeed the Mesozoic is well named as the age

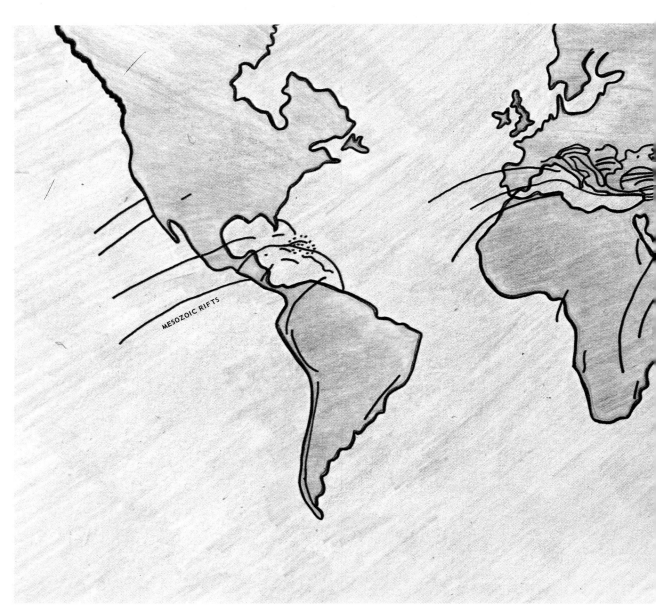

MESOZOIC RIFTS

of reptiles.

The Cretaceous (pronounced Cree-tay-shus), whose meaning is chalk, followed the Jurassic and was the last period of the Mesozoic. It has been called the fiery Cretaceous for good reason. Probably no period in all of Earth's history has been so furiously disastrous, yet the volcanism neither began with the Cretaceous nor did it end when the period had closed.

The name was given by two German geologists to certain German formations of the time which are not composed of chalk. The white substance which schools use to write upon slate blackboards is a marine deposit often to be found upon the lips of profound rifts. However, many chalk outcrops are Cretaceous in age.

At the dawn of this period Amer-Eurasia was still lying quietly about sea level. The Tethys sea had invaded the old gulf plate which for most of Earth history had been land. The rocks show that this flooding was slow and intermittent. The swamps which had been the kingdom of the Mesozoic dragons, would burn with the ashes of volcanoes, sink below sea level, and then again rise to grow another forest. It was as if some great force from the southeast was periodically pressing down the plate or gneiss shield. Then for many thousands of years the pressure was lessened while the rivers carried the silt down to grow another jungle, only to have the volcanism announce the coming of renewed pressure.

The Tethys sea, however, had invaded much of Eurasia and had cut North America in half from Canada to the Mexican gulf plate. The north Atlantic ridge was probably land due to its

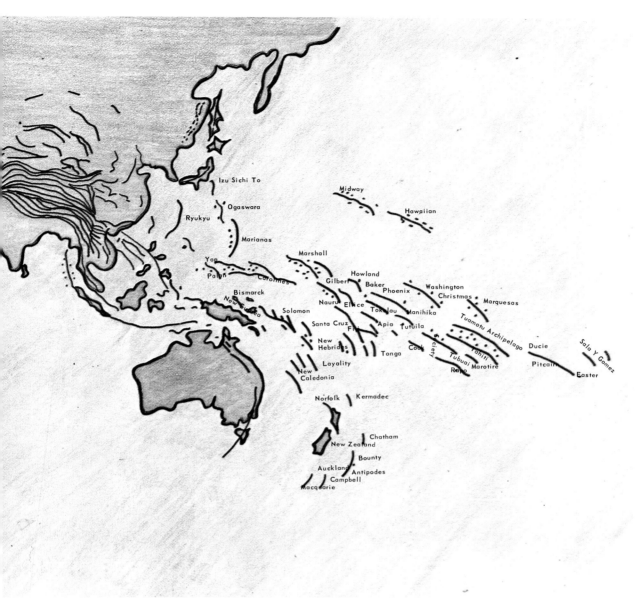

Aftermath - The Great Mesozoic Cordillera.

mountains, while the south Atlantic was land almost to the capes. We know this because the earliest primates who came into being and spread during the next period, the Paleocene, moved from South America to Africa at will.

As for the north Atlantic, the cycads or palm trees moved from shore to shore, as did the maidenhair or gingko, populating both America and Europe. Sequoias covered Greenland, Iceland and arctic America. Today these living fossils of the Mesozoic are taking their last stand in China and California. They are magnificent giants, and to walk down their aisles, now protected in small stands from the woodsman's axe, is to touch time itself. It is well worth a side trip to see the sunlight filtering down from their towering foliage roof of some three hundred feet high while through some of their gigan-

tic red trunks, in places a road has been cut in which one can drive his car. The burl or living part of the root from which often a new tree will spring, can be purchased for a very reasonable price, and if placed in water, will start a tiny forest of its own.

Upon the other hand the gingko, although at one time as warmth loving as the palm, has learned to adjust to a variety of climates, although rapidly becoming extinct. To lovers of strange trees for their homes, this fossil of the Mesozoic is to be distinguished by its leaves which are like tiny green fans. In the fall it sheds its leaves with a magnificent display of

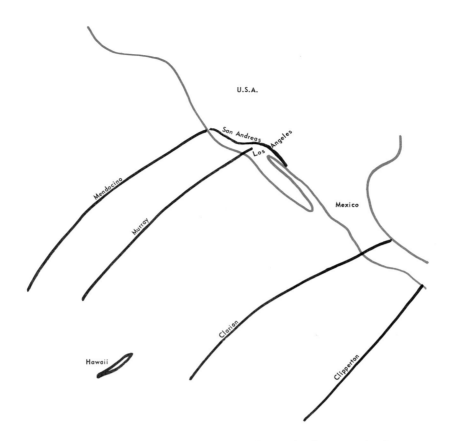

golds and reds. If allowed to grow, it will reach a very good height and give splendid shade. It is much loved in Japan. During the Cretaceous, the forests of Greenland were lush with the gingko.

Thus we know that during the Cretaceous, Amer-Eurasia had not moved very far north if Greenland, which was later to lie under the north pole, could carry the beautiful warmth loving forests of the period. A stupendous event was occurring, although no animal, not even the longest lived one, would have had the life perspective to observe such an occurrence. In fact, if man had lived then, not our entire history from the building of the Sphinx to the space-flight of Commander Shepard would give enough perspective even to guess this event in its entirety. However, it was as connected as the movement of Greenland from its Cretaceous position to that of the Pleistocene; or as connected as the automobile which skids on an icy road, turns broadside and slams into a bank or a tree. Yet only by studying the work of numbers of scientists, spending their lives understanding certain sections of the planet, and using these as parts of a moving picture puzzle, does the story begin to come into focus.

Let us again in imagination take up our positions in a space ship coming toward the planet from another island universe, at a speed exceeding that of light. In the great magnifying mirror in the front of our ship, we have been watching this planetary drama. We saw the long southern glaciation of Gondwannaland and then as the Triassic dawned, we began to see the break-up of parts of that land. We saw Polynesia rift off and slide away as Australia slammed into Asia during the Jurassic. Then the Cretaceous dawned quietly in the west, but in the east we saw the paroxysm of disasters which closed the Mesozoic, known to geologists as the Mesozoic diastrophism.

The Cretaceous dawned in the doomed length of Lemuria with the deep thunder of the whole planetary orchestra crashing in the brass section while the drum beat of exploding volcanoes ripped Earth's surface. The tremendous size of some of these vents testify to the fury of the time. The African capes in the center of the old continental mass now catch fire and lavas over a half mile in thickness well out of the great rifts from Tasmania to India. The southern tip of the Atlantic is cracking open with smoke and steam as the Pacific water seeps through to the lava.

The convulsion of fury in the Indian ended with the slide of India from its place on the northern end of the Lemurian spine, toward Asia, carrying the bed of the Tethys sea before its blunt prow in an over-riding crash which twisted up the sea bed into the planet's highest range of mountains. Many authorities do not believe that this was over until after the Eocene, two epochs later, because of the finding of an Eocene fossil upon the peaks of the Himalayas.

Now it became the turn of the other transverse ranges to go up with thrusting and fire from southeast to northwest pressure, heralding the approach of the sialic masses. The Tethys was crushed from the east to the west consecutively, and all that was left was a Mediterranean valley. Some authorities believe that these events also continued perhaps into the Miocene, in North America. At this time North America was bumped as it was approached by South America, while the Atlantic was starting to crack open at its southern end.

In North America, where Le Conte has done a splendid amount of work studying the ancient river systems as compared to modern rivers, the over-all picture of the Mesozoic "bump" becomes very clear. Mexico was pushed up ten thousand feet. The peak of the pressure raised the western United States thirteen thousand which gradually diminished to four thousand feet in the Arctic.

Above Panama, the rock mass was increased from twelve to fifteen times, and again the pressure was south and southeast to the north. It is only logical to assume that the central ridge was also pushed up, perhaps with renewed thrusting and volcanism.

As the fiery Cretaceous drew to a close, it became obvious that ancient Gondwannaland was cracking up. Australia had knifed free and was sliding away from its great rifts with a clockwise rotational partial turn toward the Pacific. South America, although still tied to Antarctica by some dragging land bridges was also attempting to slide with a clockwise partial rotation into the Pacific. Some avenue for animal traffic is necessary, and this may have been across the dragging anchor of the great central range to the ridge and thence to Antarctica. A primate connection across the southern ridge is necessary at least through the Paleocene.

In the whole picture of Gondwannaland, Australia and South America were moving away from their rifts into the Pacific, while Africa was over-riding Amer-Eurasia. Only Antarctica stood deserted at its old position, still bearing its ancient load of ice.

It is doubtful if even yet there was a south Atlantic ocean. Probably the tears from the southern end were coming north along either side of the south Atlantic ridge, but the early primates, those creatures upon our stem, were moving back and forth between Africa and South America at will and the primates did not come into being until after the Cretaceous.

The students of the lemurs also insist upon a Lemuria which lived out the Cretaceous into later times, and thus not a complete Indian ocean. Undoubtedly, however, it was fast widening, with little land now to be seen above the surface of the water, but probably with dragging land bridges which would allow the transportation of frightened animals to new homes from those which were doomed.

As Amer-Eurasia started to feel the Mesozoic "bump", the swamps which had been the homes of the dinosaurs for untold millions of years were drained of their water, and the death-march of the monsters began. One can easily imagine their bewilderment at finding the plants and animals which had always been their food, either in headlong flight from the volcanoes or buried under the ash; how they must have walked under the ash covered sun by day and by the light of exploding volcanoes by night. Undoubtedly the plant eaters fell first, sustaining the meat eaters in their death. Probably the latter lived on for some time, fighting each other to the death for food when easier prey was not at hand, and perhaps following the swift streams down toward lower land, and possibly even to a few lingering swamps in the lowlands. The greatest part of them faced starvation when their feeding grounds were drained, or were buried in the ash and lava which marked the time of their extinction.

It is certain that if they had not died, the other mammals, and eventually man himself, could never have come into being.

Thus with a curtain of flame dropping across the monstrous actors of the time, the third act of Earth's drama is ended in the fiery death of Gondwannaland which took with it the nightmare world of the Mesozoic.

Chapter 39

The Cenozoic

Or

The Age Of

The Mammals

The curtain of the drama which we have been watching now rises upon a new Earth: not that the globe was exchanged for another, but the continents began to form a new alignment. The only reason man did not discover it before the time of scientific study of the rocks is that man is such a recent creature. All his history found the continents in a similiar alignment to what they are now, and so naturally he took it for granted that the globe was always thus.

Not until it was discovered that the metals in ancient rocks pointed to the magnetic north or south in a different direction from what it is today; that the ancient climates could not be explained under the present conditions (for glaciers can no longer exist in India or coal bearing forests under the ice of the present glaciated lands), did the students of the earth sciences begin to join with the students of ancient plants and animals with their parasites, to explain these and other mysteries.

According to the theories which we have been studying, which seem to give the best answers, this was the period in which the throes of the birth of the Indian tear were almost over, or had passed their most intense fury, and the Atlantic tear was progressing from the south.

Both the tears of the Indian and Atlantic oceans began from the south along the rifts occasioned by the embattled ice fronts of Gondwannaland and, due to the sudden upsurge of lava through those rifts, the resultant steam and dumping of great amounts of water (hot water) upon the ice and its melting streams, the continents began to move away from the ice load. Thus the land which had been under the ice center from the African capes, the edge of Antarctica to Lemuria and Australia, became unstable with the loss of its lava, or magma base, under the crust, and began to sink as it was melted from the bottom and sides. At the same time the continents to every side of the sinking land, impelled by the previous shove of the ice fronts and the weight of the ice, began to move away from the doomed ice center.

For this reason, the continental fragments moved from the heavily iced lost land of the Kergulin range which once ran from the south Atlantic ridge, across the lower sunken portion of the African capes to Kergulin island and down the Lemurian spine to India. Australia moved to the northeast, Africa to the north and South America to the northwest while India, impelled by the weight of the sinking Lemurian spine behind her, was driven into Asia, smashing the bottom of the Tethys sea, and forming the shell covered, cloud soaring peaks of the planet's highest mountains.

The unbelievable fury of the collision, the greatest cataclysm Earth has ever experienced, can best be judged by the tremendous vents of certain South sea volcanoes; by the welling out of mile wide sheets of lava over the south African capes, and the moon-like craters left in the Indian ocean.

The Tethys sea was closed from the east to the west, showing the direction of impact, and Amer-Eurasia received its greatest shove northward. One may suspect that the first shove was a gentle one taking place in the Jurassic, while the earlier Triassic had already separated Polynesia (judging by its ancient plant cover) from its parent Gondwannaland. This, once more, underwrites the east to west direction of the continental impact.

Whole blocks of land now were wrenched, twisted and torn apart as lava welled out at the lines of rifting. The magmas of over half a mile in thickness which poured like hot molasses across the doomed land of Lemuria from Tasmania to the Indian peninsula during the Cretaceous, now began to move slowly north, leaving Lemuria without sufficient magma support under the Earth's crust. During the end of this age the molten wave must have reached the vents of the rising Himalayas, exploding in planetary fireworks as they had been exploding throughout the South seas, and the sinking peaks of Lemuria. It was during this time that the lemurs, the small dog faced monkeys that gave Lemuria its scientific name (which has been so misused in science fiction) began leaving their homeland, fleeing to all sides of the Indian ocean. However, Schuchert insists that some sections of the doomed land, and some sialic bridges, remained open to animal migrations until a much later date. Be that as it may, it was the terrific collision of the Cretaceous, when the continental masses came together, that explains the closing of the Mediterranean from east to west; the overriding of Asia when India folded the Tethys sea to make the Himalayas; and the raising of Earth's transverse cordillera and Earth's transverse rifts.

For this was the time of the birth of Earth's transverse cordillera. The mountains which follow the Mediterranean on both sides may be classed as members of this great cordillera of ranges which for scientific convenience may be called the Mediterranean cordillera. It would consist of the Pyrenees from the Atlantic ridge to Spain at the French border, the Alps, the Atlas, both sunken and sub-aerial (under the air) portions, running from the western side of Africa through Sicily, Italy, Greece where all the Mediterranean ranges run on to the Himalayas in one indistinguishable whole. This is what is meant by cordillera.

The word is a geological term used for convenience to distinguish all the ranges raised in the same era and running in the same general direction. For example, we have the Appalachian-English cordillera far older than these mountains of the end of the Mesozoic, which continued to raise through the first part of the Tertiary, or the time we have just been discussing. On the American side the Appalachian-English cordillera consists of: the Blue Ridge range, the great Smokies, the Crab Orchard mountains, the Black range, the Cumberlands, the Flat-tops, the Shenandoahs, the Tuscaroras, the Alleghenies, the Kittatinny range, the Taconica, the Berkshires, the Green range, the Poconoes, the White range, the Shawangunks, the Slide mountains, the Catskills and the Adirondacks. The Tennessee valley and the Shenandoah are part of the general rift associated with this cordillera. As stated in another chapter, this cordillera turns and plunges into the Atlantic where it becomes sea mounts and then crosses the central ridge, joining the continent of Europe where it comes out of the sea to cross Ireland and England and passes on through France and central Europe to end up as the Urals of Russia. It may be partly transverse, but it is, according to its rocks, one of Earth's oldest structures. Perhaps it is the relic of another great continental collision - a diastrophism too far back in time for us as yet, fully to understand.

The Mediterranean cordillera which exploded in its greatest fury at the end of the Mesozoic and continued intermittently even well into the Miocene is interesting because although science recognizes the fact that the mountains from the Atlantic to the Himalayas are one cordillera, it is not as yet certain of the ranges on either side, or those on the central ridge. If this cordillera was raised from the east to the west, as many authorities believe, then the mountainous ridges reaching from the Himalayas through the South seas could be the earliest members, and those of the Caribbean, the latest. Some authorities have given two dates to the convolutions of this latter range, calling its land "Antillia" and finding that it is very old. Dr. Henney of the Netherlands told me that in his travels over the Alps, he found some of its granites equally ancient, but showing different ages of folding. This could also be true of the peaks of the Caribbean, and those of the central ridge. The Rockies for example, show foldings of different eras from different directions as do many other ranges. However, the straight line of the great Mediterreanean cordillera would suggest that all of its members, new or ancient, were rethrust into the air by the tremendous compression from the south, and thus join the later cordillera.

Before we leave the puzzle of the distorted whorls of the Caribbean ridges, we must remember that South America was moving northwest in a partial half turn of clockwise spin and such a movement would tend to drag and pressure its sialic fragments in the Caribbean into crescent shaped strings before it breaks away from these land bridges some day in the distant future. Much the same effect is to be noted in the strings of land which still stretch from it

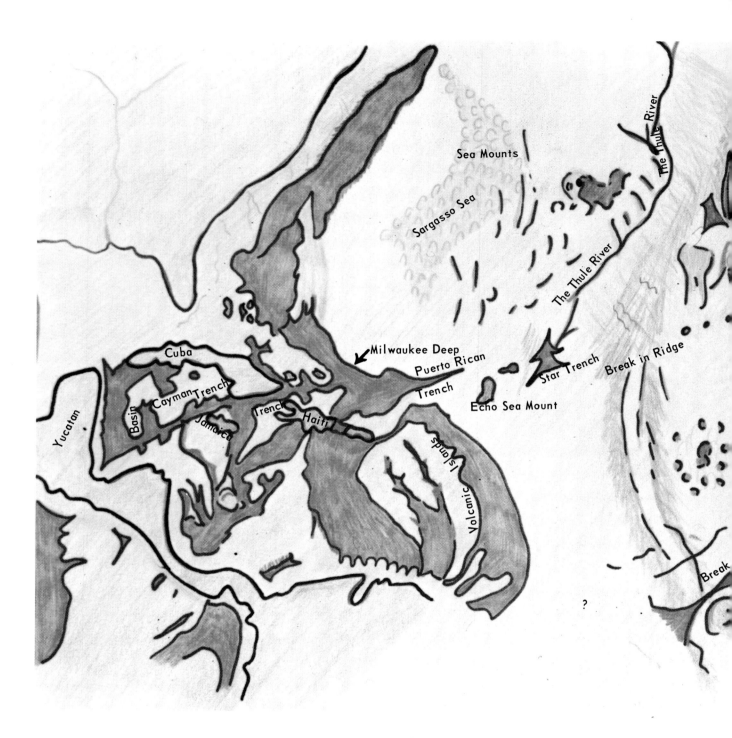

Sea Mounts

Sargasso Sea

The Thule River

Cuba

Milwaukee Deep

Puerto Rican
Trench

Star Trench

Break in Ridge

Yucatan

Basin

Cayman Trench

Jamaica

Trench

Haiti

Echo Sea Mount

Volcanic Islands

Break

?

at the southern tip, toward the point where it once connected with Antarctica.

The great Mesozoic cordillera of the Mediterranean is not the only structure of the cataclysm. We also have the great transverse rifts of the Pacific ocean. These are four giant fractures of the same age, running from the west coast of North America into the Pacific ocean and carved like monstrous knife cuts across the bed of that great body of water. They have been only recently discovered and as yet are not fully explored.

The most southerly one is the Clipperton fracture zone striking west from Central America. The next strikes out in the same direction from about the location of Mexico City. It is called the Clarion fracture zone. Striking out from the sunken land running along the coast of Los Angeles to Santa Barbara, the Murray fracture runs straight to the Murray deep just north of the Hawaiian islands. How much further it goes, we do not know. The fourth fracture zone

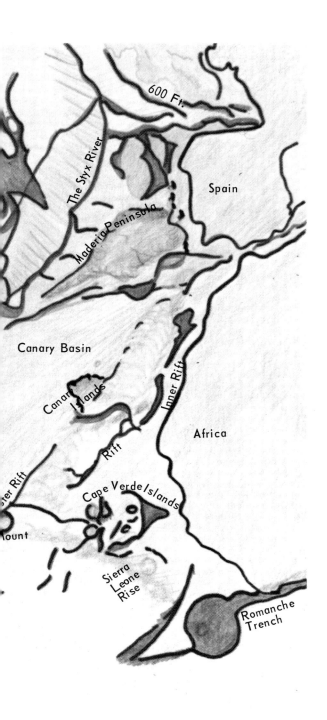

THE TRANSATLANTIC TRENCH
Thule and Styx Rivers - Trans Atlantic fracture - Possible second fracture. Both at breaks in spine of ridge. (Width of ocean is compressed.)

is the Mendocenan running like the others from the Mendocino coast of northern California straight out west into the Pacific. The Mendocino coast is where the Eel river makes an interesting bend under the sea around what had once been an island, now long sunken below the waves. We know little about these sinister cracks.

There is another enormous rift, probably of the same age, but crossing the Atlantic instead of the Pacific. This one has not been studied at all.

While using a late map of the Atlantic, together with a ruler and a magnifying glass, to trace the sunken lands on the central ridge, the present writer had a curious experience. Having been called away on other business for several hours, I left the ruler and magnifying glass upon the open atlas of the Atlantic floor. When I returned to resume the map, I saw that the carelessly left ruler ran straight from the great trenches of Central America across a transatlantic rift. I pulled the ruler away and stared at the map. There, as plain as could be, was a massive rift cutting across the Atlantic ocean. Why had I not seen it before? Probably because I was too much occupied with the central ridge. I snatched up another piece of paper and began to draw it.

The transatlantic rift begins with the bottom of the Yucatan basin, where we enter the Cayman trench which separates Cuba from Jamaica. Moving along this trench, we come to the Milwaukee deep, which in turn becomes the Puerto Rican trench. Running along this sinister structure we find ahead of us two smaller hole-like rifts which lead us to the rays of the giant Star trench. The two small rifts we have just passed, by the way, are just north of the Echo seamount - without doubt a sunken island, for it is flat-topped; and it has been learned that most flat-topped seamounts are eroded islands. The long ray of the Star trench which reaches an arm toward us is a tremendous crack which lies just west of the central ridge, and is one of the largest rifts in the much fractured Atlantic basin.

Now crossing the ridge along four minor trench-like deeps, we find that their lengthwise ruts point to three depressions which run just south of the great Meteor seamount, and from here we stare ahead at the massive trench of the Canary basin. This deep fracture in turn joins the sunken rift valley which once ran between the magnificent peaks of the Madeira peninsula and the snow capped grandeur of the Atlas range, before it became the Canary sunken ridge. The

Madeira valley was once the bed of a famous ancient river, the Mediterranean, which leads directly through the Gates of Hercules, or if you prefer, Gibraltar - into the probably trans-continental rift of the Mediterranean sea. Looking back along its well marked trail, one cannot help but wonder if this planetary crack connects with one of the fracture zones of the Pacific? But that is for some worthy young oceanographer or structural geologist to someday follow for a doctorate.

The transverse cordillera and the transverse rifts are not the only structures of this time of colliding continental masses. There is the cordillera being pushed up by the travelling land masses as they move away from the Lemurian ice center of the Paleozoic glacial, and in every case except Africa, into the Pacific. The great cordillera also of this age includes the Rockies which become the Sierras of Mexico and the Andes of South America, turning into the Antarctic Pacific range and then the Australian Pacific range.

Nor are these the only scars of the great Mesozoic diastrophism. We also have the great uplifts of the northern masses. Concerning this phenonema there are some interesting surveys from North America. It is to be suspected that the uplift of the central ridge and of Amer-Eurasia must have been proportionately greater, being closer to the point of impact, but as yet we do not have these surveys. Judging from the figures of the north American uplift, it is to be suspected that if there had been an Atlantic sea before the diastrophism of the Mesozoic, which probably reached the western lands during the Cenozoic (time of late life), or during the early Tertiary, it would have ceased to be after the collision.

As for the figures, Mexico suffered a ten thousand foot elevation to the block as a whole. The peak of the uplift was to be found in the United States with a thirteen thousand foot rise, which then slanted down to ten thousand in Colorado and dropped slowly to four thousand in the Arctic.

Perhaps in these figures we have the answer to the mystery of the undersea river channels, or at least a partial answer. Perhaps the Pleistocene's withdrawal of water into ice was the rest of the answer.

Such an uplift of the northern continental masses would also account for the extinction of the dinosaurs. These monsters who had ruled Earth for three hundred million years now found that the swamps where they had lived in the lush lands of the Dakotas and Wyoming were suddenly drained, and the plants upon which the herbivores (plant eaters) depended for a living, died in the frosty cinder filled air from the volcanoes. Undoubtedly the carnivores (flesh-eaters) lingered on as long as starving animals could be caught. Disney's film of this era, "The Death March of the Monsters", is so graphically lifelike with its color and sound, that one can never quite forget the roars of the tormented beasts as the giant upthrusts of the land separated forests and drained the jungles in whose swamp-like floors they once lived. The hopeless march of the creatures in search of food, preyed upon by the flesh eaters every foot of the road to extinction, was an epic of tragedy and horror which one cannot forget.

It is also possible, not too probable perhaps, but possible, that some of the carnivores saved themselves by stumbling down the streams to warm swamps which still may have existed in the Atlantic basin. Many of the undersea canyons of the Atlantic have rocks showing fossils of this time which would suggest swamplands, or shallow warm seas. These fossils also give this era as the very earliest possible time for the cutting of these canyons.

We know that at one time there were two rivers running down the north Atlantic basin from north to south - one to either side of the central ridge. Both were fairly steep in the north, with rapids and many dendritic tributaries, but as they continued to the south they meandered more and more and formed lakes. Is this due to the fact that through the ages since the collision they had eroded much of their bed, before the great ice sheets of the north renewed their vigor? To distinguish the rivers of the Atlantic bed, probably of Tertiary time, let us call the western one running between the ridge and North America, draining both sides, the river of Thule, and the one to the east, also running south between the continent and the ridge, draining all lands from Ireland to Spain, let us return to what was apparently its legendary name: the river Styx.

To recapitulate, we are faced with some interesting mysteries, all apparently of the Mesozoic diastrophism to Miocene date line. They are the Mediterranean cordillera, the great fractures in the Pacific stemming from the North American coastline, the circum-Pacific cordillera from the Rockies to the Australian ranges, the great downward warp of the land in the Caribbean and gulf of Mexico as illustrated in the drilling charts of the oil wells, as well as Tertiary (or later) undersea river channels in the Atlantic and the death of the dinosauria who had ruled Earth for three hundred million years. Nor must we forget the lift of the north American block.

Any geological theory must explain facts. These are facts. Under the "wrinkled skin of the drying apple" theory in which mountain ranges are simply the wrinkles of the apple, this pattern of ranges and rifting is not only unlikely, but also as many authorities have pointed out, the definite pressures which caused them are to be located in the rupture of the Indian ocean. For this reason, many geologists are now dropping the theory which ruled geological thinking for so many generations, and are casting around for another explanation. The theories which are attempting to explain these mysteries are called the drift hypotheses, because each in some fashion demands the slow movement of the continental blocks.

Let us take another look at these theories in the light of the facts which geology has learned from the rocks of the Mesozoic through the Tertiary. The western drift theory of Alfred Wegener demanded one primeval continent which he called "Pangea" and did not allow for a Tethys sea. The Tethys, being a geological fact, was a partial cause of the defeat of this theory in its entirety. Other reasons were the lack of an explanation of the Mediterranean cordillera, and the lack of an explanation for the Pacific cordillera from Antarctica through Australia. He was asked by the scientists how he could explain this part of the cordillera, if he insisted that the Americas were moving west and thus the ranges on the Pacific were wrinkled by pressure from behind, how could the ranges of Australia also on the Pacific be explained by pressures from the sea?

These same facts underwrite Taylor and Kreichgauer in their belief in two continents which clashed along the line of the Mediterranean, wrinkling up the Tethys sea to form the Mediterranean cordillera, but their explanation for the ranges of Australia and Antarctica are not much more lucid than are those of Wegener.

All of these scientists fell down on what caused the continents to move in the first place, and how they happened to move. The English scientist, Joly, came up with a practical answer on this in his studies of lavas around the Earth. He believed that the hot magmas in the Earth had radioactive elements which would periodically make them too hot as radioactivity was stored up and automatically bring about a con-

vulsion and the drifting of continental blocks due to remelting from underneath. The magmas do have radioactive elements, true, but the timetable which he gave made these convulsions of nature too numerous for the facts. However in the light of the pressures from the ice along the rifts caused by the meeting of the great sheets, we do have the motive power, and given Joly's release of vast amounts of magma, we then have the continents moving away from the icesheets. In the case of the glaciation of the Indian ocean, the movement of the fragments of Gondwannaland was into the Pacific, which would raise the circum-Pacific cordillera in Antarctica and Australia as it did in the Americas. The rest of the shove would drive Africa and India with Lemuria behind her, into a smashing collision with Amer-Eurasia; raising the Mediterranean cordillera; closing the Tethys; down warping the lands of the Caribbean as shown in the charts of the oil drilling; raising the blocks of North America and probably also the Atlantic ridge and of Eurasia, which in turn ended the rule of the dinosauria. The power of the crash would also explain the fractures in the Pacific on the western coast of North America.

However, when it comes to dates, Wegener was perhaps closer to the truth than the others. Kreichgauer insisted on many bumpings of the two continental masses along the line of the Tethys. He may be partly right, and indeed the Tethys may open again some day, but the facts do not allow as many as he visualizes. Taylor and Wegener together seem to have most of the answer. As Dr. Daly, that brilliant geophysicist from Harvard has said: "This theory of continental displacement should be called the Taylor-Wegener hypothesis."

Even in the matter of dates, these two men together seem to have the answer. Taylor saw the crash in the Mediterranean as Gondwannaland over-ran Amer-Eurasia causing the results of the Tertiary, but Wegener saw the tear of the Atlantic as not yet over and in fact did not reach Iceland or Greenland until the Pleistocene.

These two men together have given most of the answer to the mysteries of the Mesozoic diastrophism, and with reason, the combined theory has been called "the geology of the future".

The only difference in their opinions, and where each lost out to the other, is that whereas Taylor had his eyes on the Indian ocean and the Mediterranean, Wegener had his eyes upon the Atlantic.

Chapter 40

The Case For The Monsters

"There are more things in Heaven and Earth, Horatio, than dreamt of in your philosophy." Hamlet.

It was the winter of 1963, England's worst winter, and I am certain, her most beautiful. I walked across the old campus of Cambridge university toward the zoology department. In my hand I held an article from the London Times on "Nessy" the monster of Loch Ness, Scotland. The old buildings were utterly delightful in their partial blanket of snow which nestled on every stone block and covered the old walk. Overhead the trees glistened like fragile tinkling glass boughs of beauty with icicles for leaves. My thoughts flashed back for a moment to the time when, following a dog team in the far north, I had seen just such a crystal world.

There is something about England which retains a fairy tale quality. It is hard to say just what it is. At times it fades away and then again at the sight of some old building, or narrow street with dozens of ancient chimneys smoking in the snowfall, it comes back, and for a moment, you are living in another century.

I climbed the stairs worn by generations of students, and sought the zoology office. On the way was the museum. Here were relics from the Tuarak tribe of Africa which for a few moments held me spellbound. I made up my mind to return and not wait on some dull old bench for my party. So blithely, with no doubt the arrogance of the American, I asked for someone to explain the article. I was told that Dr. -------- was in class, but if I would wait, he would be pleased to talk with me. I nodded and told the young lady with the correct "Oxford accent", that I would wait before the case containing the Tuarak robes and bowls, and before she had time to recover from her surprise I was back at the case.

The bowl was strangely similar to the motif of the Troy-town maze, or the labyrinth I had seen on baskets among the Apache and Pima tribes of the Amerinds except the colors were not just softly blended with the feeling for beauty which is instinctive with the American Indian. The colors were of three only - red, black and white. I thought of Plato and the description of how Atlantean buildings were built by using these shades of rocks. Suddenly a hand was laid gently on my arm. A tall white-haired gentleman was bowing to me.

"I expected to be speaking to you about the Loch Ness so-called 'monster'. I had no idea that you might also be absorbed with the wild and mysterious Tuareg people of northern Africa."

"I have a number of interests, and one is this most fascinating group. Is the man who would understand this collection available to discuss them with me---after we finish, of course," I added with sudden diplomacy.

"No, unfortunately he is away for part of this term, but in a few months ..."

"Sorry, but by then I will be on my way back to California."

TYRANNOSAURUS REX - The king tyrant lizard. Earth's most ferocious flesh eater.

"Ah - California! You must indeed find this snow most shocking."

"Shocking? Pardon me for laughing, but that word - in the States it carries a connotation of immorality."

"Indeed? How extraordinary!"

"An example of how our languages are drifting apart. I believe it is known as time-separation?"

"Ah yes. Quite. I believe that we have other words. The connotation of naughty is as it always has been used. A thing is naughty when it is not exactly wicked, but still not exactly cricket."

"A motorist shouted that word at my cab-driver, and I couldn't help laughing."

"He didn't mean it to be amusing. He meant it as a polite rebuff."

"I understand. But we didn't come here to discuss language, did we? I have an interesting article on Scotland's 'monster'. It says that the scientists of Cambridge are convinced..."

"That the animal exists? Well the article is correct. We are."

"Why?"

"Have you ever had a course in historic zoology?"

"Yes, at the university of Illinois - some time ago."

"Then what would you say if you have interviewed hundreds of people out of the two thousand some odd sightings, to find that invariably, al-though almost none of them have ever heard of a Plesiosaurus, yet almost without fail, all of them have drawn this Mesozoic creature?"

"I would say that possibly you have one."

"That is our opinion."

"The article says that you have Loch Ness ringed with cameras."

"That we have, but unfortunately, the beast is nocturnal. This gives our cameramen a problem."

"Ah it would. But how about radar or..."

"We did not become vitally interested until it has been picked up by the screen. In fact, there may be many. We are fairly certain of at least three. We are hoping that one of these is a young one."

"To catch, no doubt, and raise in captivity?"

His eyes lit with an unmistakeable gleam as he nodded.

"How large is the creature?"

"You remember the one dug out of the Kansas swamp? That had a neck of over twenty feet."

"Then with a body and tail you would expect a fifty foot supposedly extinct lizard?"

"From thirty to fifty feet. There have been some suggestions that it may be a mammal because one observer saw eyelashes. Another thought he saw fur."

"You mean to say he got close enough to see its eyelashes?"

"Yes, we were skeptical of that also. Besides many say that the one they saw had no tail. Others saw a long serpent like tail."

"One may have lost the tail in a fight."

"Very possible. The colors are usually given as very deep brown or grey - elephant color. A few saw a smaller one with faint stripes."

"Stripes? That is a surprise."

"The young of many animals have different markings from the adult."

"Ah yes. Of course - a young one. Have you ever thought that this animal may be the sea serpent of many marine sightings?"

"Indeed we have. This creature is a fresh-water species but there well may be a marine species, possibly larger. Some of the natives of the region seem to believe that the creatures are a very dark green in the sunlight, but in spite of the small serpent like head they do not seem to remember scales. There is one definite thing about these creatures - they have a hump on the body. Sometimes these humps move - even separate."

"Then I would say that you definitely have a serpent like creature. Have you ever seen a python feed?"

"No, I can't say that I have."

"It is not a pretty sight. The pig is hypnotized. It seems unable to run. It just stands and stares and shakes. Then the serpent strikes. The pig is gradually swallowed and the hump appears. When the hump has gone down a ways the serpent makes a quick convulsive movement and the flesh of the pig is separated from the bones. The bones are disposed of and the flesh is consumed. Your animal is a close relation of habits."

"That is our opinion. By the way, we are receiving a great deal of mail from other parts of the world. It would seem that these supposedly extinct monsters are rather numerous."

"How fascinating! Where?"

"There is one or more in Idaho. I believe the location is a small lake somewhere north of Boise."

He consulted a little pocket notebook.

"Ah yes. Payette lake, a tourist spot has a 'long neck' as the people of all lands invariably call him. The color, yellow green to dark brown. The humps are reported. The animal swims with head held about six feet above the water and flippers are seldom seen unless it comes out on shore. It has been reported for ten years. The lake is mountain rimmed and more than 3900 feet deep."

"How deep have these animals been reported by sonar?"

"About 800 feet deep."

"I wonder if they have a inner air organ for storing air. They apparently come out on land, probably to hunt, and yet they stay at such depths."

"That could be the reason for the humps."

"Oh yes. In that case it might be a mammal."

"Hmm. There have been reports of triangular scales down the back."

"Ah. We have returned to the dinosaurs."

"Listen to this amazing list of sightings: Tasmania, Canada from Quebec to British Columbia, Northern Ireland, many Scotch lakes, Southern Argentina, the Montana Rockies, Sweden, Switzerland, Norway and Iceland, southern Ireland, northern Australia in similar lakes, other points in South America, New Zealand, southern Australia, Africa and Malaya. I doubt if I have them all. There seem to be several species. Of course, many of these sightings were in the papers."

"Wait a moment. Do all of these creatures have flippers - four flippers?"

"Yes. Those who were observed on land do, and interestingly enough the consensus of opinion seems to be that it is the hind pair which gives the animal its tremendous power of propulsion. It has been seen moving at rapid speeds in the water, and often compared to a freight train or fast freight."

"I notice that many of these locations are in warmer climates than others."

"True. Therefore I believe that the warmer water species of fresh water 'long neck' is another species from the longer cold water lake species. Also apparently the warmer water species is smaller, with a shorter tail."

"Do all of these animals inhabit very deep lakes?"

"Yes, that seems to be one of the necessities of their environment."

"How long do you suppose they live?"

"We wouldn't know. Recognition of their presence by the native population has come down from prehistoric times, in many cases."

"Could these be the 'dragons' of legend in so many lands?"

"Again, I would not even hazard an educated guess. However, there are some rumors of a few surviving Tyrannosaurus Rex. These are usually jungle locations in the Americas where no one can explore to find them, and the natives usually worship them. They are often suspected of throwing them human sacrifices. These, of course, may be only the rumors of science fiction followers or someone who has been imbibing more 'fire water' than he should, perhaps at some native feast."

"The ancient dragon with the Greek-Latin name which so well describes - the king tyrant lizard? Do you have any sightings on this horrible monster - surely Earth's most vicious killer..."

"With knives of steak length for teeth and the ability to probably leap over a hundred feet? No, only rumors from explorers who heard the story from Harry who in turn heard it from some native - you know the type of rumor."

"Any locations?"

"Actually no. Brazil, somewhere in unexplored rivers that end in swamps."

"Then I can locate perhaps two for you. These also are rumors - at least the first one is. The Seri Indians of Mexico are supposed to have one in a very deep cave on Tiburon island. If you investigated too closely you might become a sacrifice, which is certainly a sufficient deterrent to stop most enthusiasts from going among a rather unfriendly tribe of Indians. The location of this island is in the gulf of California. The animal was supposed to have been seen on occasions by passing fishermen when it was silhouetted against the moon, walking over the mountain ridge - probably hunting. The Seri are a fast diminishing tribe. One might suspect the reason.

"The second location is in the center of Mexico. This story was carried by the News Pilot, a San Pedro paper." (Part of this story - at least the sequel - appeared after my return to California, and I sent it back to Cambridge. Due to an accident, it apparently never reached its destination, so all the information I have is what I told the professor. If anyone wishes more they will have to look up the files of the News Pilot - I believe for 1963 and 1964.)

The professor glanced at me as if he expected me to pull out a similar book with data. Instead I only had the notes I had taken down from what he told me.

"I am sorry, but I do not have the article. There were, or rather are, two young Americans who were mining in Mexico in the mountains. They heard rumors of this monster which the Mexicans call "the cow catcher" because it devours their cattle. The descriptions and pictures tallied with the king-tyrant lizard. They were so certain that they returned to the United States to try to interest the zoology department of some university in an expedition. Personally I do not see what they could do. You couldn't capture one of those monsters. How could you subdue it? How?"

"I understand. You do not really have the facts."

"No. You see, the article in the London Times caused me to make this visit. I did not bring the article in the News Pilot with me."

"Your story of the Tyrannosaurus Rex is just rumor. I would be pleased to have it some day if you wish to send it. On how the monster could be controlled, I have no idea. To carry a suitable cage into the jungle and then get it out would be almost impossible. Suitable pictures - they would be invaluable, but such a dangerous and vicious animal would be most..."

He gave up with a gesture of helplessness. I decided to find out what I could about the Plesiosaurus, and forget this wild tale in the News Pilot.

"If you don't mind, let us return to the 'long-necks' - a very good name. What are the facts which might add up to the animal being a mammal and what facts for it being one of the dinosauria?"

He smiled with evident relief that our discussion had again gained the more solid ground of apparent fact.

"Do not forget me if you find the article on Tyrannasaurus Rex, but really it is one of these 'I heard it from Harry who was told by a native' tales. Now as to our 'long necks', as I said they are world wide and indeed they may not be the same species or for that matter even belong to the same division of animal life. The tropical species are smaller and lighter in color apparently while those of the cold water lakes are larger and darker. The marine type is the largest. We must be careful with these marine observances to be certain that the observer is not seeing a large sea elephant or a rare breed of seal not before observed. Such descriptions as a 'head like a horse' or a 'long mane about three times the length of that of a lion' puts the animal observed out of the Plesiosaurus division, and underscores that of the mammal."

"Certainly, yet there is the animal found in British Columbia's cold deep lake which the natives call 'cadborosaurus' and describe as a serpent over forty feet long, with a smaller companion, probably a young one."

"Oh yes, I have read of that one. The body is circular and no mention made of flippers. However it is only seen in the water. The color is

PLESIOSAURUS - A swimming dinosaur.

what has been described as a huge dark wet log and the swimming movement as sinuous."

"Seattle has one too, in her lake Washington", I said. "Wait, I may have some notes on that one," hunting through my pockets and locating my own note book with jottings of all kinds. Under M for monsters, I located what I wanted and read: " "Colonel Henry B. Joseph, his wife and son were cruising in their 28 foot boat in April, 1961, when their cocker spaniel saw what appeared to its masters to be a thirty-foot floating log - black and shiny. The dog barked and the 'log' began moving.

" 'In my thirty years of service on the sea, I have seen whales, giant manta rays, sharks, black fish, fun loving porpoises, but never anything like this," said the captain: 'We had shot past and turned around to go back, but the moment we came within easy viewing distance it was gone. We forgot about it and began cruising about Faben point near the north end of Mercer island. It was about 4:30 when we all spotted it again. The end of 'the log' was standing up with its head out of the water. We turned around and headed straight for it. Waves were coming from it. However when we were about 100 yards away, it must have sunk for there was absolutely nothing there."

"That is our Plesiosaurus. He rises and sinks without a ripple. But this man was silly to use his boat as a weapon. The tail of the dinosauria were powerful weapons and could crush that boat, whereupon the dog would disappear first."

I smiled. I always found the subtle British

humor delightful.

"I see that you believe the ancient Plesiosaurus may be still around."

"With every year it becomes more and more probable. Not that there are no unknown breeds of mammals you understand, but when a 30-30 bullet just ricochets from the hide and the mouth is usually described as very wide and unusually thin, the eyes often apparently lidless and staring, the head serpent shaped, the mind of the historical zoologists inevitably leaps to the supposedly extinct dinosauria. I have a few more notes, and then I must return for my next class. Listen:

" 'June 1937. Two boys named Smith and Considine paddling about in a boat on Loch Ness reported three long necked lizards about two or three feet long, with four flippers, the front pair used for steering and the hind pair for pushing. They were seen chasing each other and playing.' "

He looked over his glasses and smiled. "Wish we had been there! A baby one like this could have been caught and possibly raised in captivity."

"Captain Ron Boyce of a fishing schooner on lake Waterton in the Canadian Rockies described the animal his boat encountered as: 'In Aug. '56, the creature we saw had a neck about four to six inches thick with some eight inch thumb like prongs sticking up from the ridge down its back.' Another captain, same location, confirms this description adding that it was from thirty to forty feet in length, describing it as a serpent.

"On a July night in 1933 a couple by the name of Spicer, driving south from Scotland to

London, took a road by Loch Ness. Approaching a rise, they saw a long thin snake like neck and a good sized serpent head watching them through the trees. The creature had a ponderous body which they could not entirely see due to the rise in the road. They were not sure of a tail either, but something like one was partly coiled away from them and could be seen protruding from the other side of the huge humped back..."

"Getting ready to strike, no doubt."

"Very possible," he nodded. "But listen to this: 'The body was the length of the road's width, exclusive of head or tail, or neck. Before they could reach it, the creature seemed to jump forward and crashed through the underbrush, tearing out bushes and everything in its path. When they reached the break in the underbrush a few moments later all they saw was the edge of the lake some ten yards away.'

"A young engineer had almost the same experience. He was on a motorbike, I believe you call them motorcycles, and he was coming down the same road by moonlight. At almost the same place he first saw the long neck and serpent head looking at him through the trees. He was close enough to get a good look at the face of the creature and declared the eyes were oblong and stood partly above the skull line as is the case with some reptiles. The tail he said, was about six feet long, and clubbed on the end as if part of it had been lost in some previous accident. Without any warning it came leaping diagonally across the road giving him a good view of the flippers. The front pair were large but the hind pair definitely larger and stronger, pushing the animal forward with a leaping motion which was very rapid considering the size. Like the other sighting, the creature crashed down all opposing underbrush and went into the lake without apparently any churning sound at all.

"Dr. A.C. Oudemans of the Netherlands, who has researched quite a volume on the 'long necks', is of the opinion that these animals are mammals with air sacs in the humps. His main argument is the up and down movement is not natural to reptiles, while air sacs are, as far as we know, an unknown feature of their structure. He is probably partly right, but I cannot agree with him completely. There may be a species of mammal entirely unknown to us which is like this creature, but is is also possible that we have here a living member of the supposedly extinct dinosauria, namely the Plesiosaurus. An article in the files of the Daily Columnist, of Victoria, British Columbia reporting a sighting in their lake gave the following description:

'There were two serpents. One good view of the first disclosed the fact that definitely it was over forty feet in length, with a snake like head and a round body.' "

"Wait a moment," I said: "one last observation. I have owned both iguanas and chameleons as well as various desert reptiles. They all drink by bending their long necks to water and then raising their heads very high to let the liquid run down their throats like chickens do."

"Yes, quite," he smiled, "and it is possible that we have here some strange member of the amphibia which is equally at home in the air and in the water."

"Or perhaps all three?"

"We have much to learn about these creatures. We are only fairly certain of one thing - they exist. There has been one interesting photo taken on motion picture film which followed the creature all over Loch Ness in some amazing antics of speed and control on turns. The following day the photographer hired a cameraman, filming him in a motor boat doing the same things at the same clocked speeds, and there is no doubt of the difference, since both were filmed from the same spot. And now I must actually leave or I will be late. Thank you for coming, and do not forget the article on our tyrant dragon with the four foot head and teeth as long as your Indians' arrowshafts."

"I won't forget and thank you."

"In a year of two we may have more information on the Plesiosaurus. But I am interested in Tyrannosaurus Rex also, you know. He would certainly fit the description Plato used when he spoke of the animals which once lived on the sunken land, and then added almost as an afterthought 'therefore the animal which is the largest and most voracious of them all was to be found there.' "

I almost gasped at how he had read my mind. His eyes were filled with pleasure at my surprise and we grasped hands warmly as he hurried away.

It was snowing again when I reached the campus and crossed the paths to the old bridge where undoubtedly Shelley had often stood in the not so long ago. Nothing seemed to have been seriously changed and as I stood on the bridge of stone watching the skaters on the frozen lake below me, the only thing which was out of place was the modern costumes of the skaters. Otherwise it was a Currier and Ives painting come to life, and the crystal world of the blowing snow and tinkling trees became a fluid moment in the long stream of time.

Chapter 41

The

Mammals

Inherit

The

Earth

With the death of the dinosauria, the mammals found a brand new world in which to play; and mammals love to play.

The mammals (from the old Aryan word mamma) are all of the animals with hair on their bodies who bear their young alive and suckle them with milk. It goes without any discussion that man must include himself in this group.

With the spread of the mammals came two new aspects of intelligence - humor and imagination, as well as the pure joy of being alive. We see the young of no other group frolic in the sunshine as do the mammals. Only a cat will play with a ball of twine knowing all the time that it is a string, but pretending that it is a snake or a mouse; a dog will play with a ball, knowing it is a ball but pretending it is a rabbit, or a rat; a horse will jump in the air and run as though it were in a race. Humor and imagination, pretending that something is what it is not for the sake of fun, is typical of the mammals. The playing of tricks is another aspect of mammal humor. If you have never had a dog hide one shoe, or a cat cover up your grandmother's yarn in the trash basket, you may not understand, but the humor is there even though they do not have the ability to laugh while you hunt the object of the trick.

Of course, these traits are not altogether limited to the mammals. A small boy in our neighborhood once found a baby mockingbird (one of the world's finest singers) and brought it to me to learn how to care for it. After we built the little naked creature a nest with cotton and placed an electric light at the proper distance for heat, we then began the feeding procedure. Taking a teaspoon of warm milk and mixing in a little bread or a few crumbs of coarse flour and a few grains of sand for the digestion, complemented with worms which had the sod still clinging to them, he learned to feed the little fellow. As the days grew into weeks however, I found that I had inherited a mockingbird. After he had learned to fly, I opened the door and "freed" him; when night came, he was back at the window, hungry as usual. This went on for months, although the visits became less frequent. However, they were not always as much a source of joy to me as to him. When he felt that he was being neglected, as he sat on my shoulder and sang, he would go for my typewriter, flying away with a freshly typed page. Running after him did no good whatever. He had learned to laugh, and he did, as he changed places from one inaccessible spot for another.

Finally a choice tidbit of food would cause him to drop the paper and it could be retrieved, often the worse for wear. This was not humor? Then why did he always choose the finished page instead of a blank? And why the laughter of a mischievous child? Our neighbor's crow played his tricks on the dog. You perhaps have had similar experiences. Humor is not necessarily limited to the mammals, or the stores would not sell so many toys for pet parakeets.

With the dawn of the Paleocene (pale-ee-oh-scene), the early recent, the mammals began to spread widely and to differentiate into many types and species. It was partly due to this wide-spreading and subsequent isolation from their fellows that the differentiation followed. We are now beginning to realize what caused it. All creatures, it seems, have suffered mutations. These are hereditary changes probably caused by natural radiation from the soil or cosmic rays from space working on the genes. Some mutations are good and some are not. Natural selection at mating time usually takes care of those which are not. A six-fingered hand would not be an asset for attracting the opposite sex. In my own family the continual appearance of breech births (wrong position of the child) would soon end the line under wilderness conditions, but offers no great problem to modern physicians and surgeons.

On the other hand, good mutations which allow an individual animal better to survive in his environment, are usually kept. For example, the change of the regular coat of the fox from red to white in winter is undoubtedly a help in snowy weather to protect the animal from being seen and has saved the life of the line. The same is true of the rabbits, and it is understandable why this ability did not survive in warm lands where the white coat would be an invitation to extinction.

For this reason, the albino or partial albino is rare in all types of animals except in the far north. Fawcett, in his travels among the Indians of South America, spoke of the natural whites often to be found among the red man. He met and admired an exquisitely lovely blonde girl who had been promised in marriage to a French trader who already had three other Indian wifes. Arguing with the father that this beauty would be the toast of Paris did absolutely nothing toward changing her fate, apparently to the disgust of young Fawcett.

It is interesting that kinky or fuzzy hair in man is a mutation. In the tropics, it definitely becomes desirable, for it acts as a mattress to protect the skull from the powerful direct rays of the sun. Undoubtedly its possessors lived longer and had more children, thus causing the spread of the trait. In the north, however, it had no significance whatever, and so the few Scandinavian families who do have kinky hair, and among whom there is absolutely no possibility of negro blood, retain the characteristic as a family trait. Incidentally, the apes all have straight hair.

Similarly the retention of very black skin in the tropics is probably a mutation which became a protection against the ultra-violet rays of the tropical sun, while in the north the effect would be the opposite since man would need all the sunlight he could get. However, this has been argued by scientists who find that blondes migrating to central Africa as missionaries, etc., begin to have darker skin and hair within three generations (see "Human Geography").

Thus the rapid differentiation of the mammals, especially in the early epochs of the Tertiary when there was still an Earth fairly empty of animals, was due not only to mutations but also to long isolation necessary for the consolidation of a type.

In discussing the branch of the mammals of which man is a part, we must understand something of the manner in which Linnaeus made his famous classification. In 1735 and 1758 he published his "Systems Naturae", which is a systematic method of classifying the animal kingdom. That it has been little changed, shows how well he did the work, and also how badly the tool was needed by scientific thinkers and writers. For the terms, he chose Latin, a dead language, thus allowing any scientist talking to any other half a world apart to understand immediately the species of animal under discussion.

He decided to call the group the most similar to man "the first" - thus giving it the name primates (pry-mates). The name for man himself - homo sapiens, meaning "man of wisdom", has caused so much amusement and wry comments for both scientists and layman alike that recently the term is being dropped for "homo modernis" or modern man. The present writer will follow this classification.

The primates are the man like type of animal from the monkeys to the apes. Asking which group of the primates man most nearly resembles, Linnaeus pointed out that it was the one which do not have tails. Now we have excluded the monkeys and have the apes. Of these which most resembles man? We find that the gorilla may be our closest relative, but there are differences which keep him a distant one. He has

a skull which comes to a peak. This is due to the muscles of his very powerful jaw. The gorilla as well as the other apes have almost no chin, while their faces curve, allowing the nose to lie flat against their cheeks. The reason for this is the lack of the nose arch. Possibly the nose arch in the beginning was a mutation which remained because it allowed for the heating of the air between the wind and the lungs, thus permitting man to live farther toward the north. However, it must be noted that as the chin developed, the upper jaw retreated into line with

THE MARMOSET

Found in South and Central America.

the lengthening chin and the rising forehead. The nose arch followed as part of the "straight-facedness" which marks modern man. These developments take millions of years of time and put man's division very far back in time, indeed, from the low forehead, receding chin, protruding upper jaw and flat nose of the ape.

For these reasons we did not arise from the gorilla any more than we did from the other apes, but our stem parted company from his over some twenty-five million years ago. Since then we, as well as the gorilla and the other apes, have been pursuing our individual destinies.

Going back down the stem of the primates, we find that the apes must have arisen from the African monkeys because these have a characteristic shared only by them with apes and man. That is the opposable thumb. It is said that without this tool our hands would not have been able to grasp objects and our civilizations would never have arisen. The South American monkeys do not have the thumb, but they use their tails almost as one might use an additional finger. Farther down the stem of the primates we find the thumb among the marmosets. Descending still further down, we find the thumb among the tarsiers and even farther below, the lemurs who gave their name to Lemuria. Finally we arrive at the four-legged tree shrew with the long snout of the "smell brain" group whose eyes are on the sides of its face, thus depriving it of the three dimensional vision which we possess, along with other creatures whose eyes are in front.

Now we are faced with some problems, showing the inter-dependency of the sciences. If the primates arose in South America as some authorities believe because of their primitive monkey, then why does the lower marmoset of south and central America have an opposable thumb? Or did the tarsiers, marmosets, and lemurs actually branch from the monkeys - that is the African monkeys, since it is the Africans which also have the opposable thumb? Or, did the South American monkeys come from the Africans and the loss of the thumb must then be explained as a mutation? Yet, why would such an important asset to the welfare of the group not be retained through natural selection? And if the monkey got to South America without the thumb, how did the marmoset get there with the thumb?

Nor does the list of mysteries end here. Why are the tarsiers to be found in such vastly isolated locations as the Philippines and Madagascar? Either the primates are older than we now believe, or there was a land connection between these homelands as recently as the Miocene. Schuchert would, of course, suggest land bridges, but this does not obviate the problem of why the apparently earlier form of monkeys became isolated in South America. If they did arise in South America, and there was a south Atlantic ocean at this time, how did they get to Africa where they developed the thumb? And how does it happen that the tarsiers in such vastly isolated locations have the thumb, as well as two other lower groups? Could it be that man travelling in ships during the Pleistocene brought the monkeys to South America and there bred out the thumb for some ritualistic reason? What other answer is there? Or must we admit that the primates are older than the Atlantic? And older than the break which separated the Philippines from Asia, and Asia from the sinking Lemuria? Such answers as these are going to give one or the other group of scientists a headache. The Piri Re'is map suggests that man may have been the carrier and his ritualism to blame. We have the interesting human parasites inhabiting the spider monkey in South America which some two hundred thousand years ago lived upon men. And we have the relics of ancient religious rites among the wild tribes which have to do with monkeys. For the geologists this would be the lesser of two evils.

Furthermore, we have the problem of the lemurs. How old are they? They must have evolved on the sunken homeland in the Indian ocean to have scampered from it in all directions. Then obviously, it was a land before they left and they were evolved in something of their present form before it sank. This would bring Lemuria's final destruction into a later date than geologists like to believe. Its late sinking would indeed obviate the necessity of putting the lemurs back in the time of the dinosaurs, when the monsters were dying - namely the Cretaceous. When did Lemuria sink? Could fragments of that land with its magnificent mountain range have come down to the time of man?

Were parts of it dried off again during the heaviest retreat of the world's seas during the Pleistocene? But again, man is older than this even though today great masses of the old land do not lie very deeply below the level of the sea, and research ships are able to determine with ease that its rocks are continental, often overlain with lava.

Returning to the mammals, man had decided that intelligence was his particular gift, during the past century, but studies in the twentieth century are making this a questionable hypothesis. First there are the tests with rats. In 1958 when I returned to Redlands university for graduate work, we were shown some interesting white rats. The latter have been bred more and

THE LEMUR

From the vicinity of the Indian ocean. (Africa, Madagascar, India, Malay archipelago) Among various groups are the ruffled, bokom boulis, ring-tail, chirogales, the sloth lemur and slender loris. The lemur, as well as the marmoset and tarsier, eat nuts, insects and fruit, and are tree dwellers.

more stupid by breeding the least intelligent parents. They became so stupid that they could not even learn to feed themselves. On the contrary, the intelligent rats were obtained by breeding the most intelligent parents. One of these was put through his paces for us. He was put in a cage with a small house which had a flat roof. Above this roof, but completely out of his reach, was put a tempting morsel of food. He first tried to jump to the roof of the house and did not succeed. On the floor were several objects including a ladder. He then returned to the cage floor and looked around. Finally he propped the ladder against the house and gained the roof. Then he reached for the food. It was too high. He jumped and fell once more to the floor of the cage. Then he again climbed the ladder and after a moment of apparently going over his problem, he turned, pulled the ladder up with a hook in his tail and placing it on the flat roof, was able to reach the food.

"How far will these brilliant rats go?" a student asked.

"We don't know. The army always has the cash to get them away. What kind of tests they give them, we have never heard."

Of course, the surprise of the twentieth century is the intelligence of the dolphin. We know that his brain is not only larger than man's, but also has more convolutions. His mastery of sounds is phenomenal and apparently has a language of at least as many words as we do. Furthermore, he is excellent at imitating our phrases. The only reason we did not realize it is that they speak so much more rapidly, that we have to record their speech and then play it back more slowly. The men out in Marineland, near Los Angeles, California learned of this quite by accident. They were putting two dolphins through their tricks for the dolphin show - baseball, leaping through a fire circle - when the cry was given to stop for the day. Although it was slightly early, no one questioned the order until they reached the office. There they learned to their surprise that the loudspeaker number

THE TARSIER

Found in East Indies, Madagascar, Philippines. (Nocturnal)

which meant to close down for the day had not been given. Everyone denied being a practical joker and all at once everyone had the same thought. They determined to catch the rascals and rigged up a recorder for the next day's session. That is when they learned of the amazing ability of these perhaps most brilliant of the mammals. Teams of men are now trying to converse with them, not only at Marineland, but in other groups and places.

It is interesting to remember that dolphins were supposed to have been portrayed in the statues of Atlantis, a "hundred nereids riding dolphins" about the great statue of the sea god himself. In ancient Crete, the dolphin is again portrayed in the sea. Were these people of anti-

quity able to gain what we are so desperately trying to obtain today – communication with this most remarkable mammal?

There are two other mammals which entertain out at Marineland. One is the whale and the other the seal. If one ever sees "Bubbles", the whale, dance the waltz, it is a sight you will never forget. You will not be able to appreciate it from above where the seats of the spectators are located. The best view is down below the enormous two or three story glass tank. There you can see this huge animal stand almost on her tail and turn in perfect time with the music in the most graceful waltz you will ever see. Apparently she enjoys it tremendously, or she would never move with such grace. When it is over, and the applause begins, she surfaces and waves to the spectators with her fin.

The seals do a great many tricks, but the most amusing is when one of them takes hold of the microphone with his flippers and gives an imitation of a candidate "politiking" before an election. Then the dolphins, not to be outdone, sing "Sweet Adeline" in their fish voices, off-key like a group of inebriated choristers.

I can not close this chapter without two more mammal stories which have among other facts, one thing in common - both of the animals were wild, and adult.

The first one called "A Glimpse of Eden" appeared in the Saturday Evening Post for November 14, 1964. Playwright Nina Hooke met the seal one summer in her cliff-hung home along the shore of northern England. He had first been contacted by a small child who ran away from his screaming parents to pet him while he was sunning himself on the beach. The child hugged and kissed him while the seal returned the caresses by hugging the boy with his flippers. From that time on he was the darling of the bathers. Mrs. Hooke met him in swimming and began to frolic with him. Once she swam far out and he bounced under her and then ahead of her with wide worried eyes as much as to say: "Should you be out this deep?" However, when he found that she could handle herself in the water, he went almost too far once by pulling her down. When she surfaced she floated quietly to get her breath, and the seal floated beside her, turning his head and watching her. She reached over and held his flipper. As opposed to his liking which he gave everyone on the beach, he gave his love only to those who swam with him in the deep water. When she held his flipper for so long and he looked at her "I felt like I was looking back through time to the world before man was shunned by all other living things." The summer ended when the cold came and toward the end of September the people drifted away. Then the seal began to cry out its loneliness. One October night she heard him and went down to the sea, calling him. He came and greeted her with extravagant affection, but his eyes were troubled and he kept whining. Finally he went into the water. She decided that this must be the end of their friendship and turned away, climbing the cliff. Her last sight was his head turned watching her from far out to sea. She never saw him again.

The other story was in the December, 1964 Reader's Digest entitled "The Bear Who Came for Dinner". The author, a schoolteacher in a military school, is fond of the Canadian north-woods where he likes to fish. He was thus engaged when a huge black bear began circling his camp. He was used to wild animals. The main rule, he said, is to remember their first fears and make no swift movements, but let them see what you are doing. The bear stopped, interested. Mr. Leslie could not have stood it off anyhow, as he was unarmed. The bear eyed the big fish he pulled in and was immediately rewarded by the morsel. That sealed their friendship. The bear moved over and sat down beside him, leaning his five hundred pounds against the fisherman's boots. Mr. Leslie continued to fish until the bear was satisfied, and when he stopped and made camp the bear slept beside him. This friendship went on for months, the animal, which he called Bosco, trailing him like a dog, and sometimes wrestling with him. Leslie knew the bear's strength, and when the game became too rough, he would lie down and play dead. Then Bosco would solicitously whine over him and wash his face with his wet rough tongue. Often he got the impression that the bear was trying to communicate with him, but never as much as when the animal got into a fight with other bears and ran them off thus probably saving Leslie's life. That night Bosco kept him awake most of the night looking at him earnestly and talking to him. The following day early in the morning the big black fellow gave a piteous cry and turned away - crossing the ravine and leaving him. He never saw the bear again.

Now these two factual adventures have several points in common, apart from the friendship each human being had built up with an adult wild animal of the mammal family. Both creatures enjoyed play, sometimes fairly rough play. But more importantly, both animals had a problem to solve. They had to give up a new friend of whom they were very fond, because they lived in another world. Each creature tried to communicate his thoughts first and then solved his problem by leaving. Nina W. Hooke wrote: "He welcomed me with a great display of affection, but his eyes looked troubled. He kept shaking his head and whining. I felt that he was trying to tell me something which I already knew."

Of the bear, Robert L. Leslie wrote: "That night we sat longer than usual by the campfire. Bosco nudged, pawed, talked at full length and looked me long in the eye before allowing me to retire. In my ignorance I thought it was a rehash of that afternoon's battle." Shortly thereafter the big bear went over the hillside without looking back. "I lay awake for hours awaiting for the familiar nudge. By morning I was desolated. I knew that I should never again see big brother Bosco."

Problem solving is not limited to intelligent rats, to the dolphin or to man.

How Geology Is

Reading The Past

Chapter 42

The Eocene (Ee-oh-scene)

Little flower in the crannied wall
I pluck you out of the crannies,
If I knew what you were, little flower,
Root and all, and all in all
I would know what God and man is.
Edwin Markham.

When we speak of the ages of the past, it is hard to realize how great an amount of time has gone by on this third planet, blessed by such a comfortable distance from a fairly dependable sun. Yet nature is busily writing a record of the daily life on each stream and lake, which sometimes we are able to uncover and read. Trees also write their own autobiography; and in a much vaster canvas, so does an ocean.

Not only was the continental shelf of North America pushed up in a block, but also the wrinkling up of mountain ranges by pressure from the southeast followed. The Eocene (dawn of recent) rocks cored through by Winn parish wells and a few of the Villa Platte wells of companies drilling for oil in Texas and Louisiana coastlines of the gulf of Mexico, show that the Jackson rocks of this age were land, and that the swamps of the Cretaceous here, were raised to form the Eocene. In fact, the steepest flexing of the old plate took place at this time, for at the end of the Eocene the land was pushed down. At present it is to be found running to ten thousand below sea level and still dropping steeply when lost by the wells of St. Martin's parish. The pressure was again from the southeast.

This was a period of great change. At the start the mountain ranges were elevated from ten to twenty thousand feet. Le Conte, in his studies of river systems, tells us that the continents were almost at sea level during the Cretaceous, but the great shock of southeastern pressure made itself felt in the northern block during the Eocene. In spite of this, the plants and animals were not arctic, as one might expect from such high peaks with their resultant snows. Therefore we may suspect that the lava was not very deep below the crust.

In the forests which spread across the apparently still closed north Atlantic, the cycads (or palms) and the ghinko (or the maidenhair tree whose leaves resemble little green hands), migrated across both Europe and the United States. Modern type trees were also to be found in these lush forests. Sequoias (the giant ancient redwood tree) covered Greenland, Iceland and arctic America, while the warm forests of eastern Greenland were particularly lush with the warmth loving ghinko. By the way, the largest living ghinko tree is to be found in Santa Cruz, California, and when it drops its leaves in the fall, people come from miles around to see this living fossil in its beautiful autumn dress.

Schuchert and Dunbar state that the Cretaceous sea which had invaded from the Atlantic and peneplaned (worn down) the early Appalachians, now drained away to somewhere beyond our present coastline, and the Eocene saw them again raised up by pressure from the southeast. The Wasatch range in Utah, according to Dana, was raised at this time from steady southeast to northwest pressure and the outwelling of lava was intermittent when the flexing became too strong for the ability of the rocks to twist and bend under the pressure. Altogether North America was increasing its rock mass from twelve to fifteen times. Fontaine, in his studies of the river systems of North Carolina, finds the flexing from southeast pressure to be about twenty degrees.

A sample of how the layman can help science is the Deschutes Geology Club of Oregon. These people have graduated from mere "rockhounds" to a real interest in geology. At the bend of Crooked river where it cuts into the old folds of Prineville county in central Oregon, they found the remains of a semi-tropical forest of Eocene age. Opalized logs of giant hardwoods of four different types of leaves made them seek out the help of Dr. Ethel Sanborn, paleobotanist of Oregon state college. These logs were crowded to the edge of an old swamp. Not far from this location, a fossilized bed was examined by Dr. Ralph Chaney, paleobotanist of

Entombed leafy plant found at Lake Uinta,
showing some veining. After Bradley.

the university of California, who found the leaves of fig trees and palms as well as redwood stumps. This forest apparently enjoyed a forty-inch rainfall during its life in the Eocene. According to Schuchert and Dunbar, the Sierras were completely peneplaned during the Eocene by the tremendous run off from the high crests of the great basin range (now gone) with their then icy crests. The Pacific coast was submerged to a considerable way inland.

In the Indian ocean, we know that the highest points of the Himalayas were below the Tethys, for at least a part of the Eocene, for Eocene fossils of shell bearing animals are to be found on their peaks. The Alps received their greatest crush from the south at this time according to some authorities, but Geikie, in discussing Mt. Blanc as "the classic example", remarks that the old granite top was forced up during the Eocene and uncovered with subsequent erosion. However, Bowie, in discussing the balance of continents and oceans, points out that the Earth is eroded about one foot every nine thousand years. This would give Mt. Blanc an age of about nine and a half million years which would suggest that it was either exceedingly high in the Eocene, or else, younger than we think perhaps due to repeated upthrusts.

For a closer look at the Eocene, let us pause for a moment to peruse the ancient writing which Dr. Wilmot H. Bradley found in the varves of an ancient Eocene lake (see Smithsonian 3461 - 1936).

The lake, which Dr. Bradley has named Uinta for the nearby Colorado range, began its life during the Eocene when tremendous pressures from the south and southeast rolled mountain peaks up around it and left it a depression for the clear mountain fed streams to fall into, before it rose to the point where its water spilled down a ravine and found its way to the sea. During this portion of Lake Uinta's reign, many streams, now dead, were its tributaries, and we know that its outlet reached the sea because the presence of large ocean-going fish make us certain of this. Skeletons of herring and perch attest to the fact, though we know that they did not live their lives there, but merely came up to spawn, as only adult and very young skeletons are to be found. Today most herring live in the sea, but thirty million years ago, it may have been different.

Crocodiles shared the most sluggish section of the lake with mud turtles (of whom they are very fond), where the water lapped the warm sub-tropical forest. Figs and grapes abounded, along with aromatic shrubs and trees. Gourds, delicate ferns and palms filled the forests about the shores of the lake. We know that the lake was surrounded by high mountains, however, for there are traces of oak, maple, hickory and gum woods along with pine and hemlock.

Under the warm forest flew a swarm of insects which closely resemble those now living. Caddice flies, whose larvae build about their bodies little masonry houses of sand grains and well jointed twigs of wood, were in the shallow water on the edge of the lake. Dragon flies and crane flies and even midges were common, while crickets and beetles as well as grasshoppers filled the air. Mosquitoes, black flies and gnats flew in swarms. Spiders spun their webs in the sunshine, once in a while catching in unwary cockroach running from one fallen log to another.

Stray feathers tell us that there were birds. Loons, sandpipers and rails were numerous, but their skeletons have escaped us. Only their feathers give them away. The only skeleton found was a relative to the grouse - perhaps a visitor from the uplands.

Despite the recent aspect of this forest, the skeletons of mammals who sometimes came down to drink in the lake, tell us that this was not of our time. The horse is our biggest sur-

Petrified tree stump at entrance to Ginkgo Petrified Forest museum at Vantage, Washington. Pictographs on wall are replicas of those found along the banks of the Columbia river, now submerged by the new dam.

prise. He was a tiny creature no larger than the dog, and science has given him the name "Eohippus" meaning "dawn horse." The name "hippus" was chosen for obvious reasons. He had four slender hoofs on each front foot and three on the back foot. The weight was born largely by a heavy pad not unlike that of modern dogs. He did not eat grass in those days. His teeth tell us that he ate forest leaves. Today our horse walks on his middle fingernail.

The varves of the long dead lake changed because of the spring freshets when the melting snows of the mountains brought down more minerals from the rapid water churning over the rocks. The summers made themselves known also by the deaths of the many tiny plants and insects suspended in the water. These fell to the bottom like a gentle snowfall, marking off the seasons.

For thousands of years the lake continued, and then for thousands more. Finally came the ash of volcanoes and of burning forests. The great mountains which had fed the lake for so long had turned destructive as the red magma of the mantle below the crust belched up in fury through the peaks. That record, too, was carried to the bottom of the lake in charred wreckage.

This lake bottom ultimately changed to rock and we can count the seasons very plainly. It took one thousand, eight hundred years for enough material to accumulate on the bottom to make a slab of rock one foot in thickness. The normal rate of accumulation for similar material runs from two hundred fifty to eight thousand two hundred years per foot. Thus it is possible to estimate that Lake Uinta had a life of about seven million, five hundred thousand years.

Dr. Bradley believes that in the record of that one lake, there is reason to think that the sunspot cycle of our sun, flaring up every eleven years, does indeed influence our weather. The fewer the sunspots, the lower the level in the lake, while with the sunspots come the storms. The rings of the stumps of the trees which grew around the old lake show that cycle even better, he said, because the more sunspots and the wetter the weather, the wider the tree ring.

However even more interesting to geologists intrigued by the weather cycles of time is Bradley's belief that the lake shows a much longer

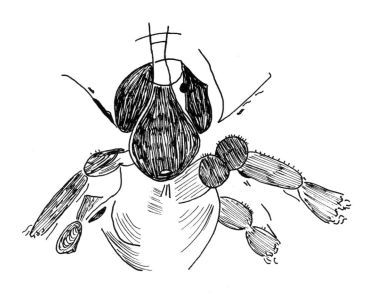

Entombed mite found at Lake Uinta.
Enlarged from 1/100th of an inch wide.
After Bradley.

cycle - a grand cycle with the eccentricity of Earth's orbit and the precession of the equinoxes.

Lake Uinta however, did not always present the picture of lush forest life. The volcanism became more and more frequent. The rain of ashes began to smother out the vegetation which tried to grow again. For long periods of time the place was a desert of wreckage and then finally the plants and animals came back as the lake began to function once more. However, renewed intervals of volcanism and cycles of devastation came. Pumice and ash brought down the embers of burned life.

Finally came drought. The source of the life-giving moisture began to dry up. The lake no longer reached its outlet and began to go stale. Fish flopped in the burning sun and died in the mulch, covered with the endless throngs of insects. Many species of plants died out entirely. At last the lake became a foul stench which seethed with flies while the water trickled in and fluctuated with the season. The flies too often remained on the mud, contributing their carcasses to the book of rock. After this period, the mulch which had been water became bitter with salt, which of itself became a sort of preservative. Delicate lacy ferns and animals were imprisoned there for the eyes of the future. Of this rock Bradley says: "As the organic ooze or gel was covered by successive layers and finally by thousands of feet of sediments, it was compressed even more and gradually hardened into a dense substance... Under the eye of the microscope, by grinding small pieces so thin as to be trans-lucent, these plates of rock suitably mounted on glass slides, show not only finely preserved micro-organisms (germs etc.) but in addition, an off assortment of wreckage - the eyes of tiny insects, spatulate scales from mosquito wings, and an abundance of pollen grains. When this hardened organic substance is heated it yields a distillate of crude oil from which may be obtained gasoline, fuel oil, and related products."

The down warp which originally caused Lake Uinta then began to cease, and gradually the tributary streams, which came back with a renewal of dampness, filled up the lake bed with sediment, and the lake ceased to exist.

In another field, hunting for the past cycles of time, Dr. A. E. Douglass of the university of Arizona, who compiled a comprehensive study of tree rings, gave a very good tool to the anthropologists and archaeologists, although it has not as yet been pushed back to the Eocene. However, that is not saying that it cannot be, especially since we know that the varves of Lake Uinta matched the tree rings of the logs found on its shores. The lake makes a longer calendar and no doubt might be used as a check on the tree ring when it is pushed back far enough for Uinta and other lakes to be used as a check. Dr. Douglass found that by placing one tree against another and matching them, a definite record of the warm and cold, wet or dry seasons could thus be made. He also found that the sun-spot cycle of eleven years was very prominent, and repeated itself again and again.

In his books: "Climatic Cycles and Tree-Ring Growths" and "Secrets of the Southwest", Dr. Douglass describes how his tremendous work began. His story reads almost like fiction. He and the scientists who worked with him started with weather marked, storm beaten trees usually to be found upon hillsides in exposed locations where little ground water could help them with their struggle to remain alive. When enough of these were cut down and their rings compared, the amount of agreement was a surprise to everyone present. Certain years and also certain cycles of years showed far more water than other cycles.

With the calendar thus started by living trees, Dr. Douglass began to push the calendar back. He hunted larger and older trees, thus adding the story of their varves. The finding of a missing portion was a thrill and a tremendous scientific triumph for the team of scientific minds working with him. Then came the discovery that a burned log still retained his climatic varves. The simple matter of burning did not destroy the record.

With this discovery published, scientists began to pick up the bits of charcoal which early man left in his abandoned fires as they were unearthed, and packing them in cotton to protect the fragile record of varves, began sending them to Dr. Douglass. This led not only to pushing back of the calendar, but also the actual dating of much of Amerind prehistory.

Then came a new tool. By using a corer, a long core could be removed from an old beam of wood which would not necessitate the cutting down of the trees. The corer could also be used on ceremonial beams in the kiva or men's house of peublos, which otherwise the tribe would never allow to be taken down to count varves. The Hopi of Arizona (pronounced hope-ee, meaning "people of peace") became very much interested and were as much amazed as the scientists when they learned that their pueblo was built before Christopher Columbus had talked with Queen Isabella about a trip to the west. In a like manner, the magnificent ruin of Casa Grande, previously thought to be about the same age as Walpi of the Hopi people, was found to date from the time of William the conqueror.

Dr. Douglass hopes to push back the time of his calendar into the Pleistocene and then into even earlier cycles of time. The present writer suggested to him that he get in touch with Dr. Leakey in south Africa who was making (and still is) some fascinating discoveries of early man. "Unfortunately for us," Dr. Douglass wrote to me later, "Dr. Leakey saw no reason for keeping these charred fragments from early camp fires and had thrown them away." Then in a happier note, he concluded: "There will come a time when the tree ring calendar will be matched with the varves of the glaciers and those of ancient lakes until there is a complete calendar of the whole Cenozoic period."

Dr. Douglass was not a young man when he wrote this letter, for I could pick up my book of Dr. Lowell on "The Canals of Mars" and read how Lowell observatory was founded in the clear air of the 90's at the university of Arizona, and how Dr. Douglass, then a handsome young scientist, had helped him with his work on astronomy. Since those days when Dr. Lowell, who had spent half a century observing Mars, chose the location at Flagstaff for its clear air while he corresponded with the great Italian astronomer upon the subject of the Martian canals, their duplicity of lines and how one was shut off when the other came on every twelve years, Dr. Douglass had lived on into the time when the foul air of our planet had made the seeing of Mars almost impossible even for the great eyes of Palomar. What astronomers can no longer see they doubt, and so the work of Lowell fell into disrepute. The present writer asked a great authority concerning Mars, rather sarcastically, I am afraid, that since he no longer had the clear air of Dr. Lowell, was he scientist enough not to doubt but rather to state emphatically that there is no intelligent life on Mars and the canals which bring the water from the snow caps and pump it (how else would it go in two directions crossing the equator each way in turn from the pole which was giving the water that season?) are simply not there? With a flush he said: "I see that you have read Lowell. True, we can no longer see, but we hope for some way to get off the Earth to see. You know that for us, all the stars are fading out."

Thus Dr. Douglass with the adventurous mind of the true scientist who, never losing the enthusiasm of youth, has turned his attention from the stars to learning more about our own planet and its fascinating history, and is busy forming a great tool of science to be one day, used to check other means of accurately reading the distant past.

Dr. Douglass has found that the trees of Alaska correspond with amazing accuracy to those of Arizona as well as New Mexico. Thus such men as Emiliani, Douglass, Bradley and Antevs as well as many others are blazing a trail for future scientists, perhaps as yet unborn, who will some day be able to say (after many more missing pages of Earth's story have been read) that on a Monday which was April the seventh, seven million years ago, while the sun was shining, Volcano Number 560, which has a cycle of five thousand years, again began its eruptions, coinciding with Volcano Number 582 which has a thousand and sixty year cycle.

Perhaps that is not probable for some time but I hope that it will be possible for man to put out a bulletin some day soon that fault #187 is due to have a tremendous earthquake where it crosses the 17th fracture zone. When we stop to think of how many of these records of the past (which definitely effect our future) we are burning up every day in the tanks of our cars and the furnaces of our homes, we may wonder. However, scientists are continually searching out the hidden pages, and undoubtedly the Creator has hidden enough of them away in such difficult to reach locations that the grey matter of "homo sapiens" may someday surpass his capacity for greed.

Chapter 43

Periods Of Rest And Periods Of Fire

(If you live near an old fault line) "the next great earthquake may take place while you are reading this book, or it may not come during your lifetime. But one thing is sure: it is definitely on the way." Robert Iacopi in Earthquake Country - Sunset Book 1964.

In this study of the land masses and oceans with their cracks and volcanic rhythms, as yet so little understood, we have reached the Oligocene (Oh-lig-oh-scene) or time of peace. Looking at the North American block and much of Amer-Eurasia, we see that the big shove came during the Eocene, but turning back to the Indian, it definitely began earlier. Now many authorities theorize that these great magmatic waves of fury move slowly, but the intensity is none the less terrible when they strike.

If the Himalayas followed the great volcanism of the Jurassic fragments in their plants, and in turn this followed the convulsion in the lands south of the African capes, spilling over from Antarctica to Madagascar and Lemuria, then the wave of volcanism which started in the ice laden continent of Gondwannaland first hit east and then came along the Tethys westward. The movement was deceptively slow, so slow in fact that scientists have often failed to see the connection. While Gondwannaland erupted in the most terrible volcanism Earth has known, Australia and Polynesia received fairly strong shoves, wrinkling up mountains. When Australia and Polynesia broke out in violent volcanism cutting them off from their parent land, the northern masses were receiving their first shoves.

During the Cretaceous, the Himalayas began to rise as long islands in the Tethys sea, but it was the Eocene before their peaks rose entirely out of the Tethys sea, and thrust up their cordillera with fire and flame.

For the benefit of the scientists who may be following this, let us go back for a moment.

Permian: The greatest glaciation the planet has seen and at its close the breakup of Gondwannaland. Steers finds that the volcanism of south and west African capes is of this time. Dana points out the volcanism at Buenos Aires range was of the Permian diastrophism. Kriedel believes that all signs point to a large land area (weighted with ice?) being down fractured into the magma between the south African capes and Antarctica. Schuchert finds that South America and Antarctica started west during this diastrophism, leaving behind sialic land bridges.

Triassic: Van Der Gracht places this as the final separation of Australia. Botanists note that the Polynesian islands are Triassic fragments in their plants, and Australia is from Triassic to Jurassic in hers.

The continents were high and seas low in the Triassic. Was this because Polynesia struck Asia just east of India's present position? Of course, the Polynesian isles are situated along cracks in the Pacific floor, but they display sialic patterns, and Darwin showed that the coral upon which they rest at present goes down to depths where no coral could live, while recent tests proved a base was below the coral. Orogeny (mountain building) was heavy in western Australia.

Jurassic: Now if the Triassic was a first contact between the southern and northern masses, the Jurassic should show southwestern pressure. The Tethys closed. According to Gerth the south Atlantic ocean was not yet open due to no Jurassic fossils. Dana finds that the Appalachian cordillera shows thrusting and pressure from southeast to northwest - a reversal of Paleozoic thrusting. Apparently the northern mass was beginning to pull away because after the closing of the Tethys during the Triassic diastrophism, it now again began to reopen. During the early part of the Jurassic, the land was high and seas low, also showing contact in Triassic diastrophism. Van Der Gracht places the Jurassic as the final break of Australia with her parent continent. New Zealand was born from the sea. The mountain building went from the west to the east in Australia, showing eastern movement. Du Toit observes that the lava flows which were all over the capes of south Africa during the early Jurassic had migrated to the north of Africa before the end of the Jurassic and by the mid Cretaceous were pouring out in sheets from one thousand to four thousand feet in thickness.

Cretaceous to Eocene: To cover this again

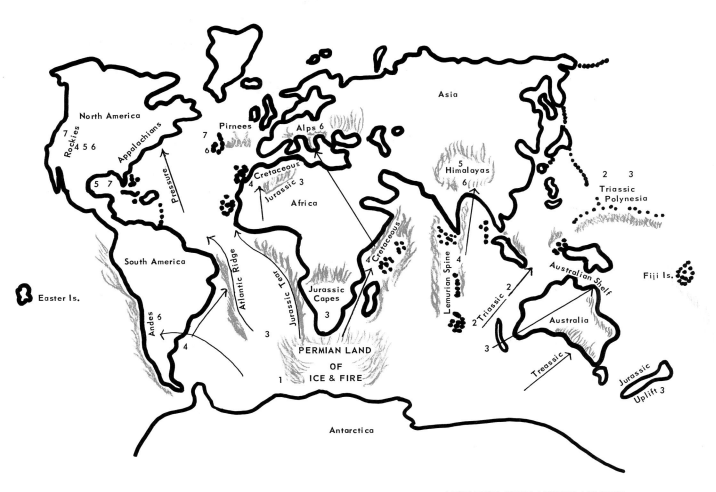

would be repetitious, but it is easy to see that the former was a period of engulfing lava in the Indian while the Eocene was a period of tremendous uplift in the northern masses. Again the Tethys was closed and with much lava.

For a moment let us discuss Antillia, as some authorities prefer to call the islands of the Caribbean. They first appear to science as islands during the Jurassic when the Tethys was reopened. Schmidt finds that Haiti, Cuba and Jamaica were isolated at this time and their plants and animals show that they are Jurassic in time. In fact the fauna (animals) is all pre-Tertiary in character. Davis agrees that the coral reefs had already been formed by the Tertiary and that the finding of an animal of the mammal species in a fossilized condition suggests raising and again subsidence. He does not think that Antillia could have remained a continent until the Tertiary since limestones of this age (an oceanic rock) are to be found in the Antigua and St. Martin's groups.

Spence implies that all Caribbean islands stood on an Antillian continent, but this is questioned by Davis. He is more inclined to believe that Antillian ranges have two ages. Those of

HOW THE FIRE MOVES NORTH

1 - Permian: ice ends in diastrophism.
2 - Triassic: fire hits Polynesia, western Australia.
3 - Jurassic: fire hits Polynesia, eastern Australia. Early Jurassic capes, late Jurassic fire hits north Africa.
4 - Cretaceous: fire all over Indian ocean, Andes rising, Rockies-Sierras rising. Lemuria sank, Tethys sea closing, ends Mesozoic.
5 - Paleocene through Eocene: Himalayas rising, north continents pushed up in blocks.
6 - Oligocene: Tethys opens in west, fire hits Himalayas-Alps. Aleutian bridge up.
7 - Miocene.

Guadeloupe, Dominican and Martinique are younger, while on the other hand, those of the Grenadines, Virgins and related groups are probably the surviving summits, much worn by erosion, which once stood upon an ancient shield.

Since these mountains, or some of them, seem to form festoons, we had better discuss this phenomena. In his studies of the East Indian archipelago, Brouwer finds much evidence for his belief that festoons of islands shows pressure upon the concave inner portion. G. A. F. Molengraaf, in the same region, agrees with Brouwer, and states that festoons are the advance and not the posterior side of an advancing continent. However, in a twisting continent, as South America is now apparently twisting in a clockwise movement, the festoons in the Caribbean would be on the temporarily advancing side, at least in the location where they are to be found.

There is another point which is most illuminating in this picture of the break up of Gondwannaland. Daly finds that the lavas of Fiji in the Pacific on the eastern shore of ancient Gondwannaland and of Easter island on the western shore of that lost continent are very similar. Both are apparently resting on a sialic or granitic base. Concerning this lava he says: "Is this remarkable glass a derivative of original basalt or is it the product of reaction between hot basaltic liquid and old crystalline granite underneath?" Easter island, a long spike of a volcano which constantly sways like a ship at sea, is standing on the (probably long sunken) Albatross plateau, off the coast of South America where that continent moves into the Pacific. Was the plateau of Easter island one of the fragments which has been down fractured into the sea? Nor is this all, for the magmas of Gondwannaland show a distinct pattern. The internal magmas, meaning all the lavas of the Indian and Atlantic as well as those along the Tethys, are sialic rich, or in other words, show mixture with con-

tinental rock, while those on the Pacific ocean side of the dispersing fragments are sialic-poor, showing little mixture of continental rock.

Also the outbreak of the lavas of Gondwannaland and her fragments show a timing pattern. As the western volcanoes or inner ones of Australia show that they are older and the Pacific ranges give evidence of being younger, indicating advances of the continent to the east into the Pacific according to Molengraaf and others, so in South America the pattern is reversed. The internal ranges are older and those to the west are younger, again showing advance into the Pacific.

So we come to the time of the Eocene. As the Paleocene - Cretaceous was the time of the first giant shove, bowing up the continents, the Eocene to Oligocene was the time of greatest lava eruption in the Himalayas, and in the Alps. Tutton, Sorby and Geikie all believe that the peaks of the Alps are composed of granite that is tremendously ancient in its structure and was forced up at this time by massive pressure from the south to southeast. In other words, they seem to be saying that the ancient shield of the continent was what was crumpled at this time, when the closing of the Tethys reached their location.

As we watched the Eocene progress, it seems that for most of the time, the Tethys may have still been open near the land of the gulf plate as shown in the drilling cores, and the lake Uinta varves which show ocean going fish.

Also the present writer has noted that the giant oyster of this period which is also to be found farther east, is found in the desert of Imperial valley in Painted canyon among other places, which is to the north of the highway running between El Centro and San Diego, California. These fossilized shells are longer than a man's hand. If any of my readers should find one, I am certain that the nearest university, or in fact any university, would appreciate the gift. (The present writer presented one to USC, Cambridge and Oxford, England.)

Before the Eocene was over, the volcanism increased as we noted, and in the gulf, the flexing of the old plate was the strongest yet, as it was down warped to plutonic depths.

In the gulf plate, the Oligocene was a time of submersion. The picture is not wholly understood because the islands of the Caribbean need more study. Jukes Brown and Harrison have called attention to the formations of Barbados

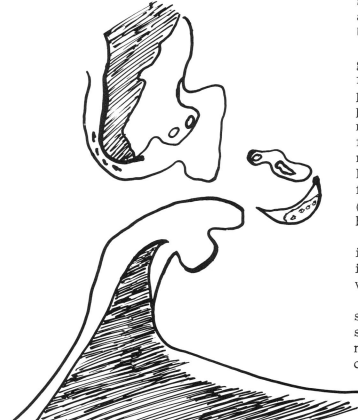

A study of Drake straits. South American and Antarctic shelves part, leaving fragments. Compiled from Croll and Wegener.

island which shows evidence of a two to three thousand fathom (or a nine thousand foot) upheaval from the sea. Globigerinal ooze underlies the coral reef to a height of eight to nine hundred feet here. Similarly Dana was interested by the discovery of the deposits of radiolarian ooze in Haiti, Cuba and Jamaica, implying upheaval during a different climatic cycle since globigerinal ooze covers the present sea bottom. We will have to leave the meaning of this in the geologists' basket entitled "unfinished business".

Returning to the Oligocene, some students believe that a new crest was pushing against the Alps during the end of the Eocene and early to mid-Oligocene. Was it the calm before this new magmatic Alpine wave which was depressing the forests of the gulf plate and drowning them periodically with invasions of the sea? If so, the long peaceful Oligocene came to an end here with the crest of the wave hitting the gulf plate early in the Miocene.

The peaceful Oligocene was a time when volcanism was at a minimum. The northern continents, apparently having reacted to the shove of the Eocene, were moving peacefully to the north. Seas were wide spread. The Tethys was again reopened after being closed at the end of the Eocene with volcanic fireworks, and a long period in which animals and plants found time to live and diversify in peace, finally came to an end. That end came at the scene of the first crush - the Himalayas and Alps.

Schuchert and Dunbar give an interesting condensed history: "In Jurassic time, horizontal compression from the south caused two or three folds to rise out of the (Tethys) sea. Although this marks the beginning of the Alpine structure, the region as a whole remained submerged during much of the Cretaceous. At the close of the Mesozoic there was further compression and some uplift, and in the Eocene came the first decided thrust, but marine water returned between rising geanticlinal folds, and persisted until the middle Oligocene. Then occurred the first great paroxysm of Alpine orogeny. Compression from the south caused great recumbent folds to rise up as mountain arcs out of the sea, and to ride forward over the old foreland, north of the geosyncline, where they piled up as a series of nappes."

Thus it would seem that the greatest magmatic wave riding out of the Indian during the Cretaceous, struck the Himalayas during the Eocene, the Alps during the Oligocene and the gulf plate's swampy jungles at the end of the

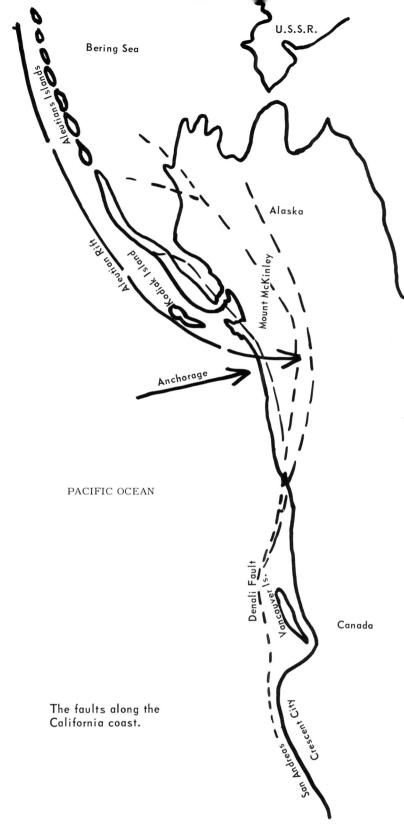

The faults along the California coast.

Oligocene and start of the Miocene.

The curtain goes up on the time when the fragments from shattered Gondwannaland, India and Africa tried to over ride the northern mass in what has come to be known as "the fiery Miocene."

Chapter 44

The Fiery Miocene

"Our conscious years are but a moment in the history of the elements which build us. Are you a bank clerk and do you live at Peekham? It was not always so.

"I know not which is the more strange, that I should carry about with me some fibres of my minister grandfather; or that in him, as he sat in his cool study, grave, reverend, contented gentlemen, there was an aboriginal frisking of the blood that was not his; tree top memories lay dormant in his mind; tree top instincts awoke and were trod down . . . but still gamboled and chattered in the brain of the old divine."

Robert Louis Stevenson

Let us enter one of the most intriguing of all the ages of time - the epoch when the Atlantic was a land, and our first certain ancestor trod barefoot through its forests.

We know that the Atlantic was land because botanists have come to realize that the great deciduous forests and ferny jungles of the Miocene must have crossed this present ocean on a very wide front. The oak came from Europe to America, meeting the great mass of American species going to Europe, where during the coming periods of ice, they were unable to escape the cold and perished. Louis Agassiz was the first paleobotanist to point out this migration when he spoke of it moving "on a wide front" across what is now ocean. Lesquiereux noted that a minimum of European species are to be found in the American Eocene, and the amazing exchange was rather from America to Europe than from Europe to America. A great number of animal species also passed back and forth between the continents. Some, such as one breed of fossilized horse is to be found in no other location at this time than on the present Atlantic shores of both sides.

The maple, which migrated across an Aleutian bridge from Japan during the Oligocene, now crossed to Europe during the Miocene. The coni-

Young dragon tree (draconis) and grasses.

Small rhinoceros (diceratherium).

Monster pig with four foot skull.
Mate lying down. (dinohyus)

Sketches by author from Drs. R. Perlman,
H. Zimn, P. Shaffer (university of Illinois)
and Dr. F. H. T. Rhodes (university of Wales).

fers, (trees having needles and cones) spread widely across the higher ranges of both Europe and America while the redwood, palm and the ghinko were to be found in the forests of Greenland, Iceland and other northern locations. Deciduous trees (those which had learned to drop their leaves in order to better endure frost) were also marching to new locations. Many of the American species which were lost in the ice ages of Europe were able to migrate in the Americas and thus survive. The fig was able to migrate to the warm forests of the Mediterranean where, until recently, man has always believed it to be a Mediterranean plant.

The dragon tree, an exotic plant of unusual beauty (perhaps cultivated by you as a potted house plant, or if you live in a warmer climate, then as a striking break against a plain wall), is a plant of the Atlantic ocean. Its species are from the various islands - either Canaries, Azores or groups of the Caribbeans. They differ in width of the spike like leaves or the color, and are hardy, making their corner of the porch or patio beautiful, but sometimes surprising their owners by blooming suddenly with myriads of lovely flowers from the top, or else growing into a sixty foot giant. If one is accidentally hurt, its sap will pour out like scarlet blood, giving the plant its legendary name of ''dragons blood'' which science has shortened to ''draconis''. The American Indian touches it reverently saying: ''This is a plant of the dragon land which once filled the Atlantic ocean.'' Who knows? He just may be correct.

One warm day in Spain where some men were digging for coal in what had been a tropical Miocene forest, they suddenly uncovered a petrified skeleton. It had been cloven in half, perhaps by the slipping of the earth in a rift. Its first appearance was that of a small ape, but when scientists were called in to view the remains as they had been found, still attached to their matrix of coal with its impressions of the ferns of that long lost day, they became very much excited. This creature was no ape. He had a nose arch, and his face was definitely much straighter than the faces of other apes. His chin, too, was longer, and his teeth smaller. Here was the first actual link on the chain of man to all the varieties of sub-men who ranged the earth during the Pliocene and Pleistocene. The scientists called him ''pro-consul'' and announced his age as ''Not less than ten million years.'' If he had been any other animal, they would no doubt have placed his age as of fifteen or twenty million because the Miocene began some twenty-five million

years ago, but a sub-human skeleton, definitely straight-faced, made them immediately very cautious. The Miocene ended about ten million years ago.

Our ancestor was a small creature, walking erect, but only about four feet in height, and therefore probably moving timorously among the giant carnivores of the day. Perhaps, for safety he moved in tribes or groups. Undoubtedly he sought the high mountains to get away at times from the huge marauding cats, or the fierce American pig (dinohyus) which was larger than the American rhinoceros (diceratherium) of the period, or for that matter the horse, or the American camel (stenomylus) which roamed the Miocene forests. The horse had become about forty inches high by this time and walked on three little hoofs instead of its present single hoof.

If little pro-consul climbed the mountains, he undoubtedly soon learned that by wearing the skins of dead animals, he could be warmer, and this fact would give him a wider hunting range, as well as a better margin of safety. In the magnificent peaks of the time, the Atlantic range of the ridge, the Appalachians, not to mention the growing Alpine-Atlas-Himalayan cordillera, snow capped and magnificent, he must have learned to love beauty. Perhaps all of us who thrill at the sight of a breath taking sunset seen from the peak of a glacial, such as the present writer once saw from the top of Glacier national park, Montana when the reflected opalescent pink glow slid along the icy pinnacles of the mountain peaks below, thrust through the purple sea of the forests. Or like the throat grasping beauty of a fierce sunrise once seen from Dante's view on the Funerals above Death valley. Here the sun slips gilded shafts of light over the frozen waves of the Devil's Golf Course below, which once a group of thirsty pioneers mistook for water, and after they had lowered their wagons down the cliffs into this death trap, discovered to their horror that it was but rock salt. Perhaps we owe our ability to appreciate such sights to our thousands upon thousands of ancestors who sat for countless hours on lonely vigils, waiting and watching either for edible game, or the stealthy approach of an enemy.

This is the reason which the American Indian gives for his exquisite sense of beauty, exemplified by the fact that many of his langauges have more than a dozen words for the exact aspect of such scenes as well as for all the various shades of color and variations of loveliness. In fact, in this respect alone, the Amerind languages surpass, for the most part, those of our so-called civilized European tongues.

While on the subject of beauty it is well to note now that if for no other reason than for the expanse of its canvasses of magnificent scenery, the Miocene is well named. In fact its name may most easily be remembered by the phrase: "Oh my, what a scene!"

Then how did the period win its scientific nickname of the fiery Miocene?

Because the magma wave which had started at the scene of the ice sheets in the southern polar regions during the Permian and had reached its greatest fury in the Indian during the Cretaceous now hit the northern block during the Miocene.

Geologists are not certain that the Atlas-Alpine-Himalaya cordillera crested this late. Most of them wish to place that event as earlier, but there is one argument which they must meet from the paleo-zoologists, and it is these questions which demonstrate the inter-dependency of the sciences.

During the Oligocene the Aleutian bridge from Asia to the Americas was dry land and functioning as a means for animals and plants to cross. This has been likened to a drawbridge which is open to traffic for one era and closed for another. It is thought provoking the Aleutian bridge was open in the Oligocene when the Atlantic Appalachian bridge was apparently closed probably due to spreading water, and in the Miocene when the animals and plants were crossing the Atlantic, the Aleutian bridge was closed probably due to submergence. However while the Aleutian bridge was open in the Oligocene, some American species made their way to Asia. Among these was the baluchitherium, a giant rhinoceros measuring eighteen feet tall at the shoulder. He was therefore four feet higher than the Imperial mammoth, and the largest land mammal. He crossed the Aleutian bridge into Asia, probably along with the palm, oak and walnut forests of Canada. At this time the deserts of Asia were still damp forests. However, before the Miocene was over, they began to dry out to their present desert state, and the answer would seem to be that the Himalayas gained their great height during the Miocene, thus cutting off the flow of damp sea air with its moisture bearing content. The mammals who had crossed and could not find their way back, and were not able to adjust to the new desert conditions, began to die off. These extinct species in Asia would certainly suggest that the Himalayas gained their great heights during the Miocene.

There is also another thought which science has not as yet entertained, but nevertheless is intriguing. The long headed and round headed races of mankind are separated by the Himalayas in their great fountain heads. When did this seperation take place? We will leave the answers to this question on the shelf entitled "unfinished business."

The Miocene began in the land of the gulf plate which is now the sea beyond Florida. At the end of the Oligocene this was again raised and a tropical forest grew. It was not unlike the forest in Spain from which we received the important skeleton of pro-consul. Then the Miocene began with deep thunder in the base and the explosion of unknown volcanoes announced its arrival. The Miocene is a mass of wreckage...in the gulf plate. Ashes and cinders from the mighty throats of volcanic giants were roaring the coming of the magma crest. The pressure from the south in the Catahoula beds which usher in that crest was the greatest ever experienced in the gulf plate in so short a period. They bear the tell-tale marks of carbonized wood, mingled with volcanic glass and ash.

By the mid-Miocene the warm wet pleasant climate of the Atlantic was interrupted with the roar of volcanoes along the Appalachian bridge and doubtless also along the high peaks of the Atlantean ridge. The magma crest had arrived. The Alps and the Himalayas broke out with fire and the thrusting was felt all the way to the Pacific ocean. Undoubtedly some of the festoon islands moved further toward the sea.

However, it was in North America where the fury of the time is the most easily studied, that the cresting magma wave of the Miocene can be seen in all of its tremendous power. It had now passed the gulf plate and had moved to the great basin range in mid-Miocene, striking it with tremendous rifts between the then worn down Sierras and the western face of the Colorado plateau. Suddenly the entire range with all of its peaks crested with glaciers was dropped in a block for the distance of three thousand feet.

And simultaneously, or what seems so to us at this distance away in time, the great peaks of the mile high mountains in Idaho were shaken in unimagined fury, tremendous rifts opened up along the valleys and sheets of lava poured out - finally completely burying the previous land to the crests of its highest mountains.

After this performance is there anyone who would dare to say that it could not have been repeated during the Pleistocene in the mid-Atlantic?

Chapter 45

The Pliocene

Now we come to the time when the continents of the northern mass of Amer-Eurasia responded to the great push of the Miocene, and began a journey north toward the pole. We would naturally find that during the millions of years of this journey, there would not be too much volcanism, as the continental masses were apparently not meeting too great a resistance. Also we would expect that the climates would be slowly cooling. Both of these expectations seem to be met by the facts.

We do not have any outpouring of lava such as the sheets of Idaho, which Schuchert and Dunbar found during the Miocene were a mile in thickness and had a 24,000 cubic mile capacity, burying the previous peaks of the Idaho range.

The fiery magmatic wave which had struck the Alps and Himalayas from the Oligocene through the Miocene; Florida and the gulf plate at the first of the Miocene; and travelled on to the great basin range, dropping that mighty structure, and then welling out of the rifts in Idaho during the mid-Miocene, was now carrying the continents northward on its crest.

The Miocene apparently ended with a cool Atlantic current, and this fact seems to suggest that the Atlantic Appalachian bridge joining Canada through the central ridge to Ireland and England may originally have been cut at this time. However, this could have been for a short period only as both Pliocene and Pleistocene saw many species of both plants and animals continue to cross from continent to continent.

This was the stage upon which our pro-consul ancestors crossed with numerous "sisters, cousins and aunts". In other words the age of man was about to dawn. But there were many experiments. I was once asked by a rather snobbish titled lady in England, if the Darwinian theory had not been discarded? My questioning look at her made her rephrase her question.

"After all, the 'missing link' has never really been found, now has he?" looking at me through her jeweled lorgnette as if I might be the long lost specimen.

I smiled disarmingly and asked:

"Which 'missing link', are you proposing to discuss?"

There was more truth than sarcasm in this statement. Let us first take up the bushman of Africa. Not that he is a missing link, but there is a mystery in his background which makes him a fascinating object to study. At one time he was not a scientific riddle. He was only a curious tiny African savage of a somewhat unprepossessing type. Then a young scientist named L.B.S. Leakey from Cambridge remembered his own great rift valley of Africa and decided to excavate there. He was not particularly interested in the bushman, but scientific mysteries seem to have a strange way of running in parallels.

Now if there is one dominant characteristic of the modern European skull, it is the fact that in proportion to the size of the head, the jaw and size of the teeth are shrinking. For example, Neanderthal man was not devoid of brain capacity, yet when taken in proportion to the size of his teeth and jaw, the brain case did not seem so large. In this matter of jaw-to-brain ratio, Dr. Arthur Keith of England has worked out a table, which takes the modern European as an example against which to measure other early fossilized forms of man for a better understanding.

About the same time that Leakey announced his interest in Africa as the possible cradle-land of man, a resident of the little inlet of Fish-Hoek, near Cape Town, South Africa asked Dr. M.R. Drennan of Cape Town university if he (an amateur) could not excavate under professional direction in a cave which he had explored with some companions. His offer was accepted with interest and the work began. Under the partial direction of the university he began taking great pains to keep meticulous notes and sift the various horizons.

When his first horizon was that of a crude culture not unlike the nearby bushmen and with a few skeletons in shallow graves which were promptly identified as the local inhabitant's ancestors (in all probability) everyone was pleased that all was going as expected.

The scientists freely predicted that the next find should be that of small brained, big jawed ancestors - allowing for the passage of time, of course. They were wrong. The next horizon was a hearth showing strong Mousterian influence with even the tools that suggested the inhabitants were not bushmen, but Neanderthaloid. Now the scientists became most intrigued. Neanderthal man had never been found in Africa. His home soil, as far as science knew, was Europe - particularly central Europe. But the young men digging could find no skeletons. They searched very carefully, but although there were the tools and other indications, the skeletons evaded them.

They continued digging down very carefully to the next horizon. Types of soil and the depth of each was kept and labeled. Then they came to a new hearth. The scientists were alerted. They had every reason now to expect a Neanderthal burial. What a find that would be! The hearth proved to be a disappointment. It had been used perhaps only once or twice. There were no tools. Perhaps it was an overnight stop or an outpost during an invasion or a war. Finally there was a burial. The scientists were again alerted. They rubbed their hands in warm anticipation. At last a Neanderthal...but no. This was no beetle browed, heavy jawed Neanderthal man. This man was tall. His face was straight. The nose was thin and arched. The cheek bones were wide and the face was diamond shaped. The chin was firm with a long upper lip . . . Cro Magnon man here in Africa? Below the hearth of his old enemy Neanderthal? Below the modern races?

Dr. Drennan of Cape Town university was much excited by this sudden revelation. They measured the brain case. True it was greater than that of modern peoples. They measured the teeth. They were proportionately small to the brain case. They looked at the thin hawked nose arch and shook their heads. This was fantastic!

Now for the first time the scientists flocked into the bush to round up the puzzled bushmen. They studied noses, brain cases, type of face, etc. They had a tremendous puzzle to unravel. This ancient petrified African from Fish-Hoek had an amazing ratio to modern man on Keith's brain to jaw scale. For every cm of palate this enigma had 66.6 cc of brain space. Modern man averages much less and runs no higher than 1:60, but Fish-Hoek man was 1:66.6.

Yet, in spite of this superiority, scientists came to the conclusion that his living descendents were bushmen. Why? Because in spite of the fact that bushmen skulls were tiny compared with their ancestor, they were of the same shape. Bushmen teeth were very small compared to those of other negro tribes, and when placed against the ancient skull, it was to be seen that the face had changed but slightly. The difference was indeed in the size of the brain case, and that is what caused the change in ratio.

Then the scientists sought out another tribe of neighboring negroes. Here they found a difference. The nose was wider and shorter, the teeth much larger, thus causing a more chinless type of face.

The scientists put their conclusions on the shelf and awaited more finds. The ancient Fish-Hoek man could have been a captive from a distance who became chief and took many wives. It may have just been a freakish occurrence. They became skeptical because, in any race, individual differences are tremendous, even among the modern low capacity bushmen. But then there was the haunting memory of that Neanderthal hearth. Was there an invasion?

Now if this was the only discovery, we would be more than justified in being skeptical. However, such is not the case. In northern Transvaal is an arid country called Springbok plains. At one time this had been a swamp - many thousands of years ago in another climatic cycle. At that time this desert had been a fertile woodland, and the swamp probably an overflow from a brook. Apparently a body had once been buried here. Later when the soil became swampy and infiltrated the dead man, the lime from the water came up through the soil from the rocks below, a layer of which had been basaltic, and the skeleton was inclosed in a rocky matrix of limestone along with the animal which apparently he had been hunting - the extinct giant buffalo. Over this rocky formation the red sands of the present desert were blowing.

Now such climatic changes mean antiquity, and science became interested as the body was freed carefully from its ancient tomb. And once more they were amazed. The petrified bones were those of a large man with great brain-capacity, a long thin nose and a strong jaw, but again with proportionately small teeth.

Then at Hagenstad in the Orange Free State a culture very similar to Europe's Aurignacian was found with the remains of this same extinct giant buffalo. The Aurignacian culture is that of Cro Magnon man.

It was about this time when Leakey graduated in anthropology from Cambridge, England, and remembered the great rift valley of his childhood. He remembered the various levels, and from all he could learn these would seem to represent the great pluvials of the ice ages. This was, of course, the Pleistocene and not the previous Pliocene (Ply-oh-scene), but anthropology must be studied in reverse. We have to dig through the later horizons to come to the earlier.

What Leakey lacked in money in 1926 he more than made up for by enthusiastic student volunteers.

Geology tells us that the three giant landlocked lakes of this tremendous rift were at one time one sheet of water. Leakey found three old

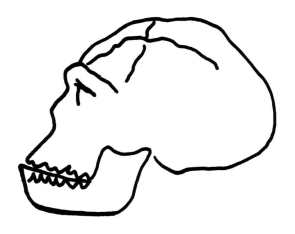

Neanderthal skull found in 1914 in Weimar valley, Germany, in the grave of an inter-glacial stream. Now regarded as early, since later Neanderthaloids gained in skull capacity.

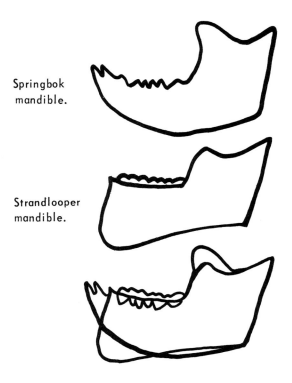

Springbok mandible.

Strandlooper mandible.

Springbok mandible placed over the Strandlooper mandible, showing the straight facedness and chin of the earlier mandible.

beaches - one at 300 feet above the present water line, one at 600 feet, and finally one at 800 feet. He was of the opinion that these corresponded with the pluvials of Europe - a rather forward looking opinion for that time. Geology is today far more willing to agree. (See African Pluvial Periods and Prehistoric Man by J. Reid Moir and Report on Quaternary Geology of the African Rift Valley by Dr. Erik Nilsson.)

On the 393 foot level of the Nakuru basin, Leakey and his enthusiastic young scientists found some ancient burials which had been disturbed by the valley being twice filled and twice drained since they were placed there. Altogether however, he found twenty-six individuals, and all were of the same racial type. They were the tall disharmonic long head with the wide cheek bones, short firm chins and noses which were the long hawked mark of Cro Magnon man.

The present writer finds it significant that there were twenty-six burials. Any American Indian of the Atlantic tribes would nod in recognition of the ceremonial number for the people who followed the Venus calendar. Of course, it may have been merely coincidental.

Leakey was intrigued by this discovery of what apparently were individuals of the old Cro Magnon race - even to the unusual skull capacity. Yet most amazing of all to him was that they were surrounded with beads, implements worked in flint, and had stone mortars for crushing grain, showing that even during the Pleistocene they had cereal food. No longer can we say that cereal eating man is recent. We must go back into the ice age to find the pluvial period when this village grew its grain, fashioned beads and buried its dead beside this lake. Beautiful bits of finely decorated pottery reminded the young workers that these men, like the pre-Egyptians, were even at this time in antiquity a people of an ancient cultural heritage.

Leakey now climbed to the 600 foot beach. Here he found a large cave where once more he and his enthusiastic supporters began their careful work just as they had been taught in Cambridge. They kept a map of the soil, and what bits of partial horizons they found. After going through several levels, the investigators found typical Mousterian artifacts and congratulated each other that they would be the first to uncover a Neanderthal man in Africa. They were disappointed. No skeletons greeted them, but their time had run out and they had to go back to England.

When they returned in 1928 and continued, they fully expected to find the skeletal type always connected with this culture. The bones of the animals which he had tossed away from his cave dinners were all the correct ones for the time of Neanderthal's period. Yet the skeleton of the elusive Neanderthal eluded him and his young scientific friends.

Finally the Neanderthal level or horizon was passed. They dug on down through drift and a few ancient bones of extinct animals and then came to an earlier horizon. With amazement the young investigators saw that this culture was Aurignacian! Cro Magnon below that of the Neanderthal? It just couldn't be! But apparently it was. Then they came to a burial. This seemed to be the answer to their puzzle. With trembling hands they uncovered the skull. There was no doubt about it. This was the skull of the tall disharmonic. The cheekbones were wide. The nose had been thin and hawked. The skull capacity was again the exceptional one of the old red race. And then, as if in confirmation, a few pottery fragments came to light. Again cereal food at this tremendous step back into prehistory?

Leakey does not attempt to answer the question which he has uncovered. He does not suggest what the strip of Neanderthal culture could mean above that of Cro Magnon, nor does he comment on the pottery again connected with the tall disharmonic.

On the very top beach level he found one skeleton whose lower jaw was partly eaten away, probably by disease. It apparently was the disharmonic. Unfortunately a well known scientist made the long trip to Africa to view the find, and when they went to the site, a flash flood had destroyed the evidence, so the scientist went away disappointed and skeptical.

Near the top of almost every work of excavation in Africa is found the Strandlooper culture, which has unmistakable likenesses to the modern negro. Was this an invasion of post-glacial time? This has been suggested. The culture has been given the tentative name of Australoid, not so much because there is any similarity to anything Australian, but purely for identification purposes.

If this Australoid culture came into Africa shortly after the end of the Pleistocene, where did it come from? To the present writer it seems that Melanesia should be considered as a homeland. This series of islands, which without doubt during the Pleistocene was larger and fairly stable, would offer a good environment for the evolvement of a distinct racial type which, though mixed, is recognizable even in the skeletal remains.

This however does not answer the questions which Leakey leaves unanswered. We find ourselves wondering if, when Neanderthal man entered Africa, as evidently he did (and in time his skeletal remains will be found), he found Cro Magnon man in possession - a possession which went back untold millennia? And then the other inevitable question: were Neanderthal and Cro Magnon both exterminated making a clean

open land for the invading Strandloopers? Or does the modern negro bear some of the blood of each? His teeth are only large. They do not have the strange type of teeth which Neanderthal had. The modern negro has a thicker skull than other divisions of modern man. But that may be entirely due to an adaptation to the killing heat of the tropical sun. Neither does the negro have the thick neck or the huge bony eye ridges.

There is of course, the possibility that the negro is entirely "Strandlooper", but then, how about the bushmen?

There are two more facts to consider in this intriguing puzzle. It is possible that Neanderthal man has not died off, but exists in the genes of most of us, as has been suggested by some scientists. Take another look at Uncle Ned or Tom at the grocery store. Does he have shaggy protruding brows under which deeply sunken eyes peer out at you? There was a time when scientists refused to believe that this cross was possible. They argued that these men could not have passed on their thick necks set so powerfully into their shoulders. But that was before they found a crossed type in an ancient cave of Syria. Now they are not nearly as certain.

So it is possible that in this racial clash of the ice age, Neanderthal may have spared some Cro Magnon females, as in Europe, Cro Magnon may have spared some Neanderthal females, if not for mates, then for slaves. However, slaves ultimately become absorbed in populations, as note in Greece and Rome, not to mention even India where the subject Dravidians have been the untouchables for so many millennia. Today they are not too far apart in skeletal type, these ancient masters and slaves.

In all this racial muddle the bushman remains the greatest anthropological riddle on the face of the Earth. Nor did we need just the one Fish-Hoek skull to start science wondering about our small modern savage. Behind this skull in time is a still more massive-brained skull unearthed in the same general locality, known as the Boskrop man.

As the great English scientist, Sir Arthur Keith, says: "...of all the evolutionary products of humanity known to us, the bushman type is the most remarkable. In the ancestral form it is the largest brained type of humanity so far discovered."

What caused this change in type? Was it the withering power of the sun? Or an attempt to stay alive among an overpowering number of enemies?

What is evolution doing to the bushman?

Chapter 46

Man's Earlier Cousins, The Apes

Man, like the captain of the good ship Pinafore, had cousins by the dozens before and during the time of the great ice sheets. We have not always thought so, but then, we have not always known about them.

Some museums, even yet, have a chart showing a tree with an ape at the bottom, Neanderthal man part way up, Cro Magnon a little further and a European at the top. Flattering, but not too scientific. Neanderthal may have had a more primitive brow with his heavy eye ridges, but modern man has more primitive canine teeth. Neanderthal had a thicker neck structure and at one time we thought he leaned forward and walked with a shuffle. Other types found since have convinced many scientists that this specimen was actually a victim of arthritis. (Some diseases have plagued man for untold ages, and incidentally also animals, since some fossil teeth have been found with what seemed to be cavities.) However, modern man has to bow to both Neanderthal and Cro Magnon in the matter of brain capacity.

We have come to realize that modern man is actually an early type which has managed to survive the rigors of time and the destruction of the elements. True, he has progressed, but possibly not as much as he could have, had events and environment been different. The result of this thinking is the realization that man is an older inhabitant of Earth than our scientists dreamed possible - say fifty, or even twenty-five years ago.

We know now that modern man did not separate from the stem of the apes during the Pleistocene or even the Pliocene. We have to retreat through millions of years to the Miocene or possibly even the Oligocene to find the earliest stem. There were many strange types of men and submen. They did not all die off immediately and allow our ancestor to take the royal path. No, they probably fought him every step of the way - through the vast ages of the Pliocene and even

during the changing climates of the Pleistocene.

To begin with, let us go back a moment and take another look at the apes. During the millions of years when the continents were locked together from their first savage crash, and were riding northward for their Pleistocene destiny with the polar ice, they not only carried the apes and man but numerous types of sub-men, as well as other branches of the mammals. It is often very difficult to date a find of antiquity because up to the time of carbon dating and other recent methods, scientists had to depend upon the animals with which the specimen was discovered in his horizon. Then instead of thinking in terms of "It must have been close to period X when this extinct animal was the most abundant," they had to take recourse to "It could not have been after Period Z because it was at this time that the animal in question found with the specimen, became extinct." This often made a difference of millions of years.

Also, as in the case of some Neanderthal types, the skull was found in the gravel of a stream bed, and could have come down from a far more ancient location. Carbon, floride and other types of dating are slowly changing this, and cross dating, or dating by other methods as a check, or by more than one laboratory, are slowly revising our knowledge of man's antiquity. The result generally is that although the ice ages are coming closer to us, man as a creature who lived through the violence of ice, earthquake and flood is retreating backward in time.

Let us take a look at the apes - much farther back on our stem than the recent Pleistocene, but who managed to survive that time of destruction. They are the gibbon, the orangutan, gorilla and chimpanzee. Most authorities agree that the gorilla, in his skeletal structure, is the most like man. However, he is not on our stem, but a separate offshoot from it, as are the others. The gorilla has many skeletal similarities, especially with some of the races of sub-man, particularly in his great overhanging eye ridges; the teeth are more those of a plant eater. The gorilla, science tells us, is not a bellicose animal except when annoyed. He lives peacefully in family groups, sometimes making his nests in trees, probably for protection but often on the ground. I once heard a lecture, probably at UCLA some years ago, in which a scientist had himself fastened into a large powerful cage with food and water, and left among the gorillas. (Unfortunately I have lost the notes along with his name). The animals were curious at first, but later paid no attention to him whatsoever. Sometimes they camped near and sometimes were gone for many days. The main fact that I remember is that he took down a vocabulary of about one hundred words which the animals seemed to recognize, and showed great interest when he repeated them back to the speakers. He had a feeling that in time he would have been accepted and perhaps kept for a pet.

The chimpanzee seems to be definitely the most intelligent of the apes. He can even be taught some of our words, but when we speak of the act of talking, we must remember that the shape of the mouth and teeth have a great deal to do with speech as we know it. If you do not think so, try pronouncing t, s, l, r, sc, and many others. Then note how the lips must work in sw, o, p, u, slow, flow, etc. The tongue must be very agile and the lips able to make various movements. Then how does a parrot talk, and a myna bird? Because of a very agile tongue. Tongue-tied is a meaningful word. I have heard dogs try to talk and even sing. Perhaps you have, too. Up in the far north on the trail when the wolves are not too distant, we would hear them. A yapping alerted the group to food (perhaps you and the dogs), but at other times there was an attempt at something like concert singing with the whole group joining in. It is a weird, wild music, but I have heard Indians declare that they like it and sometimes try to imitate some of the "songs". On the trail when you have stopped at a town and rented a cabin, often the dogs will sing. Your dog will begin. We had one wild wolf which later deserted us. She began and carried the high soprano. The others joined in, and for about three minutes they entertained. Then, as if on signal, they stopped. A moment or two later, across the river, another group of dogs began. Again in concert and again stopping abruptly. After a moment or so, a third and even a fourth group farther away would sing, and moments later when the others had finished, yours would start again. In time, one begins to see how and why the Indians enjoy it. Jack London in his "Call of the Wild" spoke of it as a sad song which spoke of "the travail of existence". I did not find the song of the huskies anything but a sort of strange attempt to make music, perhaps too different from ours for us to understand and various voices carrying different parts and running with concurrent conductivity. There are sad and dismal songs too, as when a dog has been abandoned or lost, but we must leave this byway.

We also may think that the talking of the parrot and mynah are random exercises. Most of them and I would say for the most part the great majority - are. However, I have known two which spoke intelligently. One was a parrot I heard in Mexico City. It came about as the result of an argument with a group of physicians during a party. I seriously questioned their implication and asked to be guided to this wonder bird.

Accordingly the following day I was taken to a middle class home on a rather attractive tree-shaded street where the houses were set back in gardens behind the great iron fences which kept away undesirables - either people or dogs. After the introductions, I was taken to the cage of a large green parrot of not unusual appearance and introduced to him by his mistress. He eyed me and acknowledged the introduction briefly in Spanish.

"Shall I suggest something for you to ask him?" she smiled graciously.

"No, thank you. I would rather ask my own question. I won't bother him. I will limit it to just one question."

She nodded and I asked the bird:

"Do you have a girl friend?"

He eyed me again and then answered quickly in Spanish: "Yes, I do. She lives down the block and has green feathers. They bring her here sometimes."

The other incident was with a famous mynah bird who lived in Los Angeles during the thirties. He had been on radio and seen at universities, but of course these affairs could be managed. The scientists were skeptical because the owner was always very near. However on one occasion the talking mynah was advertised in the papers as being the guest on the opening of a new market. I bribed a friend to engage the owner in a conversation when I reached "Jimmy". There was a long line of people waiting to speak to the famous mynah and the owner had been sort of hustling them along, to keep the line moving. When I was next in line my friend descended upon the owner and Jimmy turned a speculative eye on me.

Gorilla, orangutan and chimpanzee.

"Jimmy", I asked quickly, "tell me something that you particularly want and I will buy it for you. What do you want here in the market?"

He glanced around as if in thought, and then said: "Popcorn."

"I'll come back with the popcorn." I smiled, signalling my friend to step back and wait. Just outside of the market door a vendor was selling hot popcorn.

Returning again in the line, I signalled when I was to be the next. My friend dutifully buttonholed the owner once more, and I stepped up to Jimmy.

"Well here is your popcorn," reaching down in the bag and holding out a kernel.

"Thank you," Jimmy said, taking the proffered tidbit with his foot. Then came the surprise! The man behind me reached into the cage and pulled Jimmy's tail. The bird turned around, and without dropping his bit of popcorn, said in a loud voice which carried all over the store:

"Get your cotton-pickin' hands off my cage!" (Jimmy's actual salty language on this occasion is definitely unprintable.)

In the general laughter which followed, the owner saw my popcorn bag and started toward me yelling: "No one is allowed to feed my bird! Hey you!" But both my friend and I were rapidly on our way out. I had my answer. I am only sorry to have to report that a few months later Jimmy was given to the aviary for rare birds at Catalina island. I sailed out to see him again only to be informed by the keeper that he had been placed in an outdoor cage, and evidently not being used to that, contacted pneumonia, dying during the night.

If a person is to be sent to a new location where the keeping of a pet is impossible, then if a good home cannot be located by advertising, the best thing to do is to take him to a vet and have the last dose administered in your presence. There is nothing to it. The paw is pricked with a sedative and when the animal is sound asleep, the lethal injection is made. There is no struggle or pain if the sedative is given first.

But don't leave him. One never knows what may happen after you close that door. And turning him loose in abandonment is cruel. If you have ever found an animal, as I have on the desert, then it is easy to realize the terror of abandonment.

In respect to the gorilla, there is one more story which illustrates the child like intelligence of this species. My cousin Muriel, the most attractive, magnetic woman I have ever known, had a college friend at USC. One night she went with her friend to stay over night, and her friend's father, a zoology professor, assigned the girls to the guest room when they came in rather late after a party. All went well until the morning when Muriel woke up to an empty bed. Realizing her girl companion had gone down to breakfast, Muriel hurriedly dressed and started for the stairway. Arriving at the top, she let out a curdling shriek. Coming up the stairs toward her was a full grown gorilla dressed in a man's clothes. Tearing back, she slammed her door shut and bolted it against the supposed monster. The family came hurrying up the stairs after her. The father was the first to reach the bolted door.

"Were you screaming because of the gorilla?"

"Ye...es," Muriel sobbed.

"Open the door. I am sorry I didn't tell you last night. I completely forgot. He is our pet."

"Your pet?"

"That's right. We found him in the Congo jungles and adopted him when his mother had been shot. He won't hurt you. He even says a few words - that is, when you understand him."

Muriel unbolted the door and met "Congo". He conceived a great affection for the young coed. Only the door to the room must be bolted and locked behind you. Why? Because Congo had an interest in washing. He loved to launder clothes, bedding, hats, umbrellas or anything else he could get his hands on. She learned that the neighbors all brought in their laundry for Congo and he kept the back yard filled with drying clothes. This was his amusement. The other was answering the phone. Congo's guttural "Oooh?" was recognized by all the friends of the family and they simply said: "Oh hello Congo. Will you please call Mamma?" Or perhaps "Papa" or the children for whom he had his own names. He ate at the table, used the bathroom, bathed under the spray in the yard and swung from the trees to dry. All went well in the household as long as hats, coats, shoes and other unwashable objects in the upper rooms were kept locked away. He never washed anything in the lower rooms of the house. Muriel became very fond of Congo and often sat beside him on the lounge stroking his hair while she waited for her chum to come downstairs.

Then graduation came and several years passed. Muriel went to New York with her mother and father and lost touch with Congo's family. One day after she returned we were walking along the amusement pier at Long Beach. It was Sunday and there was little to do but see some of the concessions. Suddenly I felt her fingers clutch my arm.

"Look at that sign!"

"What sign?"

"That one over there: 'See CONGO, the famous man-ape from Africa."

"Oh, that's probably not your old gorilla friend."

"I'm not going to pass by. I want to see him."

"But Muriel . . ."

"Come on. If he isn't, we won't stay. Surely they would not have sold Congo!"

So we went in. A large gorilla dressed as a man was seated morosely in a chair, staring at the carpet. The crowd was filing in and we had to take a seat near the back. Then, before I could suspect what was in her mind, Muriel slipped from her seat and down the aisle. Slipping her arm into the cage around the great shoulder and furry arm, she said:

"Hello Congo. Remember Muriel?"

The great tired face turned and the eyes lit up with a tremendous unexpected joy.

"Uorll! Uorll!" and the voice broke with almost human sobs as he rubbed his face along her arm.

Then the keeper crashed over seats and dragged her away from the cage, hurling her backward to the aisle.

"You fool! Get away from that beast! That is not a child! Get away! Beat it! Get out of here!" grabbing a long whip.

Suddenly Congo reverted to the jungle. He got up and beat his breast and began to snarl at the keeper in a fashion that emptied the place as if there had been a fire.

Muriel came back toward me. She was crying.

"Are you hurt?"

"Only poor Congo. How could they do this to him?"

The keeper was now thrashing the cage, and Congo in the fury of his giant power snarled at the keeper and shook the cage until it seemed the bars could not hold him. The other keeper came over toward us - the only people now in the small theatre.

"Get out of here! If you don't, I shall call the police and have you arrested for inciting a vicious animal to fury."

With the man behind us pushing us out, we left, but at the door Muriel stopped a second and looked back. When we were on the street she turned to me.

"I shall never in my life forget his eyes - how they looked after me when we went out of the door - the most tragic . . . Oh, how could they?" We had not gone very far when a shot rang out and then several more. A crowd had gathered again and before I could stop her, Muriel turned back, running lightly to a big man coming out of the theatre.

"Yes, Madam. They shot him. He was breaking the cage and would have attacked the keeper. Would have killed him, too! He seemed to hate that keeper for some reason. I suspected that this would happen sometime. You can't trust a gorilla."

The gibbon, an inhabitant of Asia, seems to have arisen as a separate group from the primate stem during the Oligocene some forty million years ago. Since then the gibbon has pursued his own individual way, specializing in speed through the tree tops and amazing acrobatic feats. There does not seem to have been much change in his type during the endless ages from that day. Gibbons rarely reach over three feet in height, have a small brain, but their vision is good. They undoubtedly stand the greatest distance on the primate stem from man.

The orangutan (Malay for "wild man of the jungle") lives entirely in Borneo and Sumatra. He lives his life in the trees, has reddish brown hair and has a 400 cc. brain capacity. He has a strength to match his intelligence and has been observed to break the jaws of a crocodile - probably seeking him for a dinner. However the male weighs only about 160 pounds and the female seldom more than 80 pounds.

More manlike is the chimpanzee. His intelligence and smaller size makes him ideal for shows. He can be taught to be clean, eat at a table, wear clothes, guide a small car, ride a bicycle or a tricycle and speak a few words. With the latter, he must be taught with patience and love at an early age. One zoo allowed the chimps to ride tricycles if they wore clothes. This inducement finally made the chimps more amenable to putting on clothes.

In equatorial Africa, they are vegetable eaters like all the apes. The male weighs about 100 pounds while the female tips the scales at about 80 pounds. They have a 400 cc. brain capacity, have no bridge, or very slight, for their noses, their jaws are quite projective due to large teeth. Their canines are well developed. The chimps usually do not walk erect, but can be taught to do so, and if the animal wishes, he does without too much trouble. The chimp has an opposable thumb clever enough to manipulate a string. He can thread a needle and sew a fairly straight seam. The chimp is not considered to be on man's direct line. In fact none of the apes are.

The gorilla is the huskiest of the apes, sometimes weighs over six hundred pounds and has been recorded to be taller, but the average height is seldom over five and one-half feet. Gorillas are by far the strongest of all the primates. The average brain capacity is 550 cc. A good portion of this is, of course, muscle control.

Other facts on the apes are as follows: gorillas have bare chests and dark hair on the rest of their body. The orangutans can grow a mustache and beard while other apes cannot.

Only in the apes do we find the nasal rise that we do in man. Other primates do not have it, but the nose arch is still very minor in the apes and most of them have noses quite flat to their faces.

Most apes prefer to sleep in the trees, but gorillas often choose the ground for their nests, and in their case always live in tribes, sleeping together in closely made nests at night, but often hunting singly. Gorillas can be classified as land animals, although they are very adept at climbing trees.

The lips of all the apes are thin and show almost none of the mucous membrane which makes the lips of man.

The skin color of the apes differs, from white to black. The gorilla has a black face and the rest of the body is covered with hair. Other apes have coats of various shades.

The length of the limbs is one of the great skeletal differences between the apes and man. In the apes the front pair of limbs (the arms) are longer than the rear pair. This is of course the opposite of man.

As a result of the eyebrow ridges, and the sometimes seen crest through the ape's skull, the limbs, and other skeletal differences, the apes are considered to be some distance from the stem of man. Untold millions of years ago the types separated, probably during the Oligocene, and each group has gone along its own path. The present apes have many developed specialties of their own which we do not possess, and for this reason could not possibly be our direct ancestors.

Man's Other Cousins, Chapter 47
The Sub-men

It is perhaps ironical that anthropology, the most conservative of the sciences, is the one which is moving with the greatest speed. The finds made in the thirties rewrote the texts of the twenties and the finds made in the middle sixties are going to rewrite all that has gone before.

When the first Neanderthal men were uncovered, and then later the curiosity of a child chasing a rabbit into a cave (like Alice in Wonderland), came upon all of the magnificence of Cro Magnon art, and the scientists following, found the first graves of the tall, artistic disharmonic, theories and books came out by the dozen. Then followed other finds and not always of these two types of men.

One of the first enigmas was the discovery by Dubois of Wadjak, in Java, of two ancient skulls. The vault of the skull was not high, and the eye ridges were prominent. Scientists looking at the finds began to compare the ancient skulls to the modern Australian. There was one difference. The ancient skulls had a 1550 cc. and a 1650 cc. brain capacity. Decidedly above living modern man, if this was his ancestor. The discovery of these skulls in 1920 by Dubois in a mid-Pleistocene location is now one of the unexplained mysteries of science, and Wadjak man takes his place as a scientific question mark beside the African bushman and a few others.

In Rhodesia in 1921 and again in 1953 near Broken Hill, northern Rhodesia, and at Saldanha Bay north of Cape Town, south Africa, a type of skull was found which has been called Rhodesian man. He had the combined traits of the pithecanthropines (ape men), Neanderthal man and modern man, showing a distinct three-way cross. This settled for once and for all the much disputed fact of whether or not these branches of sub-men could cross with modern man. Of course, the later find in a cave in Syria of a Neanderthal-modern cross along with a modern skull now leaves little doubt. We now know that a cross was possible, and we are beginning to look upon Neanderthal man as perhaps himself a cross type.

The pithecanthropines which have been found in southern Africa and are from time to time still being found are true ape men. The skull is of a low vault and rather low capacity although higher than the apes. However they walked erect and the hip bones were more modern than apelike. They may have been a separate branch themselves from our stem, for their age seems to be too recent, in view of later discoveries, to be our ancestors. They are usually found in Pleistocene deposits with crude tools showing an attempt to use hammers of rough stone. The word pithcanthropine is made up from the Greek words of ape and man (anthropos).

Rhodesian man had not only a Rhodesian, but also a wide African range. He had a broad projecting upper jaw, eye ridges and a brain capacity of 1300 cc., which is lower than modern man, but above the apes. His palate was remarkably broad.

During the late twenties, and since, skeletons of fossil apes have been uncovered in south Africa and other places which have been named Australopithecines, a combination of words which mean "southern apes", by some authorities. Some anthropologists still believe that they may be ancestral to man, but their range in time is Pleistocene, and unless they can be proved to be earlier, in the view of later discoveries of true modern skulls in older drifts, this is a most unlikely theory. However they are a cousin of ours - many times removed, but still a relative.

The most interesting thing about these ape men of southern Africa, is that they walked erect, and the erect posture was attained before the brain case evolved to near human status. This has solved one of the main puzzles of science as to which came first. The ape men showed us that it was the erect posture. The average brain capacity of these creatures was about 500 cc. or less than 600 cc. Thus it would be necessary for them to gain a 400 cc. capacity to be equal to Pithecanthropus Erectus, the earliest known humanoid of the Pleistocene. However, as mentioned before, later discoveries have put a question mark after all the Pleistocene humanoids as being far too late in time to be on our stem. The brain cases of all these types of sub-men were too ape like in structure to be ancestral to man during the Pleistocene. The most interesting detail of these humanoids

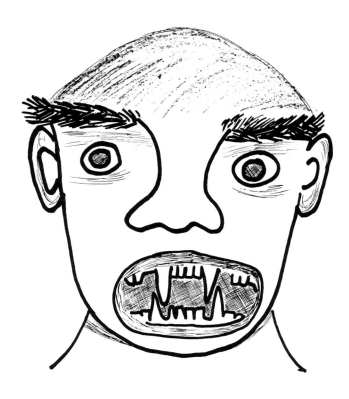

Pithecanthropus robustus (robust ape man), reconstructed from skull. Found by Dr. Koenigewald in mid-Pleistocene drifts in Java.

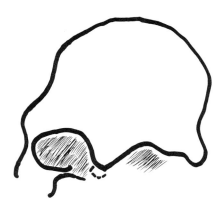

Skull of what is regarded as a modern Neanderthal cross because of the modern vault combined with the Neanderthal eye ridges. Found in a Syrian cave.

is that some of them show a crest running from the forehead to the top of the skull like the gorilla. This is apparently the housing structure for the muscles of their tremendous jaws.

In 1937 the Dutch geologist Dr. G.H.R. Van Koenigwald found a very primitive type of ape man in Java in the drifts of the mid-Pleistocene.

His discoverer named this creature Pithecanthropus Robustus, and well named he was, for he was the most powerful ape man so far discovered. Luckily the top and base of the skull were intact with the teeth still in their sockets. The teeth were essentially human other than one amazing exception. The canines were as long as those of the dire wolf. They projected downward past the lower jaw and between these canines and the lateral incisor there was a space for the long lower canines to fit in. This creature was equipped not only to tear its food, but to fight like the lion, with its teeth!

Not only do the canines strike Robustus from our direct stem, but also the late date makes it only a curiosity. The differences between the jaw of the ape and that of man is the length of the canines. We have managed to reduce ours over the millions of years we have roved the Earth, and as a result our jaw is smaller and the face straighter.

Pithecanthropus Erectus was found in Java also, the name meaning erect ape men. The remains of several individuals give us the type. His teeth were quite human and the canines much reduced in size. His skull capacity was 900 cc. which is above any ape and close to the human range. Dr. Van Koenigwald dates these discoveries to the mid-Pleistocene as well.

In 1931 central Java yielded eleven fossil skulls of a manlike creature not unlike the pithecanthropines on the one hand and Neanderthal man on the other, together with well made tools. Evidently this was another crossed type.

About 1937 Dr. Davidson Black, then of the Peking Union medical college, discovered a single human tooth in Pleistocene drifts. Since then over forty individuals have been recovered, and in 1943 additional skeletal parts were found. All were of the mid-Pleistocene. They have been named Sinanthropus Pekinesis. The brain capacity is 1-75 cc. which is a gain over Pithecanthropus, but the jaw lacks a chin, which is a very distinct feature of modern man. However, the creatures used chopping and cutting tools of a crude type which have been recovered with the skeletons.

In 1941, the Dutch geologist, again working in the drifts of the lower Pleistocene of Java, came across another ancient man. In the Sangrain district of central Java he discovered what he considered a true human type, although a tremendously powerful creature. His discovery consisted of two lower jaws. He named this group Meganthropus Paleojavanicus or giant man of ancient Java. The jaws were as powerful as those of the male gorilla, but the form was entirely human.

The most primitive types of men are found in a fossilized condition always showing great age in the Malayan region of Java and China, particularly the former. Dr. Ashley Montague in his "Man, His First Million Years" argues with reason that these finds may be older or that they could have branched off in the Pliocene and lived on into the Pleistocene, mingling with modern man probably through war and the capture of females, possibly even bringing some of their genes down to present day types of man.

In June 1954 Dr. C. Arambourg of the National Museum of Natural History Paris, France, discovered two human lower jaws in a pit at Ternifine in Algeria. The jaws were very powerful and shinless, definitely resembling the pithecanthropines. He argued that there was a difference in the teeth which warranted a new name, and called his find Atlanthropus-mauritanicus. The tools near them resembled the Abbevillian and Acheulian industries.

However, among all these types of humanoids came a surprise. In 1935 there was found in the Barnfield gravel quarry of Swanscombe in Kent, England, the left parietal and complete occipital bone of a skeleton found with the tools of the Acheulian industry in the deposits of the mid-Pleistocene. After the war, the digging in this location was continued. Accordingly in 1955 more of the same skeleton was discovered. The bones are slightly thicker than the average modern, but the Swanscombe man is entirely Anthropus Modernis! In fact if he were dressed and placed on a street of any European capital, he would not bring a second glance. This is also of the true London skull found when digging a tri-level basement.

In view of this, what must we say of the find of the primitive jaws among the tools of his culture in west Africa? The Acheulian industry is that of modern man according to English skulls. Were these two ape men captives of war by modern man or were the moderns driven out by an invasion of the ape men? Apparently the Acheulain industry was that of modern man. If this were the only case of the skull of our ancestors in the mid-Pleistocene, we might have reason to question the find and begin to look about for a possible ancient land slide or some other accident. But there is too much other evidence now piling up to refuse to recognize the fact the modern man lived through all the rigors of the changing sea levels and climates of the Pleistocene. We can hardly shrug off the find of L.S.B. Leakey

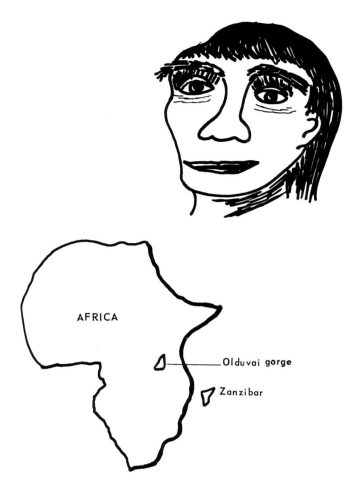

A reconstruction of the face of Zinj, a 1,720,000 year old sub-human found in Olduvai gorge, Africa, by Dr. Louis S. B. Leakey.

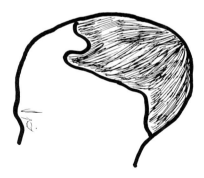

The London skull, found in a cave of very early Pleistocene time buried in a horizon below that of Neanderthal man. This skull is modern in every way. Definitely one of the long head race. Found in two portions.

in the rift valley of Africa where twenty-six individuals of the Cro Magnon race were found buried on a beach along with their tools for grinding grain and their pottery, which had twice been covered by the inundations of the pluvials and twice drained. This puts modern man very far back into the Pleistocene!

In a cave near the village of Montbrun in the department of Charente, France, in a deposit of the third interglacial are the portions of two modern skulls which have been named Fontechevade man. Apparently this was a young couple who died together in the cave. About them are scattered the artifacts of the Tayacian industry. Curiously enough this horizon is always found below the horizon of Neanderthal man. Would this indicate that this young couple were killed off in an invasion of Neanderthaloids into their land?

Fontechevade man was discovered with bones intact above the nose and in the critical facial area. In every detail this is a modern and on our direct stem. This young couple also could never draw a second glance on a street of one of our European capitals.

Now we again return to Dr. Louis S.B. Leakey who first went to east Africa along the rift valley to explore with the students of his English college - Cambridge. Among the finds mentioned at that time was his discovery in 1932 at West Kanam on the southern shores of Kavirondo gulf of Nyanza in Kenya, east Africa, in a lower Pleistocene deposit, the jaw bone of a modern man which was partly eaten away by disease - apparently cancer. Unfortunately this deposit was washed away by a flood and the scientists who came to see the fossil returned disappointed and skeptical.

This small setback in Dr. Leakey's hopes of continuing his search for early man did not stop him. Being the child of English missionaries to Africa, he was raised among the members of the Kikuyu tribe, spoke the language fluently and played with the boys who later became the tall warriors of the group. Being fully at home in both the Swahili and Kikuyu languages, he returned and enlisted the help of natives he had known all of his life. Later, on another trip to England, he brought some anthropology students back with him and ended by marrying one of them. Mary Leakey now not only helps with the digging and discoveries, along with their three stalwart sons, but also acts as doctor to the tribe for minor ills such as lion scratches. In the February issue of National Geographic magazine for 1965 are some interesting sidelights on the life of the Leakey family in Africa.

Among the finds of Leakey are a skeleton of pro-consul on the Lake Victoria islands and Kenyapithecus, regarded by Leakey as a fourteen-million-year-old stage of man's ascent. It was found by them on Fort Ternan.

However it is the late finds of Dr. Leakey which have stirred the scientific world and brought the backing of the National Geographic magazine for his endeavors to push back the horizon obscuring man's beginning.

In 1964 Dr. Leakey blasted the newspapers of the world with the headlines that man's earliest ancestor had been found. Immediately the name Olduvai gorge has become world famous.

Actually at the time of the discovery of the man science has nicknamed Zinj, Dr. Leakey was ill with fever and it was his wife Mary, along with their three dogs, who went to the gorge, all of them keeping a lookout for lions, rhino, leopards, snakes and scorpions. It was that morning she found Zinj. Leaving the find only partially dug out, she returned with the news, and Dr. Leakey, fever and all, hurried to see the ancient skull. They had been digging in the lowest strata formed a million years ago when the gorge of Olduvai had been a fertile lake shore and saber toothed tigers had lain in wait for prey much as the same animal had lain in wait for prey in the oil thick swamps of Los Angeles, California.

Suddenly she saw the skull there and had returned to get her husband, she explained as they hurried to the discovery. The Leakeys christened their find Zinjanthropus, the Zinj being Arabic for east Africa.

When samples of the minerals surrounding Zinj were checked for age by the university of California's new potassium-argon dating process, he was found to have been encased in his rocky coffin for nearly two million years - to be exact, 1,750,000, give or take a few thousand. This would make him over one and a half million years older than Peking man and immediately relieved that individual of being man's ancestor.

His face was different from ours, but not muzzled like that of an ape. It was indeed flattish and almost spade shaped, but although the vault was low and the brain case less than half the size of ours, and the eye ridges heavy, yet he walked erect and carried his head high. His palate was almost as arched as ours and his teeth were set in a jaw slightly rounded in front and the canines had no resemblance to fangs. The leg bones show that he was short and stocky, but his legs were straight and strong.

Around him were the animals of his time - the Pliocene. There were more than one hundred titans here: a pig the size of a hippopotamus, with tusks as long as an elephant; a sheep which measured six feet at the shoulder with horns of fifteen feet across. There were ostriches almost twenty feet high, with eggs which must have been as large as the soup kettles used by the pioneers of the American west.

Yet Zinj was not to be Leakey's last find. In April 1964 they again made the headlines of all the newspapers. They had found another creature, and immediately this one pushed Zinj off the dubious honor role of being man's ancestor. This one was called by the Leakeys and the scientists who were now going to Africa, "homo habilis", Latin for man having ability.

Homo habilis was three and a half to four and a half feet tall and may have had a language. In announcing the discovery to the National Geographic headquarters, Leakey said that some day this may be considered the most important find in the history of man and is "unquestionably shattering to our whole previous concept of man."

Simultaneous with Leakey's announcement of the discovery, a paper written by Dr. Philip V. Tobias of the medical school of the university of Witwatersrand, Johannesburg, south Africa, and Dr. John R. Napier of London university's Royal Hospital school were published announcing the momentous find.

Leakey announced that he and his wife Mary discovered the fossilized remains of seven individuals, one of whom was a young woman. Although the remains date as older than Zinj by about seven thousand years, Leakey insists that the two species of men lived in the same region at the same time, a statement that other scientists seriously question. However, later finds of Zinj type have caused some scientists to question his nearness to man, saying that in a million years Zinj showed little progress. On the other hand habilis may not be the ancestor the Leakeys at first thought they had found. True he is almost two million years old, has a jaw very much like ours with similar teeth. He not only ate vegetables as did Zinj, but also meat. Perhaps he took up his residence in the famous gorge because 1,820,000 years ago the land was a lush forest with all kinds of game, and the little men were hunters. The bones found with them suggest that they were particularly fond of fowl. He apparently lived in and near the gorge for about a million years. After that the Leakey's believe that he fanned out toward the Mediterranean and perhaps Europe. The hands and feet were similar in form and function to ours, said Dr. Leakey, and the jaw shows that there is enough room for a tongue to be able to form words.

Is this man's direct ancestor? Dr. Leakey is not quite as willing to say for certain now. Instead he answers: "We are going to do more

digging into a still earlier horizon," and goes on to suggest that still more types of pre-men may be found in the years to come.

Happy hunting, Dr. Leakey!

Almost simultaneously with the announcements on habilis, or "handiman" as he has been nicknamed, is an announcement by Yale university. Dr. Elwyn Simons, vertebrate paleontologist of Yale university announced in a lecture at the county museum at Los Angeles, California that the fossil remains of an ancestor of man who lived more than thirty million years ago have been found. This of course, would predate pro-consul whose remains were dated to mid-Miocene, when found in Spain. It is to be doubted if these remains were cross checked in dating and the dates may be wrong. If not, then pro-consul in Spain must yield the honor of being our ancestor to this tiny recent find dating from the Miocene.

This ancient man, less than two feet tall and found in ancient drifts of the Sahara, should make science less skeptical of these persistent legends of "little folk" who are supposed to have lived about the Atlantic shores and whose tales are carried in the legends from the Irish to the Algonkin Indians.

Jaws and teeth of this, the earliest known forerunner of man, were found on the eastern side of the Sahara desert about 60 miles southwest of Cairo, Egypt. The discovery was made by an expedition jointly made up by Yale university and the United Arab Republic.

Perhaps we should close this strange story of the fairies and giants of our species with the story of a find from China. Again we are indebted to the Dutchman, Dr. Koenigwald.

One day while exploring through old Chinese apothecary shops where from time immemorial the Chinese have been in the habit of grinding up anything extremely ancient as "medicine", the canny Hollander discovered a human tooth. Hunting further, he found two more. Now of itself, this is not strange. But the size! These molar teeth were exactly six times the size of those of modern man! What a giant this creature must have been! He would have been able to look down on Robustus and smash him flat with an outstretched palm. (The molar of Robustus was twice the size of ours.)

Perhaps truthfully, there were giants and little men or "wee folk" and those legends we heard from our grandmother's lips when we were children, whether she was Irish, Algonkin or Norse, were not so much nonsense as some scientific textbooks seemed to think.

Chapter 48

The Pleistocene And The Coming Of Civilization

As we study the early types of men and sub-men or humanoids who began to thrive during the Pliocene, and progressed into the Pleistocene, it becomes increasingly evident that modern man had a problem which time only seemed to aggravate, and it wasn't entirely the ice. The European branches of modern man told stories of the early giants which have come down to us in such tales as "Jack and the Bean Stalk", but the legends of the American Indian seem to strike much nearer to the truth.

"There were giants in those very early days who were cruel and were devouring the people. I do not mean that they were actually eating them, you understand, although there were some who stole little children for food, but in stealing and trying to mate with the women, they usually killed them. This would infuriate the lovers and husbands of these young girls when they returned from the hunt. You understand, don't you?"

"This happened here in this land?"

"No when the people lived far away across the wide water and very long ago - during the first sun age of which we have memory."

Man's apparent crowding into walled cities during the Pleistocene was not entirely due to a sudden desire for culture; it was for survival.

The Chaldean legends which come down through Babylon from the ancient Sumerians speak of these very first attempts of man at civilization. A tremendous leader of the people by the name of Oannes or Wannus, often called the first great man, is said to have gone far and wide throughout the land gathering the wandering and lost tribes of the people and leading them to a safe place where he taught them how to live together, to raise their food by growing it, and to tame the animals they had been hunting.

Undoubtedly this forward looking king was not alone in his work, but had his problems assigned to committees - although they were called together under another name, they still resemble our modern method of attacking problems. One must have been assigned to obtaining food without the necessity of the hunt which was becoming too dangerous; one to obtaining clothing to keep the people warm; one to assigning the work of keeping the city thriving; and one to suggesting even better locations; and certainly one to forming an understandable code of laws. This probably came after many accessions to the throne brought some unworthy monarchs.

Thus civilization was born out of necessity, and since there is no truer saying than that necessity is the mother of invention, man, with the help of many of his fellows, found means of taming animals to raise for food and clothing, plants to cultivate for the same purpose, and means of building shelters from the use of soil, trees and rocks instead of animal skins, and caves. Use of rocks also undoubtedly suggested the making of walls for fortifications.

Combining the ideas and suggestions as well as the skills of his fellows, caused man to make one of the great leaps toward living in cities.

Now there are many locations which lend themselves to an excellent defensive position for communal living. One is the battlement of high mountain areas. Here the problem would not be as much how to care for domesticated animals as how to care for domesticated plants. This of course, was eventually solved not only by bringing the water for irrigation down from the glaciated peaks and using the natural springs, but also by artificial terracing of the mountain sides so that cultivation would allow a greater amount of space than the sheer slope would offer. Thus grew the tremendous knowledge of terracing with imported soils used for drainage and fertility, and the control of streams by step-dams so obvious in the pre-Incan civilizations of Peru. And from whence came this knowledge so old that we trace these conduits for water to the caps of glaciers not of the present day, but of the Pleistocene? With numerous questions from tribe to tribe we always eventually end up with the same answer: "the old red land".

And where was "the old red land?"

Again the answer, if one can trust the informant, will be the same, (although the Amerind gets a keen delight in fooling the would-be authorities): the old red land, whether called

Montezuma Castle National Monument. This best preserved of all cliff dwellings in the United States is located 5 miles north of Camp Verde, Arizona.

Tla-Pallan, Itza-Pan, Aztlan or many other names, is always "in the sunrise sea".

Of course, there was a great island to the west also - the Pacific ocean's "Hawaiku" - but that is another story.

The domesticated animals chosen by these people would be the creatures which by nature would inhabit such areas. The answer is sheep and goats. Fowl of one kind or another could be tamed, and possibly deer or antelopes. There is some evidence in South America that these were tamed according to some of the very old books and legends.

In many ways mountains are ideal places for a city of a defensive location seeking people. In the terracing of the mountain sides the crops could run the gamut of climates and the inhabitants could at once enjoy the fruits of the tropics and the cereals of more northern climes.

Of course, deserts are also partially desirable, but they are not as easily defended nor as easily cultivated. In Arizona, when the Aztoutecan speaking Hopi people became surrounded by the Athapaskan speaking Navaho and Apache, they left their walled towns and fled to caves in unscalable cliffs or built their towns on top of high mesas in the middle of the desert - where some still reside. Here they cultivate their fields below in the Arizona valleys and at night scale the dangerous cliff face to their Pueblo homes. At present they no longer live within the pueblo, or rather many of them do not, but at one time they climbed ladders to their homes where each man's roof is another garden or front porch, and after pulling up the ladder, the pueblo presented an unscalable wall all around to the invader.

Still a further site for fugitive people to take refuge would be the swampland such as we have in Florida where dwell the Seminole Indians. The name means "run aways". This is exactly what happened when the United States government tried to put some of the southern tribes on what they considered undesirable reservations. The government has never had a treaty of submission on the part of the Seminoles. To all intents and purposes they are still a sovereign nation living on as they always have, in the trackless swamplands of Florida.

However, the very best location for defensive purposes is an island. That takes the knowledge of how to get out to it and back to the mainland. No doubt the earliest people seeking refuge from the raids of the ape men realized this and looked longingly to these locations, possibly even swimming to the nearest ones. But when the need became great enough, many minds were put to work on the problem and some type of boat was devised. Probably it was made by chipping and burning out the inside of a large log, but once the invention was made to float, means to make it move and guide its movements were surely not long in coming.

History dawns with ships. In the legends of the Greeks and Phoenicians, the Argonauts set out in a fifty oared ship to capture the golden fleece - a task given to Jason by his uncle, a jealous king named Aeson who ruled a city in Thessaly. Jason made the trip to the Black sea and captured the golden fleece with the help of the daughter of the king, and returning to his own land with Medea, killed the assassin of his father and seized the throne. This sounds like history, and probably is. Gods are not supposed to act like this, but kings being human and greedy for power, sometimes do. At any rate, legend is filled with ships and fleets of ships - even Amerind legend. Ships are found on the earliest tombs of pre-dynastic Egypt and on the bronze razors an unknown trading people sold to the Norse before the dawn of history, and on petroglyphs high up the Amazon river.

Once possessed of ships man became not the hunted, but the master. The seas were no longer barriers to be feared, but the highways to a world trade and colonization. Not that it happened in one century or even ten but the sequence of events was inevitable.

What islands were the first to support the cities which aspired finally to world power? There must have been three locations, judging by the maps of the era. There were probably many small islands within a short distance of each other in the Indian ocean where the great land of Lemuria had so recently gone down that even yet, the granite ridge is not very far below the surface. Then there was the Mediterranean where the river divided often to run around sunken portions which were in the process of slow submergence even then, and last of all there was the Triton sea and the Atlantic. This was also perhaps the best. In a manner of speaking, the land of the trident, which the ancients assigned to the Triton sea was the most perfect for the building of an impregnable world power. It sat athwart both the Atlantic and the Mediterranean, since there was no connection between the Mediterranean and the Atlantic. Thus ships could be allowed to come into the stronghold of the Triton and if the masters wished, could either be held or allowed to go on into the Atlantic and across the known world.

It must have been inevitable that from this seat the power went to the large islands in the Atlantic and those surrounding the Atlantic in a "league of defense and offense" which was almost impossible to overthrow, and had things continued as they were, would probably have been the masters of world destiny even today.

The people who formed these powers were, we infer from the skeletal type (even after much invasion which was post glacial), the long heads for the Indian and most of the Mediterranean as note what the Egyptian priest said to Solon. On the other hand, the race which ruled the Atlas and the Triton must have been the Cro Magnon. I, for one, have not always thought so.

I once fully believed with my friend Dr. Clarke Wissler that the Cro Magnon was the product of the Americas where he was found alive at the dawn of our knowledge of those lands. Here was his diamond face, hawk nose, long upper lip, thin lip line, high cheek bones, rounded chin, long head with its large skull capacity, tall lean body for the men with the slightly flattened thigh bones which allow them to sit on their heels for such amazing periods of

time in a resting position, smaller stature for the women who were inclined to become plump as the years advanced, and even his arrows and flints. Nor was this all, for only in the Americas are still practiced the burial rites which he practiced, and furthermore can be explained in detail by his descendents.

Wissler was of the opinion that the Americas were the cradle land of the type and the disharmonic became consolidated as a type when the ancient first long headed wandering tribes were thrown with Asian invaders across the Aleutian bridge and then sealed in for thousands of years by the advancing glacial ice.

That was before Dr. Leakey began to dig in Africa. Now the entire scientific world is reviewing its opinion. Only the Amerind who was not asked with sufficient desire to really know, has not changed his mind. He will still answer (if he can be induced to talk) that his people came from "the old red land". He will probably be as much interested and surprised as anyone to know that his ancestors once lived in Africa before the time of "the old red land" and were driven out of their homes by a strange race. He will probably not be as skeptical as the scientists have been, that is, as long as we do not try to down grade "the old red land".

"It was there that we reached our greatness when we wore the stars on our horns," Asa Delugio of the Apaches revealed to me.

"And what were your horns?"

"Could it be the sacred mountains?" he suggested.

"Ah yes, that is it!" for I suddenly remembered that king Atlas of Atlantis was known to have established the world's first observatory high on the icy slopes of Mt. Atlas, then known as the highest mountain on Earth, for the purpose of observing the passage of Venus. Was there another observatory on another mountain also established for the better checking of this important planet to the Venus calendar? Chief Asa Delugio thought there might have been, and his dark eyes, tired from the woes of his people, lit up with a hidden fire at this confirmation of a long remembered symbolical phrase handed down for thousands of centuries out of the mists of the past, and whose meaning was just now actually coming to light.

At the time I spoke to this proud chieftain, I still believed in Wissler's cradle of what he termed "the old red race". Delugio shook his head.

"No. We came from the old red land when the fire god crawled out of the caverns, and thrust his long tongue through the sea, for this land is where the earth walked, and the sea came up in mountainous waves and covered the smoking, burning temples. We came in ships, sailing to the high mountains of the southern snows. There we again built temples and buildings for watching the double star which gives us our time.''

Today, thanks to Dr. Leakey and his determination to dig in his great rift valley remembered from his childhood, we can go very far back indeed, but even so we seem to be haunted by the Venus calendar of Cro Magnon man who buried his dead in numbers of twenty-six (two thirteens - one thirteen being the years of the Venus passage and two being ceremonial because of one passage for each of the morning and evening aspects of the planet), ate cereal food and lived through the coming of two more pluvials, probably on a red island with two sacred high mountains, and caverns through which ''the fire god crawled''.

Thank you, Dr. Leakey for this one find in particular.

Furthermore one mystery of Europe is also suddenly explained by the finding of Neanderthal skulls above those of the tall disharmonic in Africa. Science has long wondered at the fury of Cro Magnon's invasion of Europe where he left no prisoners apparently, when he found Neanderthal man, for that type seems to have disappeared from the Earth upon the arrival of Cro Magnon. Was it because of what happened thousands of years before in Africa?

We do know that Cro-Magnon left his genes among the Europeans. Look at the thin hawked nose of uncle Emil, or the pretty high cheek bones of Gertrude's face which gives her such an exotic type of beauty, or the thin long lips of brother Tom, or aunt Mary's rounded chin which can say ''no'' with such firmness and conviction. Note the policemen on the corner with the tall figure and the face on the diamond. Cro Magnon is not dead in Europe, but he is much intermixed through the ages. Yet we know that the ancestors who give us those features lived through one of the greatest holocausts of all time.

Yes, history dawns with ships, and because of ships man had to learn other skills. Among these was how to guide them by the stars. The search for this information brought knowledge of astronomy and also the compass. With the help of this instrument the old red race built its observatories and pyramids across the face of the planet, always orienting the sides per-

fectly to the four directions, not only in Egypt, but also in the Americas from Ohio to Peru in untold thousands of instances. It might be argued, as has been done in the past, that the pyramids are for two different purposes in the Americas and in Egypt - one being for a temple and one for a tomb. However, these are the purposes of a culture which over the passing of millennia has forgotten the original purpose - that of star observation and for checking the calendar. Yet there are enough vestiges still remaining in all of these locations to hint the original purpose to the unprejudiced observer. I will not go into Donnelly's researches on the subject of the compass. One can always read his ''Atlantis and the Ante-Diluvian World'' for himself. Donnelly is very often right and only gets into trouble when he strays from science, but then he did not have the scientific knowledge of today to guide him, and the scientists of his time were as far from the truth as he was.

Man's greatest civilizations have been born not of the land but of the sea. I once heard a sailor arguing with a member of the long haired, barefooted, House of David sect on the flatness of the Earth. ''You are wrong'', the sailor said smilingly. ''It is not flat. It is round because I have been around it not just once, but many times, and in both directions. I can tell you for certain - it is round.''

If the skeptics among us do not believe that only ships, but the knowledge of astronomy and calendars as well as the compass was known to man previous to the dawn of our present histories, let him explain not only the long astronomical lines drawn across the plains of South America but also the countless structures oriented to the points of the compass in both North and South America as well as in the Mediterranean, and from Egypt along the Atlantic coast as far as England. And let him explain the Piri Re'is map.

Man learned from necessity, and the sea was his best teacher. Like experience, the sea has been the greatest educator of man - and the most expensive. But the lessons he learned were learned early and so well that not even the great cataclysms which he has suffered since that time has entirely wiped them out.

Man did not aspire to civilization: it was thrust upon him! And looking backward through the past one has a suspicion that he not only never really trusted either its benefits or its limitations, but rather holds against it in the recesses of his innermost soul a profound and undying resentment.

Maze stone, located approximately 4 miles west of Hemet, California.

Chapter 49

The Maze,
The Labyrinth
And The Wall

"Although once called the Father of Lies, yet the deeper and more comprehensive the researches of the moderns have been, the more their regard and esteem for Herodotus has increased."   Frederick Schlegel.

They call it the Troy-town maze, although no one knows why. Webster defines it as a "bewildering labyrinth" while Wise's Modern Encyclopedia defines it as "an edifice at amusement parks full of intricate passageways leading to inner chambers from which exit is made with difficulty." In a way both are right, but they do not have the answer.

The Troy-town maze is to be found all over the world. Children of Europe play with it as their favorite puzzle. It is inscribed on one of the walls uncovered when the ashes were removed from Pompeii. London has its maze. It is in one of the parks and the walls are hedges. Idle, laughing couples wander through and mothers go frantically calling after lost children. I heard one man exclaim with exasperation: "Blime! I have wasted three hours here and I'm not out yet. Well, I am getting out right now!" and he vaulted three hedges and caught a waiting bus.

"That wasn't exactly cricket!" a pretty girl remarked to her male companion who answered laughingly: "Not really, I suppose, but he may have had an engagement with a pretty blonde..." and their voices drifted away in the flood of other voices passing in both directions. Then one masculine voice boomed above all the others shouting out in a strong American accent: "Will someone tell me what screwball ever thought this

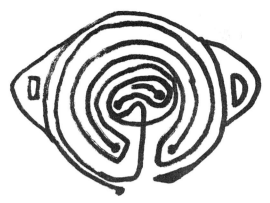

(INDIA)

This maze appears to
have a gate in the center.

Coin from Crete.

(CRETE)

Examples of ancient mazes.
Shaded portions are destroyed areas.

(ARIZONA)

thing up?"

Ah yes, the maze. Quite a few archaeologists would like to have the answer to that question.

It was dug up on a very old ring in India; inscribed on a wall of the magnificent Knossos palace at Crete when excavated; found carved in rock on one of the mountains of southern California; cut into the walls of Shipalauvi on the Hopi reservation which were erected before the coming of Columbus; carved on a giant hill side boulder in Washington state; found engraved on a cliff in the vastness of the Sahara according to Arab guides; woven into an old Pima basket, and still the list goes on. There are square ones and round ones. Some are right handed and some left. Some are only partially complete and go on into a design. What does it mean?

The name apparently was known long before the ruins of Troy were found, and evidently the maze was not upon those walls although I may be uninformed about this. However the finding of the maze in Crete would seem to pre-date Troy. The large island whose civilization was apparently unknown to Homer who wrote of the Grecian Homeric age and the Trojan war 1000 years before his time, cancels out the name of Troytown as a point of origin.

There is one fact about the Americas - at

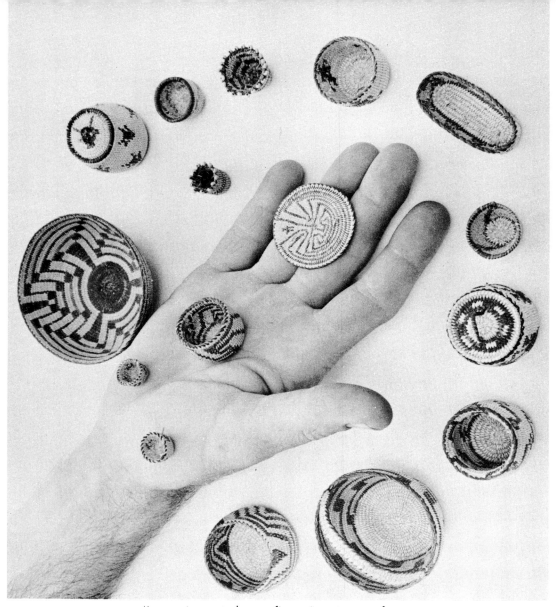

Maze coin - note human figure in entrance of maze.

least it is still true during the 1960s - and that is, there are a few erudite chiefs and medicine men who each hold a clue, even though they do not themselves always know what that clue means, yet with another clue from a distant tribe, the story can be partially revealed. There is a provision of course: one has to induce the sage to talk, or as they say, "sit down with you in council".

I began with the Pima and Papago. I found them either unwilling or unable to discuss the subject. I do not know which. I had more chance with the Navaho. There was a medicine man, the famous Hosteen Klau who was a friend of Dr. David Banks Rogers. In my hands I carried some desired green stones and shells dug up from one of the channel islands off the Santa Barbara coast. Klau was the first Navaho to weave some of the sand paintings and sacred chants, and we

owe him a debt for adding to the fairy tale beauty of Navaho weaving when he raised the old taboos, even though later it cost him his life.

After all the preliminary small talk was over and he told me something of the caves of the Santa Barbara islands as they have come down through legend, I finally edged around to the maze. I knew that the Navaho were a western tribe with Athapaskan speaking legends which ran right up to the Aleutians when they came to the Americas with their fierce red or black heavily-furred war dogs, but I was counting on the fact that like the Apache, they had conquered and married women from the Atlantic tribes and had from them learned some of the ancient eastern legends. I was not entirely mistaken.

"I know a phrase from a chant which seems to point the way, but I do not know the meaning. . ."

"Please repeat it. Perhaps together we can piece out its meaning?"

He nodded with a grateful smile.

"In the trail to the crescent where the two sparkling stars rest on the sacred horns and all the tangled troubles of the world are made to

Pima fret design.

go straight, there is a puzzle one must cross . ."

"Ah! Thank you."

"If I have said something you understand, I would be happy if you would tell me so that I can better check my own understanding."

"You speak of the old red land long sunken in the sunrise ocean. This is a direction of how to get there and it must have been given at the time that monarchy was at the height of her power and glory, which must have been world wide."

"Yes, go on," he nodded anxiously.

"The sparkling stars must refer to the twin-star, Venus, which was checked by the astronomers from observatories near the top of lost Mt. Atlas and some other mountain. It is a calendar for recording the passage of time - far better than ours today. I don't know what crescent means. Do you?"

"Unfortunately, no. But I thank you oh so much for the torch which you have lit in the darkness."

"And I thank you for helping me light it."

"What the meaning of the name crescent may be I cannot guess. The answer is totally lost in the mists of time," he said sadly as I wondered

if the old man had really known what any of the words meant.

I then took my problem to an educated Indian in the university of Mexico.

"I have been curious about that myself. Have you ever suspected that it may be a map of the labyrinth?"

"What makes you say that?"

"Because it was found in Crete and there was a vast labyrinth below the palace you know. Personally I cannot imagine those beautiful corsetted, and coiffured ladies of the court with their ruffled long dresses, sitting enthralled while some naked prisoner of war or girl captive was made to vault with a somersault through the horns of the great bull they called the Minotaur. But then my ancestors did some incredible things to my point of view, and no doubt yours did too. By the way, did you know that the Scythians, believed to be either of German or Russian ancestry, were the first known takers of scalps?"

"Yes, I was aware of the pictures of them with scalps fastened to the saddles of their horses. I wonder if that is an Asian custom? Perhaps that is why the coolies of China wear pig-tails like

Another type of Pima fret.

our red men wear scalp locks? But we are going into another byway. Let's stop right here and go back to the maze. Do you have any other reason for the connection between the small puzzle and the labyrinth, than the finding of the maze on the palace wall in Crete?"

"Yes. You have seen Mitla, have you not? That is in Oaxaca, Mexico."

"Indeed I have. There are some three hundred and sixty-five different designs of the pyramid there . . ."

"Three hundred and sixty-five and a quarter, for the number is calendrical. You may think of those designs as parts of the maze. Furthermore,

were halls, gateways, sphinxes, pillars without end and more sculptures. As at Karnak, there were ornate pillars covered with historical writing, obelisks and figures until the mind reeled at the impact. And it comes to me, an Amerind, that it is strange that in Egypt they should make the pyramid a tomb and we should make it a temple of sacrifice, while their laby-

Wall design maze, Mitla, City of the Dead, Oaxaca, Mexico.

under the ruins there is reported to be a tremendous labyrinth. It was known as 'the city of the dead'. . ."

Because the sacrificial victim was forced to enter the gates and never returned?"

"You anticipate me. However, I cannot be certain." Then turning his head, "Have you ever thought about the description of Herodotus concerning the giant labyrinth in Egypt? It had three thousand chambers, half of which were above the Earth and half below. There were courts, collonades, pyramids and statues. There

rinth is a place of history and the glory of the past as it should be; and over here it became only another means of sacrifice. The passing millennia has changed our interests in our mutual inheritance."

"You speak of the old red land?"

"Yes. Only the white man laughs at that name. The priests of Egypt do not. I have been there."

But as my eyes widened, he suddenly stopped and decided to say no more.

As I left Mexico I thought again of the labyrinth reported to be under the ancient cities of

Peru. And again I remembered Herodotus who was in Egypt to check Solon's story about Atlantis, but cast it from him when he could find no seaman who was willing to substantiate the fact that there was an Atlantic ocean. How Egypt had already lost knowledge among the common people, even though her priesthood still had the ancient histories at that time!

Then I took my problem to the most knowledgeable man I knew on the subject of the old red land - Chief Asa Delugio.

I found him at his home playing with his small granddaughter. I had but a few hours to talk and luckily we were interrupted by no one. He came up and shook hands with me warmly and than gave the Apache greeting of taking hold of my upper arm while I grasped his.

After the preliminaries, which are not to be hurried through, and the small presents I had for him and the candy for the children, we began to talk.

"No, as yet I had not copied the Popul Vuh or Chilam Balam," I said by way of apology. "I have met some interesting people though!" He listened with pleasure as I told him about the man I had just left.

"You should have had me with you. I could have told him that you are one of us concerning your belief and knowledge of the old red land. But so many Indians are bitter about white man's sarcasm - calling the old symbolical legends 'children's made up tales'!"

Finally I got around to my problem. He nodded thoughtfully.

"If you ask of me, you must tell me what you have learned. We must not keep secrets, otherwise we do not learn."

"I understand."

After describing the possible connection with the labyrinth in Crete, their civilization and that of Egypt, I leap frogged to South America. He stopped me. Of this, he apparently knew more than I did, so I went on to describe the one at Oaxaca under the ancient city of Mitla and the rumors which called it "the city of the dead". Again he stopped me.

"What have you learned from our people here about the old red land itself?"

"Only from a Navaho. I will not give his name, as I know this would not interest you and he may not wish it."

"I understand. Go on."

"It is part of a chant."

"Repeat it."

"In the trail to the crescent where the two sparkling stars rest on the sacred horns and all

Megalithic wall.

the tangled troubles of the world are made to go straight, there is a puzzle to cross . . ."

"What bothers you? Your labyrinth is the harbor's entrance where one ship only could go in at a time and must carry a guide to see it through."

"Yes, I understand that now, but what is 'crescent'?"

"I thought I told you once, but perhaps not. It is the symbol for the old red land. If the points are up, then it is living, but if the points are down, it has been covered by the sea." Then thoughtfully: "That is a very old chant?"

"It is indeed. It is giving directions apparently to a living land."

"And at the prime of its power."

"I remember now seeing the crescent on your helmet. You make things so understandable. That is almost the identical helmet of the Atlanteans pictured on the Egyptian columns."

"Have you been there yet?"

"No, but I hope to go someday, and also to the Tuareg or Tuarak people of the Sahara who many of the ancient writers called the Atlantidae (Diodorus) or Atlantides"

He sighed.

"Wish I could go with you. But there is something I had meant to ask you. Have your legends across the ocean told of the great monarch, Votan, who went down with the old red land?"

"Oh yes. We have called him Wodin, Odin, or Volcan - all depending on the nation remembering."

"Was he what you call . . . good at making things?"

"Ah yes! The clever builder! He limped sometimes."

"He is the same. When the land was sinking, he lined up the fleets, his son to go to the sunrise and his grandson to go to the sunset lands."

"We don't have that story, but I know it from over here among the Iroquois and Mexico. His book (the grandson's book), 'Proof That I am A Serpent', came down to the time of the Spanish, when it was burned."

"And your white teachers tell us that we are the savages!" he said softly. "Well no matter now. Do you have the story about the great wall? It was his wall. That is why he was called the clever builder."

"You would share this story with me - please?"

"And some day you will put it in a book where my people will read and listen as once they would not listen to me?"

"Yes indeed I will, but please do not let these legends die with you because you were angered at some ignorant teachers. These are histories beyond ours."

"I shall think on your words. If you should bring me back the chants from these two ancient books, I will give these legends to you. Now listen: Is this wall made with giant stone blocks like the great ones in our city in Peru?"

"I do not know about the wall, but the cities of these builders with giant stone are all around the Earth. They are even in the Philippines. The scientists call them the megalithic builders. That is made up of two Greek words - giant (mega) and stone (lithic)."

He nodded.

"Are their mountains terraced also and do they bring their water down from the icy peaks, and do they contain their rivers with channels, wells and dams?"

"Yes, I believe so, but I am not certain."

"Then they were built by our people, whom you call Atlantidae."

I smiled at the alertness of his mind - this old man whose tired eyes again seemed to be the mirrors of his people's troubles.

"You must listen carefully. Votan, the great monarch, had the giant wall built to contain the river of death."

"The river of death?"

"You have no legends of the river of death?"

"We have legends of the Styx (Greek legendary "river of death".) . . .ah, yes perhaps..."

"Let me describe the river to you. It ran between the high cliffs where half of it fell in thunder. It, or part of it, came down in great falls from the cliff face and splashed in roars to the river below. There it turned left with the river of death. The wild waters then went through the gorge of the swinging bridges to the sea of beauty where the ships were. Do you know this place?"

"You must be talking about the Mediterranean river which did once fall from the face of the great cliffs with the roar of a volcano, and turning left through the gorge of the swinging bridges to the sea of beauty where the ships were."

He smiled warmly.

"You speak as if you have seen it."

"I have - but only on the maps which the cartographers bring up to their drawing boards from under the sea."

"It is well. Now listen once more. Have you seen a wall?"

"No."

"Then you must look again. You understand that as the wild river of death tore around the bend of the old red land on its way to the sea of beauty where the ships are . . . I am sorry, it is hard for me to say were; I think of it as a living land."

"I too sometimes have that difficulty."

"Thank you. Now you understand as the river crashes around the jutting place, it begins to eat away the soil and the land crumbles from time to time."

"Certainly. That is obvious."

"The emperor, Votan the First, seeing this damage, ordered his engineers, or the men who work with the giant rocks . . ."

"His masons?"

"Yes, the masons, to fashion a wall which would contain the river of death. At first they said it could not be done, but he insisted, and so the work was begun. It took many years and many lives. At last, when it was completed, it became one of the wonders of the Earth. There were others: the great canals and the giant puzzle of the harbor's entrance, to mention two. Yet the wall seemed beyond the ability of man to build. It was more than a mile wide and high, and ran along the gorge to a place above the falls. It should still be there."

"Under tons of lava, earth swept out from the collapse of the Mediterranean cliffs, and a few miles of green sea?"

"I have always thought a part of it would still be there. Our people, the Atlantidae, built for all eternity."

I acknowledged his faith with a smile.

"I will try to find it. I will look very hard on the maps."

"And will you bring soon the parts of those ancient books which told of the great destruction? I mean the part which tells of how Ah-Musem-Cab crawled out of the underworld in order to close the eyes of the thirteen gods?"

"I go to Mexico soon to bring back the words. I can copy them from the books at Mexico university."

"I hope I will still be alive. My time grows short and I still have much to tell you."

"Why do you not tell your young men?"

"They will not listen. Their teachers have told them that these things are fairy stories to entertain children."

"Are you not able to make them understand that this is their heritage?"

"Perhaps your book will bridge the time of this generation to someone who wants to learn."

I have heard since that the old chieftain held the sheets containing the legends for several years, and finally giving up seeing me and knowing his time was growing short, called in his daughter, grand-daughter and another to take down his dictation of the legends. I am wondering if he gave them all, or if he still held some back to tell his own people in council?

I remember that as I climbed into my car I leaned out with an afterthought:

"What was above the cliffs of the arm of land being eroded away by the river of death?"

"Great palaces of the wealthy with their round towers topped by peaked roofs," his old hands illustrating a cone. "Also I believe there was a temple."

"Tell me, can you read any of the petroglyphs -" then as a puzzled look came into his eyes, "I mean the writing on some of the rocks throughout the broad land?"

"Yes. Much of it. Some of it is map drawing, you know."

Note ancient round towers in cave dwellings - U.S. southwest.

"Oh. I never thought of that. We have so much to talk of and always so little time!"

He acknowledged this with a warm smile, and as I drove away to California, this smile remained with me.

Chief Asa Delugio (he told me the name was Indian translated into Spanish, and I acknowledged the fact that it could not have been more appropriate), did you call that last council with your people?

Knowing that he was no longer in the land of the living, I sat watching the Mescalleros dance the crown dance in 1964. Somehow I almost felt his presence beside me as the muffled beat of moccasined feet brought in the faceless ones in the golden fringed war sheath of the ancients, the boots to the calf, the star symbol and the short swords, above which swayed the crown of the trident. I could feel my very hair raise with the thrill as they came in from the east - the direction of the lost land under the sunrise sea. Then it seemed I could almost hear him whisper "It is not only their inheritance - it is also yours - and the inheritance of us all."

Chapter 50

The Coming Of The Ice Age

The Doepping granddaughter, a modern Cro Magnon.

The Doepping daughter in her Mohaw tume, before being taken into the tribe

"To hold the same views at forty as we held at twenty is to have been stupefied for more than a score of years, and take rank not as a prophet, but as an unteachable brat, well birched and none the wiser." Robert Louis Stevenson.

The slow ride of the continents northward on the lava wave below the crust was bringing ice to the northern hemisphere. The pole was becoming land bound and whenever that happened, we have seen in our review of the ages of the past, the ice began to cover the mountain tops. Not suddenly, of course. There was only slightly less melting than the year before and the snowflakes of the centuries began to pack down into those of the millennia. There was a cooling of the entire globe, for the snows of the southern hemisphere also lengthened down the mountain slopes into glaciated tops. However, the great sheets which joined in the valleys and then moved down to the seas were confined to the north.

The creatures living their short life spans probably did not notice the difference. Gradually they grew heavier coats than their ancestors wore, and the warmth loving plants either made their way south to warmer lands, or froze in the long, cold winters. Other plants learned to live with the ice and existed on the mountains until the great white sheets crushed them under their inevitable advance.

For man, with his problem of the sub-men, it meant the lowering of sea levels and the inevitable emergence of more desirable living space protected by an expanse of water.

First we know that the people who lived in lakes moved around the entire Earth, following the sea coasts and the rivers. Such people had water transportation. They built their homes above the water and tossed their rubbish into the lakes. In these rubbish heaps we found the remains of their animals - the pig, sheep, dog, and sometimes cattle. We have also learned that these animals which were evolved in the region of the Indian ocean mark that region as their place of origin. This is double checked as correct, when we find that these Kitchen Midden people are the small, slight long heads who always buried their dead in the crouch position. The well of the long heads is also India and the Indian ocean. That they were one of the first people on Earth to use ships, there is no doubt, for the very earliest civilizations dug up in India before the inroads of the Aryan speakers, shows that they were advanced enough for ships. They lived in modern type homes in cities with streets which were lighted with street lamps; public baths of running hot and cold water; private dressing rooms; central heating, probably with oil furnaces; sewers; windows and doors and many other conveniences of modern civilization. Undoubtedly these people were once in touch with ancient Egypt as the priest of Volcan remarked that the Egyptians originally came from the east, colonizing the entire Mediterranean.

However, connecting the Indian civilization with the very early Kitchen-Midden people living above lakes around the entire Earth could possibly have been an accident, or at least so I supposed until something most unusual happened. A couple who are friends of mine came over to tell me of an odd and almost unbelievable circumstance. Their name is Doepping. He is of German ancestry, she of Finnish. I became interested in them when I learned that their daughter had married a full-blooded Mohawk American Indian. They laughingly told me that the tribe had frowned on the marriage tie and had only given their consent after the girl had entered the tribe with full blood rite adoption. I explained that this was part of the Amerind's rejection of white man. Suffice to say that this couple are now very happy with their brood of mixed blood children, who are well accepted at all white schools they attend and pass unnoticed as regular Caucasians. The Mohawk, an eastern tribe whose territory runs from New York state into Canada, is of the tall Cro Magnon type which always blends rapidly into the whites.

This had nothing to do with the problem for which the Doeppings sought a "council meeting" as they laughingly called the visit. Leona's blue eyes were dancing when she said:

"Wait until you hear the puzzle I have for you! Well, last night Bob and I went to an Hawaiian restaurant. The entertainment was great and we were having fun with the strange food, when some Hawaiians came to sit down at the next table. We thought nothing of this for awhile, but during a break in the music and chatter, I suddenly cut Bob off in the middle of a sentence.

" 'Bob! Stop talking! I want to listen to those Hawaiians.'

" 'Why? They are talking Hawaiian.'

" 'I know, but I can almost understand them!'

" 'Impossible!'

"And with that I turned around to their table and began to repeat some of the words. They stopped talking in shocked surprise. You see

these were only the root words and understanding was difficult, but still the similarities were unmistakable. Suffice to say they were as puzzled as I was. Now! Why is Finnish like Hawaiian?"

Leona had thrown me what may be called a "curve ball". For a moment I was stumped. Then I remembered the Kitchen Midden people, and how Finnish along with the Basque were two lost fragments of a language which evidently was once spoken throughout Europe. Were these the Kitchen Midden people whose village remains were to be found in the lakes of central Europe and Switzerland, which could be dated from the

Pleistocene? This language had apparently been driven to the north and west in two islanded groups by the invasion of round headed Aryan speakers evidently coming from the east. If this was true, then this ancient language had left other fragments - words or phrases - imbedded in the Aryan languages of the Atlantic from the Scandinavian Gothic and Celt of the Scotch-Irish to the Spanish. Of course, the people were overwhelmed and became part of their conquerors so that today, some five or even more thousands of years later, they can no longer be identified.

But how does that fit into the puzzle of the Hawaiian language? Then I remembered Dr. Buck's "Vikings of the Sunrise." The Polynesians, migrating across the trackless Pacific carried the pig, dog, and chicken in their long canoes. All these were evolved in the Indian ocean area. The language, which held no Aryan root words, showed that the original speakers fled before the Aryan invasion from the north which crushed their cities and wiped out their early remarkable civilization. Evidently these two invasions of the round head Aryan speakers west to the Atlantic and south to India were of about the same general period, probably triggered by some famine or other disaster in their own homeland.

What a discovery!

No truer words were ever spoken than the comment of Stevenson that a man who does not change his views from twenty to forty has been stupified for more than a score of years. However, there comes a time when one cannot walk down these fascinating by-ways, but must pass the torch of learning to some younger mind when one realizes that like Albert Einstein, one's lifetime of gathered knowledge is but that of a primer on the desk of an immense library filled to the soaring ceilings with unread volumes.

Language has its limitations as a key to the past, but the oft-mentioned premise that negro, white man, red man, and yellow man are all speaking Aryan languages in the Americas, namely English, Portugese and Spanish, is a fallacy when used against language as a clue to the past. A few hundred years ago these men were all speaking different languages and the ancient tongues are the key to the past, not the recently acquired one. I may have learned Siouan or Japanese or Swahili, but that does not make me a member of those tribes or nations of people. If you or your children learned to speak Arabic it would not make any of you Arabs. However, your ancestral language is different.

Not only the time separation of such a spread of languages as the Aryan is indicative of the original dispersal, the over-run languages of another stock are checks upon the direction of that migration forgotten in the lost fog of passing millennia.

When one begins to recognize the root word similarities, and can distinguish them from the contact words, the study of languages becomes an absorbing lifetime profession. Language is like a living, changing thing. It still bears the marks of ancient contact with another people either through trade, migration, missionary conversion or conquest. For example, scientists studying the languages of the Philippines found that, previous to the coming of the Spanish, the natives had cotton, Indian corn and other American foods, as well as old Arabian words which suggested either missionary contact or ancient trade. And this is true of the Aryan tongues even though thousands of years ago the migrating round heads, at least in Europe, have completely over-run and absorbed all of the conquered people.

Leona didn't know whether to be pleased or not at this revelation.

"All of this means that I have some of the blood of these people from India?"

I looked at the typical round head harmonic of her skeletal structure and smiled.

"From your stocky frame, round face with its small nose and large blue eyes, framed by light-brown hair above the milk white skin, I would say that perhaps way back some five thousand years ago your Aryan speaking ancestors conquered some long headed Kitchen Midden girl and perhaps settled down on her land. It only takes five generations to change the color of the skin for good. However, the skeletal characteristics are not to be dispersed so easily."

"Then it is really as if I didn't have this foreign blood at all."

"Not exactly. If your mother had been another woman or your father another man, would you still have been you?"

"I don't suppose so."

"Definitely not. The genes would have had a different pattern. There are unlimited patterns, but the genes go on and on through the centuries and the millennia. By the way, that little half-Mohawk grand-daughter of yours looks very much like you, although she has a bit of Bob's high cheek bones."

"She does, I know."

"Are the high cheek bones bad?" Bob asked.

"I am one-hundred per cent German and they run in our family."

"Also in her father's family," I reminded him. "No, I think they bring a very exotic look to the woman. Take for example the very lovely Marlene Deitrich, the queen Nefertiti, often called the most exquisitely beautiful woman in all antiquity, certain attractive Greek statues of the golden age, and "Lucky" the exotically charming siren of the Parisian fashion world who died during 1964 - they all were gifted with high cheek bones."

"How about me then?" Bob laughed. "I am neither Egyptian, Parisian or Greek. I am one-hundred per cent German."

I looked at the sinewy well knit figure, the face on the diamond, the hawk nose, the long distance between the nose and the upper lip, the long thin lips, the rounded chin.

"You may be one-hundred per cent German for some generations back, but somewhere a tall dark haired, probably beardless man of the sea who sailed the Earth in ships, read books, and worshipped the fire god, got into your ancestry. You are a typical Cro Magnon. Perhaps that ancestor of yours once fled from burning Atlantis, who knows?"

"How long ago did he do all this?"

"Perhaps when your Aryan speaking ancestors were riding their horses and tending their sheep somewhere in east Germany or Russia. However, they gave you your green-blue eyes."

"No wonder I have always liked the sea . . ."

"But all that is thousands of years ago. We Europeans are a mixed people. To me that is our greatness. Think of the richness of our heritage! There is actually no such thing as a 'pure' national type or race - except perhaps the African bushman and the Australian aborigine. But even those show some mixture. Strange is it not, Leona, that although you show less than a thousandth part of that distant ancestor of yours in your features and skeletal structure, yet the language you learned in your home may some day help to solve some great mysteries of the Atlantic ocean and the movement of the peoples around its shores. As of now it is a story still half buried in the darkness of unknown millennia stretching back through time."

The study of languages leads to another fascinating subject: the study of writing. If you have no absorbing hobby, try collecting alphabets in an "alphabet album". There are, of course, two types of writing. One is to make marks for an idea such as the Chinese still do. Thus a certain idea graph stands for "man" another for

"Lucky", a modern Nefertiti.

"house", still another for "horse" etc. This is a laborious system of conveying ideas. There are too many symbols to learn. The Chinese have hundreds. It has the advantage that no one else wants to take the trouble to learn it. However, it is utterly impractical for trade. Thus, far back in antiquity, before the time of recorded history, nations began to invent alphabets.

Taken from the first two letters of the Greek alpha and beta (a and b), the alphabet has a mark for each sound. Thus "horse" and "house" can be written with all the same symbols except one and there will be no confusion.

I tried making an alphabet album once in an idle sort of way and became interested enough to write an article on the subject which was published during the thirties by Ray Palmer, the editor of a magazine called Amazing Stories which for the most part published science fiction. Unfortunately, since then many of my notes have been lost or stolen. However, what I have left may give the interested reader an idea of how to go about making an alphabet album. It will soon become a subject of conversation if you do, and some will wish to copy it. That is well, for this is how learning progresses, but be careful that you get it back or much work will go for nothing. However, if you progress far enough, the time may come when you will wish it checked by a linguist at a university, and through it many interesting contacts may come into your life.

As you collect alphabets you will begin to find sounds which are not in our alphabet, and finally will undoubtedly start wondering why ours has just twenty-six letters (two thirteens) with duplicated sounds, and also some sounds which do not have their own symbol. Others have wondered also. Was there something about this number twenty-six which once had a special meaning?

Then sooner or later you will begin to see that the Egyptian hieroglyphic and the hieratic (popular) seem to be the basis for many other scripts. Or is it possible that a giant trading empire of antiquity was the original through which it has filtered down to us largely from the Egyptian? For example, the Phoenician definitely shows Egyptian background and so does Etruscan as well as the Pelasgian which some old authorities tell us is just another name for the Etruscan or Tyrian.

The Etruscans who once lived on the Tyrian sea and had ships which, along with their cousins the Phoenicians, sailed the length and breadth of the Mediterranean, were very similar to the ancient Egyptians. Like them, the women were elegant, banquets were held in mixed company, and entertainers danced for the guests. They had a very modern type of home with all the modern cooking utensils and furniture, but their histories and books are gone, so we cannot read Etruscan. This again was due to Rome. The Romans conquered the Italian Etruscan cities one by one, until Italy became entirely Roman. What they did not realize is that Italians today have lost their Etruscan heritage of a magnificent antiquity.

In a like manner, Mayan is today undecipherable even though their dates run to fantastic antiquity. Only one clue came to me as I noticed that the Mayan glyph for an unknown sound looked like the stylized head of a snail - it had rounded ears instead of knobs on feelers. The Egyptain

glyph for f or v was a snail crawling. This could be a clue.

It is tragic again that Mayan books, many of them history books, I am told, came all the way down to our own millennium from an unknown past only to be burned by the conquering Spanish. Once more, these conquerors might have had some student who had the divine spark of intellectual curiosity among that band. Or they could have had a Diodorus or a Herodotus who might have suspected that these ancient people perhaps could have been a contact with that legendary sunken land which lay so near to their own Spain. Alas there was not. So they merrily burned the clues to their own ancient history, as vandals usually do, for the tragedy of the vandal is that he has no vision.

There is another lost language in Crete along with an unknown alphabet. Apparently there is no recognized connection with the Tyrians, although both show many culture traits in common, along with Egypt. Once there were two languages in Crete, and two sets of writing. One was a commercial language and the other was reserved for history and the arts. There was a young English genius who was killed in war, who was able to translate and read one of the scripts, but it turned out to be the commercial one. Thus although we know how much they paid for their grain and from where they imported various goods, and at what prices, we cannot read their histories. Perhaps some day another such genius will come along who can untangle the labyrinth of the cultural script of Crete.

The loss of this alphabet was not due to vandalism since we have the books. Instead, we know now that Crete did not fall because of an invasion, but rather because of a seismic disaster. A terrific earthquake along the Aegean fault shook her palaces and temples to pieces and they burned to white heat when the stored oil used in her central heating system caught fire. These people also had tiled baths of hot and cold running water and sewers under their cities. We do not know the date, but apparently we can get a rough idea from the trade with Egypt. It was apparently not as old as the disaster which took the life of the ancient colossus of the sea. However it may have been one of the colonies of that land, since we read often that the legendary Titan, Zeus, supposed to be related to the rulers of Atlantis, was the king of Crete. What we could learn from those tantalizingly forbidden history books!

It is strange that in the Mediterranean, one civilization after another went down in flames

ALPHABET CHART FROM AN OLD BIBLE

FROM EARLY BIBLE JAMES I EDITION		Hieroglyphic	Hieratic Egyptian	Phoenician Moabite inser.	Phoenician Siloam inser.	Right to left Cadmean	Left to right Cadmean	Local Forms Greek	Local Greek	Pelasgian or Etroscan	Hebrew		Latin Early	Latin Late	English Modern (Early)		Anglo Saxon	Norse	Modern Finnish	Ogam or Ogham Early Irish + British	Tagalog Philippines Pre-Spanish
Aa	EAGLE							Alpha / Eastern													
b	CRANE							Beta Corinth / Melos Megara													
gG	BOWL							Pharos / corinth													
d	HAND							Delta													
h(e)	HOUSEPLAN, TEMPLE							Epsilon													
f,v	(Snail) CARASTES							Dig-amma													
+Tch z	DUCK							Eastern Zeta			G Formed from c										
xKh	SIEVE							Argos													
Th	TONGS LOOP							Theta													
i	(Feathers?) LEAVES							Iota													
K	THRONE							Kappa													
l	LIONESS							Lambda													
m	OWL							Mu													
n	WATER							Nu													
S	DOOR BOLT							Sigma													
a	(Sword) WEAPON												Blended in → A							
p	DOOR							Pi / Melos													
T ts	SNAKE							Psi													
q	KNEE?							Kappa													
r	MOUTH							Rho													
S,Sh	FIELD							Chi					Blended in → S							
T	ARM WITH CAKE IN HAND?							Tau													
eo	O Is generally used for W,O and U							Omikron / paros													
NG								Gamma					(NG) →							
Oe					(Eta)								(oe) →							
ae	a is also				(Phi)								(ae) (y) →							
ea or oa / U					Omega →			Upsilon					(u)	u	u	(u) →					

For o place comma below
For o no comma
For i as ca mark comma above
For i as ca mark comma below

289

By 3,000 B.C. the Sumerians had invented the first writing system.

with all their histories, due to war and the vandalism of the invaders. Each time civilization was set back for a thousand years. Almost no people were innocent of this. Greece sacked Corinth and in turn was most thoroughly sacked by Turkey. After Rome had finished with the Etruscans, she sacked Egypt and Carthage. The latter was such a thorough job that not one stone was left standing. She had little reason to cry out when the Goths, Visigoths and Vandals came down on her marble city. In the art of what she was pleased to call "vandalism", Rome had been an excellent teacher.

Yet there was one conqueror who was different. The Assyrians perhaps

"Came down like a wolf on the fold,
Their cohorts all gleaming in purple and gold"

but Ashurbanipol, who came to the Assyrain throne in 668 B.C., was one of science's first great archaeologists when, discovering a library in an unknown tongue below his wine cellar, immediately sent his wise men out to bring back dictionaries so that he might read it. If the library was a shock and a fascination to him, it is even more so to the present generation of scientists who are translating that library from Ashurbanipol's five Babylonian dictionaries. All we know as yet is that there is not only history but also drama, novels and other forms of literature. Ah yes! All we know as yet is that there are recordings of events at fantastic dates in the past.

What did the Sumerians look like? The most prominent feature about their squat, round-headed, rather unprepossessing physiognomies was their tremendous nose. Their language is neither Aryan nor Semitic, but apparently they did will the nose to some of their conquerors. The Assyrians, of course, spoke a Semitic tongue, but they and their other Semitic languages which flowed over the city and land of Babylonia may at one time before they met up with the Sumerians, have had shorter noses.

Half a world away there is another people who remind us of the Sumerians. They are the Mayans. According to their pictures of themselves they had tremendous noses and squat bodies. However, this may have been just stylish during their days of glory. What they really looked like is rather problematical since they used artificial means to reshape the heads of their infants, put heavy weights on their babies' noses to make them long, and dangled glittery objects between their infants' eyes to make them cross eyed. Despite these absurd customs, the Mayans did not seem to suffer mentally. They had four inter-revolving calendars better than ours today and used the zero long before Europe could read and write. Were the Mayans Sumerians - even displaced Sumerians? Probably not. The alphabet and writing are not the same. If the men of Sumer interest you further, read "They Wrote on Clay" by Chiera.

There was an alphabet I was most delighted to come across in an old encyclopedia. It is called the Writing of Ogham. One is reminded as one looks over this strange early British and Irish script (of which there are supposed to be some six hundred copies in various old books and apparently only ceased to be used when Christianity came to the British isles) of the fact that one of the most persistent legends of sunken lands is that of Ogham or Ogyges once supposed to have lain off Ireland on the shallow 300-foot-deep shelf that runs almost to the Atlantic ridge. Ogyges was apparently ruled by a sovereign named Og whose statue, together with his queen Magog, stood for untold generations in London until it was destroyed during the bombing in the last war. These two statues were tremendously large granite carvings such as one might expect of the Megaliths. It was comparable in size to the giant masterpieces of early Egypt or the cruder granite statue of the rain god Tlaloc whose one hundred and sixty-seven tons was recently moved from his resting place of over a thousand years in the town of Coatlinchan by the Mexican government in order to bring it to Mexico City. The people of Coatlinchan rioted before he was trussed up and taken away. They had grown fond of him and pointed out his battered face and stumps for arms as examples of Spanish vandalism. Upon arriving in Mexico City and being placed again upright before the new buildings of the Mexican Hall of Anthropology, a thunder storm such as that capitol has seldom seen broke out through the concentrating clouds, and hit the streets with flooding water over much of the city. (The story of Tlaloc and his trip is told in December 11, 1964 Life magazine.)

Pausanias, during the second century A.D., who wrote the "History of Greece", said that a ruler by the name of Ogyges became king of Boetia or Thebes, and who, according to Lycophoron of the third century A.D., was a Titan and the son of Neptune and Alistra. According to St. Theophilus of Antioch, in his letter to Autolyous, about 170 A.D. Ogyges was related to the Titans and married Daria, daughter of Oceanus. According to Donnelly, this occurred during the reign of Phoroneus the Argive, son of Inachus and grandson of Oceanus and Tethys. Their people were the Pelasgians, which means "the people of the sea". He quotes Acusilaus' "Fragmenta" as his authority.

The name Ogyges seems to be connected among the ancients with the island of Cos and with the Meropes. It is interesting to know that in the Pacific realm of island legends, the Merope usually refers to people who build pyramids or to the pyramid itself.

Theopompus in his book "The Meropidae" declared that "these were the people who invaded Europe from the sea." This is a very enlightening statement in view of the story by Plato. The Atlantean war evidently was the legendary war between the gods and the Titans. The home of the Titans was off the Irish coast? Was this the gateway of Atlantis or the Atlantic league? If this is true, then the "gods" must have been the kings of the Mediterranean league, possibly led by Zeus of Crete. It is just a wild guess at pre-history of which no doubt we shall learn more when the unknown histories of Crete are translated, and Zeus returns from legend to the stage of recorded history.

Donnelly, still speaking of Gyges, or the lost land of Cos or the Meropes, says that the Greeks of the golden age referred to this region of legend as "the sacred isle", (quoting Camden) "Nor can anyone conceive why they (the Greeks) should call it (Ireland) Ogygia, unless from its antiquity: for the Greeks called nothing Ogygia unless what was extremely ancient."

He then mentions the Irish canoine (keening wail) done for the dead, which was heard by Herodotus as it was chanted in Libya by the women. It was also chanted in Egypt and by the Etruscans in Etruria, Italy, by the Tyrenian sea, while the present writer remembers very vividly one golden morning in the Chippewa encampment beneath the cedars and pines of their "sacred forest" on the Michigan peninsula, being awakened to the scent of cedar smoke and the wailing dolorous chant of many women's voices interspersed with sobbing which came in a wavering rhythm from the depths of the forest. I leaped from my bough and skin couch and dressed in apprehension. Seeking the chief I asked in alarm for the meaning. He smiled at my concern and answered: "It is our custom. On a certain day in a certain place, once a year, we mourn for the dead. When the women have finished their chant they will return and then we shall eat. You will forget what you have heard and mention it not."

He was right. A few hours later, with the sunlight filtering down through the trees in long slanting lines, the women came back, even while we young ones were out having our morning swim, and food was waiting for us when we returned. No one mentioned the sorrowful chant and with the chieftain's eyes on me in a forbidding manner, I did not mention it either.

There seem to be strange similarities across the Atlantic. Unfortunately some of my notes were stolen in England and I will have to write from memory only. The most important loss was the Tuareg alphabet known as Tamacheck. I copied much of it from De Provok's books, one of which is "In Search of African Gods". Speaking of this Frenchman, it is too bad that he didn't use his friendship with the Tuaregs to learn more of their culture instead of merely ferreting out the location of the tomb of their ancient queen so that he could rob it. This only confirmed this people in their worst suspicions concerning the baser motives of the white man and probably forever closed the door of communication.

I did not receive all of my information from this author, although much of it duplicated what I learned elsewhere. However, there are a few words of the language which the Arab remembered that I later tried out on the Sioux of South Dakota. I found that they knew more of the Tuareg words than any other group, and the similarity here and among all the eastern tribes should be investigated. I remember that the word meaning to throw an image or cast a shadow in Tuareg, to the Sioux meant to follow and hide behind a tree so that the animal will not know you are following. It is interesting that English has both meanings for the word "shadow".

On the other hand, the Algonkin spread of languages, which evidently once covered the whole of the land north of Mexico before the invasion of the southerners from the direction of the Caribbean or the Athapaskan speakers from the Aleutians, has a peculiarly guttural tone to it. I was able to hear much of it when with the

Dragon ship, either Viking or Phoenician trireme.

O'Chippewas in northern Michigan. They had vague memories of the great ice mountains to the north where once half of their people were lost in a terrible splitting of the land. They also remembered a trading nation which came in ships to buy their copper. The name of this distant land was Pahn. I thought of the god Pan of Greece and his pipes which in South America were built into organs and again which were found in the hands of the long heads whose graves were uncovered by Dr. David Banks Rogers. But that strange gutteral tongue haunted me until I found the two volumes of "The Viking and the Red Man". These books, too were among the articles stolen. The author had found most of his word similarities by going to the outermost islands off the Atlantic from Norway and into the most isolated mountains in that land. There he heard such words as ''barsark'' (our word berserk) which on both sides of the Atlantic meant a dance that imitated a bear which had eaten poison fruit and had gone crazy.

To my questions about the possibility that they might have remembered white men coming, they either remembered nothing, or long ago a very few came in dragon ships which always went away almost immediately afterward. And there was always the inevitable physical argument: "If they had come in numbers and stayed long enough for them to teach us our language then we would have their beard!" And there was no answer for this.

Therefore the only physical possibility of such a similarity of the Algonkin and some pre-Aryan tongue such as this Gothic apparently seems to be, would be for both languages to be fragments from a lost trans-Atlantic tongue.

There are many unanswered questions. Why is our word "mangle" a word for war in so many languages including the pre-Spanish tongues of the Philippines? In French it means to chew, or eat.

The similarity of the Tuarak (the Amerind insists that this is the correct name for these people, Tu meaning "all powerful", ar or the r sound stood for the fire god and the k sound for people) on one hand, and across the Atlantic the languages of the Aruaks, Aruakians, Caribs and other tribes which later spread both north and south according to their legends, is certainly another avenue which should be investigated. Not only are the languages similar in root word

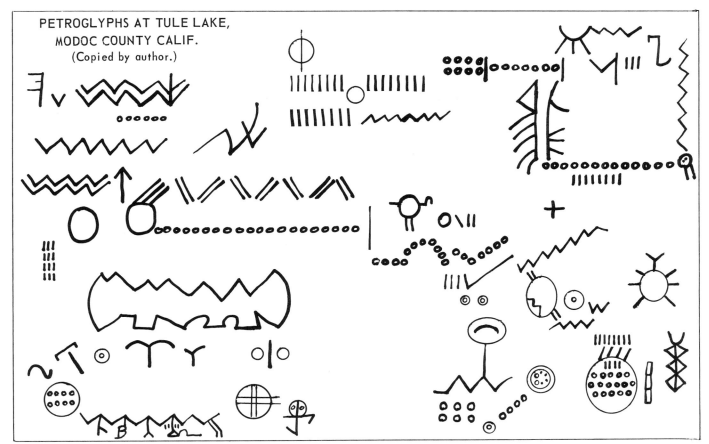

**PETROGLYPHS AT TULE LAKE,
MODOC COUNTY CALIF.**
(Copied by author.)

1) Attention is called to the thirteen circles with the eight lines below it, upper right, which is very distinct.

2) The glyph ⟋Ⰺ⟍ here is repeated at the "lava beds", a national monument about fifteen miles to the south. It is there written thus ⟋ℓ⟍

3) Note in lower right the circle with four lines and sixteen circles inside with what looks like a bit of cane beside it. This could be a primitive or earlier way of writing the Aztec day-sign "cane".

4) To the right of this sign is what appear to be the snake with the turtle at its correct place just before the head of the snake.

meanings, but the ball games played all through the Americas (especially of the hockey type and those which do not use the hands) are to be found on both sides. The Basques even have the same name as the Nahuatl for the same game. And rubber was an American product.

Again there is the war sheath of the ancients which becomes the kilt not only in Ireland and Scotland, but among the Basques, Greeks, Moroccans, and numerous other ancient peoples. The bag pipes also are ancient. They are played in Morocco, Algeria, by the Basques, etc., around the Mediterranean. Next time you hear them, notice the lifting of the hands in the dances and the duplication of the trident symbol not only on the costumes but also in the rhythms.

The Amerinds listening, that is if they are informed, are quick to notice this, also the stories of the Finnish kavella which contain the symbolism of the Amerind chants - even to the rhythm.

Among the Laplanders they point out the babies in cradle boards, and the tent which is so much like the tipi or Nahuatl tepec, whose name in both cases means "mountain". They ask me if the Laps also have twenty-six sticks to make up the house and if they know it stands for the double star? Frankly, I do not know. The language of the Laps, Finns, Gothic highlands of Norway, probably old words lost in the Gaelic of Ireland and Scotland (which by the way are still mutually understandable) as well as the Basques with the early Egyptian, stemming back to the Tuaraks and the Amerinds. A great deal could still be learned. These fragments are very old. Donnelly says that in the Greek legends, Ogygia was connected with the disaster of the first deluge. This should mean that there was a second one, perhaps when Crete was shaken and much of the land in the Mediterranean which had not gone down or been submerged in the first deluge then went down in the second. This may have been from 5000 to 8000 B.C. We will have to wait for carbon dating on Crete for this.

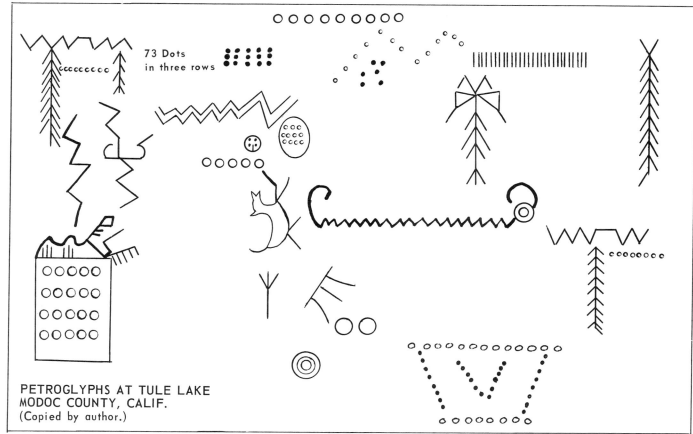

PETROGLYPHS AT TULE LAKE
MODOC COUNTY, CALIF.
(Copied by author.)

73 Dots in three rows

1) Attention is called to the upper left hand glyph which is duplicated at the right center. The main difference is in the number of dots, the one having eight and the other nine. The slight difference in placing may be but a natural writing variation on the part of the one who inscribed it. In this connection, the feathered figure above it seems to be only this part of the glyph in reverse.

2) An Indian friend from the Pueblos has suggested that the central glyph could be interpreted as "coyote defeated in fifth battle, or fifth cycle and prisoners burned in the sacred fire". It is most interesting to learn that he interprets the trident under the hanging wolf symbol as the fire sign.

3) The symbol at the lower right is without doubt a striking example of a Venus calendar glyph.

Note in this one the K symbol for the throne done in the very early dot or circle writing which most authorities now consider the very earliest of all writing. As yet not to be deciphered, although world wide.

Also note that the K symbol which is sometimes used for "throne" in the Americas is usually "people", perhaps because they believe themselves to be the people of the ancient throne? In the petroglyphs the Amerinds tell me that the sun symbol denotes the head chief. Evidently Coxon did not know this and was trying to make it calendrical, such as a day, etc.

Another loss of mine suffered in Europe was the theft of my alphabet of Irish and early English "stick writing". My grandfather once found this in an old dictionary and copied it for my alphabet album. The sounds are represented with what would seem to be a tree with various branches either on one side or the other. I often think of it when I see similar marks on Amerind petroglyphs.

And speaking of alphabets, an article in the Arizona paper from Phoenix under the date of March, 1965 (AP) mentions that fine art officials of Bangkok, Thailand have discovered an ancient city in the jungles 250 miles to the northeast of Bangkok, the Bangkok Post reporting the tale. The story said that the Buddah images found in the ruins dated back to the seventh century. Also found were some images carved in stone and a stone inscription in an alphabet believed to be of south Indian origin. A detailed study is being made of the site. It may be possible that this is the long lost writing of the ancient Dravidian empire. That would indeed be a discovery.

This city would be of the same age as carbon dating has set as the time of life (the sixth and seventh century A.D.) for the ruins in Mexico known as Monte Alban. Also the latest ideas of Mexico university concerning that site is that the stones of "the dancers", standing about the entrance to the tunnel under the pyramid in the newly excavated plaza of the ruined city, may be from a still older civilization. I mentioned in a previous chapter how they seem to be scenes from Africa, China and Egypt. The learned

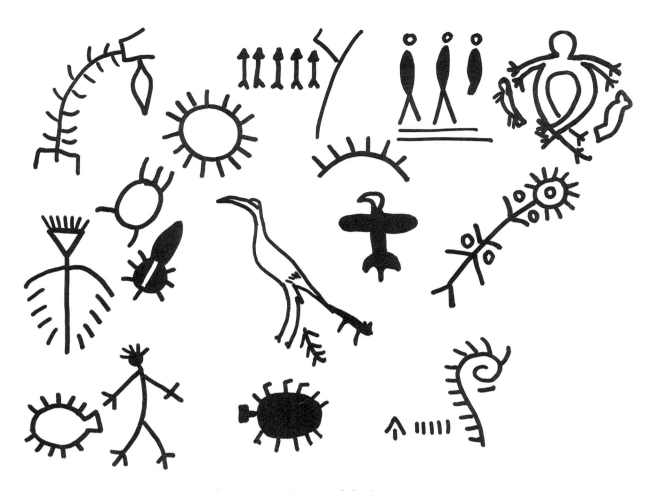

Pictographs along the Columbia river.

archaeologist who took our class in archaeology through, shook his head before them as he pointed out the details on the Pharoah's throne room. They are crudely carved and pretty worn by time, but very disturbing if you do not wish to grant the carver had no access to ships.

Before we close this chapter on languages, alphabets and writing, we should mention the hundreds of inscriptions to be found on the rocks in our western states. William Coxon gave his entire life to the study of petroglyphs (from the Greek words petro - rock and glyph - writing), and a tribute to his lifetime of study is given to him in the September, 1964 number of Arizona Highways, entitled "Ancient Manuscripts on American Stones".

Coxon was once told by an anthropologist who apparently wanted to be rid of him and his questions, that the writings were "mere Indian doodlings, and if they had any meaning at all, it perished with the individual who made them." This shocked Coxon, but as he compared the "doodlings" he found the same sign often repeated - sometimes eight hundred miles apart - and decided that the "doodling Indian" was quite

a traveller. His first great discovery was that the glyphs followed ancient streams and always upon rocks or cliff faces which reached out into the stream. He also found that standing at one and looking along the stream bed he could locate the next inscription. All this to him was a revelation that the writers had boats and were using the streams as a means of transportation. He decided that the glyphs were maps of the place and also of the animals to be found there. (Some of the signs are undoubtedly of religious or magical significance, but many are calendrical with meanings which escape us. I have often found myself staring at them in frustration and wishing for Asa Delugio.)

Coxon's greatest discovery was that the same glyphs circle the globe, always following streams of the ice age time. They are to be found in Ireland - up several rivers, through Spain, north Africa and the Nile river from the cataracts south. They are to be found in the Canary islands, certain islands like the Virgins in the Caribbean sea, the Lotun cave of Yucatan, along the gulf of Mexico from whence they enter the United States via the Mississippi and its tributaries, the Rio

Indian petroglyphs at Newspaper Rock, Petrified Forest, Arizona.

in which they were pecked out with a sharp instrument. He tried carving them out for himself in lava rocks and found that large blows shattered the rock and ruined the designs. Then he knew why they had been pecked. He found out further that island after island had been explored in the Pacific, and some of the larger ones rather thoroughly. He reasoned that the writers wished to use these for way stations on their voyages either to rest, obtain fresh food, make repairs or a combination of all three.

As Coxon found more interested parties in other lands, he found more and more similarities, many of which were absolute duplicates such as the design unearthed in Assur, Assyria (near Babylon) with a symbol on it which differed only from the one found in the Santan mountains of the pinal country, Utah, by the fact that first one which was a stone mould for metal had a four-circle design while the one in Utah was a three-circle design. The number of divisions in

Grande, on across the great divide into the west and via the rivers all through these lands. They are along the Colorado and the Gila to mention only a few. They appear along the gulf of California and throughout the Pacific ocean.

Coxon learned of this world wide spread from a letter which a honeymooning couple in Hawaii wrote him. The man, Dr. Thor Hayerdahl, knowing Coxon's interest in rock inscriptions, copied some of those pecked in the lava rocks of the island. Coxon was dumfounded because after comparing the glyph with one which he had found on the Gila river in Arizona, he discovered them to be identical. For him this mysterious design had no meaning unless it was a map of some land somewhere. The effect upon his thinking was to convince him at once that the doodling Indian theory could hardly account for this.

Like the present writer, he sought out the Pimas and the Papagoes. He learned from them that they were as mystified at the writing as he was. They declared that the inscribers in stone were extremely ancient and came to the land long before they as a tribe had wandered to what was empty land.

Coxon then worked on, contacting interested parties in other lands who were willing to copy down or photograph the inscriptions which they had found. He learned that the writings were almost entirely done on lava rock, but not always,

Shell disk from Tennessee mound. Probably calendrical.

the space between the first and second and the second and third circles are exactly the same. The sphere is also in both cases exactly centralized in the middle of the symbol. Scientists in Syria dated the artifact as 1400 B.C. and it is

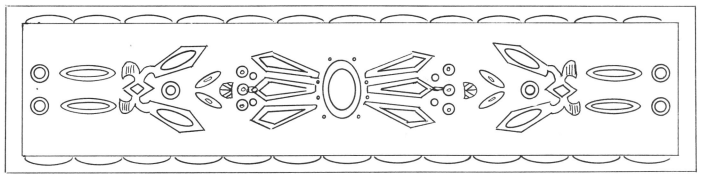

The double trident points to the altar of the sacred fire or oval of the turtle symbol. Other figures in the design are the twin gods, the rabbit and the dragon. it is hard to locate the dragon until one remembers that he is always pictured with oval pop eyes and tusk-teeth. The protruding tongue of the twin gods is a Mayan characteristic where protruding tongues are common subjects of temple paintings. It is interesting to note that the tongue has eight lines. The rabbit's whiskers are the same shape and also carry eight lines. The eight-thirteen "magic" numbers hidden in the design are carried by the double-lined symbols.

illustrated in Olmstead'd "History of Assyria". But was it Assyrian, or was it Sumerian? (My comment).

Coxon did not seem to realize that the serpent symbol stood either for water or for the people of the sea. He thought that these inscriptions were trying to tell others following them that the site was infested with snakes. In one case however, he realized his error. That was when he was hunting the sites, and found that when he saw the serpent symbol, if he counted the turns in the body and then compared that number to the turns in the dead river, he would find the next site. He sometimes believes that the number twenty-six and the number fifty-two (two twenty-sixes) means the number of weeks in our year. Evidently he doesn't know about the Venus calendar, which certainly antedates our present calendar by many centuries. And that brings up another point - why did our ancestors, choosing various gods for the different days of the week, pick fifty-two for the number of weeks or seven for the number of days? Was the seven chosen because both in Europe, the Mediterranean and throughout the Americas there were seven kings who escaped the cataclysm with their ships, and therefore seven became a more desirable number for the days of the week and fifty-two for the number of weeks even though this left a number of days dangling at the end of the year? If we had thirteen months of twenty-eight days each, we would not have so many days at the end of the year. However, the number thirteen for the Aryan speaking tribes was "bad luck" although they still held to the seven and the fifty-two. Thus they made the number of months twelve (a dozen - one of their numbers of measure) and divided the extra days around among the various months, a rather clumsy arrangement, but very interesting in the light of legend.

It is also interesting that Coxon has discovered that these inscriptions all over the world are geometrical in type. Concerning this he says: "Among the approximately four hundred characters used in the Egyptian hieroglyphics are twenty elementary signs of geometry. The same signs also present themselves in the . . . rock writings (of the Americas) . . .

"The highly significant testimony which the hieroglyphs themselves record rests in the fact

IS THIS A MAP?

Glyph found in Hawaii and Gila River, Arizona. It has some characteristics of the wrecked land on the Atlantic ridge.

that the Egyptian scholars in the art of writing, like the stone writers, used combinations of the elementary signs of geometry to construct symbols. True, they only employed the hieroglyphical repertoire which afforded maximum simplicity and speed of execution, and the minimum of size, but these fifty or more signs and symbols firmly and indelibly establish knowledge to the Egyptians of geometric symbolism.''

This statement of Coxon is provocative and shows that his theories should be followed by some other worker.

''After exhausting this limited requirement of geometric formations, the scribes of the Nile leaned mightily, for the remainder of the approximately four hundred figures making up the hieroglyphical treasure, upon pictorial characterizations. The stone writers were more consistent, for they continued from where the Egyptians vacated geometrics, developed sequences of symbols from each elementary sign and qualified those basic forms for alphabetical recognition by the creation of orderly, progressively and consecutively evolved symbolical variants - thousands in number.''

It is too bad that Coxon did not live (he died in 1963.) to follow this theory further. He may have touched upon the clue to the ancient writing from which all other forms are descended. Coxon has thrown the torch of research into the future. I pass it on to you.

Diodorus Siculus of Agyrium, Sicily, living about the time of Julius Caesar, was another great archaeologist. Perhaps he had read the ancient library of Egypt which had been burned. Perhaps he only intended to read it. As if to make up for what happened, he walked the regions of north Africa in an attempt to study the people he called ''the Atlantides'' and other writers of his time called ''the Atlantidae''. He knew what he was looking for when he saw the symbol of the trident.

Since that time two millennia have passed. We no longer recognize the ancient symbol for what it is. Perhaps the Scots put the symbol on their uniforms only because their fathers put it on theirs - in other words it is customary to do so. We no longer learn the ancestral dances of our country, or regard them as something weird. Start looking around you. Begin by asking the meaning behind the dance or festival. Perhaps you will find, like some of the towns in Germany, that a certain festival which comes once a year chooses a very beautiful woman to be the central figure. She is then brought into the village and gives out presents and for that day she is the

''queen'' from a distant golden island to the far west. In the early times she lived out these few days of glory and then no one ever saw her again. She was a sacrifice to Woden. So the festival had a sad undertone in spite of its joy. For the people knew. (See chapter 41 - Page 175, Mummies of The Norse)

In the Scandinavian north the Odin festival sacrificed a horse. In some lands at Christmas a beautiful woman is chosen to walk toward the assembled guests bearing lighted candles on her head, or on a head dress. Any Amerind medicine man will tell you that these are the flaming volcanoes of ''the old red land'' before it sank.

The next time you see the Scots or Irish dancing, note the fingers pointed up, making with head, the trident, or pointing down, meaning the land was broken and submerged. Once these arm movements had a meaning, but other religions have come in to wipe them out. However, the pipes still have three points up and above them, one chanter, to carry the often weird old melodies. If you do see the pipers march, note the boots (now leggings) to the knee or above the calf, and the skirt which was once the fringed war sheath. Sometimes the cuffs on the sleeve bear the trident. If they are true to the ancients, then somewhere above the brows there should be a feather with a bit of the downy fluff at its base. We shall learn the reason later.

If you should see an American Indian dance, note the symbols and the changing rhythms. Or if you should see the pipers, listen to the drums. If you chanced to hear and see the Kennedy funeral in Washington, you undoubtedly were as intrigued as I was by the ancient death march of the drums, and the insistent beat of three. I thought of the keening of the women who wept once a year, and the time when I asked Asa Delugio about the weeping god who held the short swords above his head points up, in the gateway which went nowhere in Tiahuanaco, Bolivia and (which he insisted was their city) - why this figure wept? And his answer was ''his tears are not for the dead of yesterday, but for the old red land.'' Somehow this haunted my memory as I listened to that strange ancient death chant of the drums - flourish,2,3,4; flourish, 2,3,4; flourish, 2,3,4; and then very slow deep drum tolling as if from a bell: Boom! boom! boom!

If you start asking questions, listening and noting the symbols, you will begin to feel a thrill as if memories were pressing in upon you just beyond the remembering. And if you do, your life will become all the richer.

Chapter 51

Who Were The Oldest Civilizations?

I was again seated in Louise's Pantry in Palm Springs, sketching an ape man, when I felt someone leaning on my shoulder. (Palm Springs is a desert village not far from Los Angeles that expands on week ends into a crowded city.) I turned partly around and looked up at Louise, with her creamy complexion which is God's gift to the Norse. Her eyes were wide with amazement.

"Who or what is that?"

"An ape man."

She swallowed as if something sour stuck in her throat.

"Where does he live?"

"He once lived in Java."

"When?"

"Perhaps a couple of hundred thousand years ago."

"I feel better already. Now I will probably sleep tonight. By the way, do you remember the people who once sat at your table? I had forgotten them, but they remembered you."

"Oh yes, indeed I do. They had travelled through north-western Africa."

"Well they have been in twice, but not too recently. They wanted to see you about some writing . . ."

"Thank you! I will go right over."

"And not wait for a slice of my home made pie?"

"Not tonight. You couldn't even tempt me with a whole pie after that message."

"That must be some writing!"

I hurried through my meal and drove over to the Sahara Court. Everything seemed exactly the same until I passed the recreation hall where again a dance was in progress. Suddenly my heart sank; the beautiful mobile home which had been standing on the corner where I had viewed the pictures of north Africa was gone, and another stood in its place. I parked my car in front, circled around the Cadillac in the driveway and rang the chime-bell. A most gracious stranger came to the door. She had never heard of my friends, and had only recently been able to acquire the empty space. I thanked her and drove disconsolately away.

Turning down highway 111 past Cathedral city and Rancho Mirage, I drove on to the desert. It was a beautiful moonlit night, a perfect time for walking through the wastelands. I pulled my car up finally slightly off the highway and strode up to the great rocks which overlook Salton sea - once the arm of the ocean, but cut off unknown centuries ago and partly dried up in the desert air. The cactus and creosote threw ghostly shadows as I walked toward the rocks. Somewhere up there, under the covering of travertine, was writing - a strange ancient script like that found on the rocks near the pre-Inca site in Peru.

The travertine covering is a rough rock-like paint of nature splashed against the boulders perhaps thousands of years ago when the waves were high and dashed up with salty spray. Under that travertine somewhere high above my head, was the writing. It had not been easily seen when last I came here sometime during the thirties and in the sunlight. I remembered that the travertine oozed itself around the curious letters as though some giant had carelessly splashed them with a paint brush full of cement. Once I had taken pictures of them, and with just the right light, could make out almost every letter. They were among the notes I lost in Europe. Now I could only remember the eight pointed star and the double cross. ✳ ☨

That they were old there could be no doubt. The travertine had been here for perhaps about twelve thousand years, according to geologists who estimated that the coast was rising about a foot a millennium, and the rocks are now about twelve feet above sea level. But that is the present sea level, so the figures on their antiquity become immediately complicated by the unknown age of Salton sea. Most scientists grant it is probably Pleistocene. What time in that interesting period, we do not know.

I stood there for a long time looking over the desert, wondering what strange type of ship had come here and why the voyagers had left writing upon the rocks. Could they guess that some day others would come and stare at that message, unable to decipher its meaning? For a moment I felt strangely close to these people of such vast ages ago. Did they have planked ships? Were they long heads who buried their dead in the crouch position, or were they the tall Cro Magnon type who have scattered their children around the Atlantic ocean, even as the lemurs of another era scattered theirs around the Indian?

Realizing that it was impossible to find the covered writing in the shadows of the moonlit night, when it was difficult to see it even in the daylight, I walked slowly back to the car and drove back toward Los Angeles.

On the way I had plenty of time to ponder my problem. Were these letters like the runes of the Norse? They certainly were neither Sumerian, Egyptian nor Mayan. What civilized people of vast antiquity had written both above the Salton sea and upon the rocks of a pre-Incan site? Who were these giants of the antediluvian world?

Did the eight pointed star stand for the Earth number in the Venus calendar, or did it stand for the compass, without which they could hardly have explored the Earth and sailed the oceans - or did it stand for both? And the double cross, what did that mean - or did it have a meaning of its own; most of our letters do not. I remembered with a laugh how a stanza of Omar Khayyam's Rubaiyat kept going through my mind as I walked away from the travertine rocks:

"Myself when young, did eagerly frequent
　Doctor and sage and heard great argument
About it and about - but evermore
　Came out by the same door wherein I went."

Then I thought of archaeology's method which was pointed out by my friend, Clarke Wissler, when he began to trace down the origin of the pole dance. He didn't live long enough to get around to figuring out the relationship of that dance to the May pole dance in Europe and the flying dance of Mexico where the Volodores drop from a sixty-five foot pole, tied by their feet and dance all the way down to the ground. But his method was worth trying. He took the culture traits and made a chart of them. The tribe which had the most was the one which either was the originator of the dance or the closest ancestrally to the originator. The answer was the Algonkin, much to the chagrin of the Siouan-speakers who declared that they, the Dacotah, had this dance from "time beyond the remembering". Was Wissler right? This could have been a flying dance; and in that case it must have originated with the totem of the bird, for it is by totems that the red man of the Americas remembers history.

There were two powerful totems in the Americas - the flying gods and the reptile gods. Each people thought his particular god favored him, which is not so unusual. All men believe that they are the "great ones," the "nobles" or "the supreme people". Ask any tribe of people the meaning of their name and you will find out, if they tell you the truth, that it has a similar meaning. So also they believe that their particular tribal god is interested in them above all others. In fact, it would be a dull sort of world if it were not so. We all have our pride in ourselves, our parents and our children. So also we must all feel that our deity has an interest in our welfare. Indeed, perhaps we are not so far wrong, for who has never had the experience of feeling, at a particularly bad moment, a lift from beyond the veil?

So with early man. He wished above all to please his tribal god. If it was a totem animal, he used the animal's weapons. He never ate that particular animal; an enemy totem, yes, but never his own. If he wished to sacrifice to that totem, then he sacrificed an enemy animal. This is the basis of all very early history. And curiously enough it is world wide. It is as true in the Europe of the religions previous to Christianity as it is today in the Americas, or the Mediterranean previous to the coming of the Semitic speakers.

The genius of the Semitic speakers is re-

SERPENT MOUND, ADAMS COUNTY, OHIO

This serpent mound in Ohio winds over a landscape covering a length of 1330 feet, at an elevation of five or six feet.
Said to have been built by the descendants of the survivors
of a tidal flood from the region of the gulf of Mexico.

ligion. Start counting up on your fingers the
religions of the world and you will see how many
were begun by these wandering tribes from the
direction of Arabia. Some, such as Moham-
medanism, were spread by the sword. With the
tribal gods, much history was wiped out. Some,
such as the Tuaraks, resisted the forward march
of the new religion, or gave it only lip service.
Apparently, according to the Arab I met in
Mexico City, the Tuaraks still worshipped the
sea god "with a pitchfork on his head". Today
you can see his dance when you see the crown
dance of the Apaches. The "pitchfork" is the
trident.

Apparently this is the fire god - oldest of all
religions. He was born in an island empire where
the fury of his fiery breath was a very frightening
reality and an ever present danger. The land was
surrounded by the serpent - water. Even today, in
the twentieth century "the great mystic ram of
the mountains" is regarded with a certain amount
of awe by most Amerind tribes.

The other all powerful totem is the bird.
From tribe to tribe the type of bird differs.
Sometimes it is the eagle. Sometimes a single
tribe has both, showing a very ancient war, conquest or mixture of peoples. This had long puzzled me until the afternoon I found the old gold-
embossed red book called "The Traditions of
Decoodah" in a second hand book shop. That

book opened a window on the past.

In my archaeology class in college I had
found that the great serpent mound of Ohio which
has the shape of a tremendous snake with gaping
jaws (heading toward the north), had definitely
made our professor hesitate when asked the
meaning.

"There is an egg in front of it," he frowned
uncertainly. "It is my opinion that the serpent
is chasing the egg." He then assigned a test for
the next lesson and further questions were silenced.

The Chinese say writing was invented by the
turtle. Decoodah said the turtle people were
the Dakotah. It would of course be a natural
thing for a totemistic people who needed written
communication in their trade to take the marks
from the shell of their totemistic animal.
Decoodah said that about 500 to 700 A.D., as
near as I can understand his dates, the serpent
and turtle came up the Mississippi from a civil
war which was causing the downfall of city after
city in the Caribbean sea. I sought out the Sioux
to ask them to clear this up.

"There is a large mound which is a giant
serpent coming up the Mississippi from the
south." Then I told them what Decoodah had
said - the invasion of the serpent was from the
war torn Caribbean. They nodded in understanding.

"That is right," the old sachem said.

Once more the young men crowded around to listen.

"Then why is the serpent trying to swallow an egg?"

"Swallow an egg?" the sachem's voice was touched with unbelief.

"On the serpent mound there is an oval just before his open jaws. Our professor told us that the oval was an egg."

There was a burst of delighted merriment.

When the laughter finally calmed down, I asked:

"Did I say something funny?"

"Very funny. The oval is the symbol of the tortoise. We are the people of the tortoise. We led the serpent up the Mississippi river from the civil war. That is why the turtle is pictured just ahead of the snake."

Of course I felt like a fool, but a moment's discomfiture of appearing to be a fool is worth the information involved.

But now it was his turn, and he too was after information.

"Have you encountered any other tribes of the turtle?"

"Not personally, but there is a book called "The Ancient Seri". They are undoubtedly tortoise. They dance on the shells of the giant tortoise, and they told the inquirers that they were of that totem - coming a long time ago from the direction of Peru or Bolivia in ships."

"What kind of ships?"

"Balsa ships; and Techuanaco on Lake Titicaca is the only place on Earth that they are found."

"Very enlightening."

"There is a strange legend that deep in an extinct volcano these Seri have a monster which they worship. It is a giant lizard - greater in size than the ones now living on Earth."

They looked at each other, but what their thoughts were, I could not tell. The leader again spoke.

"Where do these people live and are they well off?"

"They live on an island in the gulf of California. They are next to complete starvation and rapidly dying out. They have but few children and almost none of them seem to grow up."

He shook his head in pity and again they looked into each other's eyes.

"In the beginning you mentioned a book you had read about us which was written over a hundred years ago."

"Yes, that is true. Decoodah, the last high priest of the elks decided to tell a young white man his chants rather than let them die, because he wished to bridge the 'time of the destroyers'."

"They were the original people in this land. We call them Pahns. That is not a slanderous name. It is what they call themselves."

"I know that. Also it is one of the names for the old red land."

"You know that too?"

"Not only that, but in the legends of the Mediterranean sea, Pan is a goat god who plays music on the Pan's pipes. These are to be found today in the high Andes of Peru and Bolivia where the pre-Inca built with giant stones."

There was a sound as of breaths suddenly drawn in and many pairs of dark eyes were fastened on mine, almost as if held in a trance.

"We have legends of the giant rocks and this mountain city. Also the old red land was symbolized by the great horned ram of the mountains. He has not lost all his power even yet."

I nodded solemnly, hoping he would go on. Instead he murmured -

"You said that you would tell us what this man of Pahn had written down for the book."

"Decoodah mentioned the fact that the mounds were a historical writing in which one could read the story of the city once built around them until followed by the mound of extinction. Their capitol city was at a place whose Indian name I have forgotten, but which was the location of St. Louis. Then when the serpent came up the Mississippi river . . ."

"Led by the tortoise?"'

"Yes, I believe that is what he did say . . . at any rate, the people of Pahn moved further north and established another capitol. The black tortoise then established his capitol at the present location of St. Louis. . ."

"Did he say which of our seven tribes led the migration?"

"No, I don't believe that he specified which one."

"It was the Hunkapah, and today they are the furtherest north."

"Why do you have seven tribes, since you are all one nation?"

"Because there were seven kings who left the old red land during the great destruction. We are of these seven."

"Why that is what the Nahuatl people say. They live in central Mexico. Their greatest civilization was the Toltec, actually more learned than the Aztec and quite equal to the Mayans."

"We know of these Mayans. They are not entirely of our people. But I would know more about the empire of the black tortoise."

"You understand that this migration took place somewhere around 700 A.D."

"Yes. I am not confusing it with the old red land, and I see that you are not, either. So please go on."

"The black tortoise emperor established his capitol and his court on the location of the Puan or Pahn capitol and there gave each of his four sons a part of the kingdom to govern. The lines were drawn very sharply and for a time all went well. However, there were more migrations of the serpent still coming up from the southern sea which is evidently the gulf of Mexico."

"That is correct. Go on."

"In the southern court, a grandson of the black tortoise was growing up. However, he was greedy for power and he began to intrigue with the tribes now coming north, since he saw that they were his own people and would make him a fine army.

"In the meantime, the black tortoise himself was in the far west. He was extending his empire by conquering tribe after tribe or annexing them. He hoped to build a tremendous empire extending from sea to sea. One of the parts of his army left behind are the Yuma who today live on the California-Arizona border."

The sachem nodded thoughtfully, and then looked up at me expectantly. "There is more of course."

"Yes. Runners brought him news of the rebellion at home. He started back, but learned of an invasion down the coast from the far north. These were Asiatic types, bringing war dogs of heavy red or black coats. They may have been chows."

"Oh indeed yes - they had the purple tongue. We called them 'dog soldiers' and from time to time we eat them ceremonially to gain their bravery and power. I have one of the old line which has come down from the invasion of 'the dog soldiers' from the direction of what is now Alaska."

"Finally a great captain of the armies, known as Dacotah," I continued, "went to the Puan capitol and told them that the black tortoise was no longer interested in keeping the internal peace, but only in fighting in the far west. He wanted to take over, and offered them a full league partnership if they would allow him to train the Puan armies for invasion. They agreed, and then Dacotah began a march to power. The black tortoise was killed, and the kings who had been fighting the insurrection of the grand-

son were worn out from fighting each other, but turned on the captain. The war continued for years. Finally all law broke down, and about the year 1000, all tribes left their cities and took to the woods in complete anarchy, with only memories of the civilizations of the past."

"You have helped us clear up our own legends, and we thank you and Decoodah," he said graciously. "Is there another question you would like to ask?"

"Yes there is. In Egypt, the pharaohs fasten a tiny goatee beard to their chins sometimes. I can not believe them to be bearded, because they paint pictures of themselves as beardless red men. Then why the beard?"

"How large is the beard?"

"Very small and only on the chin."

"Then they are remembering the old red land."

"With a beard?"

"Certainly. The great horned ram had a tiny beard on the chin. Did not this goat god you spoke of who played the music in the Mediterranean have a beard?"

"Of course! It was a feature of the totem animal! But I still have another question. Please tell me why you use so many feathers if you were allied to the Atlantic serpent? (Note: The Dacotah are the originators of the "war bonnet" of feathers now used by all tribes. This was of old also a culture trait of the Toltecs, and in a lesser degree by the Aztecs. The mark of the full chieftain - feathers to the ground is also Dacotah.)

"We have much reverence for the eagle and other strong flying birds. They still have much power . . ."

"You have two totems?"

"This is very far back in the past . . ."

"There was once a bird-serpent war. Which side were you on - which was yours?"

"Your knowledge amazes me. This was long before the great destruction. In truth very much has happened to cloud our memories. Why do you not ask this question of the Pueblos? I have been told that their memories are more clear. Not so many disasters have clouded their history."

So I took my leave of the picturesque Cro Magnon "seven kings" and set out to find the round headed, stockier Pueblos. I was beginning to see great beams of light opening up a pathway through the tragedy and fog of the millennia. For actually, I was starting to realize that this first great global conflict might be the key to much of what had seemed a hopeless puzzle of the conflicting races of the ancient Atlantic.

Chapter 52

The Earliest Nations Of Historical Times, In The Mediterranean, And The First Global War

We are now going to leave the realm of legend for the stage of earliest history. Although there is no actual hard and fast line between the two, the solid ground of history should help us to untangle the more shadowy past which is legend.

Egypt we already know. Donnelly speaks of it as "the golden bridge ten thousand years long, glorious with temples and pyramids, illumined and illustrated for the most continuous records of human history, along which the civilization of Atlantis, in a great procession of kings and priests, philosophers and astronomers, artists and artisans streamed forward to Greece, to Rome, to Europe. As far back in the ages as the eye can penetrate, even where the perspective dwindles to a point, we can still see the swarming multitudes, possessed of all the arts of the highest civilization, pressing forward from out that other and greater empire of which even the wonder working Nile land is but a faint and imperfect copy."

Let us for a moment look at this land and note its main culture traits without going into long lists. The Egyptians spoke an agglutinating language, and were matrilinear. They looked to the totem or clan of the mother as the one from which the children inherited. In other words, the son of a king would not inherit unless he married his sister, for she carried the inheritance and probably at one time, the chanted histories. The son - her son - would succeed to the throne, and if something happened to the husband before the death of the old king, then his grandson through his daughter, not his brother or any other relation would inherit the title.

In this respect almost all of the tribes of the Amerinds, especially those of the eastern seaboard, are matrilinear to such an extent that the woman owns the children and the home.

A second trait of Egypt is that they liked to have banquets where they are pictured as reclining on long divans with a friend, while being served by slaves with trays, and entertained by professional singers and dancers.

A third main trait was that the men wore a short sheath while the women wore a long graceful robe, usually of white in Egypt, which was draped over the left shoulder.

A fourth trait is that their cities were usually supplied with fresh running water and sewers.

A fifth trait - they had ships.

Sixth - they were traders, especially of purple dyes.

Seventh - they were skilled metalsmiths, making articles of trade.

Eighth - they were amazingly modern in their

Column headers (left to right):

- Short Sheath
- Sun Face Tongue Out
- Full 2nd burial, painted bones
- Partial burial (red rust)
- Long bob-bangs hair dress (men)
- Crest cut or hanging hair dress (men)
- Circular Shield
- Long / Shield
- Reptile Gods
- Human Sacrifice
- Scarab Jewelry
- Medalion of Royalty
- Pans Pipes
- Flying Machines
- Explosives
- Silver ware on table
- Serpent, water symbol
- Trident, sea symbol
- Gold-Silver Jewelry
- Pole Dance
- Crown Dance
- Lightning of Fire Bird, Condor, Phoenix
- Lunar Calendar
- Cedar-Oak Sacred Groves
- Sacred Caves
- Advan. Mathematics
- Advan. Astronomy
- Bag Pipes
- Fire God Complex
- Sacred Fire
- Wind God Complex
- Hard Ball Games
- Ball Courts
- Head deformation to make forehead nose line
- Torches carried to Battle
- Round Towers
- Legend Land Sunken Sea
- Dentistry
- Circular War Bonnet

Row / group labels (left column):

- Gaels
- Europe
- Europe
- Europe
- Europe
- Europe
- Europe
- Europe
- Europe strong
- Europe
- Europe partial probably complete
- Europe strong
- Romans Greeks
- Europe strong
- Europe

Center annotation:

Celts, Basques, Atlantic Coastline, Romans, Greeks, Moroccans, Spanish

In-cell annotations: "complete", "Apaches", "partial" (several columns), "jade", "green stones", "strong"

Legend	Symbol
MINOR	● (gray)
LEGENDS	●
LEGENDS - STRONG	●
SUSPECTED	▶
STRONG	●

Note	TUARAK	TYRRHENIAN	CRETE	EGYPT	SUMERIAN BABYLON	INDIAN OCEAN	CRO MAGNON Spanish coast site	CRO MAGNON African gorge site	CRO MAGNON France cave	MAYAN	TOLTEC	EASTERN TRIBES	APACHE	CHAN-CHAN	PRE-INCA	Trait
	●	●	●	●	●	●				●	●	●	●	▶	▶	Agglutinating Language
	●	●			▶●					●	●	●	●			Matrilinear
	▶●	●	▶●	●	▶●			▶●		●	●	●	●	▶●	●	Venus Calendar
Later Europe	●	●	●	●	●	●				●	●	▶●	●		●	Writing
	●	●		●						●	●	●	▶●	●	●	Caste System
	▶●	●	●	●	●	●	●			●	●	●	●	●	●	Cities
	▶●	●	▶●	▶●						●	●	●	●	●	●	Sewers
	▶●	●	●	●	▶					●	●	●	●	▶●	●	Maze or Labyrinths
	▶●	●	●	●	●	●	●			▶●	▶●	●	●	▶●		Ships
	▶●			●	●	●	●			●	●	●	●	●	●	Contained Rivers
	▶●	●		●	●	●	●			●	●	●	●	●	●	Canals
	▶●			▶●						●	▶●	●	●	●	●	Irrigation
				●	●					●	●	●	●	●	●	Dams
				▶●	▶●					●	●	●	●	▶●	●	Mtn. Terraces
Europe	▶●	●	●	●	●	●		●		●	●	●	●	●	●	Cereals
Europe	▶●	●	●	●	●	●				●	●	●	●	●	●	Vegetables
Europe	▶●	●	●	●	●	●				▶●	●	●	●	●	●	Fruits
	▶●	●								▶●	●	●	●		●	Medicines
				▶●	▶●					▶●	●	●	●	●	●	Nuts
	●	●	●	●	●					●						Wine and Beer
Some Europe		●		●	●	●	●				●	●	●		●	Megalith. Large Stone
		▶●	●	●	●	●				●	●	●	●	●	●	Paved Roads
				▶●	●					▶●				●	▶●	Public Baths
		▶●	●	●	●	●				●	●	●	●	●	▶●	Metal Decor. Buildings
	●	●	●		●					●	▶●			▶●		Banquets
Gog Magog	▶●		▶●	●		●				●	●	●	●	▶●	▶●	Giant Statues
	●			▶●	▶●					▶●					●	Tunnels
		●		●	●						●			●	●	Bridges
		▶●		●	●	▶●				●	●	●	●	●	▶●	Oriented Pyramids
		●	●	●		●				●				●	●	Closed Arch
				●	▶●					▶●						Roman Arch
		▶●	●	●	●	▶●				●	●			▶●	▶●	Great Columns
		●		●						●	●			●		Cement
		●		●	●					●	●	●	●	●		Code of Laws
		●		●								●	●	●		Trial by Jury
Europe late		●	●									●	●			Bull Fight Cult
		●	●	●	●	●	●			●	●	●	●	●	●	Paved Streets
		●	●	●	●					●	●	●	●	●		Tile
	●	●	●	●						●	●	▶●	▶●	●	●	Cotton
	●	●	▶●	●	●											Flax - Linen
										●	●					Silk
		●	●	●	●					●	●	●		●	●	Embroidery
	▶●	●	●	●	●					●	●	●	▶●	●		Decorated Walls
	▶●	●		●	●					●	●	●	●	●		Stucco
Europe	●	●	●	●	●					●	●	●	●	●		Lamps
Europe	●	●	●	●	●					●	●	●	●	●		Spears
Bow & Arrow		●		●	●	●					●	●	●	●		Bow & Arrow
	●	●	▶●	▶●								●	Taos			Robes to Eyes
	●	●	●	●	●	●				▶●	▶●	▶●				Purple Dye
Europe	●		●	●	●	●				●	●	●	●		●	Woven Wool
Western Europe		●		●	●	▶●				●	●	▶●	▶●	●	●	Observatories
Europe		●		●	▶●	▶●				●	●	●	●		▶●	Odin - Votan
				●						●	●	●	●		●	7 Kings
Finland	●	●		●	●					●	●	●	●		▶●	Chanted History
	●			●	●					●	●	●	●	▶●	survival	Drama
	●	●	●	●	●					●	●	●	●	●	●	Orchestras
	●	●		●	●	▶●				●	●	●	●		●	Percussion Instruments
Europe	●	●		●	●	▶●				●	●	●	●		●	Wind Instruments
Europe	●	●	●	●	●					▶●	●			●	●	Stringed Instruments
Europe	●	▶●	▶●	▶●	▶●	▶●				▶●	▶●	▶●	●		●	Dance Dramas
Europe Beaker	●	●	●	●	●	▶●		●		●	●	●	●	●	▶●	Pottery
	●	●	●	●	●	●				●	●	●	●	●	▶●	Geometric Designs
	▶●	●	●	●	●	▶●				●	▶●	●	●	●	▶●	Circular Designs
	▶●	▶●	▶●	▶●	▶●					▶●	▶●	▶●	●	▶●	▶●	Sun a Red Circle
	▶●	▶●	▶●	●	▶●					▶●	▶●	▶●	●	▶●	●	Moon a White Circle
	●	▶●								▶●	▶●	●	●			Sacred Colors-Serpent Red, Black, some Green
	▶●				●					▶●	▶●	●	●	●		Moon - White Gold-Silver
Ireland		▶●			▶●	●				●	●	●	●		●	The Weeping Woman Crying at Night
		●	●	●				●		●	●	●	●	▶●	▶●	Basketry
		●	●	●	▶●	▶●				●	●	●	●	●	▶●	Sandles
	●	●	●	▶●	▶●	▶●				●	●	●	●	●	▶●	Leather Shoes or Boots
		●	●	●	●	●	▶●			▶●	●	●	●	●		Walled Towns
	●			●	●	▶●				●	●	●	●		●	Arm Dagger

homes and lives.

There is a list of a few of the culture traits, in case anyone might think that these nations of antiquity just happened by accident to have some of the same customs.

Suppose, for a name, we call the nations which show all of these traits and many, many others in common, the Matrilinear Complex of Agglutinnating Tongues.

First, let us take up Babylon. Although these people were over-run later by the Semitic speaking invaders, yet in the beginning they were the Sumerians. At one time it was thought that Herodotus, who lived before Plato, was simply making up a wild and fanciful story when he described the magnificence of Babylon. However, since that day, the city has been uncovered from an unpromising mound where the dry dust of the desert blew continually in whirling gusts. Then slowly the glittering ancient capitol came to light. Herodotus was entirely vindicated. He not only told the truth, but was also most exact in his measurements. For example, he had said that the wall about the city had such a broad top that two chariots, each drawn by a brace of four horses could pass each other. This was true. Of course, today the beautiful enameled work upon the bricks is gone, but standing in the ancient street with half closed eyes and the page of Herodotus open to the right place, one can walk with this eye witness and see Babylon in her glory.

As the scientists excavated the tremendous city with its hundreds of towers and temples, over fifty ziggurats (whose name means "mountain top"), they thought of the mysterious Sumerians who founded it, rather than the Semitic speakers who destroyed it, only to build again and destroy again many times. If the Sumerians had owned only libraries of paper, their books would never have survived; but "They Wrote On Clay" - the name of a most interesting book about them.

One of the most intriguing facts about this city of the Sumerians was their tremendous system of canals and the intricate maze of irrigation. The land is a desert, but the Sumerians made it produce an unbelievable amount of various kinds of foods, which since its first destruction, it has never really attained again.

Scientists uncovering these waterways were thinking not so much of the beautiful enameled work on the bricks, as of the reason for all this magnificence - the man made mountains with the stepback principle of seven terraces upon which a procession could wind around on its way to the top. Why were they so much interested in these man made mountains, some of which even carried growing trees and hanging gardens? Was it because these were originally mountain people who had learned in some other location to terrace the sides of mountains and irrigate from canals? No other people in history, with the exception of the fabulous pre-Inca of Peru and Bolivia could contain their rivers as well, and manage dams. The pre-Inca of course, even had a series of step dams - an engineering triumph which we consider quite modern.

The scientists have further speculated that perhaps the Sumerians arrived from their "somewhere" with this knowledge and immediately began fashioning metals and trading, because in these mysterious mountains of their homeland there was an abundance of metal. They also concluded that the Sumerians must originally have come from the direction of the Indian ocean because they handled such a flow of commerce from that direction. All this is logical and probable. But how about the ships and their tremendous knowledge of orienting the ziggurat so that its sides are so exactly to the cardinal points that its corners then form a giant compass? Is it not likely that the mountains from which they so reluctantly came to the flat dusty Mediterranean were actually islands in the sialic rich Indian ocean whose sunken lands of continental rocks are often only some three hundred feet below the surface?

From whence did they bring such astounding astronomy and mathematics? Such a tremendous knowledge of masonry, again in the category of the pyramid building Egyptians, and only exceeded by the fantastic megalithic builders of Bolivia and Peru?

Were they a "part of the debris", as they said that they were, "washed out of the Mediterranean mud after the great flood?" There is another legend on this score. It was told that they were brought to the location on the back of a giant water monster by the great Ouranos whose names run down through the legends of all Mediterranean peoples as the king who collected wandering and lost peoples and relocated them, possibly after some earlier flood. The curious part of this legend is that the king then went back to the great monster and spent the night within it. Undoubtedly this was a ship, (probably larger than the people who reported seeing the debarkation had ever witnessed before.)

There are other legends of the Sumerians.

Donnelly does a great deal of research among ancient writings to find out who the Meropes or the Merus are, when he found that the Phoenicians had called them by this name. He found in one case, mentioned before, that the Meropes were the people who had once invaded Europe from the sea. He furthermore connects them with the islands of Cos and Ogygia. In every case the flood mentioned seems to have been one of vast antiquity - probably the flood following the first retreat of the ice? Were these the people then who came to the Santa Barbara channel in planked ships and rode up to the tar pits in search of tar? Furthermore, the date which was suspected by Dr. Rogers and is now official, is of the first retreat of the ice. This too, then, must be the date of the submergence of the hundred-mile-wide strip of California. The villages were all disrupted and the cemeteries down faulted into the sea. Of course, it could have happened later, in the great destruction. The coast fault (the tourist resorts do not like to have it called the San Andreas when it goes through their territory), could have been triggered by the action in the transatlantic - Mediterranean fault and the ridge faults which caused the great destruction.

If the Sumerians were rescued by the Cro Magnons of the Atlantic league, then it is possible that the Sumerians were of the great bird totem which is of the Indian ocean. The strange part is that they resemble neither the long heads nor the disharmonic cross. They seem to be a small lost group of round heads whose great nose suggests a northern place of origin. Were they very anciently allied with the lost Dravidian empire? Or with the Atlantic league?

There is another people who resemble them - the great nosed Mayans who also are fantastic wizards at advanced mathematics, astronomy, calendars; had sewers under their modern yet fantastically strange ancient cities. They have a family similarity, as it were, except in the manner of clothes. The Mayans, too, arrived with a full court of nobles and a tremendous history. Both are rather short, squat of figure and burdened by an over-sized smelling organ. Undoubtedly the Sumerians thought it was beautiful. We know the Mayans thought so when they hung weights on the noses of their babies to lengthen them. Yet the Mayans have many Gothic root words. Do the Sumerians also? Furthermore if they advanced into Europe on a wide front after the flood of Ogygia, this could mean that we all probably have a bit of Sumerian somewhere. Take another look at Uncle Dick and Aunt Bertha -

when they are not looking, nor suspecting your thoughts. These Sumerians were also probably one of the most intelligent if not the most intelligent of all ancient peoples. Not that these two physical characteristics have anything to do with each other; it just happened.

Speaking of intelligence, there is a strange thing which once occurred to a Hittite city. It was massively built and with an almost impregnable defence, and placed very close to the Sumerian ancient road of trade. Perhaps these Hittites were pirates; perhaps not. We can not say for certain, but they incurred someone's ill will. Some army came out to punish them and burned the city. This in itself is not unusual, but the manner in which it was accomplished was. The great rocks were completely melted down! Did the Sumerians have explosives, magnesium, gun powder? In this regard some savants have professed to believe that the Chinese were originally a Sumerian colony, as their alphabets seem to have something in common, in their opinion. Looking at the Chinese nose, one is inclined to doubt that. However, perhaps the mysterious Sumerians have just scored another first. We have learned that they had geometry before Euclid, astronomy before the Arabs, and now, perhaps, chemistry before the Chinese. And is this also the source of the famous Greek fire the secret of which died with the defenders of Constantinople?

It is most intriguing that the name Merope or Meru is very strong throughout the Pacific ocean where the Polynesians tell some fanciful tales of these people. They were pyramid builders. The name means pyramid. Yet the Merus are far stranger than builders of pyramids. They have machines which fly without any noise, and when they held an island, they would excavate massive caves where they built their cities. These were lighted by huge lamps which burned forever without any fuel. However, the description of these Meru do not fit the Sumerians. The Meru, the Polynesians will tell you, were very small and slight of figure with pale gold skin. No mention is made of their nose, and one would hardly miss that distinguishing characteristic. So the Meru retreat to fantasy and the Sumerians to historical mystery.

However, in the Americas there is a strong clue which we must read in Amerind fashion - in totems. I have found that flying legends, canoes, ships that fly, etc, all finally stem back to the Indian ocean. Whether they actually once had three-decked ships that moved through the air and could "drop bombs", as is told in some of their fantastic stories repeated in the Vedas and other fairy tales, is a question beyond this book. The lost Dravidian empire is one of the greatest question marks in all pre-history. Undoubtedly it was given its death blow by - as the Amerinds say - the great destruction. Then there was an attempt at rebuilding, but before that even got well under way, the Aryan speakers came down out of the north, boasting that they had already "slain the great dragon", and burning cities and libraries as they came. The cities already excavated show the tremendous damage, because at the end of the streets are the piles of skeletons, dismembered, apparently of the defenders. They are the slight long heads. This is not the skeletal type of the Sumerians.

However, the lost empire may have been the Meru and their advanced civilization would without doubt cause them to be regarded as "the gods". Perhaps these were the original gods of the Titan-god war in which the gods won by means of unusual beams of light (fire?), thunder, etc. The Titans were so-called because they were so large according to the Greek legends as well as those of the Phoenicians. This would pinpoint the Cro Magnon man. Provok mentions, in his trip among the Tuaraks, that they usually measured seven feet tall, and the guards of the queen were all this height. Or perhaps I received this information from the war chief Sedillio of the Yaqui, who was himself a large man. He spent two weeks with the Tuaraks after he had finished studying with the Egyptian priesthood, always searching out the legends of the Atlantic, and their mutually understood ancient history. It is tragic that this very learned man, with degrees from two European universities, should find it necessary to throw away his life in a small Indian war with the Mexican government just because he was the hereditary war chief. If he had only lived a few weeks longer, this book might have been far more interesting, but unfortunately we had but a few hours before he went to his death. At that time I was more interested in my first book "He Walked The Americas" much of which I owe to his chants, but his quick sketchy descriptions of the galleries of the Tuaraks where he was received as a prince of the blood, because of the medallion he wore, and the similarities of their languages, I had thought to enlarge upon at our next meeting. To him I owe the quick remark that the bird- (or condor, bird of the lightnings) serpent war was of the Atlantic peoples and the lost empire of the Indian ocean. This happened, he declared, in the vast millennia before the great destruction.

The Sumerians have a statue which pictures a short dumpy figure of a scribe as clothed in a sheath of feathers. This would make him of the bird totem, but he does not fit the physical description of the long heads. However, they may have been an allied power, perhaps because they too were traders and had a stronghold in the Indian ocean.

The general time of this bird-serpent war comes to us from the memory chants of the Amerinds. "It was of the time of the first flood, before the ice mountains had all melted, and the people of the Atlantic were known as 'the dragon', partly because of the shape of the continent as it twisted down the Atlantic and partly because of the monsters which they worshipped. These lived in the swamps west of the land toward the direction of the sunset. The swamps were filled with the monsters, and it was hard to cross to the sunset land because of them. There was the one who lay deep in the water. He ate only the people and the children who played rough and fell overboard. But there was the great one who wandered down where the swamp was not so deep. He jumped on the ships to sink them. Then he could eat at his leisure. It was the twins who came back after the bird-totem war when at first the bird was defeated. The twins brought an army and attacked the monsters. Then they made their way to the old red land where they drove out the new invaders and took over the government themselves. Later the flood came and the monsters were seen no more."

Other tribes, often the Pueblos, will tell you that the hero twins were the sons of an emperor who was murdered by an enemy power. They were saved and smuggled away to the "grandmother land of the moon" (lunar calendar?) where they grew to manhood. "From there they went back to the land of the monsters where they slew the dragon which was eating the people. Then they attacked and won back the kingdom. Later however, they had a disagreement. The elder brother, who was the wiser, went away. He left his mischievous and sometimes cruel younger brother as king, and wandered far, dropping his flint blood as he went."

This story of the twins which runs from Canada through the Pueblos to Mexico and perhaps beyond, may have long lost history behind it. The anthropologists who have heard it think of it only as a tale for the edification of children which has some aspects of the Venus calendar. Of course, there is little doubt about the latter, but concerning this supposed "fairy tale" - is

The hero twin dance, symbolizing the snake-bird war, dimly remembered legend of the war between the serpent people and those of the condor totem.

it actually only that? So many times, unfortunately, the anthropologist, with his preconceived theories, goes into the "council" with a "Bastile mind", and the shrewd Amerind, who is no fool, realizes this. The result is that the supposed scientist comes out with a mouthful of dust.

Is this oft-repeated story only a child's tale to be told around the campfire on long winter nights? I determined to find out. After the preliminaries of a day's residence in which I watched some of the Pueblo dances, I was invited to the campfire where I had asked for the story of the hero twins. I had heard it often before, but I noted that at this meeting there were no children. It was explained that they were tired from the day's excitement and had been sent to bed. I was myself weary from watching the most intricate steps and amazing group movements of the tall masked Katchinas - who one could easily imagine were aliens (as the Pueblos claim) from another planet. But I was

not to be digressed from the purpose of my visit.

As the story unfolded, I realized that many pairs of eyes were glancing from time to time at my face. Perhaps it was this interest, and perhaps it was something in the way the story was worded that began to bring a new picture to light in my own mind. Finally the story was ended. The men smoked quietly while I sat across from the sachem. Both of us were staring into the fire. Finally he broke the silence.

"What are your thoughts?" he asked softly.

"I cannot believe this is a story to entertain children." Then falling into the Amerind's own manner of expression, which seemed to come naturally there before the fire which was scented with the sacred cedar, I said almost gropingly: "It seems I am looking back through immense vistas of time. There are two great powers which have clashed. I do not know why - perhaps over the right to trade on certain distant lands, for both of these powers had ships..."

The silence was so breathless that it crept around me and the ring of eyes upon me, as a lynx might upon padded toes.

"One of these powers was of the bird - I would say the condor. Being the 'bird of lightnings' means that this power had some explosive weapons which at first were not used. The land of the serpent, sometimes called the golden dragon, and sometimes the old red land, perhaps was trying to drive the ships of the bird away from some of the islands or colonies the bird had held for centuries, even though far away from their own ocean. At first the serpent succeeded. The people of the bird fled

These hero twins paintings are by the famous Indian traditional artist, Grumbo.

away in their ships, leaving their monarch or some other great leader behind as a prisoner, or perhaps dead on the field of battle. The fleeing ships of the bird carried the monarch's sons back with them to the great power which had strongholds in another ocean and counted time by the phases of the moon. Here the children were raised.

"Now comes the sequel. Another generation has come to power, but the old defeat still smarts, and either the same two boys or two allied powers of that ocean return with another fleet and all of the deadly weapons of the bird of lightnings. The surprise battle, carried on at the very stronghold of the serpent or dragon after crossing the swamps as they may have been at this time, was then turned to storming the entrance of the capitol. In the surprise attack, the conquerors won and seized the throne.

"Then, as is so often the case, the victors quarrelled, and one took his ships and went back - probably to the land of the moon. Perhaps his ships were sunk and he had to return overland, thus leaving a trail of flints.

"From other tribes I have heard that the twins were not actually born at the same time, but the elder was eight years older than the mischievous and often cruel 'coyote' or younger one, the wolf. I believe the Finns call him Fenir. This would make the Earth number (8) and might mean that the story had something to do with the Venus calendar which seems to be centered in the Atlantic.

"Some tribes tell me that the twins came back to kill the monsters. . ."

The old sachem nodded.

"Yes. They were eating the people."

"I also heard that the monsters drowned."

"There was a very ancient flood."

"Then the war must have been before that flood. And the reason that the ships of the Indian ocean could not go down the Mediterranean is because the dragon power owned the Mediterranean and they had another puzzle entrance at the Triton sea. Nor could they come around South America into the Atlantic because of the monsters. That is, until after that early flood. Some of the parts of the puzzle are beginning to fit - for me."

The old sachem reached over and tossed another twig of cedar upon the fire.

"After the flood - it must have been the Ogyges flood," I continued, actually thinking aloud, " - the Atlantic land was much narrower because much of the western part had sunk. So when the people moved back, and the monsters were gone, they called it the serpent. They then began in the Atlantic another march to power".

Suddenly another thought came to me. I looked at the Pueblo pottery standing around, the curvilinear designs, the many symbols of the giant bird. Then I turned to the pale tan faces, lit intermittently by the flames. They were rounder than the eastern tribes, but just as innocent of hair.

"Do you have any legends of the Moki river?"

The eyes of the old sachem widened, and those present looked at each other.

"We will be frank with you; this word means 'the dead', in Navaho. We would not want to be considered the dead."

"Have you ever heard of Chan-Chan?"

Their faces were like a group of gamblers looking at each other. I couldn't read a thing.

"Come now. These must have been your people millennia ago. They arrived in Peru on ships from the Pacific. They had a monarch and a full court of various castes. They built homes of stucco and tile. They made a great wall around their country as large as the wall of China. They brought water down from the mountains. They had factories for their weavers. They had paved streets. Their porches were always framed with peach trees, or some kind of fruit, judging from their pictures on their pottery. Their women did their hair in whorls like your young girls and their pottery was something like yours. The Incas finally conquered them by cutting off their water supply..."

"Where is the Moki river?" the old chief asked.

"In Peru. Chan-Chan was built on the Moki river. And there is something else. Near that place today is a poverty ridden tribe in the jungle. They are round heads like you, and they call themselves the Urus. They are very light skinned. Besides the Urus there are the Chorotegans. They built their city in Central America near the Mayans, about two thousand years ago, and had a most remarkable civilization until an earthquake wiped it out. They,too, had your polychrome (many colored) pottery, and the girls with their hair in whorls. I wonder if the Mayans . . . must have come across the isthmus by land!"

"We do have much similarity to the Mayans, if that is what you are thinking. Our houses have the same shells under the corners. That is because we were once a people of the seas."

Who was it that said: "Only in the Americas can one catch one's antiquity alive!"

"I could talk all night, but I must go, as I have a plane ticket. But let me tell you this. If you are of the people I suspect, then you had very great ancestors, although today they are all gone. You were supposed to have arrived with books. I wonder what happened? Perhaps that was when the Inca decreed the penalty of death for anyone having books?"

They were looking at me in a puzzled way.

"You must have come from the direction of the Indian ocean, though without books it is hard to say for certain."

"Did the great bird come from there?"

"As closely as I can determine."

"Then where is Hawaiku?"

"It was a very large island in the Pacific when the ice mountains were in the north and the sea level was much lower. Apparently not only the Hawaiian chain may have been one island but the south sea islands may have been very much larger."

"Many of the Pueblos have memories of it."

"I know. I have heard them say so. Also of Itiwanna which, like the Mayan Itzamna, is from the Atlantic."

The old sachem nodded, again adding to the fire. The cedar smell filled the air with the sparks which flew upward like fireflies.

"The giant bird can easily cross an ocean, you know."

"I do not doubt that," I smiled, "with a wingspread of twelve to fourteen feet, all he needs to do is catch one of the tail winds."

My thoughts at the moment were not with the condor. I glanced again at the faces and figures about me. These were mostly people of the Pacific, but they were not patriarchal! Matriarchal round heads who were beardless? Then I thought of the Sumerians. But the nose was not as domineering here as even among the eastern tribes. I thought of the Chinese colony which some archaeologists have tried to attach to the Sumerians. Then I thought of the Meru. In the great leveller of the cataclysm, could not some of these people have formed a union and mingled - then after having trouble somewhere else, sailed for America? There was one more clue. I once asked Dr. Iskihashi of Stanford university if he recognized the name Chan-Chan. He replied with a puzzled frown: "Yes, it is a Japanese name meaning enemy - but very, very ancient indeed."

So I bid farewell to the Pueblo people with a memory of the sachem staring into the fire as if trying to see through the mists of time itself. And later, as I found my seat on the plane and looked back to where the Pueblo was only a dot on the desert below, I wondered myself if we would ever know.

Chapter 53

The Flight Of The Tyrrhenians

"The great meteor and the other sea mounts appear to have been islands long ago. Another sea mount nearby was the same depth as the great meteor which reinforced the theory of subsidence. When we pulled the sled across the summit of Hyeres sea mount, we found it eroded to bare rock. On the eastern and western flanks there were fields of white and yellow siliceous sponges growing on white sand that often bore ripple marks. Moreover between the flanks the southern slope was composed of black volcanic slag like the refuse of a steel mill.

"The sinuous summit of the Atlantic ridge is deeply split by an almost continuous crack called the Atlantic rift valley, which may contain the epicenters of that ocean's earthquakes. I wanted to risk a sled in this tantalizing ravine. (A sled fitted with an undersea camera is towed by the research ship Calypso.)

"Calypso's sonar picked up the buttresses of the Atlantic ridge which arose on the graph exactly as they had been described by the outstanding U.S. Atlantic explorers Maurice Ewing and Bruce Heezen. As we sailed toward the summit, the peaks climbed to an altitude of minus five thousand feet. Then came a dramatic fall of ten thousand feet into the rift valley. Sailing on the flat sea, it was hard to realize we were on top of a staggering system of peaks and valleys doomed to eternal night.

"The stereo pairs were awesome. The camera had come upon scenes of suddenly shifting and bewildering variety as though riffling through a catalogue of geology. One shot would show a jumble of lava blocks, cut as sharply as taffy, and the next would carry you across a miniature Sahara, followed by the gray bedrock of the Alps powdered by a thin snow of sediment.

"The sled roamed over flats in which the first stretch would be pure white sediments that build at the rate of about three feet in ten thousand years, whereas the black stretch would be littered with volcanic cinders that seemed laid down by contemporary eruptions.

"The bottom water was marvelously clear and the pictures had readable details as far as fifty feet away. Some shots showed the narrow steep valley walls which were lined with basalt boulders that had recently rolled off the peaks. In two places, the photos showed barrel shaped blocks of pillow lava, ribbed with concentric patterns which appeared to have just cooled from yesterday's fiery extrusion. The pillars were so similar in size and configuration that a heap of them might be thought parts of a fallen temple column in mythical Atlantis."

From "The Living Sea" by Capt. J.Y. Cousteau with James Dugan.

The loose threads of our mammoth detective story are now being gathered together and tied in place. Of course, like the famous maze or labyrinth of which the people of the sea were so fond, there are false passages that lead nowhere, for as yet we have no answers to these mysteries. However, on the whole, the picture is beginning to clear, thanks to the historical memories of the American Indian.

Apparently, early in the story of modern man when he found he had a problem with the wild men, he sought places of refuge and soon learned the efficacy of a home on the sea. Two regions, slowly expanding, but still filled with much partly submerged land, offered ideal locations. These were the Indian and the Atlantic oceans. Because of the fact that the fertile region of the Mediterranean at this time could be colonized from the Indian only by land, or by means of the Triton sea, and therefore could be ruled by the Atlantic sea power, it was inevitable that these two trading sea giants of pre-history should come into conflict.

Possibly the power of the Indian "bird" had already traded through the orient and the eastern part of the Mediterranean before this conflict, because of the numbers of culture traits of the bird to be found in Europe. Possibly the two powers fought over England's tin supply. Of this we do not know. We do know that England was one of the greatest sources of tin from the sunken mines off Cornwall, and America was one of the greatest sources of copper from the ancient mines up the Mississippi. These two metals combined make bronze, and for untold ages bronze was an object of great demand.

Apparently the dragon land, as it was called, depended upon reptilian monsters to guard the western approach to the land through the swamps. There may have been a few of these creatures still around in the Pliocene and very early Pleistocene. The one which "lay deep in the water" must have been the Plesiosaurus which are apparently still around. (Interestingly enough

Plains Indian Chief
(Original tempera painting
by Fred Beaver, 1964)

as this goes to press a story was printed in a small magazine, by a young man studying pre-med in a Florida university. Apparently he could not get a larger magazine to take the story. Reason? A very sound one in resort areas - it might frighten tourists. It seems that five youths set out in a rowboat to do some skin diving and had one weapon between them. They were on the gulf side of Florida where one of them knew the location of a wrecked ship. During the afternoon they ran into a storm which came up quickly and blew them off their course. They made a mistake in trying to get near a marker buoy which sucked them under and overturned their boat, thus losing their weapon. They managed to swim over to the boat and turn it back again. After bailing it out with their hands and little else, they climbed in again with no means now of rowing or steering the craft. Night was coming on. The first sign of the monster was a high pitched whine. Apparently the Plesiosaurus has the ability to locate prey in the dark by sonar as does the dolphin and many other creatures of the deep. Next, there was a horrible stench. This was also noted by the many observers about Loch Ness in Scotland. Perhaps this happens

when the animal gets rid of its foul smelling feces. The young man telling the story did not connect these two events with the sea monster, showing that he did not invent the story and had not read other reports. When it first appeared like a "telephone pole standing on end" and coming toward them, they panicked and jumped overboard, trying to swim for what they hoped in the darkness was the direction of the shore. One by one the author heard the screams of his companions before he himself made the shore utterly exhausted. Besides, he was in shock from seeing his friends dived upon and dragged under. The bodies of three of the boys were never found. The fourth was found, but he was not certain of the identification. He did not say if it was mutilated, but the coast guard warned him not to repeat the story.

The animal in the swamps may have been the jumping Tyrannosaurus Rex. It was an air breather and could have been drowned. Cambridge is interested in capturing a Plesiosaurus to study how it can stay in the very deep water, as apparently it does at Loch Ness, if it is an air breather. Possibly there is some kind of an additional air bladder? At any rate, science is no longer scoffing at the Plesiosaurus.

Monsters to the west of the land in the Atlantic would protect its western side from invasion, especially if the Atlanteans themselves taught the monsters to be alert to people as food, by means of human sacrifice. Thus the reptilian god as a totem had a distinctly monetary value to these sharp traders.

Also this explains why the hero twins first attacked the monsters before the capitol of the red land. Furthermore it explains why the Mayans evidently came from the Pacific and crossed the Isthmus to their location.

Apparently, of these ancient peoples, only the Sumerians, the Mayans and the Chimu kings of Chan-Chan on the Moki river lived into historical times, each arriving in his present location with a tremendous library of historical books, literature and mathematics, by means of a fleet of ships. Unfortunately all three of these nations are now gone and we have only the libraries of the Sumerians and the as yet unreadable Mayan script, carved upon pillars and written on the walls of their temples.

Two other colonies of the great colossus of the Atlantic lived on into historical times. One is still alive: Egypt - with her ancient libraries burned, and Crete - destroyed by seismic disaster, which however, spared the libraries. But up to now they have not been read.

It is easy to see that the Atlantic, Indian and Mediterranean are unstable regions with recurring cataclysms. Perhaps the flood of Ogyges, or that which drowned the monsters, left the trading nations (what was left of them) on a far more friendly basis, since many tribes now took the combined totem. Possibly this is due to the fact that the disaster took such a toll of the island cities from both of the contestants, as well as their colonies. As is usual with humanity after a disaster which hits everyone, old enmities are forgotten. The Cro Magnon invasion of Europe may stem from this time when the refugees came with whatever they could save, and sought the caves of the land for shelter. In order to be certain about this, carbon-14 dating would have to be taken on those famous works of art done by them of the animals of the ice age, and upon the bones of Cro Magnon man himself. Until this is done we cannot date this invasion of the great disharmonic into the territory of France as coinciding with the flood of Ogyges.

Following this invasion of Cro Magnon (according to Spanish discoveries the great megalithic walls are the work of the Cro Magnon), there was another invasion from the direction of the sea many millennia later. These people wore the feathered war bonnet.

Putting this information, which is factual, together with the statement by Herodotus that Pan was one of the "ancient eight gods" and that Hercules was one of the "twelve gods" which followed much later, we have some light on the statement of Asa Delugio; "At first there were four, then eight more were added, and finally there were twelve." Delugio did not know what it meant, but swore solemnly that it was true history. I believed him, and it has been under a thousand guesses as to its meaning, but only now it is coming to light.

The people with the war bonnet of feathers who invaded both shores east and west from the Atlantic showed a mixture of totems. This must have taken place following the flood of Ogyges when the Meropes came into Europe from the sea. This early invasion is what evidently partly gave Europe its strong cultural leaning toward the totem of the bird. Also this must have been the time of the god Pan who was one of the eight gods. He lasted down to the great destruction, for Delugio gave Votan's identity, or that of the fire god, as "the mystical great ram of the mountains". Pahn or Pan was given as the name of the red land by the Dacotahs and many tribes through early legends told to the Spanish explorers before the natives stopped telling their legends. This is certainly a double totem and perhaps why the Norse Eddas say of the sea-power:

"The Sun's Heart I saw from the south coming
He was by TWO together led."
Norse Song of the Sun.

Most authorities admit that this is ancient and undoubtedly pre-Gothic, or rather pre-Norse.

The first epoch (that of the four bacabs as I have heard them called, although I do not know quite whether that means mountains, epochs of time, gods, or what) must have been the incredibly ancient dragon land, of which there is a memory in Tibet of a visit by its emperor.

The second epoch of power was that of the serpent or the old red land of whom the emperor Votan is a well remembered figure around the Atlantic and the Mediterranean, perhaps in the latter location as well as others because his people carried the memory with them and not because he himself went travelling. These must have been the people of the Venus calendar with its strong culture trait of doubles and of all the agglutinnating tongue-matrilinear complex.

The first epoch is too far back to be certain of anything much about it, but the time of Pan, the eight gods and the power of the old red land is burned into the living memories of the Amerinds. Also in the Mediterranean we find a strange later invasion of the same culture traits.

Scientifically speaking, culture traits are hardly admissable as evidence that peoples are of the same stock, and come from the same cultural center, especially when one must cross an ocean such as the Atlantic, because most archaeologists will immediately retort that it was accidental. However Elliot Smith made a most interesting study of these in his book "The Children of the Sun". True he became a bit mixed up over just who the Mediterranean people were, but the culture traits he did not miss. They were older in the Mediterranean than he had believed.

He pointed out very well that when the lists of such traits begins to lengthen, it also begins to interfere with the law of averages, and the number of possible "accidents" becomes unallowable. For example: when we say that the sea going peoples who so long ago inhabited the shores of the Atlantic and Mediterranean coastline from Norway to Africa, as well as those who built the ruined and buried cities of the Andes in Peru, just happened to terrace their hillsides for hundreds of square miles; build pyramids whose four sides face the cardinal points of the compass; wore clothes of cotten consisting of a short skirt, a long belt whose fringed ends hang in front, and a mantle draped over the left shoulder; prefer jewelry of green or blue stones; hold ceremonial masked dances; consider that black or red dogs or a dog headed god had something to do with a safe journey over a river of death; and build their cities with giant, many-tonned rocks whose edges are perfectly fitted without the aid of mortar, we are perhaps not going beyond the law of probability. However, when with further research we also find that they artificially flattened the heads of their infants to give the profile of the forehead the appearance of being a continuation of the nose line; fastened tigers to the gates of their cities (whose name, by the way is either cat, chat, or some word similar to Bal or Bel or Balaam); had a sacred fire in their holy of holies; held black to be the correct color for the garments of their priest-hood; symbolized the sun by a red pyramid and the moon by a white circle; celebrated certain feast days in common with very similar cere-monies; stored their food in round towers. . . Elliot Smith goes on and on. Even the most skeptical scientist, unless he has a bastile mind, has to admit that there seems to be grounds for a reasonable doubt about all these "accidents". Elliot Smith has not exhausted all the culture traits in common, and I have made no attempt to do so. One of the most interesting to me is the use of feathers - such as the manner in which both the Toltecs and the Dacotah use the war bonnet. The feathers are twenty-six in number and in the center is a tall pole within the bonnet itself which symbolizes the sun. This places it back in the Pleistocene when the world seemed at times to these people to be turning into a vast planet of ice. However, when I discovered the war bonnet in the Mediterranean, I began to trace the people who wore it.

They have sometimes been called the Tyrians and sometimes the Tyrrhenians from their lo-cation beside or in connection with the Tyrrhe-nian sea. The war bonnet with its circle of feathers is pictured by the Assyrians in their lists of prisoners as being worn by the Tokhari. Some authorities have identified these people as the ancient Libyans who today are the Tuareks. The other people are the Philistines. They were pictured on the columns of Rhameses III of Egypt who was plagued by an invasion of the people of the sea. When the prince of the Philistines, who came in their ships, asked the pharaoh for land,

he pleaded that the Egyptian should remember that he too had to flee the inroads of the ocean, and asked the monarch to have mercy and give them, actually his kinsmen, land of their own. Rhameses relented, withdrew his fleet, and sent them to Palestine where he asked that they pro-tect his borders from the hords of the Semitic speakers coming in from the east. They settled in seven cities of which the principal ones were Gaza, Escalon, Azotus, Gath, and Ekron, among whom there was a powerful defensive and offen-sive league in war. They fought the Israelites when they invaded, but were overcome by the Assyrians, and were absorbed by the conquerors.

Again here we note the seven tribes of these people, or "the seven kings" of the Dacotah, and seven nations of the Toltecs, Aztecs and other Nahuatl peoples. A study of these languages would prove enlightening.

Similar to the Philistines in culture are the other members of the agglutinnating-matrilinear complex - namely Egypt, Crete, the Etruscans, the Phoenicians and Carthage, or the Carthagi-nians. Is it accidental that these are seven? In all cases they picture themselves as red-skinned, wear in the beginning similar clothes, have banquets in reclining positions on divans, have a similar religion, use or have legends of the maze or the labyrinth, decorate the walls of their houses, temples and their tombs. They call themselves the people of the sea and handle ships with the skill of great hereditary know-ledge. It was probably not an accidental thing that when in 1958 an Etruscan tomb was opened in Tarquinia, it was found to have painted upon the walls a three masted vessel in full sail, with long sweeps astern. The Etruscans, when they first appeared in the Mediterranean, were a wealthy people with a strong fleet of ships.

It is also probable that the language structure of Etruscan, Cretan and Phoenician are so little understood simply because the students are try-ing to make inflectional languages of them when they are agglutinnating. Undoubtedly this happens because these students are so impressed with the high standard of living of these people that they cannot imagine that such a high civilization would spring from anything but an inflectional language. This is partly because most students now are inflectional speakers and we run into some na-tural prejudice. When these students begin to study an agglutinnating language they are often pleasantly surprised. For example there is an International Summer School of Linguistics in Bogota Columbia which trains youthful couples to go out and live with the wild tribes in order to study the language. Their reason is two-fold. They wish to preserve the language for further research and also to provide missionaries a means of communicating with the people of the jungle.

A young couple, Mr. and Mrs. Jay Salser, have been living along the upper Orinoco river. This is what they have to say: "The languages of these so-called primitive people are at once much richer and more complex than ours. All their sense of invention has been focused upon oral communication. Their fantasy (legends?) is far richer than ours and even their verbs are much more exquisitely developed." (From an article in the Los Angeles Times, November 1964.)

Who are the Tyrrhenians who have come down into history? According to the very solid historians of Egypt they came from the direction of the west in ships and were quoted as fleeing from the inroads of the ocean. Ever since that time our historians, unable to believe there was an Atlantic ocean, have been trying to place them elsewhere instead of factually looking upon them as a tremendous complex of united or similar cultures stemming from a single homeland.

While linguists are unsuccessfully trying to give them inflectional languages, archaeologists are trying to bring the Etruscans and Phoenicians from either the north or east. If old Assurbanipal had shown an inflexibility of mind, along with his wise men (all Semitic speakers), he would never have been able to read the agglutinnating Sumerian language. Actually he was a better scientist, in the true meaning of intellectual curiosity, than some we have today who only research to prove a pre-conceived opinion.

If we do follow the simple words of these seven wandering kings who wore the feather diadem of the trident, we will take another look at what geology is learning about the Atlantic ocean before we give our lives to defending a theory which science (that is the earth sciences) is about to overturn.

What do we know, or what do we suspect about these nations: the Carthaginians, Etruscans, Phoenicians, Lydians, Egyptians, Philistines, Tuaraks? They seem to have appeared between the fourth and second millennia B.C. with a fleet of ships. As for Egypt, we are talking about her delta civilization with their own people. If we examine their cultures we find an amazing likeness of traits. And as for the Tuaraks who apparently came as the Tokari, wearing the war sheath and the diadem of feathers, we have their own word as the Tuaraks that they

came from the sea and that they were many millennia older than the Semitic speaking invaders who came out of the east from the direction of Arabia, bringing sheep and riding camels. As for the Tokari, they apparently retreated again to the Sahara where they had lost their Triton sea. There they continue to hold the key to the whole puzzle in libraries no one is allowed to read.

Who were the Tyrrhenians? Let us try the names. The Phoenicians, we know, carry the Greek nickname (Phoeniki) meaning "redskins". The Tuaraks, the Amerinds have translated for us the "all powerful people of the fire god." The Amerinds have explained further that Tu means all powerful, the r sound stands for the fire god and the k sound stands for people. Turning this information against the other groups, we only find the name Carthaginians explained. Perhaps they were the Carians - a very powerful people in the early Mediterranean. In the word car we again find the k and r combination. Also it appears in the name Etruskans or Etruscans. Of course, among the Amerinds it is very strong, particularly in the Caribbean sea in which we have the Aruakians, Caribs, etc.

Apparently all of these people followed the human sacrificing religion of the fire god, where in the Mediterranean he had a second name of Bel or Baal (Balaam in the Americas) and as that deity had a cat symbol. This spreads over Europe also, for we find the Baltic, and curiously enough in Scotland the Balmoral castle which takes its name from the Balmors or Lord Balmore who can trace his name right back to the pirate chieftain, Balmor of the evil eye, who invaded Ireland in legendary times with a fleet of thirty-two ships, telling of the destruction of his home island by the sea.

However, we have some names which do not match. The name Tyrr, although the sound of r is in it, is not what we would expect. So I started to search for Tyrr through mythology. I found that not only in the Mediterranean, but also in the Gothic Eddas, Tyr was the son of Woden who lost the use of his right hand during the battle of the Tyrrhenian sea. The Gothic source says that it was bitten off by the wolf which the Finns give the name of Fenir. Just who this wolf totem may be, it is significant that both in the legends and mythology of the Egyptians and the Amerinds he is the death god. Could he have been the "younger twin"?

In my notebook, I had marked from Mediterranean and Norse legends the names of Tyr,

Balder, Atlas and Brunhilde as question marks to ask Asa Delugio. His answers were: "You say that they were Woden or Votan's children? Of course this does not mean that he sired them. It means that they were the kings of colonies of the old red land. You say that this northern queen Brunhilde 'gave away sun necklaces' according to the Norse chants? She should not have done this indiscriminately. Those are the medallions of royalty which she should have given only to her actual sons, who would have been 'princes of the blood'."

I also note that on the same page I told him that the Orkney islands off Scotland were formed largely of red sandstone, and that his eyes widened perceptibly at this, as he finally asked: "Would it be possible for you to go to this northern colony of the old red land (judging from its name) and bring me back some of the soil?" (I probably made him a promise on this which I was not able to fulfill. I hope not, but the notes do not say.)

Leaping back to the Mediterranean in our quest for the name of Tyrr, we find that Herodotus tells us that in the time of Hercules, Tyrrhenius led many of his people to Lydia and also undoubtedly to where the Phoenicians founded Tyre and Sidon. It is quite wrong for the modern archaeologists to try to place these people as invaders from the Black sea or the Persian gulf, which doubtless, being traders, they knew well, when further legends throw much doubt on this conclusion for which they have no ground.

The legends of both the Phoenicians and the Greeks tell that one of the "tasks" of Hercules was to steal the cattle of Geryon, a king who lived on the island of Erythea. In the time of Strabo, the Roman historian, there was a city named Erythea which was not far from Cadiz, Spain, and which had fallen into ruins millennia before Strabo mentioned it in his writings. He knew it only as a legend and a mound of great antiquity.

Upon the other hand, the Persians have a legend handed down to them from the conquered Sumerians that the Phoenicians had migrated into the Mediterranean from the Erythrean sea. The direction of this unknown body of water is given by the translation of the name Geryon (their mythical king), which means "light of the sunset". Furthermore, the location of the island of Erythea in the legend of Hercules or Heracles is "somewhere in the remote west". The name Erythrean sea must have been an original Phoenician or Tyrrhenian name, as it was often used by the early Greeks for the region of Spain.

Perhaps it was the sea which ponded just east of the old red land before the river of death met the Mediterranean falls? The location of Cadiz, Spain and the ancient city of Erythea, which according to Strabo had fallen into ruins long before Cadiz was founded, are both upon the Atlantic shores of Spain.

The mention of Heracles in connection with the homeland of the Phoenicians, and the losing of Tyrr's hand in the battle of the Tyrrhenian sea, causes one to ponder the possibility that this was actually a war in which Heracles not only stole the cattle, but drove the owners toward the Mediterranean where they made a stand in the Tyrrhenian sea, or what at that time probably was the colony of Tyrrhenia or Etruria?

This seems to hold the seeds of pre-history and would explain the dispersion of the Tyrrhenians to the east as far as Tyre and Sidon. Was this the time of the war which the Egyptian priest related to Solon, relating how the pre-Greek colony of Pelasgia under its queen Athenae or Minerva held back the invaders and helped to drive them back toward the sea? Or are the later migrations of the people in the time of Rhameses actually those of the fleeing people from the inroads of the sea, as they said they were, but following the path which their kinsmen had taken so much earlier to Lydia and the isle of Lemnos where scientists have found unmistakeable connections to the Etruscans?

At any rate, in this closely knit group of peoples who have such a strong cult of secrecy, especially over new lands and regions of trade, would the Phoenicians have consulted the Carthaginians after their discovery of some island, probably in the Caribbean, and then abided by the negative decision of Carthage not to use it as a base for trade, if Carthage had not been a colony of their OWN people?

The flight of the Tyrrhenians from the west to the east has been one of the mysteries of history, but with the reading of the libraries of the Cretans and the Sumerians sometime in the future, it may all be solved.

As a people, the Tyrrhenians have passed from the stage of history, but they have not passed from the minds and bodies of their descendants who dwell all around the Mediterranean and also along the shores of the Atlantic. Although today they may speak in many other tongues, yet the tragic story of these children of the fire god who sailed the Earth in their ships so many millennia ago and suffered the terror and agony of losing their homeland at last to the sea, can never be entirely forgotten.

Chapter 54

The March Of The Ar-Zawans

"Yesterday the Highlanders came skirling down the busy streets of London, and for a few brief moments, everyone stopped to listen. We all know that the pipes are older than history, take as much time to master as it does to become a surgeon, but nothing has such a strange, almost primitive effect on the blood.   Perhaps that is because they are the voice of old, old legends, of lost heroic causes and of battles - long, long ago." - The London Times.

It was well that I had given myself an extra hour to catch the train to Oxford, for when this happened, I too stopped and watched them pass with their ancient war sheaths swinging, tartons fastened to the left shoulder as the cloak has been fastened for thousands of years, and the mark of the trident upon their cuffs. So much of this was old - so very old - yet there were unmistakeable signs of Aryan speakers' dress. The woolen material was never worn by the ancient civilizations, although they would recognize the red, white and black colors as those of the fire god. Green, the Amerinds tell me, stands for the renewal of life and was used much by those of the bird totem.

All too soon they were gone and again I was on my way to Oxford. Taking a taxi I asked the driver to direct me to the oldest and most famous hotel - not the newest. That is how I found the "Mitre". Going up the carpeted stairways where Shakespeare had probably often walked when he stopped on his drive from his home to London, I was shown to my room, not large but adequate, and the price very reasonable. Strolling down the hallways, I could not help but stop to admire the priceless old etchings which filled the walls, as well as the antique furniture. Here was a room, the fireplace of which was built by masons before

America had been discovered. I thought of Keats and his

"Souls of poets dead and gone,
What Elesium have ye known,
Happy field or mossy cavern
Choicer than the Mitre tavern?"

And Mathew Arnold's

". . . steeped in sentiment as she lies, spreading her gardens to the moonlight, and whispering from her towers the last enchantment of the middle ages, who will deny that Oxford, by her ineffable charms, keeps ever calling us nearer the true goal of all of us, to the ideal, to perfection, to beauty, in a word, which is only truth seen from another side?"

That night after visiting the lovely town and the university, I sought out the halls of science. I found the professors very busy, being on a tight schedule, but I have yet to meet more cordial, charming gentlemen. That night I ate a most delicious dinner in the quaint dining hall and finally went to sleep to the singing of old songs sometimes slightly off key, in the "tavern" below. The early morning found me on the train again and back to a place I had always wanted to go - Land's End where below the waves is Ys, the lost city of yesteryear.

In addition to making some friends, I had learned something from my trip to Oxford: a most important city was being uncovered by British scientists on the mainland near Crete. This the professors at Oxford knew about and wished to discuss, but they could not at the time, and I could not come back. However, they guided me to books which discussed it in detail.

Curiously enough, I was not only sped away to Oxford by the music of the bagpipes, but welcomed back in the same way on my return to London. However, this time they were in the distance, and I stood quietly on the corner, back a bit from the crowd, listening to them. Some others stood near me. I heard one woman say: "That is how they stopped the riot at the Madrid soccer match! Apparently the Spanish didn't like the manners of the referee, for they started throwing bottles and other things. My Danny says that just then the Fusilliers started through the melee skirling 'The Road To The Isles'; and would you believe it, those people stopped and not a sound was heard until the music died? Then the cheering was deafening!"

I wondered if it were not that the Spanish were remembering that they once marched to the pipes? The armies of Julius Caesar marched to them, and it is said that when he heard them coming through the glens of Scotland, he halted his conquering armies and turned back. Also it is well known that he had no wish to hear "piobmhor" coming, as they are known in Gaelic, and decided against going to Ireland. Probably the pipes passed from Italy to Albania and from thence to Morocco. Or as in Moroccan legends, they were introduced by the legions of Heracles who marched to conquest with the pipes. After all, Albania has the kilts as well. I also remembered a tall, curly blond haired, green eyed Irish priest named Fingleton had told me that in his travels he had heard Basque shepherd lads playing the pipes with very ancient, haunting airs. Were the pipes spread by Hercules? The Greeks say yes, and that is how they learned to play them. Perhaps the Moroccans and Greeks are right. But the voice of the pig - a sacred animal to the Indian ocean? Were they spread originally thus by these traders untold millennia ago? We do not know, but today the factories of Scotland are doing a good business. The best pipes are either Scotch or Irish and have to have certain reeds, etc. etc. An expert can tell the difference immediately. At any rate, nothing is gaining so much in popularity around the globe except American twisting and the Beetles. (Re-

cently Nigeria offered six thousand dollars and a home to any capable Scot who would teach the pipes to a negro band.)

In passing, Fr. James Fingleton, whom I met in London, also told me that the Gothic people had many Gaelic customs and words. He was inclined to believe the Basques were of his people, like the Bretons of the French coast, who are big strong men like the others of the Celts (he included the Basque), but he could not see why the Welsh spoke Gaelic. They were much smaller. This suggests to me that a considerable amount of work should be done here by Gaelic scholars. A good deal could be learned about the past of Europeans and the spread of tall, handsome Cro Magnon man, of whom youthful Fingleton is himself an excellent example.

Before I began reading about the new discovery, I started reworking the traits of the ancient peoples. Not only are they important, but so also are the ones which cannot be included in their lists. These are the culture traits of the bearded peoples. I spent the rest of the day in linguistics and learned that the two inflectional tongues - the Aryan and the Semitic - tend to blend toward one another so that among the early Aryan speaking invaders of the Mediterranean region such as the Hittites and the later Persians, as well as the Armenians, show a much closer relationship to the Semitic tongues than the later Aryan. I have a suggestion for this. These people also show that they inherited the Sumerian nose. So do the Semites. Is it not possible that these words which some authorities have discovered to have similar origins, might be Sumerian contact words? Both groups came into the Mediterranean to find the Sumerians there first. True, both groups had certain culture traits in common - woolen clothes for example, and the domestication of sheep. However, the most important culture trait which marked them in a matriarchal world was that both of these bearded peoples were patriarchal. Instead of the children being owned by the clan of the woman, and taking their name from her, in these two groups the man owned the children; he gave them his name. The woman was no longer free to come and go as she had been under the matriarchal system. She was watched over, sometimes (as with the Semites) placed in harems for the pleasure of the ruler. She no longer attended banquets with the men, and indeed the Greeks and Romans regarded the conduct of the Etruscans scandalous because they ate in mixed company and had unclothed females used both as waitresses and entertainers. How startled they would be at our present society which has returned to the easy life of the Tyrrhenians!

It is intriguing to watch these culture traits of the Aryan speakers as they appeared on the different waves of invaders. One of the strangest (and it appears particularly among the early waves of invaders) was the fact that the Aryan speakers were clean shaven while the wearing of the hair was quite modern.

Now this separated the Aryan speakers from the Semitics. When the latter came in from the direction of Arabia, their hair was long and they had full beards, both of which they wore most elaborately curled. Why did the Aryan speakers appear as beardless? Was it because they were longer in contact with the civilizations of both the seas and the Mediterranean? This theory is further braced by the fact that they wore costumes not too different from those of the agglutinnating-matriarchal complex. On the other hand, the clothes of the Semitics were long robes, elaborately painted or otherwise decorated. These reached clear to the ground. As noted, both groups wore woolen clothes, but this undoubtedly stemmed from their mutual domestication of sheep. Both groups seemed to accept twelve as a particular number for the counting of time and measuring of goods. And both used the lunar calendar. This was undoubtedly inherited from the Sumerians, who also held the morning star and its 8-13 number in particular regard, doubtless due to their own knowledge of the Venus calendar or the knowledge of that Atlantean time complex used in the Atlantic regions - particularly the Americas. The Semites (some of them that is) adopted this star, but gave it six points, instead of its five or eight; five, of course, being the difference between eight and thirteen.

Let us now see wherein these two bearded races differ. The horse was tamed by the Aryan speakers, and upon his back they moved to victory. They were indeed so careful of their horses that the other peoples usually considered the animal their totem. Even today the Aryan speakers have a definite feeling of disgust at the thought of horse meat, although using it for animal food and fertilizer is not given a second thought. The Semitic peoples came into the Mediterranean area upon the camel. It is not eaten either, probably because its flesh is not agreeable to the palate. If the Semitic people had a totem, it was the tiger. However, they might have taken this from the previous Sumerians.

The earliest Aryan speakers: the Kurds,

Hittites, etc., all had the horse, attached plumes to their helmets, carried circular shields and had the wheel. In fact, the wheel came in with the horse, and chariot. For the purpose of war it carried the Aryan speakers to victory. They were the first people to use the decimal system; and in arithmetic it was a great advance. Counting by tens became a characteristic of the Aryan speakers.

Even past the time of the Greeks and Romans the Aryan speakers continued to use the war sheath with the pocket belt in front, the cloak carried on the left shoulder, and high boots. The helmet was always in the shape of the crest on top. In civilian attire they wore robes or tunics similar to those of the Etruscans, such as the Roman toga.

Later waves of the Aryan speakers began to show a change in costume and scholars feel that this was the real costume of the homeland. Trousers appeared; usually they were worn with an overblouse similar to the costume of the Russians today. Caps were worn which were peaked with the point coming forward. They also often wore shoes with the turned up toe. Today we see the costume in our brownies, faeries and leprechauns - all children of our imagination. The satyrs of the Greek myths who spent their time chasing nymphs through the woods, may be the Tyrrhenian caricatures or comic cartoons of these people. Satyrs are always pictured as small, rather dumpy, but clever. The little men who roll the balls which made the thunder in the tale of Rip Van Winkle are typical of these cartoon characters.

Later waves of Aryan speakers gave up the crest helmet for more pointed types, showing the influence of the peaked hat which persisted as a hat worn by women during the middle ages, and they tell me is still to be seen today in Wales.

The designs of the Aryan speakers were circular, after the white moon symbol which they inherited from the Kitchen Midden people of the Indian ocean along with other characteristics of the bird totem.

When we mention the Indian ocean of extreme antiquity we must remember that these long heads were slight, beardless and light skinned to a pale tan or gold shade. Since that ancient time the negroes have infiltrated from the islands of Melanesia and Africa, darkening the skin, while the bearded peoples have passed around the beard. Today the people of the Indian ocean are very different indeed, although once in awhile one sees the ancient type.

Besides the curvilinear designs, the Aryan speakers made much use of their beaker pottery, as a means of carrying this decoration as well as octopus designs. In particular they liked to paint "the Kraken", a mythical octopus-like creature of giant proportions with twelve legs. Of course, no octopus has twelve legs, but undoubtedly this was done to use the sacred number twelve. (The word octopus is Greek for eight feet). The Roman arch, which is often given as a culture trait of the Aryan speakers, was used by the Sumerians.

One of the most interesting facts I discovered is that the early people of the Mediterranean who were Aryan speakers and wished to communicate, adopted a type of writing very similar to the Sumerian. Later the Persians took on the Arabian letters and their literature flourished, as this means of writing and reading was much more simple. Scholars wishing to read prehistory might find much to interest them in these early books of the Persians.

With this information in mind, I was ready to learn what the British had found in Greece not far from ancient Crete. The first ruin was in Anatolia. It was so much like the Cretan civilization that the excavators were for awhile swayed by the belief that this was actually a part of the Cretan empire - perhaps a colony. The construction of the houses were so Cretan in type that it took some startling evidence to make them change their minds. That evidence was that these people called themselves Arzawans. Try pronouncing Aryan and then Arzawan - using in both cases the ah sound for the a.

They looked at each other amazed. They had found the ancient name for their ancestors! Probably it also meant "lords of the soil".

The site is a hundred and fifty miles up the Meander river which flows into the Aegean sea near Miletus. The ruins have been compared to the ones which Heinrich Schliemann found at Hissarlik. The architectural style is definitely Cretan, and it has been suggested that the nobles of Crete fled the doomed land to a colony of Aryan speakers with whom they had been trading perhaps for many centuries, or even for millennia.

That these were the residences of Ar-zawans and not Cretans was discovered when the stables for the horses were uncovered. Not only were they elaborate, but they exceeded in elegance the servants' quarters. So far about ninety sites have been excavated or partially excavated, and a grain store, mansions, streets, and various residences have come to light.

Now let us look back at the legends of prehistory and see what we can make of them with our added knowledge. The centaur, which was a mythical creature of half man and half horse, undoubtedly was the first idea of what a man on horseback was. It is interesting that the first ones seen by the Amerinds when the Spanish invaded with their horses, were also mistaken for centaurs, although they did not have that name for them. The American Indian had never seen a horse ridden. Back in the Pleistocene they had hunted them for food and probably killed them off, for it was in the Americas that the horse was evolved. It was tamed in Asia. So the man of the Mediterranean seeing for the first time a man on a horse, thought (like the Amerind) that he was seeing a brand new creature and carried back to his people the story of the centaur.

Other legends are not so easily explained. Let us take the figure of Saturn for example. We have the picture of him in the Sumerian literature as well as the Roman. In both cases he is a jolly old man always laughing. He has a rotund figure, a round face with a turned-up button of a nose, a pair of merry, twinkling blue eyes, and an abundance of white hair and beard. In all cases he is very fond of children, always giving them presents. Only in Rome do we have the entire story, and it is very suggestive of history. During the time of the Saturnalia in Rome, the image of Saturn was unwrapped from his year's nap and the week of his orgy began from December 21st to 28th. The slaves became the masters and wore pointed hats with the point on top tipped forward. They wore shoes which have turned up toes and were waited on by their masters. Because Saturn was an emperor of the forest and his people were of the woodlands, trees were decked out gaily, and the children were all given presents.

Perhaps by now you have recognized this ancient emperor as a much beloved elf who slides down chimneys at Christmas time, but he is such a typical Ar-zawan figure that it becomes very interesting to see what other legends say of Saturn. He is usually given the kingdom of Eirie or Ireland and his son is Zeus. Sometimes he is given the kingdom of Crete and Zeus dethrones him. He gathers an army from the northern colonies of the Atlantic, and with them marches upon the ancient empire of Tyrrhenia. For one glorious week he overcomes the defenses by surprise and turns the whole kingdom upside down. The children, who have

Gold mask of a prince found in the citadel at Mycenae in an ancient grave, 16th century B. C. Now in the National museum at Athens, Greece. Note the full beard and mustache, neatly trimmed.

often paid with their blood for the dark religion of sacrifice, are given presents. His armies, and the freed slaves, are having a tremendous orgy in the wine cellars of the palace when the armies of Zeus disembark from the ships and the battle of the Tyrrhenian sea is fought. When it is over, the Titans of the north are thrown into the prison of Tartarus, now under the Tyrrhenian sea, and Saturn himself is banished to a cave in Ireland. This not only sounds like pre-history, but it would seem to prove something else, that the Ar-zawans, as people of gathering importance, were around at this ancient date.

Do we have any other clues which might point to an old invasion of Ar-zawans before the flood of Plato's Atlantis? Yes, we do. There is the figure of Hercules who Herodotus tells us was one of the twelve gods who came out of the more ancient eight gods. He obliges our curiosity further by telling us that Pan, the goat god, and his wife Maia, are of the eight gods. Now this is in view of the fact that not only is this the name for the ancient Mayan civilization which arrived in the Americas with history and advanced mathematics, but also the name of one of the ancient dry wadis of the Sahara, which

once was a magnificent river called Maia - and the name is pronounced the same (Mah-yah). (The present Niger, also of the Sahara by the way, was anciently the Nagar, and it flowed from the highlands of the Canary ridge into the Triton sea, which is the opposite way from which it is flowing at present. Nah-gar means serpent.)

The fact that the twelve gods under the leadership of Heracles overcame the ancient eight gods and dethroned them is a link to a statement made in the Apache camp long ago when the dancers of the crown dance were listening for the first time to the words of the usually silent Asa Delugio. He had said that he knew something which he could positively say was historical, or true, but did not know the meaning, and asked me to tell him if I knew the meaning. The words were "First there were four, then eight more were added, and finally there were twelve."

I had guessed mountains, islands, even calendar numbers, but he kept shaking his head. I finally had to admit defeat, but the numbers had haunted me. Now suddenly they became clear. Not the four; that is still a mystery.

Many Amerind tribes begin an historical chant with the words: "At first, four great Bacabs held up the earth." But the eight were the eight gods of the Venus calendar of which Pan was one, and the twelve were the captains who rode to power with Hercules. Fantasy? I doubt it, but let us check further. Let us take another look at Plato's Atlantis.

We have the story of a conqueror who comes to a broken, ruined and sparsely settled island. However, it has some magnificent ruins of a canal system and a tremendous pyramid in the center. A royal couple and their daughter are living there - probably in the temple for refuge. We are not told what happens to the old king and queen, but the daughter is taken as a wife by the conqueror. Realizing, as he must, that the throne would only go through her to her progeny, he builds her an elaborate prison from which historically she does not emerge again. However, she has the fantastic number of ten sets of twins. Twins, of course, are the accepted number for rulers. "Two together led" says the Edda of the Norse.

He places these "twins" over the islands and retains the main reins himself for his own progeny. Ten is the Ar-zawan decimal system. All these "sons", supposedly having the blood of the recognized queen, would be accepted as future rulers whether they wore the sun necklace "medallion" or not.

The conqueror does not do away with the ancient religion entirely, but substitutes a sort of bull fight game as a preliminary to the feast of the sacrificed animal. The bull sacrifice is acceptable, as the bull is the totem of the Dravidian empire and not of the serpent. The kings sit around all night judging cases and put their judgments down on the columns where before the serpent had engraven his sacred laws. Note that these meetings of the kings were called every five and then every six years so as to give equal preference to both the odd and even numbers. They were being very careful not to greatly disturb the conquered people. They wore the ancient purple robes and threw the blood of the sacrificed animal over the columns, even as in the Americas the blood of the human sacrifice by the Aztecs was thrown over the columns.

For the worship of fire the conqueror substitutes ancestor worship. This reinforces the caste system, which he needs while ruling such an ancient and proud people steeped in millennia of their own history.

The fact that one of the first projects Her-

cules began was the building (rebuilding) of the canals, shows that the island had probably been entirely covered by the sea of the great destruction, and the canals were undoubtedly completely filled with debris. The manner in which the lords of the aristocracy cared for their horses marks them as Ar-zawans. The fact that they had war chariots is another culture trait of the bearded conquerors. The manner of conquest is similar to that of the march over the broken Dravidian empire. The Ar-zawans did not conquer it any more than they conquered Atlantis and the empire of the serpents. The great destruction had done that already in both cases. What the Ar-zawans did was to conquer a broken-hearted people who had crawled back to what fragments of their lost glory the sea had left for them, and in both cases were probably still in too much of a state of shock to think of war. The magnificence of their homeland was gone forever. Why fight an invader?

Among the Atlantic league, the Ar-zawans were regarded probably as a foreign power and the colonies were cool to them. They no doubt began with kindly thoughts toward the children, as Saturn had done, possibly remembering their own hard dealings with the serpent, but one Mediterranean power showed them friendship. That was Crete. However, with their wealth and power came also the realization that the land was not stable and they began to seek other lands to conquer. After being defeated in the Mediterranean, the second destruction took all of Atlantis and most of Crete.

There is one main flaw in this picture of antiquity. Plato has painted a magnificent picture of an Ar-zawan island city-state during the bronze age, but his informant gave him the wrong date for the sinking. It could hardly have been almost eleven thousand years ago. That must have been the date for the great destruction. Why? Because of the fact that the lunar and Egyptian calendars go back to that time when they were last synchronized. That must have been done on the old red land or in the Indian ocean or both. The Ar-zawans had rapidly taken to the sea and to trading as well as masonry, but it is to be doubted if they learned thousands of years of astronomy and intricate calendars in the few generations allowed to them before the great fire hammer of the giant rifts struck again.

Also this explains why Egypt did not remember the great flood; Egypt was not the Egypt of the time of Sais, when the great destruction took place. Sais was of the delta civilization

322

which came in from the Mediterranean in ships roughly somewhere around five thousand B.C. Lower Egypt entered as great civilizers and the crown of upper Egypt moved farther up the Nile. Where did they come from? Let us take a guess. There is a serpent in the crown.

Was lower Egypt remembering her own desperate misfortune when giving the date, the correct date, of the great destruction? The story told of the war in the Mediterranean between some agressing nation from the sea and the Greeks was a later war, probably just before the destruction of Crete. This was not a war of lower Egypt. It was the history of upper Egypt the old priest was remembering, and he had the dates confused.

How do we know this? Because the great destruction was the end of communication between the old red land and the Americas. The horse as a domestic animal was unknown in the Americas. The wheel was unknown. The chariot was unknown. The decimal system was unknown. Nor was there an iron age in the Americas. Iron as a metal was known. In Peru two Amerind tribes had their own ancient names for iron. In fact a large mine was opened near Lake Titicaca, but almost immediately closed. It was if a giant power, having located the metal and having expected to do a tremendous business, was suddenly completely silenced. It would appear as though the discovery of iron was a secret of the lost land, and before that power had time to set up the necessary smelters and factories, was silenced by death. The bronze age undoubtedly continued for untold centuries before the use of iron was rediscovered, and it did not happen in the Americas.

Among the Amerinds the tale of the old red land ends with the rule of Votan. Yet among the Goths, Odin or Woden, was already deified when the Goths had learned to use the runes. They said that Odin invented them. Thus the Norse tell us that the ancient writing which they used to write the Eddas was the script of the old red land which most marvelously because of the Norse has been preserved to us today. With this knowledge came down also some of the blood of the ancient power, else why would they wear the helmet with the horns which stood for "the great mystic ram of the mountains" (in other words, the fire god)? And why would they continue for many millennia to ride the seas in dragon ships? Why would they drink the mead from horns? In the Edda we read the ancient lines:

"From the north riding, I saw the sons of the Nidi.
They were seven in all, and from full horns, the pure mead they drank."

We can almost picture this lonely traveller riding his horse southward and coming upon a council of the seven kings. When I first read this fragment, I immediately sought the various Amerind sages who knew some of the old words; those who claimed to have been related to the seven. The name Nidi was puzzling, but when I added "the sons of the Nidi", a light seemed to dawn and I had several translations: "the sons of darkness", "the sons of the black cloud" and "the sons of volcanic ash."

Did they have mead and did they give it to the Goths? In the library of Sumer a story is told of King Ereck who had an island in "the far west" who was visited by his daughter for the sole purpose of obtaining the sacred laws from the columns, so that she might have them inscribed in her own city. King Ereck was hesitant and so she told him interesting tales and often poured many goblets of mead. She managed to be talking most of the time herself and thus drank less. Finally he consented and gave a copy of the sacred laws to his daughter. When she received them she pretended to go to bed, but fled instead in a ship awaiting her. In the morning he had changed his mind, and finding her gone, sent out his dragons to overtake her, but by devious means she escaped them and arrived at her city with the laws.

Speaking of the runes we also have the origin of them in the lay of Sigrdrife:

"The runes are, it is said, on the shield Graven which stands before the shining god."

One is reminded of Prescott's description of the sun temple of the Incas.

There is some suggestion of the Norse conquest of Atlantis with the other nations of the Atlantic coastline, because in the Oslo museum in Norway, there are many ancient Norse carvings. One is of a battle in which the tunics of one side have serpents embroidered or painted upon them. Also there is a skirmish pictured which is taking place upon the backs of serpents. This evidently is meant to signify serpent territory. In this carving, ships do not seem to be involved.

Also there is a hint that not all the people among the Norse were in favor of this serpent war since we have mention of horse sacrifices to Odin, not only by the Norse themselves but also by the Irish. Apparently they were afraid of that deity's anger.

(It is easy to see that not all the serpents driven out of Ireland by Saint Patrick were reptiles.)

Furthermore, we continue to have sacrifices to Odin by the Norse clear up to the advent of Christianity, at which time the Norse stopped raiding Ireland, which they did almost yearly when that land deserted the religion of the ancients for Christianity. The sacrifices of the mummies in the peat beds is an example of human sacrifice to Odin. The victim was slain by means of strangulation, which is the weapon of the wind god and not of the serpent.

All of these facts go to show the closeness of the Norse to the serpent land for many millennia. The same is also, of course, true of Scotland and Ireland, Breton on the French coast and as my friend Fingleton pointed out, also the Basque. Only the latter kept the old languages, although a better study of Gothic and Gaelic should prove interesting. I have also been told by language scholars that very old German shows some most interesting contacts with an agglutinnating tongue many millennia ago. I am not a language scholar; I am only throwing out hints for future study.

Also in the Americas we have some massive contact with the Gothic languages, especially on islanded positions in Norway, not only in the Algonkin, as mentioned before, but among the San Blas and others. As white men? No. The pure blood Amerinds do not have the beard. Then did the Goths and the Norse get their height and strength from Cro Magnon man who was of the old red land? The bearded whites with the fair skin and light eyes were small people using small weapons. The big frame of the Cro Magnon is apparently a dominant feature. The eastern tribes such as the Dacotah are big men - or most of them were before the poverty of reservation life which cut down their strength. A hundred years ago they were six feet or over when the average white American was only five feet six or seven. Also white skin is a pretty dominant characteristic as we have learned, for in two generations of marrying whites, nothing remains of the "red skin" but the Cro Magnon skeletal structure. But the most dominant feature of all is the beard.

Therefore the logical picture of the ancient world is that the serpent power was the one which worked the mines of the Mississippi for copper, Peru and England for tin, manufactured their product on their own island and sold it or traded it for food and other products. Undoubtedly some of their people settled and lived in the colonies. However, in the Mississippi they apparently brought in their own workers, or hired workers and either took them home or turned them back to their own villages.

And the date at which this mingling with the people of the old red land ended forever? At the end of Votan's empire.

There is one ruin which could be a clue to the time of Hercules and the early march of the Ar-zawans to power. That is the Amazon city told about by Diodorus. It seems that queen Merynia began aggressing against the beleagered Atlantides right after their defeat in the Mediterranean. Her armies followed the men home, put them to the sword and spared the women and children. Finally they called her into conference. They offered her a city, in fact would build it for her if she would promise to protect their borders. She was pleased and agreed to wait until after she saw the proposed city. So they built a city called Chersenesus facing the Triton sea. It was a most beautiful city and the location was magnificent. She was immensely pleased and agreed to placing a watch on their borders. Almost immediately another group of the Amazons struck from the direction of Spain. She led her armies and horse women against them, cut them to pieces and drove them into the forests of Spain where they disappeared from history. This ruin has apparently been seen by a lone traveler along the western edge of the Sahara about the same latitude as the Canary islands. If this city could be dug up and perhaps carbon dated, much might be learned. We know that Hercules was able to conquer queen Hippolita of the main branch of the Amazons and from that time on the double axe which was her symbol appeared in the crests of Europe's aristocracy. Of course, the golden dragon is also on the crests of Europe. And the double axe is to be found in the Americas, but the Amerinds insist it was a weapon of the old red land. As noted in an earlier chapter they also have legends of an army of women invading up the Amazon river. These, too, came just before or after the great destruction.

The carbon date on these ruins should pin point the time when the Atlas chain sank and emptied the Triton sea. Could this have been after the time of Hercules? These Amazons of Europe were supposed to have had horses. The complete excavation of the supposedly Chersenesus should settle this point.

And the symbol of the trident - what is it supposed to represent? Evidently "the three worlds" so often mentioned by the ancients. But what are the three worlds?

Donnelly believes that they represent Europe, Atlantis and the Americas; for many years I agreed with him - but the trident in the hands of most of the ancient hindu gods? How can this be explained if the trident means only the region of the Atlantic? However, there is little doubt that the Sumerians were in touch with the ancient powers of the Atlantic.

How do I know? It happened one day while I was musing about an antique shop on Main street, a disreputable, pawn broker thoroughfare of Los Angeles. A few coins had caught my eye and I had asked the proprieter to let me examine them.

Evidently he was disenchanted with the two coins which had attracted me.

"I bought them from an antique dealer who came from Babylon, and I am sorry that I ever saw him."

"Why?"

He cheated me out of something, but that is neither here nor there."

I picked up the two tiny oblong shaped pieces of metal and asked for a magnifying glass.

"If you are looking for writing, you won't find any. Now I have some good Roman coins right over here," pulling out another tray. But I hardly heard him. There was a faint engraving, very much worn, of a cone shaped mountain with something which looked like mist or a cloud about the top. To one side was a five pointed star. From the star, two beams came down to touch what looked like a city below.

The city was most intriguing. There were curious heavy square shaped massive buildings topped with fairy tale round towers with cone shaped tops. I rubbed my eyes and looked again. In the distance was what appeared to be a canal and perhaps a square-sailed ship. Behind the ship were others, but they were much worn away.

"Where did these come from?"

"Some old Babylonian grave, he told me. Anyhow there's no writin' on 'em."

Just then more customers came in and I waved him away to the other people. He left most willingly. I turned the bit of oblong metal over. The sides and back were worn smooth. The other coin was similar except that it had two stars - one to each side of the mountain. I thought I was going to choke. The same city was below. There were more ships in the distance, but they were worn to only a suggestive line here and there. The metal was very heavy

for such a tiny thing and it had the shine of reddish gold.

I walked over to the proprieter, and waited until he was searching for something else for his patrons, and they were busy discussing what they should purchase.

"I'll take these. How much are they?"

He looked at me in astonishment.

"Instead of that beautiful Roman coin with all the writing?"

I nodded.

"What do you suppose those things are anyhow?"

"Money of some kind I suppose."

"Well they ain't gold. The gold dealer said they're worthless."

Then as he saw I still intended to buy, he gave me a larger price than I had expected by the preceding discussion. However I paid him and he put them in a bag before going back to his arguing patrons.

I found the house full of people when I got home. Some sort of party was going on.

"Hey! Where have you been?"

"I stopped in an antique shop."

I glanced around laughing into the faces of some of my scientific friends.

"You have something. I can read your face. You have something or you saw something..."

"Yes, I have something," unwrapping the coins and putting them under the table light.

The archaeologist picked them up.

"Could be very ancient Babylonian..."

Another picked up a coin with the unenlightening remark of a long drawn out "hmmmmm."

"What is this strange metal? It's so heavy."

A geologist who had started away turned back, and took the coin and the magnifying glass I had provided.

"I know it isn't gold because the man I bought it from had one tested. . ."

"Yes he did - right here. Well I hardly think that they are . . ." carrying it closer to the light.

The archaeologist looked at me with a sidelong glance.

"Did you see any more like these?"

"No. Wish I had - especially one with the engraving a little plainer . . ."

"I presume that you have heard of the legend of the cone shaped mountain or the mist covered mountain?"

"Mt. Atlas, which is now supposed to lie on the bottom of the sea?"

The geologist scratched the corner with his fingernail.

"Well, I am mystified. What is this - orichalcum?"

Possibly the same thought passed through all of our minds, but the word itself brought no smiles of disdain.

"The magic metal of Atlantis? It would go with the cone shaped mountain and the double star. . ."

"Want to sell one?" someone asked, and another answered: "Save your breath in this case. But they are curious! So tiny and so heavy! Less then an inch long and half that width of thickness. Yet the ancient engraving is . . ."

Then some of the women strolled over and the coins were put down in a renewal of banter. I took a second glance at my two prizes gleaming like red-gold jewels in the light and started toward them to wrap them up when some ladies went over to them. So I left them and spent the rest of the evening in banter. After the crowd had at last gone on its way, I returned to the table. One of the coins was gone. It was the one with the double star. What does one do in a case like that? I am careless with my priceless things I know, but unfortunate experiences have a way of teaching bitter lessons. Later the other coin disappeared also. Whoever may have either one in his or her possession today, I only hope that they leave it to a museum.

The sight of the Atlantean coins and the realization that they came from a Babylonian tomb brought many questions to me in later days.

Was ancient Sumeria in touch with Atlantis? Perhaps the pyramids of Egypt were a compromise between the step back style and that of the smooth Atlantean cone shaped mountain so much revered by the people of Atlantis and all of her colonies. Perhaps not, however, for the first pyramid of Egypt was of the step back design.

And how did the step back design get from Sumeria to the Americas? Once this had completely frustrated me. I found fact after fact and culture trait after culture trait of the Jewish people among the Amerinds. The problem of the beard made this all the more confusing. I took my problem to the Amerinds. That is where I learned of the great white bearded prophet. Later I found that I could actually use his time as a date line for the place where they had been when he came. He never named himself, and the names which they gave him were the milestones of his journey.

Finally I had to give up in utter frustration until I had straightened out the confusion which this saintly teacher was causing in the ancient culture patterns of the Americas. I began to study him, following his wanderings and tracing him back to where he entered the land to the day he left. That is when I met Sedillio, and it was due to him that I wrote the book "He Walked The Americas" published by the Amherst Press of Wisconsin. As I began to study Kate-Zahl alone, and asked the Amerinds about him something happened. He completely captivated me for many years, until at last I had tried to capture his magic between the covers of a book. Only then could I go on with the study of the antiquities which stretched behind him for untold millennia.

And only because I have written that book can I fully understand his tremendous influence upon the Amerind people and why so many scholars become puzzled by the culture traits of a Semitic speaking people among the Amerinds, especially Jewish symbols and those of the early Christians. No wonder so many students have been confused to the point of believing that they found here "the lost tribes of Israel"! There is always one negative physical answer to these beliefs - the things which nullify such a possibility even if one could get around the ancient agglutinating language barrier and somehow explain that: there always remains the physical hurdle which nullifies great invasions by either the Aryan or Semitic speaking people - the question of the beard.

Returning to the march of the Ar-zawans which began perhaps with the unfortunate attempt of Saturn, and continued to victory with Hercules, we have a steady change of costume from the first ones who settled near Crete, through the Hittites, Kassites, Mitannians, Persians and Phrygians (pronounced Freegians) who settled near the Tyrrhenians in Lydia and adopted the Tyrrhenian religion of the fertility goddess, Cybele. In 1964 the Reuters news agency reported that U.S. archaeologists had uncovered a statue of Cybele (the Greek Ceres) in western Turkey. The statue was excavated in the ancient city of Sardis near Izmir. Sardis 2,500 years ago was the capital of the Lydian empire and was known as the "Paris of its day". Scientists from Harvard and Cornell have spent six years so far, excavating Sardis. The beautiful statue belonged to a temple which was sacked, leading to a war between Greece and Persia 2,500 years ago. The statue is of remarkable pristine Greek beauty, having probably been executed by one of their masters in sculpture. It represents the goddess as a young Greek virgin, holding a lion cub aloft. According to legends, she was in the habit of visiting her colonies from vast recesses of time, on a chariot drawn by lions. She was attended with singing and dancing eunuch priests wherever she went. We will remember that this is very similar to a beautiful youthful queen who visited all of Europe, being particularly remembered by Germany. This lovely girl gave out presents to the populace from her home which was on a distant island in the west. Later, perhaps even to the present, a young girl was chosen to represent her and was later sacrificed, giving the festival a sad undertone. Whether or not this ancient festival has been recently renewed, I am not certain.

At any rate, Lydia was founded by king Gyges (of the time of the Ogygean flood?) of mythical times and flourished to the time of king Cresus, supposed to be the one with the "golden touch", an exceedingly wealthy monarch who was defeated by the Persians before 540 B.C. While on the subject of the lovely "mother goddess of fertility," from whom we get our word "cereal", would it be possible that the Phrygians came from the Freesian islands, in the Baltic? This would connect the Danube and the Baltic with Greece and the Tyrrhenians, a most enlightening possibility on pre-history. The Kassites, on the other hand, have a name similar to sunken islands off the Irish coast - the Kassides. All of these early invaders perhaps were originally from the sunken Ogygean lands and fled inland down the Baltic and the Danube. All of them introduced the horse (along with the Hittites) as well as the circular shield, crested helmet and slashing sword (the latter being Gothic).

By the time we come to the Scythians, we have a more modern costume, as they and the Persians came with trousers. The Phrygians were the first to use iron lance heads and iron swords which places them at the start of the iron age. However, besides these weapons they also carried the double axe and arm dagger. Would this make them of the legions of Hercules? The Hittites were riding the crest of the wave in the second millenium B.C. and were over-run, along with powerful Sumer, by the invading tribes of the Semitic speakers who came in at this time. The Persians, then coming down from the north, dealt the death blow to Lydia, with its Tyrrhenian background and both these were then submerged by more invasions of Semitic speakers.

The Phrygians and later Scythians no longer were influenced by Tyrrhenian costumes. They wore trousers of wool with an overblouse, and had the peaked Ar-zawan cap with the point bent to the front.

In the legends and etchings of Robin Hood and his merry men of Sherwood forest, we see bits of the old Ar-zawan costumes, which curiously have lingered on through the millennia to the day of Robin Hood, from their first appearance among the drawings of the Hittites. To look at the pictures these people made of themselves, with their large noses, one would take them for Sumerians, yet the pointed war helmet, which became the pointed hat in civilian dress, and the turned up shoes, mark them as Ar-zawans. As with all the tribes who made their way to the Mediterranean from the Hittites, through the Kurds, Armenians and Persians to the Scythians, they were all clean shaven with modern haircuts, and cremated their dead.

We have followed the march of the Ar-zawans from legend into pre-history and finally to historical events. We seem to have here a reasonable explanation in the change of physical type, which apparently followed the invasions of the Tyrrhenians fleeing from the disasters of volcanism and subsidence brought on by the end of the ice age. The subsequent mingling of the blonde Ar-zawans with the tall Cro Magnon brought out the best qualities of each and we have as a result, the beauty of the Norse.

Armed with the dragon ships of their fathers, but retaining the blonde loveliness of their Ar-zawan mothers, and taking up the history chants which were written in the ancient runes and became the Eddas, the present Ar-zawans have a tremendously fascinating heritage of history, pre-history and legend.

There is a reason why the wailing of the pipes stirs the blood with "the voice of lost heroic causes and of battles long, long ago". There is a reason why we receive a special sense of something akin to racial memory in the words:

"Magic casements opening on the foam
Of perilous seas, in faery lands forlorn."

or hear the sad moaning of the ancient chant to "the mist covered mountain."

There is a reason for the strange joy at the approach of the Christmas season late in December when we decorate trees and plan presents for children, even though we are not fully cognizant of the story of the emperor Saturn, of his furious orgy of freedom and victory, even though that ended in defeat and inglorious punishment. Perhaps it is in keeping with the best traditions of humanity that he is not remembered through the ages for these things, but only because of his undying love for little children.

Chapter 55

Will It Happen Again? --

Could It?

"Whether or not the fires of hell lie below the surface of the earth, there is no doubt that it is hot enough there to satisfy critical requirements for that region."

Geophysicist Arthur Beiser.

The great destruction was catastrophic, but was it really so strange, so fantastic, so unheard of? Only to the civilizations developing since, whose people have lived out quiet lives on more or less stable, firm ground.

Even thirty years ago scientists might have shrugged off the tale of such sudden subsidence as a fictional story dreamed by Plato in a moment of idle fantasy. Today they are not so certain, and in ten years more, at the rate knowledge about the rifts of Earth, especially those of the oceans, is being disseminated, the mid-Atlantic ridge will become a prime object of study.

Let us take a moment's glance at some of the Earth cracks we call rifts. The knowledge of them is not an old thing. It dawned with the better mapping of Earth and particularly of the seas. It is now granted that the mid-Atlantic ridge is the site of one of the most profound cracks in the planet. No scientist knows exactly why it should be, but they have mapped it from around the base of Africa through the unstable island of Iceland, which is directly upon the ridge, and from thence through the Arctic toward Siberia. At the other end, one prong of it bends toward India and the other toward Australia where it seems to connect with the curtain of fire, which circles the Pacific. Yet on the other hand, does it? One arm seems to cross the Pacific to the great rift which runs up the gulf of California and meets with the San Andreas, as it comes down from El Centro to the gulf. Of course, the San Andreas is a part of the curtain of fire. It goes on down through Mexico and Central America to South America and the very unstable end of Chile where in 1960 violent earthquakes saw the flaming outbursts of nine volcanoes.

We know now that earthquakes are the result of volcanic tubes being suddenly swelled by a rush of lava. This may happen very deep within the earth - in other words over a hundred miles down. Especially is this true in regions where mountains are being built, such as upon the Pacific coast of the United States, or in the high ranges of the Andes, where the crush and pressure of folding layers of rocks sometimes trigger minor faults which in turn trigger greater faults.

There seem to be three types of movement in earthquakes - the horizontal, the vertical (either up or down) and a mixture of the two. The shocks which come with very slight fore-

The face of the Sierras on the eastern slope is an earthquake scarp or cut. The Alabama hills in foreground are composed of very ancient rocks upthrust along the fault. This is one of a series of parallel faults running through Owens, Panamint and Death valleys. They parallel the San Andreas fault. (Courtesy of R. Iacopi, Earthquake Country, published by Sunset Books, 1964)

shocks and then the great lurch, followed by days or even weeks of after-shocks is the horizontal type. The type which keeps building up with greater and greater ones following the lesser ones are in essence volcanic, and often herald an explosion.

Returning to the mid-Atlantic rift, we have an island upon that great sunken mountain range which is still sub-aerial and which we can study. It is definitely not a stable land - this place we call Iceland. There are a continual series of extinct and active volcanoes; Otaefa, Rauda Kamba, Hekla and another in Pico. There is also a nameless island which appeared in the ocean south of the island in 1963, building up from warm pumice and ash. Usually these new islands sink again within a few years but Nameless is still sub-aerial.

On down the ridge, the islands which are still holding their heads above the water are all volcanoes. Swedish scientists have announced to the news media recently that during 1964 they discovered shells of fresh water animals in the trench between the peaks of the ridge, that is, the submerged peaks. Thus the sandy valley found by the scientific ship "Calypso" was once a quiet lake of the lost land. The animals were Pleistocene.

Since the time of Donnelly there were a series of volcanic disasters on the string of the Virgin islands in the Caribbean which would be just west of the sunken land. These volcanic eruptions were a few days apart showing igneous activity along a sunken rift. In the Mt. Pelee disaster of Martinique only one man was spared. He was in prison and down too deep to be killed by the gases of the explosions. The Amerinds on the island tried to get away by any means available, but the governor, fearing panic among the pleasure seekers and tourists, forbid anyone to leave the island during the preliminary rumbles of the volcano. The incandescent gas had an estimated temperature of 1000 degrees centigrade when Mt. Pelee finally exploded and wiped out the population of 30,000 within a few moments. It is interesting that the man who sailed away with his half laden ship when warned by the natives of what was coming, said that the Caribs told him that twice they had lost great islands to the sea, (half chanting) because they were worshippers of the fire god who always ate his own.

On the other side of the ridge lies Lisbon,

The main street of Compton, California, following the 1933 Long Beach earthquake. The derrick in the background was used for lifting debris off the spots where cries for help were heard. (Courtesy R. Iacopi, Earthquake Country)

Portugal. On a sunny day in 1775 a long rumbling sound like tremendous thunder came from beneath the ground and then the earth began to shake with violent jolts which immediately threw down half the city buildings. In the next six minutes sixty thousand people perished. Some had fled for safety toward the sea where it seems the waves had retreated backward as if it were minus tide. Anyone acquainted with oceanography or seismology would have known that this meant "tidal wave - beware"; but they did not know. They only wanted to get away from the falling debris. There was a magnificent marble quay in the harbor which was the pride and joy of the city. The solidity of the quay was reassuring to the thousands of people who fled toward it.

Then suddenly it came - the great wave. Boats were picked up and hurled about. They crashed into each other and into the people who were washed off the pier. Then the ground gave away, and it was as if a giant whirlpool opened up. The marble quay vanished, along with all of the people and all of the boats. Not a body or a plank from a boat ever floated to the top of the waves. The shallow bay where the quay stood is now six hundred feet deep. Alexander Von Humboldt stated that the planet, from Canada to the Caribbean and from the Baltic to Algiers, felt the tremor of this giant earthquake. I am sure that we need not be reminded that this was the edge of the Madeira peninsula which ran from Portugal into the Atlantic separating the river of death from the Mediterranean falls at one time before a much greater terror came out of the earth and shook it down before it was swallowed forever by the sea.

The city of Agadir slept near the end of the Draa depression in Africa. That is, until that overnight earthquake turned it into rubble and killed over two thousand people. Need we be reminded that Agadir stands at the point where the great Atlas range plunges down into the sea? The natives of Morocco will recite the legends of that day and night of horror when the Atlas, with over a hundred cities and their ships upon the Triton lake, were swept out to sea. The action was twofold. The Atlas range - or that section of it from the present edge of the northwest corner of Africa to the Canaries, was down faulted into the

Street in San Francisco after the 1906 earthquake.
The fire can be seen coming over the rooftops.
(Courtesy R. Iacopi, Earthquake Country)

sea, and the Triton sea, having lost its great retaining wall of mountains, poured out into the ocean. Today in the minute modern maps of the sea, one can see where the water went in one vast wave. Agadir, as a site for a city, has wisely been abandoned. On a rift as gigantic as this, one can never be certain when the subterranean forge's hammer will strike again.

Several shocks have taken place in Greece and along the rift which must run through the Aegean sea toward Skopje. Both are sites of earthquake disasters. Therefore they are the site of a tremendous rift. This one is apparently connected with the trans-Atlantic rift and perhaps to others at the Caribbean end. We have not mapped out all of the rifts, but every year more teams are at work upon them, and as they work we learn more about the strange restless planet upon which we were born.

It was on Good Friday, 1964 that the big one struck Anchorage, Alaska. This pioneer city is situated near the meeting of two giant crevasses. One, the Denali fault, which passes Vancouver, goes on to connect with the San Andreas. Someday, when people are more realistic, they will recognize this great planetary crack for what it is, instead of calling all of its small forks by various other names so that "the timid

will not be alarmed". Here the Denali, or San Andreas runs headlong into the Aleutian fault, which comes around from the Aleutian island chain where it is a part of the curtain of fire.

We all read what it is like to have one's house roll down the cliff face into the sea, or have one's business sink below the level of the street, but actually this is nothing to what has happened in the past.

However, it is what this earthquake has taught us that makes it fascinating. There were sub-audible earth vibrations which continued for hours. Dr. Charles Richter of the Richter scale for earthquake intensity, reported that the Earth rang like a giant bell which was struck by an enormous gong. The first indications reached Pasadena and the Cal-Tech laboratory at 7:42 - 46 P.M., and the initial reading was 8.2, indicating a very strong earthquake. This was followed by six large after-shocks and many smaller ones. At 2 A.M. came a 6.2; 3:21 was a 6.3; 4:27 was a 6.5; 6:55 a 6.5; 12:32 P.M. a 6.2. The remarkable thing was that the intensities differed around the world on various machines. For example, the shock following, which was 6.2 at Pasadena, registered 7.0 at Honolulu and 5.5 at Berkeley university, California. Just why this should be is unknown. There are educated guesses. Possibly there are streams of magma circulating beneath the mantle all of the time. Complicating this could be the fact that the shock goes through all types of rock which differ from location to location.

There are other facts we learned from the giant Alaskan tremblor. Washington, D.C. and the entire eastern seaboard rose and fell rhythmically. New instruments recently installed at the U.S. Bureau of Standards showed that the initial shock caused the ground to rise one inch, then following this the earth sank two inches. Again it rose two inches and sank two rhythmically for hours in a diminishing scale. There was also a rolling vibration recorded at Boston, Florida and other points. It was greater in the mid-west and still greater in the far west.

Apparently no one felt this movement, because there was no jar or rending of the crust. The movement was slow - twelve seconds up and twelve seconds down - and thus there was no damage.

Dr. R. K. Cook, chief of the Sound Section of the Bureau of Standards indicated that the epicenter may have been under Unakwik volcano seventy-five miles east of Anchorage, which agreed with Dr. Langer. If this is the case, then the volcano must be on the Aleutian fault, which should be traced out toward the east. However two such giant Earth cracks as the Aleutian and the San Andreas make for an unstable location.

In the words of seismologist Michael Blockford, the Alaskan earthquake was equal in magnitude to the most powerful ever recorded in North America. It was only because the epicenter was very deep in the earth that fantastic damage was averted. Dr. Louis J. Ersele, director of the seismological laboratory at Spring Hill college, Mobile, Alabama placed the epicenter at 186-187 miles in depth.

There was no scale to record some of the other giant earthquakes. The one in 1923 recorded 8.9 on an early attempt at recording intensity. It killed 68,000 in Tokyo, while a later one killed 32,000 in a country district, with 43,000 missing. Perhaps the largest historical earthquake is the one in China in 1556 which moved mountains and killed eight hundred and thirty thousand people. There was no Richter scale at that time.

There are a few other remarks on the various points of the San Andreas. Director of the Coast Geodetic Survey, Dr. Leonard Murphy, from an analysis made of reports of one hundred stations, says that the Good Friday, 1964 earthquake of Alaska released ten million times more energy than the atom bomb at Hiroshima.

Chief Rear Admiral H. Arnold Karo says that the Alaskan earthquake was the worst ever to hit Alaska, and should warn southern California that a jolt from the San Andreas at that point is overdue.

San Francisco suffered two jolts from the San Andreas - 1868 and 1906 - which suggests that this point also is overdue for another. Dr. G.G. Shore, Jr. of Scripps Institute of Oceanography, speaking of the Japanese current which sweeps around and makes a giant whirlpool off Point Conception, in a speech in November, 1964, said: "The Pacific bottom off southern California is really a submerged piece of continent". He continues by describing the trenches which are to be found off the coast. For example, west of Santa Barbara these trenches are three miles deep, but are not easily detected because they are full of sediment once washed from high mountains. (Page Dr. Rogers) The Alaskan trench is about five miles deep in comparison. We will remember that this strip of coast over a hundred miles was dropped during or after the Pleistocene, because Dr. Rogers photographed parts of cemeteries cut off and down faulted into the sea where bones from broken graves stuck out of the columns of rock. The site of this was near Santa Rosa, about halfway out to the edge of the down-warped continental shelf.

Chile, at the other end of the San Andreas crevasse, is in a very unstable position. There was a bad disturbance with volcanism at that point a few years back (1955) and again on March 4th 1964, a Chilean volcano blew up causing hundreds to remain all night in a downpour of warm, muddy, sulphurous rain. These heavy downpours of rain occur at every volcanic explosion. They have caused scientists to wonder if the Earth is not gaining water - especially when the fumes of hydrogen and sulphur climb up to meet oxygen in the air. Hydrogen and two parts of oxygen (H_2O) are the component parts of water. This is one of the reasons why science is attempting to study the mantle, and contemplating drilling in such questionable places as the Murray rift running from Los Angeles basin past the Hawaiian islands, mainly because here the mantle is close to the surface of the sea.

When we note that this Chilean volcano blew up on March 4, 1964 we begin to wonder if this tremor triggered the ancient trans-Atlantic fault? March 13, 1964 an earthquake struck Morocco and the Iberian peninsula. The tremor was felt most sharply in the southern portion of Portugal. The shock was also felt at Casablanca, Rabat, Tavira where cracks appeared, Lisbon, and along the southern coast of Spain. In Casablanca two strong tremors were reported. Dr. Charles Richter reported the quake as moderate-

Volcanic island rising out of the Atlantic south of Iceland, shows what is happening all along the mid-ocean ridge. This island appeared in November, 1963.

ly strong, with an epicenter apparently upon the floor of the Atlantic ocean.

Chile is no stranger to either volcanoes or earthquakes. Since 1520, when the Spanish first started keeping track, there have been 43 severe jolts. Dr. Pierre Saint-Amand of the Naval Ordinance test station at China lake, California was then stationed at the university of Chile at Santiago. As a trained geophysicist, his on the spot book Los Terremotos de Mayo (The Earthquakes of May) makes most intriguing reading. On May 21, 1960 the area southwest of Concepcion, a city of about 120,000, was rocked by an strong tremor. There was much damage. The following afternoon there was a second one, but the damage was not as severe. Usually the tremblors gradually diminish after the first jolt, but not this time. Thirty minutes after this tremblor came the "killer". It lasted three and a half minutes, with the ground rising and falling in waves such as the present writer saw in 1933, coming into Long Beach, Calif. Thousands of lives were lost in this one, both from the falling debris and the tidal waves which followed. This might suggest an epicenter in the sea.

The scientist on the spot, points out that the big one was followed by thousands of aftershocks, including 120 which were strong enough to have caused damage in a more populated area. Then, north of Concepcion, another "killer" came, not in 1960 as the others, but in March, 1965. It came one year and one day after the great killer quake struck Alaska. It is interesting that Valparaiso, damaged in this latest tremblor, was almost totally destroyed a few months after San Francisco was so badly shaken in 1906. It is no wonder that the people of the United States are the first relief commissions to arrive in Chile after such a disaster, and the Chilean commission the first to arrive in California. Even the layman is beginning to sense a connection.

One of the most interesting features about this quake is that apparently the heaviest damage occurred along the highway and railway lines to Argentina, where the tremblor was strongly felt. At Los Andes ninety per cent of the houses were destroyed. (Geologists should check this fault line.) The quake was only strong enough to sway chandeliers and break crockery in Buenos Aires, which is about seven hundred miles east of Santiago, but the fact that it did is very significant.

During the unusual year of 1964 another seismic disturbance came to light in the western Pacific. At first glance this would not seem to be connected with the Atlantic, but when it comes to the great Earth cracks, we are not so certain. The details of this are given to us by a group of New Zealand scientists writing in the journal "Nature" published in the British isles.

This group of New Zealand scientists report the first details of a series of intense earth tremors and volcanic eruptions which jolted the island of Raoul in November, 1964. Geographical features were shifted around and changed. Earth sank and rock cliffs disappeared. Raoul lies about 650 miles northeast of Auckland, New Zealand. It has only eleven square miles of area, but that makes it the largest of the Kermadec islands. It is the only inhabited one and that is only because since 1957 New Zealand has maintained an aviation weather station there.

Severe earthquakes and eruptions have been recorded here in 1814, 1847, 1872 and 1887. Following the 1814 eruption a Captain Barnes aboard the ship "Stella" found a newly-formed island along the western coast of Raoul where previously the charts showed the water to have a depth of 250 feet. Shortly thereafter this island sank. Other islands made their appearance and also disappeared. Prior to November, 1964 the only fragments of the previous Denham bay islands were a reef and an island hill whose cliffs were named Wolverine Rock. On Nov. 10, 1964, Raoul was hit by a swarm of earth tremors, and by eight o'clock that night the island was pulsing with more than eighty earth shocks an hour. By November 12, the frequency of the shocks had increased to the point where individual tremors could no longer be distinguished. The most intense earthquake, Richter scale 5.7, took place at 9:58 A.M. on November 14. Survey reached the island aboard H.M.N.Z.S. (Her Majesty's New Zealand Ship) Lachlan. He found the bay frothing and blowing bubbles of gas. It was also covered with floating chunks of pumice, and discolored for a mile off shore. Raoul has two lakes. One is called "Green lake" and one "Blue lake". The eruption was taking place in Green lake. Its surface had risen more than twenty feet above normal and the water was still rising more than a half inch an hour. Also the usually cold water was becoming increasingly warm. On November 21 in the morning the crater erupted violently. Steam, rocks and mud were flung some 2500 feet into the air. The water level in Green lake was now fifty feet above normal and spilling into Blue lake, killing the vegetation. At this point the island was evacuated.

On December 10th, after the eruption had subsided, ten scientists returned to the island. They included, besides Lloyd and Healy, Drs. Banwell and Adams of the Geophysics Division, Department of Scientific and Industrial Research. They found that the water now pouring from a crack in the Green lake crater showed it to be strongly saline - about one-fourth as salty as sea water. Earth shocks were still taking place at the rate of two to four an hour. Tiltmeters installed on the island showed that Raoul was bending and swaying every ten to twenty minutes. Wolverine Rock had completely disappeared as well as the reef. Parts of Denham bay had sunk a hundred feet.

It is to be noted that though there was not a great deal of sinking about Anchorage or the near environs after the Good Friday tremblor, a short distance to the west a belt of some 30,000 square miles sank six feet, while to the east an area as much as 50,000 square miles rose locally sometimes as much as 33 feet. This has caused Dr. Richtor to remark, speaking of the San Andreas, Raoul, and the Pacific curtain of fire, that: "Generally speaking, seismic activity increases over a broad area before a major shock takes place within it." The storm to which he referred began with a major earthquake (7.5) in the Aleutians on February 1965. It was followed by a

Looking down on the San Andreas fault crossing the Carrizo plain in California. Note off-set streams. (Courtesy R. Iacopi, Earthquake Country)

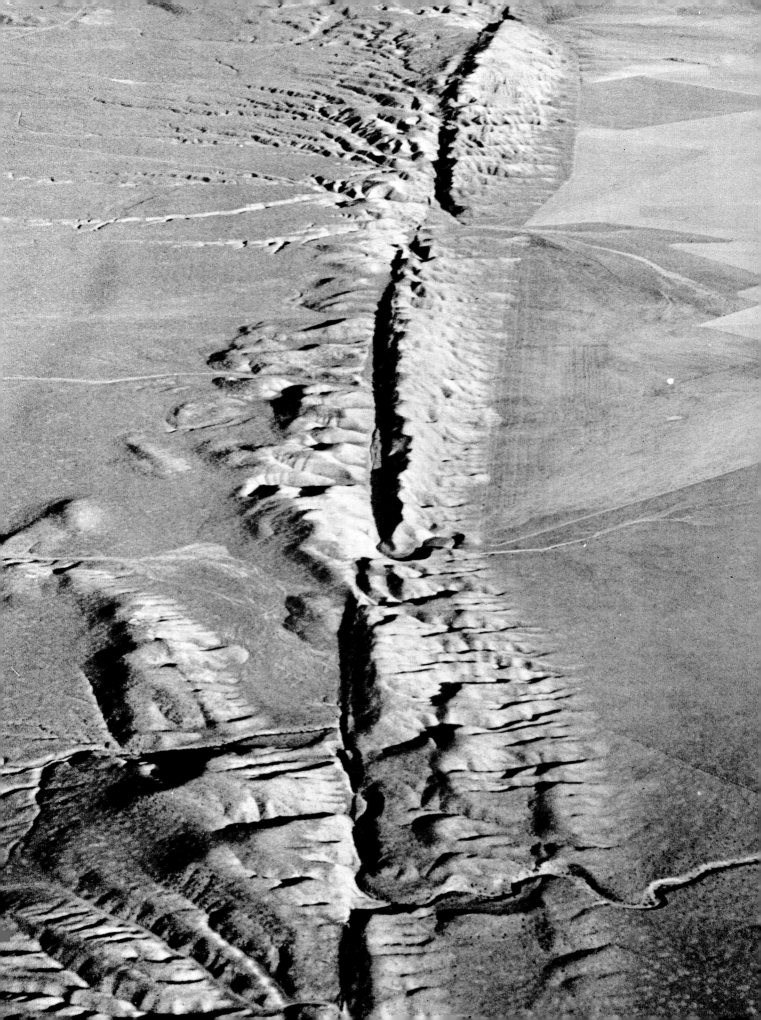

large number of after-shocks, more indeed than was expected. This was followed by an unusual number of tremors in the south Pacific. Then came the Chilean shock just one year and a day after that of Anchorage. Dr. Richter is a calm and quiet man not given to alarmist speeches; yet some time ago he remarked that the restless giant - the San Andreas - was building up great tensions in the desert region of southern California where it comes in from the gulf of California, after joining with the great crack of the world - the mid-Atlantic-Pacific rift, and turns northwest through the desert to pass out through the Salton sea and Banning on its way to the bay of San Francisco, and thence northward. An adjustment could be expected along any part of the rift, but particularly in the section below Banning.

Seismologists have made considerable progress in the last decade in recognizing potentially dangerous areas. They are usually on either island arcs or mountain arcs along the shore. The most destructive by far are the island arcs, because the epicenter of the jolt is not as deep and therefore the damage is multiplied by large figures. Thus at the present time Japan is a very unstable location, almost as unstable as was once the beautiful old red land.

There seems to be tremendous forces at work within the Earth. The whole Pacific basin reacts as if it were slowly rotating in a counter-clockwise direction. The Americas are moving north with a twisting movement, which is clockwise. It may be that contention of these two opposite movements is the force which is causing the giant Earth crack along the Pacific coast of the Americas.

This is complicated by the fact that apparently our planet is gaining more water. Not only are the glacials of both north and south polar regions melting, but there may be other reasons. We do know that the oceans are rising, or the land sinking. It seems more logical to believe the former. As reported in 1964 the Coast Geodetic Survey at San Diego finds that the ocean has risen two inches, one inch at La Jolla (about twenty miles north of San Diego) one and a half inches at Santa Monica just west of Los Angeles. Data from fourteen tidal gauges show a considerable rise in

One of the branches of the San Andreas fault crossing Baja California, Mexico. Great magnitude brings many surface movements at distant points, such as Long Beach, San Francisco and Alaska. (Courtesy R. Iacopi, Earthquake Country)

the gulf of California, but the greatest rise reported was that of Eugene island, twenty miles northeast of Morgan county, Louisiana. Here the rise was nine inches.

It would be well if the lands across the ocean would put in tidal gauges and report the inroad of the sea so that we could learn if this is world wide, due largely to melting glacials, or whether the lands are sinking. It would seem to the present writer that the movement is two-way. A great difference would suggest the sinking of the land - such as the slow subsidence of Eugene island.

In England the subsidence seems to be definite - particularly toward the south. Holland really has a problem with dykes which have to be renewed or reinforced almost yearly.

What is in store for the Earth? There is bound to be seismic activity along the rifts. As Father Fordham remarked during one of his lectures on seismology, in answer to a question: "The earthquake and volcano is nature's way of releasing dangerous strains that have accumulated in the spinning Earth, as a safety valve releases excess pressure from a boiler. Better surely, is it not, such an occasional release than a bursting planet?"

Looking at the movement of the continents following the terrible collision at the end of the Mesozoic, we seem to have South America turning in a half spin clockwise. The pressure of the opposite movement in the San Andreas coastal cleft is apparently starting to cut that continent in half about the point of greatest disturbance.

Central America would find the pressure of the twist of South America against the small neck of land joining the continents intolerable and perhaps crack free from the southern mass. North America would split off the coastal section as it did once before, only this time the amount of land should be greater, and then the other parts would continue their ride toward the Pacific. The northern lands would be caught in this twist, and again, perhaps millions of years from now, another collision of the continents in the north is inevitable, followed by a land-locked pole and another glacial age. This is so far in the future that perhaps there will be no men here to see it happen.

However, as science learns more and more about seismology, oceanography and geophysics, the men of the future will pity the men of the old red land for not being able to see just what inevitably lay ahead, and get out while there was time.

Chapter 56

The Sunken Land Of Lyonesse

From a speech to UCLA on The Cultural Arts

"Our writers have not as yet transfigured and incorporated new scientific materials into fine works of art. It is through the refracting medium of the arts that people see the world. This void in literature is more the pity.

"Science gives pure sense by particularizing, saying only one thing at a time. Literature, on the other hand, must express the inexpressible, the ineffable and render the multiplicity of our existence. Literature examines the unique case to perceive the universal. The trouble with our literature is that our men of the letters have not known how to handle the rich, raw materials given to them by science." Aldous Huxley

My little grandson, Jode, once told me that a certain place "had a sad feeling about it". I looked at this five year old lad in surprise. I had often had the same depressing sensation descend upon me in certain locations, but had brusquely put it from my mind as being due to the fact that I knew the history of the locality. For example, there is a "lake of flowers" near Mexico City where "xochil or socheel" (the Aztec word for flowers) are sold in laden barges, which so depresses me that I spend only a few moments on the lake and directed my surprised boatman to hire me a taxi. He gave me a long look, murmuring in English: "You must be Indian."

I answered him with an affirmative nod, I may be one eighth Indian through my father's family, who deny it, but that could hardly account for the black psychic cloud of this lake. Perhaps instead, it is due to having read some of the Spanish accounts of how this was the death place of the Aztec empire, where the warriors fought to the last man and so clogged the water with dead bodies that the Spanish had to retreat to far distant locations to get away from the stench. For me the passage of the centuries has not been able to wash away that stench.

Another such "haunted location" is Cornwall, England, Land's End, and the Scillies. The latter are a series of islands which today seem to be ideally separated from the hustle and worry of modern life. The charming people, for the most part, spend their lives either fishing or growing flowers. You never saw such flowers as are grown in the Scillies! There is a blue which they have been able to breed which is almost electric in its dark glow.

However, it was not always so, for this is the land of king Arthur and his knights of the Round Table; of beautiful queen Guinevere and the fascinating Lancelot; of lovely Elaine who was forced by an old curse to view life through a mirror from her tower, and the days of jousts and the quest for the Holy Grail. Only today you cannot see the storied towers or roads, or famous cities - because they are under the sea.

This was also the location of the famous tin mines which the Tyrrhenians and Atlantidae sought with their ships and brought beautiful silks, cottons, spices and a thousand other items to trade for the much desired tin and the light amount of copper to be found here. This trade was a brisk one from the old stone age through the bronze age and even into the iron age. In fact, the famous merchant and seaman of Jerusalem, Joseph of Aramathea, considered by some to be a distant relative of Mary of Nazareth, owned land here, and his name still appears on some of the ancient documents. This brisk trade must have begun with that great colossus of the sea when it became the center of metal work and the manufacturer of metal articles from domestic utensils to weapons and jewelry. After the fall of

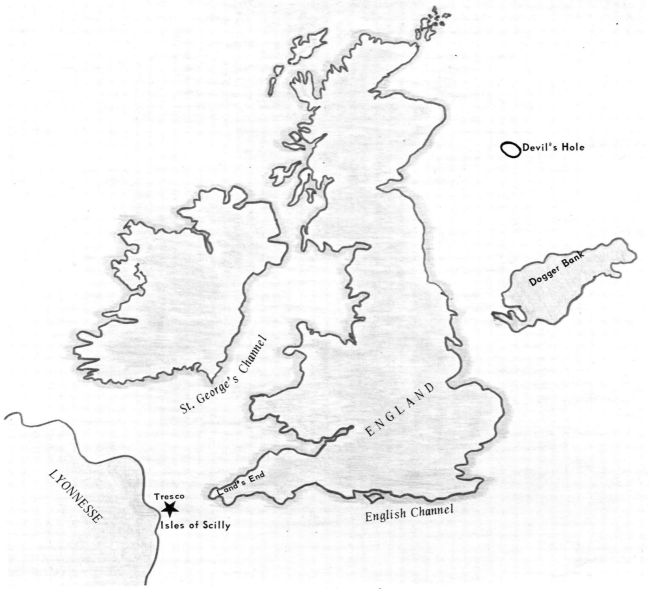

Location of Ancient Lyonesse

the giant trading center, the trade then probably went to the Tyrrhenian heirs of the old red land, until the march of the Ar-zawans when for a few generations they wore the purple robes of royalty. Today those mines, too, are under the sea.

How do we know that this land is not entirely legend? Because in the third century A.D. the Romans were busy either helping the natives hold back the sea, or sending their prisoners to the "Insula Syllia" as a place of banishment. Undoubtedly they were following the age old precedent of the banishment of emperor Saturn.

It is an historical fact that the emperor Maximus transported prisoners, one a Spanish bishop, for "heresy", to "Insula Sulina". There were similar Roman banishments and the dates were usually about 280 A.D. Tiberianus was sent to the "Insula Syllian" a hundred years later, while emperor Marcus banished a "false prophet" during the rebellion of Cassius. In this document the name was the "Insula Silis".

It is also a well known fact that the only Roman altar in England is to be found on Tresco, an island near St. Mary's (long ago called Mt. Ennor), and that a Roman road which dips down some six feet under the sea connects the two. It is the opinion of some scholars that this is not an actual causeway, but a wall against the inroads of the sea. In this case, would not the altar on Tresco have been dedicated to Neptune, the Roman god of the sea?

To the sides of this road, or wall, are to be seen the stone fences or separations of the estates, and one man flying over the location on an especially clear day during low tide was able to photograph part of a house. This is discussed by Alexander Gibson in his book "The Isles of Scilly". Mr. Gibson claims that both the altar, which is composed of large flat stones, and also

339

the Roman road, are considered by some scholars to be pre-Roman.

On the largest of the Scillies, the poet Alfred Tennyson lived for months on end at a charming hotel still serving the public. From the rose-arbor he wandered along the sea, and then returned to the shade, to write down his verse inspired by the very soil about which he was writing: "The Idylls of the King". Camelot and Arthur lived for him and through his pen, for the ages. To Tennyson this was not an island, but only the top of Mt. Ennor rising above the land of Siluria that reached from the river which separated it from France to the river of death, which separated it from another land of legend.

Today the island of Tresco is small, but even in 1538 it had a circumference of ten miles, and in the forested top were to be found numerous wild boars.

Toward Cornish there is a tract of land below the sea which once was known as Lyonesse and had a city with an acropolis. This place today is called "the town" and is marked by a lighthouse. When there is a storm and the waves are high, the people turn out by the hundreds to pick up the debris washed up by the waves. Bits of leaded glass, sometimes old coins, and once in a while a ring or other bits of jewelry are washed ashore from the drowned "city of the lions." In 1750 during a particularly bad storm, part of a column was found. It is three feet in diameter and was undoubtedly the base of a lost building. The Trevillian or Trevelyan family has for its crest the white horse which carried their ancestor to safety. In France there is a statue to a man on a white horse who is supposed to have ridden there to safety during the night when the land sank. One legend has the story that his daughter stole the keys to the locks which kept out the sea, while he was drunk, and was the first one to drown in the inrush of the ocean. In memory of the story the French toss a goblet of wine yearly over the horse and rider.

Near Sanson or between Tresco and Sanson there is an aerial photo on view at the public courthouse of Cornwall which shows the walls of a house and part of what may have been a roadway. The people of Cornwall are particularly sensitive to loss by the sea.

It was a warm magnificent day when a small boat took me on a cruise around the Scilly isles. The water was greenishly clear and I had a suggestion for the guide:

"Why don't you buy a glass bottomed boat? We have them on Santa Catalina island and you can look down as if you were yourself in the water and see what is below you. I believe that if you did this, it would be one of the greatest tourist attractions in the world."

He laughed and shrugged my suggestion away.

"We don't have the money."

"Then form a corporation and every one chip in, buying shares. Really, in good weather this should be fabulous."

He stopped my train of thought by pointing to an island which had a house and apparently part of an estate upon it.

"Sometimes we leave our passengers there if they talk too much. When we come back at the end of the day they are very glad to get back on and go along quietly."

"Why was it abandoned?"

"Perhaps because they couldn't make a living from the land. But I think that it may have been because of the noises. The place is haunted, you know, and though many have tried, no one stays. It is for sale again - cheap too."

I smiled and shook my head.

He was the next to break the silence with: "Sometimes near here you can hear the toll of a church bell."

We were quiet for some time, but I heard nothing but the slap of the waves against the side of the boat.

"Are there still families who have land under the sea?" I asked, finally breaking the silence.

"There are. They were Normans for the most part. De Barentin, Ranulph de Blanminster, William de Poer, John de Allet are the ones which come to mind first. You can look them up in the records if you like. You can't claim any land down there now. I remember that there was talk long ago about some man trying to dig from his land and then down under the sea to the old mines. A foolish idea, I would say."

In the books of A.K. Hamilton Jenkins: "The Story of Cornwall", "Cornwall and its People" and "The Cornish Miner" I learned more than I had on the trip. The people of Cornwall and the Scillies, according to Jenkin are Celts, Romans, Normans and finally the English mixed upon the basic "people of the sea" - perhaps traders, perhaps pirates who came to the isles in the hoary past. They are a tough horny-handed group who throughout the ages have made their living from the mines - a living which is being yearly taken from them by the sea. Sometimes they indulge in smuggling which they look upon as a sort of free trade. Yet it was a Cornishman who because of a terrible ship disaster in the early 1800, with the help of some others, invented the rocket and breeches buoy which hurls a rocket to a sinking ship so that the trapped crew can cross the killing power of the breakers.

The Cornishmen point out the famed castle of Arthur - Tintagel - which down steps its way into the sea. Scholars from the British Ministry of Works decided after some excavations during the 1930s, that this was not a castle of Arthur, but instead a sixth century monastery. However it is a magnificent place for the old castle, rising as it does 300 feet above the wild headland of rocks and dashing spray, and since the date is about the same, it seems to the present writer, a difficult and useless task to prove otherwise. Especially since not far away there is "Slaughter Bridge" where the armies of Arthur and the usurper Modred, clashed in 542 A.D. To me Tintagel castle is still the spot where "Arthur in Tintigel passed away" above the roaring torrent of the sea. I bow to Tennyson rather than these publicity seeking scholars who gain fame by an attempt to tear down. If a thousand years or even five hundred years were at stake, then for the sake of history - yes, but why raze the beautiful structure of Tennyson and the story of Arthur?

The subsidence of the land, which is still going on, is geologically very recent. Leaded windows in the diamond shaped style which are being washed up, are quite modern and these Tudor windows are to be seen all over England. Besides the crests which show the golden lion or dragon of Lyonesse are scarcely seven hundred years old. The difference between the date of Arthur and the supposed monastery is probably too slight to carbon date with accuracy.

The Geological Survey, which is the work of George Barrow and published by H.M. Stationary Office, London, remarks that there has been both subsidence and elevation of land. The sand bar which lies across Crow Sound and is called "Crow Bar" could not have been formed except at a time when the sea was at least twenty-five feet lower than its present level. The deposit is megalithic, (great stone builders or Cro Magnon times) because their skulls and flint instruments have been found in abundance at this point. The range of heavy metal bearing granite radiates from Devon to beyond the Scillies, and the sparkle of the veins is still to be seen below sea level, which outcrop on the surface of the sinking land.

There is a glacial deposit of flints and green sand on the highest points of St. Martins, very similar to the Eocene river gravels of Devon and Dorset, that are apparently, the last relic of an old tableland over which rivers radiating from Dartmoor flowed outward across what is now the Atlantic, to the ancient end of the shelf over two hundred miles beyond the end of the (present) Scillies. South and west of Ireland the land also went out to the edge of the shelf, which today is only about three hundred feet deep. Probably during glacial times many of these rolling hills, now submerged, were islands or even wide land. We have the legends in Ireland of the islands of Kessair or Cessair from which we get the name Cassiterides and the Castari tribes, or Kassites, or Cassides. It would be interesting if we could ever know that these may have been the Kassites who made their way to the Mediterranean during the second millennium B.C.

In the book "The Fortunate Isles" by E.K. Bowley, published by Times Ltd. Croydon, Surrey, England; we have a discussion of a recent subsidence of forty feet. This area covered much of what had been south Ireland, Wales and Cornwall, as well as the Scillies. There is an old beach level at this mark below present sea level. On the ten fathom line, or thirty feet down, says Mr. Bowley, all the Scillies become rolling hills of one large island. He also mentions that there is evidence of a forty foot elevation as well as the subsidence. At the end of this ancient island, a long peninsula projects into the sea. It was on this point that, according to legend, the extremely ancient city of Ys was located.

That this may have been at one time a powerful city-state is possible, for even in the time of the Saxon king Athelstan, when he was able to subdue Siluria with his fleet, he was so pleased that then and there he built the collegiate church of St. Buryan near Land's End to commemorate his victory.

The greatest modern subsidence was in the fall of 1478.

In a small hotel in the town of Cambridge near where the great clock chimes out the hours, the guests were in the habit of gathering before the open fireplace and exchanging stories. I found these far more entertaining than the "tele", as it is called in England. Most of the guests were salesmen, but they had an excellent sense of curiosity. I suspect that not many of them had much education, but the topics of our conversation ran the gamut of everything from unidentified flying objects and the possibility of life on Mars, to the probable efficacy of a world wide common market. One of these men was from Cornwall, and one night we happened to meet in the parlor before the others arrived. It was when I engineered him into talking about the sea. I was amazed to find out that when the others arrived they all joined in with an equal amount of interest.

"Yes, it is true that the land is sinking and it has been for centuries," he was saying. "There was a pretty general subsidence in the tenth or eleventh century."

"But the big one was in 1478, wasn't it?"

"That's right. You can see some of the stumps of the fallen trees. They were fruit and nut trees mostly, which the people were growing."

"By the way, I hear that at minus tide you can walk out along the old roads and see the rock fences."

"Quite. The people still make rock hedges between their farms you know, and there are miles of them under the sea."

"Has anyone ever tried skin diving?"

"No, that entertainment has never really taken hold of us yet. I imagine the equipment is expensive?"

"Not too much, considering the adventure. If I could choose a manner of dying when one is faced by the grim reaper, I would choose to follow one of those roads. . ."

"Perhaps some of us would like to join you, but we all have mouths to feed, you know."

"Have any of you ever thought of going together and getting a mining company which could work undersea mines - say in Cornwall, or the Scillies?"

"I tried to do just that last year," the Cornishman nodded. "You see there was this beautiful old house - very old and tumbled down, but it was built on the edge of the sea, and I had the plan of digging down through the basement until I was under the ocean and then tunnelling out to one of the veins one can see shining in the sunlight. Of course, I wouldn't break through. I would keep it all far below the sea, but it would be my own property, now wouldn't it? No bloke whose ancestor had owned it centuries ago would come around bothering. So I made enquiry and found the price very low. I saw the owner, the last son of an old family, and he was most anxious to sell. So I went home to raise the money. I didn't have a chance. The very next day, there was a tremendous storm and my charming old mansion, which I had dreamed of fixing up when I made my pounds of profit from the mines - well, the sea wall of the cliff broke and the whole cliff face, including my house, tumbled into the ocean."

For a moment there was silence. Then another man stopped stuffing tabocco into his pipe long enough to ask:

"Anyone here ever pass over Dogger bank? It's only about forty feet deep. I wonder what's down there?"

"I hear that there is a tremendous whirlpool at times," I volunteered.

"Oh yes. They call it Devil's hole," a youthful man nodded. I learned about it in the navy. What causes that, do you suppose?"

"Probably Dogger bank was once a mountain top that became an island. One of the sides perhaps has a steep canyon, and when the tide goes the water goes faster down that chasm. There are places off the California coast like that where long lost canyons suck the tides out fast and make the swimming or boating quite dangerous. By the way, there was a Captain Hull who lived next door to us in Los Angeles. He must have had adventure in his blood, for his people, like mine, were pioneers across the plains in the 1849 rush for California.

"Captain Hull told me that there is a high point in the Irish sea from which the water pours out both ways, and then the tide goes out at thirty-five miles an hour! That is pretty fast for a small boat such as he commanded."

"If your explanation is the correct one, then there is an undersea range of mountains crossing from Ireland to England. At the point where the tide goes in two directions, there must be a mountain peak?"

"Very good scientific thinking," I nodded. "And I might add that this range crosses the Atlantic from America and the English channel from here on its way to finally becoming the Russian Urals."

"Wait until the Russians and Americans find out about this!" he quipped.

So the trend of the conversation turned from the sea to other subjects and I settled back to laugh and become the listener.

When I returned to London, I looked up the Rt. Hon. Brinsley Le Poer Trench and his clever wife, Millen, who is an American. They are both writers and have often written for science fiction magazines on both sides of the Atlantic.

"Come on in," Millen was delighted when she saw me, "and come down with our Asian flu. Brinsley is in bed; the children are going back to school for the first time, and I am now staggering around."

"I only wanted to stop in to say 'bye. I am on my way back to the States."

"Oh no! But come on in anyhow; that is if you are not afraid of our germs."

"Not at all. But I do have something to ask

Brinsley. It is about his family. At the last hotel where I stayed overnight, one of the aristocrats deigned to inform me that his coat of arms is one of the most ancient, and from Ireland somewhere. I couldn't remember it all, so I thought I would ask."

"He'd love to talk to you. He may be asleep, but I'll waken him. He would be sorry if he missed you entirely."

In a moment she returned to the room and ushured me in to see the science fiction wizard. I broke the news without any preliminary hedging.

"Brinsley, is there a golden dragon in your coat of arms?"

"Yes. Why?"

"Then you know that is the crest of Arthur, or of Lancelot?"

"Well, I know that the De Poer branch of my family are, or were, Normans." Then giving me a sidelong look: "Why are you interested? Want me to lay claim to the old castle?"

"No, but it is too bad that you can't lay claim to your mines."

"Mines? Where? There are no mines on my Irish lands."

"No, but there are on the ones in the Insulum Silurian. . ."

"The what?"

"The Insulum Silurian, as it was known to the Romans. In other words, the Scilly isles; but your mines are on the bottom of the sea!"

With that I had to dodge the pillow aimed directly at my head and went out laughing. It was the last time I saw Brinsley or Millen, but my life would have been the poorer had I never known them.

Looking at Brinsley, one could easily imagine the tall, stately figure of King Arthur, a perfect Cro Magnon type, and his golden haired queen. Not long ago English scientists digging about the grounds of Glastonbury where it is said that the royal couple had been buried, discovered a magnificent tomb of a tall powerful man and his lady whose long golden hair was still as bright as when it was covered by the loam of the earth so many hundreds of years ago. Was it the legendary Arthur? Who knows?

There is only one thing more to remember about Lyonesse and that is, there was a "lake of the lyons" in legendary times of which apparently everyone was afraid. This lake had boiling water, and it was the prayer of the people that it would never boil over the land. Just before the subsidence of Lyonesse and its city of the lyons, legends tell us that the lake began to boil over.

To me this sounds like the top of a submerged volcano and what followed then was hardly due to one woman opening sea gates. It was the old, old story of earthquake, eruption and subsidence which we have heard around the Earth again and again. It happened at Santorin in 1848, when after a three months duration of volcanism and earthquakes, the population and thousands of animals were killed by the fumes of hydrogen gas and sulphur, issuing from the sea. The island then sank to over a 1200-foot depth below the waves. It happened in Tomboro in the island of Sumbawa in April, 1815. Eruptions continued until July, when submarine rifts began to open up and the most violent whirlwinds hurled men, houses, cattle and great trees torn out by the roots into the darkened skies, covering the seas with bodies, debris, floating timber and ashes two feet in thickness. It happened in the Canaries (a part of the African shelf, being the sunken portion of the Atlas range) in 1730 when on the first of September, the Earth split open near Yaira in the island of Lancerota. Cattle suffocated from the fumes which, after rising into the heavens, fell back in muddy torrents of rain. These lava flows and strange rains continued for five years. It happened in the Mediterranean near Sicily in 1831, when great cracks in the clear blue Mediterranean suddenly clouded and exploded with a waterspout sixty feet high and eight hundred yards in circumference, which carried everything before it.

It is a meteorological fact that a tornado is born of a pocket of overheated air rising through a layer of cold air. Of course, a volcanic explosion is in this situation de luxe, and tornadoes can be expected at such times. Even greatly heated pockets of air over the desert can spawn a tornado, and a waterspout is an underwater tornado.

I remember thinking of all this as I stood on the grey stones of King Arthur's old castle. The date of the first submergence of the storied land was probably the actual time of Arthur's death, and though Lancelot succeeded him to the kingship, he did not live long, but also died in the war, according to most pre-historians. However, there are legends which tell of the armies fleeing before the sea, and climbing the peaks of Siluria to escape death. Today the legends lie heavily over this part of the ocean below England, almost like a mist from the past. It is a "sad place", and for me, Arthur, with his knights of the Round table owned the castle first, even though there may have been an abbey there later. I am sure that Arthur would not object to that.

Chapter 57

The Giant Crack In The Earth

"Along the Pacific coast (of North America) the Pleistocene seems to have been an epoch of greater diastrophic changes than any other that has occurred since the middle Mesozoic."

Ralph D. Reed

Many years ago Humboldt saw that there might someday be discovered the fact that the great rifts were interconnected into one great crack in the planet. In the last decade it has been discovered that he was right. Today the whole seismic world is just catching up with what he foresaw. Scientists are no longer actually arguing over the drift theories as much as trying to explain what is happening.

Hans Stille in his "Present Tectonic State of the Earth" (1933) calls attention to the fact that the vast amount of mountain building going on in California at present is largely west-vergent, showing pressure from the east and north, noting that "on the flanks of Signal hill, (Los Angeles) the upper Pleistocene dips as much as 25 degrees." He continues, saying: "What is happening today ie, is not the normal, but the abnormal conditions of the past - that is, a catastrophic period in its decline."

Reed, in discussing the undersea gorges off the sunken land of California says: "As for the Redondo gorge, it definitely suggests that we have preserved here a river of the past, and we see the course of the stream which has since been altered. A great change in sea level would cause the same gorges to erode again. Therefore the arguments just cited are sufficient to convince many of the geologists interested, but not all, that the California mainland stood some thousands of feet higher than at present during a portion of the Pleistocene epoch. There may even have been several such periods, corresponding to the different stages of glaciation. Whether the uplift amounted to 12,000 feet in central California is a matter of less argument. The chief objection to this conclusion is that it seems 'unreasonable.' Perhaps it will seem more reasonable, or less so, when more facts are known

about the Pleistocene diastrophism."

This too, was written in 1933. Now the wave of agreement is beginning to strike the halls of science. The reason is the crack in the planet.

The curtain of fire is only a part of all the other great rifts. The great rifts of the Atlantic join those of the Indian and the Pacific. The Mediterranean rifts extend through the Himalayas. Some scholars see an arm of it going up the Adriatic into and through Germany to the Baltic. This part of the giant crack has not been sufficiently traced out. Part of it certainly runs along the Draa depression of north Africa, but it has not been well explored from here.

On the western side of the Americas, due to the efforts of Scripps Institute of Oceanography, California School of Technology and the help of geologists from the Latin American countries, the great crack is looming up as the San Andreas de luxe. It runs from the north of North America to the south of South America, making some turns around the Caribbean and being joined by the trenches of the Pacific rise, recently named the Darwin rise by the oceanographers of Scripps. One sinister fork runs toward Guatemala and San Salvador while the other fork heads into the gulf of California where it has been traced as the San Andreas, on its way to Alaska. Here as a part of the Pacific curtain of fire the mobile San Andreas crosses the Aleutian fault, one fork joining that crack and the other heading toward the Arctic. Recent discoveries have taught scientists that the sunken edge of the California coastline has its own trenches, not recognized before because they were filled with sediments from the land.

The great Earth fracture is of course, a part of the curtain of fire, or more correctly, the curtain of fire around the Pacific is only a part of the great fracture. Its age, most geologists, geophysicists and oceanographers agree, is about one hundred million years and it goes back to the time of the Mesozoic diastrophism. That it is very much alive science fully realizes. To study it and learn more about the molten mantle below the crust is the reason for drilling through that crust in Project Mohole.

Some of the modern ideas of science are that there are depressions and bulges in the mantle. The depressions are apparently the trenches and the bulges are the ridges of the oceans. These ridges are the most dramatic geographical features of the planet outside of the continents. The mid-Atlantic ridge is now acknowledged to be an average of a thousand miles wide and two miles high while its length is that of the entire

Atlantic ocean.

Nor is the mid-Atlantic the only ridge. There is also the Lemurian ridge of the Indian ocean and the Darwin rise of the Pacific. Dr. Henry Menard, Jr., who gave the name to the old Pacific ridge, is interested in discovering the reason why that ridge vanished. He understands when the ridge lost its bulge, but like other scientists cannot figure out why the lava which bulged it up for so many millennia has now drained away. The same question, of course, applies to the mid-Atlantic ridge. Why did it fall? We know that it was once land. Both locations have many guyots - those eroded islands which have the rounded pebbles of wave erosion. Also, the top of the ridges of the oceans have a high temperature in the matter of heat flow - especially the summits. What causes this? Geologists do not know, but there are theories now coming forth concerning it. Dr. J. Tuzo Wilson, geophysicist of the Toronto university is one. His remarks on the subject in his article in the Scientific American of April, 1963 entitled "Continental Drift" is indeed significant of how the modern top rated scientists are beginning to think.

"Geologists showed that some of Wegener's suggestions for reassembling the continents into a single continent were certainly wrong and that drift was unnecessary to explain the coincidences of geology in many areas. They could not, however, dispute the validity of most of the trans-Atlantic connections. Indeed more such connections have been steadily added."

He continues with some very interesting new scientific information when he discusses the finding and mapping of new rifts.

"It was the discovery of one of these connections that prompted my own recent inquiries into the subject of continental drift. A huge fault of great age bisects Scotland along the great glen in the Caledonian mountains. On the western side of the Atlantic, I was able to show, a string of well known faults of the same great age connect up into another huge fault, the 'Cabot fault' extending from Boston to northern Newfoundland."

Dr. Wilson then goes into what he terms "the compelling evidence for the existence of a Gondwannaland of the Mesozoic era - the age of reptiles - has been reinforced by the findings made in Antarctica since the intensive study of that continent began in 1955." One of the most interesting new facts recently discovered is that there is a discrepancy in gravity. He credits this discovery to the Dutch geophysicist, Felix

Great Glen fault in Scotland is named for a valley resulting from erosion along the line of the fault. About 350 million years ago the northern part of Scotland was moved some 60 miles southwest along this line. (Courtesy Dr. J. Tuzo Wilson, director of Institute of Earth Sciences, Toronto university, Canada)

A. Vening Meinesz, who was able to demonstrate that "...a submerged submarine would provide a sufficiently stable platform to allow the use of a gravimeter at sea. Over the abysmal trenches in the sea floor that are associated with the island arcs of Indonesia and the western side of the Pacific, he found some of the largest deficiencies in gravity ever recorded. It was clear that isostacy (continental and oceanic balance) does not hold in the trenches. Some force at work there pulls the crust into the depths of the trenches more strongly than the pull of gravity does."

He continues these new ideas with the words: "Arthur Holmes, of the university of Edinburgh, and D.T. Griggs, now at the university of California at Los Angeles (UCLA), were stimulated by these observations to restate in modern terms an old idea of geophysics that the interior of Earth is in a state of extremely sluggish thermal (heat) convection (movement), turning over the way water does when it is heated in a pan."

They still have not seen the connection between the weight of the ice and the pressure of lava to flow away from that pressure, forming a bulge just beyond it. Dr. Wilson admits that the

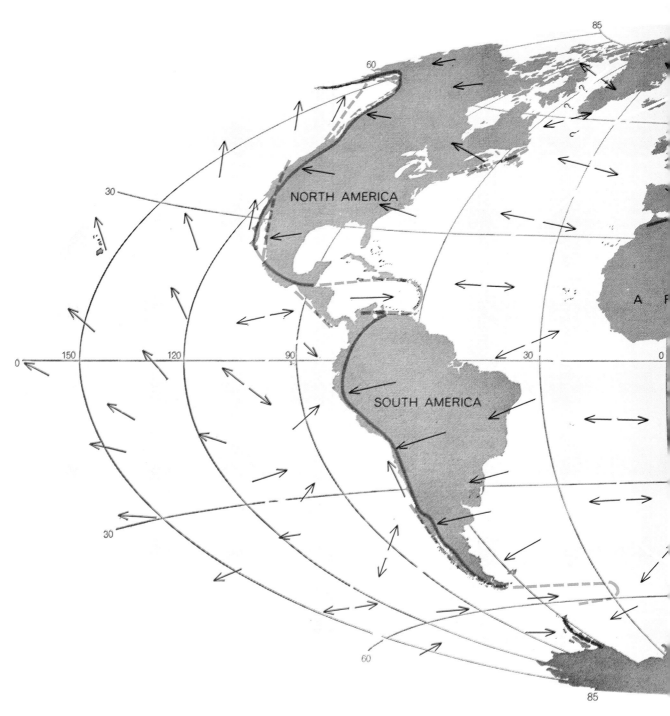

mid-Atlantic ridge is younger than the trenches, while the geophysicists of Scripps find that the Darwin ridge of the Pacific is very old indeed. Nor have any of them explained the present influx of lava creating a bulge under the recently glaciated areas of the north such as Hudson bay and the Scandinavian countries, caused without doubt by the release of pressure on the land with the melting off of the glacial weight. However, all this is a part of the reason why the relic of land left behind by the separation of the Atlantic tear was such a warm, pleasant place for the first civilizations of mankind to settle, in a rapidly cooling planet as the Pleistocene approached, and why it continued to be a fertile land with a delightful climate as long as an ice sheet weighed down the northern part of the continental masses. There was evidentally subsidence and flood every time the ice sheet melted away, but the time of the great destruction was the most dramatic, probably because by this time, the continents had drifted far enough apart for the central ridge to finally lose its base through remelting, when the rifts of the Atlantic tore open.

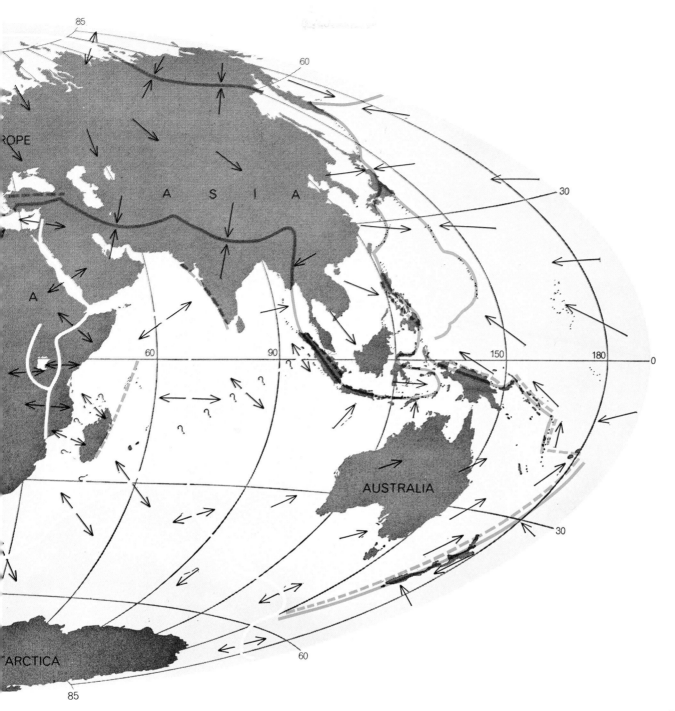

THE GREAT EARTH CRACK

Convection currents in Earth's mantle may move blocks of crustal material with different effects. Continental mountain chains and island arcs could form where currents sink and blocks meet; mid-ocean ridges where currents rise and blocks are torn apart. Arrows indicate directions of horizontal flow at present time. Solid colored lines represent mountain chains and island arcs; heavy white lines, the worldwide system of mid-ocean ridges; and broken colored lines, faults. (Courtesy Dr. J. Tuzo Wilson)

There are many of these rifts which have not yet been discovered and sufficiently traced out by science. One is that of the Draa depression which turns around the Atlas range causing the sinking of that great sialic root. Another is the parallel rift which runs up the coast of Africa on the inside of the Atlas-Canary range. Another is the trans-Atlantic rift (a ruler helped me to find) which probably connects the Caribbean faults to the San Andreas and from there to the Pacific fractures and in the other direction to the Mediterranean. One difficulty with map drawing in a region in which so little is known, as under water, is that rifts are indicated as

347

Robeson channel separating northwestern Greenland (upper right) from Ellesmere island (foreground) marks the Wegener fault. It probably joins a fault farther southwest. (Courtesy Dr. J. Tuzo Wilson)

turning in loops back upon themselves when in all probability the faults which seem to point in the same general direction are in reality parallel rifts even as those of the Owens, Panamint and Death valleys actually parallel San Andreas.

That the pressures upon the rocks is generally away from the late ice cap in the north and still away from the Permian cap in the southern continents is as yet not fully recognized. Of course, in the seas, this is complicated by the mechanics of drift. As a whole however, taking the continent of North America as an example, the eastern pressures are away from the Greenland center of the Pleistocene sheets, while in the far west along the Pacific there is a counterclockwise movement of the lands along the sea which presses them northwest, in opposition to the rest of the continent which is being moved south. This contest of continental masses lays the foundation for the most active and dangerous fault upon the face of the planet.

Fred R. Randall, cartographer for the U.S. Geodetic Survey for twenty-five years, gave some idea of the general southern pressure on most of the country when he mentioned the fact that the western states of Arizona and Nevada showed much Pleistocene volcanic activity. On his desk there was a February number of the "Arizona Highways" for 1946 and in it an article about the museum of northern Arizona, and its founder Dr. Harold S. Colton. The writer, Jerry McLain, has this to say of northern Arizona when describing the work of the museum.

"Early in the history of the museum it was discovered that northern Arizona had its own 'Pompeii'; a highly virile race of pre-historic people whose material culture was found buried below the volcanic ash from one of northern Arizona's most recent volcanoes, Sunset crater, now a national monument as a result of agitation by the museum founders.

"Research over a period of years revealed this volcano erupted between 1046 and 1070 A.D. and had a profound bearing on the lives of the natives of the region even unto the present.

"The eruption was dated by the complicated tree ring method first discovered by Dr. A.E. Douglass of the university of Arizona."

The same article mentions the fact that dozens of volcanoes near the present town of Flagstaff erupted "not more than a thousand years ago" and then describes volcanic bombs to be found in the vicinity.

Randall continued the story of other craters and finally stopped, saying: "But you are interested in faults? Right?"

I nodded with enthusiasm.

"Then print this, as a guide to some geophysicist following the illusive hunt. West of Caraco lake in Nevada, the geography slopes generally up to the west for approximately about five miles. Then it suddenly drops off sheer. This is probably due to a fault running apparently along a northwest-southeast course.

"Caraco lake is not marked on any map, but it lies approximately about fifty miles southwest of Battle Mountain, Nevada."

Few of us realize how little is actually known about our planet. Even if we make a habit of staring at the cuts made in hillsides for the building of roads, we begin to see the contorted rocks from folding and breaking on this unstable planet of ours. And looking at them makes the most boring trip more interesting.

We will not be able to go into all the sinkings in the Atlantic. Where is the Venta Silurium where Plutarch says that the ancient Irish emperor, Kronos (or Saturn?), was imprisoned after he lost the battle of the Tyrrhenian sea? Was it a land of which only the Scillies remain today?

The old records say that over a thousand people were drowned near Cork, Ireland in 830 A.D. What subsidence caused this tidal wave? Was it the Kassides supposed once to be south and west of Ireland? Or some later island now missing among the Scillies?

The Welsh Triads tell about the disaster of 500 A.D. when nineteen of their largest towns were inundated. Was this due to the sinking of Lyonesse? And this must then be the date of the death of Arthur, whose bones King Henry II removed from Glastonbury to an unknown destination. I would like to place a bet that they would carbon-14 date to 500 A.D. But there are other missing islands in the ancient lists of land which are still to be seen in England. Where is Nurcho or Nutho mentioned in document 1140-1175. Reginald de Dunstanville, Earl of Cornwall, mentions the islands of Rentman and St. Lides. Where are they? And as far as that is concerned, the Phoenicians took the morning star as the symbol of the Hesperides. Where are they?

While we - some of the skeptical among us (though not particularly the geologists or oceanographers) - are wondering whether a great mass of land could sink as a block, take a second glance at the continental shelf stretching from Mexico to beyond Santa Barbara. Furthermore the repeated sinister earthquakes along the very unstable San Andreas since the great 8.4 earthquake of 1964. In April and May 1965 it was

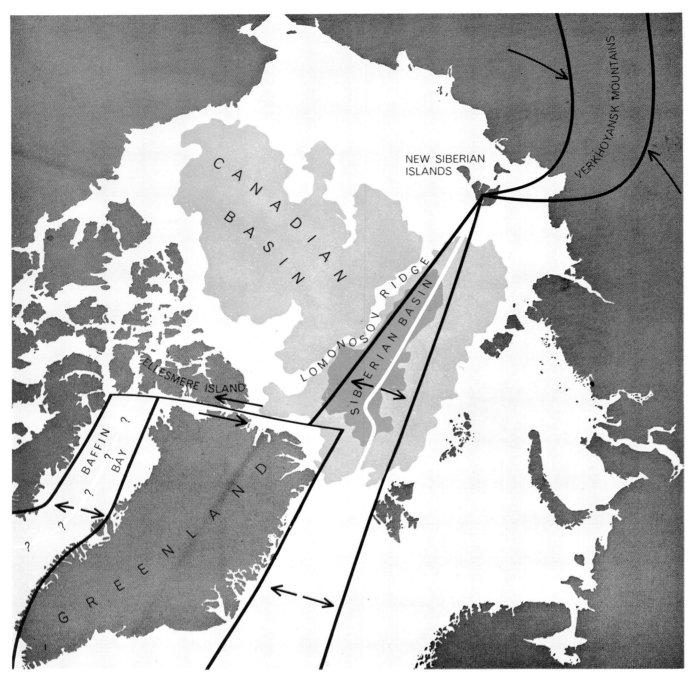

Rifting of supercontinent to form the Atlantic ocean could have produced the Verhoyansk mountains in eastern Siberia. As shown on this map of the Arctic, the rift spread more widely to the south. The opening of the Atlantic ocean and Baffin bay separated Greenland from both North America and Europe. The continents were rotated slightly about a fulcrum near the New Siberian islands. The resulting compression and uplift would create a mountain range. Opposing arrows mark the Wegener fault. (Courtesy Dr. J. Tuzo Wilson)

unusually busy. It struck Seattle with a seven-point jolt and hit South America with the same. This cut over to the Pacific, suggesting a possible crack off here, as I mentioned before. Following this it struck at El Salvador, which is directly on the large rift that the errant ruler showed me, as it pointed across the Atlantic to the Gates of Hercules. Again this is the crossroads of two rifts – the trans-Atlantic and the San Andreas. Then as if to remind everyone that

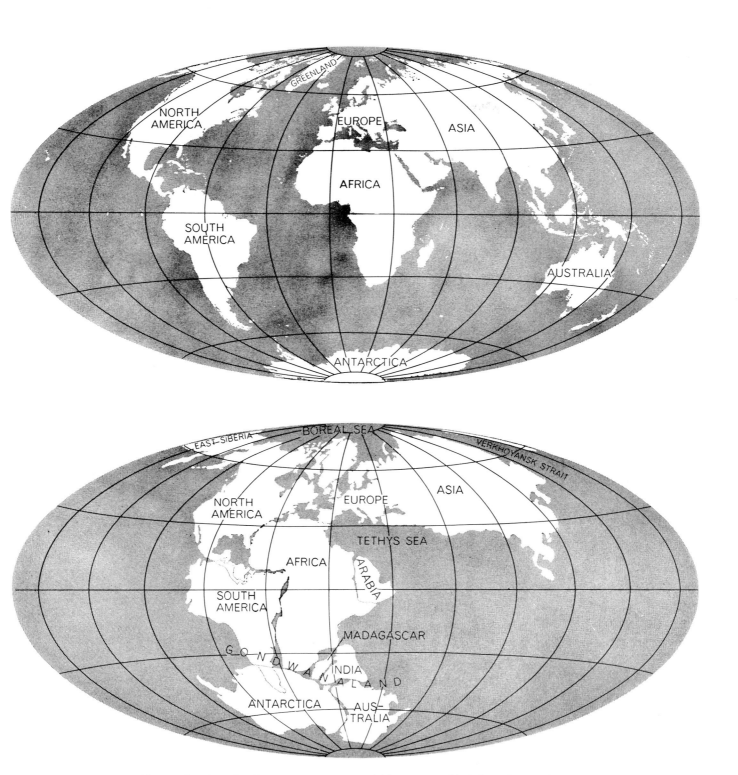

Wegener's idea. Single supercontinent would have resembled that depicted in lower map. A present-day map appears at top. Distortion is due to projection employed. Wegener's concept left no sunken land. (Courtesy Dr. J. Tuvo Wilson)

Anchorage was still in the running, it struck there again, but this time more mildly.

Perhaps it is just as well that our continents are moving somewhere. Apparently there is a region of perfect isostatic balance for a continental fragment. It is the depth at which most of the guyots are to be found. But when the island reaches this state of eternal tranquility, the sea rolls about a mile above its top, and that is definitely too deep for the abode of man.

Chapter 58

The Great Destruction

"You say that the great mountain you call Hood, but for which we have another name, is no longer in the land of the living (extinct), as I heard you say yesterday? I believe you are wrong. I can take you to a place where, by putting your ear to the earth, you will hear the growls. Unless you know now all the reasons why the great fire dragon crawled from his caves in the days before our yesterdays, you should not say that in the days after our tomorrows he will never come again."

From the statement of a Chinook guide to a group of geologists.

The land was warm and fruitful. It was world-famous for its terraced hillsides, which brought the fruits of the tropics and the staples of every clime to the tables of its aristocrats. Slaves carried trays laden with foods to the banquet tables which were always covered with fine linen and were decorated with flowers. There witty men and clever women discussed politics and travel, as they have all down through the ages.

In other locations men toiled in the staircase farms which were kept fertilized and drained by men who could give us lessons on the art and how best to rotate crops. They had all of the foods which we have today, and innumerable others of which we have but the description or the name.

In other locations the metal smiths worked at their trades, making every type of utensil which we believe is modern for the kitchen, with perhaps the exception of those which use electricity. Their jewelry is usually better than ours and they well understood plating.

On the quays the hard fisted traders watched the loading and unloading of their ships. Under the watchful eyes of the navy they carried on their work. In the private pools apparently dolphins were kept as pets to ride about women and children. Higher on the forested slopes of the mountains, there were leafy villages with quiet mansions, each with its own vista beyond the porch. Possibly various types of perfumed trees, such as the cedar or fruit trees, were grown close to the porches as an added brace to the timbers as was done in the cities of Chan Chan many centuries later.

Between some of the mountains were channels of water, for the land was not as it had been once when the only low land was the swamps to the west where the dragon lived. Now all the dragons were drowned, many centuries ago, and the smaller land was still almost like an earthly paradise. Great swinging bridges, not unlike those which swung from mountain to mountain later in Peru, connected the highways from island to island and from the main island to the beautiful Madierian peninsula running from what was Erythea, but now is lost (though the name Gadierez, a city, is today remembered in a later city called Cadiz.) Between the land of Erythea and the land we now know as the Atlas range, the blue Mediterranean river flowed over high cliffs and fell in foaming torrents to the wild stream known always as the river of death. There were no Pillars of Hercules in those days, and if you explore beneath the sea you will find the tremendous gradient of these falls and the manner in which they turned left between the two peninsulas through the glens of the swinging bridges to the "sea of beauty where the ships are." It is said that Votan had a giant wall built to contain this river so that it would not eat away the magnificent beauty of the main island. Today the men who have mapped the bottom of the sea are puzzled by what would appear to be, on their mapping boards, a tremendous curving man-made wall. Some maps have shown it in a disguised sort of manner even though the red-faced cartographers realize that such things simply could not be.

However these were the Atlantidae, as some

of the Roman historians called them, and their distant progeny who built with massive stones in Peru had not forgotten how to contain rivers, build step dams and other canals, irrigate their fields and tunnel through mountains. Therefore if the land was bulged up eleven thousand years ago, it is more than likely that they built this wall.

One side of the range, which today we call the Canaries, faced the sea of beauty and the other side faced the Triton sea where stood an island fortress with three peaks above it making the symbol of the master colossus of the seas. Here a series of locks formed a maze sometimes called the labyrinth which kept enemy ships out and allowed only the traders inside. This device had worked so well that over the years the great power it represented had become rather tyrannical. Perhaps from their ancient name, Tyrrhenians, we have the words tyrant, tyranny, tyrannies, tyrannous, tyrannize, and tyrannical? The Triton sea held closed and captive the Mediterranean, with its cities and commerce dependent because of no other outlet to the ocean. Possibly also, after the great destruction, the Tyrrhenians split purposely, sending two groups to the land near the Red sea so that they could continue to rule the Mediterranean - it would have been a very strategic move for them when they had lost the Triton with its entrance through the Canaries to the Atlantic.

The beauty of the cities of the colossus has come down to us through the historical chants and memories of her children, among whom we must all take our seat. The massive retaining walls, bright with colored rock and with orichalcum; the metal covered buildings which shone in the sun; the canals which sped the people from place to place as well as bringing food and clothing; the beauty of the sacred groves where the oak and the cedar stood, one in particular of exceeding age, watered by the fountains of hot and cold water which ran down; and the magnificent parks which were wirenetted as later they were in Tula among the Toltecs and among the Mayans where birds of rare plumage mingled with those of magnificent voices, has come down to us in legend through the ages. Is that why the canary, a long domesticated songster of a lovely golden shade, carries the name of the islands which were once a part of the ancient colossus?

The cities had sewers as had many of their later children's cities. They had tile roofs, stucco, cement and other building materials, but the Atlantidae were the world's greatest masons and when they built they built for the ages. Considering the size of the building blocks in Peru it is easier to leave them than carry away a rock weighing one hundred sixty five tons. They had observatories, and without doubt many other instruments such as the compass, since we see the evidence multiplied a thousand times.

In musical instruments they certainly had the Pan's pipes probably made into organs as they come in Peru. They may have had a type of harp which seems to be on both sides of the Atlantic, and a strange stringed instrument the modern Mexicans are developing. (Mexico has been taking the ancient instruments to be seen in old paintings on the walls of recently excavated buildings and remaking them.) The Atlantidae had flutes, all types of drums and the chorus of singers who answer from mountain to mountain, using natural echoes and filling the whole land with music. Since that time their children among the Ar-zawans seem to have the greatest gift for harmonious sounds.

In the matter of dress, the Atlantidae had three main styles and innovations which were variations of these. Both men and women wore fine linen or cotton robes draped in different ways. The women wore the right shoulder bare, probably a style started by the Amazons with whom it had the functual use of allowing for the rapid reach and use of weapons. With the men this finally became the Roman toga.

The war sheath was longer than that of the Tyrrhenians or the Ar-zawans. It came below the knee where it met the high boot, was often fringed and sometimes gold in color. The weapons most often used were either the spear, the spear thrower (the Amerinds say Votan invented it and called it atl-atl, which simply means that it was known during his dynasty), and the short swords. Later the great slashing sword was used, which was gripped by both hands. On the old Egyptian columns the Atlantidae were pictured with the short swords, one in each hand, fastened by a chain from the top of the sword to the arm band which circled the arm above the elbow.

The helmet was pictured on these columns as being of metal built in cone shape, representing the sacred mountain, with a tuft of white feathers on the top which stood for smoke. It is interesting that this was the helmet worn by Asa Delugio in the crown dance. Was that copied by the Ar-zawans? And why the point forward? Had the mountain already sunk? Will we ever know?

From the Americas we learn from tribe after tribe that their secret weapon was a metal "harder than white man steel" which has been lost. Apparently the flame thrower may at one time been used by both the bird and the serpent, but probably the bird had it first. It was lost with the fall of Constantinople.

The meaning of the trident remains a mystery. During the war games of Rome in which gladiators fought, the men of Gaul were given the net and the trident with which to fight. We seem to have lost the original meaning of both. Unless, as today, they stood for the sea? As weapons they would appear to be quite valueless against the sword.

The shield, on the other hand, was not the circular one of the Ar-zawans. It was the long triangular shield, such as we see today among the Tuaraks. Perhaps at one time it symbolized the pyramid? Could the Ar-zawans have taken their shield, like the bow and arrow, from the bird? And did this come after the conquest of the flood shattered Dravidian empire, or during the time when that empire was actively trading throughout Europe, and also probably with Asia?

To return again to the description of the lost land of the Atlantic, we have a series of high mountains to the north which shielded the gem of the sea from the cold blasts which came from the ice sheets. In Europe, that land was separated by only the river of death. The shelves of Europe, from France through the isles of Scotland and the Baltic, are the most shallow of all continental shelves. France and Ireland were one land to the shores of the famous river, bisected of course by a few rivers of their own. However, with a few good bridges, a man could ride his horse from Ireland to the end of the Madeira peninsula, and then cross the swinging bridges to the heart of the serpent empire, whose nest, the Eddas tell us, "is made of gold." Nor need he start in the hilly Ireland which the sea has left us; he could start in the fertile fields of such lost lands as Tyr-na-n'-oge, perhaps near Ogygia and Meropis? On the way he could pass through the outskirts of Ys, and even the boiling lake in the land of the lions where today the tops of the mountains are the Scillies. The underground heat should also have made of this location a very fertile and pleasant place in which to have a residence.

The end must have been heralded by a storm of volcanism lasting perhaps many years. This would be accompanied by lesser sinkings as the rifts through the center of the old red land and to each side in parallel tears, began periodically to belch forth lip volcanoes, and suffer minor sub-

sidences. Undoubtedly the dark religion of human sacrifice to the "angry fire god" was stepped up, and the bloody rites which took place largely in caverns, were also more numerous.

However the dynasty of Votan, whether he was the founder or a son of a long line of monarchs, began to foresee the end. Undoubtedly his wise men gathered the sailors and traders together for more information. He probably learned that the white hills of the north were melting in the renewed heat of the seas, and viewed the rising sea level with apprehension.

The Atlantidae were not an ignorant people. They undoubtedly had histories which told of other volcanic storms and the floods which followed. He undoubtedly had read of the fate of the dragon land when the monsters were drowned. Perhaps he read the very words that the aged Egyptian priest had spoken to Solon about the stream from the skies like a pestilence which came at long intervals of time and left only the unlettered ones to carry on the race. Perhaps this is why he stepped up his colonization activities. We know that one such expedition was sent out in 11,542 B.C., because the zodiac and Chaldean calendars were synchronized at this date. Perhaps some student of the Americas will please observe and trace back the nearest date to this for the synchronization of the Venus calendar? I realize that it was changed several times, but I leave this puzzling bit of research to someone else.

Thus the great colossus began to plan for the disaster which it sensed was coming. Books, seeds and animals were shipped out. Many colonies were set up in distant lands with new leaders being given the "sign of royalty" and to become "great suns" in turn, going to their new lands and preparing the people for a rise of the sea. These men wore the medallion or "sun necklace" and were crowned with the circlet of feathers, twenty-six in number, to stand for the double thirteen of the Venus calendar.

As can be seen by the dates, these preparations went on for some time. It is said that Votan was busy building a giant pyramid which was supposed to reach the height of the sacred mountain. He never finished. Perhaps he did not realize that the weight of this structure on the already weakened crust networked by mining operations over the centuries was asking too much of crustal balance. The massive pyramid became his funeral pyre.

We have some very ancient eye witness reports of the horror of the great destruction. The language is curiously antique, but the story that they tell and the pictures that they paint are not to be forgotten, once they have been read.

The last horror evidently came up the Atlantic from the south. In the violent shaking of earthquakes the city was crumbled, volcanoes exploded, covering the skies with ash that turned the day into night, while the red beams of the explosions mingled with the static lightning of the tornadoes engendered by the fury of the volcanoes and their red to white hot bombs. The winds of the approaching tornadoes were in many cases the warning, carrying as they did their clouds of ash.

In the land of north Africa, the great Atlas range began to crumple due to the violence of the earthquakes and the final volcanism. Here, too, the late afternoon became night, and over a hundred cities went down as the backbone of the Atlas was broken forever, and the Triton, having lost its retaining wall, swept out over the broken and sinking range, to sea. The Nagar river from that time on became the Niger and ran the other way, emptying through the southern canyon as the mountains from which it had taken its rise were also crumpled by the earthquakes and then turned to mud by the over-rush of the Triton water. (On the undersea maps made by the most recent cartographic drawings, one can see how the Triton went both west and south as the mountain wall which had held it in, crumpled. Of these maps, the best is by far the recent 1964 map put out by the Readers Digest in "The Great World Atlas". The price, considering the magnificence of the work, such as the pictures making the volume a must for scientists doing geological or oceanographical research, is amazingly reasonable.)

Apparently the great tear of the Atlantic had been piling up stresses and strains for millennia. When one point broke, that triggered the other faults which were also at the explosive point, and the result was a chain reaction.

The breaking of the Atlas range, or the sinking of the central land, whichever came first, does not really matter to us today. Together they triggered the trans-Atlantic fault which struck at the mouth of the Mediterranean. The falls were crumpled and the cliff which had held out the sea was broken. (Sometimes these points had been spoken of as "the gates of heaven".)

The first warning in the Mediterranean was a tremendous, black waterspout which heralded the splitting open of the Mediterranean rift running through the middle of that sea. Was Africa starting to move south again? We cannot guess, yet. It will take many years of research and measure-

ment before we know if the pressures engendered by the ice caps of the north are making themselves felt again at the Mediterranean line of the last collision.

The result of this was that the water poured in over the broken cliffs of the Atlantic leaving only the two relics left standing which today we call the Gates of Hercules, and covered the cities in the pleasant Mediterranean valley.

Since these faults are all interconnected, we know now that the Indian must have also been affected by the catastrophe. What happened there we will leave for some other researcher to determine.

That we have any fragments of this disaster coming down to us in writing is indeed a miracle, not only because of the violence of nature, but also because of war and man's own stupidity. It will take much international work in common, and comparison of researching teams, before we know what is happening along "the giant fracture of the world," and where we can expect it to strike next. Scientists can guarantee only one fact: disasters such as this are not all in the past, although at the present moment we seem to be living in a quiet period. It would appear to be, geologically speaking, that the Atlas rift was the first to strike, and the sudden dumping of thousands of tons of water upon the central ridge both triggered the sinking of the central land and the cracking open of the Mediterranean.

The various legends of the great destruction all have a certain pattern in common, as pointed out by Donnelly.

1) The hero is informed by a deity of an impending disaster.

2) He is skeptical, but agrees to build the ship whose proportions are dictated by the deity.

3) He is told to gather provisions, seeds and animals to again populate the Earth.

4) He carries out the orders.

5) His contemporaries make fun of him.

6) The storm begins with a tremendous cloud and waterspout.

7) Various birds are released and the last one comes back with a bit of green.

8) The ship is caught on a mountain peak.

9) The hero disembarks and offers sacrifices.

10) The hero and his wife are carried away to the abode of the gods.

In some of these stories one or another is missing but the pattern is strangely familiar; such as in the story of Berosus.

Berosus took his story from the sacred books of Babylon and introduced it into a history for the Greeks. After writing the deeds of nine antediluvian kings, he came to the time when the land was covered by a flood.

Obartes Elbaratuta being dead, his son Xisuthros (Khasisatra) reigned eighteen sacs. It was under him that the great deluge took place, the history of which is told in the sacred documents as follows:

Cronos (Ea) appeared to him in his sleep. (Note here that the Greek has translated the god's name into Greek and thus made him Cronos) He announced that on the fifteenth of the month of Daisios (the Assyrian month Sivan - shortly before the summer solstice), all men should perish by a flood. He therefore commanded him to take the beginning and ending and middle of whatever was consigned to writing, and to bury it in the city of the sun at Sippara; then to build a vessel and to enter it with his family and dearest friends, to place in this vessel provisions to eat and drink, and to cause animals, birds and quadrupeds to enter it; lastly, to prepare everything for navigation. And when Xisuthros inquired in what direction he should steer his bark, he was answered: "forward to the gods" and enjoined to pray that good might come of it to man.

Xisuthros obeyed and constructed a vessel five stadia long and five broad; he collected all that had been prescribed to him and embarked his wife, his children and his friends.

The deluge having come, and soon going down, Xisuthros loosed some birds. . .

The rest of the story follows the pattern. First the birds returned with muddy feet, but later did not return, and he stopped the vessel. He found that he was on a mountain of the Gordyan range in Armenia. He gave a sacrifice, and when he did not return to the people inside, they came out to look for him. A voice from the skies told them about the buried writings and that he had been carried away to dwell in the midst of the gods. They returned on foot to Babylonia, founding cities and restoring Babylon.

It will be noticed that this differs mainly from the bibical legend by the amount of time that the flood lasted and the amount of rain. Since most of the other tales follow this pattern rather than the bibical one, it seems reasonable to suppose that the Bible, as Donnelly suggests, was written by an inland people who could not conceive of an extensive flood without rain. In other words, volcanism, subsidence and the accompanying tidal wave was unknown to them.

The other Chaldean story, coming down from the Sumerian library of Ashurbanipal, is tremendously fascinating because it shows the volcanic elements of the cracking of the Mediterranean wall and the splitting along the rift under the river which caused the tremendous waterspout. The black cloud of ash which heralded the horror is also described, as undoubtedly the volcanoes, not only of the Pyrenees but also of the Alps, were exploding. This epoch, known as the Gilgamesh, is taken by Donnelly from several of Ashurbanipal's translations, there being missing words where sometimes the translators did not know the meaning of the ancient script, already a dead language in their day. I have found Donnelly's original 1882 translation published by Harper Brothers of New York to be by far the most complete and the most interesting of the present extant translations, although we do not yet know all the meanings for the various gods mentioned, or even for certain the name of the hero.

To be able to read the original Chaldean-Babylonian edition of unknown antiquity from the Sumerian library is in itself as much an adventure as it must have been to the first scientists uncovering the tablets. It certainly goes back to the second millenium B.C., and probably much more. Donnelly has put this story together from three of the books in Ashurbanipal's library and another excavated later from Shurippak. Thus he was almost able to make the fragments come alive.

The story begins by describing the hero, who had been attacked by some kind of disease and decided to go to his ancestor beyond the shades to find a cure. Once in the nether regions he persuaded the man to tell the story of how he survived the flood.

"I will reveal to thee O Ixdhubar, the history of my preservation - and tell to thee the decision of the gods.

"The town of Shurippak, a town which thou knowest is situated on the Euphrates - it was ancient, and in it (men did not honor the gods); I alone (I was) their servant, to the great gods... (The gods took counsel on the appeal of) Anu... (A deluge proposed by) Bel (or Bal, Tyrrhenian fire god - comment mine) (and approved by Nabon, Nergel and) Adar.

"And the god Ea, the immutable lord, repeated this command to me in a dream -- I listened to the decree of fate that he announced and he said to me 'Man of Shurippak, son of Uba, return thou and build a vessel and finish it (quickly)...(By a deluge) I will destroy all substance and life - Cause thou to go up into the vessel 600 cubits shall be the measure of its length - and 60 cubits the amount of its breadth and of its height - (Launch it) thus on the ocean and cover it with a roof". I understood, and I said to Ea, my lord - '(The vessel) that thou hast commanded me to build thus ... I shall do it...young and old (shall laugh at me)'. (Ea opened his mouth and spoke). He said to me his servant. . . (shall be punished) he who has insulted me (for the protection of the gods) is over me ... like to caverns ... I will exercise my judgment on that which is on high and that which is below...Close the vessel...At a given moment that I shall cause thee to know ... enter into it, and draw the door of the ship toward thee. Within it thy grains, thy furniture, thy provisions, thy riches, thy men servants and thy maid servants, and thy young people ... the cattle of the field, and the wild beasts of the plains I will assemble - and that I will send thee shall be kept within the door.' Khasisatra opened his mouth and spoke: he said to Ea, his lord: 'No one has made (such a) ship On the prow I will fix . . .I shall see . . . and the vessel . . . the vessel thou commanded me to build . . . which . . .

"On the fifth day (the two sides of the bark) were raised. In the covering, fourteen in all were its rafters - fourteen all did it count above - I placed its roof and I covered it...I embarked in it on the sixth day. I divided its floors on the seventh. I divided the interior compartments on the eighth. I stopped up the chinks through which the water entered in; I visited the chinks, and added what was wanting - I poured on the exterior three times 3600 measures of asphalt, and three times 3600 measures of asphalt within - Three times 3600 men, porters, brought on their heads the chests of provisions. I kept 3600 chests for the nourishment of my family - and the mariners divided among themselves twice 3600 chests of provisions. - For (provisioning) I had oxen slain; I instituted (rations) for each day - (In anticipation of the need of) drinks, of barrels and of wine - (I collected a quantity) like the waters of a river (of provisions) a quantity like the dust of the Earth - (To arrange them) in the chests I set my hand to ... of the sun ... the vessel was completed - ... strong and ... I had carried above and below the furniture of the ship, (the loading filled two thirds)

"All that I possessed I gathered together; all I possessed of silver I gathered together; all that I possessed of gold I gathered, all that I possessed of the substance of life of every kind I gathered - I made all ascend into the vessel my servants male and female, the cattle of the fields, the wild beasts of the plains and the sons of the people - I made them all ascend.

"Shamash (the sun) made the moment determined and - he announced it in these terms "In the evening I will cause it to rain abundantly from heaven; enter into the vessel and close the door" ... When the evening of that day arrived I was afraid - I entered into the vessel and shut the door - In shutting the vessel, to the pilot of the ship, Puzur Enlil the sailor, I committed the great house with its contents. . .

"I watched the aspect of the approaching cloud and terror possessed me.

"As soon as something of dawn shone in the sky a black cloud from the very foundations of heaven came up. Mu sheri-ina-namari came up. Inside it the god Adad thundered. Ramiman roared in the midst of the darkness of the cloud. Nabu and Sherru (the gods of the underworld of flame, comment mine) marched before. They devastated mountain and plain. Nergel, the powerful, tore out the post of the ship, then he went on dragging chastisement after him. Enurta came down in the advancing cloud and Adar began to overthrow everything which stood before him. The archangels of the abyss were bringing their destruction, agitating the Earth (shaking?) in their furious terror.

"Within the descending cloud the Anunmaki brandished their torches. With their glare they lighted up the land. Then the whirlwinds of Adar swept up to the heavens. Ramiman swelled up to the sky and the Earth became without lustre and was changed into a desert. (The archangels of the abyss?) broke the surface of the Earth like ... every gleam of light was turned to darkness ... the land ... as if every living thing upon the surface of the land ... the terrible (deluge) now came down on men and ascended up to the heavens. Brother no longer saw brother. Men no longer knew each other, In heaven the gods themselves became afraid of the awful waterspout. They sought a refuge. They mounted up to the heaven of Anu. The (water) attacked people like a battle. Men could not be known or recognized. All day long the flood came. Swiftly it mounted up to the mountains."

From here the story goes to the gods who "cowered against the wall like a dog, and the Lady Ishtar cried out "like a woman in travail" saying:

"How could I command evil among the company of the gods?

Command battle for the destruction of my people?

Did I of myself bring forth my people

That they might fill the sea like little fishes?"

(Is this one of the origins of the weeping woman legend? Comment mine.) The story continues:

"Six days and as many nights passed; the wind, the waterspout and the diluvian rain were in all in their strength. At the approach of the seventh day the diluvian rain grew weaker, the terrible waterspout which had assailed after the fashion of an earthquake - grew calm, the sea inclined to dry up, and the wind and waterspout came to an end. I looked at the sea, attentively observing - the whole of humanity had turned to mud. Like unto seaweed the corpses floated. I opened the window and the light smote my face. I was seized with sadness. I sat down and wept and my tears ran over my face.

"I looked at the regions bounding the sea; toward the twelve points of the horizon; not any continent. The vessel was borne above the land of Nizir - the mountain of Nizir arrested the vessel, and did not permit it to pass over. A day and a second day the mountain of Nizir arrested the vessel ... the fifth and sixth day the mountain of Nizir arrested the vessel and did not permit it to pass over. At the approach of the seventh day, I went out and loosed a dove. The dove went and turned and found no place to light so came back. I sent out and loosed a swallow. The swallow went out turned and came back. I sent out and loosed a raven. The raven went out and saw the corpses in the waters. It ate, rested, turned and came not back.

"I then sent out what was in the vessel to the four winds and I offered a sacrifice. I raised the pile of my burnt offerings on the peak of the mountain; seven by seven I disposed the measured vases, and beneath I spread rushes, cedar and juniper wood. The gods were seized with the desire of it and assembled like flies above the master of the sacrifice. The great goddess in approaching, raised the great zones that Anu has made for their glory. These gods, luminous crystal before me, I will never leave them. Let the gods come to my sacrificial pile! - but never let Bel come to my sacrificial pile! For he did not master himself and he has made the waterspout for the deluge, and he has numbered my men for his pit."

There follows here a discourse between Bel, who wishes to make a new deluge, and Ea, leader of the gods telling Bel to use other means to reduce the number of people, but never another deluge. Bel is then appeased and he takes the hero and his wife by the hand. He tells the group still in the vessel that Khasisatra and his wife were honored by being taken away to live like gods at "the mouth of the four rivers".

I may be mistaken, but it seems to me that the story up to the point where Khasisatra begins his eye witness story, to the point where he lets out the birds, is a genuine diary of what happened, but the beginning and the end are later additions to explain the possession of the diary. Could it be that Khasisatra lost his life in an accident which would be hard to explain to his company, or was murdered for his gold and power of command? It could be that the murderer then married his daughter thus ensuring himself to the crown? The fact that the gods carried the hero away would be to these superstitious people far more acceptable than any other ending. In fact this could even be the start of Bel's power in the Mediterranean, in which case the suspicion should fall upon the sailer pilot, who no doubt was a Tyrrhenian and a follower of Bel. But no matter how the book came into our hands from the distant past, its eye witness picture is priceless.

The end of this story of the Gilgamish epoch is that the entourage gained the ground in safety, walked back to the land of Babylonia, dug out the old books, rebuilt Babylon and founded other cities as a new era was begun.

The story of the flood of Deucalion is only a poor rewriting of the Gilgamish or a changing of it so that Greek names and places could be used. Deucalion Sysythes, according to Lucian in De Dea, Syria, 170 B.C., told the legend which he himself heard from the Arameans as narrated at the sanctuary of Hierapolis.

"I have heard the account given by the Greeks themselves of Deucalion, the myth runs thus: The actual race of men is not the first, for there was a previous race, all the members of which perished. We being of the second race descended from Deucalion, and multiplied in the course of time. As to the former men, they are said to have been full of insolence and pride, committing many crimes, disregarding their oath, neglecting the rights of hospitality, unsparing to supplicants, accordingly, they were punished by an immense disaster. All of a sudden enormous volumes of water issued from the Earth, and rains of extraordinary abundance began to fall; the rivers all left their beds, and the sea overflowed its shores; thus the whole Earth was covered with water and all men perished. Deucalion alone, because of his virtue and piety, was preserved alive to give birth to a new race.

"This is how he was saved. He placed himself, his children and his wives in a great coffer that he had in which pigs, horses, lions, serpents, and all other terrestrial animals came to seek refuge. He received them all and while they were in the coffer, Zeus inspired them with reciprocal amity which prevented them from devouring one another. In this manner they floated as long as the waters remained in force. Such is the account of the Greeks of Deucalion.

"But to this, which they equally tell, the people of Hierapolis add a marvelous narrative. That in their country a great chasm opened into which all the waters of the deluge poured. Then Deucalion raised an altar and dedicated a temple to Hera close to this very chasm. I have seen it. It is very narrow and situated under the temple. Whether it was once large, I do not know, but I have seen it and it is quite small. In memory of the event the following rite is accomplished. Twice a year, sea water is brought into the temple. This is not only done by the priests, but by numerous pilgrims come from the whole of Syria and Arabia, and even from beyond the Euphrates, bringing water. It is poured out in the temple and goes into the cleft which, narrow as it is, swallows a considerable quantity. This is said to be in virtue of a religious law instituted by Deucalion to preserve the memory of the catastrophe and from the benefits he received from the gods. Such is the ancient tradition of the temple at the north gate of which there stood two great columns each about three hundred and sixty feet high, and that once a year a man climbed to the top and sat there for seven days ... to signify how men had ascended to the tops of mountains to escape from the water."

Could these have been the famous Siridiac columns upon which pre-diluvial history is said to have been inscribed, asks Donnelly?

To the present writer certain elements stand out in this tale. Deucalion took horses and thus was an Ar-zawan, and this was underscored by the fact that he had a plurality of wives - thus from a patriarchal culture. Was this rewritten from the ancient Sumerian? It would seem so to me; although there might have been a second deluge in the third millennium B.C. The masses of various peoples who came into the Mediterranean during the second millennium suggests a great disaster in their homeland. The Hyksos kings, who heralded the Semitic invasions, came early in the second, as apparently did the Hittites. Was this the deluge and seismic disaster along the old Mediterranean rift which ended the glorious history of Crete with its fleets of ocean-going ships? Again the histories of Sumer and Crete will help our understanding of these events immensely.

India affords us some stories apparently from the latter deluge, for we have the tale that the giant (Titans?), Hayagriva the Strong, steals the Vedas (tales of antiquity), a demon of the race of Daityas (?) who are always warring against the gods and destroying their works. In these tales a fish is put into a dish and constantly outgrows it until finally it predicts the deluge and tells the man who has attended it to make a chest and then when the storm is at its worst to fasten the chest by the great serpent to its horns and he will be saved. Or could this be the tale of the coming of the Aryan speaking invaders? In this case the tale would be much later. At any rate it contributes but little compared to the amazing Gilgamish. Perhaps the most significant lines are when the fish speaks in the height of the storm saying: "Thou hast rightly spoken and hast known me. In a short time the Earth with its mountains groves and forests shall be sunken in the waters."

The difference mainly between the tales of the Mediterranean and Asia are in the fact that whereas in the former the deluge is brought in punishment, in the far east it is merely the ending of one age or era of Earth history and the start of another. With our scientific outlook today we cannot but help realize that Asia was probably closer to the truth.

China brings a tremendous light to bear on the study of the deluge. Not that they had an actual contact like the Gilgamish, but that two dates are given. The early history of China indicates a contact with the Fu-Hi, who are regarded as a race of civilizers. They were first seen on the tops of mountains, introduced cattle and taught the people writing. Were they invaders from the Dravidian empire? Or did the Chinese invade as wild tribes and thus contact their civilizers? The first emperor of the Fu-Hi gained his throne in 2852 B.C. His successor, Shin-nung, introduced agriculture and medical science. His reign is a long one and must be recognized as a dynasty, during which time these sciences progressed, or were introduced. The next emperor or dynasty, Hwang-ti, introduced weapons, wagons, ships, musical instruments. Could it be that they contacted their first Arzawans at this time? It is interesting that the Chinese war dog and temple guardian, the chow-chow - ancient name Fu-cah-oh or Fu-cato, "lion dog", is to be observed on some of the monuments of the Hittites. The Chinese themselves say he is older than the flood.

As Donnelly points out so well, these supposed Chinese inventions are from other nations and have been ages in the flux of development. Therefore this means contact.

The wagon would signify that the Chinese contacted the Ar-zawans, though not necessarily in the Mediterranean. Some Chinese legends say that before the flood they lived in or near the Mediterranean, and in this case the contact may have been ancient Sumer (although they certainly did not inherit the Sumerian nose). Other legends say that the first tribes of China came in from the northwest. Possibly they brought both the chow and the wagons from this direction? Winchell, in his book "The Pre-Adamites" places them as near Lake Balkat, which should give them Tyrrhenian connections, as the name signifies Bal (fire god) and kat the ancient name for lion even in the Americas - as note Tez-cat-li-poca, Popo-cat-i-petl, etc. (The cat family, lion, tiger and others were very anciently held in reverence - possibly first by the Sumerians. The domestic cat, which is not found wild, stems from Egypt historically. This would connect the interest in cats and cat-like groups with the Tyrrhenians or possibly Atlantis.) Lake Balkat lies a short distance east of the Caspian.

The third successor of Fu-Hi, named Ti-Ku, established schools, and was the first to practice polygamy. (Was this the first Ar-zawan contact?) In 2357 B.C. his son Yau ascended the throne, and it is from his reign that the regular historical records began. A great flood occurred in his reign and has been considered simultaneous with the bibical deluge. The Chinese attribute to him great foresight in being able successfully to keep the waters out of China.

However, there is little doubt that the Chinese themselves do not consider this the greatest deluge. They look upon themselves as connected with a people destroyed by water in a tremendous convulsion. This separated the higher and the lower ages of mankind at about the time when Fu-Hi and his people appeared on the mountains. This connects strangely with the Sumerian legends that the first great civilizer, Oannes, went about gathering the lost and terrified fragments of mankind. The history of the destruction of the tribes who had been their ancestors recalls the Gilgamish epoch.

"The pillars of heaven were broken. The Earth shook to the very foundations. In the north, the heavens were lowered. The sun, moon and stars changed their motions, the Earth fell to pieces. Then the waters enclosed within its bosom burst forth with violence and overflowed it. Man having rebelled against heaven, the system of the universe was totally dis-ordered. The sun was eclipsed. The planets altered their courses and the grand harmony of nature was shattered."

This could certainly refer to the emptying of the Triton sea. The sun, stars, planets, etc., could either mean that the ancient astronomers and their calendars were gone, or it could even mean a shift in the tilt of the Earth. The pillars of heaven could mean the wall of the Mediterranean valley, or the submergence of the Atlas range. The lowering of the heavens toward the north must have been the extremely rapid melting of the ice sheet due to lava in the rifts. Altogether the picture here is one of a seismic convulsion.

M. Terrien de la Couperie, of the Asiatic Society of Paris (see Squier), has this to say: "The Chinese language is related to the Chaldean. Both the Chinese characters and the cuneiform alphabet are degenerate descendants of an original hieroglyphical alphabet." Since the ancestors of the Chinese who brought their culture to China date far behind the second and third millennium B.C. when other groups were moving, in particular, the inflectional-speaking languages, this is a most interesting development. It might point the origin of such discoveries as gun powder, for example, as only one of a long list of cultural traits and their origin.

The mention here of the "three worlds" is significant when we consider one of the ancient Vedas of India. The disguised god Vishnu replies to the question of Manu as to why he had chosen to come as a fish, by saying: "On the seventh day after this, the three worlds shall sink below the ocean of the dissolution." With the trident in the hands of the Hindu gods it becomes obvious that the suggestion of Donnelly that the trident had to do with the Atlantic and the nations surrounding that body of water is not correct. Apparently the trident stood for the three worlds of water - the Indian, the Mediterranean and the Atlantic. Thus the seismic disaster which overtook the kingdoms of the Atlantic and the Mediterranean must have also caused another disturbance in the Indian.

In the Americas, Brasseur de Bourbourg translated from the Aztec language Chimpalpopoca codex, the following:

"Now the water was tranquil for forty years, plus twelve, and men lived for the third and fourth times. When the sun of Nahui-atl came, there had passed away four hundred years, plus two ages, plus seventy-six years. Then all mankind was lost and drowned, and found themselves changed into fish. The sky came nearer the water and in a single day all was lost. That day was Nahui-xochitl (four flowers) which destroyed our flesh. The year was eexcalli (one house) and the day Nahui-atl, the mountains, sank into the water."

Following this is the Aztec legend of the flood in details which much resembles the other flood patterns. I have a suspicion that the latter part of this legend is influenced by the instructions of the white prophet Kate Zahl who so often taught from the Bible.

The Popul Vuh, on the other hand, sounds much more genuine:

"Then the waters were agitated by the will of the heart of heaven, Hurukan (storm god), and a great inundation came upon the heads of these creatures ... They were engulfed and a resinous thickness descended from the heavens. The face of the Earth was obscured. A heavy darkening rain commenced by day and by night ... There was heard a terrible noise above their heads as if produced by fire. Then men were seen running - pushing one another, filled with despair. They wished to climb upon their houses, but the houses tumbled down. They wished to climb the trees, but the trees shook them off. They wished to enter into the sacred grottos, but the grottos closed before them. Water and fire contributed to the universal ruin at the time of the last great cataclysm which preceded the fourth age."

Again we see the fury of the seismic convulsion. (The Popul Vuh is the sacred book of the Mayas, which happened to escape the fire of the Spanish conquerors.)

From the Norse Eddas we see some beautifully etched pictures of this time of horror among the ancient chants which have been so heavily censored by the early monks. El, in the Tyrrhenian speech, must have meant light, as "Il" does in the Americas - particularly in South America where it also means "sun". In our own tongue we have some echoes in illustrious, illuminate, illustrate, etc., and when used as a prefix, it then has a negative meaning such as ill will, ill timed, ill tempered etc. Hel was the Greek word for the sun, and so today we have heliocentric (to be measured from the sun's center), helix, the spirals above Greek columns, helioscope (a modern device to look at the sun), heliograph (a modern device for signalling by means of movable mirrors catching the light of the sun), Helios, the Greek name for the sun to be identified with the Roman Sol. The Greeks called themselves Hellenes meaning "children of the sun". In the most ancient myths there was a city called Hel, "the city of light". From the Norse we catch a picture of its end and why

the name became identified with horror.

> "Then trembles Yggdrasil's ash yet
> Standing, and the Jotan Loki is
> Loosed.
> The shadows groan on the ways of
> Hel until the fires of Surt have
> Consumed the tree.
> Hyrm steers from the east, the
> Waters rise, the mundane snake
> Is coiled in Jotan rage,
> The worm beats the water and the
> Eagle screams, the pale-of-beak
> Tears carcasses.
> Naglfar is loosed. Surt from the
> South comes with his flickering
> Flames
> And shines from his sword the
> Valgod's sun! The stony hills are
> Dashed together!
> Men tread the paths of Hel - the
> Heavens are cloven! The giant-
> Esses totter! The sun darkens!
> Earth into the ocean sinks and fall
> From heaven the bright stars!
> Flames's breath assails the All-
> Nourishing!
> Towering fire plays against heaven
> Itself..."
> From the Edda, the Sybil's vision.

From Egypt we have no story of the deluge, but the civilizers of lower Egypt were not in the delta at this time evidently. In upper Egypt on the hills are huge pyramids, or rather were, which had their sides completely covered with ancient hieroglyphic writing. Was this the writing which Thoth was supposed to have copied in order to have it rewritten upon the columns of the temples in the delta - such temples as that of Volcan - the ancient emperor of the old red land at the time of the destruction, from whose name we get our modern word volcano?

Again we return to the Americas for another ancient book - the Chilam Balam. This book was written down by memory from the chants of the Balam priesthood of the fire god, after the original had been thrown into the flames. Simply by using the Spanish alphabet, he was able to conceal it, and it was tossed aside therefore by the destroyers.

One cannot actually blame these Spaniards when one remembers how casually every student of the antiquity of the Americas begins his studies. These strange Amerinds with the painted faces and odd costumes, especially when met in

Original painting by Rigne Boone, Zuni Pueblo Indian, conveying the following legend: "With the candles of its volcanoes beginning to blaze, the land shivers like the wings of a bird, and sinks below the waves."

war in the passion of trying to save their land and way of life, appear to be the wildest of savages, but as many a scholar has said, among them Dr. Sargent, explorer and scholar:"After twenty-five years spent entirely in probing the past of the Americas, I find that undoubtedly I know less about it today than I thought I did when I started."

They are not like the Egyptians, per se, for their memories go back behind Egypt to that vast colossus of the seas which Dr. Wissler glimpsed when he likened the various American tribes to fragments of a titanic wreck scattered higgeldy-piggedly along the shores of these continents thousands upon thousands of years ago.

When one studies the cultures of the Americas there is one tragic fact that is impressed upon your mind - the continual degeneration of knowledge. Yet it is not confined to the Americas, as I once thought it was, for during the research for this book I also discovered the same is

true of the other side of the Atlantic. We come back to the oldest civilization of the Americas in complete amazement, for there is nothing in Europe or the Mediterranean to compare to its bare ruins - for example the massive stones which have been lifted and fitted like diamonds one into the other and placed on top of mountains in one of Earth's highest ranges. But the "diamonds" are granite rocks, some weighing more than one hundred sixty tons each! There is no terracing in the world that can compare to the manner in which these farms were terraced down the mountains. The manner in which the water is conducted down in conduits from the Pleistocene glaciers, and not the modern ones, tells their age. The fact that Tiahuanaco, in Peru, supported a magnificent city at one time, where today the height of the land precludes any but a few sheep and half-starving peasants, also tells of hoary antiquity! What has happened to the human race that we

THE CALENDAR STONE

One of the most famous archaeological pieces in the world. It shows a fantastic knowledge of astronomy. It weighs 57,000 pounds and is 12 feet in diameter. The glyph at the top is the sacred maguey plant, surrounded by the thirteen circles which are star cycles of the Venus calendar. This is the "date of warning" given by the Prophet (He Walked The Americas, Amherst Press, Amherst, Wisconsin, 54406). The date is 1479. Add 13 to 1479 and you get 1492 when Columbus arrived. Add 26 (two 13s) to 1492 and you get 1518, a few months from Cortez' arrival in Mexico. Add 3 (for the trident) and you get 1521, the date of the surrender of Tenochtitlan to the Spanish. Add 52 to the date of warning and the cycle of destruction is complete - Mexico is under the heel of the Spanish boot! Sedillio laughed at the idea the calendar stone was Aztec.

have lost so much? And so long ago?

Only in the Americas does Votan, Odin, Woden, Volcan step from mythology into prehistory. Only in the Americas can we understand his terrible task when he sent his fleets away forever. Only in the Americas can we hear his words spoken to us all. Before I come to that last speech of his, I must quote from the Chilam Balam, the book which I promised to bring to Asa Delugio (the words of course), but was unable to comply before his death and thus lost out on all of the last speech of the emperor. Did he take it with him to the grave? I hope not.

When I saw his eyes widen when I started to quote the Chilam Balam, I realized its antiquity for it was he who told me that Ah-Musem-Cab meant "secret red of the earth". Then it was also that I realized that this book must have come down through the Quiches from Votan III's capital, Xibalba, and its legendary libraries. Knowing the love of the Amerind mind for hidden meanings, one wishes that the word of the Chilam Balam could have been more clear, but on second thought there is gratitude to the fates which spared it intact, untouched by the censoring hand which one feels so heavily in the Eddas. Again there is only gratitude for the fates which have spared it, like the Gilgamish, from the vandals of the ages, so that beyond the pages of all known history come the ancient words:

"Each of the tribes is talking in his own tongue and thus they have lost touch and understanding one with another. Not every truth written herein is evident, but the time shall come when all will be explained.

During the eleventh Ahau Catoun, Ah-Musem-Cab crawled out of the underworld in order to close the eyes of the thirteen gods. His name was not known. Only his sisters and his children whispered it among themselves, but they were not allowed to look upon his face. These things occurred when the Earth was to awaken to a new

STONE OF TIZOC

Aztec sacrificial stone, showing some calendar figures. Made of basalt, weighing
several tons. Found in the main temple, site of the Cathedral in Mexico city today
At the dedication of the temple, 70,000 captives were slaughtered.

age, but then no one knew what was to come.

"The thirteen gods were seized by the nine
gods. A fiery rain fell as ashes covered the
heavens and trees trembled, crashing to the
ground. And Ah-Musem-Cab shook himself, and
the rocks and trees were butted against one
another.

"And the thirteen gods were seized and their
heads were cut off, their faces were slapped and
their eyes were closed.

"Then was the great dragon who wears the
quetzal plumes ravished from the heavens, together with the rattles from its tail and its green
golden feathers.

"And the one who is eternal, covered the
thirteen gods, and bound everything together and
ascended into the thirteenth heaven. And bits of
their skin and pieces of their bones fell here and
there upon the Earth, but their heart was hidden
because the thirteen gods had not wished to leave
their children.

"Then came the fury of Ah-Musem-Cab.
Fiery arrows struck orphans, and the aged ones,
widows and little children who wished to live, but
had not the strength for life.

"And they ran to the shore where the waves
of the sea buried them in the sand. Then split
open giant cracks. Temples and other buildings
fell upon the running ones, and finally in one
great curving emerald mantle bringing its watery
blow, curled back and came the ocean.

"And when the great serpent had been ravished, the sky fell down with steam and fire,
and the dry land sank down into the engulfing
waters. The four gods - the four Bacabs who had
for so many ages held up the universe - had
fallen.

"Those who escaped came to this new land.
The men of the north came first and then the
men of the south. And the feet of the southerners
were to be heard throughout the new land."

At what age does one stop learning? I would

not know, for I have just learned something new. I remember that Asa Delugio said: "This I know to be true, but I do not know the meaning. Please tell me the meaning - first there were four; then eight more were added and then there were twelve." I have remembered it these thirty some odd years and with the help of Herodotus I learned that the eight gods were earlier than the twelve gods. Undoubtedly two calendars were the reason for the numbers. I had finally learned that the dragon was the earliest civilization and that the serpent probably followed at the death of the monsters during the first flood. I had always thought of the Chilam Balam as probably a book written or dictated by Votan III of the end of the "eight gods" in the great destruction. I copied the Chilam Balam just now from old yellow notes which I had meant to send to Asa Delugio. I copied without thinking until I came to the line "the four gods - the four Bacabs who had for so many ages held up the universe - had fallen." That struck me cold.

The four who were the first! Did Asa Delugio recognize the antiquity of this chant, and this was his way of telling me that this book was from the old red land itself? That this was the eye witness story of the first destruction? I am still gasping - but I pass on the probability.

But we were discussing the great destruction, not the first, nor the last, which China tells us happened in 2357 B.C. or a few hundred years before the Tyrrhenians as well as the Semitic and Aryan speakers began moving into the Mediterranean.

The great destruction is geologically known as the end of the Pleistocene period. There may have been a later recurrence of ice, but with the end of the great withdrawal of eleven thousand years ago, the saber tooth cat, the mastodon, the dire wolf, the great ground sloth, the giant cave bear, the antique bison (Tayloris), the giant condor and innumerable other species died off. The caves at the top of the Atlas mountains attest to the manner in which the bones of the creatures who took shelter there were hurled about by the fury of the waters. The thousands of mammoths who died in Alaska with food still in their stomachs undigested, and then were quick frozen by the icy waves, attest to the terror of the flood. This was the great destruction, and undoubtedly it was also the time when the one-hundred-mile-wide strip of the California coastline was down faulted into the sea with its villages and cemeteries, as well as its planked ships. A world wide disaster such as this could only be caused by the unexpected breaking along

the great world crack and the dumping of the Atlas with its water load of the Triton against the unstable central land and what was left of the Mediterranean wall. Once these two roots were broken, the rifts then went into a chain reaction along the crack, and the resultant lava would melt the remaining ice cap immediately, thus adding to the horror.

We do not have many other bits of these descriptions. But from the Norse comes, in "Song of the Sun", these words. The Amerinds immediately see it as a tribute to the emperor, Votan, who was the "great sun" a "living god" of the old red land.

> "The sun I saw with blood red beams beset,
>   Yet mightier now appeared in many ways -
> It seemed to me I saw a shining god, and I
>   Bowed low before the last time in the
>   world of men.
> Ah! Gioll's (the Earth) streams gushed forth
>   with much blood!"

From Sedillio, the war chief of the Yaqui, I have a few lines of Votan's last speech as he had lined up his fleets, his son to go to the east and his grandson to the west. Upon the fleet he had placed the books of the old red land, the seeds for grain, food, drink, trees, animals, and their keep, as well as the seeds for linen and cotton. Now the time had come to bid goodbye. For the last time with his court he climbed the unfinished great pyramid to give them his last instructions. He had already instructed them in the laws, in the keeping of the calendar and told them how they must meet every one hundred four years to check the passage of the double star. (The trouble was that after they had lost contact with each other for long passages of time, their languages changed so much that they could not understand each other anymore so finally the meetings about the stated pyramid were given up.)

He spoke until the great sacred mountain began to explode. Then they turned and fled for their lives. His voice was deep, they say, like thunder, and he had a small miracle which he held, that magnified his voice above the roar.

"As I, the great two horned ram of the mountains, stand before you for the last time in this world, my heart is heavy. There is much I want to say, and so little time for the saying. Yet I must tell you this - as you walk down the future turn not your back upon the beautiful homeland which nurtured your parents and their parents before them for uncounted generations. Be proud of your people and of your history. Re-

The land has gone down, but a promise of renewed life remains for its people. Symbolic painting by Roy Pablito, Zuni Pueblo Indian, referring to the sunken land.

member the greatness of the land you loved, flashing with the beauty of rubies. Try to keep track of your brethren and war not upon them. For this purpose I have instructed you to wear two small white down-feathers from the collar of the bird of lightnings somewhere above your brow. War does naught but tumble down man's greatness and makes of him a ..."

And so the voice was lost forever in the roar of the volcano and the screams of the people who stood in its hail of fire. Sedillio said: "We turned our dragons around and flew - many of them aflame."

From the Norse Eddas we have:

"That day I saw Von's dragons fleeing
Many - with their wings on fire."

So we come at last to the end of our long look through our window into the past. Perhaps we have realized by now why, in a sense, it cannot be finished. Certainly not until the floor of the oceans are as well understood as we are attempting to understand the continents. When that day comes, if it ever does, then it is probable that the history of the continents will have to be rewritten.

However, perhaps this adventure had given us some perspective and, I hope, a realization that our present - the finite - no matter how overwhelming and urgent it may seem with its problems, is in reality only one of the countless trillions of building blocks of what we call infinity. It has for me.

Chapter 59

Our
Fantastically Ancient Alphabet

Donnelly has done a great deal of research on the Mayan alphabet in comparison with the other alphabets of antiquity, showing a similarity. Since the scientists of the time discarded his theory, possibly out of emotional involvement, the recent translations of Donnelly have dropped this line of research. The present writer finds that this is unduly hasty. There are styles in archaeology due to the unusual influence of one mind, or due to the political theories of the time. Therefore in fairness to the scientists of the future who wish to pursue their studies unhampered by the prejudices of the 30's and 40's, I shall attempt to review the work Donnelly has done on our letters.

Tragically enough Landa, the misguided bigot who destroyed all of the Mayan books, is the only authority to whom we can turn for the reading of the ancient monuments. After the burning, he sent this alphabet back to the Vatican, apparently at the request of some of the more liberal thinking minds among the hierarchy. They undoubtedly wanted some means of communicating and teaching the people and looked upon this man's deeds in burning the libraries as shocking. So Landa made up this alphabet. With the help of it and the knowledge of the language, Brasseur de Bourbourg claims to have been able to read some of the ancient books still to be found in that day. In his own words: "The alphabet and signs explained by Landa have been to me a Rosetta stone." Thus does the Abbe feel about the work discovered by him in the Vatican library where it had lain neglected for so many years.

We owe most of our letters directly to the Tyrrhenians, either of Carthage, Etruria or Egypt, but largely to the Phoenicians. However when we start to study the Phoenician and the Egyptian, it becomes evident that the two nations inherited them from the same motherland. As the rather conservative Baldwin said in his "Prehistoric Nations":

"The nation that became mistress of the seas, established communications with every shore, and monopolized the commerce of the known world, must have substituted a phonetic alphabet for the hieroglyphics as it gradually grew to this eminence; while isolated Egypt, less affected by the practical wants and tendencies of commerical enterprise, retained the hieroglyphic system, and carried it to a marvelous height of perfection."

The Egyptians spoke of their hieroglyphics as having been "invented" by one of their gods. To an archaeologist this simply means that some monarch of pre-historical times brought in the writing, probably with his conquering army. Again in the words of Baldwin:

"According to the Phoenicians, the art of writing was invented by Taautus or Taut whom the Egyptians call Thouth or Thoth, otherwise called 'the first Hermes' in which we clearly see that both the Phoenicians and Egyptians referred the invention to a period older than their own separate political existence, and to an older nation from whom both people received it."

Since "the first Hermes" was known to the Romans as the son of Zeus and Maia, the daughter of Atlas, one wonders if Zeus or the first Hermes was the leader who led the people of the delta up the Nile, and also established the other colonies of the Tyrrhenians after the great destruction?

Donnelly says: "It is impossible to believe that such an extraordinary system of sound-signs could have been the invention of any one man or even of any one age. Like all our other acquisitions, it must have been the slow growth and accretion of ages; it must have risen step by step from picture writing, through an intermediate condition, like that of the Chinese where each word was represented by a separate sign. The fact that so old and enlightened a people as the Chinese have never reached a phonetic alphabet, gives some indication of the greatness of the people among whom it was invented, and the lapse of time before they attained to it."

To the Phoenicians, in particular among the Tyrrhenians, we owe the A, B, C, D, E, H, I, K, L, M, N, O, P, Q, S, T and Z. The C took the place of G in the oldest alphabets, and the Romans made the G out of the C by adding the tail sign to it to distinguish their G. The Greeks added the U (upsilon) using the present forms of V and Y indiscriminately for a time. They also added X and changed the Phoenician T to TH (theta).

The Phoenician ⊤ which had the Y sound was changed by the Greeks to its present I (iota). The Phoenician alphabet was largely made up of consonants which made of their writing a sort of shorthand. With their sense of beauty, which extended to language and the written word, this annoyed the classical Greeks and they cast about for a better way of implying sounds, calling attention to the vowels. Thus the Greek alphabet became a much clearer instrument for recording the spoken language. To this list the Romans added the Y and the various European languages, added the double V to represent the W sound.

From the Tyrrhenians we inherited the basis of our alphabet for recording sounds. All other alphabets seem to stem from these, except one - the Mayan. Yet we are told in the Mediterranean legends the Maia was the wife of Pan - one of the earlier eight gods. In the Americas we are told by some tribes that Pahn was the name of "the old red land" and by others a god of that land. Thus the Mayans become a possible division, making their way west, as they claim, under the leadership of Itiwanna or Itzamna with their

libraries of books and the priest who could read them. Was there once a connection between these alphabets? To the present writer it would seem absolutely bigoted, and a display of the worst type of emotional bias for a scientist to close his mind to the possibility, before trying every clue to find out. We are told by the very man who destroyed the libraries that this was a phonetic alphabet which the Mayans were using.

Brasseur de Bourbourg searching for some kind of clue to these books which he had, and many of which unfortunately, have since vanished, went to the Vatican library and unearthed the Landa alphabet where it had lain neglected for many years. To him it may have been the key to the histories, but he did not explain how it became so, or if he did, then the key has been lost, though the original Landa manuscript is still in existence.

Since that time one man - Ignatious Donnelly - has given a great amount of thought to the study of the alphabet of the Mayans, and even though the language was to him a barrier to deciphering the monuments to be found all over Yucatan, surely this research deserves to live on to a day when perhaps, pure intellectual curiosity concerning the past will intrigue some young mind enough to spur him to new fields of adventure.

The urging of the present writer under the editorship of Ray Palmer, in a series of articles called "Mysteries of Science" helped to change young David Kelley while a student at Harvard, from a more uninteresting major to archaeology in which he finally took his doctorate. I lost track of him in the jungles of Yucatan where the Mexicans were helping him in his explorations, and I was told in Mexico university - "We are veree proud of our Doctor Kellee. He may yet untangle the past!" Is there another to keep him company? If so, study this work of Donnelly.

Donnelly begins by noting that Mayan glyphs are largely composed of circles and faces. These, therefore, he regards as merely stylistic. He calls attention to the fact that a busy trading nation such as the Phoenicians, who were more interested in simplicity than art forms, and perhaps those of the ancient colossus, did not have time to make all of the arabesques and fancy turns which seemed to distinguish the glyphs and mark them as probably very ancient ritualistic and religious writing. Therefore the traders would take the symbol which was at the heart of the ancient glyph and with a few strokes make the letter which stood for a sound. They did not have the time to do a work of art - only to make the letter recognizable.

Donnelly remarks that:

H

"The same tendency (of simplification) is to be noted in Landa's alphabet. The original is more elaborate than the variation. In the letter H the original form is . The variation is expressed as .

"Now let us suppose that simplification is to be carried a step farther; we have seen the upper and lower parts of the first form shrink into a smaller and less elaborate shape; let us imagine that the same tendency does away with them altogether; we would then have the letter H of the Maya alphabet represented by the figure .

Now as it takes less time to make a single stroke than a double one, this would become in time . We now turn to the archaic Greek and we find the Mayan letter simplified, namely .

"Now it is known that the Phoenicians wrote from the right to left, and just as we, in writing from left to right, slope our letters to the right, so they slope their letters to the left. Hence the Mayan sign becomes in ancient Phoenician .

In some Phoenician alphabets we find the h made with the double stroke above and below as in the Mayan h. The Egyptian hieroglyphic for h is  while ch is  or  . In time the Greeks carried the work of simplification still further and eliminated the top lines, as we supposed the Atlanteans eliminated the double strokes and they left us our H.

"Now all this may be said to have been coincidence. If it is, then it is remarkable. But let us go a step farther.

M

"We have seen in Landa's alphabet two forms of the letter M. The first is an elaborate glyph, but we also see that the m when combined with o, a, or e becomes . The letter m here certainly becomes the central part of the combination or . Where does that come from?

It is clearly the heart of the central glyph wherein it appears. What does this prove? That the trading empires when they sought to simplify their letters or combine them with others, took from the center of the ornate hieroglyphic figure some characteristic mark with which they represented the whole figure. Now let us apply this rule:

"We have seen in the table of alphabets that in every language from our own day to the time of the Phoenicians, a has been represented by a circle or a circle within a circle. Where did the Phoenicians get it? From the Maya? There are two figures for a in the Maya alphabet.

"Now if we apply the rule which we have seen to exist in the case of the Maya m to these figures, the essential characteristic found in each is the circle ... And that this circle was withdrawn from the glyph, and used alone, as in the case of the m, is proved by the very sign used at the foot of Landa's alphabet which is Landa calls this ma, me, or mo. It is probably the latter, and in it we have the circle detached from the hieroglyph O•

O

"We find the precise Maya O a circle within a circle or a dot within a circle. This is repeated in the Phoenician forms of O thus ⊙ ◉ and by exactly the same forms in the Egyptian hieroglyphics; in the Runic we have the circle within a circle; in one form of the Greek O the dot was placed beside the circle instead of below it as in the Maya O• Q.

"Are these another set of coincidences?

N

"The letter n of the Mayan alphabet is represented by this sign, ᔭ itself probably a simplification of some more ornate form. This is something like our letter S, but unlike our n. But let us examine the pedigree of our n. We find in the Cushite Ethiopian the sign for na is ⟨, in archaic Phoenician it comes still closer to the s shape in ⟨ or in this form ⟨. We have but to curve these angles to approximate it very closely to the Mayan n; in Troy this form was found ⟨. The Samaritan makes it ⟨; the Hebrew is similar to the Phoenician angular type; the Moab Stone inscription gives it ⟨ ⟨.

The later Phoenician simplified their archaic

and made it ⟨. The Archaic Greek form is ⟨; then it passed into ⟨ and the later Greek ⟨ from which we inherit our N. All of these forms seem to be the representation of a serpent." (Note the ancient Tamili and East Indian as well as Tuarak name for serpent is naga. This also is the same for the snake in many American languages. Comment by Author) "We find in the Egyptian hieroglyphic that N was a serpent ⟨. The Pelasgian n was ⟨; the Arcadian ⟨⟨; the Etruscan ⟨.

"Can anything be more significant than to find the serpent the sign for n in Central America and in all these Old World languages?

K

"The Mayan sign for K is (see Landa's alphabet chart). This does not look much like our K, but let us examine it. Following the precedent established us by the Mayans in the letter m, let us see what is the distinguishing feature here. It is clearly the figure of a serpent standing erect with its tail doubled around its middle, forming a circle.

"It has already been remarked by Savolini that this erect serpent is very much like the Egyptian Ur , an erect serpent with an enlarged body - a sacred emblem found in the hair of their deities. We turn again to the valley of the Nile and we find that the hieroglyphic for the letter or sound k was a serpent with a convolution or protuberance in the middle, precisely as in the Maya, thus ⟨.

This was then transformed into the Egyptian letter ⟨. The serpent with the protuberance appears again in one of the Phoenician forms of k, to wit, while in the Punic we have these forms .

"Now suppose a busy people trying to give the sign, instead of drawing a serpent with all its details they would abbreviate it into something like this . Early Ethiopian is

 ; Phoenician . Earlier Greek when writing from right to left is . Later

when writing changed from left to right the Greek became from which we inherit our K.

T

"Turn now to the Mayan sign for T. What is the distinctive mark about this figure? It is the cross composed of two curved lines thus .

It is probable that in the Maya sign the cross is united at the bottom like a figure 8. Here again we turn to the valley of the Nile and we find that the Egyptian hieroglyph was  . In Syriac it was 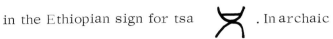 . We even find the curv-

ed lines of the Mayan T which gave it something of the appearance of the figure 8, repeated often in the alphabets of the Mediterranean. The Punic forms are  . A busy people com-

pelled to make this sign every day for a thou-

sand years and generally in a hurry, would soon stop curving the lines and it would become X. But before it had reached even that simplified a form it had crossed the Atlantic and appeared

in the Ethiopian sign for tsa  . In archaic

Phoenician it was  and  . The old-

est Greek was  and X, while the later Greeks

gave it to the Romans as our T. (theta). They also modified this into another letter 

"(which has the TH sound; thus they could write Thebes with five letters while we would have to use six. The same conservation of letters is to be found in some of the Anglo Saxon and Norse runes marking them as very early stems from the Tyrrhenian tree of alphabets. Comment Author). "The Moab Stone gives the T as X which in time came down to us as the cross and finally with the shrinking top protrusion of the stem, as

our T -  .

A

"Take the letter A. In the Maya there are three forms given (see chart). The first looks very much like a foot of a lion or a tiger; the third is plainly a foot or boot. If one were required to give hurriedly a rude outline of either

of these, would he not represent it thus:

and can we not conceive that this could have been in time modified into the Phoenician which

was  ? The hieratic Egyptian A was

 or  ; the early Hebrew was  ;

the Greek was the foot reversed in this manner

A and later it became our A.

Q

"Turn next to the Mayan sign for Q (ku): it is (see chart). Now what is the peculiarity of this hieroglyph? The circle below is not significant, for there are many circular figures in the Mayan alphabet. Clearly, if one was called upon to simplify this, he would retain the two small circles joined side by side at the top, and would indicate the lower circle with a line or a dash. When we turn to the Egyptian Q we find it in this shape .The Phoenician comes near the Mayan form in ; the Moab Stone was , while the Greek was which the Romans graduated into our Q. But a still more striking example is to be found in the other form of the Q. In the Mayan alphabet, their cu is . Now if we apply the Mayan rule to this and discard the outside circle, we have this left, . In time the curved line would be made straight and the figure would assume this form . The next step would be to make the cross on the straight line, thus: . One of the ancient Phoenician forms

is . Can this also be an accident?

C or G

"The letter c or g (for the two probably gave the same sound as in the Phoenician) is given in the Mayan (see 6 on chart). This symbol would be simplified in time into a figure representing the two sides of a triangle (comment - or a mountain--author) with the apex upward, thus . This is exactly the form found by Dr. Schliemann in the ruins of Troy. What is the Phoenician form for g as found on the Moab stone? It is . The Carthaginians gave it a more rounded form, thus: .The Egyptian hieratic was . (Comment - could this mean the mountain was falling into the sea? Author.) In the earlier Greek form the left limb of the figure was shortened thus: ; the later Greeks reversed it and wrote it: : the Romans changed this into and it finally became our C.

P and PP

"In the Mayan alphabet we have one sign for p and another for pp. The first contains a curious figure (see 19 on chart) very much like our r laid on its back. There is apparently no r in the Mayan alphabet and the Roman r grew out of the later Phoenician formed . (Comment: this is to be found in the script of Salton Sea, Calif.) "It would appear that the earliest Phoenician alphabet also did not contain the letter r. But we will find one of the curious forms of the p given thus ⌇ a fair representation of an R lying upon its face (comment - turn it around and you have R - author). Is it not another remarkable coincidence that the p in both Maya and the early Phoenician should both contain this singular sign?

"The form of the pp in the Maya alphabet is (see 20 on chart). If we are asked on the principle already indicated to reduce this to its elements, we would use a figure like this H . In time the tendency would be to shorten one of these perpendicular lines thus H and this we find is very much like the Phoenician ⌁ . The Greek ph is ⏀.

L

"The letter l in the Mayan alphabet is in two forms (see 13 and 14 of chart). If we again apply the rule which we found applies to the letter m - that is, draw from the inside of the hieroglyph some symbol that will briefly indicate the whole letter, we will have one of two forms, either a right angled figure formed thus ☐ or an acute angle formed by joining the two lines which are unconnected, thus, ∨ ; and either of these forms brings us quite close to the letter l of the Old World. We find l on the Moab Stone thus formed 6 . The Archaic Phoenician l was ∨ or ∨ ; the hieratic Egyptian ∿ ; the Greek ∧ ; and the Romans gave us our L.

B

"The Mayan be is shaped (see 4 of chart). Now if we turn to the Egyptian we see that the b is represented by the same crescent like figure which we find in the middle of this hieroglyph, but reversed in direction of the writing, thus) ; while in the early Hebrew we find the same crescent figure as in the Maya, turned in the same direction, but accompanied by a line drawn downward, and to the left, thus, c⌿ ; a similar form is to be found in the Phoenician q ; and this in the earliest Greek is changed into ꝑ ꝑ and in later Greek into our letter B. One of the Etruscan signs is ⌐ while the Pelasgian sign is ⌐) ; the Chaldaic was ⌐ ; the Syriac was ⌐ ; and the Illyrian b was ⌐.

E

"The Maya e is (see 8 on chart). This became in time [symbol] then [symbol]. We see this form on Mayan monuments. (Comment - Donnelly may be wrong about this for it may be a numeral, but possibly had both uses, Author). The dots in time were indicated by strokes, and we reach the hieratic Egyptian form [symbol].

We even find in some of the ancient Phoenician inscriptions the original Maya circles preserved in the letter [symbol]. The old Greek form is [symbol], the later Phoenician [symbol]. When the direction of the writing changed this became E. Dr. Schliemann found a form like this on inscriptions deep in the ruins of Troy [symbol]. This is exactly the form found on the American Monuments." (Comment by author: This is often taken by archaeologists to mean a stool. However, it is sometimes mentioned in Mexico university as representing a throne. Finding the sign among eastern and some western tribes I made many inquiries and found that it was either referred to as a throne, or a crown which had been sunken or ended. That is when I recognized it as the trident up-side-down or in the position of death. This would of course be a status symbol to a man wishing to prove his lineage, and thus could have been a throne.)

I

"The Maya i is (see 10 on chart) and became in time [symbol] and this developed into the simpler form [symbol] and this passed into the Phoenician [symbol]. The Samaritan i was formed thus: [symbol] the Egyptian letter is [symbol].

Gradually in all of these [symbol] the left hand line was dropped, and we have come to the figure used on the stone of Moab: [symbol] or [symbol]. The Hebrews wrote it [symbol]; the Greeks [symbol]; and the Europeans developed our capital and small I, i.

M

"We have seen the symbol for m reduced by the Mayas themselves to this figure [symbol]: if we attempt to write this rapidly, we find it very difficult always to keep the base lines horizontal; naturally we form something like this [symbol]. The distinctive figure within the sign for m in the Maya is [symbol] or [symbol]. We see this repeated in Egyptian hieroglyphics for m [symbol] and [symbol] and [symbol]; in the Chaldaic m is [symbol]. We find one form of the Phoenician where the m is made thus: [symbol].

In the Punic it appears thus: [symbol] and this is not unlike the m on the Stone of Moab [symbol] or the ancient Phoenician forms [symbol] and the old Greek [symbol] from which we get our M.

X

"The x in the Mayan alphabet is a hand pointing downward ⟨glyph⟩ . This, reduced to its elements, would be expressed something like ///\ or ⟨glyph⟩ and this is very much like the x of the archaic Phoenician ⟨glyph⟩ or the Moab Stone ⟨glyph⟩ ; or the later Phoenician which was ⟨glyph⟩ . The archaic Greek was ⟨glyph⟩ ; the Hebrew ⟨glyph⟩ ; and the later Greek ⟨glyph⟩ from which we inherit our x."

(Author's comment: It is interesting to note that our modern x is upon the sleeve of the Mayan hand pointing downward and rather strange that Donnelly did not see this.)

S

"The Mayan alphabet contains no sign for the letter S. There is a symbol immediately above the letter K (see 11 on chart) called ca. ⟨glyph⟩ . It is probable that this symbol stands for the soft sound of c as in our words citron, circle, civil, circus, etc. The Egyptian hieroglyph for s is ⟨glyph⟩ ; the Egyptian letter for s is ⟨glyph⟩ ; the Chaldaic ⟨glyph⟩ and the Illyrian for sc ⟨glyph⟩ . "The Mayan c is somewhat similar to that found in the body of the symbol for k namely ⟨glyph⟩ .

This would seem to be a simplification for ca, but turned downward. If we turn to the Egyptian letters, we find the sound k represented by this figure ⟨glyph⟩ . It is simplified again into ⟨glyph⟩ ."

(Comment by author: Are these ships?)

"The sign for k in the ancient Phoenician on the Moab Stone is ⟨glyph⟩ . If we return to the s sound, we find the resemblance is still more striking to kindred European letters. The Phoenician S is ⟨glyph⟩ , ⟨glyph⟩ and ⟨glyph⟩ . The Hebrew is ⟨glyph⟩ ⟨glyph⟩ . The Samaritan seems to be a copy of the Egyptian ⟨glyph⟩ . The European seems to hark back to the Egyptian."

Donnelly then quotes from the Proceedings of the American Philosophical Society, 1880, a speech which came to his attention just as his book was going to press:

"It is astonishing to notice that while Landa's first b is, according to Palentini, represented by a footprint, and that both the footprint and path in the Mayan dictionary of the language are pronounced Be, the Egyptian sign for be is a human leg.

"Still more surprising is it that the H of Landa's alphabet is a tie of cord, while the Egyptian H is a twisted cord ... But the most striking coincidence of all occurs in the coiled or curved line representing Landa's U; FOR IT IS ABSOLUTELY IDENTICAL WITH THE EGYPTIAN CURLED U. (Caps are his.) The Mayan word for to bend or wind is 'Uus'; but why should the Egyptians, confined as they were to the valley of the Nile, and abhoring as they did, the sea and sailors, write their U exactly like Landa's alphabet U in Central America?

"There is one other remarkable coincidence between Landa's and the Egyptian alphabets; and by the way, the English and Teutonic alphabets have a curious share in it. Landa's D or d (T) is a disc with lines inside the four quarters, the allowed Mexican symbol for a day or 'sun'. So far as sound is concerned, the Egyptian 'cake' ideograph for 1) country and 2) the sun's orbit is essentially the same."

Donnelly then goes through the amazing similarity of eleven of the ancient letters, making note of the fact that if a great many men were completely isolated from each other and given a number of curves, angles etc., and asked to invent an alphabet, the chances of such similarity in all but a very few cases would be overwhelming. And he closes his study on the alphabet with these words:

"If we add to the main eleven (which he has

so carefully analyzed) the b and U referred to in the Procceedings of the American Philosophical Society, we have thirteen letters out of sixteen in the Mayan and Egyptian hieroplyphic and hieratic alphabets which are apparently related to one another. Can any theory of accidental coincidence account for this?

"And it MUST BE REMEMBERED THAT THESE RESEMBLANCES ARE FOUND BETWEEN THE ONLY TWO PHONETIC SYSTEMS IN THE WORLD." (Caps are Donnelly's)

H.

The two Mayan glyphs for H strongly suggest a scroll of writing or two crumbling columns containing a scroll at the top. The variation somewhat resembles a tied manuscript.

We must remember that the most ancient place to put writing was upon the columns of the temples. This is not entirely the idea of Plato. Proclus, the historian, writes of Krantor's voyage to Sais, Egypt, some three hundred years after the death of Solon. There the priests of Neith showed him the temple, and finally the exact columns which still contained the Atlantean texts. The inscriptions were in hieroglyphs.

Doubtless, as time went on and Egypt drifted away from the knowledge brought in by the mysterious people of the delta who were the original bearers of her ancient culture, variations in both the way of writing the glyphs, and the meaning, must have crept in. Today these variations are puzzling to the student and scholar who depends entirely on Egypt as his clue to the past. Donnelly was wise to give Egyptian no more status than the other alphabets which came down from the same enlightened antiquity.

For this reason, it is obvious that the original meaning could have become a portal, doorway or house plan which finally evolved into our H.

Incidentally, the symbol for marimba in the Philippines is quite similar to the Mayan variation for the H; and that brings up an interesting question. How did it happen that the people of the Philippines had the American marimba before the arrival of the Spanish? Of course, they had a few other articles too, such as ocean going ships, brass and bronze cannon, but the end of a book is hardly the place to pose unanswerable questions in the realm of another ocean.

M

Since throughout the Americas our M and similar marks are recognized as mountains, I wish to add this suggestion to what Donnelly has written about the M. In fact, the main Mayan glyph has two mountains on it - one with a circle at the base which could be either a crater or a lake. Also the symbol at the top of the Mayan glyph is the identical symbol in the Chaldaic for the sound of M.

A.

The Mayan glyph for A, when shown to a few Amerind medicine men who recognize some of the ancient symbols, all pronounced it "an unborn animal". This was an intriguing new thought to me, and I am certain it would also have been so to Donnelly. Kelley was certain that the Mayan followed the Egyptian and that our A was not an entire bird but only the bill. Of course, he could have been right, as the original glyph evolved throughout the ages by various people each seeking an easier and quicker way of conveying the sound.

It is possible that if the glyph represents a foetus, it could be that of any two or three animals, perhaps a different one for each sound of A?

Incidentally, why does our small "a" resemble a water monster without a tail, or only a tiny suggestion of a tail such as a very young one might have? And which one of the sounds for A would be the name for the baby Plesiosaurus among the ancients?

X

Among the Amerinds, the symbol X usually stands for earthquake. Actually the hand pointing down, which is undoubtedly the meaning of the Mayan letter, would be an excellent way of symbolizing the sudden movements of the earth, except for one other. That is the Phoenician. The three fast horizontal jolts with the tail then pointing down is still better.

S (Or the soft sound of C)

The Amerinds translate the Mayan glyph for Ca as a ship with five kings or important people, being shipwrecked. It would therefore be symbolical of the loss of five ships or five tribes in a sea disaster.

When we take this and place it against the various other collections of Donnelly or ways of making the S sound, we see a general repetition of the ship. The number of passengers differ, as does the position of the ship, but the idea behind the letter seems to be similar.

The exception seems to be Egypt. However, we must remember again that they were not a sea people after the building of the great pyramids. Therefore we can perhaps excuse them for confusing the symbols of sea faring with what were ancient legends.

N.

The antiquity of this letter just may prove

1.   a 

2.   a

3.   a

4.   b 

5.   b

6.   c

7.   t

8.   e′

9.   h

10.   i

11.   ca

12.   k

13.   l

14.   l

15.   m

16.   n

17.   o

18.   o

19   p

20.   pp

21.   cu

22.   ku

23.   x#

24.   x

25.   u 

26.   u

27.   z

377

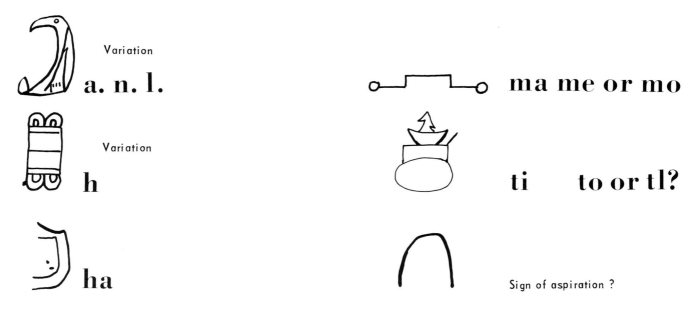

a. n. l.

Variation

h

Variation

ha

ma me or mo

ti   to or tl?

Sign of aspiration ?

After "North America of Antiquity", also
see Baldwin's "Ancient America".

the fantastic age of our alphabet as well as pin-point its original source.

To look upon the Mayan glyph of what looks like our S and find it really means N, is certain-ly very confusing, and one can hardly blame Donnelly for being puzzled. However, the East Indian and Tamali word for "serpent" is naga. Not only that, but this word is repeated over and over again in the rituals of both American con-tinents in certain distantly related tribes. In every case the word naga means snake. Possibly there might not be anything very significant about this fact alone, and it could be written off as either a curious coincidence or the possibility of a very ancient Pacific contact since naga sometimes means snake in India. However, there are a few other interesting facts to consider. Once upon a time before the great destruction, say the Tuaraks (and it is probable that in their libraries they have the historical facts) the Niger river, which today marks the southern limit of the Sahara, taking its rise in some south western relics of the vanished Atlas range and running east and south to empty into the Atlantic, was known as the Nagar. The meaning of that name? Serpent. In the times before the great destruc-tion, the mighty Nagar took its rise in the van-ished Nagar canyon, a part of the lost southern arm of the Atlas range. The Nagar canyon was situated about where the Niger empties today. From this beautiful high point the Nagar wound its way north and westward to empty into the Triton sea.

Also, say the Tuaraks, the dry wadi which is

today one of the greatest fossil rivers on earth to the north of their stronghold, was at one time before the destruction, a giant living river, taking its rise in that part of the Atlas which borders the north of Africa and emptying into the Triton sea. This is apparently about what geologists believe, for the wadi of the ancient river is un-doubtedly Pleistocene in age and ran when the Sahara region was much wetter than today.

What about this river? Its name is Maia or Mia, pronounced My-yah. This is the pronoun-ciation of the people in Yucatan whose alphabet we have been discussing.

But was there ever a tribe of Mayans living on this river?

We cannot answer that. We know that the name was not unknown to pre-Aryan India and to the early Mediterranean where Maya was one of the ancient goddesses who we are told was the daugh-ter of Atlas. By one informer she was the wife of Pan, and by another, the wife of Zeus. This un-doubtedly means that as a power the ancient queen of these people was a colony of Atlas which was at one time allied to Pan and at another, allied to Crete. Without doubt the time of her power was early, for Herodotus tells us that she was one of the eight gods and goddesses who pre-ceded the twelve. The twelve must have come in with Hercules and the Aryan or Ar-Zawan in-vasion.

What do the earliest traditions of the Mayans say? That they came in ships from the east, under a leader called Itsamna who brought not only animals, fruits and vegetables, but also books and the priests skilled in reading them. They say their homeland sank in a seismic disaster, and was covered by the sea. They admit that their eastern blood has been very much diluted by conquests of western warlords, such as the Tutul-Xiu (Too-tul-shoo) a round headed people probably from Asia, and others. However, the alphabet and writing is ancient eastern in origin. Their name comes from the refugees from the sinking "red land" untold millennia ago.

Did the ancestors of the Mayans once live along the Mia river? Some of the present day Mayans, going to college in Mexico university and becoming intrigued with the puzzle of their own antiquity, seem to think so. Even though the Mia is only a dry wadi in the Sahara desert and the twisting path of the Nagar is only a legend.

One of them stopped me, when I had challenged him in 1955 in an anthropology class to produce more facts.

"Has anyone ever told you the ceremonial name for the country where once stood, and possibly still stands underground, the vast Mixtec labyrinth?" (In Oaxaca, Mexico.)

When I shook my head, he answered:

"It is called Liboya, which means "the land of the ancient dead".

"What a fantastic coincidence!"

"I do not believe that it is a coincidence."

I stared at him in unbelief.

"What is fantastic is our ancient alphabet and our writing. It has a few internal evidences of being Pleistocene in age."

"Oh come, now!"

"Study some of the letters and one day you may see what I mean."

"With this viewpoint, have you talked to Dr. Kelley?"

"Unfortunately I have not had the honor. However, I am asking you to think in terms of the ancient world, preferably ante-diluvian, if you ever do study our alphabet. You may discover a few secrets."

He left me in a fog of frustrated confusion, and since this happened on the last day of class, and in answer to my comment on his term paper, the fog remained. That is, it remained until I began to copy the Mayan alphabet for this book. Then suddenly the N loomed out in the light of what I had recently learned, and with the help of this research I found myself looking at that glyph "in terms of the ancient world, preferably ante-diluvian".

The Egyptian glyph for N was a serpent. Therefore unless the Egyptian glyph was too far

IRISH (GAELIC) ALPHABET			
ENGLISH	IRISH	ENGLISH	IRISH
A	ᴀ	N	ᴎ
B	ᴃ	O	ᴏ
C	c	P	ᴩ
D	ᴅ	Q	–
E	e	R	ᴿ
F	ꜰ	S	s
G	ᴳ	T	ᴛ
H	ʜ	U	ᴜ
I	ɪ	V	ᴠ
J	ᴊ	W	–
K	c	X	–
L	ʟ	Y	ʏ
M	ᴍ	Z	–

adrift from the stem, the Mayan glyph should mean serpent. Then suddenly I thought of the ante-diluvian legendary Nagar river!

A civilization which once had lived on the vanished Mia river in Libya would certainly know about the Nagar and associate the name with serpent.

I placed the glyph on the map and saw immediately that it fitted the legendary bed of the Nagar, taking its rise in the twisting lost canyon of the Nagar and flowing north and west to where with another turn it emptied into the vanished Triton sea.

When the full significance of this struck me, the youthful Mayan scholar's words came back: "I am asking you to think in terms of the ancient world . . . you may discover a few secrets..."

Was the legendary Nagar river the ancestral inspiration for our letter K? And if it was, then our alphabet stemmed from the sea and the land-locked Triton over eleven thousand years ago.

Do you have a better explanation for our alphabet than this one of such fantastic antiquity?

DATES

There are two dates which should have particular significance when considered together. One is the date which Diodorus gives for the time of the Carian exploration of the Atlantic - about 3500 B.C. The second is the earliest date of the present Mayan calendar, or in their historical legends: "The day when the times were changed." That date is 4 AHAU, 8 CUMHU - the start of the present calendar. Roughly it is about 3500 B.C. Should this be written off as another coincidence?

Chapter 60

The Kerrians Or Carians

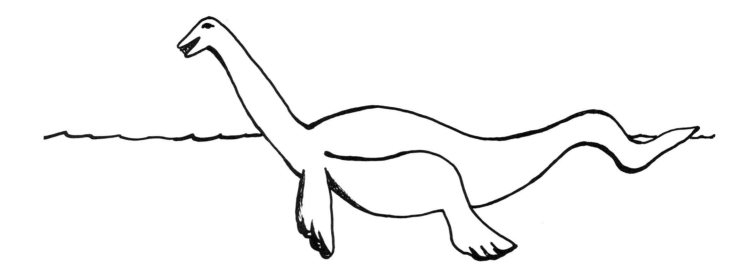

THE (SUPPOSEDLY) EXTINCT PLESIOSAURUS

This ancient dinosaur is apparently still around. Fossils give the size. A partial skeleton uncovered at Ft. Wallace, Kansas had a neck of twenty-two feet. There were twenty-five ancient species, of which apparently three types have survived. There is a fresh cold water species, a fresh warm water species (the smallest - about twenty feet) and a marine species - the largest. They apparently vary from dark grey to brown while there seems to be a very large marine species with stripes. The creature can propel itself on land with its flippers, but is awkward. Once in the water it has been clocked at twenty-five miles an hour. It is nocturnal in habits, though sometimes seen in the daylight. There have been over a thousand sightings, and some of the British universities are attempting to catch a young one (about three feet long) for study. How it is able to breathe underwater for long periods of time is the main question science now is asking - not IF they exist. Many scientists are convinced of that. The creatures are carnivorous (meat eaters) and could be very dangerous. Ordinary weapons only sting them. Looking down on one, it is easy to understand why they have been mistaken for a giant sea serpent for so many years, since when swimming, the animal is three-fourths under water.

There are several points which Donnelly missed. One is the above. Of course he could not have known that the sightings of the giant "sea serpent" even in his day had any factual basis.

As we have seen in the chapter on "The Case For The Monsters", apparently this dinosaur is still around. Also the ancients, especially the people of the sea, were well acquainted with the monster, and evidently regarded it with a certain amount of awe - even reverence. This is normal for a civilization based upon trade across long distances of sea travel, especially when the ships they used were not the sea going giants of today, nor the weapons stronger than our elephant gun, which like our spear guns would not penetrate the hide of a saurian, but merely annoy him, and possibly sting him into anger. According to legends the ancients used human sacrifice to divert the attention of the swimming dinosaur from their ships.

THE WATER MONSTER
Mayan stylized glyphs for k.

Why does this add up? Because the sea dragon of the ancients, after which they fashioned their ships, is to be found on both sides of the Atlantic in similar glyph for the letter K!

It is obvious that the sea leagues fashioned their dragon ships from the sight of him coming through the waves, with the head turned one way and the tip of the tail the other. And since the ancients always copied the assets of their totem animal, it becomes obvious also that the sea dragon was their totem. He may have shared this reverence with the giant bird (the condor), but he was probably the leading totem in the Atlantic.

Why do we say this? Because the K sound, which is his glyph, is to be found in nation after nation of the early people, when we enumerate their names. There are the Kelts with their clans, the Basques (try saying it without the K sound), and among the earliest groups of Ireland, the Formoraks who came in ships from their "sinking island". There were the Etruscans and the Cretans whom the Egyptians called the "Khefti", the Carthaginians - but above all the Carians.

Who were the Carians?

They were the Phoenicians long before the Semitic tribes invaded their lands from the direction of Arabia, riding camels and driving sheep.

As you know, the name Phoenician was a Greek nickname for the color of their skin, nor did the Greeks confine it to them, they also called the Cretans "Phoeniki" which literally means "fire skin". The Phoenicians were so flattered that they kept the name for commercial purposes, because to these worshippers of the fire god, red skin was the sacred color - the symbol of the aristocrat. They called themselves Carians. Broken down, this had the same meaning on both sides of the Atlantic. The K sound is for people, AR the initials of the fire god whose name is secret. Ian, according to the Amerinds, is one of the words for "sea" (it would be intriguing to follow up the pedigree of "Aegean"). Does Carian mean "the sea people of the fire god?" We know that almost any eastern Amerind tribe translates the name Tuarak as Tu (the all powerful) people of the fire god.

Is the name Carian the Atlantean's name for themselves?

Let us do a little research on this name. The ancient historian, Hesichius tells us that Troy was the northern rampart of "the Carian union".

THE WATER DRAGON OR WATER MONSTER
Egyptian hieroglyph for k. Representing the people of the sea and their totem animal - the water monster.

Diodorus of Sicily, who grew up hearing legends of the sunken empire, began to travel throughout Libya to learn more. Since his sources are two thousand years older than ours, it is well to listen to this Roman of Etruscan blood. He tells us that after the fall of Troy, and its people had fled to Sicily, Italy and France, the most important expedition of the Phoeniki and Carthaginian Carians was to the west beyond the Gates of Heracles. Before this happened, however, the great Triton sea was emptied in a single night of horror by a tremendous earthquake which broke the Atlas rim that held it from the sea. Following this disaster the same cataclysm struck the isles beyond the Gates and then cracked open the Gates, flooding the ancient Mediterranean valley. Thus the three disasters were related. This is very good geology. The first tearing of the east Atlantic fault, probably shearing up both sides of the Atlas chain from the equator to about the location of Agadir, emptied the Triton with block faulting to the sea, sinking the Atlas rim. This in turn struck the unstable isles with the force of unheard of waves triggering that sinking, and this in turn caused the cracking of the Gates to the valley with its sudden overwhelming flood.

Incidentally two geologists, Drs. A. Heremann and Brochard, who seem to be the only scientists who have braved the heat and other dangers of the Draa depression, say that there is ample evidence that a Lake Triton was emptied as a result of large faulting movements, but they place the date of this disaster about 1250 B.C. It seems to the present writer that this needs more research as to the time. The end of the Pleistocene with its tremendous changes would seem more reasonable.

It might be in the line of questioning to ask Dr. Geras of the university of Sind, India to seek some geological data on the date of the great civilization he is uncovering in his country. He finds a "profound knowledge of astronomy entirely pre-Aryan invasion" which was apparently ended by "a seismic convulsion".

Returning to the Carians, Thucydides was another ancient historian interested in the prehistoric Carians. He tells us that the city of Hali-Kar-Nassos, which meant "the garden of Kar", was built by emperor Kar, during whose lifetime the empire was divided into two parts. Caria, the Cilicia of Roman times, was a vassal state. Phoenicia was a part of the Carian league, as was Caria, Cara and Caron. (One wonders here about the city of Cairo, Egypt?) They were united under one ruler.

From here Diodorus again takes up the story. Emperor Kar was a powerful, but somewhat mysterious magician who built his empire up into the sea power of the world. Under him the Carians rode all the seas of the earth in their ships and traded with every known land. Also they traded with many unknown lands, or lands unknown to those outside of the league, as they kept their trade secrets to themselves. The time of emperor Kar can be considered, said Diodorus, to be the "golden age" of known history. Among the nations which sailed with the Carian fleets were the Cretans at the height of their power, Troy, and Ion. (Could this have been the real meaning of the Greek "Ionians", and the actual name for the Pelasgians, the latter again being merely another Greek nickname meaning "sea people"?) Diodorus could have explained what was undoubtedly a known fact in his time, and perhaps deemed not worthy of an explanation.

The most interesting notation of Diodorus was that the Carians, when headed for war, or for state occasions, wore a circlet of feathers in their hair above the brow. This is a great many centuries before the peoples of either Europe or the Mediterranean were supposed to have seen an American Indian!

The real breaking up of the power of the Carian union must have been the seismic disaster of the Mediterranean which ended the power of Crete. After that, the invading Greeks found Troy easy to besiege (from the Latin word "to sit down in front of") and starve into surrender - with the help of the wooden horse, of course. Thus the actual power of the Carian league was broken, not by invasion, but by seismic disaster, apparently striking again some millennia after the great destruction. Diodorus gives a date on this. After the fall of Troy, he says, the remaining Carians organized a tremendous expedition of ships to sail west from the Gates of Hercules and throughly to explore the Atlantic ocean. This expedition took place in 3500 B.C. and included not only Phoenicans, but also Carthaginians and other remaining Carians. (Thus Troy fell before 3500 B.C. and this was the date of the first Aryan invasions.)

For what were the Carians searching? Merely other lands with which to trade; or were they hunting the "lost tribes" of the "seven kings" who had sailed westward from the great destruction and whose memory must have been carried down in their legends? And is the legend of the "lost tribes" of the Semitics an echo of a very much earlier legend - the seven lost tribes of the Carians? Remember, the Carians were the ancients of the country when the Semitic tribes invaded, and in the story of Cain and Abel, Cain was "the builder of cities" while Abel was a shepherd lad. (Of course that story, as told by the descendents of Abel, carried the viewpoint of the invaders.) Today the people of the Mediterranean are a mixed people, but underneath them all, there is probably some Carian, as well as Sumerian, blood. Therefore it is high time that they drop their narrowly national, and gain a more cosmopolitan viewpoint of pre-history.

What has all this to do with the letter K?

The sages of the Amerinds tell us that the real name of a people from the red land should have somewhere in it the K sound. This was one of the points which Votan stressed in his last speech, in which they were told "always remember the signs of mutual recognition". Of course any tribe could take a nickname to fool enemies.

With this knowledge, let us briefly go back to the discussion of the K sound in names, where we were interrupted by the question of "who were the Carians?"

Among the Kelts we have the Kerry dancing, and the province of Cork. The Basques have a "real name" which is Eus-Cara or Eus-Kerri. In Europe we have Denmark, and the Baltic which not only ends with the K sound, but has in it the name for the later Phoenician type of fire god - Baal. You can probably think of numerous others in names of burial mounds and the old names for the mysterious round towers which cross the ocean apparently on the sunken ridge of the Appalachians. Is it not interesting that the Norse Vikings who wore the horns of Votan's helmet on theirs, rode in dragon ships and drank the full mead from goblets, stopped raiding Ireland and the coasts of Scotland as soon as they (the Norse) were converted to Christianity? Were they punishing the lands to the south which had forsaken the "old gods" before they did the same? Also is it not remarkable that with some of these names we can trace, if not the date, then the sequence in time?

Diodorus mentions the Carian city of Carpassos (situated on Cypress which was a Carian ship building center. Their largest ships were able to carry eight hundred passengers and were called "carpassios." Is this the origin of our words car and passenger? From this word Diodorus finds many derivations for long boats - karbas, barkas, etc. There are others of which he had no knowledge in the Malay languages and in the Philippines. There also is bark, barque, barka, etc. The Carians travelled widely, no doubt. Probably they left the massive terracing to be found in the Philippines and also the name Korea. There is little doubt that they left the names Carnac in Brittany and Karnak in Egypt.

The time of emperor Kar has been placed as during the second millennium B.C. some centuries before Moses. Now this is too late for the final dissolution of the great Cretan empire and too early for the Semitic invasions. Not that they had not started; they undoubtedly started with the Hyksos kings who conquered Egypt and ended the glory of her early dynasties, after which they were themselves conquered and enslaved. However, the Syrians, Arabs, and other Semitic speakers were pouring out of the east into the Mediterranean. From the north the Aryan speakers or Arazons were also coming.

Kar, therefore, was on the borderline of history where legend becomes fact. Evidently the seismic disaster which ended the Cretan empire also disrupted the strongholds of many of the red skinned rulers of the Mediterranean, leaving wealthy cities in a turmoil, thus offering a tempting bait to the tribes of the bearded peoples from the north and east; and so the migration rush was on. It was during this time that Kar set himself up as a savior, trying to bind together what remained of the earlier dominant powers of the sea colossus with its league of cities.

Obviously the name was not his. He chose what had been a designation for the Carians for untold centuries. It was a name guaranteed to win their attention. It was translated as meaning "sacred" and for his divinity he introduced "the great god Pan". This deity with many of the goat characteristics of Votan, was given the surname of Tu meaning "divine". Kar sent out men teachers of agriculture under the name of this deity, and women to teach the housewives how to weave. He tried in every way to brace the people against the nomadic tribes pouring in upon them.

According to Dr. Varnhagen, who was a scholar interested in the Carians, Tu-Pan was thought to be the grandson of the goddess Cybele, who seemed to be a modification of the Sumerian goddess Ishtar and possibly a successor of the "mother goddess" of the Cro Magnon times. To the Phoenicians she was Astarte, and to the later Greeks and Romans, Keres or Ceres, from whose name we get the word cereal.

At any rate, it was either under the direction of Kar or in anticipation of the great migrations, that the Carians set out to explore the Atlantic in search of their "lost tribes", and the "lost islands" of the Carians. Later on when "the people of the sea" came in their ships to Egypt, Rhameses III was too busy to help them. He recognized the circles of feathers in the "war bonnet" of the Philistines, and their red skin, when they came to Egypt in their war ships and he even fought to keep them from landing, but not with much warlike fervor, for he rescued their men who fell overboard in the fighting. Then he sent them to Palestine to settle and hold his borders against the Semitic hordes, still coming from the east.

Did the Carian expedition into the Atlantic find the people for whom they were searching? Were they able to found new colonies? Were they able to contact other lands for trade? Dr. L. Swennhagen has done a great deal of work researching the Carib tribes for this very information. He finds in their language a great many Phoenician words.

Again here I must warn researchers that they will continually run into Hebrew words and phrases, customs and ceremonies from the time of the earliest Christians, brought over to the Americas by "the white prophet", who completely confused me until I researched him alone for my book "He Walked the Americas". This one dedicated healer and teacher has thoroughly turned the Amerinds into lost tribes of the Jews (without a beard) unless you realize how one dedicated saint speaking hundreds of languages could, influence two continents by speaking a tribe's own language when he entered a tribal council, with gifts of seeds and a healing touch. Even today missionaries are sometimes shocked at a wild unchristian people with twelve "disciples" or "elders" bearing the names of the twelve disciples. And it is not the result of early contacts with monks. (This information is the result of recent letters from South American missionaries concerning my book.)

The most interesting historical information which Swennhagen uncovered was in the prehistory of the Carib tribes. They have the memory of two catastrophes in the Atlantic. The first one was an earth changing seismic disaster which took their land, and they fled westward in their seven fleets of ships. They then found another island, and after exploring it, decided it would be an ideal place to settle. They again built up their empire and their cities for many thousands of years. Then a second catastrophe struck their island which they had named Caraiba, meaning "the land of the people of Cari".

Again the people set out westward in seven fleets as before, and finding a sea, named it the Caribbean because it had many habitable islands. Part of their people went south to the mouth of a great river. (The Amazon?) It was during their stay on Caraiba that priests came teaching the religion of Tu-Pan and changed their name to Tupi which stood for "the all-glorious sons of Pan". They explained that Pan had been one of the names for the old red land, but now it became the name for the Great Spirit. He was a good god and was symbolized by the horns of the goat, as was the old land.

Dr. Swennhagen finds it intriguing that both the Guerrani and the French word la guerre, gave the same meaning to this Amerind tribe of Ecuador - namely "war", and suggests that the derivation of the name and the word should be studied for Pelasgian or Carian roots. E.O.

Thoron, writing from that same country, Ecuador, claims to have found petroglyphs with Phoenician letters. These are particularly numerous near Quito, he remarks. The Columbian, Miguel Triana, also suspects Carian contacts and suggests that the Chibchas came originally from the Caribbean.

The ending of Swennhagen's finding in Carib legends is also illuminating. The people of Cari not only settled the Caribbean because they were accustomed to mountainous islands where they could cultivate by means of terracing, but also, as their numbers increased, went both north and south. They built a city on the island of Marajo in the Amazon delta. (It is significant that megalithic ruins are to be found on the island of Maranon farther up the Amazon, as if this had been a stepping stone to the building of the magnificent lost megalithic cities in the Andes. Varhagen tells us that this latter name Maranon means "great river".

Are there any other clues to the possibility that these Phoeniki of Europe are related to the Phoeniki "redskins" of the Americas? If we take the eastern tribes, yes. The western tribes of the Americas, being round heads, undoubtedly came across the Aleutian bridge from Asia.

We know that the K sound in Carian stands for "people". Then let us look at a sizeable American list. I will not be able to discuss the Amerinds of South America, for I am not as well acquainted with them as with North America, so I will limit my discussion to the north. I will not list them all. That would take up too much time. Besides many of the names are secret and they use a nickname, as the "Black-feet" which the whites gave them because they burned their moccasins in running from the prairie fires set to drive them away from white settlements, and to burn up their food - the buffalo. However, I will take the eastern languages: the Algonkin, Caddoan, Siouan (we have for the Sioux their real name, Dakota), Muskogian and Iroquoian, the Kansan, the Tuscarora, Chickasaw, Cherakee, Chocktaw, Chiricawa (Apache), Mohawk, Comanche, Bannock, etc., etc. In Mexico we have Aztec, Toltec, Zapotec, Mixtec, Tarascaran, and Mexican, while they tell me that the name America is really Ah-Mor-Ica and far older than the explorer who is supposed to have given it his name. I have seen at one time a book which shows a great deal of research on this name, with the same end result - the name is Amerind. I have not been able to find the book again in any of the libraries where I first found it, or my friends found it, so I cannot give the author's name.

There is however, a name in North America with which I am familiar and which has been translated for me. It is OK (people) LA (sun) HOMA (redland).

Again Swennhagen finds in the legends of the Carib tribes that the "people of Cari" in very ancient times went to Venezuela and founded the city of Caracas.

Now discarding for the moment the very prejudiced theories of the scientist who went up to Alaska and, digging up a thousand graves, dumped the contents into one bin and sorted them out according to his own theories of recent Asian arrival, so that later researchers were completely frustrated by this vandalism, let us see what can be made out of the facts and legends left to us by the eastern tribes - those of the Mississippi valley and the land from there to the Atlantic.

First we have a language map showing Algonkin speakers to the north of North America and scattered pockets along the Atlantic coast, the Mississippi, throughout Wisconsin and Michigan and again in small pockets in California. These groups are surrounded by unrelated tongues (as widely separated as Arabic and English). This means that they were driven, pushed and scattered by later invasions. On the west coast these invasions were largely from the Aleutians and Asia, as the waves of Athapascan speakers swept down from the Aleutian straits - some as late as a thousand years ago. The Uto-Aztecan language in the western desert region has similarities to Mexico and suggests contact and perhaps infiltration from that region. But in the Mississippi valley to the eastern coast of the continent of North America, are two great language stocks. The Algonkin are conceded to be the earliest people and it is now more or less agreed that they once held the entire land above the Mexican border except perhaps for some very early Asian invasions. Then whence came the eastern Siouan, Caddoan, Iroquois and Muskogian speaking language groups? Late studies by many scientists have shown some linkage in the speech of these people. The similarity has been pointed out by the Amerinds themselves - that those who are college bred and interested in the past of their people particularly, thoroughly knowing one of these languages, and using the root system, can soon acquire the other tongues of this group.

These facts would hint of a long distant relationship. But who are they and from whence did they come into the land where they were dis-

covered by white man? Let us begin with the Algonkins - acknowledged now by most students of Amerind tongues to be the "ancients of the country".

The book which tells us the most concerning the Algonkins was told to a youthful white man named Pidgeon who more than a century ago went into the wilds beyond the city of St. Louis and began to map the mounds or "earthworks" as they were called. It was not long before he realized that he had interested spectators - particularly one elderly man of a proud and haughty mien. To make a long story short, Pidgeon accepted an invitation to dinner given by signs, and found himself in the encampment of Algonkin Indians whose language he diligently tried to master. The first question he was asked was: "Why do you map that which your people are so rapidly destroying?" To which he made answer: "I wish to put this on paper so that the talking words will live beyond the time of the destroyers to other generations not yet born, who will want to know."

In the previously discussed book "The Traditions of Decoodah" we mentioned very briefly the fact that the Algonkins were the Mound Builders, and that the old high priest, Decoodah, the last of his nation, began to educate the young man of another people in the location of the mounds; their history and meaning; how to read them; and how certain parts looked before they had been eroded away by the streams. We learned that the Mound Builders were a peaceful people living in cities, always communicating by river boats, and trading with nations far to the south. We learned that about four hundred to seven hundred A.D. a series of migrations began from the direction of the south up the Mississippi by people who were fire worshippers and sacrificers. These people came as four nations and built as a monument of their migration the huge serpent mound in Ohio where the reptile is coming from the south following the lead of the oval "turtle". We learned that the turtle took over their own capital at the fork of the Mississippi river where is now St. Louis, and established the black tortoise empire. The Algonkins then moved further north and founded another capital. Peace again was established. The black tortoise emperor then divided his kingdom into four parts, with the Mississippi one of the dividing lines, and placed the four kingdoms under his four sons. He himself sent armies west to try to subdue belligerent peoples and tame some of the wild tribes coming down from the far northwest. His thought was to make one strong empire from sea to sea. He was interrupted by a talented war captain growing up in his court named Dakotah who went north to the "Puans" and made a war treaty with them to join him in overthrowing the old emperor. Dakotah was fired with the ambition to conquer all the western land for himself and his allies and make one powerful world power. He succeeded partly in overthrowing the black tortoise throne, but a youth growing up in the southern court, a grandson of the original black tortoise, chose to regain the throne for himself. Making allies of brother tribes then coming into the land from the south, he marched on the capital. The other kings refused to join him and in the civil war which followed, general anarchy resulted and cities were abandoned.

Now let us look at the other side of the coin. First we have the Iroquois legends of the migration up the Mississippi in which they, taking the eastern seaboard, drove the "ancients of the country" clear to the "stinking water" probably so named because of the salty smell of fish which was a forbidden article of diet unless it was ceremonially speared by a trident. (Other tribes which have stinking water clans have this explanation.) This was true, they say, because their ancestors once were devoured by fish during the great destruction. This legend marks them as Caribbeans and probably the "stinking water" in Canada was Hudson Bay.

The Dakotah or Siouan speakers were probably the black tortoise people, for they were first to be found not too far from the vicinity of St. Louis. Soon after, being able to capture some of the horses whose ancestors had escaped from the Spanish, and had run wild, forming large herds, they tamed the animal and used them to hunt the buffalo. This inevitably led the tribe to the Dakotas where the buffalo were the most numerous. This migration was historical, as fragments of the tribe are still to be found much further south. The totem of the Sioux or the Dacotah people is the black tortoise, black standing for the sea as well as one of the colors of the fire god. (They claim to be the children of the seven kings and always keep seven tribes.) The recognition of the Venus calendar is very strong among these tall, handsome Cro Magnon type people as one can easily see in the twenty-six feathers in their war bonnet, the "dawn star" lodge of the chief, etc. although the tribe is bitter toward the white man and chary of any information. Yet Shooting Star, who has travelled far in the Americas, points to Peru as the land closest to his people!

Of the Caddoan, I am not too well acquainted, but the legends of the Muskogian speakers, the southern group and the last to come north in the migrations, are most interesting because they have been preserved from the time of the explorers when the "temple guardians" were willing to discuss the historical legends of the past even as Solon so long ago was able to obtain them from another "temple guardian" of the "fire god" a legend which curiously fits into the picture of a land so far away from Egypt.

Briefly the story told to the explorer, Du Pratz, by the temple guardian of the Natchez and their brother tribes came out of the east across the sea to the Caribbean by "following the sun", they found the land fertile and lovely, but very sparsely populated. In fact it was not until they had lived on the islands and the shore that for many generations they first met the "ancients of the country" who were traders and as surprised to see them as they were. The "ancients" were friendly and the two peoples continued to live quietly, each following their own customs without any major clashes. The people who were their brothers, who had come with their fleets, now filled the islands and the shoreline, while many went as far south as the great snows, and into the mountains of the interior. Their people were fond of the mountains, for they knew how to terrace the sides for their food. Some of these people were only heard from for a five or six year interval (to check the calendar?) while others were lost to them for years and years, and some forever.

Everything went well for many centuries and the people multiplied like the leaves of the forest - both their own people and those of the "ancients of the country". Then finally came a day when one of the chiefs of these people began to entertain ideas of grandeur and thought of conquering not only his own people but also the Caribbeans. Some of the "ancients" joined them, against this chief and his armies. Thus began the Caribbean war. He conquered many Caribbean cities as well as his own on the islands, and then the plains, but the defenders fled to the mountains for "we are the people of the mountains" and there he met defeat. However, the temple guardian continues, our great sun (the emperor) sent scouts to search out new lands. Some of these going north, found this land. The soil was rich and the animals in the forests were plentiful, so our great sun ordered all the nations who had been fighting to hold their cities on the plains, to pack up their long boats, take their sacred fire, and go north. The kings who had scouted the land gathered their tribes and came, making room for the others who might follow. We were the last tribe to come north and we have been here now for over the lifetimes of fifty chieftains each succeeding the other. We have kept in touch with our brothers to the south and in the islands. They no longer wished to come. The war was ended, and the land still warm and fertile. The last word we had is that a swarthy race in floating villages who were wearing hair upon their faces, came with giant fire and earth shaking sticks which killed as many people at a distance as grass upon the prairies. At first we sided with these strangers or our brothers did, against the "ancients". Our great sun foretold our doom for doing this, saying that our people, along with the "ancients" would be made slaves. This we understand has happened, and so we never hear from them any more.

Some of the descriptions of these explorers tell of the beauty of the wooden temples to the fire god built on high earth mounds, with gilded and painted logs, and the inside of the temple where was observed hieroglyphic writing. (It is too bad that no one thought to copy it.) It is interesting to speculate on this writing and wonder if it showed similarity to that found in Peru. The quippus for telling the passage of time, ie. the knotting of various colored strings used by the people under Inca rule, are to be found in the eastern tribes although they profess to have forgotten the meanings. Did the emperor of Peru the 78th Inca) who banished writing under penalty of death and introduced the quippu instead, do this in order to destroy the libraries of the people of Chan Chan, probably in fear that they might be older than his own? If so, he took a giant step toward wiping out the past of his own people, which may have proved far more interesting than Chan Chan. But such is ever the short sighted ignorance of the bigot.

Some of the other descriptions were of the lovely beaded costumes, the attractive mats on the floors of their houses, their beds of cane and the moss mattresses (very comfortable) and their food. The "Chickasaw plum" is noted because that tribe claimed to have brought it north with them. Our modern botanists have pinpointed its origin as Peru. (Also there are vestiges of quippu reckoning in all the eastern tribes.)

However, the firmest link to Peru is in the spring and fall festivals of the people. For example, the new year ceremony of the Chocktah (also Chicksaw and Cherakee) which was celebrated in the spring of the year when the corn first became full eared, in the time of the first new moon after the vernal equinox. Adair does not seem to recognize the origin of the ceremony which he describes and that has recently been changed to the harvest festival. All pots and houses are cleaned, houses must be repainted, the holy of holies must have a new coat of stucco, while the war cabin is repainted with red paint. All seats in the square are recovered with new mattresses, ashes must be carried from the sacred fire and the temple swept. The ceremony, the painting of the bodies, etc., etc., is very similar to the Incan Ccoya Rami of spring - September 22 to October 22. Much of the ceremony is also to be found in the Incan fall ceremony which would take place in our spring. There seems to be other links, as in Toltec, but more distant, to the Mayans and the Mexicans. The caste system is very prominent in all the eastern invaders from the south, especially in the succession of the new chief through the daughter to the grandson. In all these people the women of the tribe have a secret language which is not taught to women slaves. On occasions a woman has arisen to chieftainship and leader in war. The war chief carries before him to war "the boat of the sun" which is both Incan and Egyptian. All tribes show previous knowledge of both astronomy and mathematics. And there are enough other similarities to write a doctorate in anthropology or pre-history.

So we have travelled around in a grand circle and find ourselves back again with the totem of the Carians and the letter K. On the side of the Mayan glyph, is the Norse sign for K backward Ꝅ, and the N which is the water sign in the Cadmean letters which are essentially Pelasgian. Is this an accident, or is it as much a part of the Mayan glyph as the overturned ship with four people, while below lurks the water monster? Some of the stylized marks of the other nations for the K have a trident throne, or as in the Phoenician, the trident (𝖸), while the Anglo-Saxon for Kh has the trident in the position of death (⚕).

Only in the oldest glyphs, the Egyptian and the Mayan, do we see the origin of the glyph and the totem animal, stylized though it may be.

However, it is curious that if we take the only living (?) dinosaur, and prop him against a telephone pole (dead of course, for there is no other way we could hope to handle him) then his body would make a crude K. Ҡ. Yet perhaps this fact is not more amazing than that a hundred nations on both sides of the Atlantic know what that letter means.

Chapter 61

MOSASAURUS (Lizard of Meuse) and **TYLOSAURUS** (Knotted Lizard)

First skeleton uncovered in Meuse, Belgium. Length, to fifty feet. Tylosaurus is related to Mosasaurus, and attained a similar length. These two fit many sightings, and may not be extinct, as supposed.

"The most beautiful and most profound emotion we can experience is the sensation of the mystical. It is the source of all true science. He to whom this emotion is a stranger; who can no longer wonder and stand rapt in awe, is as good as dead." Albert Einstein.

When the discoveries once hidden in the old sheet of parchment known as the Piri Re'is map first exploded through the veil of time into the ivory tower of our scientists, those among them who still enjoyed mental adventure responded quickly to the challenge, but were almost immediately defeated by the conservatives. These men also began to glance anew over the Portolan maps, those yellowed sheets which looked not upon the globe as we do today. It took a time for all scientists to take them seriously. The conservatives refused at the outset. Those who responded to the challenge began to study the maps minutely, making the discovery that the circles with the 32 or 64 intersecting lines were centers of culture. Then they made a second discovery. These were not the maps of the globe which we have today because they were drawn for a seafaring people who only wished to go from one civilization to another for the purpose of trade. They were not maps to hang on classroom walls. They were working maps of an ancient world, a world of sea rovers.

The conservative scientists still refused to listen. There were pictures upon these maps of such mythical creatures as swimming dinosaurs,

Some Recent Cracks

Through The Mists Of Time

and long sea serpents. "Could this possibly be the work of a sophisticated ancient power? Nonsense." So the argument began.

In spite of an overwhelming response to adventure, the present writer could understand the arguments of the conservatives. Could living dinosaurs still be sharing our modern planet? It seemed impossible, yet there was so much reverence or worship for the reptile gods both in early Eurasia and Africa as well as in the Americas, that the conclusion was almost inescapable. The great water monster of the Amerinds to whom children were sacrificed until the Twins killed the monsters off in order to free the people, was an exceedingly strong legend from the north of North America to the heights of the Andes. The pattern seemed to emerge of a marine dinosaur which was the totem of the ancient people of the sea. They told legends of it, built their ships to resemble it and even reverenced its tiny desert cousin enough to decorate their pottery with its image. In Europe the Etruscan women carried serpents into battle. The Egyptian monarchs had a reptile head coming out of their crowns. The Phoenicians and others used the lizard for the letter K which in America stood for "people" and the list continued in an endless array. This surely must have been the totem of the ancient long head, and yet - in spite of the fact that the Chinese danced to the dragon and the Apache painted serpents on their arms for the crown dance - how could it be?

A trip to Cambridge university, England, to see the zoologists put the first great question mark in this book. Was the Loch Ness monster a swimming dinosaur? Yet it served no purpose to discuss the matter with the conservative scientists. In vain one could point out that the pictures on the maps were very good replicas of the giant armor plated lizard of antiquity, the Elasmosaurus, or again the Monasaur, another fifty foot monster. The answer was always the same - it ended with a lengthy discussion or lecture on the liquors used by sailors; and one must admit that liquor is as old as the oldest civilizations of antiquity.

As the zoologists of Cambridge pointed out, there was only one way to settle this argument. The Loch Ness monster must be photographed, but every time a picture was taken, the conservatives belittled it or the huge animal failed to cooperate and sank, leaving only a ripple behind. There must be a photograph; yes. But it must be of undeniable authenticity. To that end the zoologists were ringing the old lake (which is in reality a giant fault which practically cuts northern Scotland in two) with cameras. Sooner or later they were bound to get their picture - they hoped.

Just as the believers in the reality of the monster among the savants of Cambridge were becoming more and more annoyed at the manner in which all discussions upon the subject turned into dissertations upon the hallucinating effects of Scotch whiskey, the great opportunity came. The believers among the zoologists had made extensive preparations. They had even enlisted the help of the British navy. Five bombers had been stationed at a nearby field on a partial alert, waiting side by side with their great motion picture cameras. They were to fly at the distance apart which would ensure the best results to capture the illusive target from every angle. There must be no failure. Even the British people were becoming skeptical.

Then it happened.

The message suddenly split the air on a beautiful sunny July morning of 1966. "The Loch Ness monster has surfaced and is proceeding at 25 miles per hour down the length of the lake."

PLESIOSAURUS

This is "Nessie", the famed Loch Ness monster. Shown below are four frames
from a 16mm movie film taken by the British Royal Air Force, at 1600 yards.
Estimated length, 92 feet.

Immediately the five bombers started their engines and took off as one machine. They swung low over the creature and motion picture cameras whirred. They passed and turned back for another pass, but "Nessie" (the Scotch nickname for the creature which has been frightening and entertaining their people for untold generations) suddenly lost interest in these noisy birds, and sank slowly out of sight. The frustrating ripple remained behind, but this time it was different. The bombers returned to their base and within a short time the shocking news crackled out to the world over all the news media.

"The Loch Ness monster has been photographed." Then came another statement in that crisp British accent. "Further information and measurements will be released tomorrow at a news conference as soon as the films have been processed."

So the world waited for the quiet unemotional

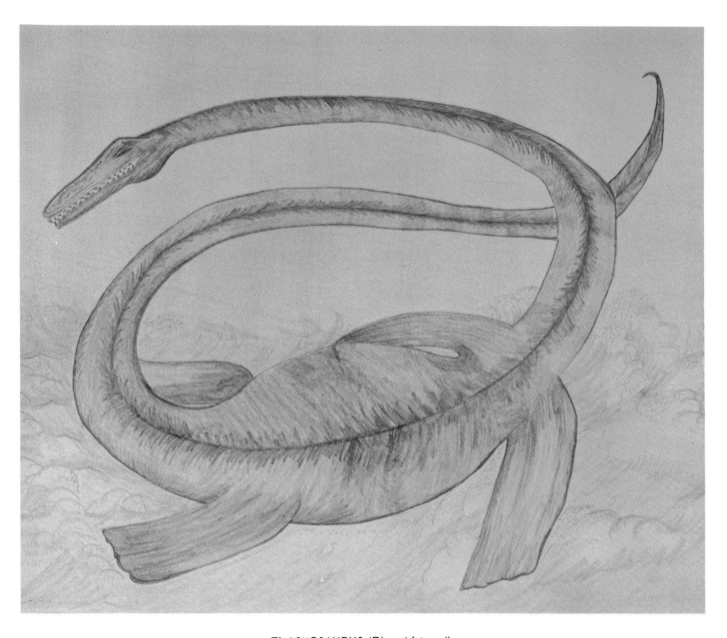

ELASMOSAURUS (Plated Lizard)

Reconstruction from a skeleton fifty feet long. Also fits numerous marine descriptions.

voice to come again. When it did the message was brief:

"Her Majesty's Navy wishes to announce that the Loch Ness monster is a possible saurian. Its measurements are as follows:

Width across the head - six feet.

Thickness of the body - fifteen feet.

Length from head to tip of tail - ninety feet."

In my memory I could again hear the well-modulated voice of the Cambridge zoologist as he laughingly answered my question.

"What will the world of science do or say? You mean if it should be ...?" Again that slightly mischievous laugh.

"I do not know about the entire world of science but I can speak for the British conservatives. They will, of course, very correctly drink their cup of tea in deathly silence, and then go quietly into shock."

Note - June 1967 - News item - An American zoologist has obtained permission of the British to shoot the monster with an exploding whaling device, supposedly to obtain a flesh sample and some hide. It will probably kill the big animal which will then sink. (He should gain much publicity which is probably his real desire.) He claims to believe it to be a giant squid! After the hundreds of descriptions of the long necks -!

Chapter 62

The War Dog Of The Ancients

THE SPHINX

They glare - those stony eyes!
    That in the fierce sun-rays
Showered from these burning skies,
    Through untold centuries
Have kept their sleepless and unwinking gaze.

Since what unnumbered year
    Hast thou kept watch and ward
And o'er the buried Land of Fear
    So grimly held thy guard?
No faithless slumber snatching,
    Still couched in silence brave,
Like some fierce hound long watching
    Above her master's grave.

Even now, methinks that those
    Dark, heavy lips which close
In such a stern repose,
    Seem burdened with some thought unsaid,
And hoard within their portals dread
    Some fearful Secret there -
Which to the listening earth
    She may not whisper forth,
Not even to the air.

Of treasures that have shone
    On cavern walls alone
Four thousand thousand years.
    Those sullen orbs wouldst thou eclipse,
And ope those massy, tomb-like lips,
    Many a riddle thou couldst solve
Which all blindly men revolve.

Would she but tell! She knows
    Of the old Pharaohs.
Could count the Ptolemies' long line;
    Each mighty myth's original hath seen,
Apis, Anubis - ghosts that haunt between
    The Bestial and Divine -
(Such, He that sleeps in Philoe - He that stands
    In gloom unworshipped in his rock-hewn
    fane -
And they who sitting on Memnonian sands
    Cast their long shadows o'er the desert
    plane:)
Hath marked Nitocris pass, and Ozymandias -
    Deep versed in many a dark Egyptian
    wile ..."

        Henry Howard Brownell (1820-1872)

Chow, the war dog.

If it had not been for Robert Beck, lecturer on Egypt, one of the key parts of this book would never have been written. Many little known facts about Egypt and other early civilizations of the Mediterranean were intriguing his audience when he finished and began to put together the notes before him. I waited in my seat very impatiently for him to be free of well wishers and then made my way to the speaker's platform. He had mentioned the Dalmatian dog which was to be seen in some of the temple paintings along with the dachshund, considered a German dog. I began with this after introducing myself, and asking casually if perhaps these animals only resembled the modern types. He shrugged his shoulders and smiled. Then I asked him about the "ancient war dog" he had mentioned so briefly. He had described it as being held by chains by the invading "people of the sea" who came in ships and were portrayed by the temple paintings of Rhameses II. These dogs were red in color he had said, and from their expression, very savage.

"Are they like any modern type?"

"Yes. Definitely they appear to be Chows. They have the same mane, the same bushy curled tail, small cat like ears ..."

"Wait a moment. Are you suggesting that these people of the sea were Chinese?"

"No. That conclusion is unwarranted. The animal may have been carried to China. In fact, it is my belief that he was carried there by Emperor Fu."

"Along with writing, agriculture, music, poetry, ships, medicine - you name it - they all come from Emperor Fu."

His cool indifferent manner was dropped immediately and he smiled.

"I see that you are acquainted with one of my favorite fantastics. I believe the modern word is culture hero?"

"I do not claim too deep an acquaintance. I know that he lived before either flood chronicled by Chinese history, and also that the Chinese point out his origin as the region of the Mediterranean, where they also claim many of their early tribes originated."

"True. And being somewhat a fancier of the Chow, I began looking over possible origins for Emperor Fu. I ran into some very interesting possibilities. Did you know the Chow was the war dog of the Hittites?"

"The first Aryan speakers? Amazing!"

"Nor is that all. He was the temple guardian of the Sumerians?"

"You amaze me!"

This was opening up another train of thought, but Mr. Beck was continuing on about his hobby - the Chow.

"Did you know further, that this animal has the heavy bone of a big cat, with claws that can cut through glass, a wrist that bends under like the cat, the lower cushion of the front paw has the half moon shape of the cat's cushion with points down as any cat. This together with the lion mane, the cat ears, and the very broad face between the eyes like the lion, brings the animal very close to the stem where the cat, dog and bear parted company ..."

"Yes, I know that the Chow is probably one of the ancestral dog types, however, excuse me for changing the subject, but have you been to the Hittite capital - the one on the trade route of the ancients which was destroyed, according to most archaeologists, by the Sumerians?"

A slight look of annoyance crossed his face, but he nodded amiably enough.

"There is not much there but ruins you know. Some digging has been done, but the final fire was too final for rebuilding."

"I have read that the fire which burned the old city was of a strange intensity - almost as if the very earth itself had melted."

"Yes. That is true."

"Was it a seismic disaster? I mean did you see any earth cracks or lava?"

"No, but I was not looking for it, either. I cannot recall that the guide mentioned anything except that the fire was extremely intense - even to melting most of the masonry. I do remember that the end was supposed to be the work of Sumerians ..."

"Or the people of the sea?"

"Why the latter?"

"They both had the Chow as a war dog, but he came to the Sumerians as a temple guardian. This may have been a later phase of his duties?"

"So?"

"If the Sumerians wiped out the Hittite capital with something or some weapon with the intensity of, let us say a modern bomb, then was it the Sumerians or the people of the sea who brought gunpowder to ancient China?"

"Oh!" and with a smile " - and just as I was beginning to think of Emperor Fu as a Sumerian!"

"This is a riddle we may never know - at least in this century. There are a few hints, however. I bought an antique red Chow made in Japan during the last century. What attracted me was that the animal had its thick, heavy paws upon a ball ..."

"Dogs enjoy playing with balls."

"But this ball had fancy circles on it with wavy lines through them in various directions and dark places. In other words it looked like a stylized ancient map of the sea rovers who traded from one port to another, but the sculptured piece had been made by a people who may have seen such maps, but did not understand the meaning of the map on the parchment upon which these lines had been drawn."

"Interesting, yes, but whose maps were they?"

"Probably those of the people of the sea."

"How do you know?"

"Because in the corner, or perhaps in several places, are pictures of the water monster which was their totem."

"Have you any other thoughts which may pinpoint this to these mysterious people of the sea?"

"Yes, I have studied the pictures of the ancient dances of Tibet. There evidently were two visits of the people of the fire god, for they appear twice. The first visit shows them coming with a cortege of glittering magnificence and wealth. The last visit shows a much poorer group. Interestingly enough, the Indians say that the costume of the fire god, who is evidently the honored guest, is all wrong."

"Do you believe that?"

"Yes, I do. It shows that the monks of Tibet wish to down grade the former religion, as do all the newer religions. If the power of a former god is too much to accept as a minor god in the new pantheon, then he is down graded as an evil spirit, or even the prince of evil. Naturely he would not be given the 'magical' clothes of his correct costume."

"Oh yes, I see what you mean. And the role of temple guardian?"

"That would be kept, if the person or animal in question had the love and admiration of the people. He would simply take over the job of guarding the new god - or his statue would."

"All this is very interesting to me, particularly so as I have been studying the coats of arms or crests of Europe. The old war dog came into contact with a great many, you know."

"This I did not know."

"Ah yes. The rampant lion (meaning the animal standing on its hind legs with front ones upraised) is often pictured as red or black, and the Chow never is any other color. Like the fox, it only throws full colored pups in either color, but never mixed or mottled ..."

Mr. Beck was again going into his subject, so I asked: "What countries have the rampant lion, and how do you know that it is not a real lion?"

"Because of the fluffy cat tail standing up (the tails of cats rise vertically when they are alarmed, angry or see prey) make the same movement. In Chows, even the shivering of the tail in excitement is similar to the cat. Sometimes the tail is trimmed to resemble the lion, but often it is simply the Chow tail, which in the male is held up the spine." I know the war dog is on the crests either as their own, or an enemy weapon, because sometimes the animal is pictured with a bar diagonally across the crest in front of the dog. This means conquest. On the other hand, the animal is sometimes pictured as standing against a sail in the same rampant position. Then as in Saxony and again in Spain, the nails of the dog are only three upraised on each paw. Probably the fourth was amputated to make ..."

"The trident!"

"Why yes, I suppose so. Strange that the animal has a black tongue, isn't it?"

"Not if he was the dog fighter for the trident or fire god."

"I do not follow you."

"He must have been bred for a black tongue. It is not a natural characteristic." (I have been told since that some breeds of the bear have black tongues. Of course it is possible that the Chow may have come from the Miocene when the stem of the cat, dog and bear separated. - author)

"But why?"

"Because the living color of fire is red. In death, the charcoal is black. Therefore black is the correct color for the mouth of the war dog. And incidentally, black is still the death color."

"Ah ha! And while we are clearing up strange facts, did you know that the Japanese regard the Chow as a mythical animal which they have never seen, but the statue of the guard dog (typical giant Chows) stand before each of their temples?"

"Is the animal elsewhere in the orient in either capacity?"

"In Cambodia, as guard before the temples, he almost resembles the Sphinx."

"And in America a similar sphinx dog is sometimes seen on the medallions of the hereditary chiefs. I have seen three or four."

He shuffled his notes thoughtfully.

"Then it was the people of the sea who carried both the Chow and gunpowder to China, according to your belief."

"It would seem possible."

"Then why did China progress no farther than firecrackers?"

"Because firecrackers were only a trade object. The sea rovers were not about to give away the more sinister aspects of gunpowder."

"That sounds reasonable. But I am not so sure but that the traders were Sumerians."

"Why?"

"Because the Sumerians, I believe, were supposed to have come from the Indian ocean originally, and we do not know actually how long ago Egypt first cut her canal through between the Nile and the Red sea."

I was puzzled. "What has that to do with gunpowder? The Egyptians are part of the sea people. They could have cut any canal through more easily with the help of gunpowder."

"Yes but are you acquainted with the rhythmic chants of India which are now considered to be pre-Aryan because of the one which tells of the "invaders" stealing them?"

"No, not really. But what a connotation that brings! The Norse runes may be also, and how about the Finnish kaleva? Finnish is, of course, a non-Aryan tongue islanded by the invasion of the Aryan speakers".

"Norse probably is also. How about the one which says that the runes were first found upon the shields which stood before the shining god?" he laughed.

"Wait a moment. I grant that the Norse are perhaps not all original Aryan speakers, but the same applies to the other people of the Atlantic coastline - the Basque, of course, and perhaps even the Gaelic people of sunken Lyonesse, which lies between France and England, probably are related to the sea rovers. I grant Greek fire must have used gunpowder, but the half Pelasgian Greeks seem to have been the only group of Aryan speaking invaders possessing the sinister secret."

"And you claim they could have gotten it from the people of the sea, rather than the Sumerians?"

"Yes because as I said they were part Pelasgian, and very close to the Phoenicians in trade, legends and even their alphabet."

"You are still ignoring the legends of the Indian ocean - the stories of the flying ships and of the bombs they dropped on their enemies."

"I suppose I have been thinking of these legends as fairy tales. That is why I never studied them particularly, except to realize that all the flying legends of the Americas seem to have stemmed from India, perhaps through the Peruvians who appear to be quite close to some of their ritual names."

"So we have come to the stone wall again. Perhaps mankind will never know which ancient power ..."

"Wait! I have a thought. The totem of the sea people is the dragon or the giant water lizard."

"So?"

"And the totem of the Indian ocean is apparently the giant bird. Undoubtedly they chose one similar to the condor who flies through the lightnings of the Andes, and in the Americas is highly revered. Curiously enough I find that American flying legends usually stem back to Peru, which incidentally has an amazing number of rituals and ancient names which hark back to India. The Sumerians probably had ships also, for you know the earliest legends of how the Sumerians came into the Mediterranean always mention Iwannos or a similar name, who travelled through the waves inside a water monster of giant proportions and who helped to rescue and help the tribes overcome by the flood."

"Yes that is true. But the bird is also the totem of Europe. How did they get it? From the Sumerians?"

"Perhaps there was an ancient contact here. The European bird seems to be an Eagle though. Someday we shall have more information from men digging with the spade of the scientists. But there is some information which they may never know unless we tell them, for this information is being lost yearly."

"You mean legend?"

"Yes. I mean an American legend which runs the continents both north and south and threads itself through almost every tribe. Once in the hoary past there were two giant powers - the great bird and the great water dragon, which finally clashed and fought with flames until the seas were red. The bird won."

"Ah ha! How very enlightening. This would seem to be a pre-flood war - way back in the ice age?"

"I would think so."

"Then where does China fit in, with its toy firecrackers? And how does it happen that they didn't admire the bird as much as the dragon?"

"Especially as China thinks that the dragon carries little children away to heaven on its back?"

"Well that's only a strange notion."

"Not exactly. The people of the sea, whose totem is the dragon, were notorious sacrificers of children."

"Oh, that is right. We have Baal ..."

"Who becomes Balaam in the Americas ..."
He checked me with a gesture.

"Speaking of the Indian ocean, did the war between the dragon and the bird have to do with a beautiful woman - a queen named Siva?"

"No. But the sea rovers were in the habit of stealing women. Helen of Troy is a case in point."

He laughed merrily.

"Well perhaps they were not the most moral people in the world, but the old half-pirates were mapping the globe when apemen were still abroad on Earth. You can't help but admire their courage and love of the sea!"

I nodded adding: "Thank you for some new thoughts and lights on an old problem. And suddenly I am thinking of a poem called "The Sphinx" ..."

"Ah, yes. I know what you mean," he nodded "you are thinking of the lines:
"Dark heavy lips which close
In such a stern repose
Seem burdened with some thought unsaid
And hoard within their portals dread
Some fearful secret there."

Then with a sigh, he added: "I am afraid the whole Earth has learned that secret now and its mushroomed cloud haunts our souls with horror ..."

Chapter 63

A Time Of Tremendous Discoveries In Geology

"Geology is in a period of unprecedented discovery. Systematic explorations of the Earth's crust by geophysicists and geologists, working in close cooperation and using new methods of investigation, are yielding wholly new knowledge about the ocean floors and the deeper parts of the continents, and a more precise understanding of regional geology. As a result, traditional views concerning the physical and chemical processes that have produced and are now molding the Earth's crust are being challenged. What processes created the contrasting formations of continents and oceans? Are they still going on, forming future continents? In the search for the answers of these fascinating questions there is an atmosphere of fascinated suspense today, such as has always marked the high points on the growth curve of a science." Walter H. Bucher of Harvard university. Author of "Crust of the Earth" and other geological volumes.

Indian artist Peshlakai Betsui's concept of the old red land's present-day remnants.

"We are living in a time of tremendous discoveries in geology" one of the warmly interested and charming professors in Oxford university, England, nodded to me quietly as he gathered his papers quickly to leave for an appointment. "Come back later and we will talk of new maps, new theories, new discoveries, which are busily shaking the structure of our ivory tower." Then with a mischievous twinkle: "I have a better idea. Come with me to another room where several other scientists are going over papers, discussing shop. We are horribly busy, but as you came in with no warning, and are leaving the same way, we must crush days of talk into a few moments, and this is the best way, for our science is as you suggest certainly exploding with new ideas right under our 'ivory tower'."

In 1946 when I spoke before the American Association for the Advancement of Science on the subject "Some Considerations Concerning the Theory of Continental Drift", they saw the number of plates I had prepared, shook heads, and cut down my original time to less than ten minutes. The reason? The theory of the moving continents was being shrugged off at this period as a ridiculous idea. Now even the conservative Bucher has apparently joined the rebellion against the stability of continents and oceans. Reason? The greatest power in the scientific world - new facts.

Fact Number One

First, word came from Sweden that Dr. Rene Malaise of Riks museum, Stockholm, that his colleague Dr. P. W. Kolbe furnished proof of the late (geologically speaking of course) sinking of the Atlantic ridge. Dr. Kolbe is an expert on the subject of diatoms, tiny marine animals. In a core which drilling machines had dug in the mid-Atlantic, shells were found at the depth of 12,000 feet which proved to be, upon inspection, of the fresh water type. Not all of them were, but the fresh water ones were in sufficient numbers at one place to warrant the conclusion that this particular location in the tropical mid-Atlantic was at one time a fresh water lake. That means that when these animals died and fell to the bottom of the lake, it was above sea level.

From this evidence by Swedish scientists, Dr. Malaise speculates that the mid-Atlantic ridge settled to its present depth as recently as ten to twelve thousand years ago. He continues with the following theory: that the ridge with its high mountain range acted as a barrier to the gulf stream, so that the Arctic ocean had become land locked from Europe to Greenland. When this land barrier was broken, the gulf stream was allowed to reach the Arctic ocean and the ice age ended. Thus the whole history of the world was affected, and the sinking became more general due to the displacement in weight of sudden warmth on the ice packs. For example, he continues, when the gulf stream broke through the barrier, its comparatively cold southern branch, the Canary island current was displaced and the Sahara became a desert.

Fact Number Two

The radio carbon method of dating rocks is causing more surprises to geologists. For example, the method which depends upon the known rate at which radioactive carbon-14 enters living matter and disintegrates on the death of that matter, is changing our estimate of the length of the phases of the last ice age as well as the duration of that era of the Pleistocene.

The rate of formation of the Niagara falls gorge brings up the estimates which had been much longer to the more modern estimates brought about by the radio carbon time clock. It tremendously shortens the period. We seem to be at the end of an ice age which began 25,000 or more years ago. It lasted through several fluctuations, reached its maximum about twenty to eighteen thousand years ago.

This would allow for the residence of man in his present form through all the fluctuations of the ice, since radio carbon has dated many of his remains in North America to these figures.

Fact Number Three

On the Washington side of the Columbia river between that state and Oregon, some four miles upstream from the Dalles dam being built across the river, scientists have finally gotten busy at excavating an ancient mound before it is forever lost to the rising stream. It is known as the Wakemap mound. Dr. B. Robert Butler, university of Washington archaeologist, believes this may be the mound of a remnant of the oldest inhabited area in the world. Its culture has been traced from 16,000 years ago to the present.

Within the mound fine carvings in bone and stone are being unearthed. "The stone artistry done in marble would rival that of Greece and Rome," says this enthusiastic archaeologist. It is very doubtful that much can be saved before the rising water drives the investigators away from their horde of treasures.

So far the skeletal type of these ancient people in the lower levels has not been released for publication, but it is the private opinion of the present writer that it may be the ancient people of the sea.

Fact Number Four

According to Ed Syers of the San Antonio News there are some great walls built of crudely hewn rock which may have formed temples of some type of culture. The great rectangular stones, almost all buried under the brush grown soil, have been estimated to weigh over a ton apiece.

Syers related that he drove out to see what little is left of the ruin. He stopped first at the town of Rockwall, Texas. Here an 80 year old resident who has been taking pictures of his ancient city showed photographs of these rocks four and five courses deep. They are plumbline straight. Between them is a fine line of mortar. The tops and mortises are beveled and the huge stones are staggered as any fine mason would stagger a brick wall. Sometimes strange designs have been found. Between Rockwall and Royse City a carved serpent head was found. There are also at the site some ancient lava flows which have cracked rock not too unlike the above. One excavator once quarried some of the rocks and found that the veins of one did not match as they should if the wall was natural. In the meantime, this site awaits further study, as one place seems to have once held a window!

Fact Number Five

Finally, years after his death, the discovery by Dr. David Banks Rogers in the Santa Barbara channel off the Pacific coast of California is now being recognized as one of the oldest cultures of mankind in the entire world. This has been uncovered, as you will remember, from notes given by the scientist himself to the author earlier in this book. Perhaps those notes are now all that may be left of Dr. Rogers' work, since the museum and all its contents were burned a few years ago.

Bones of a dwarf mammoth which he mentioned are now being dated because this six-foot animal was used as food by the early inhabitants. Radio carbon places man on Santa Rosa at more than 37,000 years ago. This was done with refinements of the radio carbon system. Undoubtedly the island was at one time a part of the mainland and was sloughed off in the general sinking of the one hundred mile wide strip, in which numerous sites were cut in two, sometimes leaving the cemetery sites visible in columns of earth left standing with the human bones protruding from the sides.

Dr. David Banks Rogers was a careful anthropologist, keeping meticulous notes and soil samples as well as numerous large photographs. The first inhabitants were the ancient dolicho-cephalic, buried in the crouch position with the red ochre and fire above which we are used to finding with the type. Pan's pipes and cigar shaped stones were also found in abundance. He placed the seeds at the site as those of a pine forest and the food source as largely that of the acorn as well as some hunting. Then came a small invasion of round heads in the second culture which were absorbed. The united people built ships, or as he suspected, foreign ships using planks caulked with tar were repaired at large yards. He had the photograph of one 100-foot ship. Of course nothing was left of the wood, but the tar lines were in the soil which he had carefully dusted out of the excavation. They showed the lines of the long dragon type of vessel. He had kept some of the tar in situ in a box awaiting the analysis of chemists to see if it was from the La Brae tar pits. Were they Phoenician ships, as he believed? Apparently now with the carbon-14 dating of the site, they evidently did go back to the interglacial when the rivers were more abundant, and the almost fossil Los Angeles river and others were running full.

Fact Number Six

Studies in six tie in with fact five. Dr. Templeton, who is connected with the Los Angeles museum, has become very much interested in the food eaten by the early mammals which were trapped by the La Brae tar pits. She tries to recover the seeds from the ancient skulls and identify them. It has been a most tedious job, and since she is the only one doing it, the work progresses slowly. However she has learned much.

"The seeds tell us that the Los Angeles area was once a series of meadows separated by small streams and pools bordered by trees and shrubs," she said. Among those seeds were the box elders which still grow along the banks of some streams, and dogwoods closely related to those now growing in damper and cooler lake Arrowhead in the nearby mountains. She found manzanitas that could not grow in this locality today without water, but manage to exist in the foggy and cooler coasts of central California. The most striking evidence were the seeds of marsh plants such as bedstraw, sedges and swamp grasses which are native to bogs. Altogether the skulls yielded more than 4,000 seeds. She also found junipers which now grow in the swamps of Texas, Louisiana and Florida - or rather the nearest relatives grow there, as the one which she found is extinct.

Fact Number Seven

Not too distant from these facts is the discovery by the oceanographers of Scripps Institute, La Jolla. Dr. G.G. Shore, Jr. says that the ocean off the coast of California from just below Point Conception to a point above the channel islands off the Santa Barbara coast is a giant deep ocean whirlpool. Speaking to the 34th annual international meeting of the Society of Exploration Geophysicists, he said:

"The Pacific bottom off southern California is really a submerged piece of the continent. The ocean doesn't really begin until you have passed a line drawn south from Point Conception.

"For many years it was thought that there were no ocean trenches off the coast of California and Baja California. Now it is known that the trenches are there, but they are filled with sediments."

He went on to explain that the trenches off Santa Barbara and San Nicholas island are about three miles deep, as compared to the five mile depth of the Alaskan trench and the seven miles of the Mariannas trench in the western Pacific. The topography of the undersea bottom is the same as the land - mountains, valleys, basins and ridges except that they are filled with sediment.

Fact Number Eight

Dr. K.O. Emery writing in the Oceanus magazine, said that fishermen are constantly bringing up teeth of mastodons and mammoths on areas which are now far out in the Atlantic ocean. He continues by saying that "This means that the continental shelf was exposed as a gentle coastal plain during the time of the elephant hunters some 11,000 years ago."

Fact Number Nine

The Pacific ocean is slowly inching up on California, the U.S. Coast and Geodetic Survey reported. Sometimes at one point it will rise two inches in 24 hours. R. Adm. H. Arnold Karo survey director, gave two explanations for the rise in sea levels along the coasts of the United States.

"The rise can be attributed to the melting of the Greenland and Antarctic glaciers, or the sinking of land which has contributed to the apparent rise elsewhere." He said that the conclusions are based on data from 44 tide gauges along the U.S. coastline which are analyzed periodically for sea level trends.

Fact Number Ten

The cliffs about Point Fermin in southern California are slowly crumbling off into the sea. The surface land began rupturing into gaps about fifty feet from the ocean. Some of these gaps are fifty- or sixty-foot cracks. The movement is not fast, but it is steady. The police are now posting signs to warn tourists that the land for one or two miles back is moving at a rate of about two inches a year, which seems to become faster as one nears the sea. This movement is more or less evident all along the coastline above Santa Monica where beautiful homes have been built above the cliffs for the view. Great walls in some cases protect the property from the sea, but fine cracks can be observed along the wall and through the cement.

Fact Number Eleven
The Alaskan Earthquake

The epicenter of this disaster was Unakwik peak, about 75 miles east and slightly south of Anchorage. The town of Anchorage is located very close to the intersection of two giant fault systems - one coming up the coast and one swinging around the Aleutian chain. This spot of crossing rifts is always a danger point. Dr. S.T. Algermissen of Washington D.C., and a team of six geophysicists, went out to ring the epicenter with seismological instruments. The information leading to the isolated peak of Unakwik was gained from information turned in by seismological stations all over the world.

In 1967 researcher Geo. Plafker of the U.S. Geological Survey, Menlo Park, studying the buildup of the quake, said that it had been going on and stresses piling up for from 930 to over 1,000 years. Other scientists disagree, believing that California has at least one major earthquake every century. The Aleutian chain has been rising for some time because Plafker found resting stages like steps in the sands of Aleutian shorelines. There have been previous announcements that the disturbance upthrust the ocean floor in the gulf of Alaska some fifty feet in history's greatest known uplift of earth mass. The horizontal displacement was up to twenty feet. Plafker is of the opinion that the quake originated in the same thrust fault that gave birth to the arc-like Aleutian island chain some thousands of years ago. He suggested that the duration build-up was shown by the Aleutian island shorelines which became progressively submerged over the centuries, by a process now linked with imperceptible earth motions constituting the prelude to a major earthquake.

There were other remarks about this earthquake. The globe rang like a bell, giving out a very low C tone. It was also revealed in Washington, D.C. that the nation's capital and much of the eastern seaboard rose about 2 inches. On Monday the new instruments in the Bureau of

Standards studied and recorded these movements. The ground where Washington, D.C. stands went up in the air about an inch and then sank 2 inches then rose 2 again. These movements went on for some two hours on a diminishing scale and finally came back to the original level. The same movements seemed to have been felt all across the continent, being strong enough to be barely perceptible to a person looking at a glass of water, in the far west. There was no great rending of the crust, said Dr. R.K. Cook of the Bureau of Standards, and therefore everything moved uniformly and thus remained rather without damage.

Fact Number Twelve
The Russian suggestion, on the subject of earthquakes

George Getze, science editor for the Los Angeles Times, is to be thanked for saving this interesting suggestion from scientific oblivion by publishing it in his newspaper.

Dr. V.I. Keilis-Borok of the Institute of Geophysics at Moscow has proposed that seismologists the world over organize a group to not only study earthquakes, but also to warn the public located at the epicenter or near the epicenter of the next giant strike. The plan is rather simple, and it seems to the present writer that it is workable if enough thought and cooperation is given to the task.

By a process of triangulation used in celestial and surface navigation which uses stars to fix the position of an airplane, we could use the same system to fix the next giant earthquake. However, instead of using stars in this case, a point of known frequent quakes such as certain points in Japan could be used. The technique depends on the measuring of the speeds with which ground waves created by these quakes reach seismic stations.

Dr. Keilis-Borok said seismographs, like the one at Caltech, California, are always receiving these ground waves, many of which pass through areas where tension is building. In these areas of building tension, the ground waves slow down. Thus by computing the differences and changes in the speed of ground waves from small quakes, the area of great tension could be pinpointed on a map, the fault lines drawn where the tension would eventually be released and the people in the area warned. He compared the tension building in a great earthquake to the tension building up in a chair which someone is trying to break. The whole piece of furniture is put under stress, but the final break with the relief of tension comes only at the point of greatest weakness.

This is the same principle working in the crust of the Earth, said Dr. Keilis-Borok as he sent out his suggestion to the scientific world.

Fact Number Thirteen

The rocks of the Earth are found to contain traces of magnetism which tell in what direction the pole lay at the time when they were formed. Thus the position of the north pole can be charted most accurately at, say, the pre-Cambrian period, some 1500 millions of years ago.

Dr. R.L. Du Bois, consultant on magnetics in Caltech's jet propulsion laboratory, has this to report on the subject - the north pole has not only been in the vicinity of Chicago, but at another time in the vicinity of southern California. At still another date the whole of North America had drifted south of the equator. This took place some 1400 million years ago. He reported this in a paper read to the General Assembly of the International Union of Geodesy and Geophysics held at the University of California.

Fact Number Fourteen

An electronic system invented by the San Diego Cubic Corporation is making the first precisely accurate maps of Earth's surface.

Dr. James H. Reid, the company's chief scientist, said a previously secret satellite had been used by the Army's map service to do the plotting. In an interview with Hal Steward of Copley News Service, he said SECOR (the company's name for Sequential Collation of Range) is receiving information from the satellite 600 miles out in space. It pinpoints the exact positions of islands, continents, lakes, cities and other landmarks around the Earth. The system uses a radio transmitter-receiver to relay information to various ground stations whose location is exactly known.

The heart of the system is a 6 1/2-pound transponder. This cost $20,000 to manufacture. The satellite is 600 miles above Earth and has a range of 4,000 miles. The total surface could be covered simultaneously with a system of satellites properly spaced in Earth orbit. Reid said that the total cost of the ground stations was less than the cost of one radar unit used in the Project Mercury tracking system. With this system we can locate and chart on a master computer every ocean.

The system could be used for locating a vessel or plane in distress and guide the victim to the nearest point of help. When icebergs are located, a transponder on them would warn away ships.

Fact Number Fifteen

Yale University has become interested in the

Portolan charts, among which is the Piri Re'is map. They have discovered that one of these was bound with a hitherto unknown manuscript by Friar John of Plana Carpini's mission to the Tartars in 1245-47. There is no relation between the two except that both were apparently included in some kind of encyclopedic work. Scholars believe that this particular map was first copied in Basel, Switzerland, from much earlier documents which have since become lost. Research has pinpointed the manufacture of the paper in the Rhine valley during the mid 1400s or in other words the 15th century, which is before the time of Columbus. This map may have belonged to Leif Ericson.

Francisco Garcia Vallejo, who was a seaman on the first voyage of Columbus, testified to the fact that the explorer had a Portolan map.

An almost amusing sidelight to this inquiry into historical facts is the rage in Madrid, Spain, where the daily newspaper ABC called the Yale scholars "feeders on carrion". The Spanish should remember that their explorer is losing none of his glory because other men came first. Indeed in their dancing of the Tarentella, the shape of their ships and their sunken ports, to say nothing of their faces, and many among them, of the entire physical structure of the body, shows their direct heritage from Earth's first navigators, the people of the sea.

Fact Number Sixteen

In the Journal for the American Scientist, Dr. Robert S. Dietz, an oceanographer connected with U.S. Coast and Geodetic Survey, has written a most interesting article on continental drift. I met Dr. Dietz when I spoke on this subject before the American Association of Science, and we had a long mutually agreeable talk. At that time he was only mildly interested. Now he has taken up the fight for the moving continents.

As recently as Feb. 28, 1964 geophysicist Gordon J.F. MacDonald of the university of California checked the growing number of physicists, oceanographers and geologists joining the ranks of the believers in drift by a headlong challenge. He said that the continents have such deep roots that they cannot move. Dietz then prepared his answer. He said that the western part of California is moving very slowly seaward. Drift on this scale makes him believe that greater drift could be occurring with the continents. He admits that he does not believe that continents plow through the mantle like ships at sea, but that they move like rocks do in a lava flow.

Furthermore, the continental slopes give further evidence of drift. The slopes of both the east and west coast of the United States, formed at roughly the same time (some 150 million years ago), have since been modified by sedimentation. Nevertheless, the Atlantic slopes off South America and Atlantic slopes off Africa had different origins from the Pacific slopes. Those along the continental edges of the Atlantic were formed when the continents split and began to move apart.

He believes that the Pacific slopes, on the other hand, are caused by sedimentation. This accumulates before the moving mass and by action of the sea causes the sediments to become new rocks.

The present writer finds agreement with the Atlantic theory but is somewhat hesitant about the Pacific slopes because of the trenches before all the Pacific shoreline around the world. Might it not be possible, Dr. Dietz, that magmatic currents, of which we know so little, might be pulling many places down? Too bad that we probably won't live long enough to find out for certain.

On this same subject, here are a few more sidelights from other scientists.

THE DARWIN RISE

The Darwin rise refers to one of the very large features in the Pacific, and in this global picture, we can hardly cut the Pacific out entirely from our understanding of the Atlantic.

Dr. Henry W. Menard, Jr. marine geologist from Scripps Institute of Oceanography at La Jolla, California, is interested in the antiquity of the Darwin rise. Its past had been overlooked before Menard and his colleagues applied some detective work on various clues which Scripps has been uncovering. The word rise here is used instead of the word ridge, because as Menard explains, these geological features run through all but the Pacific ocean. There is another peculiarity about this Pacific mountain range. It is not in the center of the ocean, following the line of the shore. According to Menard there was once a ridge in the Pacific, but it has disappeared. According to the latest theories on marine geologists, rises are caused by bulges in the mantle. The mantle of course, surrounds the core and supports the crust. It is about twenty miles below the continents and about six below the oceans. What makes the mantle bulge? Perhaps the hot material in the mantle rises in a sort of stream and raises the blocks of the mantle at adjacent edges.

Heat flow measurements are high on ridge summits. The crust is thicker toward the sides of the ridges and thinner in the middle. Both heat flow and thickness observations prove the correctness of this theory. The oceanographers went looking for the ridge, but found only volcanic lava rock on the sea floor and no ridge. Yet there were fault lines crossing the ridge which is correct for other ridges. Besides this there were round topped mountains with rounded and water worn pebbles on the upper surface and sometimes the fossils of animals which had lived about one hundred million years ago. These guyots are the very best evidence that at one time a bulge in the mantle raised the hills above the water. Then the bulge sank down and with it the islands. Why? The oceanographers would like to know.

Fact Number Seventeen

One of the most remarkable instruments of our twentieth century is the computer. In the forties, tempers grew hot in the symposiums over the subject of continental drift. The conservatives simply sat back and laughed over the whole idea and the drift theorists met frustration trying to prove anything. Today Cambridge university, England, is putting a period to this argument. As soon as the discovery was made that the poles roamed all around the Earth (not really, but in the words of a few fretful conservatives listening to their first lecture on ancient magnetism), continental drift began to pick up proponents. It was far more simple to move the continents than to swing the globe. To prove or disprove the possibility of the continents fitting together, Dr. Edward Bullard and his staff turned to a computer. He told it, in his own words "to move the continents around until they fit." The result was most startling, especially in the Atlantic. The computer discarded the continental shorelines and fit them at the edge of the submerged continental shelf. Except for some unexplainable holes, it was something less than one per cent error. Added to this fact is the expanding knowledge of the oceanic floors with their mountains and valleys. It is almost as if the ridge and the continental shelves had clung together for some thousands of years and had gradually been pulled apart while retaining much of the old markings as warm candy might have when pulled. To these strange facts, science must readjust its ideas. Was the globe always like this, or are we gaining water?

At a meeting of the Royal Society of Geodesy and Geophysicists in London, these facts won over many of the conservatives and the century old idea of rigid continents and oceans is being discarded for continental drift. There was considerable support for the idea that as the continents move, huge slabs of crust move horizontally for hundreds of miles and that Europe and America are moving farther apart constantly. It was also noted that vast new fissures are rapidly widening at two places in the globe - northeastern Africa and southern California.

The fact that ridges are to be discovered with a rift in the center and faults across them was also noted. Furthermore, near the continents there seems to be descending currents with higher gravity just as rising "fountain" currents with less gravity pushing the continents apart seem to come from the ridge. The great descending currents may be sucking continental material down into the mantle. These currents may account for the deep trenches in the ocean off South America and elsewhere. These trenches are always the scene of deep seated earthquakes and volcanoes. Of course, the contribution of the orbiting satellites were also noted. Some objections were voiced by conservatives but no alternatives were offered.

Dr. S.K. Runcorn and his staff at the university of Newcastle-on-Tyne, England, are using the information of the bulges and dents sent back by the satellites to compound a new theory. Runcorn believes that there may be convection cells inside Earth, but their number is controlled by the size of Earth's core, which is composed of iron. The core may have grown in the course of time. Perhaps there was only one convection cell at one time and then three. At each changeover, caused by core growth, a new epoch of continental drift would begin. The cracks appearing in the Red sea and along the gulf of California may be associated with these changes. Whatever the final theory will be to explain it fully, continental drift is apparently now good science and here to stay.

May the present writer suggest, Dr. Runcorn, that the weight and lateral pressure of the glacial age in Gondwannaland gave the pattern which the Indian and the Atlantic rifts followed, and the movements of the magma during the drift at the end of the Pleistocene may be due partly to these patterns, complicated by the ice patterns of the Pleistocene with their lateral pressures. Thus, the movement of the magma in fountains and suction areas may be the result instead of the cause. The pressure of the drift, a twisting movement toward a new clash of continents in the Bering sea sometime in the future could be the result of these pressures, and the building at that point of another ice age foci?

THE NEW THEORY

It is inevitable that the matching of the continents which the computers are doing with none of the passionate heat of the arguments during the thirties and forties, is not only underwriting continental drift but asking a question which finally makes its way into the consciousness of every surprised scientist. If these continents all match, will the globe upon which they match be as large as ours is today? Or is our globe becoming larger?

One of the most delightful scientific books which I have ever had the pleasure of reading is "The Expanding Universe" by Eddington. If you read it you will be as delighted by the beautiful Miltonian English as you are intrigued by the idea that the entire universe of the stars is in the process of exploding, and we as part of that universe, are also exploding. As we move out and away from the original foci we are expanding, and everything on Earth moves faster and faster. Not only do the days seem to pass faster than they did in our childhood, but they actually do. And in the end all will move faster and faster until the mad pressure of it will become unbearable.

Einstein gave us the basis for this in his theory that the force of gravity would be slowly diminished and this would allow for an enlarged Earth and the other planets of our system.

The Hungarian geophysicist Egyed calculated a rate of expansion for the Earth of about a yard every thousand years. Radioactive heat would provide the energy for this expansion. The idea of an expanding globe would allow great cracks to open up in the ocean floor and fill with lava.* This theory has some merit, but like so many other theories is not self sufficient in itself because it does not allow for the glacials and their influence on the globe. So the theories go on and the answer in its entirety still escapes us. Perhaps that is how it will always be.

"While space scientists have been shooting for the moon a group of scientists from 48 nations headquartered at the university of California at Los Angeles are probing into Earth to find out why land has shrunk and the ocean floor increased.

The inner space project is being conducted by scientists representing the International Mantle Project (IMP) according to Dr. Leon Knopoff, project secretary from UCLA.

"The purpose of the ten year international project is to find out what causes such natural phenomena as land shrinkage, expansion of ocean floors, and the make-up of the thick layer of earth called the mantle which extends 400 miles from the surface.

"The Earth probe was spurred by recent findings which indicate the mantle and crust are coupled. What happens in the upper mantle is believed directly to affect the composition of the crust.

"Since 1960 according to Knopoff, American, British and Russian scientists have revised earlier theories only to complicate the picture of the Earth by two major findings.

"One is that the sea floor of the Atlantic has apparently been increasing during millions of years. Since the Earth's total surface is constant, scientists want to know where land is shrinking.

"The second discovery is that the composition of the mantle not only differs laterally, but also sideways.

"This led to the deduction that processes by which the crust was formed may differ throughout the world.

"Verifications of these theories, Knopoff believes, will enable scientists better to understand the mechanism of earthquakes, volcanic eruptions and tidal waves.

"Scientists will also learn why minerals are concentrated in certain regions, which may lead to discovery of new mineral pockets.

"The mantle is 1750 miles deep and the biggest layer of the globe by volume when measured against Earth's 4000 mile radius."

This article shows that science is catching up to our book very rapidly and very soon it will perhaps no longer be considered fantastic. There is only one criticism of the above. Allowance must be made for the possibility that the surface of the Earth is expanding. This has not been ruled out as the reporter of this article seems to believe.

Also it should have been mentioned that the sites near the continental shelves are the trenches where the crust seems to descend into the mantle carrying cities with it as it seems to be doing in South America at the present time, and has done along the coast of Santa Barbara, as well as the civilized areas in the Atlantic.

Was there an Atlantis? Perhaps that was one name for a part of it, but there probably was an old red land, part of whose giant sandstone slabs are to be seen down warped all along the coast of the eastern Atlantic into the green waves of the ocean.

---

*From the Los Angeles Examiner, June 27, 1967.

Chapter 64
The Ancient Sunken Cities Of Ys, Hel And Asgaard – A Sea Bottom Map

The only way I can adequately express my feeling about the fascinating map of the northern Atlantic I have prepared for this chapter is to quote Keats:

> Much have I travelled in the realms of gold
>> And many goodly states and kingdoms seen;
> Round many western islands have I been
>> Which bards in fealty to Apollo hold.
> Oft on one wide expanse had I been told
>> That deep-browed Homer ruled as his demesne;
> Yet never did I breathe its pure serene
>> Till I heard Chapman speak out loud and bold
> Then felt I like some watcher of the skies
>> When a new planet swims into his ken."
>> Keats

This map of the northern Atlantic's submerged lands is gleaned from maps and descriptions in the following books: "The Viking and the Red Man" by R.T. Sherwin, published in 1942 by Funk & Wagnalls, New York and London; "Lost America" by Captain Mallory, published by Dartmonth University Library, (The Portolan Chart); "Map of the Ancient Sea Kings" published by Chilton Books in 1965; "The Earth's Shifting Crust" published in 1958 by Pantheon Books; "Great Mysteries of the Earth" published in 1960 by Pulnam.

To copy these maps into one has taken over a year, is frustrating and overwhelming, but the reader must not miss out on this thrill. Many mistakes were made. The continental blocks of Spain, the British Isles and Africa were too big. I had only intended to go to the edge of the ridge, but I couldn't stop - I had to get most of it in, because as I copied south, I found what would seem to be a city - and what a city! I looked up the ancient name of the Canaries. It turned out to be Tu-Pan-Ku, which became Tu Pan Kur after it had sunk. When it was first copied, the straight line before it seemed to be a fault, but then double magnifying glasses brought out the

impossible - tiny dots arranged geometrically on the supposed fault. Geometric dots do not happen in geology. There was only one answer - this was a city and the huge fault was an enormous sea wall, perhaps fifty miles wide! The dumping of the Triton sea was all too plain, and the sunken labyrinth in the sea before it gave that huge lake its natural name, "the Labyrinthine sea". I did not copy that. It would have taken another year!

The triangle under the Azores was named Hellas, for this seems the correct location for that lost land, somewhere on that land is the ruins of the city of Hel, "city of light". I was searching for the "Road to Hel" mentioned in the Eddas of the Norse. They must have been rivers! (At all costs the ancient names must be kept. It would be unthinkable to see "Jenkin's Corners" or some other inappropriate name on the ancient surface.)

As I proceeded a quarter of an inch at a time with magnifying glasses that make everything look fuzzy when one stops, I called the mountain ranges coming from the odd shaped horse face, "the Mane of Pegasus" only to learn months later that when the head was turned around it looked more like a lizard! Also, I had crowded the masses of terracing surrounding Hellas too much and thus had lost a strange apparition which appeared when the map was turned upside down. (See the separate section maps I have made to describe them)

Before the edge of the Irish-British shelf were the remains of two more cities - with water monsters of massive casts in the sea before them. They must have dwarfed the collosus of Rhodes (which is an actual ruin on the side that faces Turkey).

The southern city I called Ys, as I understand this city was on a point jutting into the Atlantic about here, and the wall around it against the sea is gigantic. This wall has tiny dots geometrically spaced on it which must be the great round towers where the perpetual fires burned for the seamen, so well remembered in legend.

To the north of it is the city I called after the lovely poem of Donnelly by its legendary name.

> "What was its name?" Be still - acushla,
> Thy hair is wet with mists my boy!
> Thou hast looked perchance on Tyr - na-n'oge,
> Land of eternal youth and joy."

The large square lake west of this city seems to have had two water levels, for apparently structures exist on the lower one, and then were covered with a higher rise of water. I judged that this was, in its later stages, Asgaard, the ancient Norse city and perhaps the lake was Brunhilda's pool, she being the daughter of Votan II, or as the Norse and Germans call him - Wodin or Odin. His son, Tyre or Tyr, gained much fame in the war of the gods in the Mediterranean, where he was finally killed. Probably it was his grandson, Tyr, who then led many of his people from the Tyrhennian sea east to what are now the lost cities of Tyr and Sidon. The name Tyr is unknown in the Americas, showing the break in communications followed the end of the reign of Votan I in what the Amerinds call "the great destruction".

The western shore of the Atlantic is rifted on a much deeper plane than the eastern shore, and apparently was always a morass which was called in the Americas "the morass where the dragons lived" or "the morass where the water monsters lived". There seemed to be, however, a few cultivated areas there.

THE MEDITERRANEAN GORGE

An engineer friend of mine, S.R. Gilson, MS, of the university of Illinois glanced at the map and then reached for the magnifying glasses.

"Why didn't you do justice to the water coming out of the Mediterranean? You have it diverted two ways - north and south, yet fail to show how this was done."

"But how can anything remain of that work following the seismic disaster which sank the southern half of the Atlas, cracked off the western edge of the continental shelf of Europe and broke open the Mediterranean valley?"

"Look at this and look closely," handing me the glasses.

I did and a mass of tremendous pipes or monuments that looked like pipes as well as dams appeared above the enormous earth tears.

I nodded my thanks and again began to copy while he kept muttering to himself: "Fantastic - unbelievable - perhaps some kind of a rock formation - "

"That is a good description of the whole map," I nodded. "I can hardly believe it, but it's there."

"What are all these peculiar faces? Even what must be mountains are carved to resemble something?"

"The only answer is that these sea rovers were not only talented, but also had dynamite."

"Ah! Yes ..."

He laughed as if discovering a tremendous joke.

"Well?" I asked.

"Imagine one ship's captain saying to another via megaphone: 'I'm going to the seven-headed dog' or, 'I am going to see the lady with the snakes for hair - Medusa' and then smile to see the look of astonishment in the faces of the kibitzers."

"And that same look of puzzled amazement has followed the names in the legends ever since," I added.

THE SUNKEN CITY

On July 3, 1967, English frogmen recovered a large granite ball from the floor of the English channel. The recovery of this 150 pound ball may lead to the discovery of a Roman fortress. A geological survey of the Mixon reef for the Natural History museum of London led to a submerged cliff about a mile south of Selsey Bill. Major Wallace, a geologist, had this to say: "This discovery would suggest the existence of a considerable town. The wall on the reef may possibly be the southeastern corner of a Roman fortress. The citadel's present level is submerged due to the rise of the sea level throughout the centuries since the days of the Roman occupation of Britain."

Major Wallace made two other statements that are interesting. When the tide is low, the town, or part of it can be seen. Some limestone balls discovered at a depth of eighty feet strengthens the belief that this is the location of a citadel. Many such balls have been found, capable of being hurled by a Roman catapult. These balls lie in a depression called "the hole" lying due south of the Mixon reef.

"There is a possibility that the town belonged to King Cogidumnus, an ally of Rome, and that the town thrived in 100 A.D."

The final statement made by Major Wallace is most significant when we consider other oceanic formations: "Whatever these ruins are, they are definitely not natural, but made by men. Nature could never produce such regular stone slabs as we have seen on the reef."

406

FRANCE

Tyrrhenian Sea

CORSICA

SARDINIA

PYRENEES

SPAIN

BALEARIC IS.

ATLAS RANGE

PORTUGAL

DRAA DEPRESSION

AGADIR.

HERACLES Crossing?

← City of Tu Pan Ku Tu Pen Kur?

Crossing of Charon?

HELLAS?

LAKE of the Lost terraces?

Labyrinthine Lake.

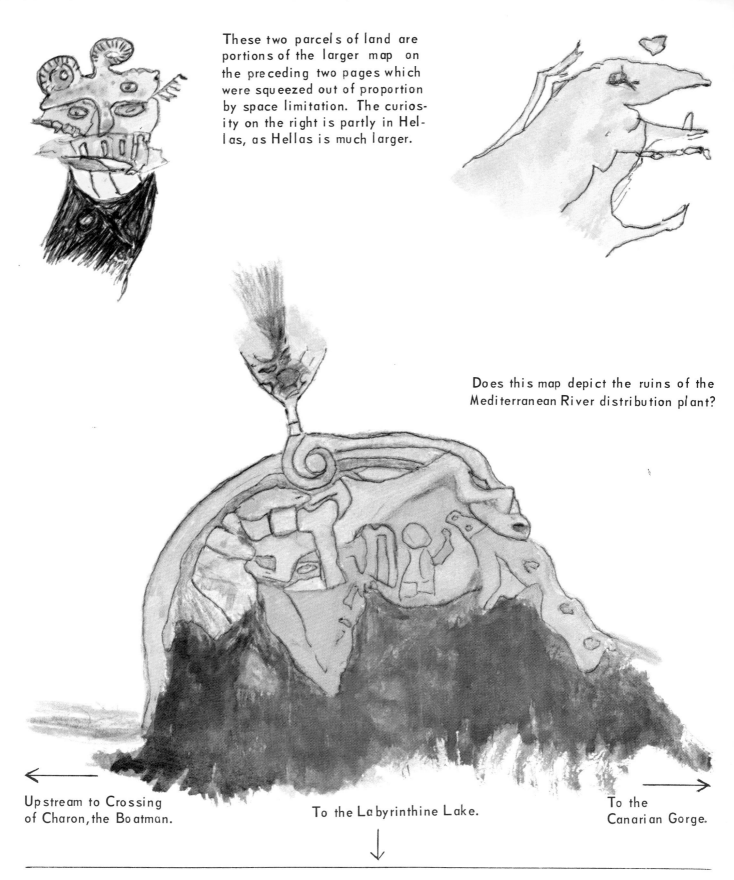

These two parcels of land are portions of the larger map on the preceding two pages which were squeezed out of proportion by space limitation. The curiosity on the right is partly in Hellas, as Hellas is much larger.

Does this map depict the ruins of the Mediterranean River distribution plant?

← Upstream to Crossing of Charon, the Boatman.

To the Labyrinthine Lake.

↓

To the Canarian Gorge. →

Pages 406-407: This map represents a composite derived from many months of study and detailed scrutiny of many old maps, modern ocean bottom surveys, and related data that have revealed the remnants of topographical features which suggest the possible location of legendary civilizations.

The map of Antarctica drawn by Oronce Fine, French geographer, in 1531. It is remarkable for its agreement with soundings charts made by present Antarctica scientific expeditions.

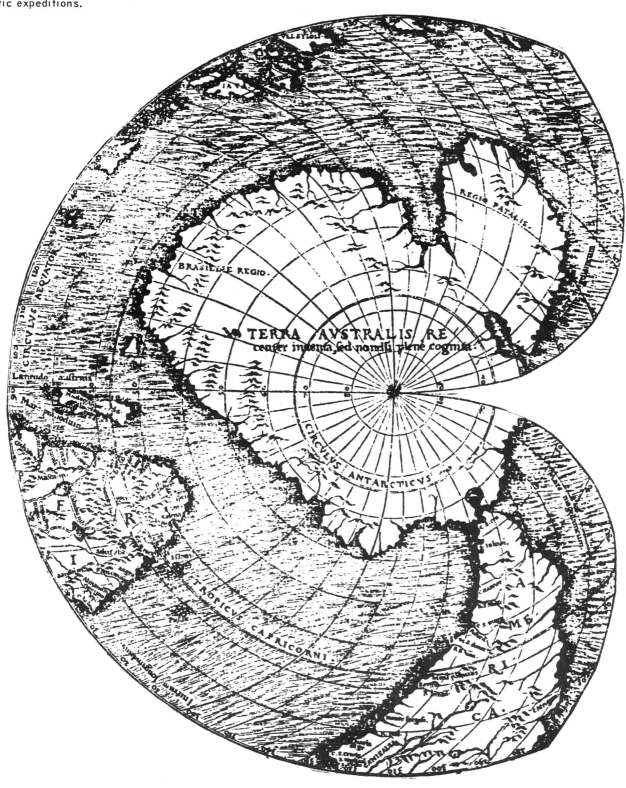

409

Chapter 65

The Ring Of Fire – Does It Still Encircle The World?

Nefertiti was the wife of Akhenaten or Akhenaton. He was the one Pharaoh who dared to defy the power of the priests of the fire god and to establish a non-sacrificing religion to a single monotheistic deity. One and a half millennia before the time of Jesus Christ, this mild youthful Pharaoh closed the temples of Egypt's many gods and started the religion of Aten, a beneficent deity worshipped under the symbol of the sun. He moved his court 240 miles north of Thebes, the ancient capital, known today as Luxor. He died mysteriously while still a young man and his lovely queen also died mysteriously not long after him. He was then succeeded by Tutankhamen (either his son-in-law or younger brother), who moved his capital back to Thebes, but who in turn died mysteriously, probably at the hands of the powerful priesthood, before he had lived very long. It was Tutankhamen's untouched tomb which was discovered by Lord Carnarvon in 1922. And his death in 1923, the first of a long line of deaths of those who had first entered the tomb, gave rise to the legend of the Egyptian curse of the tomb of Tutankhamen. It could have been the ancient poison.

"The time has come, the walrus said,
    To talk of many things.
Of shoes and ships and sealing wax,
    Of cabbages and kings."
                    Lewis Carroll.

Now has come the time for pulling the loose threads of the past into some kind of an understandable tapestry. We have scanned the lives of our millions of ancestors through the pleasures and terrors of their time; through the beauty and charm of their Earth as well as its horrors, beyond those which our time has known.

Very quickly let us class them again: the three types who haunt the northern Atlantic and its spillover into the Mediterranean and who, incidentally, haunt us. Perhaps for the first time we shall understand that suppressed pirate in us who swings his bloody sabre and whom we never recognize at fashionable dinners, but who rises sometimes in a novel we are reading or that saintly creature who surprises us when we do an unexpected good deed.

First, there are the peoples who have a recognizable culture, and the amazing thing about them is that this culture is world wide. They haunt the shores of the oceans and we can hardly deny that they must have had ships. They are the ancient dolichocephalic who have the long heads, long faces, long fingers and feet, slender build. Perhaps their most notable trait is the curving spine below the waist line which allows for rounded buttocks where any fat they acquire is usually stored, although they are not inclined to fleshiness. Their slender faces have long and wide open eyes, often with an exotic tilt. The cheekbones are high, sometimes giving the woman great beauty. Among them is Mona Lisa, queen Nefertiti of ancient Egypt, and innumerable moderns who hold fashion modeling jobs, and others who parade in beauty contests. They are the people of the tiny waist and a great love of the sea. They seem to be the well of the world's brunettes.

They were the first people in the Mimembres valley where they had no weapons, thus showing a probability that they held the land alone. They fashioned exquisite pottery with reptile designs and passed away thousands of years ago.

They were the people who lived in Mexico City before Mt. Shitli erupted and rolled a four story high sheet of lava over the land. Under this sheet, now known as "The Pedrigal", which holds Mexico university with its trees and gardens, as well as many lovely homes, is their cemetery. It was discovered when the Mexicans were digging under the Pedrigal for street

The plates on pages 412-413-415-416 are from an old Chinese play from the time of Li Po or before. The play has to do with a visit to the home of the viceroy of the fire god on a partly sunken land in the Atlantic. Costumes and scenes are the apogee of the Chinese civilization of Confucius, not the decadent civilization found by Marco Polo. It is the

China preceding the Tartar-Manchu invasion. This civilization is little known to any but archaeologists. The fox god
Hou is imprisoned on an island. He gains entrance to the
court of the viceroy. The vermillion and gold Phoenix bird
and dragon are symbols of divine descent, communication,
power and knowledge. The fox god is red and all of his

building blocks, also suitable for walls and homes. Their graves again show the pure skeletal type. They had rounded pots having three legs; were buried in the crouch position in red ochre, often holding Pan's pipes and cigar shaped rocks in their fingers.

They invaded the caves of Spain during what is now believed to be an interglacial period. Their skeletons and burial customs were identical.

Again on the islands off the Santa Barbara coast of California, they are to be found with the same burial customs, in what was probably a heavily forested area with many streams, before the hundred mile wide strip of that coastline was dropped into the sea. The huge planked ship found buried very deeply nearby could have been of the next later civilization. However this can be debated and again the time is old enough to be the last interglacial period. This awaits carbon dating.

They were the people of Europe who lived in the stilt houses over the full lakes, probably again of the interglacial period.

In the legends which precede history, we have the story from the Norse and Germans that the world was fashioned by Odin whose body at his death became the sun, stars, trees, etc.

A very similar story comes from China, but in this case the world was fashioned by Pan Ku who ruled for 18,000 years. Upon his death he became the sun, moon, stars, etc. Pan Ku sounds very close to Emperor Fu and we have a date of 18,000 years for the duration of this early civilization. Now from Herodotus of Greece, we have the statement that Pan was one of the eight gods who preceded the twelve gods. From the Americas we have the name of Pan connected with that of Maya. There is a valley called Mayapan. From the Sahara we have a fossil river called Maia which is pronounced as the Maya pronounce their name (M-ah-i-yah). The i is long in both instances and in the Sahara the Maia is one of the largest fossil rivers on Earth. From Greece again we have the information that Maia was the wife of Pan. This of course, usually means an ally or a related power.

The word Tu as used by the Tuaraks or Tuaregs of the Sahara, means "all powerful" while in the Americas it usually means "all glorious" and these must hark back to the original language. And is it not curious that the strange masked katchinas who dance in rhythmical movements for the Pueblos in the Americas, speak only the words "hu tu tu tu".

We are told by the Sumerians that originally the word Ku meant "lord of the mountain". Then Kur became "the lost land", the literal translation of which was "the land between the crust of the Earth and the all enveloping deep of the sea". It was the abode of the dead. They also said that Zui Su Dra was "the king of the mountain". He was the one who built the ship which saved most of his court from the flood. Utu with them was the sun god or god of light. Like the Greeks who had a boatman, Charon, to cross the Styx, river of death, the Sumerian had Enlil. As a boatman and like Charon he seduced a virgin in the boat. We must note that Enlil, like the later Goths in the Roman games as gladiators fighting in the arena, used a net and a trident as their weapons. All this seems to point to the civilization of the trident.

Again for more hints let us return to the Gothic legends. Odin was the father of Tyr and the son of the dragon of the sea. From our other studies in the Americas we recognize Odin as Votan the last emperor of the sunken land. If Tyr was his son in Europe, and was not known in the Americas, then he may have been the son who went east, as Votan the Third was the son who went west, and from that time on the contact with Europe was ended. Yet, we are told in the Gothic legends that Votan the Clever Builder, who walked with a limp, had a son Tyr. This son lost his life in the Mediterranean battle of the gods, but before that, lost his hand fighting the wolf.

In the Americas, the wolf is the death god as he is in ancient Egypt as Set. He is a trickster who steals the fire. This evidently means that he was successful in his fight with the fire god. The wolf in the Americas is a western totem running through the Athapascan tongue, right back to the Aleutians. Was it the totem of the Tartars in Europe? The Finnish epic seems to suggest such a conclusion. In the Americas, especially the west coast of North America, Tyr is unknown, but the wolf and the dragon fought to the death. The wolf won. It is possible that the Dene (meaning "people") of the Navaho and the Apache are the children of this western war. The Apache Dene certainly have the legends of their conquered mothers, while the Navaho Dene have far more the appearance of doli characteristics in skeletal structure, but the wolf is more feared and revered. However, they too show the eastern influence. For example, the "twin stars is the place in the center of the Earth where everything is straightened out". It is like Washington in a way, but far greater and more powerful than Washington. Neither tribe will eat fish. Once my

retinue is red - the demon shade. His hair is flame and his great mask is over his loins with teeth showing. He makes himself known by placing his own magic mask over his face. It is the one which has the breath which burns opponents. These plates probably are stylized copies of prehistoric Chinese symbols, commemorating the old red land

and sunken Atlantis, and are rich in symbolism which can tell a fascinating story to the student. The present plates were painted by Bernard Freres, engraved by Emichel Ploquin, Ruckert and Acrider, and printed by Kadar, Paris, in 1928.

friend, Shooting Star of the Dacotah, told me that all Indian tribes could be divided into those who eat fish and those who do not. This was because the fish once ate their ancestors after the great destruction. Thus, if a people like the ones of Catalina eat fish, it is because they were contacted by Tu Pan or Pan Ku of the water monster, during the time of its greatest power over the Earth, instead of being the children who survived the destruction.

This explanation has been a great help, and does seem to have a direct bearing. The avoidance of fish is the strongest in the Caribbean or among the tribes of the eastern group who are not Algonkin speakers.

Thus the vaguest outlines of the history of these ancient doli seems to be taking shape.

We know that the water monster was their totem, and since it has been found to be a living animal, instead of a figment of the imagination, the mark of the water monster on the Portolan maps shows that they were made by the doli. This was a signature in the ancient world, for most of the traders did not read. Reading and writing were accomplishments of the elite and the clergy, but all the world recognized the main totems, especially that of the reptile and his trident.

How do we know that the doli visited all of Earth's people, leaving his imprint on their skeletons, accomplishments, or customs? Because, knowing these culture traits of Earth's earliest mariners, we can recognize the giant building blocks of the Mediterranean; the canals of many cities; the terracing of the land from the Azores and Mediterranean to Peru and the Philippines; the walls of China, and Chan-Chan in Peru (which rivals that of China); the mastery of the use of cement throughout early America among other places. Even the dances of the people are significant - the dancing done with two swords from the coast of Europe to the civilizations of the Danube and the Mediterranean on through the Pacific Fili islanders to unrelated eastern and western tribes in the Americas. The long serpent line of men and women dancing either separately with arms over each other's shoulders, or done with a handkerchief to symbolize smoke, is another heritage. The sacred mountain of Ku, probably later named the Atlas, is remembered from the hats of the Welsh women to the pointed helmets of the German army. The purple robes of which these ancients were so fond, and the making of the dye which was perpetuated by the followers of Tyr in the Mediterranean from Crete to Tyr Phoenicia, and Etruria (Etruscans who carried the Tyrean name on the ancient Egyptian records) has become one of the signs of royalty in all the capitols of Europe. The building of giant causeways usually credited to Rome in Europe becomes a great mystery in the Americas because of their age. They are also to be observed sometimes off the coast of Lands End, England, Ireland and France - descending into the sea. Hardly the work of Romans, but in time, and with the help of carbon dating, they will someday perhaps be credited to their true builders.

The fantastic knowledge of eatable foods and extent of agricultural knowledge exhibited by these people or their descendents are noted by Yale university in their article "The Staircase Farms of the Ancients" in a 1916 National Geographic magazine. It was quoted here in the amazement of the scientists who found our present knowledge far below the level of the early people of Peru whose vast stores of strange and known foods far outclassed our own.

True, some of the Greek writers of a couple of millennia ago sensed these people were overbearing, and probably due to their almost impregnable capitals with their labyrinthine harbors and underground passages, were not always too honest. Yet there is something about the doli, symbolized to me by an ancestor I was tracing down through my grandfather's name, Balmor. I finally came to the cutlass swinging man with the patch over his eye who arrived with 32 ships (incidentally a Venus calendar number) and asked an early Irish monarch for land, declaring that the sea took that of his clan. When asked what he had been doing since the disaster, he remarked casually: "Pyracie". From the descriptions of him, a verse from a child's book of poems comes to mind whose author I have unfortunately forgotten:

"His conscience, of course, was as black as a bat,
     But oh! - he wore an elegant plume in his hat;
And when he walked, it wiggled - like that!
     The Pirate Don Dirk, of Dow-Dee."

My grandfather, Balmor, witty, adventuresome (in the days when that word meant the trails west of St. Louis and full of fun, was the darling of my childhood, but it was not until I had grown up that I realized part of this charm must have been due to his mother, who was a distant cousin or great granddaughter or something, to Germany's most delightful liar - Baron Von Munchhausen.

CRO MAGNON MAN

We now come to the next earlier group - the Cro Magnon. He is first noted by Leakey when he found twenty-six burials in the great rift gorge of Africa. Their bones were found with metates for the grinding of wheat or corn. The latter, by the way, has a most fantastic antiquity in the Americas and extends into many varieties. These twenty-six (a possible Venus calendar number which the Dakotas and others who hold up their tents with twenty-six uprights and wear twenty-six feathers in the war-bonnet, would claim as brothers) were found in the lowest level of the gorge, showing that the great rift had twice filled and twice emptied after their time. Thus we seem to have a people who had already domesticated plants and had the calendar for that work of plant husbandry during the first interglacial.

In Spain we find walls built below sea level by the people who left Cro Magnon skeletons behind, after the sea arose above their harbor.

In France, the caves of the interesting hunter-artist who first displayed his well executed drawings of Pleistocene animals to a startled world was the first scientific discovery of Cro Magnon. The anthropologists discovered in him a distinct race. The color of the skin and hair was gone of course, but the big size of these men with the square shoulders, straight spine line and strong hands might have been the ancestors of the Germanic tribes except that they were long heads with long hands and feet. Their women were inclined to stoutness with their straight spine line like their central European cousins, but they came only to the shoulder of their men. The nose, too, differed from that of the central Europeans: it was often hawked. Above the eye the heavy eyelid showed evidence of the Asian eyefold. The high cheek bones inherited from their doli ancestors became a very dominant characteristic placing the face on the diamond from the eyebrows of which the forehead slanted to a point. The skull capacity was excellent though much must be allowed for muscle control. They could have been the ancestors of the Norse and Gaelic coastal tribes however.

The Cro Magnon type is very strong in the eastern Americas where the complicated burial rite is found in many sections and in its entirety in some tribes. Also the thigh of the Cro Magnon is flattened so that the owner can sit on his heels for hours.

It is possible that the Cro Magnon is the well of the red heads with green or hazel eyes. The little children among some Amerind tribes show the red lights in their hair especially after washing it or coming in from a long swim and drying it in the sun. They very easily blend with the whites and in two generations their skin color is lost. An artist told the present writer that his models would warn him that their bodies had "bleached out by wearing white-man-clothes", and it would take much sun to bring back the "proper color" again.

On the other hand, it must be noted that the Norse are very lightly bearded and youths can put off shaving for more time than their darker skinned fellows.

Looking at pre-history, the Cro Magnon seems to be the Titan of legend. Now since the time of the glacials has been moved forward by science while man himself as a sentient creature handling tools, has been moved back into the Pliocene, we must be willing to grant that he could have lived through all of the glacials. It is also possible that the civilization of the doli reached such a high point because they early gained control of the seas, and that their power was broken forever as a world master, when the oceans rose with the first interglacial and drowned out their cities. Only then did they become weak enough for the Titans to take over with the war between the reptile and the bird, when the bird won. This could have been between the doli colossus of the sea and the rising power of the Titans, after the colossus was badly hurt by crumbling harbors and cities.

It is also quite probable that Hercules was a Titan and that Achilles and the goddess Hera, his mother, were Titans. Hera is identical to the sunken city on the Greek island in the Aegean sea, where she may have been the queen. In the Illiad of Homer, she clutches Achilles by "his long red hair". Here we begin to see the inroads of the Titans into Pelasgian territory. Hercules, we are told, was the son of Zeus, who had become the king of Crete. Yet the Tuaraks of the Sahara tell us that they are the followers of Hercules who invaded from the sea and established capitals with vast trade when the Sahara itself still bore the Triton sea. The Tuaregs (or however they finally decide to spell it) are very large men with comparatively small women and one of their features are their light eyes and tendency to red hair. The latter can be observed in the women, as the men are veiled. They have, however, a great respect for the large poisonous reptile they keep for a pet. It might be very wise for some new doctorate student to study them for language, writing and the chanted histories which apparently either they and Hercules brought or perhaps the Pelasgians who may be the people of Tyr, gave to the Greeks and others in the Mediterranean. Also it may be noted that all of the "tasks" given Hercules had to do with subduing other totems whose locations were largely in the Atlantic sea. Was Zeus (with the allied help) aiming at world domination, by starting on the ancient crippled colossus of the sea?

Speaking of Hercules, Thucydides who lived from 460 to 400 BC, a Greek historian who was famous for his judicial treatment of history, said that Hercules lived 17,000 years before his time. If world domination was his plan or that of Zeus, he did not count on the seismological disturbances of the Mediterranean, for Crete is now thought to have been finally overcome by a disaster of seismic origin. And it was about this time that the Cretans moved in near the invading Aryan tribes from the north to form the Greece we know today. Also perhaps about this time the religions of the fire god and that of the sun god were fusing ancient Greece, as well as Egypt, into nations. One last note on Hercules is necessary. The recent French expedition to Libya found a good many tombs of very large men which they thought might be Hercules' armies. They reported that there was not a round head among them. The tombs were made of the great rock slabs so much desired by the megalithic builders. This was thought to be another trait of the ancient doli who are credited with the work on the highest mountains of Peru, especially since the weeping god on the great gateway at Tiahuanaco has a crown of serpents, and beneath the ground is reported to be a labyrinth.

THE ROUND HEADS

The second and third millennia B.C. were times of geological change or some other type of disaster, for the round headed tribes began moving out of central Europe, or the Russian steppes, and wherever the Arabic tribes originated. The Aryan speakers came on horses and the Semites on camels. Both herded sheep, dressed in woolen clothing as compared to the linen of the previous people, and both were patriarchal moving into a matriarchal world. The early civilization of the round headed Europeans are thought by some authorities as perhaps starting with the ancient Uighurs of the Gobi desert. However, too little is known of these people to deduce any theories.

They came somewhat about the start of the iron age and with the Aryan speakers came the horse. Possibly the story of Atlantis might suggest that they were earlier, having come during the bronze age, for the picture which Plato paints of his bronze age city and its fondness for horses could imply such an early invasion. Also the Hittites, who are definitely Aryan speakers, poise a problem of very early inroads, even during the time of the Sumerians.

The Sumerians themselves are a people of mystery. Strangers into the Mediterranean. They may have been driven far by the great destruction which the Chinese say "destroyed completely the three worlds". Did they mean the Mediterranean, the Atlantic and the Indian ridges?

The round heads as a type are small people with straight spines, built on the square. They are from the forests of Europe. With them the beard came into the Mediterranean, the admiration or worship for trees, the art of wood carving and the wheel. They used the ten base for mathematics instead of the twenty base of the ancients. They showed a great love for children as opposed to child sacrifice. When Saturn invaded Italy, he established an easy rule which was soon overthrown before he was driven back and according to legend imprisoned in Ireland. From him we get our picture of Santa who decorates trees and gives presents to children. In Italy his coming was celebrated in the Saturnalia - a time of revelry when slaves were free and were waited on by their masters.

The round heads are the white skinned peoples of the Earth whose male chins are covered with beards. This beard they have now passed all over the Earth. Egypt, however, remembers it with the incoming of the Hyksos kings who conquered their land. They were amazed at the sight of the beard. Then those kings conquered Egypt and ruled for many hundreds of years. They were thrown out in the time of Amasis. Rhameses II records that in 1550 B.C. the treaty was signed by this power which had been pretty well destroyed by the Egyptian army. Who the Hyksos were has been a mystery until recently, when an American university working to unearth a city of early Israel found that the dates of greatest glory coincided with the dates of Hyksos rule and the city was destroyed when the Hyksos rulers were finally driven out of Egypt.

This was also the time of great unrest, when a wave of "people of the sea" came in their ships seeking land for themselves from Egypt. Their plea was that the Egyptians were brothers who should help them. After defeating them and their war dogs, the Pharaoh gave them land on his eastern borders where new waves of the Semites were coming in - probably the Arabs or Assyrians. The Egyptian records are interesting in listing the people of the sea. They were called red heads and were probably the Titans of pre-history. The list is as follows: The Tyrseni (the Etruscans), Libyans, Pelset (Pelasgian?), Thekel, Shakelesh, Denyans (Danes?), and the Weshesh (the Welsh?).

The records note that they raided the Euph-rates and then twenty-five years after Egypt won a war over the Hittites, this fleet wiped them out. Was this when the devastating fire was used?

There is a series of events here which is entirely historical and therefore is not open to debate. Let us recapitulate.

1. The power of the Semitic Hyksos invaders was broken in 1550 B.C. (Proved by Dr. Ernest Wright of Harvard university who spent $125,000 excavating Sechem, the Sichem or Sychem of the Bible. It is located at the east end of a valley between Mt. Ebal in the north and Mt. Gerzim in the south between Jerusalem and Sumeria. He proved the tie between the Hyksos and Israel.)

2. The invasion of the Tamahu in ships who came from the direction of the west, saying that the seas had taken their islands, took place in 1500 B.C. These people were red heads according to descriptions. In India the huge Daityas raided the land. Were these again the Danes? The names of many of the clans of the Tamahu (people of the fire god) sound Gothic or Atlantic coast. The word Tyre mentioned so often as the Etruscans or people of the sea, comprising the Tyrrhenian league, is extremely close to the ancient name for Ireland. The T ahead of the name is always (all powerful) as in Tuarak or Tuareg; the y is long, and if the e is pronounced, we have powerful Eirie which of course, is a modern nation. We must remember that religion played a large part here. The Goths raided with the Irish until the later were converted to Christ-ianity, when they began raiding both the Irish and Scotch, but the Goths stopped as soon as they themselves were converted. Similarly the Se-mites are split strictly along the lines of re-ligion.

3. To continue with our series of events, the fleets of the Tyrrhenians joined the Libyans and attacked Egypt in 1450 when they were defeated. They then begged land of Egypt, claiming ancient relationship and pleading the loss of their islands to the sea. Egypt gave them land to the east asking them to hold back the second and third wave of Semitic invaders.

It must have been in the early part of the Tamahu invasion that they raided the Hittites. Egyptian records say this happened 25 years after they, the Egyptians won a war over the Hittites. Therefore it must have been Egypt and the Tamahu who resented the Hittite hold over the trade route to the east, and the people of the sea, and not the Sumerians, who so mercilessly burned the Hittite cities.

Right here a very widespread and persistent Amerind legend running the length of the Americas could help to straighten out these tangled pre-historic threads.

THE TWINS

There is hardly a tribe in the length and breadth of the Americas which does not have their version of the story of the twins. Even the ancient Popul Vuh, early native book saved from the Spanish burning by a clever Amerind who had learned it by heart previously and who simply wrote it down in Spanish, thus causing the book burners to cast it into the desirable group with-out reading it, is again a story of the twins, and incidentally, the best.

The twins were the sons of a powerful mon-arch. They had led a happy life until their father had been invited to the court of a rival power. There he was entertained by a ball game. He had not been fully informed that these games were played for life or death. When his side lost the game he was executed. The twins were sent to the land of their grandmother, the moon, for safekeeping during the ensuing war, apparently won by the enemy power.

One curiosity about the twins is that they were not really twins. The elder one was eight years older than his brother. (Note the number 8 for the Earth in the Venus calendar). This would seem to lift them out of the pure story or fairy tale class and as the story progresses, this opinion seems to be more near the truth.

The pranks of the twins as children is more clear to the Pueblos, but their enmity to water monsters is evident from the beginning. As they grew to manhood, they determined to revenge the death of their father. Accordingly they left the land of the moon and went back to the great power where their father met his death. To shorten a long story, they killed off the monsters who were eating people and stormed the supposedly im-pregnable court. After winning the war, they fell to quarreling and fought each other. Then as the younger one won, the elder walked sadly away toward the east, dropping a trail of flint, or blood which turned to flint, as he went.

The nature of the twins is very distinctive. If one sees them in the dances of the Amerinds, you can always tell which one you are viewing. They are often clowns following the dancers.

The elder is more sedate. He is an astronomer. The younger one is a rascal. He is constantly drunk, makes questionable remarks and in all respects is a noisy funster. One curiosity is that they extend into Africa where it is possible the Tamahu also went in their conquests of the Mediterranean region. The drunken orgy of the younger twin which takes place at Siva not far from the former capital of the Ammonian kings (where my friends, the Randalls, saw the pictures in the underground passageways) is regarded as one of the wildest orgies on Earth.

Is the story of the younger twin that of Hercules, and the elder, that of Atlas? It is obvious that Plato's legendary history of Atlantis shows that Atlas came in to an almost deserted city probably after a disaster and took easy charge by capturing the rulers. He gained control by marrying the daughter, which according to the ancient doli manner of succession (that comes through the daughter) would give him legal kingship. Then he had ten sets of twins. Ten is the Aryan manner of counting and possibly that of the Titans as well. The possession of horses would allow Atlas to put his head men in charge. The fact that the elder twin studied the calendar would suggest that he was Atlas, who was determined to learn the superior calendrical system of the conquered land. The land of the moon could have been either Sumer, the Mayans or central Europe. All had the moon calendar, and this would signify the gathering of friends and allies who would help in another generation. I am inclined to place the moon in Europe because it appears that the break with the old land came as a sharp break at the start of the iron age. The quarrel between the bird and the wolf could be the war between the twins.

From these legends it becomes obvious that the destruction of Atlantic lands was not one great horror, but a continual series of sinkings here and there as the ocean widened and the central block went down. Perhaps it went down several times, and again arose when the ice returned and the magma flowed back under the central block and away from the basined blocks to each side. However, each time the rising would be less and the sea between deeper. This seems to show on the map. And again, the map does disclose the vast destruction of the Atlantic sinking when the continental edge collapsed. If that all happened at one time there would indeed be the great destruction which Votan is supposed to have witnessed, and which is given to the world in the Miltonic English of the Chilam Balam so well translated by Sr. Bolio, a Toltec book for which we

give eternal thanks that it escaped the book burnings of the Spanish. So lands cracked off and sunk, the last one was Lyonesse or Lyonnesse, recorded in verse by Tennyson. Again the disaster was seismic as is to be noted in the Lake of the Waves which the people of Lyonnesse were always afraid was going to overflow. It did with lava and flames when:

"All day long the noise of battle rolled
    Among the mountains by the winter sea,
Until King Arthur's Table, man by man
    Had fallen in Lyonnesse about their lord ..."

THE UNANSWERED QUESTIONS

1. Is the Norse helmet, like the German, the cone shaped peak so well remembered in song and story of the old land when it was at the peak of its glory? Did the horns of the Norse stand for the ram of Pan and of Votan, (explained to me by Delugie--this Apache chief told the author that the trident headdresses were called their horns), while the plume decoration of the Germans stood for the smoke which continually came from this ancient lost volcano?

2. Is the constant fighting of the bull the rite from an incredibly ancient battle with the people who first tamed him in the wilds of India?

3. Why did the Chinese use the 13-chambered Pan's pipes for measuring grain from the very earliest antiquity?

Also in China, why did they claim their writing came from the hide of the water monster? Is this their way of saying that it came from Tu Pan or Pan Ku, the old colossus of the sea? And how did they happen to have chariots with compasses in 2600 B.C.? Did they get these from the same source?

4. How did it happen that Armorica is an ancient Celtic word meaning "over the sea"? Also in the north portion of Gaul is a tribe called the Armoricans, or let us say was anciently called by this name? Also by using the French word for sea and the Amerind word ca for people, we begin to get some interesting combinations. In fact, by seeking out the non-Aryan words among the Aryan tongues, and non-Semitic words from Semitic tongues, we might find some contact words that would definitely point to the ancient mother tongue of the Atlantic. Only in this way will Etruscan, Cretan and other languages be someday read. A case in point is the English word mangle which is to be recognized in the word for mange, (an animal skin disease which chews up the skin), the French word for eating, a similar word in the Philippines, etc. This can

be followed by illi, the prefix of many English words which becomes the root word in distant languages meaning brilliant. In English we have illustrious, illuminate etc. and many in Finnish. Hel, the ancient Greek name for the lost city of light in a sunken land is to be found in Helsinki, Hellenic, etc. The Peruvian inti (leader) is similar to the English prefix in intelligent, etc. The relationship of gan (Irish Finnigan, etc., and the Greek gean (people), probably a Pelasgian word, since Pelas means sea in Rhodes. This is a field which needs much exploration by some ambitious Rh.D. scholars of the origins of early language, or a study of the language tree as it grew through the ages. It is perhaps the only key which exists to some lost tongues.

5. What is the meaning of the triangular stones with a face underneath, to be found on both sides of the Atlantic? Is this Votan? Was it a memorial to the falling Atlas range? When did this range fall?

6. Have we any right to doubt too deeply the dates of Herodotus when he would not confirm the story of Atlantis because he could not confirm the existence of the Atlantic ocean? Or his statement that two chariots drawn by four horses could pass on the wall of Babylon, when it took Robert Koldeway fifteen years digging with a crew of 200 men through a 77-foot mass of debris to prove that Herodotus was right? He was dealing with a world of totems and if we wish to understand him, we must learn to interpret him before we condemn his statements. Writing off the ancients smugly as liars only shows the speaker's inability to understand, or his distaste for study. Unfortunately this is true not only in science but also in literature, as Henrich Schliemann proved.

7. The lost land of Ogyges off the British Isles, ruled by Gog and Magog (the king and queen whose giant crude statues once stood in London) is no longer on the maps of the Earth, but a few words linger in English and other languages. Possibly orgy, ogle? In far off America the Dakota have a clan called the Ogalala. The meaning is explained thusly: "The name is a teasing nickname. They were once making much noise and we called them Ogalala. It means noisy people. Lala is noisy". Then from the Dakota we have received another name for people, evidently in the Cro Magnon tongue, to add to gan, gean, gen, etc. Similarly the early name for Troy (Illium) in Pelasgian is another word for illustrious or illuminated?

We have only two more mysteries to be noted.

First we must come back to Peru where the giant stones were placed on top of the Andes. Is this the work of the Cro Magnon who probably later joined the ancient doli; or in spite of the findings in Spain below sea level, is it the work of the doli? Let us lay our case as follows:

The weeping god with the headdress of serpents worn as the Dakota wear feathers, holds the trident within the three unraised fingers of each hand. Poznansky, who spent many years at Tiahuanaco on Lake Titicaca studying the ruins, makes the statement that this city reached its prime in power 14,000 years ago. It had a lavish plan and was intended for a master city, but was never finished. The land under it has now risen so high that no longer could foods necessary for any population except a few straggling peasants be grown. The temple, which also was never finished, was finally abandoned in 9,550 B.C. This is amazingly close to the date of Plato for the destruction of Atlantis. Poznansky obtained his date by determining which star was being studied in the forgotten observatory as the north star of that date.

The ancient Indian name for this ruin is Zichala or Tuchila. Sometimes a U added meant fort. This name is very close to the Zakala or Xicala, the great capital of Votan long sunken beneath the sea when mentioned in the ancient annals of the tiger priests. Was the Xicala of Votan III in the Caribbean as other legends have suggested? Was this the actual great destruction which also engulfed the Atlas range on the other side of the Atlantic and the red land through the center?

Did the ancient doli plan another capital which could not be overthrown in case the first was lost? Then the sea played its trump card and the splash which followed the sinking of the Atlas range, the breaking open of the Mediterranean valley and the cracking off of the whole European shelf, rolled such tidal waves over the Earth that the great unfinished new capital of the doli was also lost before it had been finished?

Was this the time when the communication between the east and west coasts of the Atlantic ended, and with the magnificent bronze age?

There are many questions which this book must leave unfinished:

Why do most Hindu gods in India hold tridents in their hands?

Where did the Sumerians learn to rotate crops? In the "fertile crescent" of the Mediterranean where it is hardly necessary?

Where did the Mayans learn to weigh and measure the Earth and use their intricately interrevolving calendars? Certainly not in the lush jungles of Yucatan Mexico, where the plants crawled like giant worms over their pitiful cornfields? Where did the Mayans learn to call the ancient Earth mother goddess by her Sumerian name? Or their priests by the name of Sumer? In other words, where did the Mayans spend the first important seven cycles of their sophisticated calendars? Where is the land that they simply designate as "somewhere beyond the sea"?

Yet there is no stranger mystery in the world than the weeping god of the Andes and those canals which run to the location of Pleistocene glaciers. The picture of this huge figure with his three-fingered hands holding up tridents, guarding the causeway which runs nowhere, from an enormous gate which guards nothing, brings back the reproving look on the face of Chief Delugie when asked: "Why is he weeping?"

"You bring me the Egyptian medallion of him with the red dust encrusted around it, and yet you must ask?"

I nodded thoughtfully. "Yes, I know. He weeps for the old red land and the time when Pan Ku held the whole Earth under the three prongs of the trident."

He nodded his satisfaction, and added: "He weeps for that part of the ring of fire, and some day, like the doomed range of the Atlas, they too would plunge into the sea, while in another location, other continents or parts of continents would arise - for such is the way of our planet."

Lucile Taylor Hansen

INDEX

Abbevillian - 269
Abercrombie - 152
Abyss - 34
Acheulian - 269
Achilles - 418
Acropolis - 30, 50
Acusilaus - 291
Adad - 357
Adair - 387
Adams, Dr. - 334
Adams, Leason - 198
Adour river - 141, 142
Adar - 356, 357
Adriatic sea - 42, 153, 344
Adriatic valley - 49
Aegean fault - 288
Aegean sea - 320, 331, 381, 418
Aeson, King - 273
Africa - 33, 35, 59, 73, 76, 80,
    81, 89, 90, 92, 96, 119, 120,
    81, 89, 90, 92, 96, 119, 120,
    153, 154, 156, 161, 162, 164
    153, 154, 156, 161, 162, 164,
    166, 168, 172, 173, 174, 178,
    183, 189, 190, 191, 215, 216,
    219, 223, 225, 226, 227, 230,
    231, 232, 239, 241, 249, 250,
    253, 259, 260, 261, 265, 266,
    231, 232, 234, 239, 241, 249,
    250, 253, 258, 259, 260, 261,
    265, 266, 267, 269, 270, 271,
    274, 275, 294, 295, 298, 299,
    313, 319, 328, 330, 344, 347,
    355, 378, 389, 401, 404, 418,
    421
African capes - 140, 211, 216,
    225, 226, 250
African rim - 154
African shelf - 139, 144, 154,
    156, 343
Afro-Lemurian cordillera - 164
Agadir - 33, 185, 330, 331, 382
Agassiz, Louis - 89, 254
Ah Hoggar mountains - 105, 107
Ah-Mor-Ica - 384
Ah-Musem-Cab - 134, 283, 363,
    364
Ahaggar mountains - 35, 178,
    185, 187
Ahau Catoun - 363

Ainu - 83
Alabama-English-Asian range
    - 211
Alabama-English-cordillera -
    211
Albatross plateau - 252
Aleutian bridge - 83, 84, 85, 87,
    93, 94, 169, 172, 173, 254,
    257, 274, 384
Aleutian chain - 331, 399
Aleutian fault - 331, 332, 344
Aleutian straits - 385
Aleutians (islands) - 86, 87, 127,
    164, 169, 174, 278, 291, 334,
    385, 399, 414
Alexandrian library - 14, 21, 42,
    55, 60
Alfonso, King - 123
Algermissen, Dr. S.T. - 399
Algonkin speakers - 103, 104,
    105, 384, 385, 417
Algonkins - 73, 102, 103, 105,
    113, 121, 271, 291, 292, 300,
    324, 384, 385
Alistra - 291
Allen - 192
Alpine - 253
Alpine-Atlas-Himalayas - 256,
    257
Alpine -Himalayas - 164
Alps - 117, 120, 145, 164, 190,
    191, 213, 217, 227, 246, 252,
    253, 258, 311, 356
Amasis - 26, 419
Amazon, queen of - 59, 106
Amazon city - 324
Amazon river - 60, 142, 274,
    324, 384
Amazons - 57, 59, 60, 106, 182,
    183, 324, 353, 384
Amen-em-het III, Pharaoh - 135
Amer-Eurasia - 193, 194, 200,
    201, 209, 211, 212, 213, 222,
    224, 225, 226, 230, 231, 250,
    258
American Association for the
    Advancement of Science -
    142, 183, 190, 191, 192, 207,
    397
American shelf - 145

Amerinds (American Indian) -
    13, 24, 25, 40, 41, 48, 53, 56,
    61, 62, 64, 72, 74, 79, 80, 81,
    82, 83, 90, 94, 98, 99, 101,
    105, 109, 110, 116, 117, 119,
    127, 129, 131, 132, 134, 135,
    148, 157, 158, 159, 170, 171,
    172, 206, 232, 249, 256, 272,
    273, 274, 280, 285, 292, 293
    273, 274, 280, 285, 292, 293,
    294, 298, 301, 304, 306, 307,
    308, 311, 313, 315, 317, 320,
    322, 323, 324, 326, 329, 353,
    361, 363, 365, 376, 381, 382,
    384, 385, 389, 405, 418, 420,
    421
Ammon (fire god) - 41, 177
Ammonian kings - 183, 421
Amnodont - 173
Ampheres - 29
Amynander - 26
Amynus - 54
Anatolia - 320
Andalusia - 125
Andes - 51, 61, 62, 63, 64, 67,
    87, 99, 115, 130, 135, 156,
    161, 164, 165, 191, 198, 230,
    302, 313, 328, 384, 389, 395,
    422, 423
Andes cordillera - 195
Andrews, Roy Chapman - 221
Anglo Saxons - 371, 387
Antarctica - 161, 162, 164, 166,
    168, 183, 190, 191, 192, 211,
    215, 216, 225, 226, 228, 231,
    250, 345
Antarctica bridge - 169
Antevs - 249
Anthropus Modernis - 269
Antillia - 164, 193, 209, 213,
    217, 227, 251
Anu - 356, 357, 358
Anubis - 51, 54
Anunmaki - 357
Apache - 62, 127, 128, 129, 130,
    131, 132, 184, 208, 232, 273,
    274, 278, 281, 301, 321, 384,
    389, 414, 421
Apache crown dance - 127, 132,
    134, 283, 301, 353, 389

Apaturia - 25
Ape man of Java - 92
Appalachian bridge - 257, 258
Appalachian-English cordillera - 193, 210, 227, 250
Appalachian-English-Urals - (App-eng-norse) - 164, 169, 173, 193, 200
Appalachians - 245, 256, 383
Appalousa - 171
Arabs - 35, 68, 87, 106, 108, 117, 128, 178, 179, 180, 181, 182, 183, 184, 185, 187, 306, 383, 419
Ar-zawans - 320, 321, 322, 324, 326, 327, 339, 353, 354, 359, 360, 378,
Arabian - 34, 43, 107, 108
Arambourg, Dr. C. - 269
Arameans - 358
Arazons - 383
Arcadian - 370
Arctic - 192, 201, 225, 230, 328, 344, 397
Argentina - Cape - Kerguelin cordillera - 164
Aristophanes - 21
Argonauts - 273
Armenians - 318, 327
Armoricans - 421
Arthur, King - 119, 340, 341, 343, 349, 421
Aruakians - 292, 315
Aruaks - 292
Aryans - 24, 34, 113, 116, 117, 121, 318, 378, 382, 419, 421
Aryan speakers - 34, 35, 41, 54, 74, 77, 81, 84, 87, 116, 117, 119, 124, 125, 284, 286, 287, 297, 307, 317, 318, 319 320, 326, 359, 365, 383, 393, 394, 395, 419
Aryan tongues - 35, 84, 121, 286, 290, 292, 318, 421
Asgaard - 405
Ashurbanipal, King - 115, 290, 315, 356
Asia - 16, 24, 27, 28, 72, 83, 84, 87, 91, 93, 96, 103, 127, 220, 224, 225, 226, 227, 250, 257, 266, 291, 320, 354, 359, 379, 384
Asia Minor - 16, 182
Asiatics - 13, 27, 34, 41, 76, 103
Assurbanipal - 315

Assyrian lunar cycle - 55, 139, 297
Assyrians - 34, 35, 52, 54, 55, 82, 107, 113, 115, 138, 290, 297, 314, 356, 419
Astarte - 113, 383
Athapascan speaking - 83, 103, 127, 130, 273, 278, 291, 385
Athapascan tongue - 414
Athelstan, King - 341
Athena-Minerva - 22
Athenae, Queen - 316
Athene - 26, 34
Athenians - 24, 25, 26, 28, 34, 42, 87
Athens - 14, 19, 20, 27, 28, 40, 41, 42, 48, 50
Atl - 124
Atlantean ridge - 257
Atlantean league - 74
Atlantean war - 139, 291
Atlanteans - 25, 34, 42, 59, 60, 63, 65, 73, 107, 110, 121, 124, 125, 128, 139, 160, 182, 183, 184, 232, 281, 312, 319, 326, 369, 376, 381
Athlanthropus - mauritanicus - 269
Atlantic Appalachian bridge - 257, 258
Atlantic basin - 229, 230
Atlantic fault - 381
Atlantic islands - 81, 120, 123, 130
Atlantic league - 59, 291, 306, 322
Atlantic ocean - 5, 7, 12, 14, 15, 16, 17, 24, 27, 33, 34, 35, 42, 46, 47, 48, 57, 59, 61, 65, 68, 73, 77, 79, 80, 81, 83, 89, 90, 93, 95, 98, 104, 105, 107, 109, 113, 116, 117, 123, 124, 128, 129, 136, 137, 138, 140, 141, 142, 143, 144, 145, 148, 149, 150, 151, 152, 153, 156, 160, 164, 166, 167, 168, 169, 172, 173, 178, 179, 180, 182, 183, 185, 188, 189, 190, 191, 192, 193, 194, 195, 198, 199, 200, 201, 209, 211, 215, 219, 223, 225, 226, 227, 229, 230, 231, 241, 245, 250, 252, 254, 256, 257, 258, 271, 274, 275, 281, 286, 287, 291, 292, 300, 303, 307, 309, 310, 311, 312, 313, 315, 316, 320, 323, 325, 330,

333, 334, 341, 344, 345, 346, 349, 350, 353, 354, 355, 360, 362, 371, 378, 379, 381, 382, 383, 384, 385, 387, 395, 399, 401, 402, 403, 404, 405, 411, 419, 420, 421, 422
Atlantic ridge - 89, 90, 144, 168, 178, 182, 189, 200, 209, 215, 222, 225, 226, 227, 231, 256, 290, 311, 397, 419
Atlantic rift - 178, 194, 311, 344, 346, 402
Atlantic slopes - 401
Atlantic tear - 194, 226, 346
Atlantic tribes - 94, 95, 96, 99, 102, 103, 105, 110, 113, 121, 260, 278, 307
Atlantidae - 124, 282, 283, 298, 338, 352, 353, 354
Atlantides - 34, 57, 59, 124, 182, 282, 298, 324
Atlantis - 14, 15, 16, 18, 20, 21, 22, 24, 27, 28, 32, 33, 34, 35, 42, 57, 59, 60, 65, 73, 74, 109, 113, 115, 117, 121, 124, 125, 136, 137, 139, 152, 153, 181, 182, 243, 274, 275, 281, 287, 288, 291, 304, 311, 321, 322, 323, 325, 326, 360, 403, 419, 421, 422
Atlantis chain - 57
Atlantis war - 22
Atlas - 24, 25, 29, 30, 32, 33, 57, 59, 80, 107, 115, 124, 182, 274, 316, 320, 368, 378, 405, 417, 421
Atlas-Alpine-Himalaya cordillera - 256, 257
Atlas-Canary range - 347
Atlas chain - 33, 57, 59, 324, 381
Atlas mountains - 59, 73, 81, 108, 164, 187, 213, 227, 274, 279, 365
Atlas peninsula - 57, 182
Atlas range - 24, 35, 42, 47, 57, 59, 89, 105, 120, 124, 178, 179, 182, 185, 187, 199, 229, 330, 343, 347, 352, 355, 360, 378, 422, 423
Atlas rift - 355
Atlas rim - 381, 382
Atlas valley - 47
Aurakians - 99
Aurignacian culture - 124, 259, 261

Australia - 161, 164, 166, 168, 169, 172, 190, 191, 194, 201, 209, 211, 212, 215, 216, 218, 219, 224, 225, 226, 231, 234, 250, 252, 328

Australian aborigine - 90, 91, 287

Australopithecines (southern apes) - 267

Australoid culture - 261

Australian Bushman - 89

Autochthon - 29

Aymans - 99

Azaes -29

Azilian-Egyptians - 105

Azilian-Tyrrhenians - 87

Azilians - 76, 80, 81, 82, 83, 86, 87, 88, 89, 90, 94, 95, 105, 117, 120, 121, 123, 125

Azores - 137, 139, 256, 404, 417

Aztec - 40, 52, 82, 102, 113, 119, 177, 302, 303, 314, 322, 338, 360, 361, 384

Aztlan - 273

Aztoutecan speaker - 273

Baal - 315, 383, 395

Babylon - 272, 295, 305, 325, 355, 356, 358, 422

Babylonia - 290, 356, 358

Babylonian - 55, 290, 325, 326

Bad Water - 65, 160

Bal - 314, 356, 360

Balaam - 314, 315, 395

Balam - 361

Balder - 316

Baldwin - 34, 367

Balmor - 315, 417

Baltic - 142, 148, 164, 193, 315, 327, 330, 344, 354, 383

Baluchiterium - 173

Ban - 113

Bancroft - 39

Banning - 337

Bannock - 384

Barrow, G

Barnes, Captain - 341

Barrow, George - 341

Basque - 33, 116, 117, 124, 285, 293, 318, 324, 381, 383, 395

Beagle, HMS - 149

Beck, Robert - 392, 393, 394

Becker, Dr. - 157

Beiser, Arthur - 328

Bel - 314, 315, 356, 358

Berber - 33, 34

Bering Sea - 85, 402

Berlieux, Felix - 59

Berosus - 355

Bikini Atoll - 150

Bingham - 67

Bird-serpent war - 303, 307

Bird-totem war - 307

Black, Dr. Davidson- 268

Black feet - 384

Black foot - 94

Blake Plateau - 115, 151, 182

Boockfor

Blockford, Michael - 332

Blue Vengeance - 35, 68, 180

Boeckh - 34

Bogoslof island - 85

Bogoslof river - 85, 140, 143

Bolio, Sr. - 44, 421

Borremose man - 261

Bosco - 244

Boskrop man - 261

Bourbourg, Brasseur de - 360, 367, 368

Bowie - 193, 194, 201, 246

Bowley, E.K. - 341

Bradley, Dr. Wilmot H. - 246

Bradley

Bradley, Dr. Wilmot H. - 246, 247, 248, 249

Brazil - 235

Breath master - 79

Brennan, Louis A. - 13

Breton - 318, 324

Bribir - 79, 99

British Isles - 148, 290, 334, 404

Britons - 38, 65

Broca

Brochard, Dr. - 382

Brontosaurus - 219

Brooks - 140

Brower - 21

Brower - 201

Brunhilde, Queen - 2

Br

Bucher, Walter H. - 142, 143,

Buck, Dr. Frank - 81, 286

Buck, Dr. Frank - 81, 286

Bushman - 258, 259, 29

Bushman - 258, 259, 261, 267, 287

Butler, Dr. B. Robert - 397

Byron - 6

Cabot fault - 345

Caddoan - 384, 385, 386

Caddoan speaking - 102

Cadiz - 316, 352

Cadmean - 387

Cadmus - 20

Caesar, Julius - 21, 22, 35, 60, 113, 176, 298, 318

California Institute of Technology - 157, 189, 344

Calypso - 311, 329

Cambrian - 200, 211

Cambysses - 183

Camden - 291

Camp, Dr. - 205

Campbell - 179

Canary basin - 229, 256

Canary island - 324, 330, 343, 397, 404

Canary peninsula - 154

Cara - 382

Caraco lake - 349

Caracas - 385

Caraiba - 384

Carbon-14 dating - 13, 294, 313, 349, 398

Carboniferous period - 212

Cari - 384, 385

Caria - 382

Carian league - 382

Carians - 315, 379, 381, 382, 383, 384, 387

Caribbean - 119, 138, 157, 182, 227, 230, 231, 251, 252, 256, 291, 330, 331, 344, 386, 417, 422

Caribbean fault - 347

Caribbean sea - 52, 102, 150, 151, 295, 301, 315, 316, 329, 384

Caribs - 157, 292, 315, 329, 384, 385

Carlsberg ridge - 168

Carnegie Institute - 46

Caron - 382

Carpassos - 383

Carroll, Lewis - 411

Carthage - 60, 124, 182, 290, 314, 316, 367

Carthaginians - 60, 65, 121, 124, 314, 315, 316, 372, 381, 382

Casnopus - 173

Caspian sea - 49, 57, 81, 360

Cassides - 341

Cassiterides - 341

Cassius - 339

426

Castari tribes - 341

Catahoula formation - 152

Catalina island - 70, 72, 183, 199, 264

Cayman trench - 229

Ccoya Rami - 387

Celtic kilt - 53

Celts - 65, 117, 121, 211, 318, 340, 421

Cenozoic age - 17, 138, 201, 230, 249

Central Atlantic ridge - 42, 47, 137, 138, 139, 140, 211, 227, 229, 230, 258, 346, 355

Ceres - 326, 383

Cerne - 57, 59

Cessair - 341

Chaldaic - 373, 374, 375, 376

Chaldean-Babylonian - 356

Chaldean calendars - 354

Chaldean legends - 272, 356

Chaldeans - 55, 113, 120, 139, 360

Challenger (English research ship) - 136, 145, 149

Chambers - 192

Chan-Chan - 39, 51, 53, 310, 312, 352, 387, 417

Chaney, Dr. Ralph - 245

Channel islands - 69, 75, 86, 156, 399

Charon - 414

Chempal popoca codex - 360

Cherakee - 384, 387

Chersenesus - 324

Cheyenne - 94

Chibchas - 384

Chickasaw - 102, 103, 384, 387

Chiera - 290

Chilam Balam - 281, 361, 363, 365, 421

Chili - 332, 333, 334

China - 79, 173, 271, 294, 310, 359, 360, 365, 395, 414, 417, 421

Chinese - 74, 271, 301, 306, 359, 360, 368, 389, 392, 421

Chippewa - 102, 135, 291

Chiricawa - 384

Choctah - 80, 99, 100, 102, 387

Chocktaw - 384, 387

Chorotegans - 310

Chows - 91, 360, 393, 394

Chronos - 54, 164, 182

Cicero - 21

Cioacoatl - 113

Circum-Pacific cordillera - 230, 231
230, 231

Clarion fracture zone - 228

Clarion fracture zone - 228

Cleito - 28, 30

Clemente - 42

Clements, Dr. - 150, 191

Cleopatra - 59

Clever builder - 282, 414

Clipperton fracture zone - 228

Co-hua-co-huatl - 112

Coatlinchan - 290

Cogidumnus, King - 405

Coleman, Dr. - 183

Colossus of Rhodes - 404

Colorado depression - 156

Colorado range - 246

Colton, Dr. Harold S. - 349

Columbia river - 16

Columbus, Christopher - 249, 401

Columns of Hercules - 27

Comanche - 94, 384

Compton fault - 157

Constantinople - 24, 113, 306, 354

Contractionist theory - 162, 164, 165, 169, 200, 201

Cook, Dr. R.K. - 332, 400

Cooper, James Fennimore - 158

Copernican theory - 20, 42

Copernican theory - 20, 42

Copernicus - 20, 42

Copts - 80

Corinth - 41, 290

Corinthians - 41

Cornwall, England - 117, 311, 338, 340, 341, 342

Cos - 291, 306

Coso - 75, 165

Couperie, M. Terrien de la - 360

Cousteau, Capt. J.Y. - 311

Cowan, Robert - 152

Coxon, William - 295, 296, 297, 298

Cranter - 42

Crater lake - 17

Cree Indian - 7

Creek Cherakee - 102

Cresus, King - 327

Cretaceous period - 144, 151, 172, 219, 220, 221, 222, 224, 225, 227, 241, 245, 250, 252, 253, 257

Cretaceous sea - 245

Cretans - 110, 120, 184, 316, 320, 381, 382, 383, 419 432

Crete - 32, 34, 110, 120, 182, 243, 277, 279, 281, 288, 291, 293, 312, 314, 318, 320, 322, 323, 326, 359, 378, 382, 417, 418, 419

Critias - 14, 20, 21, 22, 25, 26, 28

Cro Magnon man - 64, 72, 74, 87, 90, 91, 93, 94, 99, 100, 105, 113, 120, 123, 124, 125, 259, 260, 261, 262, 267, 269, 274, 275, 285, 287, 300, 303, 306, 307, 313, 318, 324, 327, 341, 343, 383, 386, 418, 422

Cronos (EA) - 356

Crool - 140

Crown dance, Apache - 127, 132, 134, 283, 353, 389

Cushite Ethiopian - 370

Cuzco - 131

Cybele - 326, 383

Cynodictis - 173

Dacotah (Turtle) - 61, 79, 95, 99, 100, 102, 103, 128, 135, 301, 302, 303, 313, 314, 324, 386, 417, 418

Dacotah-Sioux - 105

Daisios - 356

Daityas - 359, 420

Dakota - 384, 418, 422

Dalmation dog - 392

Daly, Dr. Reginald - 16, 137, 140, 143, 145, 149, 150, 192, 193, 194, 198, 199, 201, 205, 231, 252

Daly-Willis theory - 198, 201

Dana, Dr. James D. - 137, 149, 245, 250, 253

Dance of the trident - 132, 135

Danes - 420

Dante - 256

Danube - 327, 417

Daria - 291

Dark Ages - 22

Darwin, Charles - 149, 150, 151, 189, 204, 218, 250

Darwin ridge - 346

Darwin rise - 344, 345, 401

Darwinian theory - 258

Davis, William Morris - 150, 251

Dawn horse - 170
Dead sea - 50, 153
Dead sea scrolls - 185
Death valley - 65, 160, 165, 199, 221, 256, 349
Death valley rift - 164
Decoodah - 101, 102, 103, 301, 302, 303, 385
Deitrich, Marlene - 287
Delta civilization - 38, 41, 124, 322
Delta of the Nile - 40, 41, 54
Deluge - 55
Deluge (flood) of Deucalion - 26, 49, 50, 90, 182
Delugie, Asa - 132, 135, 208, 274, 281, 283, 295, 298, 313, 316, 321, 353, 363, 365, 421, 423
Denali fault - 331
Dene (people) - 414
Denyans - 420
De Provok - 180, 291
Deser, Dr. E. - 120, 121
Deucalion - 26, 73, 90, 182, 358, 359
Devil dance - 128
Devon - 341
Devonian era - 211, 212
Di Marchi - 49
Diaprepes - 29
Diaz, Bernal - 170
Dietrich, Dr. Robert S. - 401
Diogenes - 21, 50
Disney, Walt - 230
Dixon, Dr. - 96
Doepping - 285
Dogger Bank - 342
Dolicephalic - 74, 80
Donnelly, Ignatious - 15, 16, 17, 54, 55, 136, 137, 275, 291, 293, 304, 306, 325, 329, 355, 356, 359, 360, 367, 368, 369, 374, 375, 376, 378, 380, 405
Dorians - 41
Dorset - 341
Douglass, Dr. A.E. - 248, 249, 349
Draa depression - 179, 185, 199, 330, 344, 347, 382
Dravidian - 54, 107, 261 294, 306, 307, 322, 354, 359
Drennan, Dr. M.R. - 258, 259
Dropidas - 25, 28
Du Pratz - 386
Du Toit, Alexander - 140, 166,

189, 191, 219, 250
Dubois, Dr. R.L. - 267, 400
Dugan, James - 311
Dunbar - 245, 246, 253, 258
Dunstanville, Reginald de - 349

Ea - 356, 357, 358
Easter-Capes-Kerguelin - 191, 200
Easter island - 65, 77, 164, 190, 191, 211, 252
Ecuador - 63
Eddas - 124, 313, 315, 322, 323, 327, 354, 361, 363, 366, 404
Eddington - 403
Eel river - 143, 229
Eel river canyon - 86, 142
Eexcalli - 361
Egyed - 403
Egypt - 14, 16, 20, 21, 22, 24, 25, 26, 27, 29, 34, 35, 38, 40, 41, 42, 51, 52, 53, 54, 55, 57, 59, 62, 68, 74, 76, 79, 80, 95, 107, 119, 124, 125, 128, 129, 132, 165, 172, 183, 271, 273, 275, 280, 281, 285, 290, 291, 294, 298, 303, 304, 312, 314, 315, 322, 323, 326, 360, 361, 362, 367, 376, 383, 386, 392, 394, 414, 419, 420
Egyptian-Atlantidae - 80
Egyptian cycle - 55
Egyptian delta - 26, 124
Egyptian hieroglyphic - 288, 297
Egyptians - 14, 16, 20, 21, 24, 27, 28, 38, 39, 40, 41, 42, 48, 51, 52, 53, 54, 55, 59, 60, 74, 76, 79, 80, 82, 105, 107, 274, 285, 287, 288, 293, 298, 300, 304, 305, 307, 314, 315, 316, 322, 353, 362, 367, 369, 370, 371, 372, 373, 374, 375, 376, 379, 381, 387, 389, 394, 417, 419, 420, 423
Einstein, Albert - 12, 209, 286, 388, 403
Eirie - 420
El - 361
Elasippus - 29
Elasmosaurus - 389
Elbaratuta, Obartes - 356
Elephas antiquis - 92
Elk nation - 102
Ellice islands - 149
Emery, Dr. K.O. - 399

Emiliami, Dr. Cesare - 138, 139, 140, 249
Emperor Fu - 393, 414
Emperor Maximus - 339
Eniwetok - 150
England - 152, 161, 164, 182, 183, 193, 200, 210, 227, 232, 244, 258, 260, 270, 275, 311, 324, 339, 341, 342, 349, 395
Enlil - 414
Enlil, Puzur - 357
Enurta - 357
Eocene - 83, 152, 170, 172, 225, 245, 246, 248, 250, 251, 252, 253, 254, 341
Eocene lake - 246
Eohippus Borealis (dawn horse) 83, 170, 247
Equinoxes - 40
Ereck, King - 323
Ericksen, Dr. D. - 138
Ericson, Leif - 401
Ersele, Dr. Louis J. - 332
Erythea - 316, 352
Erythrean sea - 316
Espejo, Dr. - 39
Essouk - 187
Ethimen - 42
Ethiopian - 371
Etruria, Italy - 291, 316, 367, 417
Etruscans - 27, 48, 54, 65, 116, 121, 124, 182, 184, 288, 290, 291, 314, 315, 316, 318, 319, 370, 373, 381, 389, 417, 420, 421
Etruskans - 315
Euaemon - 29
Euclid - 20, 306
Euenor - 28
Eumelus - 29
Euphrates - 356, 359, 420
Eurasia - 83, 194, 201, 204, 222, 231, 389
Europe - 24, 27, 35, 40, 42, 64, 65, 76, 84, 87, 89, 90, 94, 96, 116, 117, 119, 120, 121, 137, 138, 141, 144, 151, 153, 154, 167, 172, 183, 184, 189, 200, 204, 209, 211, 223, 227, 245, 254, 256, 258, 259, 260, 261, 271, 275, 276, 285, 286, 290, 297, 304, 306, 311, 313, 315, 324, 325, 327, 354, 362, 382, 383, 384, 395, 402, 405, 414, 419, 421

European shelf - 144, 422
Eus-Cara - 383
Eus-Kerri - 383
Ewing, Dr. Maurice - 140, 143, 311

Faroe island - 192
Fasching - 177
Fawcett - 239
Fenir - 54, 309, 315
Field, R.M. - 193
Finaeus, Oronteus - 43, 46
Fingleton, James, Fr. - 318, 324
Finns - 116, 117, 124, 309, 315, 422
First Dynasty - 128, 132, 139
Fish-Hoek man - 258, 259, 261
Flemming beds - 152
Flood of Noah - 16, 73, 90, 356
Fontaine - 245
Fontechevade man - 270
Fordham, Father - 337
Forel, Dr. F.A. - 142
Formoraks - 381
France - 141, 152, 164, 173, 182, 227, 340, 354, 381, 395, 418
Freesian islands - 327
Frio sands - 152
Fu-cah-oh - 359
Fu-cato - 359
Fu, Emperor - 393, 414
Fu-Hi - 359, 360
Funafuti Atoll - 149

Gabes, bay of - 33
Gabes, gulf of - 35
Gadeirus - 29
Gades - 29, 185
Gadierez - 352
Gaea - 27
Gaetulae - 59
Galley the - 74
Gates of Hercules (Heracles) - 107, 230, 350, 355, 381, 382
Geike - 192, 193, 246, 252
Geophysics division, Department of scientific and Industrial research - 334
George III - 43
Geras, Dr. - 382
Geronimo - 128, 132
Gerth - 250
Geryon - 316

Getze, George - 400
Gibralter - 107, 230
Gibson, Alexander - 339
Gilgamesh - 73, 90, 356, 358, 359, 360, 363
Gilson, S.R. - 405
Glastonbury - 38, 343, 349
Glob, Dr. Peter - 176, 177
Gobi desert - 173, 220, 419
Goddard, Dr. Pliny - 82
Gog - 422
Gonds - 168, 190
Gondwannaland - 168, 169, 172, 190, 191, 193, 194, 195, 200, 201, 209, 210, 211, 212, 213, 214, 215, 216, 217, 218, 219, 224, 225, 226, 231, 250, 252, 253, 345, 402
Gondwannaland glacial - 165, 191
Gorgons - 57, 59
Goths - 117, 290, 306, 318, 323, 414, 420
Gracht, Van Der - 193, 201, 250
Graff, Van Der - 154
Great American rift - 158
Great league - 41
Great pyramid of Egypt - 38, 40, 53, 67
Great serpent - 121, 359
Greece - 20, 22, 24, 41, 42, 47, 54, 57, 59, 68, 87, 153, 183, 227, 261, 290, 304, 320, 331, 414, 419
Greeks - 17, 18, 20, 21, 22, 24, 26, 27, 28, 32, 33, 34, 35, 40, 41, 42, 47, 48, 49, 50, 52, 53, 54, 55, 57, 73, 96, 107, 116, 123, 129, 142, 170, 192, 210, 267, 273, 287, 291, 293, 306, 307, 316, 318, 319, 320, 323, 355, 358, 359, 368, 369, 370, 371, 372, 373, 374, 375, 381, 382, 383, 395, 414, 417, 419, 422
Greenland - 161, 165, 172, 194, 201, 223, 224, 231, 245, 256
Griggs, D.T. - 345
Guerrani - 384
Gutenberg, Beno - 137, 189, 193, 195, 198
Guyot, Arnold - 144
Gyges, King - 291, 327

Hades - 34

Hali-Kar-Nassos - 382
Hamilton, Dr. Edward - 144
Hancock - 86
Hansen, L. Taylor - 7, 148
Harrington, Dr. - 67, 73, 96, 119
Harris, Shorty - 159, 160
Harrison - 152, 252
Hawaiian islands - 78, 228, 332
Hawaiku - 78, 273, 310
Hawkins, Dr. Gerald S. - 38
Hayagriva - 359
Hayerdahl, Dr. Thor - 296
Healy - 334
Hebrew - 370, 371, 373, 374, 375, 384
Heezen, Dr. Bruce - 143, 311
Hegel, Georg Wilhelm - 116
Heidelberg man - 92
Hel (god of light) - 176, 361, 404, 422
Helen of Troy - 24, 395
Heliopolis (sun-city) - 42
Helios - 26, 361
Hellas - 404
Hellenes - 41, 361
Hellenic - 27, 29, 422
Helsinki - 422
Henney, Dr. - 227
Henny, Dr. - 158
Hephaestus - 27
Hera - 359, 418
Heracles - 27, 107, 109, 187, 316, 318, 321
Hercules - 22, 27, 41, 57, 68, 107, 182, 313, 316, 318, 321, 322, 324, 326, 327, 378, 418, 419, 421
Heremann, Dr. A. - 382
Hermann, Dr. - 182
Hermes - 367, 368
Herodotus - 21, 22, 40, 52, 53, 54, 60, 68, 73, 276, 280, 281, 288, 291, 305, 313, 316, 321, 365, 378, 414, 422
Hesichius - 381
Hesiod - 26
Hesperia - 57
Hesperides - 57, 59, 183, 349
Hess, Dr. Harry - 144
Hierapolis - 358, 359
Hill, Dr. Robert T. - 154, 156
Himalayas - 150, 164, 173, 190, 191, 194, 225, 227, 246, 250, 252, 253, 257, 258, 344
Hippolita, queen - 182, 324

Hissarlik - 320
Hittite - 84, 306, 318, 319, 326, 327, 359, 393, 419, 420
Hodgson - 198
Hoggar - 106, 107, 108, 110, 178
Holarctica - 190
Holmes, Arthur - 345
Homer - 22, 24, 26, 53, 54, 117, 277
Hopis - 56, 62, 113, 131, 249, 273, 277
Homes - 198
Homet, Dr. Marcel F. - 64, 65
Hrdlicka, Dr. - 103
Hull, Captain - 140, 342
Humboldt, Alexander Von - 34, 330, 344
Hunkapah - 99, 302
Huntington, Dr. - 96
Hurukan (storm god) - 361
Huxley, Dr. - 94
Hwang-ti - 359
Hyeres - 311
Hyksos kings - 41, 52, 54, 359, 383, 419, 420
Hudson - 145, 148, 193, 346

Ian (sea) - 381
Iberians - 116, 117
Igharghar river - 185
Illiad of Homer - 418
Illium - 22, 24
Illyrian - 373, 375
Imhotep - 53
Incas - 51, 64, 65, 74, 96, 125, 310, 323, 387
Incan - 63, 64, 99, 125, 387
India - 81, 161, 162, 164, 166, 168, 172, 173, 190, 191, 192, 194, 211, 225, 226, 227, 231, 250, 253, 261, 276, 284, 286, 328, 359, 360, 378, 394, 395, 421
Indian ocean - 81, 93, 94, 137, 142, 150, 154, 164, 168, 173, 190, 191, 192, 193, 195, 198, 199, 201, 211, 212, 215, 216, 225, 226, 227, 231, 241, 246, 250, 251, 252, 253, 257, 274, 284, 286, 300, 305, 306, 307, 309, 310, 311, 313, 318, 319, 322, 345, 355, 360, 394, 395, 402, 419
Indian tear - 226, 344
Insula Siles - 339

Insula Sulina - 339
Insula Syllian - 339
Insulum Illurian - 152
Insulum Silurian - 343
International Geophysical year (IGY) - 142, 148
International Mantle project - (IMP) - 403
Inyo county - 73, 74
Ion - 382
Ionians - 41, 42, 382
Iroquois - 94, 102, 282, 384, 385, 386
Ishtar (goddess of the moon) - 113, 357, 383
Iskihashi, Dr. - 310
Isle of Lemnos - 316
Italy - 47, 54, 57, 211, 227, 288, 381, 419
Itiwanna - 310, 368
Itsamna - 378
Itza-Pan - 273
Itzama - 78
Itzamana - 78, 79
Itzamna - 310, 368
Iwannos - 395
Ixdhurbar - 356

Japan - 144, 167, 172, 195, 219, 224, 254, 337
Jason - 273
Jefferies - 198
Jenkins, A. K. Hamilton - 340
Johnson, Joe - 178, 179, 180, 183, 185, 187
Johnson, W.D. - 143
Johnstone, Paul - 177
Joly - 140, 189, 198, 199, 204, 205, 208, 216, 231
Joseph, Colonel Henry B. - 238
Joyce, Dr. - 100, 160
Jurassic - 209, 219, 221, 222, 224, 226, 250, 251, 253

Kansan - 384
Kar, Emperor - 382, 383
Karo, Chief Rear Admiral H. Arnold - 332, 399
Karnak temple - 52, 280
Kassides - 327, 349
Kassites - 326, 327, 341
Katchinas - 308
Kate-Zahl - 326, 361
Kavella - 117, 293

Keats - 317, 404
Keith, Sir Arthur - 82, 92, 93, 258, 259, 261
Kelley, Dr. David - 368, 376, 379
Kelts - 381, 383
Kenyapithecus - 270
Keres - 383
Keresian speaker - 77
Kerguelin island - 164, 168, 190, 191, 211, 226
Kerguelin range - 191, 226
Kessair - 341
Khamissa - 187
Khasisatra - 356, 357, 358
Khefti - 381
Kielis-Borok, Dr. V.I. - 400
King, Dr. - 92
King Aeson - 273
King Alfonso - 123
King Arthur - 119, 338, 340, 341, 343, 349
King Ashurbanipal - 115, 290, 315, 356
King Athelstan - 341
King Cogidumnus - 405
King Cresus - 327
King Ereck - 323
King Gyges - 291, 327
King Mestor - 29, 54
King Sent - 51
King Vikar - 176
King-Tyrant lizard - 235
Kitchen Midden - 76, 105, 117, 284, 285, 286, 319
Klau, Hosteen - 278
Knopoff, Dr. Leon - 403
Kober - 193, 209
Koenigwald, Dr. G.H.R. - 268, 271
Kolbe, Dr. P.W. - 397
Koldeway, Robert - 422
Kraken - 320
Krantors - 376
Kreichgauer - 190, 231
Kriedel - 250
Kronos - 349
Ku - 414, 417
Kuenen, Dr. - 143
Kulp, Dr. J.L. - 138
Kur - 414
Kurds - 319, 327

La Brea tar pits - 72, 73, 86, 95, 172, 398

La Chapelle - 88, 92
Ladd, Harry - 150
Lady Ishtar - 357
Lagarto formation - 152
Lake Balkat - 360
Lake Titicaca - 61, 302, 323, 422
Lake Triconis - 33
Lake Uinta - 246, 247, 248, 252
La Llorona - 112, 113, 115
Lamberts - 193
Lamont - 145
Lancelot - 343
Landa - 367, 368, 369, 370, 375
Langer, Dr. 332
Latham - 80
Leakey, Dr. Louis, B.S. - 249, 258, 259, 260, 261, 269, 270, 271, 274, 275, 418
Le Conte - 225, 245
Lemuria - 168, 172, 213, 217, 224, 225, 226, 227, 231, 241, 250, 274
Lemurian river - 168, 215, 216
Lemurian ice center - 230
Lemurian ridge - 168, 172, 190, 191, 201, 211, 215, 216, 217, 345
Lemurian spine - 191, 211, 215, 225, 226
Lemurs - 225, 227, 241, 300
Leslie, Robert L. - 244
Lesquiereux - 254
Leukippe - 28
Libby, Dr. Willard - 138
Liboya (land of the ancient dead) 379
Libya - 16, 27, 28, 124, 182, 291, 379, 381, 419
Libyan sheath - 53, 57, 128, 132
Libyan lake - 57
Libyans - 52, 53, 57, 68, 110, 124, 182, 184, 314, 420
Lilliputian stars - 207
Lindenkohl, A. - 143
Linnaeus - 239
Lizardo, Dr. - 40
Lloyd - 334
Loch Ness monster - 232, 233, 236, 237, 312, 389, 390, 391
London, Jack - 263
Longfellow - 64, 148
Lost city of Peru - 67
Lost land - 24
Lowell, Dr. 249
Lucian - 358

Lunar calendar - 40, 307, 319, 322
Lycophoron - 291
Lydia - 316, 326, 327
Lydians - 315, 326
Lyonesse - 340, 341, 343, 349, 395, 421
Lyonnesse 421

Mac Donald, Gordon, J.F. - 401
Macchu-picchu - 64, 67
Macelwane, James E. - 198
Machairodus - 172
Mackenzie river - 16
Madeira gorge - 89
Madeira peninsula - 152, 154, 182, 229, 330, 354
Madeira valley - 230
Magog, queen - 54, 290, 422
Magus - 54
Maia - 321, 368, 378, 414
Malaise, Dr. Rene - 397
Mallory, Captain - 404
Maltese cross - 67
Manco-Kapac - 64
Mane of Pegasus - 404
Manson, Marsden - 199, 204, 205, 216
Manu - 360
Marajo - 384
Maranon (great river) - 384
Marcellinus, Armmianus - 42
Marcus, Emperor - 339
Marineland - 242, 243
Markham, Edwin - 245
Mars - 249
Martin, Joe - 111
Master Builders - 68
Matriarchal round heads - 310
Matrilinear complex of Agglutinating tongues - 305
Maximus, Emperor - 339
Maya - 361, 374, 378, 414
Maya alphabet - 369, 370, 371, 372, 373, 374
Mayans - 40, 53, 78, 79, 105, 119, 288, 290, 300, 302, 306, 310, 312, 321, 353, 367, 368, 369, 370, 371, 372, 373, 374, 375, 376, 378, 379, 387, 421, 422, 423
Mayapan - 414
Mayas - 361
McLain, Jerry - 349

Medea - 273
Mediterranean - 17, 24, 33, 34, 35, 39, 41, 47, 48, 50, 52, 54, 55, 57, 59, 62, 65, 72, 73, 74, 76, 77, 81, 84, 87, 89, 90, 93, 94, 96, 107, 110, 116, 117, 120, 121, 124, 125, 138, 142, 148, 150, 154, 156, 172, 182, 185, 192, 213, 227, 228, 230, 231, 271, 274, 275, 282, 283, 285, 288, 293, 297, 300, 302, 303, 305, 306, 309, 311, 313, 314, 315, 316, 318, 319, 320, 322, 323, 324, 327, 330, 341, 343, 347, 352, 353, 355, 356, 358, 359, 360, 362, 365, 368, 371, 378, 382, 383, 392, 393, 395, 405, 414, 417, 419, 421, 422
Mediterranean cordillera - 213, 227, 230, 231
Mediterranean league - 34, 139, 291
Mediterranean rift - 344, 355, 359
Mediterranean valley - 42, 47, 87, 182, 225, 355, 360, 381, 405, 422
Medusa - 405
Megalithic (giant stone) builders 67, 125, 282, 305, 341, 419
Megaliths - 290
Meganthropus Paleojavanicus (giant man of ancient Java) - 268
Meinesz, Felix A. Vening - 345
Melanesia islands - 261
Menard, Jr., Dr. Henry W. - 345, 401
Mendocean - 229
Mendocine river - 142
Mendocino strip - 86
Merina, Queen (Merynia) - 59, 324
Meropes - 291, 306, 313
Meropis - 354
Merus - 306, 307, 310
Mescalleros - 128, 208, 283
Mesozoic age - 17, 162, 164, 190, 191, 192, 194, 200, 213, 217, 218, 219, 221, 222, 223, 224, 225, 227, 228, 230, 231, 233, 253, 337, 344, 345
Mesozoic diastrophism - 142, 191, 224, 230, 231, 344
Mestor, King - 29, 54

Mexican - 68, 80, 111, 112, 128, 158, 159, 164, 222, 235, 368, 375, 384, 387, 411
Mexico - 39, 60, 62, 79, 81, 100, 102, 104, 112, 131, 157, 158, 170, 180, 193, 209, 225, 230, 235, 245, 280, 282, 283, 302, 328, 349, 353, 368, 384
Mia - 378, 379
Mid-Atlantic - 257, 345
Mid-Atlantic ridge - 13, 136, 137, 138, 145, 152, 204, 328, 344, 345, 346, 397
Mid-Atlantic rift - 329
Mid-Atlantic-Pacific rift - 337
Mid-Miocene - 257, 258, 271
Mid-Oligocene - 253
Mid-Pacific - 150
Mid-Pleistocene - 267, 268, 269
Milton - 206
Mimembres - 77, 87, 95, 411
Minerva, Queen - 34, 316
Miocene era - 89, 93, 150, 152, 167, 170, 172, 173, 201, 225, 227, 230, 241, 253, 254, 256, 257, 258, 262, 271, 394
Mississippi river - 102, 103, 121, 301, 302, 311, 324, 385, 386
Misor - 54
Mitannians - 326
Mitla - 39, 280, 281
Mixon reef - 405
Mixtec - 384
Mixtec labyrinth - 379
Mnemosyne - 28
Mneseus - 29
Moab Stone - 370, 371, 372, 373, 374, 375
Modoc tribe - 77
Mohawk - 285, 286, 384
Moir, J. Reid - 260
Moki river - 310, 312
Molengraaf, G.A.F. - 251, 252
Monasaur - 389
Montague, Dr. Ashley - 269
Monte Alban - 294
Moors - 80, 123
Mortimer, Sir - 177
Morton - 121
Mound Builders - 39, 53, 385
Mt. Atlas - 279, 325
Mt. Blanc - 246
Mt. Ennor - 339, 340
Mt. Mazama (fire god) - 17
Mt. Parnassus - 26

Mt. Pele volcano - 157, 329
Mt. San Gorgonia pass - 156, 158
Mt. Shitli - 411
Mousterian - 90
Mousterian influence - 258, 260
Mu - 357
Mu sheri-ina-namari - 357
Munchhausen, Baron Von - 417
Murphy, Dr. Leonard - 332
Murray, Sir John - 149, 168
Murray banks - 168, 191
Murray deep - 228
Murray fracture - 228
Murray rift - 332
Muskogian - 384, 385
Muskogian speaking - 102, 386
Mya - 379
Mya river - 108
Myohippus - 172

Nabon - 356
Nabu - 357
Nagar - 321, 355, 378, 379
Nahuatl - 293, 302, 314
Nahui-atl - 360, 361
Nahui-xochitl - 361
Nakuru basin - 260
Napier, Dr. John R. - 271
Natchez - 102, 386
National Geographic magazine - 62, 270
National Geographic society - 67
Navaho - 56, 60, 62, 135, 273, 278, 281, 310, 414
Navaho Squaw dance - 56, 60
Naval Electronics laboratory - 144
Neanderthal-Cro Magnon - 91
Neanderthal man - 82, 87, 88, 89, 90, 91, 92, 93, 94, 258, 259, 260, 261, 262, 267, 268, 270, 275
Neanderthaloid - 90, 91, 92, 93, 94, 258, 259, 270
Neanderthaloid-modern - 91, 267
Nefertiti, Queen - 287, 411
Neith, Queen - 26, 34, 53, 123, 376
Neptune - 25, 33, 55, 107, 164, 291, 339
Nereids - 30
Nergel - 356, 357
Nerthus - 177

Nessie - 232, 390
Nidi - 323
Niger - 35, 321, 355, 378
Nigeria - 59, 318
Nile river - 24, 26, 41, 42, 53, 54, 55, 295, 298, 323, 368, 370, 371, 394
Nile valley - 55, 304, 375
Nilsson, Dr. Erik - 260
Niobe - 26
Nizar - 358
Noah - 73, 90
Normans - 35, 340
Norse - 22, 48, 54, 74, 83, 116, 117, 120, 121, 124, 176, 271, 273, 300, 313, 315, 323, 324, 327, 361, 365, 366, 383, 387, 394, 395, 404, 414, 418, 421
Norse mummy - 176, 177
Nurcho - 349
Nutho - 349

Oakville sandstone - 152
Oannes - 25, 47, 164, 272, 360
Oceanic League - 31, 34, 42
Oceanus - 25, 291
Ochlaip - 42
O'Chippewas - 292
Odin - 33, 48, 54, 124, 176, 177, 282, 298, 323, 324, 363, 405, 414
O'Donnigans, Pat - 56
Og - 290
Ogalala - 422
Ogham - 290
Ogygean flood - 327
Ogyges - 290, 291, 313, 422
Ogygia - 26, 54, 291, 293, 306, 309, 354
Ogygian - 327
Oligocene - 152, 172, 173, 250, 252, 253, 254, 257, 258, 262, 266
Ollantay-tambe - 64, 68
Olmstead'd - 297
Olympus - 34
Opert, Dr. M. - 55, 138, 139
Orannes - 47
Oranos - 55
Ordovician era - 211
Osage - 94
Osiris - 79
Otlantay-tambe - 64, 68
Oudemans, Dr. A.C. - 237

Ouranos - 305
Owen, Robert - 151

Pacific - 77, 81, 83, 93, 95, 103, 137, 138, 145, 149, 150, 156, 164, 165, 168, 189, 190, 192, 193, 194, 195, 198, 199, 201, 204, 209, 210, 211, 215, 218, 219, 225, 228, 229, 230, 231, 246, 250, 252, 286, 291, 295, 306, 310, 312, 328, 332, 334, 337, 344, 345, 346, 349, 350, 378, 399, 401, 417
Pacific complex - 194, 195, 199
Pacific cordillera - 168, 231
Pacific islands - 76, 218
Pacific slope - 401
Pacific ridge - 345, 347
Pahn - 73, 292, 302, 303, 313, 368
Pahnee - 73
Palentini - 375
Paleocene - 219, 223, 225, 239, 252
Paleolithic age - 124
Paleoscene age - 152
Paleozoic (ancient life) epoch - 209, 210, 211, 213, 214, 216, 217, 230, 250
Palestine - 52, 314, 383
Pan (goat god) - 68, 73, 113, 121, 292, 302, 313, 321, 322, 368, 378, 383, 384, 414, 421
Pan-ilic - 121
Pan Ku - 414, 417, 421, 423
Panamint valley - 160, 165, 199, 349
Panathenaca - 34
Pangea - 192, 193, 194, 200, 201, 231
Pan's pipes - 61, 68, 72, 73, 302, 353, 398, 414, 421
Papago - 278
Papagoes - 296
Pateneit - 42
Pausanias - 291
Pauns - 73, 303
Pawnee - 73
Payette lake - 234
Pedrigal - 80, 411
Pelasgia - 316
Pelasgians - 34, 41, 42, 47, 48, 54, 87, 116, 171, 184, 288, 291, 370, 373, 382, 384, 387, 395, 418, 419, 420, 422

Pelasgus (man of the sea) - 26
Pelset - 420
Penck, Albrecht - 149
People of the sea - 35, 41, 42, 47, 48, 52, 107, 109, 110, 116, 121, 124, 128, 131, 139, 291, 297, 310, 311, 314, 340, 379, 383, 389, 392, 393, 394, 395, 397, 401, 419, 420
People of the veil - 106, 108, 109, 110, 116
Perce, Nez - 171
Permian cap - 200, 201, 212, 213, 217, 250, 257, 349
Permo-Carboniferous times - 165
Persians - 54, 84, 316, 318, 320, 326, 327
Peru - 24, 38, 39, 61, 67, 70, 72, 73, 117, 121, 125, 128, 130, 131, 144, 171, 272, 280, 282, 299, 302, 305, 310, 313, 323, 324, 352, 353, 362, 386, 387, 395, 417, 422
Peruvians - 38, 39, 51, 61, 68, 73, 117, 119, 121, 395, 422
Phaethon - 26
Philippines - 77, 142, 164, 219, 241, 282, 286, 292, 376, 383, 417, 421
Philistines - 52, 76, 82, 124, 314, 315, 383
Phoenicia - 382
Phoenicians - 34, 35, 42, 47, 48, 54, 59, 60, 65, 72, 73, 120, 121, 123, 124, 160, 171, 172, 273, 288, 306, 307, 314, 315, 316, 349, 367, 368, 369, 370, 371, 372, 373, 374, 375, 376, 381, 382, 383, 384, 387, 389, 395, 398
Phoeniki - 381, 384
Phoenix - 115
Phoroneus - 26, 291
Phrygians - 326, 327
Pidgeon - 101, 102, 385
Pillars of Hercules - 27, 28, 29, 138, 352
Pima - 232, 277, 278, 296
Piri Re'is - 43, 46, 241
Piri Re'is map - 22, 42, 43, 46, 47, 121, 241, 275, 388, 401
Pithecanthropus Erectus - 267, 268
Pithecanthropus Robustus - 268, 271

Piute - 160
Pizzaro - 60
Plato - 14, 18, 19, 20, 21, 22, 24, 25, 28, 32, 34, 35, 40, 42, 47, 54, 59, 63, 65, 68, 74, 113, 117, 124, 125, 138, 153, 181, 182, 232, 237, 291, 305, 321, 322, 328, 376, 419, 421, 422
Plafker, George - 399
Pleistocene age - 13, 16, 17, 62, 63, 69, 72, 73, 75, 80, 82, 83, 84, 85, 86, 87, 88, 93, 94, 105, 115, 117, 137, 138, 140, 142, 148, 149, 152, 154, 156, 158, 160, 161, 170, 171, 172, 178, 192, 194, 199, 200, 201, 218, 219, 224, 230, 231, 241, 249, 256, 257, 258, 259, 260, 261, 262, 267, 268, 269, 270, 272, 286, 300, 311, 314, 320, 329, 332, 344, 346, 349, 362, 365, 378, 379, 382, 397, 402, 418, 423
Pleistocene diastrophism - 17, 142, 344
Plesiosaurus - 233, 235, 236, 237, 311, 312, 376
Pliocene - 93, 150, 152, 173, 256, 258, 259, 262, 269, 270, 272, 311, 418
Plutarch - 30, 32, 42, 60, 349
Pluto - 182
Po river - 47
Point Conception - 332, 399
Point Fermin - 399
Polynesian - 81, 218, 224, 226, 250, 286, 306
Pompeii - 59, 276, 349
Pomponius Mela - 59
Pontius Pilate - 101
Poole, R.S. - 54
Popo-cat-i-petl - 360
Popul Vuh - 281, 361, 420
Portolan chart - 401, 414
Portolan map - 388, 401, 417
Poseidon (sea god) - 25, 28, 30, 31, 33, 55, 107, 113, 164
Poznansky - 422
Pre-Aryan - 116, 120, 292, 378, 382, 394
Pre-Incan - 68, 70, 72, 73, 125, 272, 299, 302, 305
Pre-Semitic - 120
Pre-Tartessian - 124
Pre-Tertiary - 200, 251

Prescott - 24, 323
Priam - 24
Pro-consul - 256, 257, 270, 271
Proclus - 42, 376
Project Mohole - 344
Proterozoic diastrophism - 209
Proterozoic glacial - 209, 210
Prouty, Dr. W.E. - 169
Provok - 307
Puans - 303, 386
Pueblo - 77, 79, 128, 273, 303, 307, 308, 310, 414, 420
Punic - 371, 374
Pyramid of Egypt - 53
Pyreness mountains (fire mountains) - 67, 68, 105, 173, 227, 356
Pyrrha (fire goddess) - 26
Pythagoras - 20, 42

Queen Athenae - 316
Queen of Amazons - 59, 106
Queen Brunhilde - 316, 405
Queen Hippolita - 182, 324
Queen Merina (Merynia) - 59, 324
Queen Minerva - 34, 316
Queen Neith - 26, 34, 53, 123, 376
Queen Nefertiti - 287, 411
Queen Siva - 395
Queen Tinian - 180
Quilaztli (the one who always bears twins) - 112
Quillay - 121

Ra (sun god) - 41
Rama - 99
Ramimam - 357
Randall, Fred R. - 349, 421
Raoul - 334
Red man - 77
Red sea - 153, 156, 168, 353, 394, 402
Redondo gorge - 344
Reed, Dr. Ralph D. - 142, 344
Reiber, Dr. Dean - 13, 17, 135
Reid, Dr. James H. - 400
Retzius - 80
Revelle, Dr. Roger R. - 152
Rhameses II - 392, 419

Rhameses III - 42, 52, 121, 314, 316, 383
Rhinoceros Mercki - 92
Rhodesian man - 267
Richter, Dr. Charles - 137, 157, 331, 332, 334, 337
Richter scale - 137, 157, 331, 332, 334
Ridge - 16, 25
Rio Grande - 79
Rio Tinto river - 125
Robustus - 268, 271
Rockies - 164
Rogers, Dr. David Banks - 69, 70, 72, 73, 74, 75, 76, 86, 94, 278, 292, 306, 332, 398
Romans - 73, 116, 124, 129, 170, 172, 176, 180, 182, 288, 304, 318, 319, 320, 325, 339, 340, 343, 368, 371, 372, 373, 381, 383
Rosetta Stone - 367
Ross, Dr. Patricia - 119
Royal Society of England - 149
Rubin, Dr. Meyer - 138
Runcorn, Dr. S.K. - 402
Runic - 370
Russia - 164, 211, 227, 287

Sacsahuaman - 64
Sahara desert - 33, 35, 52, 57, 59, 68, 105, 106, 107, 108, 124, 135, 179, 185, 187, 271, 277, 282, 311, 315, 321, 324, 378, 379, 397, 414, 418
Saharides - 213, 217
Sahhua-yacu - 64
Saint-Amand, Dr. Pierce - 333
St. Theophilus - 291
Sais - 15, 16, 24, 38, 40, 42, 54, 124, 184, 322, 376
Salser, Jay - 315
Salton sea - 67, 156, 158, 171, 181, 299, 300, 337, 373
Samaritan - 370, 374, 375
San Andreas - 156, 157, 160, 306, 331, 334, 337, 344, 347, 349
San Andreas rift - 156, 158, 165, 178, 328, 332, 350
San Blas Indians - 96, 98, 324
San Gorgonia pass - 156, 158
Sanborn, Dr. Ethel - 245
Santa Barbara - 74, 75, 86, 306
Santa Cruz island - 69, 70

Santa Rosa island - 69
Sardis - 326
Sargent, Dr. - 362
Saturn - 320, 321, 322, 326, 327, 339, 349, 419
Saturnalia - 320, 419
Savolini - 370
Scillies - 182, 338, 340, 341, 349, 354
Schliemann, Heinrich - 22, 24, 320, 372, 374, 422
Schmidt - 251
Schuchert, Charles - 140, 169, 172, 173, 174, 213, 227, 241, 245, 246, 250, 253, 258,
Scilly isles - 152, 340, 343
Sclater - 168, 190
Scripps Institute of Oceanography - 142, 152, 332, 344, 346, 399, 401
Scythia - 183
Scythians - 57, 183, 279, 327
Sebonnytus - 42
Sechem - 420
Sedillio - 80, 307, 326, 365, 366
Seminoles - 115, 273
Semites - 318, 319, 419 420
Semitic - 24, 34, 48, 54, 124, 290, 318, 420
Semitic invasion - 52, 359, 383, 420
Semitic speakers - 34, 41, 48, 52, 54, 74, 77, 87, 117, 120, 300, 305, 314, 315, 326, 327
Semitic tongues - 107, 290, 318, 421
Semitics - 124, 319, 381, 382, 383, 420
Senehis - 25, 34, 41, 42, 54
Sent, King - 51
Sequoias - 245
Seri Indians - 235, 302
Serpent - 301, 302, 303, 307, 308, 354
Serpent mound - 302
Set (god of death) - 79, 414
Seychelles bank - 168, 191
Shamash - 357
Shapley, Dr. Harlow - 207
Shelley - 237
Shepard, Commander - 224
Shephard - 140, 150
Sherru - 357
Sherwin, R.T. - 404
Shetland island - 192
Shin-nung - 359

Shooting Star - 61, 62, 99, 100, 386, 417
Shore, Jr., Dr. G.G. - 332, 399
Shrovetide - 177
Shurippak - 356
Siberia - 16
Sichem - 420
Siculus, Diodorus - 57, 59, 60, 124, 183, 282, 288, 298, 324, 379, 381, 382, 383
Sidon - 48, 54, 316, 405
Sierras - 160, 164, 199, 230, 246, 257
Sigrdrife - 323
Sillurian Insulum - 182
Siluria - 340, 341, 343
Silurian era - 211
Simons, Dr. Elwyn - 271
Simpson, Dr. George - 165
Sin (Summerian moon goddess) - 176
Sinanthropus - 92
Sinanthropus Pekinesis - 268
Siouan - 384, 385
Siouan speakers - 105, 300, 386
Sioux - 52, 56, 61, 79, 82, 94, 99, 100, 105, 291, 301, 384, 386
Sippara - 356
Siva, Queen - 395
Siwa - 183, 185, 187
Skakelesh - 420
Skopje - 331
Smiledon - 172
Smith, Dr. P.A. - 85, 143
Smith, Elliot - 313, 314
Smithsonian Institute - 80, 96, 98
Snake (Iroquois) - 94, 102, 282, 302, 384, 385, 386
Snider - 189
Socrates - 18, 19, 20, 21, 25
Socsa-hu-man - 135
Sol - 361
Solon - 14, 20, 21, 22, 24, 25, 26, 27, 28, 30, 32, 34, 40, 42, 54, 55, 82, 107, 124, 138, 139, 274, 281, 316, 354, 376, 386.
Sorby - 252
South Atlantic ridge - 168
South sea islands - 185, 198, 191, 201, 218
South sea - 226, 227
Spaeth, Dr. - 20
Spain - 54, 59, 64, 68, 76, 81, 89, 115, 120, 123, 124, 125, 152, 154, 161, 182, 211, 212, 227, 230, 256, 257, 271, 288, 295, 316, 324, 394, 404, 414, 418, 422
Sparta - 41
Spence - 81, 123, 251
Sphinx - 224, 394, 395
Spicer - 236
Star trench - 229
Stella - 334
Steers - 250
Stevenson - 286
Stevenson, Robert Louis - 254, 284, 286
Steward, Hal - 400
Stille, Hans - 344
Stonehenge - 38, 64, 65
Strabo - 182, 316
Strandlooper culture - 261
Styx (river of death) - 230, 282, 414
Suess, Dr. Hans - 138
Suess, Otto - 139, 189
Sumer - 290, 323, 327, 359, 360, 421, 423
Sumeria - 326, 420
Sumerian Library - 87, 115, 323, 356
Sumerians - 34, 55, 94, 120, 129, 272, 290, 297, 300, 305, 306, 307, 310, 312, 3p5, 316, 318, 319, 320, 325, 327, 359, 360, 382, 383, 393, 394, 395, 414, 419, 420, 422, 423
Sunken land - 15, 35
Survey - 334
Swanscombe man - 269
Swennhagen, Dr. L. - 383, 384, 385
Sychem - 420
Syers, Ed - 398
Syriac - 371, 373
Syrians - 383
Sysythes, Deucalion - 358

Taaut - 51, 54
Taautus - 367
Tabor - 154
Tacitus - 176, 177
Tafassaset - 187
Tamacheck - 291
Tamahu - 420, 421
Tarascaran - 384
Tarsarus - 123
Tartars - 401, 414
Tartarus - 34, 42, 47, 54, 120, 321
Tartessus - 123, 124
Taunge skull - 92
Taut - 367
Tayacian - 270
Taylor, Frank Bursley - 168, 190, 191, 192, 193, 194, 200, 201, 204, 231
Taylor and Wegener theory - 139, 192, 193, 194, 199, 200, 201, 205, 231
Taylor - Wegener - Daly - Willis (TW-DW) theory - 199, 204, 205
Tayloris - 365
Techuanaco - 302
Tehuanas - 60
Tehuantepec (People of the land of the ancient glory) Isthmus - 60
Templeton, Dr. - 398
Temple of Karnak - 52
Tennyson, Alfred - 340, 341, 421
Teotihuacan - 39
Termier, Pierre - 139
Tertiary - 84, 145, 150, 164, 168, 191, 201, 227, 230, 231, 239, 251
Tet - 51
Tethys sea - 150, 164, 168, 190, 191, 192, 193, 194, 200, 204, 211, 212, 213, 215, 216, 217, 219, 222, 225, 226, 227, 231, 246, 250, 251, 252, 253, 291
Teutonic alphabet - 375
Tez-cat-li-poca - 360
Thebes - 184, 291, 371
Thekel - 420
Theopompus - 291
Thoron, E.O. - 384
Thoth (God of letters and history) - 51, 53, 54, 55, 361, 367
Thouth - 367
Thucydides - 382, 419
Thule river - 230
Ti-Ku - 360
Tiahuanaco - 298, 362, 419, 422
Tiberianus - 339
Tibet - 129, 313
Tibetians - 129
Timaeus - 20, 25, 34, 42, 68
Tinian, Queen - 180
Titans - 34, 35, 42, 54, 120, 121,

123, 125, 288, 291, 307, 321, 359, 418, 420, 421
Titicaca lake - 62, 302, 422
Tla-Pallan - 40, 273
Tlaloc - 290
Tobias, Dr. Philip V. - 271
Tokari - 82, 315
Tokhari - 52, 121, 314
Tokuda, Dr. - 84
Tollund Man - 176, 177
Toltecs - 40, 113, 302, 303, 314, 353, 384, 387, 421
Tonga deep - 195
Tonga island - 195
Tortoise - 103, 302, 303
trans-Atlantic fault - 332, 355
trans-Atlantic rift - 331, 345, 347, 350
Travertine rocks - 300
Trench, Brinsley Le Poer - 38, 342
Tresco - 339, 340
Trevelyan - 340
Trevillian - 340
Triads - 349
Triana, Miguel - 384
Triassic - 201, 218, 219, 221, 224, 226, 250
Triassic diastrophism - 250
Triassic fragment - 218, 250
Triton lake - 33, 120, 330, 382
Triton sea - 57, 59, 107, 108, 178, 179, 181, 182, 183, 184, 185, 274, 309, 311, 315, 321, 324, 331, 353, 355, 360, 365, 378, 379, 381, 382, 404, 418
Trojans - 24
Trojan war - 22, 136, 277
Tropical calendar - 40
Troy - 22, 24, 136, 277, 370, 372, 374, 381, 382, 422
Troy-town maze - 73, 181, 182, 232, 276, 277
Tu-Pan - 383, 384, 417, 421
Tu-Pan-Ku - 404
Tu-Pan-Kur - 404
Tuarak - 52, 60, 106, 107, 108, 109, 110, 117, 121, 130, 135, 182, 232, 282, 292, 293, 301, 307, 314, 315, 354, 370, 378, 381, 414, 418, 420
Tuaregs - 52, 68, 80, 106, 117, 128, 130, 131, 179, 180, 181, 182, 183, 185, 187, 232, 282, 291, 414, 418, 420
Tuareks - 314

Tuchila - 422
Tula - 353
Tule Lake - 77, 210, 211
Tupi - 384
Turks - 22, 24, 95
Turtle (Dacotah) - 61, 79, 95, 99, 100, 102, 103, 128, 135, 301, 302, 303, 313, 314, 324, 386, 417
Tuscarora - 384
Tutton - 252
Tutul-Xiu - 379
Tyr - 35, 48, 54, 124, 315, 405, 414, 417, 419
Tyr Phoenicia - 417
Tyre - 35, 48, 54, 316, 405, 420
Tyrannosaurus Rex - 73, 79, 209, 219, 234, 235, 237, 312
Tyrean - 417
Tyrenian sea - 291
Tyrian - 288, 314
Tyrian sea - 288
Tyrnonoge - 354
Tyrr - 315, 316
Tyrrhenia - 27, 29, 34, 35, 54, 316, 320
Tyrrhenian league - 420
Tyrrhenian-Phoenicians - 54, 74
Tyrrhenian sea - 34, 35, 42, 47, 54, 120, 291, 314, 315, 316, 321, 349 405
Tyrrhenian valley - 47
Tyrrhenians - 35, 48, 54, 59, 60, 87, 116, 124, 314, 315, 316, 319, 320, 326, 327 338, 339, 353, 356, 358, 360, 361, 365, 367, 268, 371, 420
Tyrrhenius - 316

Uba - 356
Uighurs - 419
Uinta lake - 246, 247, 248, 252
Unakwik peak - 332, 399
U.S. Hydrographic survey office - 42
U.S. Geodetic survey - 349, 399, 401
U.S. Geological survey - 138, 150, 399
U.S.S. Cape Johnson - 144
Urals - 164, 227, 342
Uranes - 55
Urannes - 47
Uranos - 55
Uranus - 25, 164

Ureanus - 25
Urus - 310
Uto-Aztecan - 385
Utu - 414

Valdez Cove - 72
Vallejo, Francisco Garcia - 401
Varhagen, Dr. - 383, 384
Varuna - 55
Vatican library - 367, 368
Veatch - 143
Vedas - 74, 307, 359, 360
Venta Silurium - 349
Venus - 40, 131, 208, 218, 274, 275, 279
Venus calendar - 25, 40, 128, 131, 132, 260, 274, 275, 297, 298, 300, 307, 309, 313, 319, 322, 354, 386, 417, 418, 420
Venus cycle - 82
Verrill - 63, 64, 68
Vesuvius - 59
Vikar, King - 176
Viracocha - 64
Virgin islands - 329
Vishnu - 360
Vodan - 33
Volcan - 24, 25, 27, 33, 107, 138, 139 282, 285, 361, 363
Vons - 366
Votan - 35, 48, 124, 132, 133, 177, 282, 313, 316, 323, 324, 352, 353, 354, 363, 365, 382, 383, 414, 421, 422
Votan I - 405
Votan II - 405
Votan III - 363, 365, 414, 422
Vuh, Popul - 361
Vulcan - 27

Wadjak man - 267
Walking hills - 159, 160
Wallace, Major - 405
Wannus - 272
Wegener, Alfred - 166, 167, 168, 192, 193, 194, 200, 201, 204, 231, 345
Weimar skull - 88, 92
Welsh - 420
Weshech - 420
Wharton - 152
Wilkins, Otto - 139

Willis, Dr. - 140, 198, 199, 201, 204
Wilson, Dr. J. Tuzo - 345
Winchell - 360
Wishaw, Elena - 123, 124
Wissler, Dr. Clarke - 92, 94, 96, 98, 99, 100, 103, 104, 274, 300, 362
Wodin - 33, 48, 176, 177, 282, 298, 315, 316, 323, 363, 405
Wolverine rock - 334
Wright, Dr. Ernest - 420

Xibalba - 363

Xicala - 422
Xisuthros - 356
Xitli - 80

Yahpisahs (hairy ones) - 98
Yama - 129
Yaqui - 98, 157, 307, 365
Yaquis - 80
Yau - 360
Yequa - 151
Ys - 317, 341, 354, 404
Yucatan - 39, 60, 148, 295, 368, 378, 423
Yucatan basin - 229

Yuma - 159, 160, 164, 303

Zahl, Kate - 361
Zakala - 422
Zapotec - 384
Zeus - 26, 30, 32, 34, 182, 288, 291, 320, 321, 359, 368, 378, 418, 419
Zichala - 422
Zinj - 270, 271
Zinjanthropus - 270
Zodiac calendar - 354
Zodiacal cycle - 55
Zui Su dra - 414